AFFECT
IMAGERY
CONSCIOUSNESS

Volume II
THE NEGATIVE AFFECTS

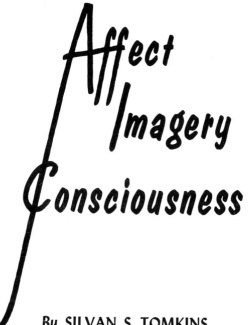

Affect
Imagery
Consciousness

By SILVAN S. TOMKINS

Professor of Psychology, Princeton University

With the editorial assistance of

BERTRAM P. KARON, PH. D.

SPRINGER PUBLISHING COMPANY, INC., NEW YORK

Copyright © 1963
Springer Publishing Company, Inc.
44 East 23rd Street, New York 10, New York

Library of Congress Catalog Card Number 62-16410

Type set at The Polyglot Press, New York

Printed in U.S.A.

To My Mother
Rose Tomkins

Contents

Acknowledgments

ACKNOWLEDGMENT is gratefully made to the following for permission to use copyrighted material: William Heinemann Limited, London, for quotations from the Constance Garnett translation of Fyodor Dostoevsky's *Notes from Underground*; W. W. Norton & Company, Inc., and Hogarth Press, London, for excerpts from Sigmund Freud's *New Introductory Lectures on Psychoanalysis*; Arvid Paulson, Mrs. Anne-Marie Wyller, the Strindberg Society in Stockholm, and the publishing houses Natur och Kultur and Albert· Bonnier, Stockholm, and Grosset & Dunlap (Universal Library), New York, for portions of *Letters of Strindberg to Harriet Bosse*, translated by Mr. Paulson; McGill University Press and University of Toronto Press for material from Dr. Lee Salk's paper, "The Importance of the Heartbeat Rhythm to Human Nature: Theoretical, Clinical, and Experimental Observations," published in *Proceedings of the Third World Conference of Psychiatry* (1961); E. P. Dutton & Co., Inc., New York, for drawings from the book *Siné Qua Non* by Maurice Siné, Copyright ©, 1961, by Siné; Random House, Inc., for a quotation from Robert Penn Warren's poem, "Original Sin"; Charles Scribner's Sons for a quotation from Allen Tate's poem, "The Wolves"; Alfred A. Knopf, Inc., for an excerpt from Philippe Ariès' *Centuries of Childhood*.

Volume II

THE NEGATIVE AFFECTS

Chapter 14

Distress — Anguish and the Crying Response

DISTRESS—ANGUISH: CRY, ARCHED EYEBROW, MOUTH DOWN, TEARS, RHYTHMIC SOBBING

What is the response?

The crying response is the first response the human being makes upon being born. The birth cry is a cry of distress. It is not, as Freud supposed, the prototype of anxiety. It is a response of distress at the excessive level of stimulation to which the neonate is suddenly exposed upon being born.

In the cry the mouth is open, the corners of the lips are pulled downwards, rather than upwards as in laughing, and vocalization and breathing are more continuous, rather than intermittent as in laughter. In addition there is an arching of the eyebrows which accompanies crying, which, if it appears without crying, gives a sad expression to the face. As Darwin suggested, crying leads to an engorgement of the blood vessels of the eyes, and the arching of the eyebrows is due to the contraction of the muscles around the eyes to protect them from the excessive blood pressure. The spasmodic pressure on the surface of the eye and the distention of the vessels within the eye, according to Darwin, reflexly activate the lacrymal glands.

Darwin reported that, although the anthropoid apes do not weep, certain monkeys do. According to Ashley Montagu, man is, however, the only creature who weeps, i.e., who sheds tears when he cries and when he is distressed. We have not yet been able to resolve this difference in opinion. The neonate, however, does not weep when he cries. The first appearance of tears is

3

somewhat variable. Montagu suggests that it is not usual for the infant to cry with tears until six weeks of age.

He also suggests that weeping became established in man because natural selection favored those infants who could produce tears, since tearless crying by human infants, with their extended dependency period, would have caused dehydration of the mucous membranes, and this would have rendered them vulnerable to the insults of the environment. The mucous membrane has marked bactericidal and bacteriostatic capabilities. Montagu reports Schlagel and Joyt's finding that 90 to 95 per cent of viable bacteria placed on the nasal mucous membrane are inactivated in about five to ten minutes. If, however, a jet of dry air is placed upon the mucous membrane, the ciliated cells are destroyed, and there is a piling up and drying of the mucus with an increased permeability of the mucous membrane. Since the gelatinous mass of dried mucus is a good medium for bacteria, these may then more easily pass through the more permeable nasal mucosa, with not infrequently fatal consequences, according to Montagu. Crying without tears would produce such dangerous drying of the nasal mucous membrane. Crying with tears would keep the mucous membrane wet. In addition, tears contain lysozyme, the same enzyme that is secreted by the mucous glands of the nasal mucosa. This enzyme is highly bactericidal, and therefore weeping further protects the infant against a variety of invading organisms. According to Montagu, tears also contain sugar and protein, which nurture the eye as well as the nasal mucous membranes. Finally, weeping activates the mucosa, increases the blood supply, and activates the mucosal glands to secrete additional lysozyme.

So much for the immediate biological function of weeping. Although tears commonly accompany crying, it should be noted that the distress cry, especially if it is brief, need not be accompanied by tears, and weeping with tears need not be accompanied by the distress cry. We have therefore distinguished the weeping response from the crying response. Weeping, like distress, is activated by a general level of density of stimulation, but somewhat higher than either distress or aggression. One can weep therefore in distress or in rage, or even in joy, if there is a high enough density of stimulation despite a sudden reduction.

Since we emphasize the distinction between distress–anguish and fear–terror, and since this distinction is not commonly made, we should at this time examine the distinction between these two responses as they appear on the face. One of the critical distinctions between distress crying and fear is the difference between the wide-open eyes of fear versus the characteristic contraction of the 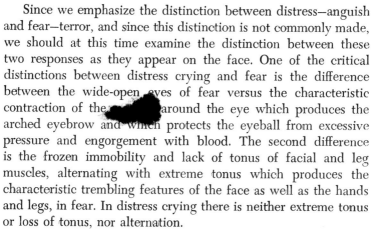 around the eye which produces the arched eyebrow and which protects the eyeball from excessive pressure and engorgement with blood. The second difference is the frozen immobility and lack of tonus of facial and leg muscles, alternating with extreme tonus which produces the characteristic trembling features of the face as well as the hands and legs, in fear. In distress crying there is neither extreme tonus or loss of tonus, nor alternation.

Darwin's assumption was that crying expresses suffering "both bodily pain and mental distress," and we are in agreement with him. In our view, however, the awareness of the feedback of the crying response *is* the experience of distress or suffering. If this is so, then there are numerous variations in the duration and intensity of crying which will be experienced as quite different degrees and kinds of suffering. The brief outcry which is evoked by a sudden, intense but brief, stab of pain is quite distinct from the moderate crying evoked by a slowly rising moderate pain of longer duration. Both of these are different from the cry of hunger which continues to mount and remain unsatisfied. It should be noted that with distress–anguish, as with every other affect, there are radical differences in the total phenomenological experience of distress when the feedback of the distress cry enters into different central assemblies of components of the nervous system. As an extreme instance, the cry of pain when I step on a tack with bare feet may be the same cry of distress I emit upon hearing of the loss of a love object, yet the total experience of distress is quite different in these two cases. This is not because the affect is different but because the two total central assemblies and, consequently the total information being transmuted in the two cases, differ so much that the feeling of distress–anguish in each case is experienced differently.

The same phenomenon occurs, as we have seen before, in the interaction between distress and pain. The same pain may be more or less tolerable depending upon how much concurrent distress is experienced at the same time. So with the distress of sudden grief compared with the distress of sudden pain. In the latter case there may be a concurrent realization of the transitory nature of the pain and distress, whereas in sudden grief the same distress response may be accompanied by an awareness of the greater distress th........ to follow and of the permanence and irreversibility .... loss as well as its future consequences. In short, the accompanying cognitive content may radically transform the total conscious experience when that experience is the transmuted information or set of messages in a central assembly which contains as one component of that information the feedback of a distress cry which is indistinguishable from the same component or a sub-set of messages in another central assembly containing different cognitive contents.

It is important to remember both the small number of primary affects and the great number of combinations with other information in differing central assemblies which are possible for the affects. The evolution of an innate affect requires hundreds of years, and one should not lightly assume that there are different affects for the great variety of experienced feelings. The experienced feelings vary not only by virtue of varying combinations with different memories, thoughts, perceptions and actions, but also because of varying combinations of primary affects, as well as because of varying transformations of the affective responses themselves. Lacey has presented persuasive evidence that there are somewhat idiosyncratic ways in which each individual eventually comes to express his affects. One individual may characteristically feel fear in the stomach, another in an increased heart rate. Finally, it happens that the innate affective response is itself unmodified, but its conscious correlate is radically modified. As with any other perceptual information, increased skill in recognition may change the percept despite constancy of the sensory feedback.

General biological function of crying

The general biological function of crying is, first, to communicate to the organism itself and to others that all is not well; second, to do this for a number of alternative distressors; third, to motivate both the self and others to do something to reduce the crying response; fourth, its function is to negatively motivate with a degree of toxicity which is tolerable for both the organism that cries and for the one who hears it cry.

Since the cry is an auditory stimulus, it can be heard by the mother at a distance, which provides a considerable safety factor for the otherwise helpless infant. It is also a much more distinctive stimulus for purposes of communication than are the various thrashing-about movements of which the neonate is capable. It is conceivable that, in the absence of the auditory cry, the human mother would be quite as unable to detect the distress of the neonate as is the chick's mother when she sees but is prevented from hearing the cry. This is also likely because of the number of alternative ways in which the cry can be activated. A mother who could detect distress if a diaper pin were sticking into the infant might be unable to do so if the infant were distressed at being alone, in the absence of a distress cry, since much of the thrashing about of the infant is very similar whether the infant is happy or unhappy.

What the distress cry gains in specificity as a distinctive communication, it somewhat sacrifices because it is a signal of so many possible different distressors. When a mother hears an infant cry, she characteristically does not know what it is crying about. It might be hungry, or cold, or in pain, or lonely. She must try each of these in turn, to find out, and even then the test does not always remove the ambiguity. Since infants will stop crying for many reasons, quite unrelated to what started them, the mother may easily misdiagnose the nature of the distressor. For example, an infant who is hungry may stop crying upon being picked up but start again when it is put down. The mother at this point cannot be sure whether the child is crying from hunger or loneliness.

This degree of ambiguity is a necessary consequence of the generality of activation of the distress response. In lower forms, the cries are more specific in nature. It is an unanswered question how specific the cries of the human neonate may be, although some mothers are confident they can distinguish different types of cries from their infants.

One method of answering such a question would be to record a sample of the cries of a neonate during its first week. Then, at moments when the infant was not crying, subject it to a distributed series of playbacks of its past cries, and record the fresh crying which the infant emitted in response to hearing itself cry. The infant should cry to the sound of its own cry, since the cry is a quite contagious response. One could then examine the degree of correlation between each cry which was used as a stimulus and the contagious response to that cry. If the neonate does emit distinctively different cries, then it should respond differentially to its own distinctive cries; therefore the variance between pairs of cries should exceed that within pairs of cries. To our knowledge such a test method has not yet been employed.

Although the number of alternative activators of the cry creates some ambiguity concerning its significance, it is this multiplicity of activators that makes the cry a response of such general significance. It enables general suffering and communication of such suffering. It is as important for the individual to be distressed about many aspects of its life, which continue to oversimulate it, and to communicate this, as it is to be able to become interested in anything which is changing.

Although the communication of distress to the mother is primary during infancy because of the infant's helpless dependency, the significance of communication of distress to the self increases with age. Just as the drive signal is of value in telling the individual when he is hungry and when he should stop eating, so the distress cry is critical in telling the individual himself when he is suffering and when he has stopped suffering. Awareness that all is not well, without actual suffering, is as unlikely as would be the awareness of the threat of a cigarette burning the skin which had no pain receptors. This is to say that, over and above the motivating qualities of pain or of the distress cry, there are important informational characteristics which are a consequence of their intense motivating properties.

The cry not only has information for the self and for others about a variety of matters which need alleviation, but it also motivates the self and others to reduce it. In contrast to fear, which is activated by anything which is so novel that it produces a relatively sharp gradient of density of neural firing midway between what will trigger startle and what will trigger excitement, distress—anguish is a self-punishing response designed to amplify those aspects of the inner or outer world which continue to stimulate neurally with an excessive, non-optimal level of intensity. So long as this non-optimal state continues, the individual will continue to emit the distress cry and suffer the stimulation of this self-punishing response, added to the already non-optimal level of stimulation.

Both the non-optimal level of stimulation and the distress cry may be masked, or reduced, in awareness or in general, by competing stimulation which is more intense and more sharply increasing in intensity and by the affects of startle or fear or excitement which may be activated by such competing stimulation. Despite such competition the coupling of distress and its activators enjoys the competitive advantage of endurance in its claim upon consciousness. Both the activator and the distress cry are long-term motivators, requiring no novelty to keep the individual under a perpetual bind.

Toxicity of distress—anguish and of fear—terror

It is because of these very properties that the toxicity of distress had to be kept low if it was to be biologically useful. The problem of toxicity has not received the attention it deserves in the theory of motivation. The problem is a commonplace one in pharmacological therapeutics. Every year hundreds of drugs are discovered to have properties which destroy biological enemies of the human being. These are often valueless in the conquest of disease because their toxicity for the host is as great as it is for the bacteria or virus against which it is effective. The problem was similar in the selection of self-punishing responses for the protection of the organism which was to use them to alarm itself.

If negative affect is too punishing, biologically or psychologically, it may be worse than the alarming situation itself, and it may hinder rather than expedite dealing with it. The evolutionary solution to such a problem was to coordinate the toxicity of the self-punishing response to its duration and to the probable duration of its activator. In the fear or anxiety response, therefore, we are endowed with a transient response of high toxicity, both biological and psychological, and in the distress response we are endowed with a more enduring self-punishing response of lower toxicity.

Fear is a response which, psychologically, is very toxic even in small doses. Fear is an overly compelling persuader designed for emergency motivation of a life-and-death significance. In all animals such a response had the essential biological function of guaranteeing that the preservation of the life of the organism had a priority second to none. The biological price of such a response was also one of high toxicity. Physiological reserves are squandered recklessly under the press of fear, and the magnitude of the physiological debt which is invoked under such duress has only recently been appreciated to its full extent.

Nor has such toxicity restricted to one affect entirely solved the problem. The compelling quality of fear—terror, which in general safeguards the existence of the organism, can lead to its destruction. Occasionally the overly anxious animal is so frozen in fear that he is eaten before he can flee the predator. Particularly in man do we witness excess in both biological and psychological toxicity, such that the individual so freezes in fear that he thereby loses his life rather than saves it. Panic may cost an individual his life not only if he freezes, but also if under its duress he surrenders all but the most primitive use of his capacities. For example, many individuals have died in fires because all tried to escape at once and in so doing trampled each other to death. Soldiers in combat have lost their lives in panic, either because they could not pull the trigger of their guns, could not run away or because they ran wildly into the face of enemy fire.

Despite the toxicity of the fear response, there can be no doubt of its over-all biological utility so long as it is a transient response and so long as it is activated only by truly emergency situations. As we shall see later, it is extremely difficult to make the lower forms suffer chronic anxiety in the way in which it is possible for this to occur in human beings. The development of complex cognitive capacities, in our opinion, made possible the continuous activation of negative affect and required that negative affects be differentiated in terms of toxicity so that less toxic negative affects may be activated. The linkage of high-powered skills of anticipation with massive, overly toxic panic was to make possible both rapid and slow suicide. We have seen before, in the phenomenon of voodoo death, that continuous high-level anxiety sustained for only a few days is sufficient to produce death. Such responses in lower animals are invoked usually only by direct assault or threat of assault.

In man the multiple linkages of such a toxic affect to a variety of internal and external cues makes possible the chronic anxiety neurosis. This disease we believe is a consequence of one of the mistakes of the evolutionary process. Fortunately the infant is spared this danger of the experience of excessive prolonged anxiety, since its anticipatory skills take considerable time to develop. Secondly, the infants appears to be so sensitive to two other competing affects that the anxiety response is minimized. These are startle and the distress cry. The infant's first reaction to being born is not to become afraid, but to cry; its most common reaction to novelty is not fear, but surprise or another type of surprise, the Morro reflex, which is eventually displaced by the startle response. The distress cry is considerably less toxic than the anxiety response and is therefore much better adapted to serve as a self-punishing response (and punishing to others) for long periods of time and to direct attention to activators of prolonged duration.

Thus in the so-called three-month colic the infant may cry more or less continuously the first three months of its life. Although the biological and psychological price of such crying is not trivial, since the baby may become cyanotic, yet its overall toxicity is sufficiently low so that the infant can survive despite this ordeal. There can be little doubt that three months of panic would place such a severe burden on the infant's physiological reserves that its survival would be extremely unlikely.

There is another aspect to the problem of toxicity which has also received insufficient attention. The crying response has the general biological function not only of communicating to the mother that all is not well with her infant, but also of motivating her to do something about alleviating this distress. This has been achieved by making the sound of the cry a sufficient activator of the distress cry for anyone who hears it. Its sound is within the spectrum of greatest sensitivity of the human ear, and while it does not destroy tissue (so far as we know), it is, along with pain and other types of noise, entirely adequate as a distress activator.

Here again we are faced with a critical toxicity problem. If it is too disturbing to listen to the cry, the infant's life may be endangered, insofar as the mother might either run away from the overly punishing stimulation or become aggressive and hurt the child. Many human mothers do indeed respond to their own distress at hearing their infant cry by essentially abandoning the infant either temporarily until it stops crying, or permanently. Less well known but not uncommon is violence to the point of killing the crying infant or child. Within the United States I have noted within the past fifteen years no less than one and sometimes two or three murders each year of an infant or child by a parent or nurse, because the crying of the child could not be tolerated.

Although the distress response itself is not so toxic as this would suggest, it must be remembered that added to the un-relieved distress response are those additional affects which may have been employed in socializing the crying of the parent or nurse. To the extent to which the parent or nurse was made to feel shame, or fear, or anger or all of these when he or she cried as an infant or child, this burden will usually be redintegrated upon being exposed as an adult to the crying of his or her own or other children.

The combination of the crying of the infant, the adult's own distress, plus other recruited negative affect, is often sufficient to raise the general level of neural firing so that anger is activated. If the crying cannot be stopped, this anger then feeds upon itself until the overt act of violence occurs. The most recent incident of such a kind was in an Associated Press dispatch from Sacramento, California, early in April, 1961: "Donald Mike Johnson, 26, was booked for investigation of murder yesterday after he admitted punching his two year old son to death be-cause the child would not stop crying." Characteristically the parent or nurse has been exposed to several hours of uninter-rupted crying, and then has the adult equivalent of a crying tantrum himself.

The problem of toxicity then has not altogether been solved by evolution, even in the case of the distress response, with respect to the punishment of the parents whose care of the infant the cry is designed to evoke. Granting these and other exceptions under particular circumstances, it is generally true that distress is a self-punishing (and punishing to others) response of acceptable toxicity even in intense and prolonged crying, and that fear is much more toxic and therefore tolerable only for very brief periods of time. This increased tolerability of the distress response means that the individual has increased time and degrees of freedom in coping with its alleviation. Obviously, high-intensity distress, or anguish, is more toxic than low-intensity distress; and high-intensity fear, or terror, is less bearable than a low level of anxiety. But for comparable intensities, it is clear that distress is considerably less toxic than fear, and anguish is considerably less toxic than terror.

Fear and terror evoke massive defensive strategies which are as urgent as they are gross and unskilled. Further, they motivate the individual to be as concerned about the re-experience of fear or terror as he is about the activator of fear or terror. In contrast, the lower toxicity of distress permits the individual to mobilize all his resources including those which take time (e.g., thinking through a problem) to solve the problems which activate distress.

Thus if I am distressed at my poor performance as a public speaker, I can usually tolerate this sufficiently to work upon improving my skill. But if I become stage-frightened, I may freeze so that I cannot speak; or so that I then avoid the entire public-speaking situation lest I re-experience panic. Again, if failure in work is very distressing, I can try again and succeed. But if failure activates intense fear, of whatever content (e.g., that I never will succeed, or that I will be punished severely), then if I try again, it is with competence impoverished by the excessive drain on the channel capacity of the central assembly which the toxicity of fear entails.

If I am completely intimidated by fear, then I will not try again, and there is no possibility of solving this particular problem. What is more serious, my development as a general problem-solver is thereby jeopardized. Again, if in general social relationships an individual is rebuffed or is left alone and responds with distress, he can re-examine this particular instance, and decide to seek friendship elsewhere, or tolerate the distress of loneliness or change his own behavior to please the other. If, however, the rebuff or the indifference produces intense fear, the individual may more readily generalize his experience so that there is a withdrawal from interpersonal relationships of any kind; or, in attempting to master such anxiety he may provoke more rejection and then more anxiety because of the grossness, incompetence and craven submissiveness obvious to those towards whom such overtures are made.

In short, fear is an affect designed to rapidly minimize acquaintance with its source, whereas distress is designed to reduce such acquaintance but with less urgency and therefore with more mobilization of the best resources of the individual and so with more competence. Under emergency conditions, distress would be a luxury which most organisms could not afford. Only the helpless neonate, who must and is able to call upon the skill of others to survive, can rely exclusively on the distress cry; and only adult human beings who with the aid of their society have managed to cope successfully with the major threats to the physical integrity of life can afford the luxury of primary reliance on the low-toxicity affect of distress.

This is not to imply that distress is not very unpleasant, nor that fear may not be counteracted. Some human beings cannot tolerate distress even in the smallest doses, and some human beings counteract their most intense panic. Upon closer inspection however such cases usually show complex affect combinations. Those who cannot tolerate distress most often have in their past suffered great shame, or anger, or fear along with or consequent to distress, which summates with distress. Those who master fear may have in their past also experienced joy in the progressive mastery of negative affect, or do so for the sake of some goal or value the lure of which can reduce the affect of fear with a competing affect such as excitement; or finally because to be governed by fear produces shame and self-contempt which is adequate to initiate counteractive behavior which reduces fear. Despite these complications, it remains the case generally that one affect is much more tolerable, much less toxic *per se*, than the other.

Although in man there are a number of distinct affects, these evolved only gradually in the evolutionary series. As mentioned previously, Ambrose has shown that what is differentiated in man as laughing, crying and smiling appeared earlier as just one facial posture of crying and threat with teeth baring. Gradually laughing was differentiated from crying, but still resembled crying in the anthropoids, until in man all three are quite differentiated.

One of the consequences of the lack of differentiation of facial affects in simpler forms is that the simpler mode of affective expression may express a broader spectrum of feelings than its analog in man.

Distress vocalizations similarly seem to express a wider spectrum of feeling in lower forms, although the activators seem to be more specific. Howard has shown that the typical bird song is a territorial cry which serves as a warning to other males. Any particular species has at least six or seven different calls, indicating danger, hunger, presence of food and so on. The distress cry of birds is but one cry of many, is uttered only in threatening situations, and is responded to by other birds of the same species as though they understood its specific significance. It is perhaps more accurate to describe it as a cry of alarm as well as of distress, since it probably serves the functions which in man would be served by both fear and distress.

Frings and Jumber tape-recorded the distress cries of a starling which it uttered when caught. They then played this at high volume over a loudspeaker in a town where there were many starlings. The effect was to drive the starlings away permanently.

There are also distress cries of birds which have exactly the opposite effect on the parent bird who hears them. In species of birds in which the mother does no feeding, the cries of the infant birds bring the mother and prevent their getting lost.

The extraordinary specificity of such responses was shown in a study by Bruckner who found that the domestic hen responds only to the sound of the distress call of the chick. When he fastened a chick to a peg behind a screen, the mother would come to its rescue when she heard the chick crying. But when he put the chick under a glass dome so that the mother could see it struggling but could not hear its distress cry, she was entirely indifferent.

Further examples of the specificity of the releasers or activating stimuli of the distress call have been reported by Tinbergen. The distress call is released in many birds, ducks, and geese by any model of a bird which had a short neck like a bird of prey. Many other characteristics such as the shape and size of wings and tail were shown to be irrelevant.

In addition to cries to specific predators, in animals other than man there appear to be quite specific stimuli to the distress cry. Whether these are truly "releasers" in the ethological sense is not altogether clear. Thus, according to Tomilen and Yerkes infant chimpanzees will cry if they are prevented from clinging to their mother.

The cry of the distress has been studied in some detail in puppies. Scott and Marston have reported that young puppies under twelve weeks old emit whines and yelps at rates up to and over 100 per minute. It has been called "distress vocalization" and is produced by a variety of discomforting situations such as hunger, cold, confinement and isolation. Yelping behavior is highly variable between individuals. The behavior of individual puppies is much more consistent, there being "high" yelpers and "low" yelpers. Individual reaction to the experimental factors is consistent.

Fredricson reported that confining an isolated puppy (six to ten weeks old) in a small box outside the home pen produced high rates of distress vocalization. He was able to reduce this yelping rate 50 per cent or more by placing a second puppy in the box, whereas substituting a small box in place of the puppy had no effect on the yelping rate.

Fredricson also reported that puppies separated from other puppies and confined alone in a small box gave a mean number of 211 yelps per puppy for a five-minute period, in contrast to puppies who were placed in confinement together with another puppy who emitted a mean number of 30 yelps for the same period. Causey reported that puppies isolated in a strange room showed more vocalization than those isolated in a familiar room. Roos, Scott, Cherner and Denenberg reported that young puppies, three to six weeks old, yelped more when restrained than when not restrained, and when alone than when together. When isolation and restraint are combined, there is an increase and a significant interaction effect. Undisturbed puppies in the home cage with their mother and litter mates characteristically show little or no distress vocalization.

There is a differential effect of the presence of the mother and all litter mates, on yelping, compared with one litter mate. Thus the puppies which were placed alone in the pens gave some yelps in every case, with a large range from 7 to 687 in a given five-minute period. When puppies are restrained, the range was from 485 to 969. Placing a litter mate with the puppy reduces the yelping but doesn't return it to zero as does restoring the mother and all litter mates. Whether this represents an innate preference for the mother or a learned one, or a combination of both, is not clear.

Although there appear to be innate differences with respect to the amount of yelping, yet the interactions between learning, habituation and innate thresholds are quite complex. The importance of first experiences was shown in Fredricson's experiment in which a reversal of conditions for the two groups led to an only partial reversal of results. Puppies who had been confined alone in the first three experimental sessions yelped roughly half as much when later confined with another puppy (an average of 134 yelps together versus 211 yelps alone). Puppies who had been confined with another puppy in the first three experimental sessions yelped approximately six times more when confined alone (an average of 286 alone versus 30 together). This is consistent, but the difference in means for the two groups of puppies in the initial trials is more striking (211 versus 30) and is statistically reliable, while the differences in means for the two groups in the later reversed conditions is less striking (286 versus 134) and falls just short of statistical significance at the 5 per cent level.

First experiences, namely, "alone" for one group and "together" for the other, apparently modified all subsequent reactions to some extent. The initially "alone" group produced a larger total number of yelps for all combined trials (6 trials; 9,322 yelps). The initially together group produced in 6 trials 7,625 yelps.

The first experiences were, according to Fredricson's assumptions, more stressful when undergone alone. The significance of first experiences for future behavior in that an earlier stress contaminates what might otherwise have been a relatively tolerable experience is shown concretely by the difference in means for yelping (134 versus 30) when both groups are confined together with another puppy. Puppies which started out with the more stressful experience yelped approximately four times as much under less stressful conditions than the second group, for which these more benign conditions represented the first experience. The difference in means is significant at the 2 per cent level of confidence.

There seems to a critical period of socialization for dogs in the early weeks of life during which, if there is an opportunity, the responsiveness to other dogs is developed; if there is no opportunity, the responsiveness does not develop. Thus, the reactions of excessive vocalization does not appear in older puppies which have been reared alone in small boxes from before the time of the critical period of socialization, according to Fisher. Such animals were both restrained and isolated.

Further, the distress cry habituates somewhat over time. In an additional experiment, Roos, Scott, Cherner and Denenberg studied the effect of adaptation to the two extreme conditions of their first experiment, restrained and alone versus non-restrained and together. They were given one ten-minute test per day for ten consecutive days. The yelping decreased over the ten-day interval for both groups. The alone-restrained group decreased from a mean of 1,128 to 920 on the tenth trial, compared to the non-restrained and together group mean of 348 on the first trial to 128 on the tenth trial.

UNLEARNED ACTIVATORS IN DISTRESS—ANGUISH

The unlearned activator of distress is a high-level of density of neural firing. Such neural firing itself may be produced by either internal or external sources. These include pain, hunger, cold, noise, heat, loud speech, very bright lights or overly intense or enduring affect, including excessive distress itself.

The extent to which unlearned crying at separation is characteristic of the human neonate or infant is not clear. As we shall see, for birds it seems clear; but for the puppy, distress crying in response to separation seems to be dependent on experience during a critical period of socialization. For the human infant the facts are difficult to establish.

They are difficult to establish because of the numerous ways in which the human cry can be activated. There is recent evidence from Schaffer which raises a question whether crying at separation as such is based on an unlearned mechanism, and indeed whether crying upon separation occurs at all, on either a learned or unlearned basis.

Schaffer reported the responses of twenty-seven generally healthy infants, aged under 12 months, to admission to a hospital for surgery. Those sixteen infants who were over 28 weeks of age cried a great deal. Of those nine infants who were 28 weeks and younger, seven did not protest or cry, appeared to accept the new environment and showed awareness of the change only through unusual silence. One of the two exceptions was already 28 weeks of age, and the other was thought to miss his dummy.

In response to visitors, those over 28 weeks were demanding and clung to their mothers, rejecting strangers. Those under 28 weeks hardly differentiated beween the strangers' visit and visits by the mother, except that there was somewhat more vocal activity during their mothers' visits.

On returning home those over 28 weeks clung to their mothers and cried if left alone by her. Those under 28 weeks did not respond by crying, but appeared bewildered, scanning their environment with a blank expression.

These results are consistent with Levy's report that infants under six months of age do not cry just before receiving a second injection given at repeated intervals under the same circumstances but that they do cry in anticipation of the injection with increasing frequency as they become older; by the end of the first year most children remember enough of their earlier experiences to cry at the sight of the doctor and needle.

In general it would not be inconsistent with the known

greater dependence of human development on learning that crying at separation from the mother would be innate in the lower
animals and would depend more on learning in the case of the
human infant.

One of the most important and somewhat neglected sources
of distress is the low-grade pain or discomfort of the low-energy
state. The phenomenology of the state of fatigue is well known.
Its exact physiological substrate is less clear. It is well known
that there are diurnal body rhythms in which, as the body temperature waxes and wanes, the individual feels energetic and alert
or sleepy and tired. These variations in temperature are also
related to the intake of food. Also immediately after the intake
of food, following several hours of not eating, there is a relatively
rapid rise in internal temperature. The low temperature of the
low-energy state appears also to be accompanied by a set of
signals of low-grade pain or general discomfort, which are
very close to the level of neural firing adequate to activate the
distress cry. Frequently, as the state of fatigue deepens, it is
sufficient to activate distress, and then the combination of fatigue
and distress is often sufficient to activate anger. This sequence
is classic in the late afternoon experience of millions of mothers
of tired children. It is equally familiar to adults, but is frequently
masked by the custom of tea or cocktails at the mid-afternoon
or end of the day.

Since the fluctuations of energy level are inherent in the life
of any animal, their effect on the thresholds of the affects is a
matter of considerable significance which has not yet received
the attention it deserves. As we have previously mentioned, it is
our impression that children are least responsible, most given to
tantrums with minimal or no provocation when overly tired.
Unfortunately, precisely the same thing is true for his parents
at about the same time of day. When, therefore, all members of
any family require the most gentle and delicate soothing of
ruffled psyches, each one is most likely to increase the probability
of distress and anger on the part of others by himself emitting
the cry of distress and then of anger or rage.

If, as we believe, these responses are primarily activated and
sustained by a constant bombardment of low-grade pain and
discomfort from the low-temperature, low-energy state, usual

at the end of the day, then the psychic elaborations by all members of the reasons for their conflict, children as well as parents, are in large part rationalizations of distress. Interaction should therefore be minimized and discipline in particular avoided at such periods. Instead, every effort should be made to reduce or mask the physical discomfort and its concurrent distress.

Warm soothing baths, cocktails, tea, snacks, music—these are the time-honored ways in which human beings have coped with their own fatigue-distress states for centuries. This wisdom, however, may soon be improved upon by modern pharmacology. It is quite within the realm of possibility that we may be able to iron out the peaks and valleys of energy utilization for a more sustained but less intensive positive affective experience, or exaggerate them for a more intense experience of alertness, high energy, and positive affect, for periods which alternated with a deeper sleep, thus eliminating the intermediate low-energy states, which are essentially being asleep on one's feet.

Not a small part of the problem of human happiness is hidden in these daily variations of free energy. By free energy we refer primarily to a state of blood chemistry and temperature optimal for human functioning. For example, blood-sugar level may be grossly reduced at a particular time because sugar is not being released into the blood stream from body reserves. Ordinarily, this is a consequence of homeostatic control mechanisms which are governed by both short-term and long-term criteria, as we have noted before in the case of the hunger drive mechanism. It is entirely possible, however, that the present largely social regulation of eating is not optimal for the minimizing of distress. It has been reported that a greater number of smaller meals would produce a more sustained blood-sugar level and that the American custom of a small breakfast and a large supper is the reverse of an optimal schedule for the maintenance of a steady output of energy. It has long been known also that there are great individual variations in these requirements and in the relative proportion of fats, carbohydrates and protein required.

Diet is of course but one of a complex of physical factors critical for the maintance of the state of well-being. Anything which disturbs the requisite number of hours of sleep indirectly increases fatigue and pain and therefore distress. Frequently psychological problems become much more distressing than they need be, because they interfere with sleep. This then increases the distress of the individual, and summates with the original problem to magnify it in a spiraling build-up. In a few cases I have observed this spiral terminated in a psychotic episode. Sullivan was one of the first psychiatrists to stress the destructive effects of the cumulative loss of sleep preceding the psychotic break and the reparative function of drug-induced sleep in warding it off. Psychosis apart, an individual with the same "personality" may be a very different person at the peak of his energy cycle and at the bottom of his daily variations in free energy.

Much of the prejudice against the reliance on tranquilizing and energizing drugs in the treatment of the mentally ill depends on the assumption that one must change the personality structure of the individual to cure mental illness. It is our belief that two individuals may have identical personality structures, and one be relatively sick and the other relatively well if one, for whatever reason, suffers continual activation of his negative affects and the other does not. Drug therapy is one way in which the affects may be controlled. The effects of affect control may be quite profound without altering in any way the basic personality structure. The most radical consequences of present pharmacological advances may be in the realm of minimizing negative affect and maximizing positve affect, for the normal human being.

Another source of distress, uncommon in nature, is the repetitive rhythmic stimulus. Doust, Hoenig and Schneider reported that the use of a flickering light on twenty-five normal subjects, at frequencies between 3 and 32 flashes per second, produced marked changes in oxiometrically determined arterial blood oxygen-saturation values. Flicker rates between 3 and 9 per second, and also between 12 and 17 per second, produced a decrease of blood oxygen-saturation values, while this was normal at 9-11 flashes per second, and elevated at frequencies of 18-22 per second.

Using 109 subjects, 58 normal controls and 51 hospital patients, they showed that the arterial oxygen saturation levels vary very consistently for normal subjects regardless of the type of rhythmic stimulation used—whether photic, auditory or cutaneous. Maximum anoxemia occurred at 5 and 15 pulses per second in the normal subjects, and they showed in addition a summative effect of simultaneous sonic and photic stimulation.

By depressing the oxygen levels by the choice of optimal stimulation frequencies, spontaneous comments by the healthy subjects revealed considerable changes in affect and levels of awareness; among the patients, repressed unconscious material was brought into consciousness. Some of the spontaneous comments made during the anoxemia periods included "concentration poor, feel slowed up, tired, drowsy, sleepy, irritable, annoyed, fed up, desire to stop machine or break it, headache, dizziness or giddiness."

That excessive heat or humidity of the atmosphere directly affects the well-being and the consequent distress and aggression of the individual is well known. There is also evidence which is beginning to accumulate that the proportion of positive and negative ions in the atmosphere may be significant in the maintenance of optimal functioning and the minimizing of distress and aggression. Rheinstein, working under the direction of Knoll at the Electronics Institute at Munich, has reported that subjects breathing negative atmospheric ions, under double blind conditions, show the effect of such stimulation on reaction time within 45 seconds. There is an approximately 30 per cent decrease in reaction time due to breathing negative atmospheric ions. Continuing work at the University of Pennsylvania under the direction of Kornbluh suggests that fluctuations in frequency of crimes of aggression vary as a function of barometric and atmospheric conditions and the relative precentage of positive ions in the air.

That somatic factors play a prominent role in human well-being or discomfort has been known from the beginning of time. The indifference of personality theory to this domain is largely a consequence of the presumed secondary role of affects and the customary polarization of specialization of knowledge, in which it is assumed that reality is organized after the model of departments of instruction in institutions of higher learning. If man is at once a physical, biological, psychological and sociological entity, as we believe him to be, then a unified general theory of the human being must ultimately cut across these our present specializations.

Distress—anguish from skeletal muscle feedback:
interrupted or inhibited action

Another source of high density of neural stimulation sufficient to activate distress is the feedback from the peripheral skeletal musculature. This musculature may itself be innervated on either a learned or unlearned basis, in the interests of action or as a part of affect arousal. There is one affect, the startle response, which is largely constructed of the feedback of the sudden contraction of the skeletal muscles. The continuation of such contraction would in all probability produce distress and perhaps unconsciousness and exhaustion, since the epileptic attack is in large part just a series of large muscle contractions. Any behavior which requires continuous massive muscular exertion may activate distress if the feedback of this effort continues at a high level of density of neural stimulation.

This is how "trying" very hard to do something may become distressing, if the effort is unsuccessful and continually increased. This distress activated by failure will most often be activated if the individual does not give up but continues to maintain high tonus in his muscles.

Further, any action which is unfinished by virtue of being interrupted in such a way that the individual does not relinquish his goal may increase peripheral muscle tension so that distress is activated. When this happens, the significance of the interruption is enhanced, since present distress is now added to the continuing attractiveness of the original goal to further increase impatience and peripheral muscle contraction. Much of the increased memory for interrupted activities in the Zeigarnik effect may have been due to the distress which was activated by heightened muscle tonus in response to interruption.

Any action which is contemplated or intended but which is inhibited for any reason can also produce sufficient increase in peripheral muscle tonus to activate distress. A hungry man who wishes to but does not reach for something to eat, a sexually aroused individual who inhibits his wish to grasp a provocative sex object, an angry man who does not hit the provacateur, a talker who inhibits his speaking, a looker who inhibits his voyeuristic wish—all may generate sufficient muscle tonus sufficient to activate distress and enhance the punishment of self-imposed inhibition.

Distress–anguish from interrupted or inhibited affect

The role of feedback of the skeletal muscle responses in activating distress is important not only as a by-product of action or intended action, but also as a by-product of the activation of affect of any kind. We distinguish the affect of anger from the wish to hit, the affect of excitement from the wish to look or embrace a sex object. Similarly we distinguish conceptually the source of distress from the interruption or inhibition of the con-current affect, which may support an action or intended action, from the source of distress which results from the interruption or inhibition of the action *per se*. We make this distinction even though the sole cause of the interruption of the affect may be the interruption of the action, and even though the distress from both sources is fused as part of one total phenomenological experience.

As an example, the affect of anger may produce sufficient contraction of the skeletal musculature to activate distress by virtue of the high density of neural stimulation in the feedback of such muscular expression of anger. However, the contraction of particular muscles of the fist and arms preparatory to hitting someone in anger is a different, although related, source of potential distress.

The interruption by parents of activity of their children is as likely to be an interruption of the expression of affect as of any particular activity. Redl was the first to call attention to the negative affect generated by the interruption of any ongoing activity, such as games, in the case of children with weak egos. The interruption of excitement, e.g., by forbidding a child to continue to play, may produce sufficient muscular contraction to activate either distress or aggression directly or distress followed by aggression. In such a case the excitement is ordinarily intensified by prohibition sufficient to activate the cry of distress, which when added to the ongoing stimulation then becomes capable of evoking anger. If the interruption of excitement recruits wide-spread muscular contractions, the total density of stimulation may be sufficient to activate aggression directly and immediately. The phenomenon which Redl describes is a general one. Excitement which must be inhibited often produces a stiffening of the body.

The intense muscular contraction when affect is interrupted or inhibited is itself produced in different ways and for different reasons, depending in part on what affect is being inhibited or interrupted. Thus the indirect, substitute cry which occurs, we think, in clenching the fingers, or the toes, or the diaphragm, or in the drumming of the fingers or in the wiggling of the feet, may continually reactivate the distress response, because the impulses which would normally have gone to the throat in the cry are diverted to another muscle system which produces enough feedback to reactivate the cry rather than reducing the tendency to cry.

There is of course a similar self-perpetuating, high-inertia characteristic in the distress cry proper. The cry once begun has the potential of producing sufficiently dense feedback to reactivate the cry. It is our impression, for which precise evidence is still to be obtained, that the clenching of the fists as a substitute cry is more self-perpetuating than is the cry proper, since the cry eventually is self-reducing through exhaustion. Not only are indirect cries reactivators of distress through skeletal muscle feedback but so are the muscular defenses against the cry. It may stop the overt cry to keep a stiff upper lip, but the feedback of this muscle contraction is somewhat self-defeating with respect to the experience of the affect of distress. This is because it is likely to continually reactivate distress which though it may not produce an overt cry, since the mouth is held firmly tight, yet sends the characteristic pattern of muscle responses of the cry to the face again and again, as the feedback from the attempted defense of the stiff upper lip continues to reactivate the cry. This is why the attempt to hold back the cry may eventually produce a heightened distress which breaks through the attempted defense.

Distress, however, is not the only affect which may activate further distress by an increase in neural bombardment via the feedback of skeletal muscle contraction. Anger can activate distress and tears of rage through excessive muscle feedback bombardment, when it is not reduced by being expressed overtly. Intense anger which is somewhat reduced by appeasement by the provacateur may still be sufficiently strong to produce muscle contraction which activates distress. An explanation to someone who is furious, which is sufficient to take the edge off his anger, may yet leave him somewhat distressed simply because the anger itself has produced enough bristling in the muscles to activate distress after the anger has somewhat abated.

In general the long-term suppression of the overt expression of any affect can produce residual affect hunger for overt expression which will maintain sufficient skeletal muscle tension to activate chronic distress.

Feedback from skeletal musculature as a component of the activation of distress—anguish by pain

Such feedback from the skeletal musculature may also be a component of the activators of distress produced by pain, since very commonly one contracts the muscles in response to pain, and this adds appreciably to the density of neural stimulation. Indeed one of the ways in which the experience of pain may be minimized is by minimizing the skeletal response to pain. Gardner, Licklider and Weisz have reported a procedure with music that has been effective in suppressing pain in 5,000 dental operations—by music which promotes relaxation, and by noise which directly suppresses pain. The importance of relaxation is high-lighted by their preliminary observations, with other clinical medical situations, that this aural procedure was effective in over two-thirds of their cases, and that when it was not effective, the patient was not relaxed, or the pain was well developed before the sound was turned on, or it was not feasible to continue intense stimulation throughout the operation because of possible damage to the ear.

In their procedure the patient wears headphones and controls the stimuli through a small control box in his hand. Before the pain begins he listens to stereophonic music and as soon as he feels pain, or anticipates it, he turns up the intensity of the random noise stimulus, which is somewhat pleasant but less so than the music. The main function of the music is to relax the patient, and it is the noise which primarily drowns out the pain. The noise sounds somewhat like a waterfall and also has a relaxing effect. When both music and noise are presented, however, the music can be followed only through concentration. The major effect of pain suppression appears to be produced by interference with the pain by a stimulus of greater density of neural stimulation. It is probably for this reason that the interference effect is greatest with pain which is deep and of the slow onset. Sharply localized pain, e.g., at the time of incision, or when the suturing needle passes through the skin, is not usually suppressed. Although this competing auditory stimulation is dense enough to interfere with the central assembling of pain messages, it is chosen to provide a compromise between analgesic effectiveness and pleasantness of quality. Otherwise it would certainly also activate distress and the total discomfort might not be very different from the suffering of pain.

These preliminary experiments have not given a clear picture of the differential role of muscular relaxation in the suppression of pain, compared with its role in the suppression of the distress response to pain, but it is clear that it plays some part in both the experience of pain and pain-evoked distress. The pain of incision, which was not suppressed by the noise was nonetheless small and inconsequential under these conditions. Here it would appear that the general state of relaxation prevented the distress response, which might otherwise have amplified the pain and set up reverberation which would be further amplified by the deep, slow onset pain of the rest of the operation. Wolff has noted that once a circular reverberating circuit of pain is set up it has an inertia of its own which requires only occasional new pain stimulation from external sources to be maintained indefinitely, but that once such a reverberating circuit is interrupted it is finished as a self-sustaining circuit.

Distress—anguish from continuing dense neural stimulation from central sources

A very high density of neural firing may emanate from central rather than peripheral sources. We have already seen in the case of startle, in the double-take and in the unexpected tap on the shoulder that the recruitment of interpretation from central sources may be at such a rate that the individual startles just as easily to an idea as to a gunshot. Such recruitment and emanation of messages from within may not only have a steep gradient of arousal, but it may also maintain a sustained level of neural stimulation. Just as a blindfolded chess player may emit detailed visual imagery sufficient to play the game and to activate the affect of excitement, so he may indulge in imaginary conversations with himself or recollections or anticipations which if sustained too long may activate distress because they attain too high a level of stimulation. Frequently when such a level is attained, the individual turns it off or down, and thereby avoids or reduces distress.

It also happens that the individual cannot turn off such stimulation from central sources and so suffers distress which he cannot reduce. Quite apart from the positive or negative quality of such imagery, excessive central stimulation may activate and maintain distress. It is not uncommon for enforced preoccupation with what was actually a highly rewarding experience to produce acute distress through excessive reliving of the moment of great excitement or enjoyment. This is most likely to occur where such experience had been preceded by long periods of distress and longing. The individual who falls in love after having been long deprived of intimacy may recollect in his mind's eye the intense moment of initial intimacy so many times that eventually he suffers distress from the satiation of excessive repetition.

If the excessive repetition of external stimulation can provoke intense distress, so too can the same repetition of imagery emitted from central sources, whether that experience was itself rewarding or punishing. Such repetitive inner preoccupations are capable not only of producing distress, but also of producing insomnia, whether the accompanying affect be excitement or distress. Any unfinished business of the day or of the whole life history is a potential candidate for such repetitive intrusion into the central assembly and awareness.

The most striking instance of such intrusion, which produces both intense distress and confusion because of the density and high velocity of ideation, occurs in the acute, initial stages of a schizophrenic episode. Under these conditions the individual may be suddenly confronted, from central sources, with an overwhelming number of images, impulses and ideas changing so rapidly and reaching such a high level of density of stimulation that intense distress is activated, punctuated by sudden terror at the suddenness of increase of stimulation. Some patients frequently resort to writing down this ideation with the explicit intention of reducing the velocity and density of ideas and their impression of chaos by ordering their thoughts, sometimes half of them on one side of the page, and half of them on the other side. The schemes for achieving order and reducing the excessive bombardment of inner experience vary considerably, but all involve the reduction of confusion and distress by some simplification and ordering of ideas. Such patients believe that their future recovery depends on their reducing the number and velocity of ideas by which they are being bombarded. The normal individual ordinarily knows such central bombardment for only brief periods of time. When it proves excessive he is able to turn it off or down. In the acute psychotic phase it is not possible to turn down the density of such stimulation so that distress is activated and very frequently also terror at the sudden experience of being overwhelmed.

Nor are psychotics alone in facing such inner bombardment. The creative individual, suddenly bombarded with a whole new set of ideas, and their fanning out implications, ordinarily experiences excitement. But if this production of ideas continues at a very high rate and continues to evoke excitement, the combination of ideation and excitement may eventually produce a density of stimulation which activates distress and finally weariness and exhaustion.

Innate differences in the distress—anguish threshold

In addition to the unlearned relatively transient internal and external sources of stimulation which may activate distress, the innate threshold of the distress cry must be considered. Several years ago Friess reported that the testing of neonates during the lying-in period showed a high correlation between their general activity level, the magnitude of their startle response and the amount of their crying. She further reported a relationship between this total complex and characteristic responses to frustration during the fifth to the tenth day of life.

These children were tested in the following way. First, the breast or bottle was presented to the infant. After he had been sucking well for one minute, the nipple was removed. After one minute, it was restored to him. The quiet child when wide awake may take it at once but if drowsy or asleep may require some help to grasp it. When the nipple is removed, such an infant is quiet, continues the act of sucking and then falls asleep. When the nipple is restored, the characteristically quiet infant keeps his mouth closed, and there is considerable difficulty in reinserting it. The moderately active child usually takes the nipple right away when it is presented. When the nipple is removed, the moderately active infant remains awake and may move his head or arms and legs. When the nipple is restored, the moderately active infant sucks at once. The highly active child, when the nipple is presented, may continue his activity or take it right away. When the nipple is removed, the highly active infant may have a startle response or cry. When the nipple is restored, he may continue his activity and/or cry before sucking. Friess studied these children for several years following these initial observations, and found that this early activity pattern was modified only within certain limits.

What is of interest here for us is that as the congenital general level of activity rises, so does the tendency to startle or cry and so does the tendency to persevere once frustrated. The quiet, less active child appears to suffer less from deprivation and to go to sleep in response to the withdrawal of the nipple. We would account for this difference, by our theory of the activator of the distress cry, as due to the lower level of general stimulation consequent to less feedback from a lower general activity level. The more active child, in contrast, is bombarding himself with a higher level of neural stimulation and is therefore more vulnerable to distress. The more recent findings of Lipton and Richmond have in general supported Friess' findings of congenital differences in autonomic responsiveness. They have also reported that if one cuts down the feedback of the infant's own responses

by swaddling, that the perturbations of heart rate, in response
to a gentle air blast on the skin, are reduced.

The relationship between body type and affect thresholds
generally has not been determined. The relationship between
distress and body type would be somewhat complex. Using
Sheldon's system of classification, we should expect the greatest
vulnerability to distress for the ectomorph, since the ratio of
surface receptors to mass of the body is greatest in his case.
The vulnerability to distress should be next for the mesomorph
and least for the endomorph, who has the smallest number of
surface receptors per unit mass of body. In general this would
be consistent with the classic picture of the high-strung ectomorph
and the jolly endomorph. Unfortunately it has not yet been
possible to demonstrate reliable differences in personality between individuals with different body types. It may, however, be
possible in the future to demonstrate differences in the tendency
for one or another affect to become central in the development
of ectomorphs, endomorphs and mesomorphs. On the other hand,
it is possible that there are no simple relationships between
affects and body types.

The reason we believe that the relationship between body
type and affect may also prove to be somewhat complex is not
simply because of the radical transformations of these innate
relationships by later learning. There can be no argument that
whatever the strength of the original relationship, it may be
grossly attenuated by later learning; and this presumably accounts for the paucity of established findings in constitutional
psychology. We refer rather to the complexity of the simplest
innate relationships. For example, although the endomorph would
be least likely to be excessively bombarded with external stimulation and therefore distressed, yet the mesomorph appears
peculiarly insensitive to pain, compared both with the ectomorph
and endomorph, and would therefore be least likely to experience
distress from this source.

Inasmuch as distress may be activated by different kinds of
excessive neural stimulation, it might be that each body type
would be more or less vulnerable to different sources of distress
so that the more general relationships between body type and
affect in general would be quite low. On the other hand, the

finding, reported by Lois Murphy, of a strong relationship between sympathy and aggression such that those children who were most aggressive were also the children who showed the greatest sympathy for other children is suggestive of a possible high general affective responsiveness which later learning may differentiate, as appears to be the case with general intelligence.

The unlearned basis of distress reduction

The major unlearned basis for the reduction of the distress response is the reduction of the unlearned activators such as hunger, thirst, pain, loud sounds, insupport or any excessively dense neural bombardment. The infant who cries from hunger will ordinarily stop when he is fed. The infant who cries because of pain will ordinarily stop when the source of pain is removed or reduced. The infant who cries because of sounds too loud will ordinarily stop when these are turned off or down. The infant who cries because he is insufficiently supported will stop when he is well supported. What we have said, however, is not always strictly true, since crying itself can set up a level of neural bombardment sufficient to continue to activate the crying, which began in pain, after the pain has been reduced.

Another unlearned basis for the reduction of the distress cry is interferences from other stimuli which reduce crying by activating competing affects. For example, a neonate who is crying may be stopped by being distracted with a bright shiny object. Shirley reported that at five weeks half of her sample of babies would be quieted by being picked up, talked to, caressed.

PARTIAL RESTORATION OF THE PRE-NATAL ENVIRONMENT

There are great changes which occur in the transition from life in the womb to neonatal existence that may interact with and amplify hunger pain and other discomforts and so reduce the threshold of the distress cry. One of these is the change from the muffled sound of the heart beat of the mother to the more varied, louder sounds of the nursery and the home. This includes, in the nursery, the cries of other infants and from time to time the cries produced by the infant itself. Salk has shown that, when the muffled sound of the mother's heart beat is continually reproduced over a loudspeaker in the nursery, the neonates cry less and gain more weight than normal controls while they are in the nursery.

Table 1 shows the weight changes he found from the first to the fourth day of life in newborn babies exposed to the simulated heartbeat sound, compared with a control group.

TABLE 1

WEIGHT CHANGE FROM FIRST TO FOURTH DAY OF LIFE IN
NEWBORN BABIES EXPOSED TO HEARTBEAT SOUND
(Experimental Group)

Birthweight (grams)	Gained Weight			Lost Weight No Change or	
	No.	%		No.	%
2510–3000 ...	27	72.9	...	10	27.1
3010–3500 ...	32	71.1	...	13	28.9
3510 and over ...	12	60.0	...	8	40.0
Total ...	71	69.6	...	31	30.4

WEIGHT CHANGE FROM FIRST TO FOURTH DAY OF LIFE IN
NEWBORN BABIES NOT EXPOSED TO HEARTBEAT SOUND
(Control Group)

Birthweight (grams)	Gained Weight			No Change or Lost Weight	
	No.	%		No.	%
2510–3000 ...	11	37.9	...	18	62.1
3010–3500 ...	19	40.4	...	28	59.6
3510 and over ...	7	19.4	...	29	80.6
Total ...	37	33.0	...	75	67.0

The heartbeat group showed an average (median) increase of 40 grams, whereas the control group showed an average (median) decrease of 20 grams from the first to the fourth day of life.

During the heartbeat phase of the experiment, one or more babies cried 38.4 per cent of the time; in the control phase, one or more cried 59.8 per cent of the time.

Since there was no difference between the heartbeat group

and the control with respect to food intake, it is likely, according to Salk, that the weight gain for the heartbeat babies was due to their decrease in crying. Salk has reported that a replication of this study on newborn infants conducted by Reed at the United Hospitals of Newark, New Jersey, confirmed the original findings. Salk also reports that Reed was able to decrease the heart rate of an infant from 146 beats per minute to 114 beats per minute by exposing it to the normal heartbeat sound. When he discontinued the sound, the infant heart rate returned to 138 beats per minute. Reed also found that a child with 20 per cent second-degree burns slept soundly for six hours in the presence of the heartbeat sound. The sound, when used with pre-operative pediatric patients, was found to enhance sedation so that children seemed to be more relaxed on the arrival in the operating room.

Salk first became aware of the possible significance of the maternal heartbeat rhythm while observing the behavior of a mother rhesus monkey and her newborn, in the Central Park Zoo in New York. He noted that she showed a marked tendency to hold it on her left side, frequently with the newborn's ear pressed against her heart. He thereupon began more systematic observations and found that on forty-two occasions the newborn was held on the left side forty times and on the right side only twice.

Salk then observed human mothers with their newborn babies and found that among (32) left-handed mothers, 78 per cent held their babies on the left side and the others on the right side. Among (255) right-handed mothers, 83 per cent held their babies on the left side. Clearly, both left- and right-handed mothers have a significant tendency to hold their babies on the left side, close to the heart, as was the case with the rhesus monkey observed.

In pursuing this research, Salk also examined paintings and pieces of sculpture produced during the past several hundred years that included a child being held by an adult. Among 466 such works of art, 373 (or 80 per cent) showed the child on the side closest to the adult's heart.

Salk considers that the foetus is imprinted to the 72-per-minute heartbeat of the mother during its intra-uterine life, and that "under natural conditions the imprinted stimuli serve to bring the developing organism into proximity with conditions that enhance its survival. . . . Imprinting compels the organism to seek continued sensory stimulation by coming into contact with its environment and by so doing enhances the development of behavior patterns through associative learning, that have adaptive value."

The idea that humans are imprinted to the mother's heartbeat was tested by Salk by determining the effect of the simulated heartbeat on the time it took children to fall asleep. He argued that when in the presence of an imprinted stimulus "an organism experiences a relative lack of anxiety and the presence of what might be called a feeling of security. Such a stimulus, if existent at bedtime, would lend itself to relaxation and sleep." He therefore expected that children would fall asleep quicker when exposed to a heartbeat sound of 72 paired beats per minute than they would when exposed to no sound or to a metronome sound of 72 beats or to the sound of recorded lullabies.

The result was that young children exposed to the normal heartbeat sound fall asleep in approximately one-half the time required under each of the other three sound conditions; and that there is essentially no difference between these three conditions. Tables 2 and 3 show these results. It should be noted that these children are not newborn but range in age from 16 to 37 months (except for one of 50 months).

Salk interprets these results as evidence that the mother's heartbeat is an imprinting stimulus on the foetus, and that it therefore "has effects which are not obtainable with other sound conditions. The fact that the metronome sound, set at the same frequency and being very similar to the heartbeat sound, produced no effects at all indicates all the more that the normal heartbeat sound has very unique qualities for the human."

This evidence is very impressive, and there should be added to it one of Salk's earlier findings, that when a heartbeat rhythm at 128 beats per minute was presented for a short period of time, there was a noticeable increase in crying and restlessness and that this was also the case when a gallop heartbeat rhythm was presented.

TABLE 2

Time* Taken for Each Child to Fall Asleep During Each Observation in Relation to Various Sound Conditions At Bedtime

NAME	AGE (mos.)	NO SOUND USED (minutes)	Av.	HEARTBEAT (minutes)	Av.	METRONOME** (minutes)	Av.	LULLABIES (minutes)	Av.
Donna	23	60 60 50 60	57.50	15 10 10 20	13.75	25 55 60 50	47.50	10 60 25 60	38.75
Orlando	27	60 25 35 45	41.25	15 40 35 20	27.50	50 40 45 40	43.75	30 60 60 55	51.25
Gladys	35	60 60 55 60	58.75	15 25 15 60	28.75	25 25 60 50	40.00	40 60 20 35	38.75
Israel	24	25 30 30 --	28.33	25 25 -- --	25.00	-- -- -- --	-----	-- -- -- --	-----
Nilsa	25	60 60 60 60	60.00	35 60 20 35	37.50	60 60 55 60	58.75	10 30 60 10	27.50
Kim	21	60 20 30 45	38.75	20 15 10 10	13.75	35 50 15 25	31.25	10 20 60 20	27.50
Michele	25	35 60 40 45	45.00	30 15 15 20	20.00	35 40 60 60	48.75	15 60 60 30	41.25
Bernard	23	10 15 55 55	33.75	40 60 30 5	33.75	-- -- -- --	-----	-- -- -- --	-----
Dolores	23	25 20 20 55	30.00	25 10 5 20	15.00	30 50 55 40	43.75	20 35 50 50	38.75
Jimmy S.	50	60 60 25 60	51.25	20 60 15 35	32.50	60 50 60 30	50.00	60 60 60 60	60.00
Diana	21	15 55 50 60	45.00	20 20 50 10	25.00	25 35 25 25	27.50	45 55 40 40	45.00
Jimmy O.	24	60 45 40 50	48.75	10 50 25 10	23.75	40 40 60 50	47.50	-- -- -- --	-----
Reginald	20	15 30 20 60	31.25	25 15 20 --	20.00	-- -- -- --	-----	-- -- -- --	-----
Elton	22	25 30 20 55	32.50	15 15 15 20	16.25	45 50 60 60	53.75	35 15 30 60	35.00
Mario	20	15 10 15 25	16.25	15 5 15 5	10.00	35 30 25 60	37.50	50 30 60 45	46.25
Evelyn	28	60 60 55 50	56.25	20 15 10 50	23.75	25 60 60 60	51.25	60 60 60 60	60.00
Manuella	32	60 60 40 60	55.00	30 35 15 15	23.75	60 60 60 40	55.00	60 35 60 60	53.75
Jasmine	28	50 60 30 45	46.25	15 25 10 30	20.00	60 60 60 60	60.00	60 60 60 60	60.00
Debra C.	27	60 60 45 45	52.50	35 30 20 55	35.00	60 60 60 60	60.00	60 60 60 60	60.00
Kim L.	32	60 60 50 30	50.00	15 30 10 35	22.50	60 60 60 55	58.75	60 60 60 60	60.00
Thomas	26	40 60 60 60	55.00	5 5 5 25	10.00	60 60 60 60	60.00	60 60 60 50	57.50
David	24	50 60 35 55	50.00	40 20 15 35	27.50	25 60 60 35	45.00	50 60 60 45	53.75
Alvaro	31	40 45 50 60	48.75	5 5 5 35	12.50	-- 50 60 60	56.67	60 50 60 50	55.00
Chauncy	16	60 60 55 30	51.25	15 10 25 45	23.75	25 60 50 60	48.75	60 35 60 55	52.50
Larry	24	55 60 -- --	57.50	35 20 25 --	26.67	-- -- -- --	-----	-- -- -- --	-----
Raymond	37	60 60 60 50	57.50	50 10 10 55	31.75	60 60 60 60	60.00	60 60 60 60	60.00

* Observations were made at 5 minute intervals. Where time taken to fall asleep is 60 minutes, in most cases it was considerably longer; for practical purposes systematic observation was stopped at that point.
** Metronome — set at 72 beats per minute with same sound qualities as heartbeat.

TABLE 3

AVERAGE TIME* (MINUTES) TAKEN TO FALL ASLEEP FOR
A GROUP OF CHILDREN (16 TO 37 MONTHS OF AGE**)
UNDER VARIOUS SOUND CONDITIONS AT BEDTIME

Sound Conditions at Bedtime	Average Time Taken to Fall Asleep (minutes)	Number of Observations
No sound used (usual conditions)	46.04	101
Normal heartbeat sound (72 paired beats per minute)	23.00	100
Metronome sound (72 single beats per minute)	49.25	87
Recorded lullabies (played continuously)	48.69	84
	Total	372

* All children were observed at five minute intervals from the time they were put in bed. Observations were stopped after 60 minutes; If the child was still awake at this time, it was nevertheless considered asleep at 60 minutes.
** One child was 50 months of age.

Before we can consider the evidence conclusive, however, it would be necessary to stimulate children with simulated heartbeats ranging from a rate of a few per minute to one hundred or so, as well as a continuous sound of the same frequency and intensity. We cannot at this point be certain of just how specific the response to the exact rate of 72 heartbeats per minute is until its rate is more systematically varied. Salk understandably hesitated to use the very rapid rate of 128 beats for fear of disturbing the newborn; but one might, by using many infants each stimulated for brief periods of time, plot a function of the impact of variations in rate on the activation or reduction of the distress cry.

In addition to the question of the specificity of such stimulation and its relation to imprinting, there are two additional alternative interpretations which one might place upon these results.

One rests upon the possibility of redintegration. To the extent to which the foetus was relaxed in the womb, it might be argued that any stimulation which closely resembled that stimulation might via redintegration produce the same response of relaxation in later extra-uterine life. Sontag has shown that the heart rate of the foetus can be conditioned *in utero* to auditory stimulation that is produced outside the mother's body. It is not unreasonable, therefore, to assume that some learning occurs to the sound of the heartbeat while the foetus is in the womb, and that similar stimulation outside the womb after birth might produce the same relaxation of the body and decrease in heart rate as occurred before in the womb.

A second alternative explanation is that the infant relaxes and stops crying to the sound of the heartbeat outside the womb for the same reason that it does so in the womb—namely, that this represents one of the many alternative optimal kinds of stimulation for the human organism in general. It is well known that adults and infants alike are soothed and relaxed by rhythmic sounds—be they lullabies, the sounds of the ocean or of crickets in the country; by rhythmic motion, both passive motion as in the cradle and active motion as in swimming or in being walked in the arms of a human being; by warmth, as in the bath or in sunbathing; and by rhythmic stimulation of the skin, as in caressing and stroking.

It is also clear that stimulation of any kind—photic, thermal or auditory—has a bandwidth within which stimulation is optimal and usually pleasurable (or at least not painful) but outside of which it is not optimal and is usually accompanied by pain and a distress. Therefore, too rapid motion, too intense tactile stimulation of the skin, too bright light, too loud sound, too hot stimulation can be extremely painful and/or distressing.

Since in the evolutionary process the conditions of the womb are likely to have evolved an internal environment which is optimal for human function, the test for the specificity of rhythms and intensities of stimulation, either via imprinting or via redintegration, is complicated by the possible confounding of generally optimal conditions with these specific other mechanisms. In other words, if the mother's heartbeat is normally soothing while the foetus is in the womb, it can also be so outside the womb—whether it has been imprinted or whether the neonate remembers the earlier condition or neither.

There is some support for the second alternative in the disturbance which Salk reported as occurring when the simulated heartbeat was increased to 128 beats per minute. One might argue that such a rhythm probably disturbs the child, both *in utero* and as a neonate, because it is innately disturbing whenever and wherever it is experienced.

One ideal test which would resolve the argument whether reduction of distress in the neonate is via redintegration or via optimal stimulation would be the demonstration that there is a kind of stimulation which is not disturbing in the womb, which is not optimal for the child in the extra-uterine environment, but which would nonetheless stop crying in the newborn child. The upside-down position of the body might provide such a test case. If it were the case that putting the neonate in the upside-down position reliably stopped crying, it would constitute evidence for the assumption of reduction of distress via redintegration, unconfounded by the common factor of optimal stimulation.

This assumes that the human animal is designed for the right-side-up or prone position, rather than the inverse posture; and that the inverse posture is not an optimal one for man. That redintegration may be operating in such a case is suggested by the preference of adolescents for assuming the position of head back and down with legs stretched up against the wall while telephoning or reading, and for the use of such postures in yoga exercises to induce relaxation.

Yet despite the possibility that Salk's results might be interpreted on the basis of an optimal stimulation hypothesis, a redintegration hypothesis or a combined optimal stimulation-redintegration hypothesis, his evidence for specific imprinting is impressive evidence for his interpretation, inasmuch as lullabies and a 72-beat metronome did not relax the children. A conclusive answer must await the determination of the effects of systematic variation in the simulated heartbeat itself to determine just how specific the effects of the exact rate of heartbeat is upon the child.

Finally, we would disagree with Salk's equation of distress crying with anxiety. The distressed child will not gain weight as rapidly as the non-distressed one, despite equal food intake, as Salk has shown; he will not sleep as readily as the relaxed child. But neither of these necessarily argues that the distressed child is an anxious child.

The other change in the transition from life in the womb to neonatal existence is the loss of the predominantly non-visual, interoceptive world in which the infant is gently supported in a space which is in constant cushioned motion. Not only is the neonatal posture quite different in adding rudimentary vision and other exteroceptive bombardment, but characteristically the constant support and motion is absent. The effect of adding vision and other exterosensory information would in itself have radically changed the nature of the conscious field. Particularly it would attenuate the former awareness from the vestibular receptors and from the proprioceptors. One can experience the nature of this shift by closing the eyes when slightly intoxicated by alcohol. Under these conditions one will suddenly feel quite unsteady and dizzy. The vestibular stimulation responsible for this is ordinarily masked by the greater density of visual stimulation. The same effect may be experienced by lying down with eyes closed in the back seat of an automobile in motion. The sudden amplification of auditory and proprioceptive and vestibular stimulation unmasked by the removal of the interfering visual stimulation produces a heightened awareness of suspension with movement in space which must be similar to the reverse shift from womb to extra-uterine existence with respect to awareness of body support and motion.

It is our belief that this change, added to hunger pains and other body discomforts, in effect lowers the threshold of the distress cry. In addition to the use of the cradle and its motion to calm the crying infant, which is some evidence for the view that the reduction of the difference between intra-uterine and extra-uterine stimulation will raise the threshold of the distress cry and frequently stop the crying of the neonate, we have found, as we have noted before, more evidence for this hypothesis. One day when I heard my son, age one month, crying, I lifted him out of his crib and held him in my arms while sitting in a chair beside his crib. He continued to cry. Still holding him in the same position I stood up, preparatory to walking the floor with him. To my surprise this was sufficient to stop the crying and was thereafter a reproducible phenomenon. He would stop crying not as a function of motion, but of being held in about the same position as if he had been in the womb. The exact position proved not to be critical. What seemed critical was the approximate reproduction of the pull of gravity on the body, suspended by human muscles in a state of moderate tension.

In the case of both the reproduction of the auditory environment through the loudspeaker and the reproduction of the state of being gently supported in space, there are at least two distinct ways in which distress may be reduced, in addition to Salk's suggestion of the possibility of imprinting. One is by a reduction in the density and variety of neural bombardment, and the other is by a return to a more familiar environment in which the infant presumably was more relaxed and in which he did not respond with distress either because of the more low-keyed stimulation, or because his threshold of awareness was very high or because the threshold of the distress response was very high. It is also possible that the way in which this mimicking of the intra-uterine environment affects the distress response is through the synergistic effort of both a reduction in actual sensory bombardment as well as a return to a more familiar environment in which the neonate is accustomed to relax rather than to cry.

In either event it is clear that the cry may be reduced for some time by reducing some of the background stimulation which accompanies other stimuli capable of evoking the cry, such as hunger or pain.

Oral activity

Another way in which distress may be reduced, or at least attenuated, is through competing oral responses. The almost universal reliance, among both children and adults, on oral automatisms to relieve distress and/or other negative affects is well known. Beginning with the pacifier, the thumb or the blanket, and ending with the cigarette, there are few human beings who do not derive solace from sucking or biting something in their mouths.

Despite the universality of this phenomenon its rationale is still somewhat opaque. Freudian theory suggested it was essentially a derivative of the hunger drive, and by extension, of the symbiotic mother-child relationship. While this is a plausible explanation, it places too great a burden on the satisfactions inherent in the feeding experience. As we have seen from Harlow's work with monkeys, the clinging to the more pneumatic surrogate mother was preferred over dependence on the surrogate mother who fed the infant monkey. David Levy some years ago offered an alternative theory to account for excessive finger-sucking and other oral automatisms. This was that there was an oral activity need over and above the hunger and thirst drives, and when this former need received insufficient gratification during feeding periods, it would continue to press for satisfaction after feeding and so produce oral activity which was independent of hunger and thirst.

Levy presented persuasive evidence for this theory in a series of experiments in which he varied the amount of oral activity during feeding. Two groups of young puppies were bottle-fed the same amount of milk but with different sized holes in the nipples. Those puppies who had nipples with small holes had to suck hard for their milk. At the end of this meal they neither sought nor accepted additional sucking from fingers or other suckable objects. Those puppies who had nipples with large holes received the freer flowing milk with relatively little sucking effort on their part. These animals did seek and accept further sucking experience, on fingers or other suckable objects.

Levy also presented evidence that excessive finger-sucking in children was associated with mothers whose breasts were relatively free-flowing and presumably failed to sufficiently satisfy the need for oral activity. He demonstrated a related need in chickens, the need to peck. When he raised chickens on the ground so that they could peck on the hard surface as they ate, there was no residual pecking activity. When he transferred these animals to a wire mesh, so that there was no hard surface on which to peck as they ate, they responded by pecking on a scapegoat chicken and denuded him of his feathers. When he placed these animals back on the ground, this pecking stopped.

Despite Levy's impressive evidence, Sears' test of this hypothesis with human infants failed to confirm it. Infants reared on milk from cups did not develop the residual sucking which

Levy's theory would have predicted. However, even if Levy's theory were entirely confirmed, there would still remain the question why such a need should provide such general solace against distress, and why it should become so insatiable a phenomenon (in many cases to the point of addiction), since a biological need should be self-limiting.

A theory of sucking response as innate reducer of distress

Our theory is that sucking on something in the mouth is a competitor and therefore a reducer of the use of the mouth as an emitter of the cry of distress. It is superior to such a strictly defensive maneuver as keeping a stiff upper lip, because it moves and relaxes the mouth rather than increasing the tonus of the mouth and thereby increasing the level of density of stimulation from feedback from the mouth. Most other competitors of the cry, such as drumming the fingers, clenching the toes or fists, or stiffening the lip, or the whole face, run the risk of further heightening distress through excessive stimulation. Sucking, however, reduces muscle tonus and thereby interferes with the activation of the distress cry or reduces it, if it has already been activated. Since any sudden reduction of stimulation, of distress or any other affect activates joy, smoking and other oral needs first become rewarding by changing negative affect to positive affect and then produce insatiable monopolistic addiction by the generation of negative affect when sucking is not possible, and by the reduction of this negative affect when sucking is possible, in a circular, spiraling intensification of both postitive and negative affect.

The consequences of prolonged crying

In addition to the reduction of an innate activator of distress, the partial return of pre-natal conditions, the instigation of competing affect and the instigation of competing oral activity, another unlearned basis for the reduction of the distress cry is the state of relaxation which may be produced by continuous crying. Crying may continue for long periods of time without apparent habituation, either of its activators or of the crying response itself. However, if the activator of crying is a source which is of just above threshold value of density of neural bombardment, the crying response itself may be capable of producing sufficient relaxation of skeletal musculature ultimately to turn itself off.

Another circumstance under which crying may be self-limiting is when the inhibition of the crying response has become a major component in the conditions which activate the cry. If in response to an adequate stimulus to the cry, the individual attempts to suppress it, the density of neural stimulation may increase radically. If then the cry breaks through this attempted inhibition, the total density of stimulation is suddenly sharply reduced. This sudden gradient of neural stimulation reduction may even be sufficient to produce the smile of enjoyment of what has been called a "good cry." In any event the elimination of the additional load of excessive stimulation involved in the attempted inhibition of the cry may be sufficient, along with some relaxation of skeletal musculature, to make the cry self-limiting.

Further, the cry may be innately self-limiting when it has produced a state of exhaustion and depletion of physiological reserves. How much such a burning-out of the distress cry is due to exhaustion and how much it is due to the attempt to avoid the pain which excessive and chronic crying may entail, we do not know. There is evidence against the entire self-limiting, burning-out hypotheses, however, in the phenomenon of the three-month colic. This is a loud continuous crying with a somewhat cyanotic face. Crying sometimes ends abruptly only to begin again. This crying is almost invulnerable to interference by holding, feeding or whatever—and if the crying is stopped, it is ordinarily only a temporary cessation. The abdomen is distended and the legs are flexed on the chest.

As Lakin has shown, the mothers of colicky infants are more insecure, less well-adjusted to their husbands, have greater competitiveness with their mothers, and have more ambivalence about their role than do mothers of non-colicky infants. Despite the continuing ministrations of an ambivalent mother, the colicky infant nonetheless usually stops by the end of three months. It is not likely that the mother's basic attitudes have changed, nor that all such mothers would feel more positively towards their colicky infants at about the same stage of their development.

Ambrose has argued very persuasively that the termination of colic at the end of three months is due to the fact that by this time the cognitive development has reached a crucial stage: the infant becomes capable of responding positively to the mother, discriminating her not only from strangers but in effect discriminating the rewarding, good mother from the punitive, bad mother who causes crying. He supports this argument further by evidence from Piaget and others that at this age there appears the coordination between two or more schemata.

Against Ambrose's argument is the fact that the infant has not by this time yet learned to discriminate the mother's face from the face of a stranger, using the criterion of shyness in the presence of the face of the stranger and smiling restricted to the face of the mother. If this differentiation has not been achieved by three months, it is questionable whether a differentiation between the good and the bad mother could have been learned by this time. It is of course entirely conceivable that the maturation of the nervous system reaches a level by three months which reduces the excessive responsiveness of the infant to stimulation. Ambrose's hypothesis is not entirely implausible, but further research would appear to be in order to settle this question. Whatever turns out to be the determinant of the sudden reduction of the three-month colic, the phenomenon itself argues strongly against exhaustion or depletion as a major factor in the limiting of the crying response. The response would appear to be extraordinarily resistant to self-limitation, unless additional, costlier affects such as fear are concurrently activated. What has been called "stress" is an indeterminate amalgam in terms of affect. The word has been essentially used to characterize whatever negative affects are activated under circumstances which are not optimal for human beings. The self-limiting characteristic and the state of exhaustion are both reached much more quickly when terror, with or without distress or anger, is produced by stressful circumstances.

Chapter 15

Distress – Anguish Dynamics:
The Adult Consequences of
the Socialization of Crying

THE UBIQUITY OF SUFFERING

Distress—anguish is a fundamental human affect primarily because of the ubiquity of human suffering and the consequent universality of the cry of distress. Anxiety, by contrast, is properly an emergency affect. When life and death hang in the balance, most animals have been endowed with the capacity for terror. This is appropriate if life is to be surrendered only very dearly. The cost of terror is so great that the body was not designed for chronic activation of this affect. A human being who responds as if he had reason to be chronically terrorized is properly diagnosed as ill. This is as unnatural a state as perpetual hunger would be, since both of these are incompatible with optimal existence. Whereas the lower forms lack the cognitive capacities to create a chronically terrifying environment, in the absence of a continuing present danger to life, man is quite capable of linking terror with imaginary threats.

To recapitulate our argument, it seems very likely that the differentiation of distress from fear was required in part because the coexistence of superior cognitive powers of anticipation with an affect as toxic as fear could have destroyed man if this was the only affect expressing suffering. What was called for was a less toxic, but still negative, affect which would motivate human beings to solve disagreeable problems without too great a physiological cost, without too great a probability of running away from the many problems which confront the human being, and which would permit anticipation of trouble at an optimal psychic and biological cost. Such, we think, is the human cry of distress.

Because trouble is ubiquitous and because anticipation is perennial, man is forever courting suffering. Although the world might be made safe enough to minimize terror, it is inconceivable, given the inherent uncertainty of the world in which we live, that man's existence can be proofed against suffering.

There are three general sources of human suffering—the ills of the body, the frustrations of interpersonal relationships and the recalcitrance of nature to human striving and achievement. The body is inherently vulnerable and mortal. Interpersonal relationships at the very best are also mortal, incomplete and labile. Finally, the distance between aspiration and achievement is a perennial source of distress.

No philosophy which does not make its peace with human suffering can long satisfy. One of the central human needs fulfilled by religion is a recognition of the reality of suffering. Indeed it may well be that the recognition of suffering was a more critical function of religion than its promise of salvation. Melioristic philosophies dedicated to the progressive reduction of suffering have failed to satisfy the chronic needs of the human animal for confrontation, recognition of and sympathy for his suffering.

Nor should any theory of personality fail to address itself to this domain. This is because distress is suffered daily by all human beings, as they become tired, as they encounter difficulties in solving problems, as they interact with other human beings in ways which are less than ideal. Distress is as general a negative affect as excitement is a positive one. Between them they account for a major part of the posture of human beings towards themselves, towards each other, towards the world they live in.

DISTRESS ABOUT OTHER AFFECTS:
THE ARCHAIC INFANTILE TABOOS IGNORED
BY PSYCHOANALYSIS

Although distress is ubiquitous, the human being nonetheless enjoys some freedom with respect to the objects about which he will suffer. Among the objects which can be learned to activate distress are the other affects. Not only does the interruption of excitement or enjoyment produce distress, but we may be taught to be distressed at the activation of any positive or negative affect.

In the past history of most adults is a very archaic set of taboos produced by punishing and making the child cry, utterly inappropriate for any adult by most cultural norms and ordinarily outgrown in normal development. These are not to be confused with the furniture of Freud's superego, or their somber derivatives in Melanie Klein. They concern neither sex, nor aggression, nor eating nor being clean.

We refer to taboos frequently appropriate to preserve the life of the very young, or the comfort of his parent. First is curiosity. The very young child sometimes must be restrained in his philosophic excursions into the nature of things, lest he destroy himself and the objects of his curiosity. Second is the fact of self-injury. Whenever a child has in fact injured himself, many parents add punishment to this already disturbing fact by their concern and further punishment lest the child not appreciate how he might avoid what he has done to himself.

Third is the impulse to cooperate and help his parents. A mother who is cleaning the house may be so slowed down by her cooperative child that she punishes the child for his misguided help. Fourth is the identification impulse. There is no single wish possessed by the normal child that is stronger than the wish to be like the beloved parent. Such a wish, however, produces a great variety of behaviors which may jeopardize the child's life or discomfort his parents. Not all or even much of such behavior is so motivated. Punishment for identification is often punishment for something other than the impulse itself, as far as the parent is concerned; to the child, it may produce a taboo on his deepest wish.

Fifth is the smile and laughter of joy. Because the child's delight is noisy and boisterous it may be punished. Sixth is the generation of noise in general. Apart from explosive laughter, there are numerous occasions when the child's spontaneous high-decibel level discomfits his parents who may respond with punishment sufficient to produce distress crying.

Seventh, there is the taboo on the most intense form of curiosity, staring into the eyes of the stranger. Although the child is initially shy in the presence of the stranger, once he has over-come this barrier he is consumed with the wish to explore the face of the new person. Since this may be a source of unease both to the parents and to the guest, this if often forbidden with sufficient severity to induce distress in the child.

Eighth is shyness in the presence of a stranger. Just as often as a child is made to cry because he insists on staring at strangers, so he may also be punished for his shyness when confronting either strange peers or adults. A child can be made to suffer distress because he feels shy and will not shake the hand of the guest or play with the child of the guest. Ordinarily the parent may increase the intensity of the shyness or shame in the presence of the stranger, and later, when the guest has left, evoke distress by some form of punishment for his shyness.

Ninth is the linkage of fear and distress. A child who is afraid to go down a dark hall into his dark room may be spanked and made to cry, so that showing fear is learned to be a source of distress.

In addition to distress evoked by other affects, these affects are further tabooed by the punishment for the very impulse to cry in response to punishment for the original affect. A child whose loud excitement has provoked a spanking which produces crying may be spanked again for the crying. In effect, this produces additional punishment for his excitement. This set of taboos is ordinarily masked by later learning designed to circumvent the watchful eyes of the parents.

The compacts of the young have, among their chief aims, the satisfaction of many of these human impulses which parents have appropriately thwarted at certain ages. Parents may never repeal or sufficiently attenuate such prohibitions, and they may never appreciate their collective weight. To the extent to which they are not circumvented and outgrown, these prohibitions produce a residual affect hunger with a vulnerability to massive intrusions.

In the extreme case the outcome of the imposition of such a set of taboos may be catastrophic—an individual unable to explore, to tolerate his own injuries or sickness, to express tenderness by helping another, to identify with those closest to him, to express his dissatisfaction in further crying, to express his delights, to raise his voice at any time or to achieve intimacy by looking into the eyes of another person.

The social inheritance of distress about affects

These taboos are, of course, not the only way to learn to be distressed about one's own affects. There is also a social inheritance of distress inasmuch as the child will be distressed by that which distresses the parent, as Freud has shown us in the case of specifically sexual excitement, and curiosity and anger. In Psychoanalytic theory, however, distress plays a very minor role, and sexuality and anger were assumed to be controlled not by distress but by the threat of castration and the anxiety this was presumed to evoke. We say presumed, because, as we shall show later, the threat of castration is as much an activator of shame as it is of terror.

Whether sexual excitement and curiosity are controlled by fear or distress, or both, will depend on the severity and type of sanctions invoked by parents. If a child is spanked for masturbation, much will depend on how severe the pain is, and on what kind of verbal lecture accompanies his punishment for sex play, and particularly on what the affect of the parent is. He may suffer no more than the distress which would ordinarily accompany pain, or he may suffer more shame than distress because of what he feels to be the indignity of being spanked or because of the alienation from the parent which this creates; or he may indeed be terrorized at being suddenly overwhelmed by an apparently monstrous, enraged punitive parent.

The same options hold for the socialization of anger. The display of anger by a child towards his parent, by facial expression, speech, or in aggressive action may be inhibited by punishment from the parent which produces the cry of distress, or fear or shame depending upon the severity and the nature of the punishment. In any event, anger is, of all the affects, one of the prime objects of distress because it is difficult for any parent to respond to anger from the child with indifference or reward. In response to the anger of the child, the parent is very likely, at the least, to produce in the child distress, if not fear and shame.

With respect to which affects are learned to evoke distress, all may; although more commonly parents vary in which affects they socialize by evoking distress and which affects they socialize in other ways. A child may be made to cry if he becomes angry and defiant, but made to hang his head in shame for shouting too loud in his excitement, and be frightened if he is found masturbating. Another parent may use shaming techniques for the control of all affects including shyness itself; and still others may generally terrorize children by threats of physical punishment. As a consequence, distress may be experienced about any other affect or group of affects or about no affect.

Other objects of distress and other influences

In the discussion above we have included, in addition to the affects, some actions which are closely linked to affects: such as the exploratory behavior powered by interest, the destructive behavior powered by anger, helping behavior, and imitative behavior powered by excitement or enjoyment, timid behavior powered by fear and sexual behavior powered in part by excitement.

However, with respect to the impact of socialization the possible objects of distress are limited only by the imagination of the parent who cares enough to make the child distressed about whatever it is which he wishes to discourage in the child. Clearly this usually encompasses the control of behavior and belief as well as the control of affects. Historically, at some time or place, every variety of behavior has been made the object of suffering. Parents have made it distressing to be overly active or passive, to be bold or cautious, or to be overly friendly or too reserved. One child's delight can be another child's distress.

Not only do parents enjoy some freedom in what they may choose to make the child distressed about, and thereby to some extent to make the future adult distressed about, but they may employ very different methods in producing distress. These vary from the infliction of punishment through physical pain, drive deprivation, verbal scolding, leaving the child alone to the parent's crying out in distress himself.

Further, the objects of distress are not limited to what we

have learned to be disturbed by in childhood. The major sources of distress throughout life arise from the body, its pains and illnesses, from work and its problems, and from the vicissitudes of interpersonal relationships. The environment is constantly also creating new disturbances and challenges which create distress. Development necessarily entails the meeting of new challenges and, even within a constant environment, a growing sensitivity to challenges which were unappreciated earlier in development.

Not only does the spectrum of sources of distress grow wider with development, but there are many sources of distress which so much depend on environmental vicissitudes as to be essentially independent of personality and personality development. Thus serious economic depressions, wars, illnesses and injuries of the self and of love objects, deaths of love objects, and similar misfortunes may subject children, adolescents, and adults alike to severe distress over which they can exercise little control. Neither personality nor life ends in childhood and there is no certain way of guaranteeing that a child who has experienced only excitement and enjoyment may not, beginning in adolescence, be vulnerable to severe distress the rest of his life through circumstances over which he can exercise little control.

Distress as a necessary condition for the formation of stable objects

What an individual will be distressed about depends in part, but only in part, on what he is excited by and what he enjoys. To the extent to which he has enjoyed anything or been excited by anything, he is vulnerable to distress at any interruption to the continuation of such enjoyment or any barrier to repetition or increased contact with it. As we have noted before, however, it is equally the case that what one has been made to suffer for can also become the object of intense enjoyment when that distress is suddenly reduced. Suffering and enjoyment are not only activated by each other, so that one can suffer most about what one enjoys and cares for, and can enjoy most what has cost one suffering, but these two affects are capable of mutually so increasing each other's intensity that intense and enduring affective investment can be centered on particular objects. We have already examined the dynamics of such spiralling affective and cognitive constructions in connection with the affect of enjoyment. If one wishes to guarantee commitment to any object, be it a person, an institution, a profession, or a way of life, one must not only provide intense rewards but also sufficient distress, in the form of challenges, separations, and deprivations so that excitement is continually sustained by these sources of uncertainty, and by the continual redefinition of the object, and enjoyment heightened by the overcoming of these impediments, by reunion with the love object, and by the attainment of the redefined "new" object now seen in another perspective following distress.

A WIDER SPECTRUM OF OBJECTS OF DISTRESS AS A PRE-CONDITION FOR THE ACTUALIZATION OF HUMAN POTENTIAL

Because of the freedom of objects of distress, and because distress is a necessary condition for the formation of stable commitment to objects, distress can continually enlarge the spectrum of objects which can concern the human being. The objects of distress are in no way limited to what we have learned to be disturbed by in childhood. Development necessarily entails new objects of distress as much as it entails new objects of excitement and enjoyment. If I do not learn to become distressed by what can happen to my friends, to my wife, to my children, to my profession, to my community, to my nation, and to my world, then I have certainly failed to become completely human.

Distress is not a toxic crippling affect which necessarily generates avoidance strategies, but rather promotes remedial strategies which can attack the sources of distress. The presence of distress indicates a potential for remedial action either by the individual, or with his support. Therefore one might assess the level of normal development by the width of the distress spectrum. To the extent to which there are many kinds of distress insensitivity on the part of any individual, there is developmental retardation. Such retardation is not inconsistent with otherwise normal development. A profile of distress sensitivity might also be used as a measure of the development of a society. Any society which is not distressed by its illnesses, its injustices, its discrepancies between abilities and achievements, its lack of excitement and enjoyment, or its fears, humiliations and hostilities is an underdeveloped society. If remediable conditions cause no distress and therefore no remedial action, a person or a society is in a condition analogous to one who is sick but who develops no temperature, or no other strategies to deal with its disturbance. Although a person or a society in continual distress is not in an optimal condition, the total lack of distress when non-optimal conditions could be remedied if there were distress is a more serious deviation from optimal functioning.

Although distress-anguish is more tolerable than fear-terror, it is sufficiently unpleasant that human beings would rather not experience distress if it is possible to avoid the experience. If development requires a widening of the spectrum of objects of suffering, then the education of the young as well as of the adult requires exposure to more and more sources of distress. If this is not to founder on increasing resistance against the experience of empathic distress, it must be preceded and accompanied by experiences which create excitement and enjoyment in connection with the objects of distress and by experiences which create excitement and enjoyment with the potential affective rewards from remedial action. In the case of one of our most serious remediable problems, the plight of the Southern Negro citizen, emphatic distress should first be built upon delineations of his life and character as he existed here and now which excite and delight his fellow white, which stress that which the white admires, enjoys, or respects, and which enhances communion and identification, and upon glimpses into a future America in which there is mutual respect and enjoyment between all persons. If and when positive affect is experienced by whites about Negroes, then the distress and anger which are necessary to mobilize remedial action will be more easily activated and sustained. No one has to urge distress upon anyone who becomes aware that a beloved is suffering.

ADULT MODIFICATIONS OF THE CRY OF DISTRESS

The reader must be puzzled at our earlier affirmation that distress is suffered daily by all human beings. Nothing seems less common than to see an adult cry. And yet we are persuaded that the cry, and the awareness of the cry, as distress and suffering, is ubiquitous. The adult has learned to cry as an adult. It is a brief cry, or a muted cry, or a part of a cry or a miniature cry, or a substitute cry, or an active defense against the cry, that we see in place of the infant's cry for help.

First, it is not altogether true that the adult does not cry. Under the pressure of sudden unexpected pain the adult may be caught sufficiently defenseless that he cries out in pain. But characteristically this cry is a brief one. Immediately following the pain, even if it continues, the adult erect defenses against the continuation of the cry. Whereas an infant suddenly feeling pain might cry out and continue to cry long after the pain has abated, the adult will minimize the duration of the overt cry once he has emitted it. The first adult transformation of the innate cry then is on the duration of the response.

Another transformation on the cry is on its intensity or loudness. Even when unexpectedly pained, the adult's cry may be muffled and muted. A patient in a dentist's chair may be heard to emit soft, low cries of pain, sometimes immediately followed by appropriate verbal expression—"ouch!"

A more complete transformation of the cry is the whine, in which one can hear the plaintive tones of the cry embedded in speech, usually divested of the facial grimaces of the cry. There are individuals who cry to each other in the complaint, "Did you hear the latest? I think it an outrage. I can't understand it—someone should do something." Such a cry may indeed be a transformed tantrum, the combination of the cry of distress and the cry of rage. This type of shared crying in and through speech has powerful adhesive properties. The shared, verbalized cry-complaint can weld dyads and larger groups into very stable, cohesive alliances against common enemies. If you and I cry about the same things or people we can enjoy each other.

The mute facial cry

Another transformation in which it is a part of the cry which carries the burden of communication to self and others is the facial cry, stripped of sound. This may be a transient, or a chronic, frozen cry. In the transient facial cry, there is a sudden turning down of the corners of the mouth, and a raising of the inner ends of the eyebrows which produces oblique eyebrows, and a contraction of the central fasciae of the frontal muscle which produces quadrangular furrows, shaped like a horseshoe in the middle of the forehead. The adult who is suddenly distressed may emit the entire innate facial response which accompanies the cry, except that he has learned to control the vocal part of the cry, and so he cries silently.

If the reader will "send" such a set of messages to his face, the feedback from this set of facial responses can be experienced as sadness without the vocal components. In the frozen cry this same set of facial responses has become habitual and chronic. This face always looks sad, and we think the individual behind this face feels sad whenever his attention is caught by this perpetual bombardment. Since we believe the sensory feedback produced by the muscular responses may or may not be transformed into conscious reports, it is not necessarily the case that the chronic, frozen cry is a chronically conscious experience of sadness. Our observation of faces has also disclosed a third type of facial cry which is neither transient nor chronically frozen, but what we have called sub-clinical.

In this case there appears to be a chronic readiness for the facial distress response, which appears whenever the individual is not otherwise engaged. These appear to be individuals of manic-depressive personality structure. Their faces are highly animated when engaged in conversation with others, or when interested in their work, but who when alone and unoccupied characteristically assume the expression of the frozen cry. Not infrequently individuals may also show this expression when they are in public places, but feel alone, as in a subway train in a metropolitan area, where there is such anonymity that the individual may feel that he is quite alone. Over the years we have observed thousands of such faces in repose, which are crying silently.

Another variant of the mute facial cry is the miniature, readiness cry. In this case the facial muscles are readied for the full facial cry in the manner of a runner who sets himself for the gunshot which will start the race. The runner is perfectly still, but his muscles have been placed in a position such that he can start to run in the shortest possible time following the signal. We have observed facial responses which are miniaturized cries which, either with further amplification or with reduction of countervailing responses, or both, would become a full-fledged facial cry. In such cases there is a tightening of the mouth, eyebrow and forehead muscles, which if further contracted would result in the facial cry. In addition there may be a tightening of muscles antagonistic to these, which guarantee that the readiness will not be translated into further overt responses, in much the same way that the runner prevents himself from running at the same time that he sets himself to run at the signal. This miniature, readiness cry may itself be transient, chronic or sub-clinical. If it is transient, it may appear very briefly in the course of a conversation, and the one who sees it may be only vaguely aware that something has momentarily disturbed the other one. If it is a chronic, frozen set of the muscles to be ready to cry, such a face is less obviously sad than one with the chronic frozen, full facial cry, but nonetheless gives a predominant expression of sadness just below the surface. If it is of the sub-clinical type the impression is identical with that of the more chronic type, but the element of contrast to the preceding animation is suggestive of a deeper split within the personality, i.e., a surface-depth split as well as a sharp positive-negative affect polarization.

The substitute cry

Next, there is a substitute cry, in which there is no sound and no facial responses, but in which the massive set of motor messages which would have been sent to the face and vocal cords are sent to some other set of muscles thus providing some expression of the original cry. Thus in pain, instead of crying many individuals clench their fingers, or toes, or calves or thighs. Indeed, there is no part of the body which may not be the recipient of the set of motor impulses which would ordinarily produce the distress cry accompanying pain. Such a set may be added to some usually less intensely activated accessory responses, such as a tightening of the muscles in the fingers, or added as a competing pattern of responses to an organ usually otherwise activated, as in tightening the muscles of the diaphragm. To repeat an example, the adult who sits in the dentist's chair and attempts not to cry out in pain commonly braces himself against this innate affective display by a substitute cry which is emitted in advance of the pain. He may tightly squeeze the sides of the dental chair with both hands, or tighten the muscles of his stomach and diaphragm or tightly curl his toes and feet. He senses that if these muscles are in a stage of massive contraction before and during the experience of pain this will help to drain off the massive motor discharges of the cry and interfere with the innate contractions of the diaphragm and vocal cords which would normally constitute the cry of distress. Whether by interference or substitution this enables the individual to cry as it were in his hands, or feet, or diaphragm, and not to cry in his face and throat. This is a variety of what we have termed defensive accretion. In contrast to positive accretion, substitution, like all defensive accretions, is a motivated technique of defense expressly designed to prevent the display of the innate affective response, to reduce its visibility either to others, to the self or both.

The contraction of the muscles of the diaphragm is an illustration of the fact that an organ which might be used simply to suppress or interfere with an affective response, such as crying, may also be used as a substitute. Contracting the muscles of the diaphragm in a pattern opposed to the crying responses might suffice to suppress or inhibit it. But it is our view that pain innately activates a very dense set of motor messages, which give rise to crying. When this set of messages is sent to some other organ system instead of activating the crying response, we term the reaction of that other organ system a substitute cry. When the diaphragm is being used as a substitute cry, it overcontracts beyond the point necessary to interfere with the crying response. The same overreaction, providing a substitute expression for the cry, may be seen in the overly stiff lip and jaws which may not only be held so as not to cry, but in part to express the discharge of the cry in the increment of tightness with which the facial muscles may be held.

The same argument holds for normally activated accessory responses such as gripping the hands in pain. This is often an overflow phenomenon which may accompany pain even when one does cry out in pain. If, however, this response becomes involved in substitution, then the hands are contracted more intensely than would otherwise be the case and this is why we think that one may utter a substitute cry in the hands. That substitution is involved is, of course, most clear when the response does not normally accompany the affect in question. We have found that under pain stimulation there is no part of the body which may not become the target of substitute cries. Some individuals report characteristic contractions of the thigh muscles, others of the calf, others of the sac which holds the testes, others of one shoulder blade, and so on.

Rhythmic response, agitation and laughter as substitute cries

Further, this set of substitute messages may be sent in series in such a way that the site is activated somewhat rhythmically. Under continuing provocation the distressed individual may substitute drumming his fingers on top of a table, swinging his folded legs, tapping his feet on the floor, or chewing gum.

Drumming the fingers has been described also as a substitute for anger. Inasmuch as these affects can so easily pass into each other because of the similarity of their innate activators, it is not surprising that they may be expressed by the same substitute reactions. Nonetheless, it is our view that there is a different set of motor messages being sent to the fingers, and that the drumming of the fingers as a substitute rage has a more "pointed" and more staccato articulation which is distinguished from the drumming of the fingers as a substitute cry.

Even pacing the floor may provide a substitute for the distress cry. Much of the "agitation" of the agitated depressive may indeed be a set of substitute cries. We are not yet certain however that this is the case, although anxiety as such is minimal in many depressives, there is frequently evidence of anxiety such as deep sighs in the midst of agitation in agitated depressives. Agitation, unaccompanied by anxiety, is more likely to be seen in the distressed normal who may not cry but who switches these massive motor messages to some substitute site.

Although smoking is not a substitute for the cry, but rather a technique of defense and interference, nonetheless ongoing smoking may become the site of additional motor discharge in the case of the individual who suddenly puffs very much more rapidly than is customary for him. This is an oral equivalent of drumming the fingers.

The sudden nervous laugh may also be used as a favored site to which to switch the excessive motor messages. The laugh being one of the few uncensored channels of affective expression may become the prime vehicle of the expression of any and all affects which suffer inhibition. Thus there is the frightened nervous laugh, the dirty laugh of contempt or hostility, the ashamed laugh, the surprised laugh, the laugh of enjoyment, the laugh of excitement and the laugh of distress, the substitute cry.

Interference—the defensive face

The next type of transformation is related to substitution and similar to it, but utilizes a different principle for controlling the overt cry of distress. This is the technique of interference. Although substitution does in fact interfere with the cry by switching it to some other organ, interference is a more suppressive transformation. The most simple kind of interference is to send inhibitory messages to the lips—the stiff upper lip or tight lips, both upper and lower, designed to keep the mouth closed and to prevent the cry of distress. A more general defense is the frozen face, in which the entire facial musculature is kept under sufficiently tight control so that all affects, including distress, are interfered with at the site of expression. Such a general technique of interference with all affective expression is sufficiently radical that it is also most commonly a chronic condition. Less commonly it is seen as a transient reaction to threat which seems temporary but severe. It may even be observed in the course of a conversation as a brief tightening of all facial muscles, when something very distressing or frightening or shaming has been mentioned.

Another technique of interference is the atonic face, in which all the muscles of the face suddenly lose all apparent tonus, giving the face and the eyes in particular a dull vacant look. This is often seen in the faces of children or adults who are in the presence of strangers and are uncomfortable. A child who is intensely shy in the presence of a stranger may not express his shyness by hiding his face, or lowering his eyes or head, but rather by what may be a human equivalent of the so-called sham death reflex in animals.

Certain animals when suddenly feeling overpowered by a mortal enemy defend themselves by losing all tonus in their body and appearing motionless and dead. In these animals this appears to be an innately endowed strategy. In man its origins are less clear, nor is it certain that the mechanism is related. At the present time for human beings in our society, the extreme case of loss of tonus in fainting and the loss of consciousness, usually involves not the affect of distress—anguish but rather overwhelming fear—terror. This is consistent with the sham death reaction in animals. However, in the late nineteenth and early twentieth centuries, ladies' swooning was not so uncommon as it has recently become.

Although fainting with the loss of consciousness and the upright posture is generally now restricted to extreme emergencies, the less generalized lack of tonus in the face as a defense against crying and other negative affects is more frequent. It should be noted that both the frozen face and the atonic face are quite radical defenses against the distress cry and that such extreme defenses are ordinarily powered by a negative affect much more toxic than distress itself, usually terror and/or shame. In such cases the distress cry itself is defended against because the consequences of emitting it have been taught to be extreme terror or extreme humiliation.

Interference—self-inflicted pain or pleasure

Not all techniques of interference however, involve direct inhibition of the motor messages to the face. There is also interfer-

ence by responses which produce competing, masking stimulation, positive or negative in quality. Consider first the time-
honored strategy of masking by self-inflicted pain, which is more
intense than the pain of the medical or dental procedure being
undergone, the distress and fear that would ordinarily be induced
by the doctor or dentist. This is clearly not a strategy designed
to reduce pain per se, since its success depends on producing
more intense pain which will mask both the less intense pain
and its associated distress and/or fear. This strategy aims at reducing the cry and the fear by substituting a greater self-inflicted
stimulation for a lesser one which is passively suffered and which
as a consequence of passivity activates an increment of distress
or fear to that which the pain alone would have activated. By
inflicting the greater pain on oneself one achieves greater control of the experience of pain. This will radically reduce that
part of the distress or fear which was a reaction to supposed
helplessness and may even activate enjoyment. In this case it is
the awareness of the self-imposed greater pain which is interfering with the awareness of the inflicted pain and its associated
distress.

A similar strategy is involved in the less dramatic self-inflicted
responses produced by someone who is distressed when he does
the variety of things to his face which he may do to interfere
with distress. These begin in infancy and childhood and include
head banging, nose picking, ear pulling, hair pulling, face rub-
bing, tongue rolling, lip biting and fingernail biting. All of these
produce mildly disturbing stimulation which can interfere with
the impulse to cry by taking up most of the limited available
channel capacity of consciousness.

Not all competing stimulation by self-inflicted responses
need be painful or unpleasant. The same principle is involved
in the self-administered oral stimulation of sucking on a finger,
blanket, or pacifier or later a cigarette. As we have previously
noted, these produce mildly pleasant stimulation which becomes
rewarding insofar as it is capable of reducing distress by interference, and by producing muscular relaxation and the smile
of enjoyment. Indeed this form of control of crying is often
taught in the first few days of the neonate's existence, in the
hospital nursery. We have observed nurses who put the infant's

thumb into the infant's mouth, when he was crying, as a way of stopping crying. This is sometimes done to large numbers of neonates at the same time. Governesses also occasionally link the reduction of distress to sexuality by stroking the genitals of the crying infant to soothe him by competing stimulation. Children and adults alike also learn the technique of interfering with distress by masturbation.

Anger in place of distress—anguish

Finally, anger may be learned as a substitute affect. Since we believe that anger—rage is an affect which is innately activated by the same type of stimulation as is distress—anguish, except that it is a somewhat higher level of density of neural stimulation which is involved, it easily happens that distress itself, experienced unrelieved for some time can produce sufficient increment of stimulation to innately activate anger. If there is no further punishment for the expression of anger, then this sequence may be telescoped so that the beginning of the distress cry becomes the learned activator of anger. The tantrum represents the unlearned progression from distress to rage but there are adults who become permanently irritable or angry whenever they might have become merely distressed. It is our belief that such perpetually irritable or easily angered individuals have learned to respond to their own implicit distress cry with anger. If this is so then if one were to interfere with or inhibit the anger, these individuals should suddenly find themselves with a strong impulse to cry. It should also be possible to expose such past learned sequences from residues of sequences of facial responses by means of high-speed moving picture photography. At 5,000 frames a second or upwards we should be able to trace the momentary turning down of the corners of the mouth and the momentary obliqueness of the eyebrows before the frown and the tightening jaw of anger are expressed, if such indeed has been the learned sequence of affects.

It is our belief that ultimately the principal components of the personality structure as well as the development sequence may be diagnosed from the sequence of brief facial affective responses to a variety of affects used as stimuli. These would include the sound of crying, the sound of the tantrum, the sound of laughter, the smile of a face, the look of excitement of a face, the sneer of contempt, the cry of fear and the look of fear, and the face lowered in shame. The series of facial affective responses to the affective responses of others contain the critical information we need to evaluate the present status of affects as well as the developmental sequences if these are still reflected in miniaturized form, as we believe they are.

So much for those modifications of the crying response itself which account for the rareness of the observed cry, despite the ubiquity of distress and suffering. There are of course numerous strategies which all human beings engage in to avoid and minimize suffering. In this section we have, however, been concerned with the more restricted question—given unavoidable distress, how may the human being cry without being heard or seen?

LEARNED ACTIVATORS OF DISTRESS–ANGUISH: ANTICIPTION, MEMORY AND INTERPRETATION IN THE ACTIVATION OF DISTRESS–ANGUISH

So much for the unlearned activators of the distress cry. The learned activators of distress, as of any other affect, are without limit. There is in fact no kind of circumstance, historically speaking, which some human beings have not learned to cry about, and to suffer from. The ready linkage of the distress cry to a wide variety of activators can convert the world into a vale of tears. Men learn to suffer more than they need suffer. A major aspect of the problem of human happiness is to be found in the history of learning how and about what to cry, since unhappiness is the genus of which distress is a prime species.

One may learn to be distressed by and about anything in different ways. First, any anticipation or memory of any innate activator of distress may evoke distress: the sight of a needle which has once given pain can activate the distress cry in any child over a year of age. As we have seen before this involves the cognitive construction of an object. Younger infants characteristically do not anticipate pain and do not cry under the same circumstances.

Distress can also be learned to be activated from anticipation or memory of the distress experience itself. Thus, if an adult interrupts a child's game and the child cries (which he may not) he may learn to be distressed (and angry) at that adult, quite apart from his behavior in this particular situation. This is another instance of the general case in which an affect is learned to be activated to a cognitively constructed cause. Critical here is the conceptual linkage, either at the time it occurs or later in reflection, between the affect and its cause as construed by the individual who is experiencing the affect.

There is never a guarantee that such cognition is either accurate or precise. Consequently one may learn to be distressed at the wrong person, or at too many people, or at the entire situation or at life in general. Since the memory or anticipation of the experience of a negative affect can be a sufficient activator of that same affect, the human being is very vulnerable to the self-confirming prophecy in this domain. If he mistakenly identifies a person as the source of his distress, he may nonetheless experience distress first in thinking about this person, then in anticipating meeting him and for the third time actually seeing him again. By this time it has indeed become true that this person distresses him, apart from whatever else he may do. The same dynamic holds for anger, fear and shame—the person, activity or circumstance which it is believed is responsible for the suffering of distress, or fear, or anger, or shame (whether this is so or not) easily becomes the source of distress or anger or fear or shame, in fact first through hypothesis formation, then through anticipation and finally through confrontation with the constructed dread object.

A theory of the neurotic paradox

This constitutes a major neglected component of the so-called neurotic paradox, the resistance to extinction of irrational fears and other negative affects. Mowrer has correctly stressed the critical role which the avoidance of anxiety plays in rewarding the neurotic who continues throughout his life to defend himself against dread objects which no longer exist or which no longer threaten him. Under such conditions of continuing reward

for avoidance, it becomes difficult for him to reacquaint himself
with the original source of his anxiety and thereby to learn not
to be afraid.

But even when the neurotic "knows" that as an adult he need
no longer fear what might have constituted a real threat for him
when he was a child, this knowledge rarely helps. We would
suggest that a major part of this invulnerability to relearning is
due to the fact that negative affect is usually learned not only to
the innate or even learned activators of negative affect, but also
to the experience of negative affect itself. It is as frightening to
be afraid as to be threatened. It is as distressing to experience
distress as to be in pain.

Since the neurotic is one who has had the continuing experience of severe negative affect about experiencing negative affect,
it is insufficient to demonstrate that he need no longer fear or
be distressed by the *object* which presumably originally frightened or distressed him. He is in fact now quite as afraid or distressed of re-experiencing the fear or distress which has happened to him hundreds of times in the absence of the supposed
cause of fear or distress. We are suggesting that the fear or
distress has long ago ceased to be activated by the original activator, therefore the knowledge that this activator no longer has
the power it was once endowed with is not therapeutic. The
neurotic must now be taught to tolerate his own negative affect,
since it is the anticipation of his own fear or distress which has
become the major activator of further fear or distress.

Interpretation and reinterpretation

It should be noted that for any individual, neurotic or normal,
whether his interpretation of the cause is correct or incorrect,
precise or diffuse, an act of interpretation is necessary to *learn* to
respond to any object with any affect. In the situation in which
the child cries at the sight of the needle, we are dealing with an
object that primarily causes pain, which then causes distress, but
here too interpretation is involved. The infant under six months
does not cry at the sight of the needle, because he lacks the cognitive capacities to achieve the requisite conceptual linkage.

Because an act of interpretation is necessary to link any affect with an object, the ultimate effect of any experience is never static or determinate but continually susceptible to reinterpretation. An experience which was not distressing when it happened may later become very distressing. Something said in jest which was so regarded by both parties, at the time, may later be reinterpreted and thenceforth regarded as a very distressing experience, if the relationship between these individuals later becomes strained, and the picture of the personality of the jester is restructured to account for the distress more recently suffered at the hands of that individual. By the same dynamic the straw that breaks the camel's back is ordinarily a blow made heavy by being compounded of straws, each of which may have been benign enough, but which gathered together in memory and thought can produce an insight which then provides the basis for a reinterpretation of each "straw" so that the weight of each experience is multiplied many times, and their cumulative significance so exaggerated that only a single further intimation is required to confirm a theory that the world has become too intolerable to endure. Suicides and psychotic episodes are not infrequently precipitated by events which seem to dot the "i" and cross the "t," because, as in any crucial experiment, the questions have been put to nature with extraordinary clarity.

Anticipation or postication which links affects to their supposed objects, then, involves some degrees of freedom in such amalgams not only at the time of their formation but at any time thereafter.

AFFECT CONSTRUCTS: SIGNS, SYMBOLS, ANALOGS
AND POWERS

This same freedom of construction of affect and its objects makes possible a variety of transformations of both affect and learned activators and their combinations. We have distinguished four major types of such constructs achieved by transformations: 1) signs, 2) symbols, 3) analogs and 4) powers.

A sign-affect construct is one in which something which had preceded affect now directly activates the affect. Thus if a child learns to cry at the sight of a needle which has previously given pain upon injection, the sight of the needle has become a sign which directly activates the cry which first was produced by the pain following injection by the needle.

A symbol-affect construct is one in which a linguistic description directly activates affect. If one says to a child "I don't like you" and the child responds to this with distress, this is an example of a symbol-affect construct. It should be noted that what Freud meant by a symbol is discussed under analog affect constructs, and is not what we mean by the word symbol. We use the term exclusively to refer to linguistic symbols. Since language may refer to signs, analogs and powers, it is also the case that a symbol-affect construct may also be instances of other types of affect constructs. Thus if a physician says "Now I'm going to give you an injection," this may also function as a sign-affect construct. Let us defer the use of language in analog-affect and powers-affect constructs until we have defined these.

An analog-affect construct is one in which a state of affairs that is sufficiently similar to that which activates an affect or sufficiently similar to the affect itself, directly activates the affect. What Freud meant by symbolism is included in our definition of analog-affect constructs. Thus sexual excitement which is aroused by, or expressed by, a banana would be an example of an analog-affect construct. Further, a TV program turned on by a child may not in fact be loud enough to cause distress, but is sufficiently similar to a distressingly loud blaring program to activate distress. The mechanism by which something similar to a sufficient activator itself becomes a sufficient activator of affect, we will examine in the chapters on Memory and Transformation Dynamics. Another example is the frown on the face of a parent which may appear to the child to be a similar to a learned symbolic activator, such as the verbal expression "I don't like that," which in turn has been learned to activate distress. The frown is of course also similar to one's own frown. Examples of an analog-affect construct in which it is the similarity of the activator to the affect itself that is critical include music, which is "sad," weather which is gray and somber, the slow movement of a tired person, the slightly sad expression on someone's face, the somewhat plaintive sound of someone's voice. In all of these cases, we believe, there is enough similarity between these stimuli and the cry of distress to activate the latter in the one exposed to it who has become sensitized to and learned these similarities by an analog-affect construct.

A power-affect construct is one in which anything deemed instrumental to the activation of an affect is learned to directly activate that affect. Thus, if a child has suffered distress at the hands of another child who beat him up, and he conceives of his own muscular skill and strength as instrumental in preventing further distress, and his own muscular weakness and lack of skill as instrumental to suffering more distress from the same source, then he may learn to become distressed at his own weakness or failure to achieve skill in self-defense. In such a case the failure of competence or power is learned to activate the same affect as the original circumstance which the power was designed to remedy.

Returning now to symbol-affect constructs (verbal instigators of affect), a symbol power-affect construct would be one in which a linguistic reference to a power condition sufficient to activate distress would also activate distress. An example would be the circumstance in which a communication of the form, "You're skinny," said by the self or by another, would activate the same distress as would the awareness of this fact in non-linguistic form, and the same distress as would a painful defeat in a fight with another child.

A symbol-analog-affect construct would be one in which a linguistic reference to a condition similar to that which activates an affect, or similar to the affect itself, directly activates the affect. An example would be the learned activation of distress to a statement of the form, "I like rock-and-roll music," when this produces imagery of vividness and loudness sufficiently similar to stimulation intense enough to innately activate distress. An example of a symbol-analog-affect construct when the similarity is to the distress affect itself would be the learned activation of distress to a statement of the form "What a dreary day."

The power of words

It is all but impossible to exaggerate the extent to which modern man lives and has his being in a medium of words.

Words may symbolize signs, analogs and powers which activate affects. But above all language is the lens of thought through which affects can be brought to a magnifying, searing, white-heat focus. The worlds which have been constructed out of words have promised the wildest excitements, the deepest enjoyments, the most abysmal distress and the ultimate shame and terror. From God, heaven, and the angels, through the bourgeoisie and the proletariat, to hell and the devil, man has been fascinated, dedicated, alienated, humiliated, terrorized by his own linguistic inventions. The theater is a very special case of catharsis by word.

There is no affect which cannot be activated and maintained endlessly by the magic of the word. In part this is because a word can, under particular conditions, symbolize a lifetime of experience. The word "no" to the question "do you love me?" can evoke distress of a depth and endurance without equal. The world created by words includes words about affects. When one person says to another person, "I love you," or, "I hate you," such communications have properties which may be quite different from the affects which they are intended to communicate. The statement, "I hate you," may never be forgotten although the feeling which it communicated was no more than a sudden flash of anger as significant an indicator of the emotional climate of an interpersonal relationship as a momentary flash of heat lightning is an indicator of the enduring climate of a particular geographical area. In part this is because words are at once capable of great compression of reference and at the same time capable of endless expansion, and through memory can be preserved indefinitely. How words acquire the capacity to dominate the affective life we will examine in the chapters on memory and transformations.

Signs, symbols, analogs and powers as reducers of affect

It should be noted that although we have emphasized the role of words, and signs, analogs and powers in the activation of distress, the same definitions also hold for maintenance and reduction of distress. If a word can be learned to activate distress, so can a word maintain or be learned to reduce distress. If a verbal expression of disapprobation can distress, a verbal reassurance can equally well reduce the same distress. If a sign precedes an activator of distress a sign may also be learned to precede the reduction of distress. Similarly with analogs and powers. The TV program which distressed though it was not really so loud can also be the occasion of reduction of distress when it is turned down in volume just a bit. This may be interpreted to be enough difference to be quite tolerable though in fact the difference may be very slight, but similar enough to a distress-reducer to have the same effect.

With respect to power-affect constructs, any indication of increased physical prowess achieved by a child distressed by an aggressive attack of another child may reduce his distress in the same way that a successful counterattack would reduce his distress. Similarly, if a child suffers considerable distress at the hands of his parents and regards identification with them as instrumental in reducing his vulnerability to further distress, then any indication of achieved similarity between himself and his parents can be learned to reduce the distress suffered from parental punishment.

PARENTAL ATTITUDES TOWARD CRYING: TECHNIQUES OF REWARD AND PUNISHMENT FOR THE REDUCTION OF DISTRESS CRYING

The reduction of the distress response has concerned all societies. Despite its central significance and its impact on child development, empirical investigations of the vicissitudes of the distress response itself are scattered, halting and atheoretic. In part this is because Freud misidentified the birth cry with anxiety, and because he attributed so much significance to oral phenomena and to weaning that the cry itself was regarded as a secondary consequence of oral deprivation.

The socialization of this response is likely to involve the socialization of the distress cry of the socializer. Although to some extent this is true of the socialization of any response, this is inescapable with the crying response. This is because hearing the distress cry of the child almost certainly reactivates the distress cry in the parent and this in turn reactivates all the circumstances connected with his own early crying experiences. This is not always the case with every critical response in which control is taught by the parent. Thus the child's hunger does not necessarily activate the parent's hunger. The child's masturbation does not necessarily activate the parent's sexual excitement. But the child's distress cry can and does distress the adult and threaten the reactivation of the very response which he is attempting to control in the child. He is therefore faced, essentially, with reliving this part of his own past history and with the option of remaking history by repeating with the child precisely the strategy by which he was socialized, or treating the cry of the child as he wished he might have been treated.

Whether there is exact repetition or defense against repetition, the degrees of freedom of the parent in this matter are rarely very great. His strategy ordinarily is not chosen from the full range of alternatives, dispassionately examined. This is usually because the socialization of his own distress cry was itself achieved in the crucible of his parent's passion about crying. It is our impression that few responses of the child engage more intense feelings on the part of the parent, and few responses have been more rationalized. As we shall attempt to show presently, most human beings develop an articulate philosophy about crying and the display of suffering. Generally speaking there is a polarization of ideology in which one is for the human being who cries or one is against the human being who cries. Coordinate with this polarization of ideology there is a polarization of action. One either punishes and tries to suppress the crying of the child, or one tries to reduce the crying of the child by removing the source and also by further rewarding the child with sympathy, to soothe the child.

Although there are many parents who are generally for or against the cry and the child who cries, there are also some who are conflicted and who oscillate between sympathy and punishment and back again. This lability of affect about crying is not uncommon in manic-depressive parents, who thereby create future labile manic-depressives in their own image. There are still others who are also in deep conflict about the distress cry, but who have achieved a stable differentiation of the conditions under which they will attempt to help and reward the child who cries and those conditions under which they will further punish the child just because he cries. Thus a parent may sympathize with an infant who cries, but not with the same child after the age of 2. Another may sympathize with a child who cries in pure distress but not when the cry has an undercurrent of anger and complaint. A parent may sympathize with a child who cries because he has been physically hurt, but not with a child who cries because he has been disciplined. A parent may sympathize with a child who cries because he is lonely, but not with a child who cries because he doesn't want to go to bed. A parent may sympathize with a child who cries if he has been hurt accidentally, but not if he cries upon injury when he had been warned of danger. A parent may sympathize with a child who cries in the privacy of his home, but not with a child who cries in public. A parent may sympathize with a child who cries about anything so long as it does not involve distress at some parental dictate or behavior. Such differentiations are without limit, and they account for the social inheritance of such distinctions from generation to generation. Despite these differentiations, however, there appears to be a polarization of attitudes in which there is something closer to a multi-modal rather than a normal statistical distribution of attitudes.

Reducing crying by punishment: pain, terror, shame, loss of love or indifference

Let us consider first the varieties of punitive techniques for the control of the crying response. Their aim is not to alleviate present suffering. The aim of these techniques may be threefold; first, to stop the crying itself; second, to stop the behavior for which the child may have been punished and made to cry; and, finally, it may be the intention of the parent not only to make the child stop crying but to increase his suffering because he is crying. In this latter case the act of crying may seem to require the same kind of punishment as the immoral behavior for which he was punished and which then initiated the crying. In this case the child is judged responsible for two offenses.

Punitive strategies are numerous. The child may be slapped on the face or beaten. Some American Indians control the response by holding the nose of the crying child. In either case it is pain which is the primary motivation.

Terror is another strategy. Here the threat of a severe beating may be used to incite fear, or a command "stop it," in a sudden shrill tone, is sometimes used to frighten children out of the cry of distress. I have seen a mother, ashamed of her son crying in a barber's chair, and concerned at the distress of others in the barber shop, quiet the crying by suddenly shouting a blood-curdling "stop it" which at the same time startled all those it was designed to protect from the child's crying. A more common variant is the expression, "If you don't stop that crying I'll give you something to cry about."

Shaming or contempt by the parent is commonly used to activate shame in the child to reduce the crying, e.g., "You ought to be ashamed of yourself, a big boy like you, crying like a little baby." Shame may be linked to moral strictures, e.g., "Good little boys don't cry, it's not nice to cry." Morality may also be introduced by way of the harmful effects of crying on the parent, e.g., "You'll make mommy cry if you don't stop crying." Its more extreme form may be, "You'll be the death of me with your crying" or "Stop it, I can't stand it." Loss of love may be used as a threat, e.g., "Mommy doesn't like little boys who cry," or, "You're more trouble than you're worth."

Finally, the parent may indicate that he is going to do nothing about the crying, that the child can "cry it out." Or, the parent may say nothing but pretend complete indifference, or pointedly turn away from the crying and leave the room or begin to pay attention to someone else. In the case of the infant the parent simply does nothing about the crying. We consider this a punitive response since, although the parent hopes to thereby reduce the crying, he is quite prepared to wait it out whatever the cost to the infant. In the case of the child, this may also involve a refusal to do what the child asks of the parent. A child who requests aid of the parent may cry when this is refused. The child's continued crying under these conditions involves a compound punishment when the parent permits the child to cry it out.

Reducing crying by remedial help or comfort

Let us consider now the major varieties of rewarding techniques used in reducing the distress cry. First, every attempt is made to find the source of distress and remedy this. If the infant is crying from hunger he is fed. If he suffers gas pains, he is burped. If he is crying because he is cold and wet, he is re-diapered. If he is crying because a diaper pin is hurting him, it is found and closed.

Second, the infant is in addition rewarded by being picked up and held and patted or hugged, or by being looked at, or smiled at, or talked to, or all of these, in an attempt to increase his positive affect, to soothe as well as reduce his distress. Indeed these tactics are often sufficient to reduce crying by interference, even before the original source is remedied. If it is a child rather than an infant who is crying, verbal reassurance as well as help in remedying the source of distress is offered.

It should also be noted that remedial help may be offered without sympathy, and sympathy may be offered without remedial help. Indeed a parent may be quite hostile about the act of crying at the same time that he tries to get at the source of the crying and offer remedial help or encourage the child to help himself. The consequences of such dissociation between sympathy and remedy we will examine presently. The attitude of a parent who says, "There, there, that's enough of that, let's see what the problem is," is something short of pure reward for the crying child. Even closer to a punitive posture is that of a parent who responds, "If you just keep on crying you'll never be able to do anything about it."

Jollying

Still another variant which is something less than rewarding to the crying child is a jollying attitude on the part of the parent who regards the source of distress and the distress cry both as trivial enough to be reduced by laughter. So much for the variety of ways in which control of the distress response is attempted. We turn next to the consequences of such strategies.

THE IMPACT OF EARLY DISTRESS EXPERIENCE
ON ADULT DISTRESS EXPERIENCE

The relationship between early and later experience, whether it refer to distress in particular or to all negative affects or to all affects, cannot be understood apart from a theory of memory and thinking, which we will present in later chapters. The present discussion is therefore necessarily somewhat incomplete, and we will present now only the general outlines of these theories. This discussion may also be taken to apply to the more general question of the relationship between any early affective experience and any later affective experience.

According to our view of memory, there is a long period of incompetence enforced by the slowness of learning how both to perceive and how to remember. There are somewhat antithetical consequences of such a view. First, any human being deprived of the opportunity to do this work will be relatively incompetent to recognize the simplest objects and to respond to them with affect when first given the opportunity; he will at this later date require a long period of experience before elementary perceptual and motor skills will be achieved. Second, by virtue of the necessarily long period of incompetence enforced by the slowness of learning how to remember, the impact of experience in early infancy will be limited both with respect to later infancy and childhood as well as with respect to adulthood. The effect of earliest experience will be greatest on immediately following experience and will become progressively attenuated as the time gap increases.

We have seen in Shaeffer's and Levy's reports that neither separation from the mother nor the sight of a needle which has previously given pain distress the infant under six months of age. Pain, of course, distresses any animal of any age, but the anticipation of pain is a quite different matter.

Despite the lack of relatively long-term effects in early infancy, there is evidence that if crying experience is tested for later effects within a relatively short period of time, these effects may be considerable. It will be recalled that in Fredricson's experiment with puppies, the condition of the first three experimental trials affected the response to later trials in the experimental series. Being confined alone was more distressing than being confined with another puppy. If in the initial three trials the puppy was confined alone, this added an increment of distress to the experience of being confined with another puppy in the later experimental trials. Nonetheless, this was a short-term effect, and the long-term effects were not studied.

If, as we have said, the impact of any particular early experience may become more attenuated the older the individual becomes, this is not necessarily the case. Early experience is continually being transformed by the experience which follows it, just as much as later experience may be transformed in terms of the memory schema of earlier experience. Particularly during infancy and childhood, it is the case that we do not understand what has happened to us until it happens again and again with sufficient clarity and intensity that stable objects and relationships between objects can be constructed. One of the consequences of such a view of the nature of early learning is that one can never specify whether any particular experience will or will not have consequences pathologic or otherwise in the life history of the individual, since this will depend on the extent to which later experience amplifies or attenuates the significance of the earlier experience and the cognitive constructions which are placed upon the entire set of experiences as they are lived and experienced in memory and thought.

Every life history has a theme, but it is truly indeterminate until the entire melody has appeared and been repeated often enough so that the individual can recognize it, construct it and then begin to recognize further repetitions of it as he develops. The young human being is a relatively open system, because each new experience plays a vital role in the interpretation of the growing cumulative images of past experience. Indeed, human development might properly be defined as that phase of experience in which the analysis of past experience and future possibilities is conducted in the light of present experience. Development ceases when the contribution of present information becomes primarily illustrative, as a special case of past generalization.

It is not unlike the relationship within any science, between what is established and its frontier. Those congealed bits of information called "laws" can be incorporated into testing instruments so that precise values of any particular situation can be simply established, as for example by a voltmeter. The growing edge of that science, however, is where the theorist puts questions to nature with great uncertainty and fear and trembling, and where the results of observation and experiment are truly new information which will inform the science and the scientist how he should choose between plausible alternatives and what he should believe. Theories within science also ultimately become senile and cease to struggle with genuine uncertainty. Development, in short, is characterized by a state of information processing in which there is a ratio of pronounced retro-action over pro-action, and senility is that state of information processing where pro-action dominates retro-action.

For this reason, we argue that the distinction between learned and unlearned sources of distress is soon swamped by the more critical distinction between the relative influence between past and present information in the interpretation of both. In the chapter on transformation dynamics, we will examine in more detail how cumulative experience is successively transformed, and how past experience comes to influence future experience and behavior. We wish at this point only to note that there is true indeterminacy with respect to the future because the human being is an open system and only gradually begins to impress his individuality upon the world in which he lives.

For the question of the nature of human suffering, and of its learned activators, this means that for some time the answer is being continually changed in such a way that what once caused little distress may come to cause great distress, and what once was very distressing may ultimately be not at all distressing, or what once caused some distress causes increasing distress over time. There is in short no necessary relationship between early and late experience because each is capable of being changed in the image of the other. And yet, despite the fact that it takes many repetitions to strengthen any particular early experience into a monopolistic frame of reference by which later experience is evaluated, it is also the case that much early experience is available for retrieval under very specific conditions and that it can intrude itself forcefully against the will of the adult, who may regard this reminder of early experience as entirely alien to his adult personality.

Applied to the problem of the impact of early distress socialization on the adult personality, this means that in addition to early distress experiences which are selected, reinterpreted and strengthened as trends which become stabilized in adulthood and which constitute the selected and somewhat created continuities in development, there are also discontinuities in which early and later modes of dealing with distress co-exist in memory. In the latter case the adult reactions to distress ordinarily dominate behavior even when infantile and childhood distress experience was quite severe and different from later experience, but under very specific conditions the individual may be suddenly overwhelmed by intrusions from earlier distress—anguish experiences. The nature of the specific conditions under which long isolated early experience reappears we will describe in the chapter on memory.

The snowball model of affective development

Let us consider briefly now a few examples of these possible relationships between childhood and adulthood distress experience. Consider first what we have called the snowball model. Let us suppose that, in the individual's childhood, distress crying is socialized by parental contempt which produces shame. In later childhood and adolescence let us suppose that this individual experiences more and more shame because he cannot compete successfully with his peers. Let us further suppose that his image of himself becomes more and more clear and stable—he is an inferior person. As this happens, any suggestion of inferiority begins to activate heroic attempts at counteraction. However, this counteraction becomes more and more difficult, because as he encounters difficulties, distress is aroused. By now the distress-contempt-shame complex has been reinterpreted and much amplified by virtue of the present strongly held belief in the inferior self, so that impediments to counteracting shame encounter distress, which further activates shame, which thus ends in further defeat and strengthening the image of the self as inferior.

In such a case it will prove relatively simple to demonstrate that the early mode of socialization of distress is continuous with and influential in producing an adult who becomes ashamed whenever he becomes distressed by any difficulties. Further it will be obvious that this trend became much stronger as he developed. What may not be so clear, because of the prevalence of the oversimplified Psychoanalytic model, is that the early mode of distress socialization was not only continuously confirmed but reinterpreted and reintegrated into an image which had some of the properties of a snowball rolling down a mountain.

The iceberg model of affective development

Second, consider what we have called the iceberg model. In this case the individual also begins with the same contempt from parents for crying, which teaches the child that whenever he feels distressed he should hang his head in shame instead. However, these parents otherwise are a source of much reward. They give the child much loving attention and enjoy his company so long as he does not cry. Further, they much applaud any show of achievement. This child begins then with a relatively sharp differentiation between affects of his own which elicit positive affects and affects of his own which elicit negative affects.

Let us suppose now that he responds to such socialization with a determination to accentuate the rewards and to minimize the punishments. In contrast to the first hypothetical case, let us postulate here a continuous history of successful achievements through childhood and adolescence, marred by only occasional experiences in which he reexperiences the distress—shame sequence, which serve only to strengthen his counteractive efforts to maximize his positive experiences.

As he enters adulthood this individual has a firm sense of his own identity as the master of his own destiny, as one capable of achieving what he wants, of eliciting respect from others for his efforts and of generally enjoying his interpersonal relationships. However, he may be suddenly confronted with distress which he cannot counteract, produced, for example, by a long siege of enforced passivity through illness or by loss of a child or of his wife, or by the loss of his savings and business in the event of an economic depression which does not permit his customary counteraction, or by senility and retirement which undermines his customary activity and productivity and confronts him with the imminence of his death. Under any one of these or similar circumstances he is confronted with deep and enduring distress for which he has learned only one reaction, that of shame and humiliation. In such a case the iceberg of childhood learning may suddenly intrude itself as an utterly alien experience, so disturbing as to produce further negative affect and depression or withdrawal. It is just because this individual never experienced protracted distress and its associated shame that he developed no gradations of such affects and therefore no psychological immunity to these negative affects.

The iceberg effect may be extraordinarily labile in its appearance and disappearance. Psychotic episodes have been observed to be produced by enforced passivity after incapacitating injuries, which just as suddenly disappear, to be replaced briefly by the normal dominant personality, and then displaced again by a psychotic reaction. In one such case of an acute psychotic episode with a past history similar to the hypothetical paradigm of the iceberg, the individual upon being moved from a diagnostic ward in a mental hospital to a ward of severely regressed schizophrenics was galvanized into violent, counteractive self-righteous aggression upon being visited by his wife and children. He bitterly, and with much contempt, challenged their right to take unto themselves the right to place him in the company of such human beings. So complete was his sudden apparent recovery that the attending psychiatrist then placed him in a convalescent ward preparatory to imminent discharge. Within two hours of this change, however, there was a return of the psychotic reaction. One week later, against the advice of the psychiatrist, his wife, in response to pleas from her sick husband that he not be taken back to the hospital following a weekend at home, refused to return him to the hospital. A warning was given by the psychiatrist that there was a very high risk of suicide. Upon return to his family, however, the dominant personality reappeared and was never seriously disorganized again by such intrusions in the following fifteen years, despite the fact that the last five years of his life were marked by painful terminal cancer.

The late bloomer model of affective development

A third type of developmental pattern is what we have called the late bloomer model. In this case affective experience is differentiated from the start and is either unintegrated or produces such conflict that integration and a firm sense of identity, singleness of purpose and philosophy of life can be achieved only relatively late in life. In contrast to the iceberg model, the very same kind of challenges which disorganize the dominant personality and produce regressive intrusions here become the vehicle of long delayed integration.

Protracted illness, loss of loved ones, economic depressions, severe failures or any circumstances which throw into relief the individual's values and which challenge and test the personality can be the occasion for a renunciation of part of the self and a radical reinforcement of another part of the self in a conversion experience or series of conversions in which values are revalued and ultimate decisions attained which thereafter result in commitment and dedication to a particular way of life.

With respect to the socialization of distress let us return to our hypothetical case of the child who was shamed into the control of distress. In contrast to the snowball model and the iceberg model, let us assume that the late bloomer was also so socialized but somewhat inconsistently so. Let us assume that every time he cried he was made to hang his head in shame by his father but was given love and sympathy by his mother. Under such conflicting treatments let us further assume that he develops a masculine identification which regards the expression of distress as infantile and contemptible, which is to be counteracted by self-discipline.

In adolescence this pushes him in the direction of competence in body contact sports. In college he concentrates in one of the natural sciences since he feels that this is a demanding difficult field dealing with the "real world." However, he also identifies closely with his mother and he secretly enjoys his distress experiences with her, because when he cries in her presence she feels closest to him and gathers him up in her arms and together they return to his infancy. As a consequence of this type of distress socialization, his strongest positive feelings of love and communion are inextricably linked to the reduction of distress. This generates an adolescent passion for girls, an interest in art through which such feelings may be expressed, and as an undergraduate in college an election of courses in fine arts, literature and music, in psychology and in philosophy. He is particularly interested in psychology and philosophy because he cannot integrate his masculine shame–distress socialization and his feminine love–distress socialization, his hard and soft selves. He thinks that if he learns more about human beings from psychology and more about the meaning of life and the nature of value and morality from philosophy, perhaps he can come to a firmer sense of identity.

But he learns that there is much difference of opinion in these very fields of knowledge to which he looks for illumination and guidance. He drifts through college alternately disciplining and indulging himself, incapable of completely committing himself to the hard, real world of masculine competition or to the soft, warm, outstretched arms of the eternal mother. The masculine world cheats him and the feminine world shames him. This failure in integration may be deepend, and a decision further postponed by the election of a medical career. He will become a surgeon, the most masculine species of a profession committed to answering the cry of distress. As a surgeon in training, he learns to disregard the distress of his patients and to try to master the skills of surgery. At times he can scarcely conceal his contempt for the helpless distress of his patients, behind the façade of the professional manner. At other times he is overcome with empathic distress at their suffering. He eventually practices medicine with only moderate distinction because of his failure to completely commit himself to his chosen profession.

Then in his late twenties or early thirties he suffers a crisis. He loses his beloved mother or his respected father, or one of his children; or he is bedridden with a serious injury or illness for a year; or he goes to war and is appalled at the mass carnage; or there is a serious economic depression and he suffers a great loss of income and sees millions of others in perpetual distress.

He may lose a patient because of negligence, or because he thought there was little danger involved in delay of therapy, or because he was simply mistaken in his judgment. Whatever the nature of the challenge, he is suddenly confronted for the first time with sustained suffering and distress which he cannot entirely regard as an object of contempt inasmuch as it is unearned and somewhat enforced suffering. Nor can he regard it as offering him love and support since, if he is himself stricken, he may find himself suddenly alone, e.g., in the death of his mother; if it is the suffering of others with which he is confronted, it is they who ask for help rather than give to him. Further, what they ask for and need is not only sympathy and love, but also competence and good works. In short, in terms of his socialization he now conceives that it is a compound of the loving mother and disciplined competent father that is called for, if human suffering is to be alleviated.

Under such a crisis, self-confrontation can produce the late bloomer who achieves a creative synthesis of the warring parts of his own nature, arising from two types of socialization of the cry of distress. Thenceforth he is a surgeon dedicated to the alleviation of human suffering through both his skill and love. Thus he finally achieves a joint identification with the best characteristics of both parents. He has become a human being he is proud to be and one who receives love from others because he has given help in a spirit of compassion.

The impact of early affective experience in general on adult affective experience

There are, of course, numerous other types of complex relationships possible between early and late experience which we will not pursue at this point. It was our intention only to show that how the individual is socialized when he cries for help is critical for his personality development, but that the precise influence of any particular modes of distress socialization is indeterminate until later experience either reinforces earlier modes, as in the snowball model, or inhibits them almost entirely, as in the iceburg model, or integrates them in a creative synthesis, as in the late bloomer model.

The same arguments hold for the development of any affect in the personality. Positive affects are equally capable of coming into conflict and resisting integration. They are equally capable of being selectively reinforced until they become monopolistic in the adult personality. They are also capable of being submerged, to intrude themselves suddenly as long forgotten, welcome or unwelcome selves.

Thus positive identifications with both the mother and father, quite apart from motivation through negative affect, may produce a conflict very similar to the last paradigm. In such a case the father might excite the respect of the child sufficiently to make him wish to be an ultra-masculine human being, whereas the mother might evoke an equally strong wish to become ultra-feminine. Again, an early excitement produced through identification with a father who has a monopolistic affective investment in, say, mathematics, does in certain cases produce an adult completely dedicated to mathematics. Finally, other early interests, e.g., in play or in becoming as nurturant as one's mother, may be submerged by a later dominant identification with the father and peer group.

But when this later, almost monopolistic affective investment no longer pays the same dividends, the early submerged interests may intrude and accelerate disenchantment with the dominant adult values by restoring the intensity of lost excitement. This can happen in two distinct ways. If an individual "succeeds" too visibly and too completely, he may be robbed of a reasonable return on any further investment of his affect and energy in a particular mode. This is most likely in the event that his goal has been defined in terms of a particular visible achievement. More commonly the basic goal is so defined that it is either unattainable or continually redefined. The other way in which the sub-dominant interest may swamp the personality is in the event that there appears to be an impermeable barrier to further progress, either because the individual suddenly thinks he lacks the ability necessary to achieve his ultimate goals, or thinks that external circumstances have conspired to defeat him. Either of these enforced reductions in dividends from monopolistic affective investments can dry up the mainsprings of adult motivation and release the long masked subterranean interests of early childhood. The individual then is captured by a second child-hood, or more properly, he for the first time exploits, deepens and completes his childhood.

Similarly with the other negative affects: early fears, early humiliations, early angers may be deepened and reinforced, they may be submerged to intrude themselves sporadically, or they may coexist side by side with competing unintegrated aspects of the personality indefinitely or until a creative synthesis is finally attained. In the discussion of the other negative affects, therefore, we will assume the same general possibilities to hold between early socialization and later experience.

THE RELATIONSHIPS BETWEEN LEARNED AND INNATE ACTIVATORS OF DISTRESS—ANGUISH

The distinction between learned and unlearned sources of distress, important as it may be for some purposes, eventually ceases to be a critical distinction. This is because distress which is activated on an unlearned basis is stored in memory, and learning to retrieve these and other stored memories means that these experiences will be integrated with other experiences from quite different sources and together constitute a dossier on suffering. Thus if one child of two has experienced a great deal of pain which has provoked sustained crying, and another child of the same age experienced the same sustained crying, but in response to scoldings by his parents who communicated their anger verbally, both children may thenceforth wear the sad face of one who has cried excessively and who expects the world in general will continue to be a vale of tears. In such a case general-ization from excessive crying, one from an unlearned source, the other from a learned source, has resulted in the same dis-tressed posture towards all future experience.

If we consider a third hypothetical case in which one third of the second year of life was spent in crying from physical pain, one third spent in crying due to verbal scolding by parents and one third spent in crying due to the inability of the child to reach objects that he wanted but which were just out of reach, then again we think that the life space of such a child with respect to the predominant affective quality of its second year and the optimism it might have for the future would be very similar to the two other hypothetical cases. In short, so long as past suffering is available from memory for further recall, analysis and reorganization, it does not matter so much to the suffering individual that the source of part of his suffering was essentially unlearned and another part based on his own efforts, and still another part perhaps needlessly provoked by someone who wished to teach him to suffer about matters of social significance.

CONSEQUENCES OF THE PUNITIVE SOCIALIZATION OF DISTRESS–ANGUISH

Assuming that parents may choose to produce distress for the greatest variety of behaviors which seem offensive, the same parent is then faced with the option of how to further respond to the distress cry itself. In addition all parents are faced with the problem of the socialization of the distress cry whether or not they are personally responsible for making the child cry. Although some parents respond quite differently to the cry which they produced as a result of punishment, and the cry which is the consequence of an accident to the child, nonetheless there are many parents who adopt consistently punitive postures towards the cry, regardless of the reason the child is crying.

In the following discussion we will consider some of the possible consequences of the punitive socialization of distress–anguish. We say possible consequences because of the essentially indeterminate status of the ultimate effects of early experience on later personality. To recapitulate, we consider socialization of distress–anguish punitive whenever the distress cry itself is punished or rejected or whenever there is a failure of help in remedial action to reduce the source of distress, or both. This punitive socialization may or may not be consistent or general. If it is not general, that is, if the parent punishes one kind of crying but does not punish crying of another kind we regard this as a mixed socialization of distress which we will discuss later. In contrast to the previous sections where we were concerned with the objects of distress, or the sources which activate the cry of distress, we are here concerned primarily with the effects of the techniques of distress reduction.

To the extent to which the distress cry itself has been further punished, the original cry of distress for whatever reason is ordinarily increased in intensity and duration through the further punishment administered for responding with distress in the first place. Every type of offense then has a higher priced distress penalty than would accrue to it without the further punitive response to the distress cry. In this way violations of the norms of the parents, and later of authority in general, become more serious in distress consequences. Further, distress which is produced by illness or injury is also exaggerated. If a child has been spanked for crying after having injured himself he is vulnerable as an adult to reactivation of severe distress whenever he experiences pain or the possibility of pain, injury or illness. He can as an adult make a mountain of suffering out of a molehill of pain, if the innate cry to pain is further linked with more pain and punishment. Such a child may become one of those adults whose face is frozen in a perpetual silent cry, or who continually complains in a whining voice, which is one of the adult forms of the cry. In such cases there may be no strategies of avoiding or minimizing distress because the individual has been essentially taught that the world is a vale of tears and that he is destined to suffer much of his life. This is the lesson which is taught when the original wishes of the child are continually punished, and when the cry in response to this punishment is further punished and so a further source of distress. If, in addition, every attempt at protest or resistance in anger at this further distress is further punished, then the child is taught not only that everything he wishes for produces suffering, but every attempt to counteract and reduce this suffering produces further suffering. Thus can be produced what we have called a multiple suffering bind.

Multiple suffering bind

We have defined the multiple bind in general as the case in which negative affects are so organized that any one of this set of negative affects activates the remainder of the set and thereby greatly amplifies the intensity of each component of the set.

When the cry of distress activates further distress from

punishment for crying, and still more distress as a result of anger and aggression against this distress, then each of these separate experiences of distress constitute a special case of the multiple bind, that of the homogeneous multiple bind, when distress begets more distress. A homogeneous multiple bind for other affects would be the circumstances in which fear begets more fear, or anger more anger, or shame more shame. In contrast, a heterogeneous multiple bind is that type of inhibition of affect in which a different affect constitutes the major source of inhibition. An example of a heterogeneous multiple suffering bind would be one in which crying had been reduced by the arousal of fear or shame. In such a case the adult would be inhibited in responding with distress or would avoid so responding because he had been earlier taught to feel afraid at the possibility of crying. If, having been slapped on the face for crying, he had attempted to run away from the punitive parent and then been pursued and further lectured to on the importance of taking one's punishment like a man, he might then have been shamed out of his fear, or at least out of acting on it. If now, hanging his head in shame before the punitive parent, the child is further lectured on the importance of a stiff backbone in the face of discipline, the shame response itself may be bound by further shame. The final consequence of such a distress-distress-fear-shame-shame multiple bind might be the frozen face which would solve the entire problem at once.

Distress—fear bind

Distress we have argued is a negative affect of much less toxicity than fear, and so enables the human being more easily to confront and solve his problems. We have also argued that distress is ubiquitous, whereas fear is properly an emergency reaction. If I may feel like crying many times during every day, when I am confronted with very difficult problems whose solution is not at once apparent, when I feel tired or sick, when someone is less than kind or is indifferent—then if under all of these circumstances I were to become afraid rather than distressed I would indeed be sick. Under such conditions it would become very much more probable that I would quit trying to solve difficult problems, that I would dread the normal diurnal variations in energy as if they were mortal illnesses and that I would become very cautious about trusting and liking human beings. Avoidance of the distress experience itself and of the circumstances which provoked it would become a much more likely strategy than attempting to control the sources of distress. A generalized pessimism which contaminates achievement motivation and communion enjoyment, and which produces a pervasive hypochondriasis, is not infrequently the consequence of the linkage of distress to fear.

Such a bind may be created early and become more and more severe and generalized with development, as in the snowball model, or it may be limited to infancy to reappear only sporadically as the iceberg model. We have investigated one such case of the latter kind. The patient's father was a scientist with a hypertrophied sense of rationality, who believed that crying was an irrational response, as unnecessary and undesirable for the infant as it was for the parent. He was determined, so he told me, to stamp it out in his children at the earliest possible moment. His wife was not prepared to witness his training program so he asked her to leave the house for a few days, and this she did. Thereupon every time the two-week-old infant cried his father hit him until he stopped. This was continued for four days and by this time the infant no longer cried and the mother returned.

The consequence of this experience appeared to be therapeutic. As an infant and through late adolescence this individual was a jolly, happy human being. His mirth and good spirits were indeed so contagious that it appeared to the father that he had established an important new principle of child-rearing. I knew the son from earliest childhood and could not have guessed at such a punitive socialization.

It should be noted that the same principle somewhat attenuated was consistently used thereafter. There was in this household a general taboo on distress and on anything which might provoke distress. Sickness for example was met with indifference or hostility lest anyone receive sympathy for suffering. For all of this, as far as one could see, the outcome was a delightful and happy human being. If we had known of the extremely punitive attitude toward distress, we might have interpreted this as not daring to cry because he was afraid to cry. Nonetheless, in the absence of this information everyone, including myself, regarded this individual as one to be envied his love of life. He had been literally forced to seek out the wellsprings of excitement and enjoyment.

We are not suggesting, nor do we believe, that this development was necessarily altogether defensive in nature. It is quite possible that the later general taboo on suffering, reinforcing the earlier fear of suffering, did produce a quest for positive affect which was sufficiently rewarding to powerfully reinforce this quest so that it became quite autonomous of its original defensive character. According to our iceberg model, earlier experience may well be swamped and isolated by later experience whether or not the latter represents an avoidance of the earlier experience.

Ultimately, however, beginning in early adulthood, this individual was to pay a severe price for his socialization. When he was first confronted with sustained suffering in the economic depression of the 1930s, which he could not avoid or reduce, he became anxious and self-punishing in the extreme. He became the target of his own hostility and contempt, apologizing continually for his own existence to such an extent that he made others as well as himself extremely uncomfortable. I was very puzzled by this radical conversion and it was only accidentally that I heard from his parents the account of his socialization. Whereas he had been distinguished by excessive positive affect for the first twenty years of his life, he was to be equally conspicuous for his exaggerated negative affect of beating and shaming himself for the next twenty years. In recent years however there has been a diminution in part because his economic status has improved sufficiently to make the quest for positive affect again a possible goal. The period of this self-punishment however far outlasted the economic depression which initiated it.

When distress is early linked to fear and there is a selective reinforcement in a snowball effect, this is one of the ways in which we may produce an anxiety neurosis or schizophrenia. In either pathology the vicissitudes of everyday life are learned to activate fear as well as distress. In a later chapter on humilia-

tion we will examine paranoid schizophrenia as a prime example
of a psychosis produced by terror.

The problem of physical courage

One of the further consequences of the punitive socialization
of distress through the evocation of fear is the complication of
the problem of physical courage. The human being responds
innately to pain from his body with the cry of distress. If this
innate response is inhibited by fear, the individual's fear of pain
will be greatly increased. As we have noted before in the chapter on drive–affect interactions, the total experience of pain is
an amalgam of pain, distress and/or fear. A placebo acts
primarily by reducing the affects associated with pain, and the
total suffering may thereby be appreciably reduced. Although
pain is not easy for the human being to tolerate, it can produce
panic the more distress itself has been linked with fear. The
practice of medicine is greatly complicated by the struggle of
the adult patient not to cry out in pain, and the anticipatory
fear or shame or both which he may experience at the prospect
of loss of control of the cry. It seems likely that the greater
tolerance of pain, in our culture by women and in Oriental
cultures by both men and women, is due to the less punitive early
socialization of the distress cry. It is more permissible for an
American female, young or old, to cry than it is for an American
male. In the case of male Orientals, it is more permissible for
the young to cry than for the young American male. Since the
control of the cry can thus be more gradually learned by the
Oriental male child without the complication of early fear and
shame added to the problem, he is later able to tolerate more
pain more stoically. We have been told by hospital physicans
in New York City that by the time an Oriental patient is admitted to the hospital, he is likely to be at death's door.

The problem of frustration tolerance

The linkage of fear to distress also increases radically the
problem of frustration tolerance. Although distress is not so toxic
as fear, it is nonetheless so unpleasant and the child may become

so distressed that he has a tantrum whenever he meets problems which he cannot solve immediately or whenever he is deprived of anything which he wants. If now fear is added to this burden, we may produce a very weak ego which is incapable of sustaining the distress of any frustration whether it be met in trying to solve problems, in fatigue or illness, or in deprivation or discipline of any kind.

Again, such intolerance of distress and frustration may be overcome in adolescence or adulthood, to reappear whenever there is great similarity between adult and childhood experience, or as in the snowball model, it may simply become more and more aggravated as the individual matures.

The problem of toleration of loss of love and of individuation

The linkage of fear to distress also radically increases the difficulty of solving the essential problems of individuation and the sense of identity and the toleration of loss of love. It is difficult, because distressing, to tolerate the threat of loss of love and communion, which is part of the price of achieving a firm sense of one's own identity, that is to say, a part of the problem of becoming individuated from one's parents, from one's wife and friends, and from humanity in general. The addition of fear to distress favors more radical strategies of submission and conformity or rebellion and deviance, lest one experience the terror of loneliness and difference. Loneliness and alienation are no doubt distressing to most human beings, but they need not be terrifying if fear has not been closely tied to distress. The child who has been made to experience fear whenever he feels like crying is peculiarly vulnerable to the threat of separation from the parent who produced the distress—fear bind.

Nor is the impact of fear on distress limited to an increased sensitivity to the threat of separation from others. In addition, any sign of distress in others may also arouse anxiety in the self. Thus such an individual may become anxious if another person gives expression to his tiredness or illness, if another person expresses his discouragement and apparent failure, or if another person expresses his feeling of loneliness. All such attempts at communion through the expression of distress may evoke from the distress-frightened listener not sympathy but fear.

Further, since the experience of fear is so toxic, repeated distress-fear sequences can eventually power massive defensive strategies lest such experiences be repeated. Thus a person who is distress-frightened may deny that he or others are ever tired or sick, are ever defeated or seriously challenged in competitive striving and problem-solving, or ever lonely. Such a linkage may also power compulsive athleticism or withdrawal from the risks of life, compulsive achievement or passivity, and compulsive communication or isolation.

The punitive socialization of the distress cry then not only produces the serious problem of learning how to cry without being seen and heard, but may add to this problem, the even more difficult one of coping with affects, such as fear, which are more threatening than distress.

Distress—shame bind

If, whenever a child cries, he is the recipient of contempt or rejection or indifference from his parents, he may be taught to hang his head in shame whenever he feels like crying. While shame is not the toxic, emergency affect that fear is, it it nonetheless quite unpleasant and indeed sufficiently so that it may evoke fear lest it be re-experienced. In this way distress may become bound in the sequence distress, shame, fear, in the absence of any terrorizing tactics by parents. It can happen that although it is not sufficient to evoke fear, and although shame might by itself be insufficient to evoke fear, the experience of combined distress and shame produces a sufficiently rapid increase of density of neural firing to activate fear on an essentially unlearned basis. This can happen despite the fact that the activation of shame by distress has been learned.

Even without the addition of fear, the experience or threat of shame every time distress is activated or anticipated constitutes a radical increase in the toxicity of the distress experience. Everything which we have argued accrues to the distress-fear bind may happen in the distress-shame bind. Sickness or fatigue, difficulties in problem solving, threats of loss of love or any occasion of loneliness become doubly difficult to tolerate when shame is added to distress. Under such conditions the individual is prompted to constantly apologize for his own existence, heaping contempt upon himself and others whenever anything is in any way distressing. He may further try to avoid such experiences by denying that there are any reasons either for himself or others to feel distress. Such an individual will find it doubly difficult to tolerate physical pain or frustration in problem solving or loneliness. He may in attempting to minimize such experiences avoid risks of any kind, physical, mental or social.

If because of shame we suppress the cry and the feeling of distress, the same factors operating within us will make us incapable of awareness of the distress–anguish of others, or when the other's distress–anguish is overly obtrusive, will produce the same reaction to the other as our own distress produces within the self–avoidance of the other, or contempt, and some attempt to suppress rather than recognize the feeling. The reality of the suffering of the other becomes as difficult to appreciate as is the suppressed suffering of the self. Under these conditions the real troubles of the individual, and those of his wife, children, friends and associates are muffled, sedated and rebuffed. Their reality is denied.

When someone complains to him, he becomes bored or turns the conversation towards another direction or nods a perfunctory "hmm," vows to avoid this person in the future, frowns, lifts his lip in disgust or tries a more direct suppressive tactic. "Well, what did you expect–any damned fool would have headed that off." The implicit cry may be recognized and ridiculed:– "Stop it, you're breaking my heart–can I get you a crying towel?" or, if he is more mellow, he shakes his head in brief acknowledgment of the suffering of the other and then voices his own impunitive philosophy, "Well, those things happen. That's life."

Shaming the cry of distress may be combined, in socialization, with an emphasis upon remedial action. In such a case the parent is impatient with the child's crying and says something as follows: "Let's not be a cry baby. Crying never solved anything. Stop crying and let's see what can be done. If you stop crying I'll help you." The child is thus made to feel ashamed for two things. First, he is shamed just because he is crying. Only babies cry. Second, he is shamed because he is passive and crying rather than being active and doing something constructive about what he is crying about. This combination of shame and distress plus help in remedying the source of distress may produce an externalization of distress affect.

What are the consequences of externalizing affect? In the case of distress the individual is concerned only with the troubles and complaints of himself and others. The consequence is an excessively litigious way of life—if only these circumstances could be altered, life might be worth living. In response to the distress of others there is no awareness of resonant distress in the self. Rather, every attempt is made to help the sufferer by encouraging him to be articulate in his complaints so that something can be done about them. If the complaints are unreasonable or unrealistic, then they are responded to as such. The implicit plea of the other for sympathy is unrecognized because his affect is unrecognized. The same is true for the self. The continually unrecognized distress within will sometimes seek new objects and occasions for complaint because externalization is the only way in which the individual can express distress. The paradoxical power of the technique of recognition of feelings discovered by Rogers is due to the equally paradoxical phenomenon that it is entirely possible for an individual to spend a lifetime in complaint, in litigation and remedial action and to be only dimly aware that he is continually on the verge of crying in distress. Such an individual would be surprised to hear himself described as an unhappy person. In his own mind he is perpetually coping with one minor crisis after another, but these have nothing to do with his inner life of feeling or with his personality. It is no more than a reflection of the nature of the world he lives in.

The language of a distress externalizer reflects his unawareness. He never says, "I don't like X" or "I'm concerned about X" or "X troubles me." Rather, "Did you hear what happened about X? Isn't that a terrible thing—I don't know what the world's coming to when such things can happen. I'm going to give them a piece of my mind. They won't do that again if I have anything to say about it."

If someone comes with a complaint there is no recognition of the feeling of the other but rather a good-neighborly sharing of outrage: "You don't say! That's terrible! You know what I'd do? I'll tell you."

Externalization of affect cheats the individual and those with whom he interacts of one half of the positive response to suffering. The one who is so helped is usually only vaguely aware that something is missing.

Another variant of the distress—shame bind is that produced by "crying it out." In such a case the parent ordinarily is hostile toward crying or the child in general or both. Since this is a pointed turning away from the cry of help, the child upon finishing his crying may or may not be exhausted and apathetic, depending upon how long he cried and with what intensity. Searles noted many years ago that such a sequence of wish, crying and exhaustion could ultimately produce the most severe withdrawal of affect from all objects, since what was learned was that wishing produced pain and exhaustion.

It has frequently been reported to us that upon encountering difficulties in problem solving many adults suddenly feel quite tired and even exhausted to the point of falling asleep. In addition many also report that when they feel this way under these circumstances they also feel somewhat ashamed and that their head is likely to drop a bit. We would suggest that although the apathy and fatigue are probably related to earlier crying to exhaustion, that this sequence may on an innate basis be sufficient to activate shame and the feeling of alienation between the self and the one who was punitive. This is similar to the experience of mourning, in which distress and anger are produced when excitement and longing are increased by the death of the love object. Whenever these positive affects become attenuated, frequently after crying, then the head is hung in shame and defeat. Depression is therefore an oscillation between increase and decrease of positive affect which alternately activates distress or anger and shame. This is because, in our view, shame is activated by an incomplete reduction of excitement or joy, so that a child who wishes to look at or smile at a stranger but who is also reluctant, will respond with shame or shyness. When a child has cried to exhaustion because his parent would not help him, the interest in the parent is sufficiently attenuated, we think, to evoke shame and the child feels that the parent is in a real sense a stranger to him. It is because of this type of innate activation of shame that the adult whose distress has been socialized in this way so frequently experiences shame along with weariness and sleepiness when he might otherwise have simply felt distress in response to illness, or failure, or loneliness.

Ultimately also, such socialization of distress is capable of producing a profound resignation to destiny because of an awareness that when one needs help most, one's cry for help will not be heard, or if it is heard it will make no difference. Much of the pessimism which Freud attributed to the vicissitudes of the early oral stage can be accounted for by the long continued and repeated sequences of the lonely crying to exhaustion which has been permitted by parents whose posture towards distress is essentially punitive.

As we have noted before, the consequences for the adult may range from an intensification of such resignation, to occasional intrusions, to massive intrusions, or to complete masking but with an underlying vulnerability.

Intensification of power strategies

As we have noted before, there is a very high probability, given the rewarding and punitive characteristics of positive and negative affects, and given the automatic registration of all conscious experience in memory, and given the analyzer mechanisms, and finally given the feedback circuitry of the human being, that there will emerge, as a resultant of the interaction of these sub-systems, certain general ideas and strategies.

These general strategies are in one sense learned. They are not found in the neonate. On the other hand the probability of their being learned is so great, despite great variation of environmental stimulation and experience, that we have labeled them General Images. These include the general strategy of maximizing positive affect, minimizing negative affect, minimizing affect inhibition and maximizing power. By power we mean the ability to achieve a maximum of positive affect and a minimum of negative affect and a minimum of affect inhibition. The application of this to the affect of distress is that no matter what the particular socio-cultural matrix may be, all human beings will inevitably develop the strategy of minimizing the experience of distress and maximizing their power to do so. Further, if they suffer chronic unexpressed distress, they will attempt to express it and to maximize their power to do so. As we have also noted before, each of these strategies may interfere with the others.

Such a power strategy will be intensified to the extent to which the individual has suffered a punitive socialization of his distress. This is so because the increment of punishment for the distress cry, when added to the innate punishment of the response itself, increases the total punishment and therefore increases the attractiveness of the power which would be necessary to reduce or minimize or avoid further punishment.

If identification with the punitive parent is at a minimum because the parent continually generates and also punishes distress while providing insufficient compensatory positive affect, there are at least three power strategies open to the child. First, the child may elect to break through the constraints and do precisely that for which he suffered distress. So in response to the request to lower his voice, he may after punishment which produced distress, elect to shout just as loud as he did before. In this he is testing and reaffirming his power to minimize distress, in this case by flouting the power opposed to him.

Second, he may elect to break through the constraints by doing more than that for which he suffered distress. This strategy is similar to the first except that it is ordinarily conceived in response to constraints which, for a variety of reasons, appear to the child to be a more serious threat to his general power to minimize distress and indeed often also as a threat to his ability to maximize his positive affects. In short, the ambitiousness of the counter-strategy is proportional to the interpreted seriousness of the constraints on his powers to maximize his positive affects and his powers to minimize his negative affects. So, if he has been punished and distressed for making noise, his response, under this strategy, would be to make much more noise than he ever really wished to make. He is involved in a declaration of principles, the right to the pursuit of happiness.

His third alternative in breaking through the constraints

which produce distress and which limit his power to limit his distress is the strategy of retaliation. The second strategy comes close in intent to this, but stops just short of it. In the second strategy there is a testing of the limits and an affirmation of greater power than was originally thought necessary. In the third strategy the threat to the child's power is conceived to be so serious as to require retaliation, a reversal of power roles to guarantee his own basic power. The rationale here is that if I have power over you, you no longer have power over me. Hence the child now dedicates himself to recovering his power by successively limiting that of the parent who originally undermined his own power. He will now shout even if he doesn't wish to, if he can be sure this will distress his parent. Further he will become inventive and devise new ways to limit the power of his parents by increasing their suffering in such a way that they cannot control their distress, but become dependent on the child for deliverance from suffering.

If, however, the punitive parent encourages identification by providing positive experiences which somewhat attenuate the punishment of the distress socialization, other power strategies are open and ordinarily preferred to the flouting of authority and to retaliation. The principal alternative strategy is identification with the parent.

Identification with parents, we think, has two quite distinct sources. One source is based on excitement and enjoyment. The other source is the suffering of distress and other negative affects at the hands of parents. In this latter case, the power to minimize suffering is frequently conceived to lie in being as similar as possible to the models who are responsible for the suffering. Indeed, the models themselves not infrequently teach this strategy directly. But whether parents directly suggest this or not, children are not slow to diagnose their vulnerability to suffering to be a function of their childlike condition. It is a readily achieved insight that if they only possessed the characteristics of the parent, they would have solved most of the problem of minimizing distress and other negative affects. Thus begins that identification with an aggressor who is sufficiently rewarding to encourage identification rather than an open opposition of wills.

If the attempt at identification is itself punished, the child may be forced into the more hostile power strategies. A child made to cry for shouting too loud may experience a great intensification of distress and the generation of a more hostile power strategy if he asks to be permitted to set the dinner table and is refused, or if he attempts it and is criticized for his failure to correctly imitate his parent.

If by adulthood, the investment of affect in the power to minimize distress has continued to grow, the individual may sacrifice much positive enjoyment in the interests of guaranteeing that he will never again suffer distress. Such a posture is itself much exaggerated if distress has been further increased through multiple binds. In such a case the stake of the individual in the power to minimize distress is multiplied many times over, since the power to minimize distress has become the power to minimize negative affect in general. Under such conditions the strategy of power can assume monopolistic proportions. It becomes a wish, in the extreme case, not only to make the other suffer distress, but also to humiliate the other, to terrorize him and to destroy him.

Intensification of the strategy of minimizing
distress—anguish inhibition

The strategy of minimizing the experience of distress—anguish is a very general one which all human beings adopt. However, the strategy of minimizing the inhibition of distress might never be activated except for the fact that most societies impose some restrictions on the free expression of distress—anguish. When such restriction is punitive, the attempt to minimize inhibition of distress is intensified. Indeed, chronically suppressed distress produces what appears to be a quest for maximizing rather than minimizing negative affect. A person who has been unable to cry in distress much of his life will seek opportunities to cry, e.g., in sad plays or movies, in the crying released by alcohol, or in funerals. He wants to cry and welcomes the opportunity to do so.

This wish to cry also generates a further power strategy

designed to make it possible to express the distress which the punitive parent has inhibited through punishment. If an individual has been severely and consistently punished for crying, then the individual must ultimately conceive the strategy of doing whatever led to his crying and also violating the specific prohibition against crying. This involves an exaggerated power to undo, and to reverse the power of the other to forbid crying. Thus is generated excitement about the fantasy of crying out in public, without further distress or fear or shame about crying openly. Not uncommonly such a wish may be combined with other taboos into a single fantasy, e.g., the sado-masochistic sexual fantasy of mutual sexual excitement by hurting and making the partner cry while one also cries. In such a fantasy, the aggressive act, for which one might have been punished and made to cry and then punished again for crying, is committed again, but the crying now goes unpunished and the other is hurt and punished instead and also made to cry and suffer.

The activation of such fantasies also appears in the uninhibited crying of two intoxicated individuals, who are able to cry publicly without dread of punishment. In the tavern a good cry is as satisfying to those who may not otherwise cry as a good fight is to those who may not otherwise fight.

CONSEQUENCES OF THE REWARDING SOCIALIZATION OF DISTRESS–ANGUISH

By a rewarding socialization of distress we refer to the case in which the distress of the child evokes sympathetic distress in the parent who then communicates his own distress, his sympathy and his love for the child and who attempts to reduce distress by comforting the child. Insofar as it is possible, he also offers remedial help to cope with the circumstances which provoked the distress. The parent is concerned about reducing both the suffering of the child and its source. The consequences of such socialization for the personality of the child, and eventually for the personality of the adult, are antithetical to the consequences of a punitive socialization of the affect of distress.

Attenuation of distress—anguish

Because the distress experience is not permitted to last very long or to become very intense, and because it becomes the occasion of, and eventually a sign of, communion, intimacy and help from the parent, there is a radical attenuation of suffering for the child who is so socialized. In contrast with the doubling of penalties of all offenses in the punitive socialization, here penalties are halved, even when it is the parent himself who has spanked the child and made him cry. Having taught the child a lesson and discharged his own hostility, he is likely now to be seized with distress at the suffering he has inflicted on the child and to rush to the aid of his own victim. He will then offer not only sympathy but constructive help in how to govern himself in the future so that he does not again provoke unnecessary punishment. Thus a child who has been impulsively spanked for running headlong into the path of an automobile will be comforted, the love of the parent communicated and reaffirmed and connected with the rationale for the punishment. Further, every attempt will be made to produce insight in the mind of the child concerning the real dangers inherent in such behavior and the importance of modifying his behavior in the future in his own interest and for the sake of his parents.

Multiple suffering freedoms

In contrast to the multiple suffering binds produced by punitive socialization of distress, rewarding socialization has the cumulative effect of enlarging the freedom of the individual to express, to deal with and to reduce his distress. These freedoms derive not only from the lack of binds from fear or shame or further distress about crying itself, but also from the repeated experience of successful remedial action in coping with numerous sources of distress.

Increased trust in human help

One important type of freedom which is a consequence of the enjoyment of repeated help from parents in coping both with the experience of distress and its sources is a general trust

in the parents and in human beings. Basic trust has two components. First is the firmly held conviction that when one is in
trouble that this matters to someone else, that my distress is
your distress, that you are your brother's keeper, and that you
will offer sympathy and good wishes. Second, it is the equally
strong conviction that when I am too troubled to help myself,
you can and will help me directly or help me to help myself.
The individual who suffers punitive distress socialization, however, is haunted all his life with something akin to the ultimate
human predicament, the necessarily lonely confrontation of his
own death which is inescapable. He senses that if and when he
meets trouble he must meet it alone, and he must suffer in
silence lest he evoke more misery. He feels he can count on
neither sympathy nor help and that he is forever vulnerable to
contempt, to hostility or to rejection if he were to surrender to
the cry for help.

In contrast, rewarding distress socialization strengthens basic
trust and makes possible a depth and strength of interdependence which is impossible with punitive distress socialization. It
also generates confidence in the efficacy of the remedial action
taken by others on one's behalf.

Increased willingness and ability to offer sympathy and help to others

Inasmuch as every important response of the parent provides
an identification model for the child, rewarding distress socialization produces in the child empathic distress at the suffering
of the parents and others, a willingness to communicate felt
sympathy, a willingness to help the other and a belief that it
is possible to do so. This set of positive attitudes towards the
sufferings of others, combined with the belief that this is
reciprocal, is necessary if enduring and intense social ties are
to be generated and maintained.

Depending upon the nature of the socialization, this positive
syndrome may be differentiated and fragmented. The child
and later the adult may be taught, through identification, to feel
distress at the distress of the other but be unable or unwilling
to communicate it. He may be willing to communicate his

sympathy but unwilling or unable to offer remedial help. Finally, as we have noted before, he may insist on offering help, but in a way which is punitive toward the experience and expression of distress itself.

Further, in addition to identification as a basis for increased sympathy and helpfulness, there is also an intensification which derives from past enjoyments of the experience of distress. The rewarding distress socialization has not only attenuated the experience of distress but has made it the occasion of two kinds of enjoyment. First, it has been learned to be an occasion of the deepest intimacy and affirmations of love and concern. Second, it has been learned to be an occasion of additional enjoyment when something has been done to reduce distress at its source. Since the sudden reduction of distress is an innate activator of the smile of joy, this incremental reward becomes firmly linked with the affect of distress, which then becomes a sign of enjoyment to come.

Identification is therefore reinforced by two additional sources of enjoyment in the case of reward distress socialization.

In contrast, punitive distress socialization encourages contempt for, muffling of or sedation of the distress of the other, lest the individual re-experience fear or shame.

Increased willingness and ability to offer sympathy and help to the self

That posture of the parent symbolized in the stricture, "God helps those who help themselves," may or may not generate a self-reliant, self-helping individual, but it rarely produces an individual who offers himself sympathy. In punitive distress socialization it is as sinful for the individual to sympathize with himself as it is to express distress. "Don't feel sorry for yourself" is the prelude to "God helps those who help themselves." The taboo on distress has ordinarily this twofold character in punitive distress socialization.

In rewarding distress socialization the child is taught, through identification, to feel sorry for himself as well as for others. Such self-sympathy is not only an inevitable and appropriate response to any source of distress. It is also a necessary condition of its reduction both through habituation, and through a direct attack on its source. In contrast the muffling and sedation of the distress cry ordinarily intensifies it, and the addition of fear prevents both its habituation and a frontal attack on its source.

Rogers has noted that one of the early signs of movement in psychotherapy is an increased sympathy for the suffering of the self. Such sympathy for the self may also be a necessary condition for the repair of self-respect, since a self which can sympathize with its own suffering can more readily forgive its failures.

Further, sympathy for the suffering self is a sufficient but not a necessary condition for self-help, since self-help may also be a consequence of punitive socialization. The individual who was simply punished for the expression of distress is more likely to have sympathy for himself but yet remain sorry for himself and do nothing to help himself than one who was punished for the expression of distress but who was also punished for any failure to conform to some norm, or to help himself by a frontal attack on the source of his distress. Punitive distress socializations vary in their relative emphasis on the undesirability of the distress response alone, and in their emphasis on this and also on behavior which is either conforming or self-helping. Punitive socialization may under the latter conditions produce a very self-reliant, self-helping individual.

It has sometimes been urged in defense of punitive distress socialization that it is only by such a "sink or swim" strategy that the inherent overdependence of the child can be overcome. This argument is often further buttressed with the assertion that rewarding distress socialization will in fact further heighten this dependency by fixating the child on a complete reliance on the overly helpful parent. Such an argument overlooks one of the salient characteristics of the child, his innate eagerness to explore, to master and to identify with the parents he loves and respects. Passivity is not the primary problem of childhood unless the positive affects have been bound by fear or shame or distress. As we noted before in Harlow's experiments with young monkeys, those reared without benefit of the affection and solace of the surrogate mother ran in terror from the frightening object. Those who had enjoyed the benefits of mother love ran to her for protection, and after experiencing the reassuring contact, shortly thereafter turned to explore and do battle with the object which had a moment before paralyzed the young monkey.

While self-reliance may be bred by adversity and by punishment, many other not so desirable consequences also issue from such socialization. Self-reliance and self-help may also be bred by rewarding distress socialization without paying these other costs of punitive distress socialization. The arguments against the sympathetic response to distress are however sound under certain special conditions. If the child has been terrorized, and/or had his sources of excitement and enjoyment severely limited, and/or the other parent was a source of severe negative affect, and if further sympathy is offered without either help or instruction in self-help, then the child may be further infantilized by loving kindness shown to him only when he cries. In short, if the world of the child is made both very dangerous and very barren of reward, then the tender arms of an overprotective mother may indeed become the only mode of at once reducing terror and finding satisfaction. But for such a child the choice is not between normal development and being overindulged. The choice has been narrowed to one between schizophrenia and infantilism or perhaps neurosis.

However, the critic of the rewarding distress socialization has nonetheless a telling rejoinder. He may insist, properly, that even when development is otherwise normal, too much sympathy, especially if it follows punishment which the parent has administered with wisdom, will defeat the purpose of the punishment. If one is not prepared to follow through, why cause distress in the first place? Or again, the critic may say, if a child becomes distressed while studying because the material seems too difficult, of what help is it to seduce him with sympathy when what he must do is try harder? The critic is correct if sympathy is offered as a substitute for constructive effort to cope with the source of distress. Sympathy without remedial action may ultimately prove as punitive in consequences as an overemphasis on remedial action while punishing the distress response itself. The latter, as we have seen, leads to the externalizing of affect and the muffling of affect and to a failure to recognize the plea for sympathy. The former may lead to an equally unsatisfactory neglect of effort to cope with the numerous sources of distress while the individual is smothered and seduced by sympathy.

A complete and truly rewarding distress socialization necessarily therefore involves guidance and aid in learning to help the self, as well as balm. Given such a socialization the individual not only sympathizes with himself, but also has achieved self-trust in his ability to help himself out of his distress.

The nurturance of the idea of progress

In addition to strictly personal and interpersonal trust and confidence, there is the consequence of the belief in the general idea of progress. It has been affirmed that necessity is the mother of invention. More often we think invention is the mother of necessity. It is only after something has been demonstrated to be possible that similar novelty becomes psychologically possible, urgent and often even necessary. Only those who have enjoyed the amenities of modern civilization must have more of the same. The primitive feels none of the necessity to be inventive that modern man cannot escape. With individuals as with societies, the idea of progress and the demands as well as the sacrifices in the interest of progress are acceptable only to those who have enjoyed progress.

This begins with the circumstances which make one cry. To the extent to which one has had the experience, again and again, of remaking the world closer to the heart's desire, the idea of progress is born, takes root and grows. Neither meliorism nor revolution grow out of unrelieved suffering, in the nursery or in society. Historically, revolutions have occurred in those societies when improvement of social conditions begins to be enjoyed. Revolution springs from hope which has been nurtured by some relief of distress. Similarly with meliorism and the idea of progress generally. It occurs only after suffering has been ameliorated and provided a model for more relief. The essential dynamic is similar in man as in society. It is the repeated experience of progress in coping with the sources of distress which generates the idea of the possible, transforms it into a probability and finally into a necessity.

This is not to say that the idea of progress which has played such a central role in Western industrial society is a simple derivative of a rewarding distress socialization. Indeed it seems more likely that the influence might well have operated in the other direction, and that a general idea of progress in a society or the lack of it might trickle down and determine the strategy and tactics of dealing with crying crises in the nursery.

Favors the development of physical courage

Since pain innately activates distress, the rewarding socialization of distress favors the development of courage in the toleration of bodily pain. This is why, we think, American women are less disturbed by bodily pain as such than are American men. Their distress socialization less commonly relies on shame to inhibit the cry of distress. The paradox is that because they have not been shamed into bravery—they are braver. The same dynamic holds for those societies which permit the child to learn the control of the distress cry gradually and without reliance on fear or shame. Many such societies however insist on severe tests of physical courage in puberty rites. It would be of interest to compare societies which are consistently punitive with societies which introduce such discontinuities, with those which are consistently rewarding with respect to pain-induced distress. We would expect an increased ability to tolerate pain in that order.

Favors the development of frustration tolerance in problem-solving

When children encounter difficulties in doing what they would like to be able to do, they are vulnerable to distress of tantrum proportions. Rewarding distress socialization first soothes the child sufficiently to attenuate the intensity of distress and then encourages him to try again. Although distress—anguish is not so toxic as fear—terror, it may nonetheless overwhelm the child if he is not taught how to reduce and grade its intensity and again address himself directly to the sources of his distress. Tolerance for distress—anguish depends essentially on how many intermediate intensities of the response are available to the child, and how readily he achieves control over the intensity of the distress response by transforming it to successively lesser intensities. Such transformations depend critically on the minuteness of the transitions and these are a function of the number of intermediate intensities of distress—anguish with which the child has had experience. It is a general principle that mastery of any negative affect is facilitated by a rewarding socialization which allows the individual to experience the negative affect in graded intensities varying from weak to strong as it increases and then gradually decreases in intensity. Thus he learns many fine gradations of intensity and duration.

Such gradations of distress are capable of being learned and providing a bridge back from the tantrum to a sufficiently low key distress cry so that problem solving can be attempted again.

Punitive socialization produces severe negative affect about negative affect which amplifies the affect, instead of producing fine gradations, in intensity and duration. Such amplified affect is usually mastered by strategies in which the major aim is to avoid the possibilities of distress rather than directly confronting the source of distress and coping with it.

Favors individuation and a sense of identity

Because distress has been rewarded rather than punished, the loneliness of individuation can be better tolerated and the achievement of a sense of one's own identity is thereby favored. The pain of loss of love, or of the separateness which is occasioned by the confrontation of real differences between oneself and one's identification figures and love objects, either by virtue of maturation and the assumption of adult responsibilities or by virtue of the death of loved ones, are borne more readily when distress has not been linked with shame or fear and when it has been softened by linkage with sympathy and help.

SOME CONSEQUENCES OF THE INCOMPLETE REWARD SOCIALIZATION OF DISTRESS

By incomplete reward socialization of distress we mean any socialization in which the parent attempted to reduce distress crying by some type of reward, without attempting to remedy the source of distress or to help the child help itself to remedy the source of distress. The parent might, for example, pick up the crying infant, rock it, feed it, speak to it, sing to it, look at it, smile at it, kiss it or pat it. If the parent continued throughout childhood to emphasize the rewarding reduction of distress, without reference to the source of distress, the individual as an adult will tend to seek sedation whenever he experiences distress. Thus when he feels lonely or is baffled by a difficult problem, is tired or sick, or when his wife or child or friend suffers, he will seek to re-experience the particular mode by which his distress was characteristically reduced. He may seek solace in eating or being fed, in conversation, in listening to singing or music, in some form of motion akin to being rocked, in exhibiting himself so that he will be looked at, in some form of body contact, in sexuality, or in some retreat into an enveloping claustrum reminiscent of his mother's arms. Any one of these may make him feel better, after which he may or may not return to his original problem. To the extent to which the individual has been taught primarily to sedate himself rather than to solve his problems, there will be a continuation and strengthening of such a trend, if the snowball model describes his development, and there will be intrusions of such phenomena even though they have been outgrown if the iceberg model describes his development.

These strategies of distress sedation also becomes salient, even for those who have learned to cope directly with the sources of their distress, under the special conditions in which it is not possible to attack the source directly, or is assumed not to be possible. So an individual who characteristically counteracts barriers of all kinds which might have occasioned distress may nonetheless seek solace in eating or talking to others, if and when he is confronted with what appears to be an insoluble problem.

Such strategies may also be sought when the psychologist contrives to limit the freedom of his subjects to deal realistically with their distress. This we take to be the limitation on the generality of Schachter's conclusions that "the affiliative tendency is positively related to the states of anxiety and hunger." Let us review his experiments at this point.

SOME EVIDENCE ON THE USE OF SEDATION STRATEGIES AS A FUNCTION OF ANXIETY, HUNGER AND BIRTH ORDER

In a brilliant series of experiments, Schachter showed that when human beings are made to suffer the anxiety of anticipation of a series of painful electric shocks, and then given the choice of waiting for this ordeal alone or being with others until the experiment began, 63 per cent of the subjects wanted to be together while they waited. When they were told they were going to receive only very mild shocks, this on the average produced a lower anxiety response; only 33 per cent wanted to be together with other subjects while waiting for the shocks. Schachter found that this wish was highly directional in that anxious subjects, who were also subjects in this experiment, wanted only to be with those in a similar plight and not simply with any other human beings, and that the wish remains even when no verbal communication is permitted.

There were large individual differences in the strength of the wish to be with people under such conditions, and it was ordinal position which appeared to be the critical determinant of these differences. Early-born subjects were more anxious than later-born subjects, and anxious early-born subjects chose to be together with other subjects whereas equally anxious later-born subjects did not do so. In support of the generality of these findings Schachter showed further that first-born are more likely to become alcoholic, are more susceptible to psychotherapy and remain in it longer, and are less effective fighter pilots than later-born individuals. Schachter interprets these findings to indicate that first-born individuals are more dependent than later-born individuals.

Thus far we have been describing anxiety and togetherness. When Schachter dealt with distress produced by food deprivation, the results were in the same direction, although the relation between ordinal position and sociophilia under these conditions did not hold up. In part this may be because we are dealing with distress rather than anxiety, or because when a child is hungry there is less difference in the attitude of parents toward first- and late-born children, that is, all children may be fed when they cry whereas more first-born children are the object of concern when they cry about other things, or are frightened.

Limitations on the generality of Schachter's findings

While these findings represent an important contribution, there are two limitations on their generality. First, the subjects in the original experiments were all girls. The difference between the sexes in personality experimentation is one of the most strik-ing unintended findings in the entire literature. Well over a few hundred experimental tests of personality have foundered on the sex difference. Girls would be more likely to feel and reveal their dependence on others under the threat of electric shock than would boys. Secondly, the conditions of these experiments are such as to evoke sedative strategies, since there is nothing that can be done in the waiting period to directly attack the sources of fear or distress. If the subjects were to be given the choice of doing something remedial about their anxiety or distress or of being together with others, the differential choices would under these conditions be more determined by the punitiveness or the rewarding characteristics of early distress socialization. Further, we should expect differences between affiliation under anxiety and under distress. Counteraction of distress need not be related to counteraction of fear because of the gross differ-ence in toxicity of these two affects.

SOME CONSEQUENCES OF A MIXED
DISTRESS SOCIALIZATION

Distress socialization is of course not always consistent or uniform. The parent may punish crying severely one day and shower love on the child when it cries tomorrow or even imme-diately after punishment for crying. The consequences of the latter strategy we have already examined. The consequences of the day-to-day change in parental reactions are a lability of the child's own internalized attitudes toward, and his expectations of, others' attitudes toward distress, producing hot and cold postures in the child and later in the adult.

When the split between rewarding and punishing socialization of distress is embodied in the difference between the mother and father, there may be serious conflict which makes personality integration impossible, or which results in a retarded integration as we saw in the analysis of the late bloomer model. It also produces an enduring sensitivity to clashes of personalities and to the difficulties of communication, and an interest in promoting communication and resolving social conflict. Finally, apart from these socially useful consequences, it may also produce what we have defined as social restlessness, the inability to be alone for long, or together for long, and a tendency to maximize the shifts from solitude and togetherness.

Another source of such a split derives from a punitive socialization of distress, in which, however, the parents provide much reward for anything other than crying. The consequence of such socialization is a muffling of distress with an accentuation of the positive affects, to the point of denial of suffering with the ever present possibility of severe intrusion effects as we saw in the extreme case of the child who was beaten until he stopped crying.

Finally there are those varieties of mixed socialization of distress which depend upon the circumstances under which crying occurs. The consequences are as numerous as the varieties of distinctions which govern whether a child will be punished or rewarded when he cries. It will also depend on the extent to which these distinctions are learned by the child, and this in turn depends in part on how self-conscious the parent is and how explicitly he communicates his philosophy of suffering. However, distinctions between types of distress can be taught and learned without either the parent or child achieving the ability to verbalize the basis of the learned distinctions. Thus, if the individual has been rewarded when he cried as an infant, and punished when he cried as a child, he may generalize this and later repeat this with his own children without knowing why.

A parent may reward crying which is pure distress, but not crying with an undertone of complaint, blame and anger. As an adult such an individual may deal sympathetically with human error and the distress it produces, but respond ruthlessly toward any distress which carries a hint of blame or anger, whether toward himself or others.

If the parent rewards the child when he cries in pain after having been hurt accidentally, but punishes him if he had been previously warned, the individual may generalize such a distinction so that he responds very sympathetically to any distress the source of which appears to have been beyond the control of the individual, but harshly whenever the individual appears to have displayed poor judgment in heaping trouble upon himself.

If the parent rewards the child when he cries after physical injury but not after he has been disciplined, the individual may as an adult startle his associates and friends by an island of softness in a personality otherwise bounded by firm contours.

If the parent punishes crying whenever authority is challenged, for example, when the child will not go to bed upon the request of the parent, but rewards crying if it is a consequence of loneliness, this can produce an adult who is generally authoritarian but with a soft spot for social isolates, or for any of those in need of human companionship.

If the parent punished crying in public but rewarded it in private, this may produce an adult with a tough public façade, but a childlike family man. A similar consequence may issue from punitive socialization of distress by the father and rewarding socialization of distress by the mother. A further generalization would produce a sharp dichotomy between sympathy for an extended in-group, which might include one's own family, own friends, and own company, but harshness towards anyone not included in the extended in-group. Such a consequence can also be produced by a split in distress socialization when the family rewards distress, but the out-group punishes it, as happens when a child is a member of a punished minority group. However under these conditions in some cases the adult may respond with intense sympathy to a very extended in-group, which may even include humanity, and exclude only oppressors, which in the most extreme case may be restricted to that small part of the self of the oppressor which has not been regenerated.

Finally, if the parents punish crying whenever the source

is within the family, but reward it whenever the source is outside the family, the consequences for the individual as an adult is to maximize sympathy for any distress suffered from outsiders, but to minimize sympathy for any distress which occurs in intimate interpersonal relationships within the extended in-group when the distress is a response to the behavior of members of the in-group.

IDEOLOGICAL CONSEQUENCES OF DISTRESS SOCIALIZATION

How a parent responds to the distress of a child may be governed by a philosophy of suffering and may produce an internalization in the child of such an ideology, or an internalization in the child of a philosophy which is in radical opposition to that of the parent. The latter indeed may be produced by extreme distress socialization, or inconsistency of distress socialization even if the parents themselves have no organized ideology of suffering. We will consider these problems in the chapter on ideology and affect. We will therefore defer our discussion until we consider the ideological consequences of punitive shame socialization.

Chapter 16

Shame – Humiliation versus Contempt – Disgust: The Nature of the Response

If distress is the affect of suffering, shame is the affect of indignity, of defeat, of transgression and of alienation. Though terror speaks to life and death and distress makes of the world a vale of tears, yet shame strikes deepest into the heart of man. While terror and distress hurt, they are wounds inflicted from outside which penetrate the smooth surface of the ego; but shame is felt as an inner torment, a sickness of the soul. It does not matter whether the humiliated one has been shamed by derisive laughter or whether he mocks himself. In either event he feels himself naked, defeated, alienated, lacking in dignity or worth.

SHYNESS, SHAME, GUILT AND SELF-CONTEMPT

Shyness, shame and guilt are not distinguished from each other at the level of affect, in our view. They are one and the same affect. This is not to say that shyness in the presence of a stranger, shame at a failure to cope successfully with a challenge and guilt for an immorality are the same experience. Clearly they are not. The conscious awareness of each of these experiences is quite distinct. Yet the affect that we term shame–humiliation, which is a component of each of these total experiences, is one and the same affect. It is the differences in the other components which accompany shame in the central assembly or, in other words, which are experienced together with shame, which make the three experiences different.

The relationship between shyness, shame about inadequacy and moral guilt is similar to the relationship between the smile of triumph and the smile of love. In one case the smile accompanies hate and injury inflicted upon an adversary; in the other the smile accompanies the most tender intentions. Yet in both cases the underlying affect is enjoyment, the awareness of the smiling response. One person enjoys love, and the other enjoys hate. So with shame; the total field in which shame is embedded in the central assembly of components of the nervous system at the moment will give quite different flavors to shame depending upon its intensity and upon the objects which appear to activate it and the objects which appear to reduce it.

These differences in intensity and in objects have important consequences for the nature of an individual's shame response and the role that it plays within his personality. But the failure to grasp the underlying biological identity of the various phenotypes of shame has retarded our understanding of these consequences as well as of the magnitude and nature of the general role of shame in human functioning.

While the affect of shame–humiliation encompasses shyness, shame and guilt, it is distinct from the affect of disgust–contempt. In its dynamic aspects, however, shame is often intimately related to and easily confused with contempt, particularly self-contempt; indeed, it is sometimes not possible to separate them. Therefore, contempt–disgust and shame–humiliation are discussed in the same chapters.

It is the purpose of this chapter to make clear the fundamental natures of these two affects, including their critical differences. While in many regards the effects of someone else shaming one and holding one in contempt may be similar, and one's own feelings of shame and self-contempt may co-vary, in this chapter the basic biological difference between shame and contempt will be discussed, as well as some of the differential dynamics.

SHAME–HUMILIATION: EYES DOWN, HEAD DOWN, BLUSHING

The shame response is an act which reduces facial communication. It stands in the same relation to looking and smiling as silence stands to speech and as disgust, nausea and vomiting stand to hunger and eating. By dropping his eyes, his eyelids, his head and sometimes the whole upper part of his body, the individual calls a halt to looking at another person, particularly the other person's face, and to the other person's looking at him, particularly at his face. The child early learns to cover his face with his hands when he is shy in the presence of a stranger. In self-confrontation the head may also be hung in shame symbolically, lest one part of the self be seen by another part and become alienated from it.

It may be speculated that clothing originated in the generalization of shame to the whole body, and the consequent need to cover it from the stare of the other. In different cultures a cover may be worn over the genitals or the face or both, whichever are felt to be the most private parts of the body.

Blushing

Paradoxically, there is a response auxiliary to the shame complex, which has the effect of increasing facial communication, even though the response is instigated by the feeling of shame and the wish to reduce facial visibility. This is blushing, the awareness of which ordinarily increases shame because it has defeated it.

As Darwin described this affective response in his *Expression of the Emotions in Man and Animals:* "Of all expressions, blushing seems to be the most strictly human; yet it is common to all or nearly all the races of man whether or not any change of colour is visible in their skin. The relaxation of the small arteries of the surface, on which blushing depends, seems to have primarily resulted from earnest attention directed to the appearance of our own persons, especially of our faces, aided by habit, inheritance, and the ready flow of nerve-force along accustomed channels; and afterwards to have been extended by the power of association to self-attention directed to moral conduct."

As Darwin further noted, attention directed to any part of the body may interfere with the tonic contraction of the small arteries of that part, which then become relaxed and fill with arterial blood. Since this may and does happen to any part of the body, the question may be raised whether we are dealing with an innately patterned affective response or whether blushing might not better be conceived more simply as a reaction to heightened self-consciousness. We are inclined to make the latter assumption.

IS SHAME—HUMILIATION AN AFFECT OR A LEARNED RESPONSE?

There is the further question whether the shame response proper, the dropping of the eyes, face and head, and the conscious experience of the resultant feedback, should properly be called an affect in the sense in which the smile of joy and the cry of distress are facial affective responses whose feedback is, innately, the conscious experience of these affects.

In these latter cases there is reason to believe we inherit the neurological instructions which are stored in sub-cortical centers, which when stimulated send an appropriately patterned set of messages to the face. Is the same true for what we are calling the shame response?

It may be thought, on the contrary, that because the aim of shame is to reduce facial communication, it is less probable that it is an innately patterned response; that it is more like silence in speech, i.e., a self-conscious strategy designed simply to stop communication which calls for no special innate program.

The reduction of visibility of the face and the dropping of the head appears in animals other than man, most notably the dog. The dog appears to be as capable of responding with shame as man. While this occurrence of shame in lower animals might be taken as evidence for the view that shame is an innately patterned affect, it is nonetheless consistent with the alternative interpretation that shame is a highly probable strategy which will be learned in order to reduce communication whenever this becomes distressing or frightening.

Hebb and Riesen have shown that disturbance at strangers in chimpanzees is spontaneous. At four months the nursery-reared chimpanzee is disturbed by what they call "shyness," which may become much more violent than that term would usually imply.

However, this shyness, although spontaneous, does not develop without much previous general learning. This might be taken to indicate that shame is a learned strategy. Nissen reported that chimpanzees reared in darkness and brought into light at an age when fear would normally be strong were not disturbed either by friend or stranger.

Nissen's interpretation is that the chimpanzee in some sense cannot "see," that a certain amount of perceptual learning is required before the chimpanzee can recognize objects. Again, his observations are consistent both with the view that shame is itself a learned response and with the alternate view that shame is an innate response which nevertheless requires a perceptual response that has to be learned.

In human infants too, as we have noted in discussing the smiling response, there is no shyness until the infant can learn to distinguish the mother's face from the face of the stranger, at which point he first begins not to smile, to look away and sometimes to cry and even to fall asleep.

These reactions to the stranger by the infant are first of all reactions of not smiling. Infants appear to vary in what else they do when confronted with the stranger for the first time. Some infants cry, some turn their eyes away, some stare with intense interest at the unfamiliar face, some appear to freeze in fear.

This variability, while suggesting a learned response, does not necessarily argue against the innate patterning of the shame response, since there is a variety of ways in which the stranger might activate affects other than shame, either on an innate or learned basis, and the alternative affects may account for the variability of response. Thus, if the infant were to startle at the face of the stranger, the aftermath of the startle response might produce such contraction of the general skeletal musculature as to raise the level of neural bombardment sufficiently to activate the distress cry, and thus interfere with the shame response.

Another alternative is that the suddenness of recognition of the stranger might be sufficiently rapid to produce fear but not sufficiently rapid to produce a startle.

Nonetheless, the argument that shame is a learned response rather than an affect is persuasive until we examine the parallel with another set of mechanisms by which intake is reduced—

disgust, nausea and vomiting—to be described later in this chapter. Here there is no question that these auxiliary defenses
attached to the hunger drive are innately patterned responses,
whose major function is to interfere with and reduce the intake
of food just when the hunger drive is at its peak. Disgust is a
mechanism which excludes intake at the moment when another
mechanism is insisting on intake. The parallel of disgust and
nausea with shame appears to be quite close. Just when the
infant might establish communication by looking and smiling
at the familiar face of the mother, the perceived difference reduces the excitement somewhat, and this reduction appears to
activate an affect designed to interfere with the ongoing excitement and enjoyment.

A THEORY OF SHAME—HUMILIATION

We are inclined to favor the theory that shame is an innate
auxiliary affect and a specific inhibitor of continuing interest
and enjoyment. Like disgust, it operates ordinarily only after
interest or enjoyment has been activated, and inhibits one or
the other or both. The innate activator of shame is the incomplete reduction of interest or joy. Hence any barrier to further
exploration which partially reduces interest or the smile of
enjoyment will activate the lowering of the head and eyes in
shame and reduce further exploration or self-exposure powered
by excitement or joy. Such a barrier might be because one is
suddenly looked at by one who is strange, or because one wishes
to look at or commune with another person but suddenly cannot
because he is strange, or one expected him to be familiar but
he suddenly appears unfamiliar, or one started to smile but
found one was smiling at a stranger.

Once shame has been activated, the original excitement or joy
may be increased again and inhibit the shame or the shame may
further inhibit and reduce excitement or joy. Thus a shy child
may suddenly break into an unashamed stare, or he may turn
away completely from the stranger who evokes shyness.

The exact nature of the innate shame response is still to be
determined. With high-speed moving picture cameras it should

be possible to delineate the precise nature of the response as it first appears upon the recognition of the unfamiliar face.

The nature of the shame—humiliation response:
Engel and Reichsman's observations

Until now, empirical studies of the shame response have been few and these have been indirect. It has been studied more as an instance of failure to smile than as a response in itself. As previously described, after the human infant learns to distinguish its mother's face from strange faces, indiscriminate smiling ceases and shyness begins. Only relatively recently has the shame response proper become the focus of empirical investigation. Engel and Reichsman studied the depressions of a hospitalized fifteen-month infant, who had a surgically produced gastric and esophageal fistula soon after birth because of a congenital atresia of the esophagus. They observed this infant for nine months. Although the shame response was not the focus of the investigation, what was observed included, we think, such responses.

This infant, named Monica, after recovery from a marasmus and depression, showed a striking set of responses which Engel and Reichsman called the depression-withdrawal reaction. Whenever the infant, between 15 and 24 months old, was confronted alone by a stranger, there was a characteristic reaction of muscular inactivity, hypotonia, a sad facial expression, decreased gastric secretion and eventually sleep. The depression-withdrawal reaction occurred only when the infant was confronted alone by a stranger. These were people she had never seen before or persons who in their first contacts remained aloof or disinterested. There was only one occasion when a stranger did not evoke the response, and he happened to physically resemble her father. When a familiar person was also present with the stranger, the reaction was milder and briefer but still occurred. The reaction developed immediately upon perceiving the stranger and lasted as long as he remained—in some cases up to three hours. The reaction was never observed when the baby was alone.

If the stranger remained inactive the baby immediately lost muscle tone, the limbs literally falling where they were. Thereafter the baby was immobile, movements being restricted to glancing at the stranger from time to time. She first turned her head away, but later gave this up and merely stared past him. Finally she would close her eyes, at first intermittently, then after ten to thirty minutes they would remain closed.

The face sagged, the corners of the mouth were down, the inner corners of the brows were elevated, which with a furrowed brow produced the "omega of melancholy." The mouth usually was slightly open.

If the stranger remained more than twenty to thirty minutes, the infant would go to sleep. If the stranger was still there when she awoke, she responded again with the depression-withdrawal pattern.

When the stranger made no overtures and repeatedly reappeared on succeeding occasions, the infant eventually lost her shyness and made efforts to establish contact by small touching movements with the fingers or feet. When this happened gastric secretion generally tended to increase.

This infant was far from normal. She had suffered a severe depression in her first year of life, and when hospitalized was severely underweight and underdeveloped. Her muscular development in particular was severely retarded, varying between the 5-to-8 month level. At 15 months she was unable to sit up or even turn over in bed without help, nor did she speak.

Inasmuch as the reaction to the stranger was complicated by the past history of a depressive state serious enough to have involved general retardation of development, we cannot rely upon this evidence as necessarily representative of the response of a normal infant to the stranger. At the least it is the shame of a depressive. Despite this there appear to be important communalities between her response and that of infants and young children generally. First, it is clear that the avoidance of interocular interaction is salient—since she turned her head away at first, stared past the stranger and finally closed her eyes completely until she fell asleep. Although Engel and Reichsman do not report the most characteristic components of the childhood and adult shame response, namely the momentary dropping of the lids and head, it is nonetheless clear that the infant is trying to reduce interocular experience. It is possible that the severe depression which preceded this period of testing produced both a complication and an exaggeration of the shame response, so that the conscious voluntary intention to reduce interocular interaction somewhat modified and masked the earlier innate response.

Despite these complications, Engel and Reichman's observations are important in revealing an aspect of shyness which deserves further investigation. This is the sudden loss of tonus in the facial and other muscles and the correlated reduction in the secretion of hydrochloric acid by the stomach. We have often observed the loss of tonus of the facial muscles with an apparent dullness of the eyes in children who are shy in the presence of a stranger. It is quite possible that this is an innate component of the shame affect when it is most intense. Both affects and drives become quite different in form as intensity or duration of the affect or drive increases. Such differences may be either innate in origin or learned modifications of the innate responses.

The further association of hypotonia and shyness with reduced gastric secretion of hydrochloric acid deserves further study in a series of normal children. It may or may not be a general finding. It is entirely possible that shyness was so intense and generalized in this deeply depressed, marasmic child, that it became the occasion of the refusal of both interocular interaction and the taking in of food, and still be possible that in normal children shame is restricted to the inhibition of interocular experience without generalization to the gastric response.

Engel and Reichsman labeled this set of responses depression-withdrawal, and they are undoubtedly right that this is more than a simple shame response, even though it includes shame components. Prominent in it is also distress. The infant sometimes cried and more often looked sad and about to cry. This infant had suffered a severe depression. We will consider later the affects specific to depression. Here we wish only to call attention to the confounding of the simple innate affect of shame by depression.

We conceive depression to be a syndrome of shame and distress, which also reduces the general amplification of all impulses. This reduction of amplification is both neurological and humoral. In relative hypoglycemia we noted the failure of normal adrenal support when the zest for life is impaired. In depression there is a more general reduction in amplification, probably mediated through the reticular formation and other amplifier structures. The observed hypotonia, therefore, is a consequence of that reduction in amplification which is characteristic of intense and enduring shame which has been accompanied by equally intense and enduring distress, which together constitute depression.

The question whether shame *per se*, mild or intense, in the absence of depression, necessarily includes hypotonia, must be considered a question for further investigation. Certainly when the head drops forward this may be due primarily to loss of tonus of the specific muscles involved. It is also possible that the lowering of the eyes and the lowering of the eyelids are due to a specific loss of tonus in specific muscles rather than to the more usual neurological program of a contraction of one set and a relaxation of the antagonistic muscles.

Height of the apparent horizon as a measure
of shame–humiliation

A series of experiments by Werner and Wapner have also provided a promising technique of investigation of the development of the shame response. They employed the angle of regard of the eyes toward the horizon as a measure of the effect of different experimental treatments. This technique appeared to provide a sensitive measure of changes in mood, and, we think, of the shame response. Krus, Wapner and Freeman found that success elevated the apparent horizon, compared with failure, that manic patients had a higher horizon than depressed patients, and that excitatory drugs elevated the apparent horizon, compared with tranquilizing drugs.

Werner and Wapner reported that the apparent horizon was located significantly higher than the objective horizon (physical location of eye level) in the youngest children (aged 6) and that is systematically shifted to a position below objective eye level with an increase in age (to 20 years).

The significance of this latter finding is not altogether clear. It may be due to the fact that children must look up to adults and that their gaze is lowered as they become as tall as those they look at. It is, however, possible that the characteristic taboo later imposed on interocular interaction also plays a role in the gradual lowering of the gaze of the eyes.

CONTEMPT–DISGUST: SNEER, UPPER LIP UP

In contrast to shame, contempt is a response in which there is least self-consciousness, with the most intense consciousness of the object, which is experienced as disgusting. Although the face and nostrils and throat and even the stomach are unpleasantly involved in disgust and nausea, yet attention is most likely to be referred to the source, the object, rather than to the self or the face. This happens because the response intends to maximize the distance between the face and the object which disgusts the self. It is a literal pulling away from the object.

Contempt–disgust is fundamentally a defensive response which is auxiliary to the hunger, thirst and oxygen drives. Its function is clear. If the food about to be ingested activates disgust, the upper lip and the nose is raised and the head is drawn away from the apparent source of the offending odor. If the substance has been taken into the mouth, it will be spit out and the head drawn away from it. If it has been swallowed, it will produce nausea and it will be vomited out either through the mouth or nostrils.

According to Darwin, "Disgust would have been shown at a very early period by movements round the mouth, like those of vomiting—that is, if the view which I have suggested respecting the source of the expression is correct, namely that our progenitors had the power, and used it, of voluntarily and quickly rejecting any food from their stomachs which they disliked."

If disgust and nausea were limited to these functions, we should not define them as affects, but rather as auxiliary drive mechanisms. However, their status is somewhat unique in that disgust and nausea also function as signals and motives to others as well as to the self of feelings of rejection. The awareness of disgust and nausea is not limited to offensive tastes and smells but readily accompanies a wide spectrum of entities which need not be tasted, smelled or ingested.

In contrast to such affects as fear and excitement, however, the linkage with a specific drive is much more intimate. Whereas excitement lends itself equally to the support of thirst or hunger or sex, nausea would appear to be more specific in its relationship to hunger than is excitement in its relationship to hunger. This is not to say that a feeling of nausea could not interrupt the consummation of sexuality as well as the consummation of hunger. The difference here is that the site of the nausea response is such as to provide direct interference with the act of oral or nasal consummation, whereas its interference with sexual consummation is more remote sitewise, even if it is no less effective an inhibitor of sexuality than of orality. Further, it would appear to differ fundamentally from all other affects in a second way.

The stimuli which primarily activate disgust and nausea are those which are relevant to hunger, thirst and breathing.

From an evolutionary standpoint, one would suppose that what was too noxious to be ingested with safety was information which came to be built into the mechanism of disgust and nausea. As such, this mechanism evolved in the form of an affect more specialized for the intake drives than for the other drives or for any other purpose. In short, because of its specialization in the interest of particular drives, it could not so easily serve as a dissociable affect in the service of rejecting other kinds of non-drive information. In this respect this affect represents a more primitive type of affect-drive organization.

In the lower animals it is clear that affects which in man are highly dissociable from drives, and which are as capable of activating drives as of being activated by drives, are more closely linked to drives. Thus the hormonal arousals of female sexuality in many of the lower forms necessarily arouses associated excitement, but not conversely. In the human, however, stimulation of excitement can produce sexual erection and tumescence as easily as tumescence and genital stimulation can activate excitement. In the human also this excitement is readily dissociable from the sex drive. Olds has shown that in the rat there are several joy centers, each of which is located in the area specific to the drive which it supports. We would suggest that the sense of smell, which is in the older brain, still retains in man the more primitive drive-affect organization. Disgust and nausea therefore have some of the characteristics of the other human affects, but are more similar to the more specific linkages of affect and drive found in the lower animals.

Contempt appears to be changing now in status from a drive-reducing act, i.e., the rejection of vomiting of noxious food, to an act which also has a more general motivating signal function, both to the individual who emits it and to the one who sees it.

Contempt—disgust for objects which are not taken into the mouth

Whether there exist innate activators for disgust in the more general characteristics of stimulation such as we have postulated or the other affects seems problematic. It seems more likely that disgust is learned to be emitted to objects which are neither taken into the mouth nor smelled, on the basis either of similarity of the stimulus characteristic of the new object to other disgusting objects or of the similarity to other disgusting objects produced by the similar constellation of an underlying wish to incorporate an object close to it, when there are also wishes to maximize the distance rather than minimize it.

Thus if an object is dirty, it may be experienced as similar enough to a malodorous object to excite disgust. Similarly, if an object or activity is disorderly, it may seem to an individual with a low contempt threshold to be also dirty and smelly, so that it should be cleaned up.

Similarity may also be based on an underlying wish to incorporate the object or come closer to it. Thus disgust may be aroused by a very attractive sex object, if there is both a strong wish for and fear of sexual contact. In such cases, paradoxically, the less disgusting the object, the more disgust may be felt if fear exceeds desire.

Similarly, if one has been humiliated for being lazy and passive, then the more tired one becomes, when someone else visibly indulges himself in his passivity, the more disgust will be felt as the wish to imitate the other increases. Again, the puritan is vulnerable to disgust whenever he is confronted with those who enjoy their pleasures. In these last two examples similarity is even more attenuated in that these are acts which the individual would like to imitate but which he dare not imitate.

Disgust is primarily nonetheless an act of distancing the self from an object, and it is felt primarily toward objects which are purely negative in quality. It is possible to be disgusted at attractive objects only under the condition that imitation of them, or increased closeness, or incorporation of them is also tabooed.

As Angyal has shown, intimacy of contact with a repulsive object is a prime factor in the arousal of disgust. It is much more disgust-arousing to touch a repulsive object than to see it or hear it. If any sticky, soft, slimy substance were compressed into a solid block like wood or metal, there would be less disgust in touching it because no visible particles could attach themselves to the skin. By analogy anything which has had contact with disgusting things itself becomes disgusting. Many disgust taboos, including dietary rituals, can be understood as a minimizing of contact between clean and malodorous, disgusting objects. In this sense they are essentially handwashing compulsions at a distance.

Contempt—disgust and blocked pregnancy in mice

Although disgust and nausea in man seem primarily to subserve the intake drives, more recent evidence has shown that at least in the lower animals it may also subserve the sexual drive. Bruce and Parrott have shown that pregnancy is blocked in a high proportion of recently mated female mice exposed to strange males. This reaction is virtually abolished by the prior removal of the olfactory bulbs of the female. The smell of the strange male appears to be the primary stimulus in the exteroceptive block to pregnancy in mice. A high degree of discrimination is shown by the female because if she is returned to her original stud male 24 hours after separation from him, her pregnancy is carried to term.

To what extent there may be disgust reactions based on differences in body odors among humans, which would restrict exogamy, is not known. It is clear, however, that disgust lends itself readily to activation by objects which originally aroused no disgust.

Contempt–disgust, feces and the anal character

It remains an unanswered question of some interest whether the odors and excreta of the human body are innately disgusting or whether these are learned responses. While there can be no doubt that Freud's classical anal character constructed an extraordinarily elaborate classification system through learning, which enabled him to put in one filing cabinet all the clean objects and in another all the dirty disgusting objects, yet the question about the biological basis of this nostril sensitivity remains. It appears that the infant is not disgusted by any of its smells. But the infant also vomits easily, and does not later. There is a reasonable doubt whether the characteristic disgust of the adult at human feces, rotten eggs and the like is or is not an innate response. Certainly the eating of putrefied matter would not be a matter of biological indifference. It may be that the anal character, whose primary affect is disgust, is an anal character because humans are innately disgusted by the odor of their feces. If the human feces were not innately disgusting, however, it would still be relatively easy to teach the child to be disgusted at his own feces, by identification with the parent who lifted his lip and drew his head away from the child's feces.

THE GENERAL SIGNIFICANCE OF SHAME– HUMILIATION

We have said that a philosophy or a psychology which does not confront the problem of human suffering is seriously incomplete. But there is no claim which man makes upon himself and upon others which matters more to him than his essential dignity. Man above all other animals insists on walking erect. In lowering his eyes and bowing his head, he is vulnerable in a quite unique way. Though not so immediately strident as terror, the nature of the experience of shame guarantees a perpetual sensitivity to any violation of the dignity of man.

Men have exposed themselves repeatedly to death and terror, and have even surrendered their lives in the defense of their dignity, lest they be forced to bow their heads and bend their knees. The heavy hand of terror itself has been flouted and rejected in the name of pride. Many have had to confront death and terror all their lives lest their essential dignity and manhood be called into question. Better to risk the uncertainties of death and terror than to suffer the deep and certain humiliation of cowardice.

Why are shame and pride such central motives? How can loss of face be more intolerable than loss of life? How can hanging the head in shame so mortify the spirit? In contrast to all other affects, shame is an experience of the self by the self. At that moment when the self feels ashamed, it is felt as a sickness within the self. Shame is the most reflexive of affects in that the phenomenological distinction between the subject and object of shame is lost. Why is shame so close to the experienced self? It is because the self lives in the face, and within the face the self burns brightest in the eyes. Shame turns the attention of the self and others away from other objects to this most visible residence of self, increases its visibility and thereby generates the torment of self-consciousness.

Since shame is primarily a response of facial communication reduction, awareness of the face by the self is an integral part of the experience of shame. Blushing of the face in shame is a consequence of, as well as a further cause for, heightened self- and face-consciousness. As previously noted, individuals may blush in any part of the body to which attention is directed. The face is the most common locus of blushing because the face is the chief organ of general communication of speech and of affect alike. The self lives where it exposes itself and where it receives similar exposures from others. Both transmission and reception of communicated information take place at the face. The mouth talks, the eyes perceive; and the movements of the facial musculature are uniquely related to one's experienced affects and to the affects transmitted to others.

But even when it is granted that the face and the eyes are where the self lives, because (as described in previous chapters) all affects emanate from the face, how does this account for the peculiar intimacy between the self and the affect of shame? If all affects are expressed through the face and eyes, then why are all affects not equally implicated in self-consciousness if all the affects and the self share the same site?

Face of the self is most salient in shame—humiliation:
a comparison with other affects

Although the face is the site of all the affects, the face is experienced as most salient in shame. Just as it is possible to suffer an injury but be unaware of the pain messages which are sent to but are not selected for the ongoing central assembly of components of the nervous system, so it is also possible for any message to be contained in a component of the central assembly but to achieve minimal articulation and visibility.

It is quite possible for an individual to be lost in admiration and excitement about another person, but with a minimum of awareness of one's own face and one's own self. The feedback from the face and chest constitute the awareness of excitement, but such excitement appears to envelop the object of excitement and not to be localized on one's own face. One has only to look at the faces of a theater or TV audience to see that excitement can lift the individual out of his seat, his skin and his face, and place him experientially in the midst of the world created by the artist.

In the smile of enjoyment in response to the smile of the other, it is the smile of the other which is mostly likely to be figure to one's own smile as ground. It is the awareness of one's own smile, transformed and projected around the visual smile of the other, which often lends such apparent warmth to that visual experience.

In the cry of distress in response to pain the affect is also experienced as the surround of the pain, making it seem much more intolerable than it would otherwise be. The placebo effect depends on the attenuation of this referred affect.

In fear, it is the dreaded object which is salient and seizes consciousness. Only in free-floating, objectless anxiety is the self entirely bathed in terror. But even here the individual ceaselessly tries to find an object appropriate to his affect.

In disgust and contempt it is also the object of disgust or

contempt which is salient. Although I may be contemptuous of myself, ordinarily when I feel disgust it is the object of disgust of which I am most clearly aware. The disgustingness of the object of disgust is partly the affect which is referred to the object like an envelope of slime. Even when the self becomes the object of disgust, there is a minimum of self-consciousness of the self as subject. Indeed the distinction between shame and the other affects is nowhere clearer than when one compares shame with self-disgust, in which the self splits itself into subject and object.

If I have done something which violates my own deeply held values, it is possible for me to respond either with self-contempt or with shame or both. If I respond with self-contempt, part of the self assumes the role of a judge who lifts his upper lip in a sneer, pulls his head and nose away from the offending psychic odor which is experienced as emanating from that other self, or part of the self, which is the object of contempt. The self is experienced as part subject and part object, or as two different selves at different times. Under such a bifurcation the offending self or part of the self may also be punished by the judging self. The judge may even feel self-righteous enough to conduct an inquisition on the hapless self.

In contrast, when the self is ashamed of itself, the judge and the offender are one and the same self. The head that is hung in shame is experienced as the head and face of the entire self. The individual is ashamed of himself. It is not possible to be ashamed or humiliated in this way without self-consciousness. The self is completely salient in the face that blushes or hangs down.

This is not to say that an individual may not both be ashamed of himself and hold himself in contempt. We have seen a child slap an offending hand which was reaching for illicit cookies with a running verbal condemnation, while the head was hung in shame. The adult too may express self-contempt by a part of the self while the condemned self hangs its head, but the distinction between the self experiencing affect in which the object is salient (disgust), and the self experiencing affect in which the self is salient (shame) is still maintained in self-disgust at the self, which is then ashamed.

One may also compare shame, in its apparent localization to the face and self, with pain. Pain, especially felt on the skin, is ordinarily correctly and vividly localized at the site where it originates. Shame, similarly, is usually correctly and vividly localized at its facial site. Referred pain, in contrast, is localized somewhere other than the site from which it emanates. Most affects other than shame are similarly referred to sites other than the face from which they emanate.

It may be objected that the relative salience of the face and the self in shame is what is to be explained rather than an explanation. This is so, and we must next inquire why, despite the fact that all affects emanate from the face, shame more than any other affect is localized in the face experientially. Nonetheless the experiential salience of the face in shame is a partial answer to the question why shame is so central a human motive inasmuch as the salience of the face involves the salience of the self and exaggerated self-consciousness.

Shame—humiliation response heightens facial visibility and is a further stimulus to shame—humiliation

Shame is both an interruption and a further impediment to communication, which is itself communicated. When one hangs one's head or drops one's eyelids or averts one's gaze, one has communicated one's shame and both the face and the self unwittingly become more visible, to the self and others.

The very act whose aim is to reduce facial communication is in some measure self-defeating. Particularly when the face blushes, shame is compounded. And so it happens that one is as ashamed of being ashamed as of anything else. Thus occurs both the taboo on looking directly into the eyes of the other and the equal taboo on looking away too visibly. In short, self-consciousness and shame are tightly linked because the shame response itself so dramatically calls attention to the face.

Shame—humiliation involves an ambivalent turning of the eyes away from the object toward the face and the self

The shame response is literally an ambivalent turning of the eyes away from the object toward the face, toward the self.

It is an act of facial communication reduction in which excitement or enjoyment is only incompletely reduced. Therefore it is an act which is deeply ambivalent. This ambivalence is nowhere clearer than in the child who covers his face in the presence of the stranger, but who also peeks through his fingers so that he may look without being seen.

In shame I wish to continue to look and to be looked at, but I also do not wish to do so. There is some serious impediment to communication which forces consciousness back to the face and the self. Because the self is not altogether willing to renounce the object, excitement may break through and displace shame at any moment, but while shame is dominant it is experienced as an enforced renunciation of the object. Self-consciousness is heightened by virtue of the unwillingness of the self to renounce the object. In this respect it is not unlike mourning, in which I become exquisitely aware of the self just because I will not surrender the love object which must be surrendered. The ambivalence in shame is clear when it involves a curious child confronted by an interesting stranger, or a reluctant lover confronted by an exciting love or sex object. What of the case when shame is produced by contempt and derision from the other, when it is produced by defeat in problem solving, when it is produced by contempt or reproach from the self for the self?

Shame—humiliation in response to disgust—contempt

It is our belief that contempt becomes an activator of shame only insofar as it represents an impediment to or a reducer of excitement or enjoyment. In other words, one must have expected good things to have come from the other person before the other's contempt produces shame.

Unless there has been interest in or enjoyment of the other person, or the anticipation of such positive feelings about the other, contempt from the other may activate surprise or distress or fear or anger, rather than shame.

The humiliated one under these conditions still wishes to look at the other with interest or enjoyment, and to be looked upon with interest or enjoyment in a relationship of mutuality. It is just this tension between the positive affect and the heightened negative awareness of the face of the self that gives the experience of humiliation its peculiar poignancy. In this case the residual positive wish is not only to look at the other rather than to look down, but to have the other look with interest or enjoyment rather than with derision.

The same dynamic holds if the other simply looks away. One can be shamed by another in whom one is interested, just as easily by indifference, i.e., by a failure to hold attention on one's self and/or on one's face, as by derision. In either case, contempt or indifference, one has been forced unwillingly back into self-consciousness by the impediment to communication.

Shame—humiliation and defeat or failure

What of the feeling of shame following defeat? Suppose one has struggled long and hard to achieve something and one suffers failure upon failure until finally the moment is reached when the head gives way and falls forward, and, phenomenologically, the self is confronted with humiliating defeat. We would argue that cumulative failure might activate anger or distress or even fear, but that in order to activate shame there must be a continuing but reduced investment of excitement or enjoyment in the possibility of success. Defeat is most ignominious when one still wishes to win. The sting of shame can be removed from any defeat by attenuating the positive wish.

Guilt and conversion experiences

What of the self-alienation which comes when one has violated deeply held values, moral or otherwise? It will be recalled that it is our view that guilt is another form of the affect of shame—humiliation.

One may have inadvertently hurt or shamed a love object, and the self becomes ashamed of the self. In this case the impediment in communication is endopsychic. The self cannot be interested in and cannot enjoy itself. It has become a stranger to itself and is alienated from itself in much the same way that separate selves may become alienated. One of the critical conditions here as in the dyadic humiliation is the maintenance of interest or enjoyment in and of the self.

To the extent to which I maintain interest in myself or enjoy myself, I can be ashamed of myself. If, however, I reject myself completely, then I may respond with contempt and disgust for myself. Here, as in the dyadic relationship, contempt can be quite complete with no residual interest or enjoyment to produce painful ambivalence. Shame for the self, as for another, is two-valued and therefore deeply disturbing in contrast with contempt, in which the object whether it be the self or another is completely rejected.

If I have no interest in yesterday's self, I cannot become ashamed of that self today. Any conversion or experience which radically increases the difference between my self of yesterday and my self today will reduce the shame I can feel about the behavior of my old self. Whenever cumulative debt of shame from unfinished business, from moral violations, from the indifference or derision of others, from unrelieved defeats reaches a total which cannot possibly be paid out of esteem income, shame bankruptcy may be resorted to by a conversion experience in which a new self is created which is free to renounce past humiliations and to start anew. The same dynamic compels the dissolution of marriages in which mutual contempt and shame force a declaration of bankruptcy and limited liability.

Shame—humiliation and positive affect

In the response of shame, be it to the stranger, to the censor external or internal, or to defeat, the self remains somewhat committed to the investment of positive affect in the person, or activity, or circumstances, or that part of the self which has created an impediment to communication. This continuing unwillingness to renounce what has been or might again be of value exposes the face of the self to pitiless scrutiny by the self or by others. To the extent to which such renunciation is possible, the self can condemn itself wholeheartedly in contempt, or can meet the scorn of the other with counter-contempt or with hostility.

One of the paradoxical consequences of the linkage of positive affect and shame is that the same positive affect which ties the self to the object also ties the self to shame. To the extent to which socialization involves a preponderance of positive affect the individual is made vulnerable to shame and unwilling to renounce either himself or others. To the extent to which contempt has been used as a major technique of socialization with a minimal display of compensatory positive affect, the individual will be more readily able to renounce parts of himself, and others.

Democracy versus hierarchy: political counterparts of shame—humiliation versus contempt—disgust

Shame—humiliation is the negative affect linked with love and identification, and contempt—disgust the negative affect linked with individuation and hate. Both affects are impediments to intimacy and communion, within the self and between the self and others. But shame—humiliation does not renounce the object permanently, whereas contempt—disgust does. Whenever an individual, a class or a nation wishes to maintain a hierarchical relationship, or to maintain aloofness it will have resort to contempt of the other. Contempt is the mark of the oppressor. The hierarchical relationship is maintained either when the oppressed one assumes the attitude of contempt for himself or hangs his head in shame. In the latter case he holds on to the oppressor as an identification object with whom he can aspire to mutuality, in whom he can be interested, whose company he can enjoy, with the hope that the oppressor will on occasion be interested in him. If, however, the predominant interaction is one of contempt from superior to inferior, and the inferior internalizes the affect of contempt and hangs his head to contempt from the self as well as to contempt from the oppressor, then it is more accurate to say that the oppressor has also taught the oppressed to have contempt for themselves rather than to be ashamed of themselves.

In a democratically organized society the belief that all men are created equal means that all men are possible objects of identification. When one man expresses contempt for another, the other is more likely to experience shame than self-contempt insofar as the democratic ideal has been internalized. This is because he assumes that ultimately he will wish to commune with this one who is expressing contempt and that this wish is mutual. Contempt will be used sparingly in a democratic society lest it undermine solidarity, whereas it will be used frequently and with approbation in a hierarchically organized society in order to maintain distance between individuals, classes and nations. In a democratic society, contempt will often be replaced by empathic shame, in which the critic hangs his head in shame at what the other has done, or by distress in which the critic expresses his suffering at what the other has done, or by anger in which the critic seeks redress for the wrongs committed by the other.

The polarization between the democratic and hierarchically organized society with respect to shame and contempt holds also in families and socialization within democratic and hierarchically organized societies.

Shame–humiliation, contempt–disgust and the fantasy of being one's own mother or father

Despite the importance of the distinction between contempt and shame, it is not always or necessarily so absolute a distinction. When shame proves too painful to be tolerated—as, for example, when the love object heightens the gulf between himself and the one he shames or the shamed one despairs of ever achieving communion again, as, for example, in the jealousy provoked by the birth of a sibling—then the shamed one may defend himself against his longing by renouncing the love object and expressing contempt for the person he cannot have, and becoming in fantasy his own mother or his own father.

The fragility of this defense is exposed whenever a person who has substituted himself for his parent is confronted by a new love object that provokes longing for communion and identification. Under these conditions such a person can be overwhelmed with a newer version of the love and shame which initiated the defense of counter-contempt.

THE EARLIEST UNIVERSAL SHAME—HUMILIATION EXPERIENCES
GENERATE SELF-FULFILLING PROPHECIES: SHAME—
HUMILIATION IN RESPONSE TO STRANGERS

As soon as the infant learns to differentiate the face of the mother from the face of a stranger (approximately seven months

of age), he is vulnerable to the shame response. Even when the
child is reared by many mothers, as in an orphanage, there is
still a differentiation between familiar and unfamiliar faces,
though the gradient is less sharp under these circumstances.
Under any schedule of socialization which is conceivable, the
infant will sooner or later respond with shame rather than with
excitement or enjoyment. After the first experience in which a
strange face evokes shame, usually unexpectedly, this easily
becomes a self-fulfilling prophecy, since with the next stranger
the infant is forewarned that he may experience shame if he
acts towards him as he does spontaneously towards his mother.

The expectation of an impediment to communication somewhat attenuates the excitement he experiences the next time he
sees another stranger. Shame is then evoked again, and the child
has taken the crucial steps in constructing in his imagination the
class of people in whose presence one feels shy. Future experience in which this expectation is confirmed will then produce a
learned shyness which is much more severe and generalized
than the innate response to innate activators. Such learned shyness is not as predictable a phenomenon as the original response
to the unfamiliar face, but given the general cognitive capacities
of the human infant, the construction of a class of people who
make you feel shy is highly probable. This construction gradually
reinforces the taboo on unashamed looking and being looked at.
As soon as it is achieved the child has been driven out of the
Garden of Eden and must thereafter somewhat guard his face
and his eyes from looking and being looked at.

There is an Image of shame in the presence of strangers
which we may be confident will be constructed on the basis of
the almost certain universal innate response to the stranger. It
will vary in strength and significance depending upon the
strength of its numerous competitors among other Images,
particularly the Image of the good mother and the Image of the
excited and exciting human being and the Image of the smiling
human being who makes one smile. All human beings inevitably
have interpersonal experiences in which others express the
primary affects and in which these are activated in the self. This
is the basis for the construction of a whole series of Images in
which the other is excited, or smiling, or ashamed, or contemp-

tuous, or angry or afraid or crying and in which the self is made to feel one or another of these primary affects. The significance of each of these constructions for each individual depends on the relative weights of each Image, which in turn depends on the extensiveness of the transformations and generalizations supporting each Image.

Not all affects, however, are capable of generating self-fulfilling prophecies. Thus the fact that I experienced excitement in listening to a joke and experienced enjoyment or laughter at its completion does not mean that I will necessarily be excited by or enjoy either a repetition of this experience, or hearing another story.

In contrast, if and when I experience shyness and shame when I first am exposed to a stranger, this experience may generate expectations and fantasies which will intensify my alienation from him the next time I see him and also make me more shy of the next stranger I encounter. This property is a characteristic of all negative affects, particularly of fear. However, it is also true for fear and shame, as or excitement and enjoyment, that the intervening cognitive activity between exposures to the same potential affect provoking objects can produce habituation rather than sensitization.

Putting aside for the moment the critical question of the differing conditions that lead to sensitization or habituation, it is our argument at this point only that the sensitization of the self-fulfilling prophecy is one of the ways in which self-consciousness can be painfully intensified, and in which shame may become a central motive for human beings.

Thus ends our answer to the question, why is shame so central, so mortifying and so self-conscious an affect. Our answer has been that the eyes both receive and send messages of all affects and thereby increase the ambivalence about looking and being looked at; that the awareness of the face is more salient in shame than in other affects; that the shame response itself heightens the visibility of the face; that shame involves an ambivalent turning of the eyes away from the object toward the face and self; finally, that the earliest universal shame experiences generate self-fulfilling prophecies.

THE LOOK OF SHAME–HUMILIATION AND CONTEMPT–DISGUST: ADULT MODIFICATIONS

As we have seen, the adult rarely cries and we had to scrutinize the face closely to find the residues of the cry of distress. So with shame, the frank dropping of the eyelids, the lowering of the gaze and the dropping of the head are also modified by the adult, though it is our impression that the shame response is less modified than the cry of distress. It is rather the open stare which comes under the most severe inhibition. Nonetheless it is not altogether acceptable for the adult to express shame too openly, with too great intensity or too frequently.

Abbreviation

The first transformation which many adults perform on their shame response is that of abbreviation. Immediately following lowering the eyelid, or the eye or the head, the adult erects defenses against the continuation of these responses, so that often the response is over almost as soon as it has been made. Whereas a child might stand before a stranger for a minute with his head bowed, the adult may look downward to avoid the gaze of the stranger, but only momentarily.

The faces of shame–humiliation: prolongation

Another transformation is the chronic frozen face of shame. This is also a transformation of the duration of the response, but a prolonging rather than an abbreviation of the response. Such a face looks perpetually humble, but it usually escapes complete detection by virtue of its chronicity. The lids or the gaze may be held sufficiently low or the head may be bent forward sufficiently, or all of these together so that there is an over-all appearance of reticence.

Sub-clinical readiness

The sub-clinical look of shame is another transformation. Here there is a chronic muscular readiness to drop the head and eyes down and forward. This readiness may often be observed to be translated into an overt shame response when the face is in repose, alone and not otherwise occupied, or in public places when the individual feels that he enjoys sufficient anonymity so that his face is less on guard and less involved in interactions with others. A very common face in repose is the look of depression in which the head is not only allowed to drop forward, but at the same time expresses the frozen mute cry of distress, so that the face is both sad and humble.

Facial defenses against shame–humiliation

THE FROZEN FACE

Another transformation is the frozen face, in which the entire facial musculature is kept under sufficiently tight control so that shame, along with all other affects, is interfered with at the site of expression. This may be a chronic or a transient defense against shame and other affects.

HEAD-BACK LOOK

A more limited and specific defense against the shame response is the look in which the head is tilted back rather than forward and the chin juts forward. In this anti-shame posture the eyes also look down, but as from a height. This compliance with the injunction "Keep your chin up" is a defense against the chin dropping in shame, similar to the anti-distress injunction "Keep a stiff upper lip" as a defense against crying. The anti-shame look can be differentiated from the contempt response. In contempt the whole face is pulled back and the upper lip is lifted, as well as the nostrils, to avoid the bad-smelling object. In contrast, this anti-shame look may bring the face and particularly the lifted jaw nearer to the face of the other in defiance of his contempt, or possible contempt. We say his possible contempt because we have found this posture a chronic one among those who have dedicated their lives to fighting for unpopular causes. It would seem in these cases that there was a chronic expectation of contempt from others which was countered by an equally chronic anti-shame posture of the head and face.

Another specific anti-shame posture is the use of the contempt response, either as a transient or chronic posture with which to combat one's own readiness to feel ashamed. The anti-shame response is not necessarily a response against the other's contempt. It may be rather a defense against one's own shame. That shame might have been produced by an otherwise loving parent who was too busy to give a child the attention he wanted. In contrast the contempt response can be a response not only to one's own shame, but also to the contempt of the one who shames.

Affect combinations and affect sequences involving shame—humiliation

Still another channel for the expression of shame is laughter. There are many kinds of laughter other than the laughter of joy, just as there are many cries other than the cry of distress. The embarrassed laugh is easily recognized as something other than pure joy, though its characteristics have yet to be precisely described.

The look of shame is also transformed by other affects which are also chronically dominant in the personality, or are characteristically expressed concurrently with shame. Thus the face may express both fear and shame, or distress and shame, excitement and shame, enjoyment and shame or anger and shame. These may be either chronic or transient expressions.

In fear and shame the individual's face looks both humble and terrified. The head may be bent forward, and the eyes frozen forward or oscillate from straight forward to sideward. Or the eyes may go to the side in fear, but also down in shame, so that they move in an angle which is a resultant of both affects.

In distress and shame the individual looks both sad and defeated. The face has any one of the adult variants of the distress cry, and at the same time the gaze is downward or the head is down.

In excitement and shame, as in the furtive sexual look, the eyes may track the object only very briefly and with a somewhat lowered gaze, followed by a dropping of the eyes still lower after visual exploration ceases. In its more chronic form the eyes stare forward and are lively and mobile in tracking, but the head may be permanently lowered, so that the eyes appear to be looking up from underneath the lids. "Bedroom eyes" are eyes which combine excitement and shame.

Enjoyment and shame is seen in the face which has a smile, in one of its variants, combined with lowered eyelids or a downward gaze. The modest but willing maiden of the Victorian era commonly presented the shy smile which promised modest enjoyment.

Anger and shame is the expression of one who has suffered defeat unwillingly. The jaw is tightly closed though the head hangs down. He appears as one who curses his fate.

Combinations of the look of shame with other affects are also found in sequences which are stable enough to constitute facial styles. Thus, one individual may frown frequently and follow this by a lowering of his eyelids and his gaze, indicating both a chronic anger and shame as a controlling affect inhibiting the anger. Another's face is continually alive with excitement, punctuated rhythmically by shame. Here the offending affect of excitement may be linked to sexuality, or be excitement in general. For another, there are frequent grimaces of distress followed by lowering his head in shame. Such a one may have been ashamed primarily about his unceasing complaints. Another's face is seized with the frozen stare of fear, and this is followed by lowering the eyes. The feeling of this fear and helplessness makes him vulnerable to yet another serious insult to his integrity.

From the face we may learn not only what affects produce shame, and are controlled by shame, but also how one copes with shame, once aroused. Thus we may see that one individual characteristically follows the shame response with a frown and a tightening of the jaw. He is one who intends to fight the shamer. Another follows the shame response with one of the variants of the distress cry. His face tells us that to be ashamed is ultimately to make him sad. Yet another follows the look of shame with the look of fear. This individual is frightened lest his own shame response betray his inferiority to the world.

Another follows the shame response by a smile. He is prepared to be impunitive either toward himself or others. He will forgive and forget the insult to his dignity in the interests of mutuality. Or if the shame is from within, in response to a violation of his own norms or in response to failure, it signifies a willingness to forgive himself in the interests of inner harmony. Another follows the look of shame with the look of excitement. For him we would suppose shyness, defeat, alienation or guilt are short-lived, are counteracted, and the original object again pursued.

The adult look of contempt—disgust

So much for the look of shame. What of the look of contempt? It appears in general to suffer relatively less transformation than any other affect, with the exception of the smile. Only the most intense disgust reactions of childhood are ordinarily entirely unacceptable in the adult. However, the major inhibitions are imposed according to circumstance. It may be entirely appropriate for an adult in American society to show extreme disgust at a gross moral offense, or at the sight and smell of putrefaction, but entirely inappropriate in response to the taste of one's host either in food or in painting. It is also a more acceptable affect in a hierarchically organized society than in a democratically organized society. Even within the latter it is considered a more appropriate affect among the upper classes than in the middle class. The ability to establish a distance between oneself and one's inferiors is necessarily valued by any society or class which must preserve hierarchical distinctions.

The look of contempt, as of shame, may be brief or it may be chronic and frozen with a slight lift to the upper lip and nostrils as though one were constantly in the presence of offensive odors, or it may be a readiness to respond with contempt in which the facial muscles are set so that they may the more readily respond with disgust. This gives to the face the look of arrogance of the perpetual critic. As with shame, the laugh may also become the vehicle of contempt.

Affect combinations and affect sequences involving contempt—disgust

There are also numerous combinations of contempt with the look of other affects. Thus the face may look disgusted with lifted nostril and afraid with staring frozen eyes if one is threatened by a lower-caste person, or an alien-rejected impulse. In the combined look of distress and contempt, the mouth is drawn down while the lip is drawn up. Such a look is common when one is fed up with circumstances which are frustrating. In enjoyment and contempt, the smile is marred by the retraction of the upper lip, as the mouth is pulled to either side. This is the nasty nice smile of one who is attempting to be a lady or a gentleman, who is as pleasant as it is possible to be when confronted with a mess. In anger and contempt the jaws are tightly closed, but not so tight as to conceal the look of disgust in the nostrils. This is the look of self-righteous anger.

There are also sequences which are aroused after disgust has been aroused. Contrary to shame, disgust is not ordinarily preceded by and aroused by one's own affects as these appear on the face, but rather by the affects of others. If disgust is followed by the look of anger, we may suppose the individual is active in fighting what appear to him to violate his norms. If the look of disgust is characteristically followed by the look of distress, we may suppose the individual is usually passive and unhappy about what offends him. If the look of disgust is characteristically followed by the look of fear, we may suppose the individual is one whose reaction to norm violations is such that the experience of disgust itself arouses such expectations of punishment or censure that the individual becomes frightened.

If the look of disgust is characteristically followed by the smile of enjoyment, we may suppose the individual is impunitive with respect to what offends him, in the interests of mutuality. If the look of disgust is characteristically followed by the look of excitement, we may suppose the individual is fundamentally ambivalent about matters which first offend and then excite him. In contrast to the sequence shame—excitement, there is more lability and ambivalence in the sequence disgust—excitement inasmuch as disgust commonly distances the self more from its source than does shame.

Relationship between shame—humiliation, guilt and internalized contempt—disgust

We are using the word shame in a manner sufficiently different from contemporary usage to warrant some repetition of distinctions we have drawn before. Some will be puzzled at our usage of the word shame when they would have used the word guilt. Thus we use the word shame to refer to the underlying affect when a parent lectures a child on his badness for having done something wrong, and the child hangs his head in acknowledgement of his immorality.

We also use the term shame to refer to the child hanging his head if the parent, rather than lecturing the child, had beaten him for the same offense. It will be noted that we are focusing on the affect of the child rather than the nature of the parent's behavior which evokes the shame response. Similarly we use the term indiscriminately if the child has internalized the shame response, so that later he is ashamed of the same response, whether or not the parent is aware of his norm violation, or if the child is only ashamed lest the parent discover what he has done, but would not feel shame if he were certain his crime would go undetected.

It is not that we regard these distinctions, which have been drawn by many theorists, as unimportant. We do not. It is rather that they are differentiations of the varying conditions under which the same affect is evoked or reduced, and under which it is included as a component in varying types of central assemblies. Like a letter in an alphabet, or a word in any sentence, the other sub-systems of the nervous system with which shame is assembled, and the messages in those sub-systems at the moment, as well as components of the preceding and following central assemblies, are capable of radically transforming the apparent quality and meaning of shame.

This view flies in the face of contemporary usage which

always distinguishes shyness from feelings of inadequacy and both from guilt.

For some purposes it may indeed be more convenient to use another word such as guilt to refer to shame which is about moral matters, or shame which is about moral matters and which has also been internalized, to distinguish it from a wide variety of other types of shame experience, such as shyness before a stranger, or shyness about a strange sexual impulse, or the feeling of shame when one has been defeated, or the feeling of shame when one has been rejected or another makes fun of one, or one punctures one's own pretentiousness.

It is not our purpose to blur or lose these distinctions, but rather to express them in such a way that further differentiations not now recognized either in common speech or in theory can more easily be detected and communicated. It is analogous to a reference to table salt as NaCl or as salt. To describe it in terms of its components, while it is more awkward for some purposes, is more efficient in enabling one to order this substance to some in which there is only chloride, and to others in which there is only sodium.

Thus with shame, for some purposes it may prove profitable to treat together all those individuals whose shame response is internalized rather than externalized, whether the content be morality or achievement. In such a case one would examine the communalities of socialization which produced either an internalized moral piety or an internalized wish to achieve lest one be ashamed. For other purposes it might be profitable to examine the differences in socialization which produced shame about morality and which produced shame about achievement. In this case it might be necessary to disregard the distinction between internalizing and externalizing of shame. Again it would be profitable to compare the differences in experienced shame and consequent behavior between those who were beaten into shame and those who were shamed by parents who expressed only distress at "shameful" behavior, e.g., "that makes mommy very unhappy." Again for some purposes it would be profitable to examine the socialization and consequences for the adult personality of the differential shaming of one impulse compared with another, e.g., shaming for sexuality but not for aggression, or shaming for aggression but not for sexuality. It is both more economical and productive of finer differentiations to be able to generate such shame syndromes than to be permanently governed by the more visible compounds of common speech.

We used the term shame—humiliation rather than guilt to refer to the underlying affect because shame is closer to the broader meaning we wish to communicate than is the word guilt. Thus we commonly speak of being ashamed of moral infractions, but we do not ordinarily speak of feeling guilty for our inferiority.

Despite the fact that we have used the word shame to refer equally to shyness, defeat, alienation and guilt, we have drawn throughout this chapter another distinction which has not been commonly made. This is the distinction which we think is a radical one, that between the affects of shame and contempt. Much of what has been called guilt we would call internalized contempt. There are several kinds of self-contempt. If a parent shames a child by expressing disgust or contempt for him, the child may learn to expect such contempt again when he is considering repeating the offense or after he has done so. Whether or not this restrains the repetition, it provides a type of punishment for norm violation which is to be distinguished from an expectation of being shamed again. Indeed, the response to the expectation of parental contempt may be counter-contempt, fear, aggression, distress or even excitement or enjoyment that one will probably evoke attention from the aroused parent.

SELF-CONTEMPT—SELF-DISGUST AND THE DYNAMICS OF THE BIFURCATED SELF

If this expected parental contempt is internalized, so that the self is split in two, with one part of the self a judge, and the other the offender, this same drama may be played out as an endopsychic conflict. In this case the judge in the self finds the accused self disgusting. The accused self may react in one or more of the following ways. The accused self may fight back and accuse the judge of excessive piety, holding him in equal contempt. The accused self may become afraid of the judging self and that perhaps the accuser is correct. In this case he fears himself as he once may have feared the tongue lashing he received from his parents. To turn the tables on the judging self, so that the judging self is stripped of his power to condemn the accused self, the latter may repeat and exaggerate his offences to prove his invulnerability to contempt, whether from the other or from the internalized other within the self. He becomes not shameless but contemptless in his behavior.

The part of the self which becomes the object of the contempt of the judging self may not fight back, but passively accept the judgment of contempt and respond in one of two ways. The condemned part may respond with shame and hang that part of the head which belongs to it before that part which lifts itself back and away from the offending part in scorn. In this case the self is ashamed of its own contempt, and suffers the same shame as if the parent were expressing disgust. Although the self is ashamed, it is nonetheless to be distinguished from that self-shame in which there is no part of the self which is disgusted with the other part. One of the critical differences between these two is that where there is contempt for the self there can easily be contempt for others, in contrast to the case where there is unified shame for the self. As we shall presently see, this is also the case where one may project shame, and protect the self from contempt by finding the offense in the other.

The second general way in which the accused self may respond to internalized contempt which it accepts is by rejecting the offending part of the self. If thine eye offend thee, pluck it out. Since contempt is an affect which distances the self from the offending source, it indeed encourages suppression of the offending part of the self as well as atonement and reformation. If one can take toward the self the attitude that there is a part of the self that is truly disgusting, then one can the more easily destroy that part of the self, and promise oneself to reform. In shame the self still loves itself despite its shame and finds the renunciation of the offending part much more painful.

This rejection and suppression of the self followed by reformation, in self-contempt, is also frequently accompanied by a similar program for others. There are few more zealous for the eradication of the comtemptible in man than those who have performed such psychosurgery upon themselves. The only case in which such piety is more unrelenting is that in which the offending self cannot be entirely excised or suppressed unless it is eliminated from the lives of others, particularly those with whom one is closely identified. If one has contempt for one's own procrastination, for one's own passivity, for one's own distress, for one's own disorganization, and these affronts to the self are contained only through the greatest vigilance, then their appearance in others, and particularly those with whom one is most closely identified, is most likely to call forth prompt and ruthless contempt. In contrast, if such characteristics evoke shame in the self, they will evoke vicarious shame in the self when they are detected in others. The further affects that shame will evoke will then depend on how one has learned to deal with one's own shame.

The distinction between what one is shamed and humiliated for and for what one feels shame—humiliation

We may feel shame for many things for which no one has shamed us. We may not feel shame though another tries to make one feel ashamed. We may be shamed by another, though the other does not intend we should feel ashamed. We may be shamed because the other expresses negative affect toward us, though he does not wish to shame us as such. Finally, we may be shamed only because another tries to shame us.

Consider each of these. If I try very hard to achieve something and fail, or if I violate my own standards, moral or otherwise, I am vulnerable to shame. No one has shamed or need shame me in such a case.

If someone expresses contempt for me, I may become angry and counter with contempt for him. The intention of the other to shame me does not necessarily mean I will experience shame.

If someone to whom I am speaking is so busy and preoccupied with other things that I feel an impediment to mutuality, I may become ashamed though the other has no intention of producing shame. Or the other with whom one is closely identified, such as a wife or a child or a friend, may produce shame in oneself unwittingly, by behavior which would have evoked shame had one done it oneself.

If another is angry with me, or distressed by my behavior, or says that what I have done has frightened him, I may feel shame even though he does not try to shame me as such, but does intend to communicate some other negative affect.

However, the other may intend to shame me, and succeed only because of this, his intention. If I am doing the best I can and am reasonably satisfied with my progress but someone says he is disgusted with what he regards as a miserable performance on my part, then he may succeed in making me feel ashamed when otherwise I would be satisfied.

Because of the somewhat independent variability of what one was shamed for and of how one responded, and because there are also delayed and indirect consequences of having been shamed, and because one feels shame for much that no one shamed one for, the description of the socialization of shame is complex. It should refer at once to the attitudes of others and to the total effect of these attitudes upon the self, as well as the endopsychic sources of shame.

THE MAGNITUDE OF THE ROLE OF SHAME– HUMILIATION IN PERSONALITY DEVELOPMENT

Since shame is one affect among several, despite its centrality and despite its significance for the sense of identity, its role in the personality depends to some extent on the intensity, the frequency and the duration of shame and its activators relative to fear, distress, anger, contempt, excitement and enjoyment. Those who find many and deep sources of excitement and enjoyment, or who find the world terrifying, or those for whom the world is a vale of tears are the less likely to feel ashamed, defeated and alienated. But this is a gross oversimplification of the role of shame.

It would be an illuminating type of analysis in those special cases where one affect or another assumes monopolistic proportions relative to all other affects, or where each affect is quite separate from every other affect in what activates it and in the consequences which follow the activation of each affect. As we shall see, however, the more common state of affairs is that shame is often mixed with other affects so that affects are also experienced at the same time as shame, other affects become the activators of shame, shame becomes the activator of other affects, and other affects are utilized as anticipatory defenses and ways of coping with shame after it has been aroused.

The question of the role of shame—humiliation in a particular personality is further complicated by varying degrees of dominance, relative to other affects, over time. A person who is almost entirely captured by shame in childhood may come to terms with this affect in the course of development and become concerned with and organized around different negative or positive affects as an adult. As we noted before, in the case of distress, the early experience of any negative affect may be so reinforced and generalized during development that we may speak of a snowball effect. Or it may be submerged, and outgrown but with vulnerability to intrusions so that we may speak of an iceberg effect. It may continue to co-exist with conflicting other affects to be finally integrated so that we may speak of the late bloomer. There is in the latter case also the common fourth life course of a continuation of personality conflict of varying degrees of severity and disturbance. Thus could a Chekhov characterize his life as spent in squeezing out of his blood the last ounce of servility. The importance of the individual's struggles with his shame, the incessant effort to vanquish or come to terms with the alienating affect, his surrenders, transient or chronic, have too often been disregarded by personality theorists in their quest for a static structure which will describe a personality.

Chapter 17

Shame – Humiliation and the Taboo on Looking

Man is, of all the animals, the most voyeuristic. He is more dependent on his visual sense than most animals, and his visual sense contributes more information than any of his senses.

Despite and in part because of this, there exists a universal taboo on looking. This taboo is most severe when two individuals become intimate and look directly into each other's eyes at the same time. There are also taboos on looking and being looked at only slightly less severe than the taboo on shared interocular intimacy.

The taboo on mutual looking has many sources. First, it is a taboo on intimacy. To the extent to which mutual looking maximizes shared intimacy, whatever taboos there may be on intimacy as such are immediately enforced on interocular exchange, just as they are enforced on sexuality. We will try to show later that intimacy is in fact greater in interocular experience than in sexual intercouse *per se*.

Second, in every culture there exist some contraints on the direct expression of some affects. Since the face is the site of the affect, mutual looking becomes tabooed insofar as it might violate whatever cultural contraints there may be on the expression and communication of affect. The relationships between the taboos on intimacy and affect are complex.

Intimacy necessarily involves the sharing of affect, though it may also involve more, as in the sharing of sexual pleasure. The expression of affect, *per se*, need not involve intimacy. In the expression of contempt, for example, far from increasing intimacy, such affective interchange, if it is mutual, increases

157

the psychological distance between two individuals even if they are aware of their mutual contempt for each other. There are taboos on the expression of affects which are quite independent of the taboos on intimacy, but both of these taboos, nonetheless, contribute to the taboo on looking.

The taboo on mutual looking, because of the taboo on expression of particular affects, arises in part because of the unique capacity of the look-look with respect to the expression, communication, contagion, escalation and control of affects. Thus if I glare at you with my eyes and you see this, I have first of all expressed an affect, anger, which is in itself tabooed. From early childhood I have been admonished against both feeling and expressing such anger. Second, I have also suffered taboos on communicating such affects through my eyes to your eyes. Not only is there a taboo on the expression of this and other affects but there is also a taboo on communicating it to you. Third, my angry eyes are contagious, so that your eyes may respond with an especially angry look. Because of the extreme contagion of affect in the shared interocular exchange, taboos arise lest affects not only occur but spread. Finally, such affective contagion occurring through the interocular exchange readily leads to escalation. Each of us in turn responding to the other's angry eyes can become much angrier, so that control of affect is seriously undermined.

Nor is the loss of control of affect the only source of the taboo on mutual looking. The free expression of affect on the face which the other can see also enables the other to achieve control of the one who wears his affects on his face. To the extent to which social and interpersonal relationships are hostile or competitive, it becomes advantageous to wear a poker face and not to look too intimately into the eyes of the other.

Third, the taboo on mutual looking is reinforced by its specific linkage with sexuality. To the extent to which there are taboos on the free expression of sexuality, mutual looking, which is an important part of sexual exploration and contagion, also comes under taboo.

Psychoanalysis, surprisingly, had little to say about this taboo. It generated the concept of the eye as a symbol for the penis, as in the classical interpretation of the Oedipus myth.

This, we think, underestimates the role of the eye itself in sexual experience. It also interpreted the eye as a symbol for the mouth. Above all, Psychoanalysis related man's voyeurism to the primal scene, the accidental witnessing by the child of sexual intercourse between his parents. It is our view that witnessing the primal scene deeply disturbs the child but that it is not primarily a sexual experience. Further, while the primal scene contributes to the taboo on looking, it is by no means its only root, or even its most important one.

In this chapter we shall examine the taboo on looking and its obverse, the taboo on not looking. We shall briefly review the classic expression of this taboo in the belief in the evil eye. Also we shall describe a simple experiment which clearly reveals not only the existence of this taboo but also how we maintain the taboo without becoming aware of it. The sexual aspects of the eye will be considered, the meaning of the primal scene discussed and a reformulation of the meaning of the Oedipus myth presented. Finally, we shall consider the meaning of the taboo as part of the shame response resulting from the taboo on intimacy and the inhibition of affect in general.

HISTORY OF THE EVIL EYE: CLASSIC EXPRESSION OF THE TABOO ON INTEROCULAR INTIMACY

If magical beliefs are projective systems which reflect the source of an individual's or a culture's primary affects, then there is abundant evidence of a taboo on looking and on being looked at. There is a voluminous literature, from earliest antiquity, which reveals an enduring preoccupation with the eye. In the following account we are indebted to Edward S. Gifford, Jr., for his survey of the folklore of vision, *The Evil Eye*.

The most ancient and universal belief is that the eye of an evil one will injure wherever its gaze happens to fall. This force may emanate from the eyes of animals, demons, even from the painted or sculptured eyes of inanimate objects, as well as from the eyes of human beings.

The belief in the possibility of injury from the evil eye appears in the earliest written records. A popular myth on one of the clay tablets excavated in Iraq from a civilization in the third millenium B.C. gave Ereshkigal, goddess of the underworld, the power to kill Inanna, goddess of love, with a deadly eye. Other cuneiform tablets from the ruins of the library of the Assyrian King Assurbanipal (669-626 B.C.) at Nineveh in northern Mesopotamia showed that they feared *utukku*, demons who haunted deserts and graveyards; and who could injure by a glance.

Jesus also, according to St. Mark (7:21, 22), believed in the evil eye. "For from within, out of the heart of men, proceed evil thoughts, adulteries, fornications, murders, thefts, covetousness, wickedness, deceit, lasciviousness, an evil eye, blasphemy, pride, foolishness." Here the evil eye expresses not only hostility but all manner of wickedness.

Gifford reports that this universal belief has received a special name in all languages. For the ancient Romans it was *oculus fascinus,* for the ancient Greeks *baskania,* for the Hebrews *aynhara,* among the Syrians *arnabisa.* In modern languages the Italians call it *mal occhio,* the French *mauvais oeil,* the Spanish *mal ojo,* the Germans *böser Blick,* the Dutch *booze blik,* the Poles *zte oko,* the Norwegians *skjoertunge,* the Danes *et ondt oje,* the Scotch *cronachadt,* the Irish *droch-shuil,* the Persians *aghashi,* the Armenians *avascama,* the Hungarians *szemveres,* the Morroccans *l'ain,* the Ethiopians *avenat,* the Southern Indians *drishtidosham.*

The belief in the evil eye received partial support in the Greek theory of vision that visual rays emanated from the eyes to strike external objects from which the rays were reflected back to the eyes. This theory persisted, despite criticism, until the seventeenth century. In the Middle Ages attempts were made to convict criminals by the soiling of a mirror exposed to their guilty vision. As late as 1739 the Academy of Paris recorded an experiment in which an old woman had looked into a mirror. Upon examination of the mirror there was found a film of filth which was pronounced poisonous.

The evil eye appeared in two forms, the voluntary or moral and the involuntary or natural evil eye. The voluntary or moral eye was possessed by witches through a pact with the devil and used maliciously with conscious intent. Thus Martin Delrio, a Jesuit of Louvain, wrote in 1603: "Fascination is a power derived from a pact with the devil, who, when the so-called fascinator looks at another with an evil intent, or praises, by means known to himself, infects with evil the person at whom he looks."

The involuntary or natural evil eye was ordinarily a congenital affliction which might be visited upon innocent well-meaning individuals. The involuntary evil eye might be a punishment for disobeying the Lord, according to the Book of Deuteronomy (28:54): "So that the man who is tender among you and very delicate, his eye shall be evil toward his brother, and toward the wife of his bosom, and toward the remnant of his children . . ."

More commonly those who suffered the involuntary evil eye had been cursed at birth. The Hindus believed it unwise to deny pregnant women their strong desires for candy or fruits lest their children be born weak and voracious and with an evil eye.

Pope Pius IX, though very popular, was believed to have an evil eye. After his election in 1846 he looked at a nurse who stood in an open window with a child in her arms. A few minutes later the child fell from the nurse's arms to the pavement and was killed. Pope Pius IX was thought innocent of evil intent but nonetheless responsible since it was presumed the death was due to the glance from his evil eye. It was believed that nothing was so fatal as his blessing. His successor, Pope Leo XIII, had the same reputation and was believed responsible for the death of a large number of cardinals and for the assassination of King Humbert of Italy.

The evil eye was not restricted to human beings. Danger from the eye was particularly feared from wild animals. In Ethiopia, said Pliny the Elder, there was an animal, the catoblepas, which could kill with a glance. In Libya, he claimed there was a serpent, the basilisk, which was capable of killing with its eyes.

The belief in the basilisk and its power continued through the Middle Ages and became confused with an animal called the cockatrice, which had wings, a long tail, a cock's comb, and a deadly eye, and was said to be incubated by a toad from the egg of an elderly cock. Sir Thomas Browne dismissed the cockatrice but believed in the danger from the eye of the serpent, the basilisk. In Brazil there is a legend of a bird that could kill anything it beheld.

The eye was considered one of the most powerful instruments of those who fascinated victims. Fascination might include speaking and touching, but a look was enough. Francis Bacon believed that to fascinate was to bewitch and that "fascination is ever by the eye." According to the Talmud, the Rabbis Simeon ben Yohai and Johaanen could, with a look, turn men into stone, and when the Rabbi Eliezer ben Hyrcanus was dismissed, he burned to ashes everything on which he turned his eyes. The Bantu Negroes of British East Africa believed an envious gaze would cause a spear to break. In Katanga, Africa, only those immediately concerned may watch the smelting of copper because an evil eye might spoil the process.

It has been believed that any disease could be transmitted by an evil eye; the danger is greater if it is an eye disease with which the fascinator is himself infected. On this basis Plutarch thought sore eyes the most infectious of all diseases. Montaigne thought that an agitated imagination could emit infection through the eyes. In addition to being a source of evil influence, the eyes of the healthy have been thought to be vulnerable to whatever they see. Thus Ovid supposed that while the eyes are looking on the wounded they themselves are also wounded. Roger Bacon wrote, "I saw a physician made blind while he was endeavoring to cure a patient with a disease of the eyes."

Statistical estimates of the consequences of the evil eye vary but most agree it is a potent killer. Rab, a Hebrew scholar of Babylon in the third century A.D., held 99 out of 100 deaths attributable to the evil eye. In Morocco two proverbs give different estimates: "The evil eye owns two thirds of the graveyard," and "one half of mankind die from the evil eye." In the Persian sacred book, the Avesta, Ahriman the god of evil is credited with creating with his evil eye 99,999 different diseases.

The evil eye was not only conceived as the instrument of an evil person, but was also thought to be capable of corrupting the person by its reflexive emanations. Thus according to St. Matthew (6:22): "The light of the body is the eye: if therefore, thine eye be single [that is, sound], thy whole body shall be full of light. But if thine eye be evil, thy whole body shall be full of darkness."

The evil eyes' danger was also conceived to be capable of being redirected against its owner. Pliny reported that the glance of the serpent, the basilisk, was so deadly that, if reflected back by a mirror, it could kill the animal itself. Roger Bacon also reported that Alexander the Great once attacked a city which was defended by a basilisk placed on the city wall. Aristotle advised him to use large polished surfaces to reflect the poisonous glance, and thus he destroyed the serpent by its own venom.

The danger of the reflected look for the one who looked at his image in the water or in a mirror has often been noted. Plutarch thought it possible for a vain person to thus fascinate himself, citing the case of Eutelidas, who lost his beauty and health by looking at his own reflection in the water. Ovid's account of Narcissus is similar. Narcissus wasted away and was turned into a flower by looking too long at his own reflection.

The evil eye was held capable not only of hurting human beings but also other living things. Crops could be ruined by the evil eye, and in early Roman law there was a penalty for enchanting the harvest.

The belief in the evil eye has not disappeared in modern times. In 1934, Pennsylvania Germans have been reported as believing that by pinning the eye of a wolf to the inside of a sleeve the wearer would be saved from accidents. Carleton Coon reported that, in 1947, most Mediterranean ships still carried eyes painted on their prows as protection against the evil eye. According to Gifford, amulets against the evil eye are found today in Africa and South America. The London *Daily Express*, in January 1934, reported that a man in Dorset had been fascinated and was slowly wasting away while modern medical science was unable to make a diagnosis or effect a cure. In 1935, the English *Spectator* published an account of two magic rites designed to cure children ill of the evil eye in southern India.

In 1948, the evil eye was still operating in Germany. On May 13, 1948, the United Press sent the following dispatch from Frankfurt:

"A twentieth century witchcraft trial, featuring testimony about eerie light, midnight visions and mysterious 'anti-evil pills' was held at nearby Sarnau today.

" 'He bewitched our cattle,' one farmer said, glaring at Burgomaster Werner Boldt.

"Five Sarnau citizens were sued for slander after a year of spreading reports that the Mayor of Sarnau was a sorcerer. All were acquitted because German law provides no penalty for people who say other people are enchanted.

"Sarnau's 200 residents have been avoiding the burgomaster for a year. They refused to enter his home or visit him at his office. Some of them said they suffered from a 'mysterious illness' after the burgomaster looked at them.

" 'I'm just taboo,' the burgomaster told the court today. 'I have heard that there is even some plot to remove me from office.'

"The people of Sarnau began to feel sure their burgomaster had strange power after some cattle died. 'Nobody could explain what it actually was,' one elderly woman testified, 'but lots of our cattle died after Boldt strolled by and looked at them.'

" 'It's because of his dangerous look,' one of the defendants explained today."

The *Countryman,* an English quarterly, reported in 1956 that elderly people living in Somerset were still telling stories of how the evil eye had caused a pig to run wild, bedbugs to invade a cottage, a pony to go lame and cattle to die.

Gifford reports that in the United States the belief in the evil eye is also ordinarily confined to rural districts and to the foreign sections of large cities. He reports that in South Philadelphia the fear of being "overlooked" is widespread, and that there are many women there who know the appropriate prayers against fascination and who are willing to relieve the attacks of the evil eye without remuneration.

When the labor-rackets investigating committee interviewed a racketeer from New York, the committee was told that the evil eye had been used to keep dissatisfied employees on the job. An Associated Press dispatch from Washington, dated August 15, 1957, reported: "He was hired by one employer [said the committee's lawyer] to come in once or twice every week or so and glare at his employees." He said the employer found it was "enough to have him come in and look at them to keep them at their work."

Even in modern times, in Western Europe, public figures have been feared because of their evil eye. According to Gifford, usually a concatenation of calamities coincidental with the presence of the public figure is a necessary condition for the emergence of such a belief. The most striking case is that of King Alphonso of Spain in 1923 on his state visit to Italy to pay his respects to Mussolini's new government. As his ship neared Genoa, an Italian fleet went out to meet it. As the Spaniards approached, the weather, which had been clear, changed to one of the worst storms in years, washing four Italian sailors overboard to their deaths. Also an air compressor on an Italian submarine in the escort exploded and killed a sailor. This started the rumor among the Italian people that Alphonso was a *jettatore* (fascinator with evil eye). This was reinforced when, as he entered the Bay of Naples, the old bronze cannon which was fired in salute exploded and killed the crew. All doubt was dispelled after a naval officer in the reception committee at Naples collapsed as soon as he had shaken hands with King Alphonso, and died in a hospital later.

The modern method of protection against the evil eye, in Italy, is to touch a bit of iron, such as a horseshoe. At his public appearances there were cheers, but also the sound of iron. At the end of his visit the royal train passed the dam at Lake Gleno. The next morning the dam broke, drowning fifty people and making five hundred homeless.

King Alphonso lived with this reputation thereafter. Mussolini refused to receive him and carried on negotiations through underlings who had no choice. The servants kept iron keys in their pockets and avoided catching his eye. Whenever he went to the movies, it was after the lights were dimmed lest he be greeted by rattling of iron keys. On one occasion with a large group in a restaurant he rose and shouted, "Now look at me, look at me! Do I look like a *jettatore*?" In a short time only one companion remained since it is believed that a *jettatore* increases his powers by referring to them even to deny them.

Who are the fascinators? According to Gifford, they were

most likely to be those with most reason for feeling envy and hostility. According to Francis Bacon, "Envy emitteth some malign and poisonous spirit, which taketh hold of the spirit of another. . . . Deformed persons, and eunuchs, and old men, and bastards are envious. For he that cannot possibly mend his own case will do what he can to impair another's."

Any deviation of the appearance of the eye was sufficient to establish a diagnosis. Any drooping of one or both eyelids, a missing eye, an inflammation of the eyes or a squint has been considered presumptive evidence of the evil eye. Pliny the Elder believed that fascinators have a double pupil in both eyes, or a double pupil in one eye and a figure of a horse in the other. Differences of color between the two eyes either as a congenital anomaly or as a result of iris infection has seemed to be presumptive evidence for the evil eye. In the Northern countries dark eyes are suspect, whereas in the Mediterranean countries blue eyes are feared. Gifford cites a Moroccan proverb in this connection: "Don't marry a blue-eyed woman, even though she has money in her box."

Those who live alone in seclusion were also suspected, as were those who were unconventional. Byron was presumed to possess the evil eye not only because of his lameness but because of his sexual freedom.

The eye of the camera has been presumed evil, as have eyes adorned by monocles. The English Ambassador to Siam in the late ninteenth century is said to have created panic by his use of the monocle.

The ambitious are feared. In the Book of Proverbs (28:22): "He that hasteth to be rich hath an evil eye." Where there is belief in the evil eye, praise and flattery are feared because of the envy which is presumed implicit. Thus a Hindu mother is said to be alarmed at any compliment concerning her child.

In many societies there is fear of the evil eye particularly from the stare of foreigners and strangers.

In the Middle Ages many monks were thought to have the evil eye. In 842 Erchempert wrote: "I knew formerly Messer Landrelf, Bishop of Capua, a man of singular prudence, who was wont to say, 'Whenever I meet a monk, something unlucky always happens to me during the day.'" This superstition persisted till the end of the nineteenth century in Italy. In Scotland the people of the parish of Kilmory, fearful and resentful of Presbyterian discipline, believed their minister had an evil eye so powerful that he injured his own cattle and horses.

More women than men have been endowed with the evil eye. Indeed, according to Gifford, only in recent times have men become conspicuous as fascinators. Although brides have always been held particularly vulnerable to the evil eye, in Morocco they were presumed also likely to emit the evil eye themselves, particularly on their wedding day. The veil therefore protects the bride from harm, but also protects anyone she might see before arriving at her new home. Menstruating women and women in childbirth have been generally regarded as dangerous, and they have frequently been isolated so that, as with the Kolosh women of Siberia, they "may not defile heaven with a look." Pliny believed that the look of a menstruating woman would tarnish a mirror, as did St. Thomas Aquinas. From antiquity to the present, old women have been thought more likely to have an evil eye than young and attractive women. Cartagena believed this because the menstrual blood is retained in the veins of the older women. St. Thomas Aquinas believed it because older women were more likely to be wicked.

The beliefs in witchcraft, fascination and the evil eye have been associated from antiquity to the present. In Scotland in 1597, Janet Wischart, notorious for her evil eye, was convicted of so influencing Alexander Thomson that one half of his body was roasted as if in an oven, while the other half was melting with a cold sweat. At the trial of Bridget Bishop for witchcraft at Salem, Massachusettes, in 1692, it was testified if the prisoner "did but cast her eyes" on the bewitched girls "they were presently struck down." Cotton Mather added to this testimony the following which helped hang her: "As this Woman was under a Guard, passing by the great and spacious Meeting-house of Salem, she gave a look towards the House: And Immediately a Daemon invisibly entring the Meeting-House, tore down a part of it; so that tho' there was no Person to be seen there, yet the People, at the noise, running in, found a Board, which was strongly fastened with several Nails, transported unto another quarter of the House."

It was also believed that the judges themselves were vulnerable to the evil eye. *Malleus Maleficarum,* a guide book written in 1486 for judges involved in cases of witchcraft, states that "there are witches who can bewitch their judges by a mere look or glance from their eyes, and publicly boast that they cannot be punished."

Witches who did not have the evil eye nonetheless had strange eyes. In the Middle Ages, a sorceress could be recognized by her inability to weep under any circumstances. King James I of England, in his *Daemonologie,* opined that witches could not shed tears "thretten and torture them as ye please." In Grimm's "Hansel and Gretel" the witches have red eyes and cannot see far. The Kuwai Papuans of British Guinea recognize a sorcerer by his bloodshot eyes. In Greece vampires were said to have blue eyes, in northern India copper-colored eyes. Most vampires have green eyes, but the Lamiae, a special kind of vampire, were described in the 16th century *Nomenclator, or Remembrances of Adrianus Junius* as "women that were thought to have such eyes, as they could pull out and put in at their pleasure." The original Lamia had been a beautiful queen of Libya who had attracted Zeus, to whom she bore several children. Zeus' wife Hera carried the children away, and Lamia, embittered and turned to ugliness, stole and killed the children of others. Later she ensnared young men and drank their blood. To spite Hera and to help Lamia in her efforts to terrorize, Zeus conferred the power of removing the eyes and replacing them at will.

It has also happened that entire groups of people have been supposed to possess the evil eye. Telchines were all noted for their ability to bring down rain and hail and blast their neighbors' crops with a glance. According to Ovid, Jupiter finally got rid of them by driving them into the sea. Pliny believed that the whole tribe of the Hibii in Pontus had the power of fascination.

The ancient gods also were known for the evil eye. Juno had an evil eye, and so did her bird, the peacock. Mercury, the messenger of the gods, needed protection against Juno and other fascinators and therefore carried the caduceus—a staff of olive wood with a pair of wings, topped with a pine cone and two snakes coiled about it. According to Gifford, this was introduced in the sixteenth century as the emblem of the medical

profession by Sir William Butts, physician to Henry VIII, not as
a protection against fascination but because it was thought that
the two snakes were symbolic of Aesculapius, the Greek god of
medicine. Gifford noted, however, that the symbol of Aesculapius
is a single serpent twined around a plain, rough-hewn staff, and
not the caduceus of Mercury. It would appear that the widespread fear of the evil eye might have contributed to this added
protection which medicine thus made available through this
misidentification.

In addition to Juno, the Egyptian goddess Osiris was reputed,
by Plutarch, to have killed a small boy by looking at him in anger.
Swa the Destroyer is one member of the Hindu holy trinity who
has a third eye in the center of his forehead. It is usually kept
closed since when it opens everything within range is destroyed
by fire.

Since the sun and the moon were regarded as deities, it is
not surprising to find the evil eye attributed to emanations from
them. The rays of Luna, goddess of the moon, have long been
regarded as the cause of lunacy. Roger Bacon believed "many
have died from not protecting themselves from the rays of the
moon . . . especially is this true when a man is exposed to the
rays of Saturn and Mars." An outbreak of the plague in Nepal
was attributed to the evil eye of Saturn and other planets which
came together secretly in one sign of the zodiac. According to
Gifford, even in modern Greece mothers are careful during the
first eight days, or even the first forty days, after the birth of a
child to be at home and shut up in a room by sunset, lest the
light from a star cause the death of both mother and child.

If the eye is active and perhaps malignant, who uses it first
becomes a matter of some moment. Pliny recorded a Roman
belief that if a wolf sees a man before the man sees the wolf,
the man will lose his voice. This was repeated again in treatises
on witchcraft in the twelfth and fifteenth centuries.

If the eye is potent, it is a small step to appropriate it for
one's own advantages. Jerome Cardan (1501-1576), professor
of medicine at Padua and Bologna, presumed that one could keep
all the dogs in the neighborhood from barking by taking the
eyes of a black dog and holding them in the hand.

Another consequence of the potency of the eye was its

capture by evil ones. Some Christian metaphysicians argued that demons used the eyes of their creatures as instruments.

THE TABOO ON LOOKING AND ON
NOT LOOKING: AN EXPERIMENT

The widespread belief in the evil eye does not establish the existence of a taboo on looking in modern non-superstitious individuals, nor does it explain how there can be such a taboo when we look at each other every day. Further, how can such a taboo be maintained without our being aware of it? Nonetheless, we will maintain that the taboo on mutual looking is more stringent even than the taboo on sexuality. That even modern enlightened adults suffer a serious interocular taboo is relatively easy to demonstrate. Ask the members of any group to turn toward each other and look directly and deeply into each others' eyes. It then becomes apparent that to exact compliance with this instruction is all but impossible. It is similar in its impact, to the fundamental rule of Psychoanalysis, to associate freely, to say whatever comes to mind. One can not realize the extent of censorship until one tries to suspend it. When the individual is asked to stare directly into the eyes of another person, he does so if at all only briefly and then looks away. He looks away, however, in a rather subtle way. He stares at the top of the nose or the tip of the nose, or at one eye, or at the forehead, or he fixates on the face as a whole, and his partner will ordinarily reciprocate in so attenuating the interocular intimacy. And this is also how in daily interpersonal contacts, intimacy is attenuated and the taboo on the look-look is maintained.

The taboo is, however, more complex than it appears. Apart from special cultural taboos which require women to wear veils on their faces all or part of the time, the taboo on the interocular interaction ordinarily is a secret one, which is maintained by a defense against a too obvious defense against looking into each other's eyes. One may not defend oneself against looking into another's eyes by looking away or by hiding one's face. The expression of shame or shyness is quite as shameful as shameless looking. This is why, under the conditions of our experiment, we rarely encounter subjects who hide their face in their hands, or grossly look away from their partner. They are caught between the shame of looking and the shame of being ashamed to do so.

The taboo on looking and not looking: a partial answer

The origin of both of these taboos would appear to be the shaming of the child, first for his shame in the presence of the guest who is a stranger to the child, and then for his frank excited staring into the face of the same stranger. Characteristically when confronted with a stranger, the child's shyness shames his parents. If the child hides behind his parent, or covers his face with his hands, the parent becomes ashamed and counter-shames the child for his shyness, urging him to shake hands with the guest. Once the shame has yielded, the same child will fix his eyes unrelentingly on the face of the guest. Now the parent is ashamed because the child has no shame, and because he is concerned that the guest will become ashamed because he is being too directly observed. The parent therefore then shames the child into not staring at the guest.

Our explanation suggests that if parents themselves were freer to be intimate, their children might grow up to enjoy a similar freedom. This is clearly true in some degree. There are large variations in the willingness of individuals to expose themselves and to look at others, and different societies vary in the severity of these taboos.

But yet the explanation is somewhat circular. Why is the parent ashamed both at the child's shyness and at his boldness? It is no answer to say that he is acting on behalf of the guest who is made uncomfortable by the child's behavior, since then we would have to ask the same question about the guest and give the answer that that was how the guest had been socialized when he was a child.

The sexual eye

In a culture which taboos sex, any connection between looking and sexual excitement would lead to a taboo on looking, and indeed the connection between the eyes and sexuality is close.

But this again is only a partial explanation, since the taboo on interocular intimacy is stronger than the sexual taboo. Since our reinterpretation of the Oedipus myth and the primal scene involves more than the sexual meaning of the eyes, that discussion will be deferred until after the presentation of the general meaning of the interocular taboo. At this point we shall confine ourselves to the sexual meaning of looking.

The eye can communicate any feeling, including those which are tabooed. It is particularly well suited for the expression of sexual intent.

However, the eye expresses not only the tabooed affects, but also serves as an auxiliary to the mouth, to the hand and to the genitals. If one wishes to bite or touch or have genital contact at the same time that one looks at another person, one can feel much the same shame for looking as for biting or touching the body of the other or pentrating the genitalia. Phenomenologically the eye and the hand, or the mounth or the penis can become as fused as the fork and the hand do in eating.

The eye as an adjunct of sexuality has been recognized from the earliest times. Bernard de Mandeville, a Dutch physician who settled in London in the eighteenth century, was one among many who cautioned gentlemen against the too bold use of the eyes:

"The Man . . . may talk of Love, he may sigh and complain of the Rigours of the Fair, and what his Tongue must not utter he has the Privilege to speak with his Eyes, and in that Language to say what he pleases; so it be done with Decency, and short abrupted Glances: But too closely to pursue a Woman, and fasten upon her with one's Eyes, is counted very unmannerly; the Reason is plain, it makes her uneasy, and, if she be not sufficiently fortify'd by Art and Dissimulation, often throws her into visible Disorders. As the eyes are the Windows of the Soul, so this staring Impudence flings a raw, unexperienc'd Woman into panick Fears, that she may be seen through; and that the Man will discover, or has already betray'd, what passes within her; it keeps her on a perpetual Rack, that commands her to reveal her secret Wishes, and seems design'd to extort from her the grand Truth, which Modesty bids her with all her Faculties to deny."

One may indicate sexual intent by looking at the genital area or the erogenous zones such as the breasts or buttocks or by a sweeping motion taking in the whole body. Such looking is ordinarily understood by both parties to be equivalent to sexual exploration. The eyes can be used to "undress" as the hands might be used. The sexual intent may, however, be communicated quite as directly by staring into the eyes of the other. Indeed, this is frequently more effective since it guarantees a mutual awareness of the sexual intent of the looker which may be sufficient to excite the recipient of the sex look. If this happens, there is immediate awareness by both that it has happened and that each party is aware of his own excitement and that of the other. Such mutuality commonly is a sufficient condition for intensifying the excitement of each partner, which is in turn communicated in both directions, to and between each party.

The rapid acceleration of sexual excitement by such recruitment is one of the primary reasons why sexual control is instituted very early in ocular interaction. The one looked at may lower his or her eyes and lids in shyness or look to the side in fear. These responses themselves are so well known that the sequence, direct stare followed by a sudden looking down or to the side, has become a technique of indicating to the other that one is looking with sexual interest. It is equivalent to the message, "I am looking at you in a way that will excite you and make you shy or afraid."

A variant of this is the sexual look with the lids held somewhat lowered in a steady gaze into the eyes of the other. These are the "bedroom eyes" which indicate a more general and enduring sexual interest than the momentary quick look and lowering of the eyes. This is because the duration of this look presumably began before it fell upon this particular sex object and will presumably continue after this encounter. In the stare with sudden lowering of the eyes, the intent is at once more specific with respect to object and more limited in time.

The seductiveness of the downcast eye is duly noted in the book of Proverbs (6:25): "Lust not after her beauty in thine heart; neither let her take thee with her eyelids."

Parson Weems' pamphlet of 1805, "Hymen's Recruiting Sergeant," to encourage the young to marry and propagate, described the wife's "love beaming eye" with its "soul melting

look." The eyes were "heaven's sweetest messengers of love."
Propertius—"I like not to have the joys of Venus spoiled by
darkness. Let me tell you, if you know it not, the eyes are the
leaders in Love's warfare."

Martial, the Roman poet, also complained, in a poem to his
wife, that she preferred to wanton in darkness while he liked to
play by lamp light.

Clement of Alexandria, a second century father of the Church,
gave the following intsructions for Christian eyes: "But above
all, it seems right that we turn away from the sight of women.
For it is sin not only to touch, but to look . . . For it is possible
for one who looks to slip, but it is impossible for one, who looks
not, to lust."

Inhibitions of the sexual look

If ocular interaction and awareness thereof is a prominent
component of the sexual experience and particularly of the fore-
play, then there are three distinct ways in any one of which
affect inhibition may operate with respect to the ocular response.
First there may be a taboo on looking. One who cannot tolerate
sexual looking at the other but can tolerate its sequel, intercourse,
may not begin mutual sexual enjoyment until darkness makes it
unnecessary to inhibit the impulse to look. Second, there may be
a taboo on being looked at; third, there may be a taboo on mutual
looking.

Moreover, the inhibition of the look may be general or specific.
One may be unable to look with sexual intent at all; or be able
to look at the bosom, the buttocks, or the whole body, but not
into the eyes, or conversely into the eyes but not at the body,
or at the body in general but not at the breast; or at the breast
but not the whole body. Ordinarily the inhibited look will be of
that part of the body which is of greatest interest to the individual. Thus one who longs to devour the breast with the eyes
may be able to look at the body as a whole, or at the face, or the
stomach or the buttocks, but his eyes sweep quickly over the
breast, pulled back again and again only to be lowered in shyness or moved swiftly away in fear.

Lest it be supposed that such looking is necessarily a "substitute" for the wish to touch or suck or bite the breast, such an inhibition has been reported in one case where there was no inhibition of the act of caressing, sucking and biting the breast. This individual suffered no inhibition on handling the breast, sucking it and biting it—but this could only be done in the dark despite an overwhelming wish to look at the breast while handling it and putting it into his mouth. This component was so important that the manual and oral activity alone instigated incomplete excitement. This inhibition arose from a childhood in which his mother slapped his face as a punitive technique to discourage his curiosity about her body. I have found the same inhibition, however, in the absence of this particular technique. It would appear that any punishment, most frequently verbal scolding, which caused the child to lower his eyes in shame is enough to provide the model for transfer to the sexual look when this comes under taboo by whatever method of punishment.

We do not know exactly how the child is taught not to look with sexual intent, but the sexual look is sufficiently inflammatory to motivate society and parents to inhibit any sign of it in children, if and when it does appear. In all probability this is a lesson which is learned before the emergence of sexual motives. As previously mentioned, relatively early the child is taught, usually verbally, that it is impolite to stare earnestly at the face of a stranger. In some cases the training not to stare probably generalizes to the sexual stare. What parents do if this general training is insufficient to control the sexual look, we do not as yet know.

There is reason to believe that in many, if not all, societies there is a more severe training of the female than the male with respect to sexual looking. The female learns to be visually more shy, we think. Kinsey found that only 12 per cent of his female subjects felt any sexual response to portrayals of nude figures of the opposite sex, whereas 54 per cent of the males responded. To burlesque and floor shows 14 per cent of the women and 62 per cent of the men felt a response, and to pornographic drawings 32 per cent of the women and 77 per cent of the men.

That the inhibition of the female's sexual looking is not universal, however, is clear. Even the Old Testament attributes sexual looking to females (Genesis 39: 6-7) ". . . Joseph was a goodly person, and well favoured. And it came to pass . . . that his master's wife cast her eyes upon Joseph; and she said, Lie with me."

Early in the sixteenth century the Florentine artist Fra Bartolommeo painted a nude St. Sebastian which, according to Vasari, was praised for its beauty and especially its flesh coloring. But the picture had to be removed. The friars discovered through the confessional that some women sinned in their thoughts when they looked at it.

Although this inhibition is far from universal among women, even in our society, yet it is certainly not a modern invention. When Casanova told a woman how he was excited by a voluptuous picture, he was disappointed to hear from his companion that she was unmoved by such a stimulus.

Pierre de Brantome (1535-1614), who described the French court of his time, wrote of a prince who owned a silver cup on whose inner surface he had engraved copulating figures. He would offer it, filled with wine, to a woman guest, watching her expression as she discovered the copulating figures. He would ask, "Now feel ye not a something that doth touch you at the sight?" Most of the female members of this otherwise bawdy court replied, "Nay, never a one of all these droll images hath had power enough to stir me."

This last combination of general sexual license and specific looking inhibition illuminates a general phenomenon of some importance. This is the fact that it is possible for an individual to suffer specific inhibitions in the sexual sphere which may coexist with a general freedom in the remainder of this domain. The lustiest sexuality may be enjoyed despite severe restrictions on specific types of sexual behavior. A case in point is the restriction on looking among lower-class American males (i.e., the taboo on nudity) reported by Kinsey. He illustrates this with the case of a lower-class man who had had intercourse with a different woman each night for some time, except for one night when the woman removed her clothes. The man refused to have intercourse with her because she was immoral.

Eye disease and blindness have long been supposed to be associated with excessive sexuality. In treating inflamed eyes Paul of Aegina, the seventh century Greek physician, prescribed abstinence from venery as the most important factor in the cure. Francis Bacon noted that ancient authorities believed "much use of Venus doth dim the sight." The author of an English textbook on eye disease, published in 1854, thought blindness could result from the weakness incident to the loss of body fluids "as in the loss of seminal fluid from excessive venery."

But if the eyes can be damaged by excessive sexuality it has been believed they can also be healed by love. John Bakansi, a blind priest of Cairo, prayed every night before a picture of the Virgin Mary that his sight might be restored. After a year of prayer he had the following dream: the Virgin "drew nigh unto him and took out her breasts from inside her apparel and pressed milk out of them upon his eyes; then she made the sign of the cross over him with her holy hands and disappeared into the picture." John awoke to find that his vision was clear, and his eyes full of milk.

The primal scene and a reformulation of the Oedipus myth

The significance of the eye in mythology needs no further underlining. Its significance in the Freudian mythology has not been appreciated. The major crime of the family romance is presented by Freud as though it were a purely sexual matter, and yet, if we examine the play of Sophocles which so impressed Freud, we see that this is but another version of the law of talion, an eye for an eye.

Despite the fact that the son presumably sexually possesses the mother, if the punishment fit the crime, the crime was also looking at and being seen by the mother, since the retribution is blindness. The punishment is for the ocular rather than the genital response.

The single most disturbing experience in the life of the child is the discovery of the primal scene, the witnessing, the looking at the parents. This is not in life a sexual act *per se*, any more than in the Oedipus myth. The significance of the witnessing of the primal scene varies somewhat from child to child, depending in part on the relative importance of the different primary affects in the parents and in the child.

The primal scene may be interpreted as a discovery that the

pillars of society and morality are themselves immoral and corrupt, with a disenchantment similar to that which attends any discovery of corruption in high places in government. The parents have been at once legislators, policemen and judges—writing the moral laws, apprehending the youthful violator and also meting out the punishment to fit his crimes. These crimes have included oral greediness and anal dirtiness, as well as strictly sexual masturbatory offenses, and so the control of bodily impulses in general becomes a critical part of the meaning of goodness. When both parents are discovered to indulge themselves in what seems complete license and bodily abandonment, then the basis of morality and government by the parents as well as by the self can suddenly be completely undermined and crumble.

This is but ont of the many interpretations which children commonly put upon the primal scene. It often happens that the primal scene is interpreted not as an immorality of both parents but as a betrayal by both parents. In such a case the child feels that the parents have become too interested in each other to the exclusion of what he thought was their individual interest in him. He wishes then to make them stop and pay attention to him.

Again it may be interpreted as a betrayal and infidelity by the favored parent. Thus the mother may be seen as a whore who bestows her love promiscuously after having assured her son that he possessed her love exclusively. Similarly, if the attachment to the father is exceptionally strong, he may be found guilty of equal infidelity and faithlessness.

If the child is particularly anxious, he may be more disturbed by what appears to be the overly intense affect which he hears emitted in the excited breathing and sexual moaning of both parents. Or the child may interpret the father's posture to be angry and cruel and fear lest he hurt his mother. In one such case reported by Murray and Morgan, the witnessing of the primal scene was responsible for an idiosyncratic rescue fantasy in which the son would become a surgeon who would operate on his patients in such a way as to spare them the needless pain and harm which they would otherwise suffer at the hands of an unskilled and brutal father.

The apparent fusion of anger and excitement in the father and fear and excitement in the mother may critically influence the unique conditions under which sexual intercourse may later be enjoyed. If the child identifies with the father's role, so interpreted this may produce a sadistic sexual need. If the identification is with the mother's role, so interpreted this may produce a masochistic need.

Further, it is not uncommon that the primal scene is interpreted in terms not of anger and fear but in contempt and humiliation, in which both parents are thought to be degrading the other. Identification with either parent's role, so interpreted, can produce a sexual need in which there can be no excitement apart from humiliation.

Again the mother may be presumed to be crying in distress which can generate either a rescue fantasy or an identification with the mother in which the individual requires the experience of distress as a precondition of sexual excitement. The other must make him cry before he can be deeply excited.

These represent a sample of the variety of interpretations which children commonly put upon the primal scene. It is only partly a sexual affair. It is much more a sudden strengthening or weakening of excitement or fear or anger or distress or shame.

As such the importance of witnessing the primal scene derives from the significance of looking and being looked at when one's face and the faces of the others communicate intense affect as well as sexuality.

THE MEANING OF THE EYE-TO-EYE SCENE

Although the face as a whole is critical in the communication of affect both to others and through feedback to the self, it is the eyes which are the windows of the soul. Man is predominantly a visual animal. No other of his receptor systems provides such continuous and abundant information as the optic system. In this wealth of information it receives and also sends messages concerning the affects. The movements of the eyes and the musculature surrounding the eyes express and communicate joy, excitement, fear, distress, anger and shame. So the eye receives affective displays not only from the face of the other but also from the eyes of the other, and at the same time one's own eyes and face communicate affect to the other. It is this rich, two-way, simultaneous transmission and reception which make man the most voyeuristic of animals. Only through the eyes can a human being express his excitement at another human being, see that this excitement is contagious and responded to in kind by the other, and see that the other is also aware of the excitement in both of them, and aware of their mutual awareness of their mutual excitement.

The same mutual awareness can occur through mutual looking, whatever the affects experienced by each person. If we see that we are smiling at each other, then we share the knowledge that we enjoy each other's presence. If we see that we are both crying, then we share the knowledge of our common grief. If we see that we are both angry, then we share the knowledge that we hate each other. If we see that we lower our heads, then we share the knowledge that we are both ashamed. If we see that we both are sneering, then we share the knowledge that we are both disgusted, either with each other or someone else. If we see fear in each other's eyes, then we share the knowledge that we are afraid of each other or someone or something.

Nor is mutuality of awareness limited to homogeneity of shared affect. If I smile at you and you frown at me, we share the knowledge that I like you but you hate me. If I show interest at you and you respond with contempt, we share the knowledge that my interest in you disgusts you. If I show anger at you and you show fear, we share the knowledge that I am intimidating you. If I show distress and you show surprise, we share the knowledge that my unhappiness comes as a surprise to you. If I show shame and you show contempt, we share the knowledge that my shyness repels you.

Because of the possibilities of such shared awareness there is no greater intimacy than the interocular interaction. It is an incomplete intimacy when one is looked at, without seeing the other, or when one looks at the other without being looked at. Our argument so far has been that the face is where affects are both sent and received, that the eyes are most critical in mutual affect awareness, that the self is therefore located phenomenologically on the face and in the eyes and the consequent intimacy of interocular interaction results in a universal taboo on direct mutual looking.

The closest approximation to the shared look-look is the sexual intimacy, in which analogously pleasure is simultaneously given and received by the same act. Affect may also be shared during intercourse through the voice and through speech, but paradoxically just the interaction which would deepen and complete the experience of sexual intimacy, the shared look, is usually tabooed. Sexual intercourse is characteristically conducted in the dark. Facial interaction is not only more intimate than sexual intercourse inasmuch as it involves more sharing of one's affects and of one's phenomenal self, but it is typically excluded from the experience of intercourse because it is felt that it would intensify the shame of sexual intimacy if ocular intimacy were added to it.

Taboos on affect increase the ambivalence and hence shame–humiliation about looking and being looked at

Although shame is innately produced by the incomplete reduction of the positive affects of interest and enjoyment, through learning one can be taught to be ashamed of the witnessing or expression of any affect. Since, as mentioned above, the eyes not only can witness any affect in the face of the other but also express one's own affect to the other, and since this can be a shared experience, interocular intimacy becomes the occassion, for the adult, of experiencing shame about any affect. Given any restraint on the expression of any affect, when such restraint is not completely accepted, then complete interocular freedom must evoke shame, since the residual wish to look, to exchange affect, will also come under inhibition.

If I am ashamed to be angry or to be seen as angry, then I will also be ashamed to look at and to be seen by you when I am angry. If I am ashamed to cry, then I will also be ashamed to look at you and be seen by you with tears in my eyes.

Since we think any affect inhibition generates a wish to break through affect control, we must assume that there is a universal wish behind the taboo to look and be looked at simultaneously, to be mutually aware of the expression of any and every kind of tabooed affect, including shame. We are all necessarily would-be both voyeurs and exhibitionists of all those affects we. are inhibited in expressing, witnessing, and sharing.

Since the face and particularly the eyes are the primary communicators and receivers of all affects, the linkage of shame to the whole spectrum of affect expression may result in an exaggerated self-consciousness, because the self is then made ashamed of all its feelings and must therefore hide the eyes lest the eyes meet. We may then not look too closely at each other, because we cannot be sure how we might feel if we were to do so. Indeed, many of us fall in love with those into whose eyes we have permitted ourselves to look and by whose eyes we have let ourselves be seen. This love is romantic because it is continuous with the period before the individual lovers knew shame. They not only return to baby talk, but even more important they return to baby looking.

The eyes are used to express, receive and share experience of every kind of affect and are therefore vulnerable to whatever controls these affects suffer. To the extent to which any affect has been controlled by shame, then the eyes become the site of further shame. But the universal taboo on mutual looking is based not only on shame but on the entire spectrum of affects. The reciprocal look-look may be tabooed by fear with or without shame, and by distress with or without shame. It may be too frightening to look and be looked at, or too distressing rather than too shaming.

Thus in the paranoid and others who have been terrorized rather than simply shamed, the eyes may blink in fear at the direct gaze of the other or be rolled to the side away from the confrontation of the gaze of the other. Although there is a universal taboo on interocular intimacy this taboo is radically heightened in the paranoid condition so that there is an exaggerated awareness of both being looked at and the terrifying and humiliating consequences of such visibility. In contrast, in depression there is an exaggerated awareness of the humiliating consequences of not being looked at and of losing the attention of the other.

Our argument for the universality and inevitability of the

taboo on interocular intimacy therefore rests in part on the fact that in every culture there seems to exist some constraints on affect and the mutual communication of affect, in part on the constraints on sexuality, in part on the constraints on intimacy as such. Intimacy, sexuality and affects all use the eyes as their instruments.

The visibility of the eyes make them unique organs for the expression, communication, contagion, escalation and control of affects. To the extent to which intimacy, sexuality and affect necessarily suffer inhibition, there will inevitably appear taboos on interocular intimacy.

Chapter 18

The Sources of
Shame – Humiliation,
Contempt – Disgust and
Self-Contempt – Self-Disgust

This chapter is concerned with the major conditions, innate and learned, which give rise to shame—humiliation and to the closely allied affects of contempt—disgust and self-contempt—self-disgust.

It should be noted that although for theoretical clarity these affects are discussed separately, they rarely exist separately, inasmuch as shame can be reduced by self-contempt which totally rejects that portion of the self of which one is ashamed, and the wish not to lose part of oneself inevitably leads to shame in response to self-contempt.

Included in this chapter are descriptions of an empirical investigation of the relative importance of work, other people and one's body as sources of shame as a function of age; of the concepts of affect-shame binds and of shame theory, that is, the learned inhibition of affects by shame and the individual's own organization of his experience in terms of its relevance to shame; and of how seemingly innocuous, well-intentioned and socially approved reactions by parents to a child can lead to a multiple affect-shame bind, where every affect is inhibited by shame.

The chapter concludes with the dynamics of self-contempt, including the internalization of contempt from others, the magnification and multiplication of the internal persecutor, the coping with the internal persecution by obeisance and rebellion and the process of apparent objectification of the internalized contemptuous other and the acceptance of self-contempt.

THE MAJOR SOURCES OF SHAME

We have argued that shame is an affect of relatively high toxicity, that it strikes deepest into the heart of man, that it is felt as a sickness of the soul which leaves man naked, defeated, alienated and lacking in dignity .We have also argued that the toxicity of an affect is directly proportional to its biological urgency, but ordinarily inversely proportional to its relative frequency of arousal. Thus, anxiety is more toxic than distress, and, correspondingly, anxiety is ordinarily aroused by life and death emergencies which are relatively infrequent, whereas, distress is ordinarily aroused by a wide variety of situations which deviate only moderately from optimal conditions. If shame is so mortifying, it is ill adapted to serve as a general broad spectrum negative affect. Despite its high toxicity, however, there appear to be a multiplicity of innate sources of shame, since there are innumerable ways in which excitement and enjoyment may be partialy blocked and reduced and thereby activate shame. Man is not only an anxious and a suffering animal, but he is above all a shy animal, easily caught and impaled between longing and despair. When one adds to the innate sources of shame those which are learned, the normal human being is very vulnerable to a generalized shame bind almost as toxic as an anxiety neurosis. We will now examine some of the major sources, both learned and unlearned, of shame.

"I want, but—": the varieties of barriers which incompletely reduce any of the varieties of interest—excitement or enjoyment—joy

The experience of shame is inevitable for any human being insofar as desire outruns fulfillment sufficiently to attenuate interest without destroying it. The most general sources of shame are the varieties of barriers to the varieties of objects of excitement or enjoyment, which reduce positive affect sufficiently to activate shame, but not so completely that the original object is renounced: "I want, but—" is one essential condition for the activation of shame.

Clearly not all barriers suspend the individual between long·

ing and despair. Many barriers either completely reduce interest so that the object is renounced, or heighten interest so that the barrier is removed or overcome. Indeed, shame itself may eventually also prompt either renunciation or counteraction in asmuch as successful renunciation or counteraction will reduce the feeling of shame.

We are saying only that whatever the eventual outcome of the arousal of shame may be, shame is activated by the incomplete reduction of interest—excitement or enjoyment—joy, rather than by the heightening of interest or joy or by the the complete reduction of interest or joy.

When an individual encounters a barrier to his interest or enjoyment, the positive affect may be heightened, remain the same, or be reduced or extinguished. Shame is activated by the attenuation of excitement or joy, but the effect of barriers may also involve affects other than interest, enjoyment or shame.

The individual may, in addition, be distressed, angered, frightened or provoked to contempt by any barrier to the attainment of the object of interest or enjoyment. Either the heightening or complete reduction of interest may activate anger or distress or fear or contempt. Counteraction of the barrier may be angry counteraction or distressed counteraction or counteraction in disgust or even in fear. Renunciation of the goal may also be renunciation in anger or distress or disgust or fear. Thus anger, or any of the other negative affects, leads to successful counteraction against the barrier to wish-fulfillment when anger is aroused as a result of interest being heightened and leads to renunciation of wish-fulfillment when interest has been reduced by the barrier. This is another instance of the relatively independent variability of affect, object and behavior in the central assembly.

In one case one is angry because one wants the object and does not have it, or in the other case one is angry because one had to give up the object. The same feedback from muscles which are in a state of hypertonus can activate and sustain anger, on the one hand, when the individual is prompted by heightened interest to storm the barrier, and, on the other hand, when he has been forced to turn away from the barrier in chagrin.

We cannot tell from the nature of the barrier alone whether

shame will or will not be produced, because the same barrier may produce in different individuals, or in the same individual at different times, counteraction or renunciation or that incomplete reduction of interest and enjoyment which activates shame. It is the differential effect of the barrier on interest and other affects which is critical for the prediction of shame or some other response to the barrier to the object of interest.

Thus a barrier which heightened interest and counteraction in the morning when free energy was high might produce a partial reduction of interest and shame when free energy was less abundant, and produce complete reduction of interest and renunciation at the end of the day when energy was at its lowest ebb.

The prediction of shame as a consequence of encountering a barrier to interest cannot be made on the basis of knowledge of the nature of the barrier not only because one must know whether interest or enjoyment is likely to be sustained, or heightened, or reduced, or incompletely reduced, but also because, as we have seen, the barrier may arouse other affects which may enhance, attenuate, or reduce interest or enjoyment. If an individual has learned to respond to the slightest interference with intense anger, he may readily renounce his initial goal to express his anger at the individual he holds responsible for the interference. If the slightest interference activates fear, such an individual also may be incapable of sustaining enough interest to become ashamed.

We have said that we cannot tell from the structure of the barrier whether shame or some other affect will be activated. In this we have assumed that we can easily identify what constitutes a barrier and distinguish it from what is the goal and the means thereto. But what seems like an unexpected barrier or difficulty to one individual may appear to another to be an integral part of the problem with which he is involved.

At one extreme is an individual who cannot see the difference between walking straight to the outstretched arms of the beloved, and an elaborate campaign to win the love object. Both may appear to him to be equally exciting and rewarding encounters. At the other extreme is an individual who interprets any reticence of his beloved as a barrier and a rebuff.

It is the difference between an individual who expects that he will make rapid progress in the solution of any problem, who interprets as a barrier any deceleration in the progress of problem solving, and an individual who assumes that problem solving proceeds at a variable rate in chunks and slumps and is not aware of the difference between rates of progress as a difference in barriers. In the latter case effort may be increased proportionately to the increasing and decreasing difficulty of task, but with no interpretation of such variation as interference or barriers. It is analogous to the increased pressure on the accelerator of an automobile by the driver as he encounters hills and valleys on the road. Such a driver is aware that more effort may be required to go up than down a hill, but there may be no interpretation of such an increase in effort either by his foot or by the engine as a response to an interference or to a barrier, but rather as different parts of the experience of driving an automobile.

If shame is dependent on barriers to excitement and enjoyment, then the pluralism of desires must be matched by a pluralism of shame. We have examined the extraordinary range of objects of excitement and enjoyment. Insofar as there may be impediments, innate or learned, to any of these objects, there is a perpetual vulnerability to idiosyncratic sources of shame. One man's shame can always be another man's fulfillment, satiety or indifference. Further, within each person will be numerous objects which are pursued to fulfillment or renounced, coexisting with other objects which the individual cannot achieve and yet cannot renounce, which are a deep source of enduring shame, of unfinished business.

Let us now examine the varieties of barriers, innate and learned, universal and idiosyncratic, to the varieties of objects of excitement and enjoyment, innate and learned, universal and idiosyncratic, which are capable of arousing shame.

Work, love, the body, the self as major objects of investment of interest—excitement and enjoyment—joy and as a major source of shame—humiliation

Insofar as any human being is excited by or enjoys his work, other human beings, his body, his self, and the inanimate world around him, he is vulnerable to the variety of vicissitudes in the form of barriers, lacks, losses, and accidents, which will impoverish, attenuate, impair, or otherwise prevent total pursuit and enjoyment of his work, of others, of himself and of the world around him. Insofar as his life in the world is not exactly as he would like it, he can experience the defeat, the alienation, the indignity and unwelcome intrusion of shame—humiliation into the otherwise unalloyed excitement and enjoyment of his life. The pluralism of excitement and enjoyment is without limit, and hence shame, too, knows no bounds.

Sources of shame connected with work

If my investment of interest and enjoyment is in work which has a characteristic level or difficulty, I can be shamed by any radical deviation from this optimal level. If my work becomes either too easy or too difficult, there may be just enough reduction of positive affect to evoke shame. It should be noted that in this case and the others which follow, any great increase or decrease in difficulty might reduce interest entirely rather than merely attenuate it, or it might even intensify interest or enjoyment. When some work becomes much harder, I may invest more affect, that is, become more interested, or enjoy it more, or I may liquidate my interest, or my investment may be reduced incompletely but sufficiently to evoke shame.

If I wish to have my work remain private, I can be shamed if it is opened to public scrutiny. If, however, I wish my work to be widely known and it remains unknown, this can evoke shame because affect is still invested in publicity but encounters the wall of the unconsciousness of others of my work.

If I wish the initiation or continuation of my work to be demanded by others, their indifference can evoke shame. If, however, I wish the initiation or continuation of my work to be entirely my own decision, even the enthusiastic clamor of others for my work may seem coercive and evoke shame.

With respect to the reception of my work, if I wish to have it evaluated by others, whether positively or negatively, and it is not evaluated, shame may be evoked by such a barrier to completion. If however my interest is in completing my work according to my own ideas, then I may be shamed by the evaluative acts of others, whether these evaluations are positive or negative, since they may transform the significance of my work, making me more other-directed than I might wish.

If I wish to diversify my investments of affect in many objects, in family, in friends, in art, in travel, in addition to work, then I may be shamed if there is disproportionate time and energy demanded by my work which threatens the liquidation of other affect investments. If, however, I wish to dedicate all my energies to work, the demands of family, friends and play may evoke shame because they interfere with the monopolistic pursuit of work.

If I wish my work to be in the mainstream of contemporary efforts, I may be ashamed if my work is judged to be somewhat deviant. If, however, I wish to be creative, I may be ashamed if my work is judged to be in the mainstream of contemporary opinion.

If I am a bright housewife, I may be ashamed because too much of my work is too exclusively muscular. If I am a mesomorphic academic, I may be shamed because my work is too much cerebral and too little somatotonic.

If I am very sociophilic and would enjoy team work, I may be ashamed if I have to work alone. If I enjoy solitary labor, I may be ashamed if and when I have to consult with others in connection with my work.

If I am a pure scientist but I also wish my work to make a direct, immediate contribution to social welfare and my work seems to have little such application, I may feel ashamed. If, however, I am an applied scientist who wishes also to make a contribution to knowledge but whose work is in fact more useful than illuminating, then I may also experience shame.

If I am an individual whose work is very imaginative, rich and suggestive, but who wishes also that his work be precise, rigorous and beyond question, then I may be shamed by any suggestion of error. If I am an individual whose work is precise, rigorous, and correct, but I also wish it to be imaginative, rich and suggestive, I may be shamed by any suggestion of sterility or restriction of scope.

If I wish my work to have an impact on the widest possible

audience and only the specialists take note of it, I may experience shame. If I wish my work to have an impact on specialists and it turns out to be a popular success, I may also experience shame.

If I wish my work to have an immediate payoff, but I am a policy maker, I may be shamed by the failure of others to adequately implement my decisions. If I am a worker with some aspiration to participate in the decisions which govern the conditions under which I work, I may be shamed by the requirement to execute decisions which I did not make.

Jung's dilemma of middle-age depression despite success

It should be noted that in some of the above cases the major work interest is the source of shame by virtue of a direct barrier, and in others the source is from a residual interest despite the fulfillment of the major interest. As we have learned from Jung, such sources of shame from a residual interest may be delayed in appearance until late in life, just at that point when the self has apparently fulfilled itself by success in its major work investment. Under such conditions it is likely that shame arising from barriers to the major work investment prevents the emergence of other sources of shame until the former are finally overcome. At such turning points the individual may become vulnerable to residual wishes and their lack of fulfillment in sufficient vividness to produce intense shame and profound depression.

Frequently of course, such depressions arise not from a frustrated residual work interest but from some other interest which may have been submerged by work. It does happen that a middle-aged scientist suddenly wishes he had been an artist or a philosopher, or conversely, and that he does turn away from one career to another very different one. It also happens, however, that the middle-aged scientist may discover ways of life remote from commitment to work altogether. He may now become fascinated with modes of experience in which the cognitive element is minimal—in which it is the play of the senses, or of the gross muscles, or of affect, which capture him. His awareness of past neglect of such domains, combined with present longing, may provide entirely new sources of shame to a person at such a point of crisis in development.

Shame—humiliation from love, friendship and close
interpersonal relationships

Let us consider next the varieties of sources of shame which
arise from love, friendship and close interpersonal relationships.
If I wish to touch you but do not wish to be touched, I may feel
ashamed. If I wish to look at you but you do not wish me to, I
may feel ashamed. If I wish you to look at me but you do not,
I may feel ashamed. If I wish to look at you and at the same time
wish that you look at me, I can be shamed. If I wish to be close
to you but you move away, I am ashamed. If I wish to suck or
bite your body and you are reluctant, I can become ashamed.
If I wish to hug you or you hug me or we hug each other and
you do not reciprocate my wishes, I feel ashamed. If I wish to
have sexual intercourse with you but you do not, I am ashamed.

If I wish to hear your voice but you will not speak to me, I
can feel shame. If I wish to speak to you but you will not listen,
I am ashamed. If I would like us to have a conversation but you
do not wish to converse, I can be shamed. If I would like to
share my ideas, my aspirations or my values with you but you do
not reciprocate, I am ashamed. If I wish to talk and you wish to
talk at the same time, I can become ashamed. If I want to tell
you my ideas but you wish to tell me yours, I can become
ashamed.

If I want to share my experiences with you but you wish to
tell me your philosophy of life, I can become ashamed. If I wish
to speak of personal feelings but you wish to speak about science,
I will feel ashamed. If you wish to talk about the past and I wish
to dream about the future, I can become ashamed. If I wish to
be praised by you and you wish to be praised by me, I may feel
ashamed.

If I wish you to become like me but you wish me to become
like you, I can become ashamed. If I wish to control you but you
wish to control me, I can be ashamed. If I wish that you would
control me but you wish that I would control you, I am ashamed.

If I can't smile at you until you smile at me, and if you can't
smile at me until I smile at you, I am ashamed. If I wish to
listen and you wish to listen, then I can feel shame if neither

of us can talk. If I wish to kiss you but I require a show of affection before I can do so, and you can show affection to me only after you have been kissed, then I will be ashamed. If I wish to express my ideas but I require that you first express your ideas, and you have the same reticence, then I will feel ashamed.

Another major source of shame in interpersonal relationships is the loss of the love object, through separation or death. Not only is distress produced, but the head is hung in shame. This shame may be experienced in different ways depending upon the imagery and the interpretation which is concurrent with the shame. It may be felt as an alienation, as a rejection, as a defeat, as intolerable loneliness, as a temporary distancing between the self and the other, as a poignant, bitter-sweet longing. Here as elsewhere the same affect may be experienced in ways which are totally different depending upon the concurrent other responses in the central assembly at the moment.

Still another source of shame in interpersonal relationships comes not from the increase in distance between the self and the other, but from the decrease in such distance whenever there is any taboo on intimacy. In any such interpersonal relationship it is the sudden loss of distance or the threat of it which may provoke shame. Thus, the threat of sexual intimacy either by act or by increased desire when there is a hierarchical social relationship between two individuals can evoke shame in either party.

In the constrained relationships between white and Negro Americans, it is the loss of distance which can shame either party. There is a difference between the North and South with respect to what constitutes a loss of distance. In the North the Negro is much freer to achieve excellence and higher status as a professional and as an entertainer. The Northern white can tolerate excellence by the Negro, since there is little intimacy with him. Increased enjoyment and admiration of his skill as an athlete or as an entertainer carry with it no increase in mutuality or in longing for intimacy which might threaten shame.

In the South, however, there appears to be much greater intimacy between white and Negro. If the Negro in the South were permitted to achieve and display excellence, to become a respected public figure, intolerable shame would be provoked in part because intimacy is already enjoyed and so would be transformed from the intimacy of a hierarchical relationship into the intimacy either of egalitarian mutuality or of a reversal of upper and lower positions in which the Southern white would desire the love and respect of the Southern Negro.

Shame—humiliation from the body

Let us consider next the sources of shame in the body, which arise from impediments to bodily excitement and enjoyment. First are the frustrations of the primary drives. If I am forced to wait unduly for food or water or for sexual satisfaction, I may feel shame. Next is loss of energy arising either from diurnal variations or from illness or accident. This ordinarily results in sufficient reduction of interest to evoke shame and, in addition, may produce sufficient distress from the bombardment of low-level discomfort to result in a state of depression. Depression, in our view, is a state in which there is conjoint shame, distress and reduction of level of amplification. For this reason diurnal variations are capable of producing temporary depressions.

The body is also a source of shame insofar as it fails to support interpersonal communion or self-regard. If the body is considered unattractive, the individual may feel shame because of the attenuation of his interest and pride in his own body, and because his body may fail to sufficiently excite others to maintain desired interpersonal relationships.

The body may also provide a source of shame insofar as it is incompetent to be used to produce excitement. Thus, if the individual loves to be active and to be highly mobile but his body is incapable of sufficient agility or activity, excitement will be so attenuated that the individual will feel shame. This source of shame becomes critical when the individual is immobilized through illness or accident. It also appears when socialization radically restricts the free movement of the child.

Negativism is only one outcome of early severe parental restrictions on free movement. Shame, and compensatory fantasies of flying through the air with the greatest of ease, are also conspicuous outcomes.

The free movement fantasy and **France**

It is our impression that this shame and free movement complex appears as a major preoccupation in French literature and philosophy. Beginning with the French Revolution, the wall recurs again and again as a symbol of shame which must be stormed as the Bastille was breeched. But the imagery of the wall and free movement are not only symbols of social status, shame and isolation as in Stendhal, but also signify life and excitement as against death and sterility.

In Bergson, for example, the immediacy of time and movement is put into the starkest opposition to science which abstracts and kills the object as it chops the flow of time into dead chunks. In the contemporary French cinema, there is a film in which a set of balloons is the hero, escaping into the air and floating freely out of all threats of constraint. In another contemporary film, the camera is focused much of the time on the legs of the hero as he moves about in space. In a recent French revue "La Plume de ma Tante" not only do individuals move about with extraordinary speed and facility, but a group of monks are shown pulling the ropes which ring the bells of the monastery. At a critical moment each monk becomes airborne, lifted by the rope from the bell which now sends him wildly up and down through space.

In Saint-Exupéry all human relationships are translated into the imagery of movement, free or constrained: "He was free, infinitely free, so free that he was no longer conscious of pressing on the ground. He was free of that weight of human relationships which impedes movement, those tears, those farewells, those reproaches, those joys, all that a man caresses or tears every time he sketches out a gesture, those countless bonds which tie him to others and make him heavy."

In Sartre's play, *No Exit,* claustrophobia is maximized and linked to enforced interaction and restriction of movement. The setting is Hell, and is conceived of as a huge, windowless hotel. Three people, newly dead, are ushered into a grim, windowless, single room. They are not only unable to die but they cannot move or escape into aloneness. They are eternal shut-ins. There is no way out, and they are doomed to the mutual suffocation of being unable to move out of their common jail.

Among contemporary French cartoonists Siné expresses most clearly the restraint of the free movement of the French child, the revenge he wishes to take by restraining the movement of adults and animals, his delight in free movement as an adult and his expectation that he must ultimately be stopped if he moves too fast and too freely through space.

In Figure 1 a child is shown shackled at play, while an adult is about to fly through the air from the diving board. It is the child who will shoot and stop his free movement. In Figure 2 the child's revenge is more explicit. He buries the adult in the sand so that he cannot move. In the second of the drawings here, he moves the adult who is also buried in sand; and in the third, he has tied knots in the tentacles of the octopus, an otherwise free-moving animal, whom he has on a leash and whom he is taking for a walk. In Figure 3, which is the last cartoon in Siné's book, *Siné Qua Non*, the adult who moves freely through space is finally stopped.

It is the opposition of the dead hand of authority, whether in science or religion, with the life-affirming excitement of free movement which seems to us peculiarly French. It suggests a convergence of a socialization in which there is much early constraint of movement and behavior in general with a radical discontinuity permitted for the French adult who therefore rebels against authority, against walls and particularly against any contraint on the free movement of his body through space.

After first noting the frequency of the theme of free movement in French art and thought, we turned to descriptions of the socialization of the French child for evidence of early and sustained restriction of free movement. It should be noted that we looked for *both* early and sustained restriction of free movement. It is not our belief that any early restriction on free movement, such as the swaddling of Russian and some American Indian children, is sufficient to sensitize the child to restraint and the need for freedom of movement. It is rather our belief that early socialization must be sustained for some years if it is to leave a relatively permanent and enduring influence on the adult personality. The rationale for this we will explain later.

Figure 1

Figure 2

Figure 3

We expected that French socialization should have restricted the free movement of the French child for several years to account for the continuing adult preoccupation with breaking through constraints on free movement.

Such indeed appears to be the case, according to Wolfenstein. Her description of how French parents take their children to the park shows clearly the restraint on motor activity. She writes:

"To an American visitor it is often amazing how long French children stay still. They are able to sit for long periods on park benches beside their parents. A typical position of a child in the park is squattting at his mother's feet, playing in the sand. His hands are busy, but his total body position remains constant. Children are often brought to the park in quite elegant (and unwashable) clothes, and they do not get dirty. The squatting child keeps his bottom poised within an inch of the ground but never touching, only his hands getting dirty; activity and getting dirty are both restricted to the hands. While sand play is generally permissible and children are provided with equipment for it, they seem subject to intermittent uncertainty whether it is all right for their hands to be dirty. From time to time a child shows his dirty hands to his mother, and she wipes them off.

"Among some children between two and three I noticed a particularly marked tendency to complete immobility, remaining in the same position, with even their hands motionless, and staring blankly or watching other children. A French child analyst suggested that this is the age when children are being stuffed with food and are consequently somewhat stuporous. Occasionally one could see children of these ages moving more actively and running about. But the total effect contrasted with the usual more continuous motor activity which one sees in American children. Also, French children seemed more often to walk where American children would run.

"The relation between restraint on aggression and on large-muscle activity was remarked upon by another French child analyst, who had treated both French and American children. She observed that an American child in an aggressive mood would throw things up to the ceiling, while a French child would express similar angry impulses by making little cuts in a piece of clay.

"Forceful activity on the part of children is apt to evoke warning words from the adults: 'Gently, gently.' Two brothers about nine and six were throwing a rubber ball back and forth. The younger had to make quite an effort to throw the ball the required distance; his throws were a bit badly aimed but did not come very close to any bystanders. His mother and grandmother, who were sitting near him, repeatedly cautioned him after every throw: *Doucement! Doucement!* I had the feeling that it was the strenuousness of his movements which made them uneasy, though they may also have exaggerated the danger of his hitting someone. Similarly, when two little girls about four and five were twirling around, holding each other's hands, an elderly woman seated near by kept calling to the older girl: *Doucement, elle est plus petite que toi.* To which the child answered that they were not going very fast. The implication here seems to be that any rapid or forceful movement can easily pass into a damaging act. . . .

"On the same occasion the play of another boy whom I observed, with a paper airplane, seemed to demonstrate very nicely the feeling about remaining within a small space. When American boys make planes out of folded paper, these planes are generally long and narrow, with a sharp point, with the aim of their being able to fly as fast and as far as possible. In contrast to this prevailing American style, the French boy had folded his paper plane in a wide-winged, much less pointed shape. It moved more slowly through the air and did not go any great distance, but within a small space described many elegant and complicated loops."

Despite the importance of this early socialization, we do not think that its impact would continue to be felt as pervasively as appears to be the case except for its further reinforcement by an educational system which is equally restraining. Philippe Aries, the brilliant French cultural historian, himself hypersensitive to movement and constraint, has traced the history of the relationship between the child, the family and society in terms of freedom versus "claustration":

"In the Middle Ages, at the beginning of modern times, and for a long time after that in the lower classes, children were mixed with adults as soon as they were considered capable of doing without their mothers or nannies, not long after a tardy weaning (in other words at about the age of seven). They immediately went straight into the great community of men, sharing in the work and play of their companions, old and young alike. The movement of collective life carried along in a single torrent all ages and classes, leaving nobody any time for solitude and privacy. In these crowded, collective existences there was no room for a private sector....It had no idea of education.

"Between the end of the Middle Ages and the seventeenth century, the child had won a place beside his parents to which he could not lay claim at a time when it was customary to entrust him to strangers. This return of the children to the home was a great event: it gave the seventeenth-century family its principal characteristic, which distinguished it from the medieval family. The child became an indispensable element of everyday life, and his parents worried about his education, his career, his future. He was not yet the pivot of the whole system, but he had become a much more important character.

"Family and school together [in the seventeenth century] removed the child from adult society. The school shut up a childhood which had hitherto been free within an increasingly severe disciplinary system, which culminated in the eighteenth and nineteenth centuries in the total claustration of the boarding-school. The solicitude of family, Church, moralists and administrators deprived the child of the freedom he had hitherto enjoyed among adults. It inflicted on him the birch, the prison cell—in a word, the punishments usually reserved for convicts from the lowest strata of society. The old society concentrated the maximum number of ways of life into the minimum of space and accepted, if it did not impose, the bizarre juxtaposition of the most widely different classes. The new society, on the contary, provided each way of life with a confined space in which it was understood that the dominant feature should be respected and that each person had to resemble a conventional model, an ideal type, and never depart from it under pain of excommunication. But this severity was the expression of a very different feeling from the old indifference: an obsessive love which was to dominate society from the eighteenth century on.

"Nowadays our society depends, and knows that it depends,

on the success of its educational system. It has a system of education, a concept of education, an awareness of its importance. New sciences such as psychoanalysis, pediatrics and psychology devote themselves to the problems of childhood, and their findings are transmitted to parents by way of a mass of popular literature. Our world is obsessed by the physical, moral and sexual problems of childhood."

Here we see again the intimate relationship in the mind of the Frenchman between physical immobility in a small space and the demand for social conformity. The French love of freedom and privacy was threatened not only by the "total claustration of the boarding school" but no less by the "obsessive love"— the world "obsessed by the physical, moral and sexual problems of childhood." Even in the past in which "the movement of collective life carried along in a single torrent all ages and classes" there was the same price: "leaving nobody any time for solitude and privacy." The golden mediaeval age is one in which there was more freedom to move, though even here a maximum number of ways of life are pressed into "the minimum of space."

Shaming—humiliation and aging

Finally, the body becomes an increasing source of shame as old age and illness and the imminence of death looms large. This is one of the reasons why, we think, depression is primarily a phenomenon of old age. The depressive has usually had numerous, transient attacks of depression before he succumbs to so deep and enduring a loss of joy and zest for living that he requires hospitalization. It is, we think, the convergence of multiple pressures such as the reduction of vital and sexual energy, the increase in bodily discomfort, the imminence of death, the loss of physical attractiveness, often also a loss of status, of competence, of friends or spouse through death, that together deepen and prolong depressions when they occur in old age.

Old age is the prime occasion of shame, with or without the accompaniments which together constitute depression, because there is both a heightening of the zest for life and a heightening of all the impediments to the enjoyment of life to which the aging body is vulnerable.

Despite the fact that the body with its increasing infirmity in old age is a prime source of shame, distress and fear, it is also true that concern with the aging or ailing body is a consequence as well as a source of shame and other negative affects.

This appeared in our investigation of the waxing and waning of hypochondriasis in the American population, which is presented later in this chapter. Hypochondriacal concern with the body does not simply increase with old age. It is highest when the individual is at the prime of his life, in late adolescence, from ages 14 to 19, and second highest between the ages of 55 to 64, just before retirement. It would appear that two critical transition points in social role, the prospect of joining the labor force and the prospect of leaving it, constitute crises of sufficient magnitude to force the individual back upon himself and into a hypochondriacal concern with his body.

Shame—humiliation from loss of enjoyment of the self

This brings us to a fourth source of shame, the loss of excitement and enjoyment of the self by the self. In large part this is a derivative of failures of positive affect investments to be maintained and rewarded by work, by interpersonal relationships and the body. These in turn have numerous sources, not the least of which are conflicts between work, communion and body as major objects of affect investment. Thus, as we shall see, the prospect of a necessary shift of interest from communion to work in late adolescence, just before the individual joins the labor force and assumes adult responsibility, produces a hypochondriacal concern with the body as a major source of shame. Again when the individual is faced with the prospect of retirement and of leaving the labor force, he is also forced in upon himself in shame and concern with his body.

Quite apart from these critical rapid changes of status, the individual is continually involved in trading on the bourse of affect investments. How much positive affect is invested in work, in family, or in friendship, in one friend or another, in hobbies or entertainment as against work varies not only from hour to hour and day to day, but from year to year and decade to decade. Since this is so, not only does the image of the self change, but sources of shame constantly shift.

To the extent to which I have reinvested my positive affect, there may be too little interest remaining in the older account to evoke shame. Renunciation of affect, as we have seen, not only reduces the possibility of shame but can be used as a technique of defense against longing and shame if these become intolerable. Cumming and Henry have characterized old age as a period of disengagement. It is our position that this is a special case of the more general phenomenon of affect reinvestment which occurs constantly.

If we knew the dominant affect investments over the whole life span, we would also know the dominant shifts in potential sources of shame, to the extent to which these derive from barriers to interest and enjoyment.

POSITIVE AFFECT INVESTMENT: SOCIOPHILIA AND WORK AS A CONSTANT

Although the ebb and flow of affect investment is highly variable, being divided between positive and negative affects, there is nonetheless reason to believe that there may be a constant in the domain of positive affect investment. We will present more detailed evidence for such a constant in a forthcoming volume by Tomkins, Schiffman and McCarter, *Age, Education, Intelligence and Personality*. It is our view that all human beings split their investment of positive affect between interpersonal communion (or what we have called sociophilia) and work.

Further, there is a conservation of positive affect such that increases in investment of positive affect in one domain require decreases in investment of positive affect in the other domain. To the extent to which I interest myself in work, I will interest myself less in people, and conversely.

This constant is subject to two limitations. First, all positive affect is in competition with negative affect so that it is possible to be so bound by negative affect that there can be excitement or enjoyment in neither work nor people. Second, there is a type of personality structure, which we will examine in Volume III, in which one works *for* the love and respect of people such that one cannot be achieved without the other. Such a one must work in order to evoke love and respect, and he must be loved and respected to work.

In general, however, we have assumed that sociophilia and work are negatively correlated. A derivative of this assumption is that whatever increases the investment of positive affect in one domain will decrease the investment of positive affect in the other domain. Thus if education should increase the work interest, it should decrease the interest in people. If increasing age should decrease the interest in work, it should increase the interest in people. In general these predictions have been confirmed. As education increases, Americans become more and more interested in work and less interested in people; but as they get older, they become less interested in their work and more and more interested in interpersonal relationships. Further detail will be found in *Age, Education, Intelligence and Personality.*

We will now present some additional preliminary findings.

Investment of affect in work, in relations with other people, and in one's own body as a function of age: an empirical study

We have used the Tomkins-Horn Picture Arrangement Test (PAT) to measure the waxing and waning of the dominant investments of affect in work, in interpersonal relationships and in the body.

The investment of dominant affect in work as reflected in the "work" scales, investment of positive affect in interpersonal relations is reflected in the "sociophilia" scales, concern and negative affect about one's body is reflected in the "hypochrondriasis" scales. We have examined the relationships between hypochondriasis, work and sociophilia in a representative nationwide Gallup sample of the American population. Our particular interest was in their relative strength as a function of age, education and intelligence.

Since the PAT responses are particularly sensitive to differences in the intelligence and education of the subjects, these two factors had to be controlled if we were to expose the impact of age on the strength of these variables. In our sample, as in the total population of the United States, the distributions of intelligence scores are comparable for different age groups, but the distribution of amount of eductation for different age groups are systematically biased.

This is because in the present American population the younger members have received more education than their parents. We therefore selected a sub-sample in which the relative ratios of college, high school and grammar school graduates at every age range were constant, and equal to that found in the population which is now 25 to 34 years old. This is a conservative estimate of what the educational background of Americans will be thirty years hence, if and when we test another representative sample of the American population on the PAT, on the assumption that the increased opportunities for education following World War II represent, at the least, a permanent change in the relative proportion of the population who will achieve higher education, and, at most, a base line for even further increases.

For those who are unfamiliar with the PAT, it may be helpful to note that the test consists of twenty-five "plates," i.e., each plate is a set of three pictures. The task of the subject is to place the three pictures in order so that they "tell a story that makes the best sense" and then to narrate that story briefly.

The "scales" consist of all arrangements (orderings of the three pictures in a set) from all twenty-five plates which have the same possible interpretation. If an individual gives a sufficient number of the arrangements which comprise a given scale, he is scored as "rare" on that scale, i.e., as possessing the characteristic measured by the scale: otherwise he is scored as "not rare" on that scale. Thus the final score of an individual on a scale is "0" or "1" and is not a continuous variable.* Hence, group comparisons are not comparisons of the means of distributions of scores but are comparisons of the percentage of extreme cases. Ordinarily we use the ninety-fifth percentile as a criterion of "rareness."

In the figures we will now present, there is a slight modification of this criterion in order to increase slightly the number of cases. The criterion we used to compare groups of different ages was the percentage of the population at each age who gave that

* Recently we have added a continuous score in which component responses are weighted inversely to their probability.

number of responses which was, on the average, the ninety percentile level of responses. In other words, the high general work
key has fourteen possible responses on fourteen of the total test
of twenty-five plates.

In the total population of 1500, the ninety-fifth percentile is
nine or more of these possible fourteen responses. We therefore
used in this case a criterion of at least eight responses, or approximately the ninetieth percentile score, for the entire population.
What is plotted, therefore, is the percentage of the population, at
each age, who give at least eight of these responses.

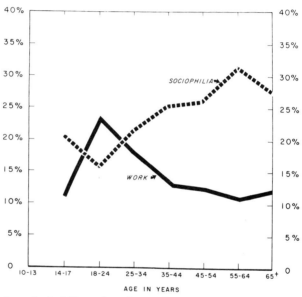

Figure 4   Sociophilia and work as a function of age: sociophilia reaches
its peak in the 55-64 age group, while interest in work declines from its
peak in the 18-24 period. (Note: percentages in this and the following
graphs denote the proportion of people tested who responded with an
extreme score on the characteristic under consideration.)

Figure 4 reveals a marked inverse relationships between the
percentage of individuals responding with an extreme score on
High General Sociophilia (Key 97a) and High General Work
(Key 218a).

In part, this is a function of some overlap between these two keys, that is, on some plates one can give one arrangement which would indicate work interest, and an alternative arrangement which would indicate sociophilia. However, in eight of the fourteen plates dealing with work there is no such overlap between the interest in work and the interest in being with other human beings. In four of the ten plates dealing with sociophilia, there is no overlap with the interest in work. Thus, of the twenty-four plates in the test which deal with either work or sociophilia, twelve, or fifty per cent, are strictly independent choices, and twelve, or fifty per cent, represent *some* degree of forced choice. Of these twelve plates, only one is a strictly forced choice in which *any* choice of six alternative responses must be either sociophilic or work oriented, but not both. In the remaining eleven choices two of the six alternatives are independent of *both* keys. It is possible for us to remove this element of overlap and determine to what extent affect investment in one or the other of these domains has the properties of a constant. This analysis is being done and will be reported elsewhere when completed. Preliminary findings seem to confirm our assumption that the age trends are valid despite the partial contraint in the two measures.

Let us first examine the varying strength of the work motive. The surprising trend we find is its relative constancy throughout the life cycle. There is a sharp increase in its intensity just as the individual enters the labor force from ages 18 to 24. However, after this six-year period it begins to drop sharply and eleven years later, at 35 to 44, it has returned to about the adolescent level.

Sociophilia, as we have said, presents an essentially mirror image. Sociophilia is at its lowest ebb during the ages 18 to 24, just when commitment to work is at its maximum. From 25 to 64 it climbs steadily in importance reaching a peak just before retirement, at 55 to 64. In the years following retirement, from 65 on, it decreases slightly. It is somewhat surprising to find that in late adolescence there is not so strong an interest in human interaction as in later life.

In Figure 5 is presented a comparison of work and hypochondriasis.

Turning to hypochondriasis, we find in general an inverse relation to work motivation and a positive relationship to socio-

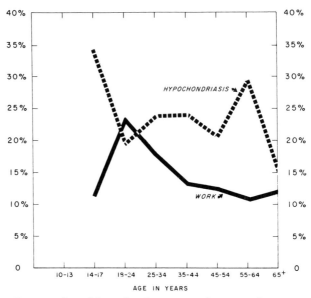

Figure 5   Work and hypochondriasis as a function of age: interest in work is highest in the 18-24 age group, while hypochondriasis is highest in the 14-19 period.

philia. The true relationship between sociophilia and hypochondriasis is even closer than it appears, since two of the five choices for hypochondriasis are somewhat forced choices between these two.

There are peak elevations in hypochondriasis at the two critical transition points, late adolescence, from 14 to 17, and late maturity, from 55 to 64. In the first case, despite optimal physical health, there is intense preoccupation with and pessimism about the body just before one is to enter the labor force and the assumption of adult responsibility. In the latter case, hypochondriasis reaches an absolute peak just before retirement, when one is to leave the labor force for good.

It is the imminence of any radical change in status and its threat to the sense of identity which we regard as the common factor in these two crises. In both cases hypochondriasis drops sharply once the new status has been consolidated. From 18 to 24, when achievement motivation reaches its peak, hypochondriasis is second lowest of any period in the individual's life. Turning the attention outward to work apparently cures the hypochondriasis of the average American. The absolute low

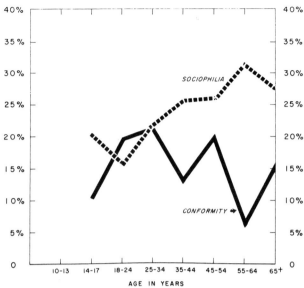

Figure 6   Sociophilia and conformity as a function of age: sociophilia
is at its peak in the 55-64 age group, at the same time that interest in
conformity is lowest.

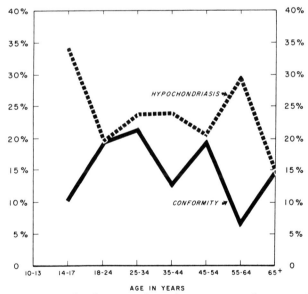

Figure 7   Hypochondriasis and conformity as a function of age:
hypochondriasis reaches a second high level when interest in conformity
is at its lowest point, in the 55-64 age group.

point of hypochondriasis comes, however, immediately following its absolute peak (ages 55-64), in the period of retirement from 65 on.

Paradoxically, when the body is most vulnerable to death (65+) the person is least hypochondriacal, and when the body is least vulnerable (14 to 17) the person is most hypochondriacal. The lowest hypochondriasis for the average American comes as noted above, with retirement. The second lowest period (18 to 24) is at the time of the assumption of adult responsibility and entering the labor force. It is not, therefore, work itself which is the cure for hypochondriasis but rather, we think, a firm commitment to any new status, whether that be active or passive.

It may be that the open acceptance of dependence and passivity in senility is as therapeutic as the acceptance of responsibility is in early maturity. Indeed the problem of death is in part the problem of the change of status associated with retirement and senility and the shame provoked by the enforced, unwilling surrender of lifelong commitments in work. Death is unique in being not only a universal source of shame but necessarily a multiple, conjoint source of shame, that is, it always involves shame from many sources.

In contrast, for example, work may provide a source of shame to an individual through barriers to his interest or enjoyment in work, but this shame does not in every case also involve, for example, shame based on contempt from others.

In an analysis which will be reported elsewhere, we have also found that there are significant systematic relationships between sociophilia and background parameters other than age. For example, in the American population it is the case that sociophilia is inversely related to education. The higher the education, the less interest in being in the presence of other people.

In Figures 6 and 7 there is presented the relationship between sociophilia and conformity, and the relationship between hypochondriasis and conformity. Both sociophilia and hypochondriasis are inversely related to conformity. Our measure of conformity is an entirely statistical one based essentially on the same rationale as the Rorschach popular response. It is composed of all those responses which are very common in the total population (from 40 to 88 percent average frequency). Whenever an extreme number of these is given by a particular group of the same age, it represents an increasing consensus without communication, i.e., a growing tendency within the group to think alike when faced with the same problem. Conversely it also represents a dropping out of individualism in the group.

The paradox of our findings is that the more people wish to be together (increase in sociophilia), the less they tend to think alike, and the more they tend to think alike, the less they enjoy each other's company. Our findings support Asch's contention that overconformity is negatively related to a genuine interest in others.

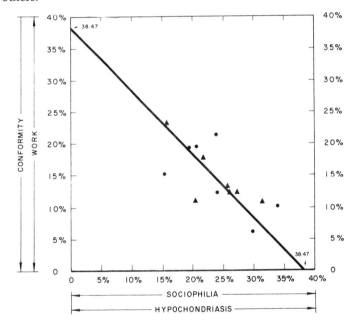

Figure 8   The relationship between sociophilia and work (represented by triangle symbols) and between hypochondriasis and conformity (represented by circles) is strongly inverse.

Figure 7 shows that there is also a trend toward an inverse relationship between conformity and withdrawal into hypochondriasis. It would appear that wherever stress forces the average American in upon his body, it also heightens his individualism and lowers his tendency to think as others do.

In Figure 8 there is presented a plot of the relationship between sociophilia and work and between hypochondriasis and conformity. This shows that there is a strong trend toward an inverse relationship between each set of these variables.

We have thus far considered the varieties of barriers which incompletely reduce any of the varieties of excitement or enjoyment in work, in interpersonal relationships, in the body as these may occur at any time in the life span of the individual, and examined their relative importance at different stages of life. We will now consider briefly that part of the developmental sequence in which parent-child interactions provide the main source of shame by the incomplete reduction of excitement and enjoyment.

SOCIALIZATION AND SHAME-HUMILIATION FROM THE INCOMPLETE REDUCTION OF INTEREST— EXCITEMENT AND ENJOYMENT—JOY

Parents provide multiple sources of shame for their children, and we will consider these multiple sources presently. Now we wish to examine only that special type of shame which is evoked by barriers to interest or enjoyment. Such is the restraint on exploration, lest the child injure himself. Such is the frustration of curiosity by parents who for one reason or another do not answer questions raised by their children. Another source of shame arises from the frustration of the child's wish to be with or interact with the parent when the parent is otherwise occupied. Another source is the disinclination of parents to allow their children to "help" them.

More generally, any barrier the parent may place before the passionate wish of the child to identify with and to act like the parents, whether it be because of concern for the child's safety, indifference, hostility or self-hatred by the parents, is a major source of shame. This is so because there is no other single wish of the normal child more important that the wish to be like the beloved parent. Any impediment to such identification evokes shame and longing and ultimately may heighten the investment of affect in becoming more like the parent who has created barriers to such identification.

Next, there are numerous sources of shame because the child's delight and laughter is noisy and boisterous and may fall under parental taboo. Nor is such restraint limited to the external expression of enjoyment. The interest and excitement of the child is often the occasion of sufficient generation of noise to evoke parental prohibitions which reduce the felt affect of interest or enjoyment enough to evoke shame, and the shame is learned as a response to the experience of positive affect.

Finally, there is the almost universal taboo taught by parents against the stare of a child into the eyes of the stranger, which was discussed in the previous chapter. Although the earliest shyness to the stranger is not taught by the parents, later curiosity is commonly prohibited if the child stares too long and too openly into the eyes of the stranger.

The numerous prohibitions against the varieties of interests and enjoyments of childhood may produce not only shame, but also in many instances an eventual heightening of excitement and enjoyment in the very activities and objects which have been tabooed. The significance of these objects has been heightened by the interference and prohibition, and the reward value of that which is tabooed is reinforced further by the smile of enjoyment which is innately invoked whenever shame is reduced and pursuit of and communion with the object is resumed.

Shame—humiliation of the other as a source of shame—humiliation

A second major source of shame, in addition to barriers to excitement or joy, is the shame response of the other. If another individual with whom I am identified or in whom I am interested or with whom I have experienced enjoyment lowers his eyes or head to me as an object of his interest or enjoyment, then my own positive affect can be sufficiently reduced to evoke my shame.

I may respond to shame with shame for different reasons. Shame by the other is first of all a barrier to mutuality, to shared excitement and enjoyment. Second, the visual appearance of shame in the other can evoke shame through redintegration in which the visual message is unconsciously translated into motor messages which produce an imitation, as a yawn may produce a yawn. The feedback of this imitation is then experienced as shame of the self.

Third, the ashamed look of the other may be internalized and act as an endopsychic source of shame to which the rest of the self responds with shame. Just as I may hang my head in shame because you say that you are ashamed of me, so I may hang my head in shame because the internalized you hangs his head in shame at the rest of my self. In this event the self is experienced as two-headed, both hung in shame. When next the other in fact hangs his head in shame and there is also an internalized head, the individual then finds himself at the intersect of three heads, all ashamed. Often the intensity of the counteraction against shaming may be understood as a response to such a hall of mirrors of shame.

Fourth, the shame of the other may have the properties not only of interfering with ongoing mutual excitement and enjoyment, but of being an identification threat.*

As mentioned above, every child's passionate wish to identify makes him vulnerable to intense shame at a threat to this identification.

In this case the one who sees his identification model ashamed interprets this as a disenchantment of the other with him. This endangers his identification with the other. If you are ashamed of me, then it must be that I have failed to imitate you.

Fifth, the identification threat may be in the opposite direction. If you are ashamed of me, surely then you do not wish to be like me. Sixth, the shame response of the other may be interpreted as a loss of love. If you are ashamed of me, you cannot love me anymore. Seventh, the shame of the other may be interpreted in such a way that guilt-shame is evoked. In this case the shame of the other is interpreted as arising from great

---

* I am indebted to Michael Nesbitt for the concept of identification threat, which he first presented in my seminar, and later incorporated in his own work on friendship.

disappointment, disenchantment or suffering, and the self is held morally responsible for hurting the other.

Eighth, the shame response of the other may evoke guilt because the hung head of the other is interpreted as a response to an immorality by the self. In such a case the other is inferred to be ashamed because oneself has committed an immorality, and the self is guilty, or should feel guilt or both. In the case of individuals with a hypertrophied internalized sense of guilt, the shame of the other is readily converted into a gesture of moral accusation, whatever the actual source of the response of the other.

Ninth, the shame of the other may be interpreted as an accusation not of moral turpitude but of general inferiority and incompetence. Indeed, a parent may in fact hang his head in shame because he feels that his child is a hopeless incompetent, and the parent's gesture arises from a feeling of defeat and hopelessness. This may evoke a contagious shame response in the child who has just suffered defeat and further amplify shame which has already been experienced. If the ashamed, defeated, hopeless parent is internalized, the child's shame response may be continually activated by the discouraged, ashamed, internalized face and head of the parent. Such a child is ever ready to interpret shame in the other as a symptom of his discouragement at the child's incompetence, and as accusation.

Tenth, the shame of the other may be interpreted as a symptom of impression mismanagement. Since every interaction carries with it a possible misfire of an impression which it is intended to communicate to the other, the lowering of eyes or head may be interpreted as a sign that the other has seen through the mask. If one tries to produce an impression upon the other of something which is untrue, then the shame response of the other may evoke shame because one has been unmasked. But one may also be shamed by the shame of the other when what one is attempting to communicate is true. Thus, if I feel and express sympathy with another's distress, but he drops his head in disbelief and shame at what he regards as insincerity on my part, I may respond with shame because of the failure of communication and the disbelief of the other in the sincerity of the affect which I have communicated.

*Shame—humiliation in response to shame—humiliation of the
other as a pressure of social norms, and of in-group solidarity*

Quite apart from the interpretations which the individual
may place upon the shame of the other, it should be noted that,
by virtue of the readiness with which one individual responds
with shame to the shame of the other, the sources of shame are
radically multiplied. The individual can now be shamed by
whatever shames another. This one in turn will have transmitted
a shame he may have learned from someone else's shame response to him.

When these three actors are child, parent and grandparent,
this mechanism provides a perfect vehicle for the transmission
and preservation of social norms from generation to generation.
It also provides a mechanism for the preservation of social norms
among adult members of a community, inasmuch as the evocation of the shame of the other and its evocation of the shame of
the self provides powerful negative sanctions against the transgression of shared social norms.

Further, the fact that the other identifies sufficiently with
others to be ashamed rather than to show contempt strengthens
any social group and its sense of community. Just as contempt
strengthens the boundaries and barriers between individuals and
groups and is the instrument par excellence for the preservation
of hierarchical, caste and class relationships, so is shared shame
a prime instrument for strengthening the sense of mutuality and
community whether it be between parent and child, friend and
friend, or citizen and citizen. When one is ashamed of the other,
that other is not only forced into shame but he is also reminded
that the other is sufficiently concerned positively as well as
negatively to feel ashamed of and for the other.

Let us next consider shame in response to the contempt of
the other.

*Necessary conditions for and intrapsychic consequences
of contempt—disgust from the other as a source of
shame—humiliation*

If the other expresses contempt for me, I may respond with
counter-contempt, with self-contempt, with anger, with fear, with

distress, with surprise, with interest, with enjoyment or amusement, with indifference or with shame. In order for the contempt
of the other to evoke shame rather than one of the above alternatives, the other must be an actual or potential source of positive
affect, which is incompletely reduced by the contempt of the
other.

Such contempt may also be internalized and yet responded
to with shame rather than complete self-contempt. In this case
there is an internal representative of an ambivalent parent, one
who sometimes loves and sometimes sneers. The self which lives
with such a representative has two options. It may side with
the sneering, contemptuous internalized parent and totally reject as disgusting the behavior on the part of the self which
aroused contempt. In this it is likely to be supported by the
parent who may, in his disgust, insist on complete renunciation
of the behavior which offends.

The parent may require this renunciation by the child either
as unconditional surrender, or as a condition for the re-establish-
ment of a positive relationship. This resembles warfare in which
the victor may call for unconditional surrender with no promises
of mercy, or for surrender with the promise of the ultimate
resumption of the prewar relationship after some reparations
are paid. In the latter case, the internalized contemptuous self
insists, as the parent originally did, that the offending self be
totally rejected and sloughed off before the judging self can love
the remainder of the self so purified. The judging self here
regards the rest of the self as unfit for self-love until some atonement and restitution has been made, along with renunciation
of the former offending part of the self.

There is, however, another option open to the condemmed
self which is the object of internalized contempt. Just as one may
respond to the contempt of the other with shame, when one does
not completely surrender one's investmnet of positive affect in
the other, so one may respond in the same way to internalized
contempt. This produces a very complex affective state in which
part of the self has disgust for another part of the self, but this
latter part responds with shame and a continuing interest in the
self which has contempt for it. Such a self is not prepared to
totally surrender its self-respect and to reject itself in deference

to the self which condemns. It is wounded by that self enough
to lower its head and eyes, but it hopes for eventual communion
and inner harmony, without renunciation either of the offending
self, or the judging self, as originally it responded to the contempt of the rejecting but loving parent.

Although it is always possible for the contempt of the other
to arouse shame rather than self-contempt, yet it should be noted
that this is inherently difficult. This is because the contempt of
the other constitutes a total rejection. When the other shows
contempt, there is a presumption that the self which so offends
the other is disgusting and should be just as disgusting to the
one who offends as to the other. Insofar as one responds to the
contempt of the other with shame, one has not entirely accepted
the disgust of the other. It is not difficult for one who is treated
with contempt to respond with anger, or with counter-contempt
to the other or with self-contempt. To only partially accept the
judgment of the other, however, by hanging the head in shame
but not responding with self-disgust and revulsion is a difficult
discrimination to maintain. Only someone who is extremely
impunitive with respect to the self and the other can respond
with shame to the contempt of the other. Much the most common
response is anger and counter-contempt or self-contempt or both.

Contempt is as we have said a powerful instrument of discrimination and segregation. By means of contempt, the other
can be kept in his place. If however, the response to contempt
is shame, this characteristic consequence of distancing is much
attenuated.

Any negative affect of the other as a source of shame—humiliation

I may hang my head in shame because the other is angry
at me, because he is afraid of me or because he is distressed
by me. If the other is angry with me, I may, of course, respond
with counter-anger, with fear, with distress, with excitement, or
with contempt or even enjoyment, if I have tried to provoke
him to become angry. If, however, his anger represents only an
interference or a temporary interruption of an otherwise positive

relationship, I may respond with shame, hanging my head in partial defeat but with the residual wish to look positively at the other. The lovers' quarrel, ending with both parties ashamed, is the classic instance of such a dyadic interaction.

As with contempt, however, the anger of the other is not ordinarily a major source of shame unless it is used very sparingly along with predominantly positive affect. Anger too readily evokes counter-anger or fear to be a prime source of shame. If a child responds to a spanking not by crying, nor by anger, nor by fear but by shame, he is not only a child who is fearless, proud, and slow to anger, but also one who loves himself as well as his parents. Such was the case for example with Chekhov, who was daily beaten by his father.

Though the anger of the other is not a prime source of shame, the distress of the other is. If a parent complains that the child's behavior causes him great distress, the child can easily be made to feel ashamed or guilty for the suffering he has inflicted.

Nor is it necessary that the one who is distressed blame the other to evoke his shame. Thus a wife who is in perpetual distress about life in general can readily evoke shame and guilt in her spouse, if he loves her, whether or not she holds him responsible for her misery. This may be either because her distress is a barrier to mutuality based on the exchange of positive affect, or because the husband holds himself responsible for his wife's loss of her zest for living.

Essentially the same dynamic evokes shame in the child or spouse if the parent or mate is overly fearful or ashamed. A parent may shame a child by telling him that his behavior will be the death of his parent, that he is responsible for the parent's needless and excessive anxiety. A wife may shame her husband by a continual display of shame and feelings of worthlessness with or without recrimination and the accusation that this is the fault of the spouse. The beaten, defeated posture of the mate is a prime source of shame in the spouse who is concerned for the welfare of the other. It has been assumed thus far that the negative aspects of any relationship must be balanced by positive feelings if there is to be shame. Let us now examine this assumption more explicitly.

Bipolar affect from the other as a source of shame—humiliation

An individual may suffer the contempt of the other and not feel shame, and he may be praised by the other and yet feel shy (which we equate with low intensity shame—humiliation). But whenever the other one is bipolar in his display of affect, this has a high potency for evoking shame in the target of this display. This is a prime way of capturing and intensifying both positive affect and shame. Such bipolarity may take many different forms.

First is an oscillation between praising and showing contempt. In such a case contempt is likely to arouse shame because of the continuing but attenuated wish for praise. After the shame response runs its course, the just dampened wish for praise is likely to become intensified over its original level, producing an addiction to praise. This is the source of the great power of the critic who can be both lavish in praise and harsh in condemnation. Be he parent or scholar, he is capable of producing a strait jacket which the other is willing, with some reluctance, to wear.

Second is an oscillation between praise and no praise. As Adler first noted, children who are raised with abundant praise are not thereby freed from a sense of inferiority, since the absence of praise, for a child or an adult whose major affect income has been high praise, is experienced as a loss sufficient to evoke shame and then the renewed quest for further praise. A parent may oscillate between praise and no praise either accidentally, when competing interests take his attention from the child, or because the child has done nothing which appears praiseworthy, or because the child has done something which displeases him, to which he responds with a studied indifference rather than with censure or to which he responds by leaving the scene.

Such oscillation may however also represent a strategy of control either by the parent over his child, or by one adult over other adults. This strategy may also arise from an anti-shame ideology which urges that one should say only good things about others and that, if one has negative feelings, it is better to keep them to oneself. Whatever the motive of one who has bipolar affects, he nonetheless controls the other through the evocation of shame and the quest for praise.

Third is an oscillation between praise and a variety of negative affects which range from anger through distress, fear, shame and contempt. In this case there is also an oscillation, but the negative pole is fragmented, depending upon the nature of the offense. The parent who ordinarily is lavish in praise of the child may explode in anger, show great distress or fear at what the child is doing, or shame or contempt. Under such conditions shame may be evoked by any display of negative affect by the other and praise becomes the balm for healing the shame of many types of wounds to pride.

Fourth, there is an oscillation between the mutual excitement and enjoyment of the parent and child, and a variety of negative affects by either the parent or the child or both. In this case the parent does not lavish praise on the child but is simply excited by the child and enjoys his company sufficiently to evoke the same affects from the child. If either the parent or the child becomes distressed or angry or afraid or contemptuous, the child may become ashamed at the rupture of mutually rewarding interaction and then motivated to renew such interaction which may in turn be further heightened in value by the reduction of the shame.

Fifth is an oscillation between mutuality and unilateral control, in which the parent oscillates between enjoying the child and dominating him. When such a child is ordered to do something he does not wish to do, he is caught between shame, the wish to please the parent and the wish to return to a more mutually rewarding relationship.

Sixth is the oscillation between mutuality and severe constraints. Here it is not coercive dominance which is at issue, but restraining dominance. The parent does not try to tell the child what he is to do. The parent permits the child to be generally self-governing except when he does particular things which offend the parent or endanger the life of the child. Again, the child may be shamed by such sanctions and is caught by the conflict between his positive feelings for both self-regulation and mutuality with the parent and the barrier to both of these created by unwanted unilateral prohibitions.

Seventh is an oscillation between mutual excitement and enjoyment between parent and child, and indifference or withdrawal of the parent from interaction. Whenever this occurs again and again and the child has the repeated experience of residual wishes for communion, he may be shamed by such indifference or withdrawal and long for renewal of communion. In contrast to the praise-no-praise polarity, this is much less likely to produce the particular overachievement syndrome in which love, praise for achievement and shame are tightly bound together. It is more likely that there will be an exaggerated sociophilia under these conditions, free of the admixture with overachievement which often accompanies the praise-contempt, or praise-no-praise polarity.

Eighth is a contempt-no-contempt oscillation in which the absence of contempt is the rewarding state, providing relief from the shame which is experienced when the other expresses contempt. Although a parent who oscillates between contempt and no contempt may not be loved, he may be respected enough to be capable of generating shame and a wish to resume a relationship with such a parent which is at least free of scorn.

Ninth is an anger-no-anger oscillation which has much the same structure as the contempt-no-contempt polarity, except that this is an overly irritable, irascible parent rather than one given to contempt. Again, the relief from the temper of the parent and from the shame it generates provides the primary lure despite an absence of positive affect from the parent.

Tenth is another polarity of the same general type of distress-no-distress. Here the parent is either overly concerned about the child or not concerned. The child is shamed by the parent's suffering expressed usually as having been caused by the child's thoughtlessness.

Finally, there is the polarity of fear-no-fear, in which the parent is excessively timid and conveys this to the child who is thus shamed for worrying the parent. If there are periods in which the fear of the parent abates, this can provide the major reward for the attempted resumption of the relationship by the child.

In all of these polarities the power of the non-shaming pole derives from the conjoint power of its opposite to generate shame and from its own power to reduce that shame.

Shame—humiliation from vicarious sources
(empathy and identification)

We have said that the shame of the other, his bipolar affect, his contempt and his negative affect are all sources of shame in the self. These are all instances of shame from an essentially dyadic relationship. But the human being is capable of being shamed by another whether or not the other is interacting with him in such a way as to intentionally shame him, or interacting with him at all. The human being is capable through empathy and identification of living through others and therefore of being shamed by what happens to others.

To the extent to which the individual invests his affect in other human beings, in institutions and in the world around him, he is vulnerable to the vicarious experience of shame.

Thus if a child or spouse or friend experiences difficulties in work, in love, in friendship, in his self-esteem or in his sense of identity, a person may feel vicarious shame. One may feel shame because the other feels shame, but also under circumstances in which the self would feel shame, even if the other does not. Thus if a child is doing poorly in his school work, a parent may feel ashamed even though his child does not.

Indeed, the parent may feel shame about his child, or a friend feel shame about a friend, just because the other does not feel shame about circumstances under which one thinks shame is appropriate. Shamelessness in a child or spouse or friend may evoke deeper shame than the circumstances themselves, since this is often interpreted as a character defect in the other. If a child fails an examination, a parent might feel ashamed, but this is a limited reaction to a remediable state of affairs. If, however, the child is not at all concerned about his failure and cannot understand the concern of the parent, the latter may be much more ashamed than he is about the failure itself.

If a child or friend is disappointed by a friend or lover, he may feel vicarious shame. If someone close to me has an identity crisis in which he struggles desperately to find himself amidst his many and changing selves, I may hang my head in vicarious shame at his self-alienation and hopelessness.

Nor does the shame of the other necessarily have to be the shame of someone close to me. I may feel shame at the indignity or suffering of any human being or animal to the extent to which I feel myself identified with the human race or the animal kingdom, and have reverence for life as such. To the extent to which I am identified with institutions such as my profession, with the educational system, with the judicial and legislative systems, with the presidency, the nation or the community of nations, I am vulnerable to the vicarious experience of shame if I detect regression or failure of development in these institutions.

I can be shamed vicariously if someone suffers shame because another is ashamed of him. If my child's teacher is ashamed of my child and my child is thereby shamed, I too can be shamed. If one of my friends is shamed by another friend of his, who is disappointed and ashamed of him, I can be vicariously shamed. If a group of scholars to whom I feel some affinity is ashamed because another group has expressed disappointment and shame about them, I can be vicariously shamed. If a nation which is affiliated with my nation is shamed when the United Nations expresses shame at the action of that nation, I may be vicariously shamed by this transgression of the emerging international law.

I can be shamed vicariously if someone else is shamed by another's contempt. If a teacher scolds and shames my child, I too can thereby be shamed. If one scholar shows contempt and thus shames another scholar, I can be shamed. If my countrymen travel abroad and are shamed by the contempt of others, I can thereby be shamed. If one friend of mine is contemptuous of and shames another friend, I can be shamed. If one government contemptuously and ruthlessly dominates and subdues another government for which I have sympathy I can be shamed.

Then there is the vicarious shame generated by invidious comparison. Shame can be experienced vicariously not only through the failures of those who are close to one, but also through the successes of others. If the success of the other increases the distance between the self and its goals, then shame may be evoked by his success. This is particularly so when two individuals or two groups or two nations are in competition. The progress of one necessarily means the defeat of the other in any competition which has but one victor. To the extent to which any individual so defines his relation to others, he is vulnerable to shame and envy when the other enjoys progress or success. From sibling rivalry, through the Oedipus rivalry, to games, academic and business rivalry, the individual knows shame and envy. When shame becomes more monopolistic, as we shall see later in shame theory, there is no kind of human relationship which is exempt from the shame of invidious comparison.

Vicarious shame can also be evoked by any act of one person toward another which stimulates longing and at the same time heightens the awareness of what is lacking in one's own experience. Thus, an elderly couple may be shamed when their friends receive a gift or some other symbol of affection or respect from their children. Under such conditions they may suddenly become acutely aware of their dependence upon the love and esteem of their own children, who seem to have forgotten them. Wives and husbands may be shamed by displays of affection between other wives and husbands if there is affect hunger in their own marital relationship.

Another form is the vicarious shame at the shame of another which is generated by the other's affect inhibition. If he is angry towards me or anyone else and must swallow his anger and this generates shame in him, as in the case of a Southern Negro confronted by a Southern white, then I may feel vicarious shame for him. Similarly, if my child feels forced to inhibit the expression of negative affect toward me, and he further feels shame because of this, I can experience vicarious shame. I can also feel vicarious shame at affect inhibition whether or not the other feels ashamed of this. Thus a Southern Negro may suffer severe inhibition of his anger but be relatively unaware of this and feel no shame about it, and yet I may feel vicarious shame just because he is under such restraint that he is relatively unconscious of the degree of his defense against the display of anger.

I may experience vicarious shame if someone controls another individual through the self-conscious use of bipolar affect. If a friend of mine is encouraged by someone to become more and more intimate and then is shamed by indifference or withdrawal, and then seduced again and shamed again, and this cycle repeated continually, I too may be shamed by my friend's shame or by his vulnerability. Similarly, if my child is so exploited by his friend, or my spouse by her friends, or my parents by one of their children or friends. I may be shamed if my government permits itself to be so exploited by another government which blows hot and cold, alternately seducing and then chilling the unwary and uncertain leaders of my own government.

The vicarious experience of shame, together with the vicarious experience of distress, is at once a measure of civilization and a condition of civilization. Shame enlarges the spectrum of objects outside of himself which can engage man and concern him. After having experienced shame through sudden empathy, the individual will never again be able to be entirely unconcerned with the other. But if empathy is a necessary condition for the development of personality and civilization alike, it is also a necessary condition for the experience of shame. If there is insufficient interest in the other, shame through empathy is improbable. How much shame can be felt at remediable conditions is one critical measure of the stage of development of any civilization.

Ambivalence toward affect inhibition as a source of shame—humiliation

As we have noted before, any learned restraint on the expression of any affect, when such restraint is not completely accepted, will evoke shame. Under such conditions there will be a residual wish to look and be looked at in an exchange of affect combined with a wish not to look and not to be looked at. If I wish to glare at you in anger, but I also do not wish to do so, or I am afraid to do so, or I am afraid you will see this, then this is a sufficient condition to evoke shame at looking at you in anger or being seen by you when I am angry. It is the learned inner restraint on any affect in competition with the wish to express the original affect which constitutes the stimulus to shame. We will consider the dynamics of affect inhibition at length, later. Now, we wish only to briefly indicate how affect inhibition generates shame about a variety of affects other than excitement or enjoyment per se.

If my fear is inhibited, I am ashamed lest I display fear but

I am also ashamed that I cannot. If my anger is inhibited, I am ashamed not only lest I display anger but also because I cannot show my anger and must suppress it. If my contempt is inhibited, I am not only ashamed lest I show contempt but also because I cannot. If my distress is inhibited, I am not only ashamed lest I cry publicly but also because I cannot do so. If my excitement must be inhibited, I am ashamed lest I betray my excitement and because I must not show it. If my smile and laughter of enjoyment is inhibited, I am ashamed if I show enjoyment and also because I must not.

Finally, if I have been constrained not to hang my head in shame, I may feel further shame whenever I lose control of this affect as well as because I must observe this taboo.

AFFECT-SHAME BINDS

As we have noted before, many affects are socialized by shaming techniques. When affect-shame binds are thus created, the individual may experience shame to a wide variety of situations, if these activate affects which are bound by shame. The significance of such binds is the indirect and powerful control of behavior through shame evoked by mediating affect. Let us review briefly the major affect-shame binds.

If the noisy excitement of childhood has been controlled by shaming the child, the resultant excitement-shame bind can evoke shame to a wide spectrum of exciting experiences, sexual and otherwise.

If the noisy laughter of childhood has been controlled by shaming, the resultant bind can evoke shame to any source of enjoyment.

If the cry of distress is controlled by shame, the resultant bind can evoke shame whenever the individual is distressed whether by hunger, pain, fatigue or failure or frustration of any kind.

If anger has been controlled by shame, the resultant bind can evoke shame or guilt whenever anger is provoked.

If fear has been controlled by shame, the individual becomes vulnerable to shame whenever he senses danger or any threat which frightens.

If contempt has been controlled by shame, the individual responds with shame whenever he is in the presence of anything which disgusts him.

If the outward show of shame has been controlled by further shaming of the child, the resultant bind makes the individual further ashamed if he has been provoked into hanging his head in shame.

If surprise and startle are bound by shame, the individual becomes ashamed of responding to novelty with surprise. This bind is created by parents who tease and surprise the child and then shame the child by laughing at his surprise.

Thus far we have considered each affect as it is individually bound by shame. We will now consider a more general shame bind in which all of the major affects are bound by the same affect of shame. In such a case the parent uses the shame of the child to control and modify the display of every affect, in what we have called a total affect-shame bind. This deepens and prolongs the experience of shame, since it is met at every turn and eventually is elaborated into what we have called a shame theory. The nature of such cognitive amplification we will examine later.

Production of a total affect-shame bind by apparently innocuous and well-intentioned parental action

Let us now consider how a total affect-shame bind can be produced. Our hero is a child who is destined to have every affect totally bound by shame. We see him first with his age equals. He is a friendly, somewhat timid child, who is being bullied. He is not angry with the bully, indeed he is a little afraid of him. His reluctance to fight evokes taunts of "sissy," "chicken," "yellow" from those who themselves may be shamed by this timidity. Rather than tolerate his shame he will permit himself to be coerced into flying in the face of fear and fight the dreaded bully.

The same timid one, coerced into tolerating fear by his age equals and into fighting the bully, may return home to be shamed into mortification for having fought. "Nice little boys don't fight like ruffians. Mother is ashamed of you. Whatever got into you? You know better than that."

The timid one may now start to cry in distress. The feeling of shame has passed a critical density, and tears well up in the eyes and add to the intensity of his sobbing. At this point his father, attracted by the childlike, even effeminate display of tears expresses manly contempt for such weakness: "What are you crying for, like a two-year-old? Stop it—you make me sick."

Our hero stops crying and sits down with his family for dinner. The first course is a fruit cup which he detests. Rather than un-obtrusively putting it aside, he lifts his upper lip and gives every manifestation of struggling with overwhelming nausea. He is disgusted and has given the customary biological sign of this affect. Both parents immediately fight fire with fire. Disgust is opposed by disgust, calculated not to express rejection of food but to arouse shame intense enough to inhibit the disgust re-action in their pride and joy. "Don't ever make that face again at the table—it's disgusting—you don't see us making such ex-pressions, do you?"

The child subsides with head bent low until the next course which is roast beef—his favorite food. His excitement overflows into action. "I love roast beef," he blurts out as he reaches across the table to pull off a small, weakly attached sliver from the end of the roast. Father's nostril and lip lifts, the boy's name is emitted in tones saturated with revulsion. The offending hand is withdrawn, the eyes lowered, their excitement contained.

After an eternity of waiting, the beef is before him. His excitement is confirmed. It does taste as good as he expected. He shouts his joy so that the neighborhood and the larger com-munity may share in his delight, "Oh boy! This is good!"

This time mother defends the elementary decencies upon which Western civilization rests: "Oh Robert, you'd think you hadn't eaten in a week, really!" Father's eyes reinforce the message till the joy is contained and the head drops in shame. Dinner proceeds on uneventfully until both parents become uncomfortably aware that their dinner companion is endangering their appetite by the removal of his face from view, and by the limpness of his posture suggestive of complete surrender to the affect of shame.

Our vignette draws to a close with shame turned against shame: "Robert, where are your manners? Sit up. It's not polite to sit like that at the dinner table." Robert sits up with face and limbs wooden lest they betray shame. The parents are temporarily appeased, but eventually the apathy and listlessness of their child becomes distressing. In the final scene shame is turned against apathy: "Robert, you could be a little more attentive, you don't have to sit there like a bump on a log. Say something."

So is our hero taught that affect *per se* is shameful, that shame itself is caught up in the same taboo and that even affect-lessness may be shameful.

Shame from shame theory

Any stimulus or stimulus field to which the individual is exposed is multidimensional. Even the simplest of stimuli presented under controlled laboratory conditions has multiple dimensions. If it is a visual stimulus it has intensity, hue, shape, duration, size, and numerous other sensory gradients. As the pool of information from stored past experience is brought to bear on the interpretation of input information, the number of alternative dimensions, and alternative selective interpretations of sub-sets of these dimensions, increase radically.

When any stimulus is perceived, that is, interpreted within the central assembly and simultaneously transmuted into a conscious report, it may activate amplifying affect on an innate basis by virtue of the gradient and level of density of the neurological stimulation of the stimulus which is reported. It may also recruit from memory further information concerning past affects experienced when the same or similar stimuli were encountered before, which in turn may activate further affect.

What will be thus recruited depends upon prior theory. After much cumulative experience, information about affects may become organized into what we term "theories," in much the same way that theories are constructed to account for uniformities in science or in cognition in general. An affect theory is a simplified and powerful summary of a larger set of affect experiences. Such a theory may be about affect in general, or about a particular affect.

Shame theory is one such source of great power and generality in activating shame, in alerting the individual to the possibility or imminence of shame and in providing standardized strategies for minimizing shame. Although shame theory provides avoidance techniques, it is also one of the major sources of the experience of shame, since it provides a shame interpretation of a large number of situations, which if there had been a powerful distress theory might have aroused distress, given a fear thory of equal generality and power might have aroused fear rather than shame, and given a monopolistic enjoyment theory might have altogether attenuated the negative aspects of the situation.

In short, whether one experiences shame or distress or fear or enjoyment in a given situation is in part a function of the cognitive organization of past experience with each of the primary affects, and of the relative weights and probabilities assigned to different kinds of in-put information. The existence of a shame theory guarantees that the shame-relevant aspects of any situation will become figural in competition with other affect-relevant aspects of the same situations. We will later examine in some detail the consequences of such an organization for the affective sensitivities of the individual. At this point we wish only to call attention to the differential weighting of shame-relevant information when the isolated traces of past experience are organized into the form of a theory.

Shame—humiliation from social norms and ideological sources

In contrast with the idiosyncratic shame theories which are the result of the cognitive organization and summarizing of one's own past shame experiences, every individual is ordinarily vulnerable to shame experience whenever he violates the social norms which he inherits by virtue of his membership in society or whenever he violates the norms of a particular ideology to which he may be committed. The Catholic, the Communist Party member, the Christian Scientist are each vulnerable to shame not only should they violate general social norms, but also if they transgress the dictates of their religious or political ideologies.

Social norms and ideologies are ordinarily supported by and are capable of evoking a total matrix of both positive and negative affects. Shame is but one of many affects which are enlisted in support of conformity to norms and ideologies.

Shame is an equally critical pillar of convention or revolutionary ideology. Whenever an ideology is revolutionary, shame is pitted against shame. The shame of social norm violation is flaunted by the revolutionary. Thus the Marxist fortifies his conscience and his enthusiasm by contempt for the bourgeois mentality, which lurks deep hidden within the middle class revolutionary. Shame is used as a powerful sanction against bourgeois backsliding and bourgeois sentimentalism. Any attenuation of the severity of the class struggle because of conflict with the social norms of the established order is controlled in part through the shaming of the reluctant revolutionary who backslides. Any deviation from party discipline in the other direction is also controlled in part by shaming the ultra-radical as a left-deviationist.

The role of shame and contempt in revolutionary political activity has yet to be fully appreciated. The threat of shame and contempt in such movements is scarcely distinguishable from the threat of shame implicit in excommunication in the Middle Ages.

Nor has the relative reliance on shame and contempt in preserving social norms and the social order been systematically measured and compared with the relative weight with which, and the particular conditions under which, social norms and the social order is buttressed by excitement, by enjoyment, by terror, by distress, and by anger, in those who support and in those who violate social norms and threaten the social order. The structure of affect components into organized patterns of social sanctions is similar to the patterning of the carbon rings in organic compounds. So much for the general sources of shame. We will next consider the general sources of contempt.

THE SOURCES OF CONTEMPT–DISGUST

"I don't want": the drive basis

Contempt is primarily an auxiliary response to the hunger drive designed to prevent the ingestion of noxious material or to achieve its total rejection and regurgitation if it has been ingested. The nature of this mechanism does not change when it is recruited to defend the self against psychic incorporation or any increase in intimacy with a repellent object.

"I don't want": the psychological basis

In radical contrast to the shame response which has the structure, "I want, but," the contempt response has the structure, "I don't want." Instead of barriers which incompletely reduce excitement or enjoyment as in shame, the reduction of excitement or enjoymnet is complete in learned contempt. When an individual learns to respond with disgust to some object which does not have a malorodous taste or smell, this is generally mediated by some similarity to the biological conditions under which the drive mechanism of disgust or nausea is ordinarilly activated.

The learning of disgust can also be mediated by seeing the look of disgust on the face of the other through redintegration. Just as the yawn and the smile, visually perceived, can be a sufficient part of the total matrix of the feedback of the past experience of the face to redintegrate the yawn or smile, so the visual appearance of disgust can provide the cue to redintegrate the translatory messages from the visual look of disgust to the motor messages to trigger the disgust reaction in the self.

The disgust of the other can provide a basis for imitation when there already is identification with the one who is disgusted. This identification may result in either relatively conscious efforts to imitate or the imitation may be relatively unconscious, as in any empathic imitation in which attention is fixed on the other rather than the self. In contrast to the learning by redintegration, here there is necessary some identification with the other.

In redintegrated disgust the individual may even hate the other if the other is expressing disgust or contempt towards him, but nonetheless respond with the same disgust whether he wishes to or not, as any part of a cliché redintegrates the remainder as in "Now is the time for all good men to . . ."

In imitation based on identification, however, there must be positive affect which motivates the mimicking of the response.

Indeed, one can tell from the greater similarity of the responses of a child to the responses, affective and otherwise, of one or another parent, which of these parents is the primary object of identification.

Similarity as a basis for the learned generalization of contempt–disgust

Let us return now to similarity as a determinant of disgust learning. Similarity in disgust learning may be based either on the odor of the object as such or on the reduction in distance between the repulsive object and the self. This is so since disgust learning is innately activated by a noxious object, whatever the distance, so long as it has particularly malodorous characteristics or by a reduction in distance between the self and a noxious object. In the latter case it is possible that, prior to learning, the basis for disgust in response to a reduction of distance may be simply that a malodorous object whose odor is too weak to activate disgust may become an adequate stimulus when it is brought nearer to the nostrils. Further, certain disgust reactions are based more on taste than smell, and in such cases, too, the object may have to be placed in the mouth to evoke disgust.

It should be noted also that the disgust at slimy objects at a distance, or the disgust at a non-smelling but bad-tasting object (which have been tasted before) are based on learning. It is highly improbable that any visual stimulus has the properties of innately activating disgust. Therefore even when an object has been disgusting to taste, the response of disgust to this object when it is next seen, but not smelled or tasted, is a learned disgust reaction. The response of disgust to a slimy object which is seen but not touched is also a learned response, based on the similarity principle, since the fact that it exudes oily or otherwise moving substance suggests that it might touch the skin even though one does not move toward it, and its potential for dirtying and clinging to the skin is similar to bad-smelling material.

Thus, any characteristic of an object which is similar either to the malodorous quality of an innately disgusting object, or to this plus closeness to the person, is capable of evoking a learned disgust response. Let us examine first generalization through similarity of the object to a malodorous object.

First, it is relatively easy to learn to give the disgust response to any object which emits any intense odor. This odor need not be innately offensive to be learned to be responded to as if it were so. It need only be intense and strange to be capable of interpretation as possibly malodorous and disgusting. We have noted before that in certain mice strangeness of odor can be an innate basis for disgust and even a block to pregnancy.

But in man disgust to strange odors is usually a learned response which is supported by social norms. Thus racial prejudice may sometimes be fortified by the readiness with which any slight difference in odors between individuals can be learned to be responded to as if this were disgusting. It is not unlikely that the disgust response to human faeces is in part learned though it is also probably an innate activator.

Depending on the strength of the affect of disgust compared to other affects, on the degree of cognitive elaboration of past disgust experiences compared with the degree of cognitive elaboration of other affect experiences, in short depending on disgust theory and other affect theories, objects which have varying degrees of similarity to malodorous objects will be responded to with disgust. Such a similarity dimension might extend from any strong odor as such all the way to any semblance of randomness, noise, or disorder in the world.

Learned contempt—disgust in response to intensity

It is a relatively easy generalization which abstracts the communalities in offensive odors, strong odors, and intense stimulation of any kind, e.g. very bright colors, very loud sounds, very intense tastes, very cold or hot stimuli, excessive humidity, intense pain, overly rapid visual stimulation, very rapid movement of the body through space, very radical changes in acceleration or deceleration of the bodies movement through space. It should be noted that none of these types of intense stimulation necessarily produce disgust, but that they are all candidates for generalization on the basis of their similarity to malodorous odors by virtue of their intensity.

In the case of extreme vulnerability to nausea from motion as on board ship, or in automobiles or in aeroplanes, it is very difficult to disentangle the malaise and distress which is an innate response to such stimulation from the nausea which is learned to such stimulation. That learning eventually plays a more and more prominent role in motion sickness is clear from those who become seasick in their staterooms when their ships have unexpectedly remained tied to the dock and when the queasy one has assumed that he awakes from his sleep far out on the high seas.

Such intense stimulation would innately activate distress or anger if it were continuous at a particular level of density of stimulation, or it would activate startle or fear or excitement in its beginning phase if the gradient were steep enough. When, however, an individual responds to continuing loud sounds with disgust rather than distress or anger, it is certain that the innate affective response has been displaced by a learned response, and that the latter is a derivative of a relatively powerful disgust theory which supports a low threshold for the disgust response, since it is here capable of inhibiting the innate response to non-optimal intense stimulation.

Indeed, a good measure of the strength of the disgust theory is a widespread generalization of disgust to otherwise insignificant but overly intense stimulation which would innately activate distress or anger. In the extreme case such an individual responds with disgust to fully saturated and to bright colors of any kind, to loud sounds, to any food or liquid which has a strong flavor, to any fast movement of himself or any other object which he sees, to any pain or to any intense hunger or thirst or sexual deprivation or sexual pleasure or intense pleasure in eating or drinking. Such an individual has learned to be disgusted with intensity as such, as a generalization from intense malodorous odors.

This is not to say that any disgust at any intense stimulation, e.g., at sexual pleasure, may not also be learned in a quite different way. Anyone may learn to be disgusted with intense sexual stimulation because a parent showed disgust at the child's masturbation rather than through generalization through similarity. Indeed, disgust to any extreme may be learned through indoctrination of an Appollonian anti-Dionysian ideology. Finally, it is not uncommon that disgust recruits disgust so that the same object is learned to evoke disgust in more than one way from more than one source.

Learned contempt–disgust in response to the unexpected: oral contempt–disgust.

Another generalization gradient is based not on the similarity of intense stimulation to intense odors and bad odors, but on the deviation of stimulation from the expected range of stimulation. Just as a bad taste is unexpected when it is first experienced in chewing a new food, so anything unexpected may become generalized as a stimulus to disgust. In the vernacular this has been expressed in the phrase "it left a bad taste," meaning not only that it was a bad taste, but that contact had proved unexpectedly disappointing.

Whenever disgust imagery is about taste rather than smell, we may infer that the individual is more oral than anal in character structure, both in our and in the classical Psychoanalytic sense, and that he is an ambivalent individual with a low threshold for disenchantment, that is, he is easily attracted to objects and easily disillusioned with that to which he has been attracted.

In contrast to a generalized disgust theory, in which there is a generally low threshold for anything disgusting, as in the so-called anal character structure, here the individual has a positive affective posture towards the world, but has learned that closer contact with objects which excite and promise reward will ultimately be disappointing, disenchanting, and leave a disgusting aftertaste. His heroes will inevitably turn out to have feet of clay. His world again and again will turn to ashes in his mouth. This is an individual whose hope is as irrepressible as his taste buds are overly sensitive. The milk of human kindness never satisfies completely, because the good mother's milk too readily and too often has turned sour in the mouth of the innocent child made greedy by past disappointments.

The orally disgusted one more resembles the ashamed one who is caught between longing and shyness than his totally rejecting disgusted brother who readily identifies impurity at a distance through his exquisitely sensitized nostrils.

In preliminary studies we found that obsessive individuals could be readily differentiated from those with a depressive character structure on the basis of the locus of disgust. The overly perfectionistic, obsessive individual when asked to say whether in disgust something is more likely to smell bad or taste bad is certain that it will be an experience of a bad smell. The individual with a depressive character structure describes the experience of disgust as something which is likely to leave a bad taste in the mouth.

THE INVIDIOUS COMPARISON

A special case of learned disgust at the unexpected is the disgust for the counterfeit, for the imposter, for the poor imitation. In this case what is being imitated must evoke positive affect, and, when the difference between the original and the imitation is discriminated to the disadvantage of the latter, there is disgust.

The power of the invidious comparison to evoke disgust was shown when condensed milk was first marketed. Consumer reaction was negative because it was regarded as an inferior type of milk. At the advice of a marketing research group the same product quickly won consumer acceptance after advertising stressed the novelty of the taste of the new product and its difference from the taste of milk.

The possibility of such differentiation attenuating the invidious comparison and disgust also highlights the possibility of the complete reversal of the invidious comparison. Whenever a variant of an esteemed object can be interpreted as superior to the original object in *any* respect, the latter can become the victim of disgust through generalization of the unexpectedly bad-smelling object. Paradoxically it is now the original object which is cast in the role of the poor imitation.

This is a bit of Platonism in which the essence of beauty or goodness is preserved eternally in the Divine Bureau of Standards, and the variant is adjudged more similar to the ideal than last year's model. It is on this basis that the length of skirts, the shape of dresses, hats, and shoes, automobiles, and now even refrigerators and other appliances can be changed from year to year. Consumers will draw their noses and palates away from last year's automobile in disenchantment as they eagerly drink in with their eyes this year's closer approximation to the heart's desire which dwells eternally as an experimental model in the mind of the great designer. Planned obsolescence is possible whenever the invidious comparison can be made to the disadvantage of last year's model.

It should be noted that such learned responses of disgust at invidious comparisons are not only made possible by heightening the significance of the difference between the variant and the original, but that here, as with all learned disgust, there is a circular recruitment which amplifies and magnifies both the disgust and the perceived differences which sustain the disgust. Once having learned to respond with disgust at the difference, this total experience now supports a magnification of the scale by which the objects are measured and compared and the greater difference leads to greater disgust.

Such a learned disgust reaction is commonly a condition for the self-fulfilling prophecy. After the initial disgust response, the next encounter with the disgusting object confirms the cognitive work which has intervened. The object is now perceived to be more disgusting than it was before, the disgust response is appropriately magnified, and the individual has now fallen into disenchantment by the same circular cognitive-affective recruitment process whereby he previously fell in love with the object.

One who falls in love must also fall out of love whenever excitement and enjoyment fail to be sustained or are captured by another object in invidious comparison. This other object need not be an ambulatory rival, so long as it is enshrined in memory. Indeed, whenever past affective experience has been so sharply bifurcated that the individual has either suffered intense disenchantment or has himself been an object of disenchantment, he is ever ready to sense the invidious comparison, whether it be of the same object at two different times, or one object with another. Such oral disgust, that is, attraction and then disenchantment, analogous to tasting and spitting out, is a prominent feature of the depressive posture.

DEVIATION FROM THE NORM

Perhaps the most critical similarity upon which disgust is learned and generalized is any deviation of the object from any norm, from the true, the good, and the beautiful. Depending upon what the society, the parent, peers, or the individual himself has come to regard as true, good, and beautiful, an endless variety of objects and behavior become capable of evoking disgust. These have ranged from contempt for lying, deceit, ignorance, and error upon which there has been some consensus, to the contempt of some for empiricism and the contempt of others for rationalism, and to the warring contempts for the slavish adherence to the facts against that for the unbridled use of imagination.

A history of learned contempt as it appears in philosophy and science, in manners and morals, and in esthetics would be nothing less than the story of civilization. Human beings have always buttressed their uncertainties by totally rejecting some of the chief competitors for their primary affective investments. The obsessive who insists that the world be ultra-clean and orderly is but a special case of the almost universal learning to detect some analogues of impurities of smell and taste in the entire spectrum of objects which have pretensions to represent our norms of truth, of morality and of beauty.

*Learned contempt—disgust in response to a
decrease in distance*

Disgust may be learned because the object is presumed to be similar to a malodorous or bad-tasting object, but also on the basis of the similarity to a decrease in distance between the repellent object and the self. An object which is not sufficiently malodorous to arouse disgust at a distance may evoke intense disgust as the distance between it and the person is reduced. This is the nature of the innate disgust response to objects which have weak but offensive odors, or which have much more repellent tastes than odors. Analogously, any reduction in distance between the self and the object which threatens the inviolacy and privacy of the self can be learned to evoke disgust.

Thus, whenever an individual of lower caste or of lower status comes too close, the higher caste or higher status individual commonly learns to respond with disgust or with increased disgust. Many eating and sexual taboos are based on the idea of the pollution of the pure by the impure through contact which disgusts as it contaminates. Not only may individuals be contaminated by the intimacy of eating together, but analogously pure foods also may be contaminated by failure to keep them apart from impure foods, as in the Jewish dietary laws.

Many contact taboos are undoubtedly based upon the supposed repulsiveness of the tabooed objects, but it is just this quality which often radically complicates the maintenance of distance and so increases the severity of the taboo. To the extent to which the individual has learned with some reluctance to renounce with disgust what initially was a delight, there lurks a positive affect about much towards which the individual also feels disgust. Therefore, lower caste or lower status individuals have a potentiality for evoking resonance in the heart of the upper caste or upper class individual who sees in the disgusting one a symbol of what originally he had to renounce with much reluctance. The lower status individual under these conditions is seductive, luring the upper status one back to the state of innocence, to the Garden of Eden before he knew shame and disgust.

Some of the harshness of caste and class sanctions must be understood as an endopsychic struggle against the great attractiveness of the repellent object, a symbol of all that had to be reluctantly renounced. This is why so often the lower class individual is endowed with heightened sexual prowess, with impulsivity, with unashamed laziness and passivity. One can diagnose the strains within a particular class or caste by noting the characteristics which are attributed to the lower classes or castes.

There are numerous ways in which the distance between the repellent object and the self may be reduced. The repellent object may attempt to become closer or more intimate. This may be done physically or through speech. Many languages have different words for the control of intimacy and distance between speakers. In addition, there are numerous conventions which serve the same purpose.

Thus the use of the first name is a common convention of intimacy which may be used by the upper status individual in speaking to the lower status individual, but which the latter may not use in responding to the upper status individual. In America the child may not ordinarily use the parents' names, but refers to them as father and mother, though the parents ordinarily address the child by his first name. The shift from a last name to a first name usage ordinarily signifies a critical reduction in psychological distance. If the one who is being so approached is repelled by this intimacy, his look of disgust is universally understood to convey his disinclination to accept this increase in intimacy.

Status contempt—disgust permits love or respect but not both

In hierarchical relationships distance may be maintained despite the presence of either love or respect, but not both. If the lower status individual is to be kept at arms length, he may be permitted greater respect and psychological distance is nonetheless maintained. Thus the Negro in the Northern states can rise to positions of respect more readily than in the South, in part because there is a taboo on intimacy between whites and Negroes. If, however, he is permitted more intimacy, he may not be permitted any increment in respect. Thus many Negroes in the South are loved as children are loved, but they are not permitted to become objects of respect. This split between love and respect permits both the Northern and Southern white to escape shame for being intimate in the South and for being respectful of the Negro in the North, and to escape the contempt of other whites as well as to minimize the contempt which is evoked by Negroes.

In our previous discussion we emphasized the minimizing of shame for the whites by this split. We are now considering the further consequences with respect to minimizing contempt for the Negroes and for minimizing self-contempt for the whites.

From the point of view of the minority group, any significant decrease in distance has the consequence of exposing them to more contempt to which they in turn may respond with shame, self-contempt or both.

An individual or a class or a minority may be discriminated against, may evoke contempt if they come closer to those who discriminate against them either by a rise in status if they are somewhat loved, or by an increase in attempted intimacy if they are somewhat respected. It should be noted that neither love nor respect are total when there is also contempt, but one may nonetheless predominate over the other so long as both are not to be maximized at once.

This scarcity of the love-respect economy is not limited to the more visible types of discrimination. It is found in some parent-child relationships in which a child is loved, but not respected and not permitted to be independent or to challenge parental authority in any way. Similarly, employees may be respected by an employer so long as there is not too great an intimacy, or they may be permitted considerable intimacy provided they are not too independent or egalitarian in their relationships. Teacher-student relationships may also be governed by a love-respect constant in which the teacher may respect a student provided the relationship is formal, or may become intimate with a student if he does not assume the status of an equal.

The motivation behind such a split in the love-respect economy is that to maximize both attitudes would entail an egalitarian relationship of complete mutuality. Since the relationship is hierarchical and maintained by the implicit contempt of the higher status individual for the lower status individual, it is assumed that maximizing of both love and respect would produce not an egalitarian relationship, but a reversal of positions. It is assumed that the one who was initially high and contemptuous would become low and the object of contempt. Hence in the South there is great contempt for the "nigger lover." All who challenge the position of the upper status individual expose that one to the threat of reversal of contempt. So long as the lower status individual makes no claim to complete mutuality, he may enjoy the respect of the higher status one, or the love of the higher status one, but not both.

*Learned contempt—disgust in response to a heightening
of conflicted desire*

But the action of the other is not the only way in which
psychological distance can be reduced so as to evoke disgust
in the one approached. Whenever there is ambivalence toward
any object, the heightening of positive affect, or the weakening
of negative affect, or both, can sufficiently decrease the psychological distance to evoke disgust.

Of course, the ambivalence may also lead only to shame.
Nonetheless if one has both a strong wish for sexual contact,
but also shame or fear of sexual contact, an unusually attractive
sex object may so heighten the sexual wish and disturb the
customary equilibrium that one is overwhelmed with disgust
at the sudden decrease in psychological distance between the
self and the other. Disgust may also be aroused if the sex drive
is greatly increased in intensity, regardless of the attractiveness
or even the availability of a sex object. Paradoxically, the wish
for sexual contact can also be heightened, and disgust thereby
evoked, by an increase in the distance between the self and the
other, especially when the other is trying to heighten desire by
provocative alternations in increasing and decreasing distance.
Even outright rejection may sufficiently heighten sexual desire
so that disgust is evoked in the conflicted lover.

Sexuality is only a special case of the evocation of disgust
through a heightening of conflicted desire. Whenever one is
confronted with something one wants and doesn't want and
the equilibrium is disturbed, one may learn to become disgusted,
as though this were similar to a bad-smelling object moving
nearer the self. Thus, if someone is hostile toward a person I
dislike, or the latter is hostile toward me but I am ambivalent
about expressing my hostility, I can be disgusted by such an
expression of hostility because my own anger is thereby stimulated. If someone easily establishes close interpersonal relationships with others or tries to do so with me, I may be disgusted
if this heightens my own inhibited wish to do likewise. This is
the classic revulsion and envy which the introvert feels in the
presence of the extrovert. If someone is lazy and passive and

enjoys himself without residual conflict about his self-indulgence, I may be disgusted because his example heightens my own inhibited wishes to do likewise. If someone is frankly exhibition-istic, I may feel disgust if this now stimulates similar wishes which were once renounced with reluctance. If someone cries in distress and this stimulates empathic sympathy and the wish to cry, I may feel disgust if my own distress was inhibited by internalized self-contempt. Let us now examine some other ways in which contempt may be learned, sources other than similarity to the innate stimuli to disgust.

Redintegration and translation from the visual to the motor as a source of contempt—disgust

Just as the sight of another yawning is a contagious stimulus to one's own yawn, so the sight of the look of contempt of the other can be a powerful stimulus to the translation from the visual to the motor domain.

As we will show later, the relationship between visual and motor messages in the nervous system is essentially translatory. Just as an individual may learn to write with his hands the words he reads with his eyes, or hears with his ears, so he learns how to produce visual effects generally by translating the de-sired effect into the appropriate motor messages. As a conse-quence of innumerable translations from the visual world to the motor as he moves about in space, he becomes skilled in the technique of visual motor translation. He is like a touch typist who converts visual displays into their equivalent motor messages which in turn produce responses which duplicate the original visual display by means of the typewriter.

Indeed, the human being has so practised visual motor trans-lation that he resembles a typist who has overlearned his skill to the point where he automatically moves his fingers when reading, even when not at the typewriter. Given the child's overwhelming need to identify with the parents, and years of practice, visual-motor translation of affect becomes an over-learned skill which tends to run itself off automatically unless interfered with by other ongoing practices. Thus, if one walks about with a smile on one's face, one will be responded to with a smile by at least half of those he accidentally encounters walking about.

Returning now to the learning of disgust, when a human being, having learned the general skill of visual-motor translation, sees the look of disgust, he also has the ability to send the appropriate motor messages to his own face which will reproduce the equivalent of what he has seen. Barring other competing interfering affective responses to the look of disgust, this translation will produce a disgust response the sensory feedback of which will be experienced as one's own disgust. This is one of the reasons why the more extreme nausea reaction on board ship is often contagious.

To the extent to which a child is exposed to frequent displays of disgust by parents, he may learn to show disgust rather than other affects. This is most likely to occur when the parent very frequently shows disgust toward servants and other individuals in the presence of the child. This is so because when the parent shows disgust towards the child, the child may be overcome with shame or fear or distress, and so interfere with the redintegration of disgust by translation. If on the other hand, the parent is sufficiently supercilious towards others in general, the child may very early learn the skill of translation, and his face freezes into a perpetual set to sneer or becomes frozen into a slight lift to the upper lip. Just as the perpetual smile or readiness to smile of the parent may be frozen on the face of the child, so too with anger, or distress, or excitement, or fear, or shame, or disgust.

Such permanent mimicry of the face of the parent, however, rarely occurs without identification with the parent, and a parent who perpetually expressed disgust toward the child would discourage the identification of the child with such a parent. For permanent mimicry of this kind to occur, the parent would have to provide a model of continuing contempt for others but not for the child. The arrogant nobility and royalty of yesteryear who trained their children, in part by example, to have contempt for those beneath them, constitute the clearest example of such mimicry of contempt. Let us consider next the mechanism of imitation of disgust from identification.

Imitation of contempt–disgust from identification

Imitation of the disgust of the parent is a much more important source of learning of disgust than is redintegration through translation. Imitation like redintegration also employs translation of visual into motor messages, but it is a less automatic process, requiring as it does conscious trial and error in the production of the imitated behavior. Further, it generally requires positive affect for the model (we will consider the exceptions to this presently) as a motive.

By identification we mean the wish of the child to be like the other. In redintegration there is an automatic zeroing in and retrieval of the whole message from the perception of a distinctive part, just as a cliché is completed upon perception of a sufficient and distinctive part of the whole cliché. In trial and error modelling, the individual both wishes to be like the other and tries to be like him. In redintegrative translation the individual may or may not wish to do what he sees. The contagion here may be quite unwelcome, as when one yawns inappropriately because another yawns.

If the child wishes to be like the parent, he may nonetheless not know how to act like him. He may therefore practice behaving as he does and so learn to be disgusted as the parent is disgusted, and at the same objects which arouse the disgust of the parent.

He may be assisted in this learning by his parents, who wish him to be disgusted at particular objects. Racial prejudice is often taught in this way. The parent may also teach his child to share disgust at certain behaviors, whether those of the child or of others.

This training may go on with or without identification on the part of the child. If the child generally wishes to be like the parent, then clearly such teaching and learning to imitate the disgust of the parent is much easier than when the child has no such wish.

The exception to which we alluded earlier is hostile imitation in which the child is frightened of the parent or angry with him, or both, and tries to master his negative affect by imitation. In such a case there is no identification but there is a wish to defeat the parent, by imitation, by borrowing his strength in order to turn it against the parent.

Identification therefore may or may not result in imitation, depending upon the age and skill of the child, and imitation may be motivated by hostile wishes against the other rather than by the wish to be like the other.

Despite the wish of the child to be like the parent, the mimicking of the disgust reaction ordinarily encounters considerable resistance, the more disgust is directed against the child himself. The child surrenders his numerous delights reluctantly if at all, and no matter how much he may love the parent, the aping of the disgust response encounters formidable competition from the child's investment of the world with his positive affect. We will examine this question again when we consider the sources of self-contempt.

The child is much more ready to learn to mimic the disgust of his parent about the behavior of others, so long as he is not too closely identified with them. However, should a beloved parent express disgust at an equally beloved friend, the child is placed in the greatest conflict, and he is reluctant to surrender one love for another, to share disgust. Disgust learning by imitation from identification is most powerful when it is directed toward objects about which the child has no prior competing affective investments. Thus, members of a minority group with whom contact is distant or minimal are a ready source of learned disgust from parents who provide a model. Republicans in the South, Democrats in upper class communities are ready objects for the transmission of disgust reactions from parents.

IN-GROUP SOLIDARITY AND LEARNED CONTEMPT—DISGUST

Such disgust learning does not of course end with the early parent-child interactions. Shared disgust is a powerful source of cohesion and identity for the tight in-groups formed in adolescence and adulthood. Freud's observation that every group requires an enemy upon which to discharge its aggression is more properly translated into the proposition that group cohesiveness and identity depends heavily on the sharing of a common object of contempt—those who are different from us, who do not understand us, to whom we would never permit membership, who, in short, disgust us. The beatnik and his odious square is but a contemporary version of the recurrent learned shared object of disgust, by which each member of a group learns his identity and the identity of the group to which he belongs, a phenomenon which recurs whenever a major investment of positive affect is made by the individual in a distinctive group which must differentiate itself from competing groups. The Cartesian formula is here transformed: "We are disgusted, therefore we exist."

Whereas the disgust which the parent provides as a model encounters competition from positive affects, the adolescent or adult can gain a sense of identity and community from learning to be disgusted at a rival business corporation, country club, university, or even a rival scientific theory. Such piety not only draws close the true believers, but purifies the spirit of any residual doubt about the worthiness of one's self and one's identifications.

The relationship between uncertainty and contempt is quite close. Within any science, contempt increases directly with uncertainty and with the rate of change of information, and within the hierarchy of sciences, contempt is proportional to uncertainty. The newer the science, the more strident the derogation of colleagues in book reviews and in the gossip which is exchanged within the scientific community. Several years ago we sampled a hundred book reviews from the technical journals in physics, biology, and psychology and found an increasing use of contempt words in the less well-established branches of science. This is not to say that physicists were less argumentative than biologists or psychologists, but that they were less derogatory in their criticism.

Imitation from hostility

One of the prime ways of teaching the child to respond with disgust is to show him much disgust, but without terrorizing the child to the point where he cannot respond in kind, and without loving him so much that he must respond with shame to parental contempt. Under these conditions the child readily learns to throw back to the parent the look of counter-contempt.

On the playground, insult and counter-insult between peers is a commonplace: "Oh yeah!" "Yeah!" can be repeated endlessly, with the hostile sneer thrown back and forth as though it were a ball. The logic of such an exchange is that the look of contempt wounds. Therefore the wound can be undone if it can be inflicted on the one who wounded one, as a hand grenade can become a weapon if one throws it back quickly.

Since disgust is innately ejective and projectile, it readily lends itself to such a strategy. You won't dirty me, because I will dirty you. The bronx cheer which is an imitation of anal flatus with the mouth is a symbolic extension of the disgust reaction, in which the dirtying of the other is magnified by the importation and ejection of mimicked bad anal odors in disgust.

Generalization of imitation from hostility to contempt—disgust to any negative affect from the other or any negative affect produced by the other in the self

Once the individual learns to respond to disgust with counter-disgust it becomes possible to learn to respond with the same disgust to a wide variety of equivalent conditions. These range from any negative affect of the other to any negative affect produced in the self by the other.

Thus, if the other expresses anger, the individual who has learned to respond to contempt may now generalize his counter-contempt to the anger of the other. If the other expresses distress or fear or shame, it may also be met with contempt. It is as though the individual had learned to be nauseated by any display of affect by the other which was negative in any way.

Through generalization the same contempt may be learned as a response to any response of the other which produces any negative affect in the self. The other need not intend to express negative feelings to arouse them. Thus he may ask for help, but if this arouses any negative feelings, the disgusted one may respond to the other with contempt rather than sympathy. The other may tell the disgusted one what to do. If this arouses any negative feeling, this latter may become the equivalent through generalization of the original hostility which prompted the learning of counter-contempt to contempt. Let us next consider the more general case of such a spread of learned contempt.

Contempt—disgust theory

Whenever the experience of disgust is recurrent and becomes central, there is likely to be a cognitive elaboration which organizes these experiences into a relatively unified theory. Such theory thereafter sensitizes the individual to contempt-relevant information and provides ready-made strategies for coping with these paradigms.

Depending upon the power and generality of the contempt theory developed, any kind of situation may be responded to as though it contained an implicit insult to which there is a ready-made response or set of alternative strategies. The nature of such a theory is idiosyncratic, differing from individual to individual. We will later examine some examples of such theories in detail. At this point we wish only to note that there is no kind of situation which does not lend itself to restructuring in the direction of offending the individual whose contempt theory renders him overly sensitized to insult and disgust. The only competitors of such disgust vulnerability are other affect theories which transform the same information into other paradigms which evoke competing affects. We will next consider the special case of contempt learning in which the self learns to have contempt for itself.

THE SOURCES OF SELF-CONTEMPT—DISGUST

The remembered contemptuous other

The beginning of self-contempt is the internalization of the contemptuous other. This is seen most clearly in l'homme escalier, the prolongation of controversy in the mind of the defeated one who continues the controversy until he has turned the tables with the reply which crushes. Contempt is met with counter-contempt, albeit delayed and imaginary. Even when the con-

temptuous other is finally put in his place, it should not be
forgotten that he has been both internalized and magnified.

One has fallen in contempt with the contemptuous other
to the extent that the imagination is caught up in continuing
preoccupation with him. This can be as self-punishing as falling
in love can be self-rewarding since the original source of contempt is greatly magnified by such preoccupation, whether or
not he is finally defeated in the mind's eye.

This is clearly not yet self-contempt, though it is a contempt
for the self which is ever ready to sting and wound the self which
carries its oppressor within its memory. Depending upon the
frequency and intensity of such experiences, the self can easily
be victimized by the necessity of dealing with the snowballing
unfinished business of settling accounts with contemptuous
others.

The self which is under the duress of such remembered
contempt will deal with the accusations differently depending
on who is showing contempt and what is the nature of the
general relationship with that other. The incident may be suppressed and forgotten if it occurred in the heat of an argument
with someone who is otherwise friendly or loving. However, if
the contempt is from a much beloved person and if the affront
was both serious and unique in the relationship, it may wound
much more deeply than if it came from someone whom it is
easy to hate. Shame, of course, may be the primary response to
contempt from the beloved, but insofar as there is identification
with the beloved, there may also be contempt which is internalized or self-contempt of the contemptuous other who continues
to sneer at the self. Under such circumstances the wound may
be healed only by renunciation of a part of the self by atonement
and by changing the self so that it no longer offends the beloved
other.

Even though the contemptuous look and voice of the beloved
other may induce the self to renounce part of itself to please
the other, this does not yet constitute self-contempt, but phenomenologically it is rather a variety of appeasement of another.
When the remembered contempt of the other is fought off, it is
even less experienced as self-contempt proper. Despite the fact
that this is not self-contempt, it may nonetheless be a major

determinant of behavior. The look and voice of conscience need not be the self's own conscience to control the self, so long as it continues to be heard and seen from memory. One can be quite as derogated by the remembered other as by self-recrimination.

Indeed one might argue that the self more readily comes to terms with its self than with a remembered oppressor who is continually magnified through bitter inner dialogue. In certain cases much of the behavior of the individual can be understood as an attempt to defeat the remembered oppressor by exhibiting qualities which fly in the face of the accusations of the oppressor. Such is often true in the flight into heroic achievement, the flight into heterosexuality, the flight into daring and the confrontation of death, and a variety of apparently masochistic phenomena calculated to give the lie to the scorn and contempt of the remembered oppressor.

Such engagement with the remembered oppressor is rarely an engagement with that one as he was, but rather with a more heroic adversary. What the individual must prove by his behavior depends upon what the other scorned and how he is to defeat the oppressor. If the other had contempt for his immorality, he must be ultra-pious if he is simply to disprove the allegation, but if he supposes he must meet contempt with contempt to defeat the other, then he will become contempt-less in an exaggerated show of defiance. In certain individuals we may even observe an oscillation between grossly psychopathic and ultra-moral behavior, calculated first to defeat the oppressor by showing one couldn't care less for his opinion and then to prove, in addition, that one is an extraordinarily good and moral individual.

If the oppressor's taunts question the achievement rather than the morality of the individual, he may become a hobo or unusually defiant about regular employment to show that the attitude of the oppressor concerns him not at all, or he may become an over-achiever driving himself mercilessly to give the lie to the other. Again, both strategies may be used. Certain artists and writers have self-consciously defied the demands of society with respect to supporting themselves by their labor, but at the same time they demonstrate to themselves that they are capable of much more heroic labor and achievement than the common man. When both strategies are used, conflict may arise, since the effort to flout the scorn of the other conflicts with the efforts to prove him wrong.

Depersonalizing of the remembered contempt—disgust of the other into the generalized other

What began as a specific insult from the other may not only be much amplified through internal dialogue, but also further transformed so that the look and voice of contempt and conscience becomes that of the generalized other. The look becomes the face of every man, or the people, the voice that of mankind, or God, or the angels. "They" now oppress me, hold me in contempt. They are no less formidable an oppressor for being no one in particular.

Such a transformation indicates an increased helplessness in dealing with the internal oppressor. The contemptuous one has either been so magnified in internal dialogue that his increased intensity is translated into an increase in numbers; or repeated contacts with the oppressor, each more painful than the preceeding one, have snowballed the effect; or contacts with others have further reinforced the impression that the individual is surrounded by hostile critics. Whatever the route the individual has taken, he now has to deal with more internal fellow travelers who find him disgusting and contemptible, but they speak with a single voice.

The dynamics of such a transformation differ in no essential way from any other class formation. After viewing many dogs, the generalized dog which the child may attain as a concept is all dogs but no dog in particular. In the construction of a generalized internal oppressor many of the instances of the class have never been perceived, but have also been constructed through inner controversy.

Yet without some reinforcement from similar experience with others, it is unlikely that a generalized other would be constructed on the basis of interaction with a single person. Consider the analogous case of romantic love—the lover too has multiple instances of the beloved through the exercise of his imagination. Yet he never depersonalizes the internalized face of the beloved, even though he may transform it in other ways.

The internal oppressor may form the basis of a self-fulfilling prophecy that others in general are likely to be contemptuous, and when such an assumption receives any confirmation, as is very likely to happen given the intensity of the feelings involved, then the construction of a contemptuous generalized other may be very rapid. A straw will readily break the back of such a feeble camel. Such circular reinforcement continues to occur once a generalized contemptuous other is constructed, so that the individual becomes increasing sensitized to new instances of the generalized other in repeated self-fulfilling prophecies.

The formation of a depersonalized contemptuous other may also be encouraged by the way in which the parent expressed his contempt and disapproval of the child. If the parent expresses pure contempt through the lifted lip with or without verbal accompaniment such as "I'm disgusted with you . . . I'm shocked at you" or amplifies the basis of contempt in a purely personal way, such as "You ought to be ashamed of yourself, you little hoodlum, don't let me ever catch you doing that again," then the remembered contemptuous other is likely to be that specific look and voice and those specific words.

If the parent expresses contempt in a more abstract and impersonal way along with the look and sound of contempt, then half of the transformation has been made by the parent. Thus a parent might say, with upper lip lifted and with un- mistakable revulsion, "Nice children don't make messes." It is a relatively simple transformation to construct from such a message, spoken at a particular time and place by a particular person, a categorical imperative good for all eternity, which appears to emanate from a contemptuous generalized other. Let us consider the next transformation which is possible with the contemptuous other.

Identification of the self with the contemptuous other or with the contemptuous generalized other

A critical transformation occurs when the self identifies with either the contemptuous other or with the generalized con- temptuous other. Such an identification can occur through the externalization of his contempt of the other. Nothing is more rewarding for the child who has been scorned for his dirtiness than to play the role of the contemptuous parent toward the first child he encounters who is also dirty. "You're dirty and disgusting" the pot calls the kettle. If the contemptuous other has been generalized, his victim is likely to be judged in more universalistic terms, "Dirty children are not nice." In either case the child has been unwittingly seduced into becoming a representative of the inner oppressor.

Having acted as a representative of a higher authority, he himself is now capable of coming under the same jurisdiction. He can become his own judge. It has often been noted that the self protects itself against the internal oppressor by finding fault with others, but it is also true that this is a two-edged sword. which once sharpened against the other, can also be turned against the self by the self.

The self may also identify with the contemptuous other because the parent exacts such identification as a price of continuing the parent-child relationship. Such a parent after having expressed his contempt may force the child to confess his sins, to express self-disgust, and to promise to reform. When the oppressor is now recalled in memory, there is also the memory of the self saying, "I was bad, I'm sorry, I won't do it again." The remembered contemptuous other is joined by the remembered contemptuous self, a reluctant ally of the other who is nonetheless on the road to setting up a judicial system which the self and the contemptuous other enforce alike. Eventually, both the self and the other may be replaced by a generalized other and finally by a completely impersonal norm.

An identification of the self with the contemptuous other may be produced by virtue of the love of the child for the parent. Here it is "we," at first, who disapprove of the bad part of the self, and of the bad parts of other selves. Such a child is deeply wounded by the rupture in the relationship between the parent and himself and readily assumes complete responsibility for condemning whatever the other condemns. It is a relatively small transformation from this cooperation to identification with the generalized other and finally with an abstract norm.

Such identification with the contemptuous other may be motivated by fear of the parent. In such a case the self is reluctant to disagree with the condemnation and disgust of the parent. The child is forced into such complete appeasement that he may not know that he hates the lawgiver within. He willingly allies himself with the other and condemns himself to reduce the fear of the contempt of the other judge within. He not only obeys the other, but must agree with him totally lest his loyalty be questioned.

Identification of the self with a norm

The self may identify itself with a parent who holds him in contempt, with a generalized other who holds him in contempt, but also with a norm which he has violated and for which he holds himself in contempt. Such a source of contempt may be nothing other than the final depersonalizing of the contemptuous other and the generalized other, but this is not the only way in which the individual may learn to condemn himself for norm violation. Internalized norms are, of course, also a source of pride, excitement and enjoyment as well as the occasion of negative affects other than self-contempt when they are violated. Inasmuch as norms may be constructed by the individual rather than borrowed from others, their violation may produce self-contempt which is endogenous, not distilled from a depersonalized contempt of others which has been internalized.

Internalized contempt from others and idiosyncratic norms and their violation are not the only source of self-contempt as we will see. Just as similarity to bad odors and to reduced distance between the self and the malodorous or bad-tasting object is a source of learned disgust, so may it be a source of self-disgust.

Similarity to bad odors as a basis for self-contempt–disgust

Whenever the self detects something about itself which seems similar to a bad odor or bad taste, the self may learn to have contempt for itself. This can provide a source of self-contempt which is quite independent of the contempt of others.

Thus, if the body seems unattractive or becomes unattractive, the self may respond to that part of itself with disgust. If the self is compared with other selves and found distasteful, the self can learn to have contempt for itself. If the achievement to which an individual dedicates himself is measured and found wanting by the individual, he may learn to have contempt for himself. If the self is confronted with a challenge and fails to meet the challenge, the self may be disgusted with its failure as with a bad taste. If the life pattern seems to have no order and no significance, the self may find itself repelling. Unresolved conflict within the self may evoke self-contempt because of its disorderliness and similarity to dirtiness.

Similarly, if one is ever tempted to do something which would disgust one, this reduction of distance may be sufficient to arouse self-disgust in the manner in which any reduction in distance between the person and a malodorous object provokes disgust. The passive sufferance of unwanted negative affects may evoke self-disgust by virtue of the similarity to the enforced experience of something malodorous coming too close to the self.

Any of these self-condemnations may arise from the violation of norms learned from others, but they may also evoke self-contempt by virtue of their similarity to bad odors, to dirtiness, to disorder, or to any of the more remote derivatives of the innate stimuli to disgust.

It should be noted however that when a parent is an anal character, he may not only teach his child to internalize his own disgust at bad smells, and their derivatives, but he also teaches him to become exceedingly sensitive to the detection of faint resemblances between any kind of psychological disorder and fecal odors. When the second generation anal character has learned this skill, he is enabled to achieve new sources of self-contempt by analogy with bad odors in ways which may never have been taught or internalized from his parents. Just as a gifted student may leave his teacher far behind once he has been given the tools of exploration, so may an individual who has been taught to have contempt for himself learn new sources and new discriminations within old sources, by which he can disgust himself. Unhappy as this skill may be, it is nonetheless a skill which may grow with practice.

Negative affect from the other as a source of self-contempt–disgust

Just as bad odors provide a basis for generalization through similarity, so too may the contempt of the other generalize to other negative affects as a source of learned self-contempt. I may feel self-contempt not only if you show contempt for me but also if you are angry, if your anger seems equivalent to your contempt. I may further learn to hold myself in contempt if you are distressed with me or if I frighten or shame you. In these cases the generalization becomes increasingly remote in that I may learn to hold myself responsible for any negative experience of the other when originally I felt self-contempt only when the other showed contempt for me.

Negative affect of the self as a source of self-contempt–disgust

As self-contempt generalizes, any negative affect may become the unwanted state which offends the self. Under these conditions I may be disgusted by the fact that I am distressed, disgusted with my timidity or any fear I experience, disgusted with my own irritability and even with my shyness or shame.

Such a state of affairs has been incorrectly defined as self-hatred. It is rather the contempt of the self for the self and its feelings.

Ordinarily generalization of self-disgust is not so indiscriminate. The self may tolerate its own fear but not its distress, or conversely. It may tolerate its anger but not its shame, or conversely. In order to achieve such a widespread generalization of self-contempt, a higher-order cognitive organization into a self-contempt theory is necessary.

Self-contempt–disgust theory as a source

When the experience of self-contempt is intense and frequent, the set of such experiences ordinarily is transformed by cognitive work into a higher-order self-contempt theory. By means of such a theory, the most varied experiences are quickly and skillfully scrutinized, filtered and transformed to extract what is relevant for the confirmation and activation of self-contempt, and at the same time activate strategies designed to minimize, avoid or escape the anticipated self-contempt contingencies. Depending upon the scope of the theory, the individual may be put under a constant alert for the signs, within and without, which force the self to reject itself.

Chapter 19

The Impact of Humiliation:
General Images and Strategies

In this and the following chapters, the word humiliation will be used as a generic term including both the affect of shame–humiliation and the affect of contempt–disgust. Indeed, in later chapters we will be centrally concerned with compounds of both shame and contempt with other negative affects, such as shame–humiliation, contempt–disgust and distress–anguish in depression, and shame–humiliation, contempt–disgust and fear–terror in paranoid schizophrenia.

All human beings have idiosyncratic characteristics which depend upon the variable winds of doctrine and circumstance, and characteristics which are general and inherently human. Human beings are innately endowed with positive and negative affects, which are inherently rewarding and punishing, with a mechanism which automatically registers all conscious experience in memory; and with receptor, motor and analyzer mechanisms organized as a feedback circuit. The combination of these innate endowments in a creature who is capable of moving freely in space, who is capable of reflecting on his past experience and of anticipating his future so as to achieve states which are rewarding and to avoid states which are punishing, will, we think, inevitably generate certain general aims, strategies or General Images.

As previously mentioned, an Image is any centrally generated blueprint which controls the human feedback mechanism. This mechanism will be described in Volume III. At this point it will suffice to recall that we conceptualize a purpose, a goal or an aim as an Image; that is, a criterion by which feedback is monitored and discrepancies measured until the Image is attained by successive reductions of the differences between the feedback and the aim or Image. Many of these Images are transitory and idiosyncratic, never again appearing in the aims of other human beings or of their originator. But some of them will be independently and continuously generated not only over the life span of one individual, but also by all human beings, with so high a probability that we regard their appearance as virtually inevitable in the development of all human beings. We have called them General Images to refer to this generality of their appearance among human beings. It is analogous to the game of dice in which we may distinguish the variable sequences of combinations of faces from the more general phenomenon that on almost every throw the dice will land on their sides rather than on their edges. Occasionally a die may land against a wall or some object which supports it so that it fails to come to rest on one of its flat sides. Despite these occasional exceptions it can be confidently predicted that for all the environments and conditions under which the game of dice is now played, the probability of landing on a side rather than an edge is extremely high. It is conceivable that an individual might not develop any of what we have called the General Images, but it is as unlikely as a dice game in which the dice never came to rest on one of their flat sides.

There are four General Images: 1) positive affect should be maximized; 2) negative affect should be minimized; 3) affect inhibition should be minimized; 4) power to maximize positive affect, to minimize negative affect and to minimize affect inhibition should be maximized.

THE CONFLICT BETWEEN MAXIMIZING POSITIVE AND MINIMIZING NEGATIVE AFFECT

We have seen before that each of these strategies historically has made a strong case for itself. The clamor of one General Image gives way only to the more coercive clamor of another General Image.

The individual who must minimize negative affect at any cost may pay the price of surrendering not only the maximizing of positive affect but even the price of abandoning completely all excitement and enjoyment. There is no zest in his life, because its pursuit might entail punitive negative affect. He dare not seek positive affect lest he become afraid, and lest this turn to terror and panic. He dare not seek excitement nor enjoyment lest it entail risk, which threatens utter humiliation or overwhelming anguish or blind rage. To pursue the strategy of maximizing positive affect under such conditions is to so jeopardize the strategy of minimizing negative affect that reward is renounced as a General Image.

Conflict between the first and second strategy may, on the other hand, be settled in favor of maximizing positive affect rather than minimizing negative affect. When the individual is captured by hope, by love or by excitement, whether it be for science, for art, for the beloved or for humanity, he may fly heedlessly, or with full awareness, in the face of great risk of certain defeat and even of death. Love of life may be surrendered out of fear, or life itself may be surrendered out of love.

The conflict between maximizing the positive or negative affects is most poignant in the case of shame and contempt. In shame there is an unwilling, partial and temporary renunciation of positive affect. In contempt the renunciation is complete and permanent, and the object which once might have excited positive affect is now the occasion of total negative affect. From shame there is always a way back to the object and to the positive affect which was only incompletely and temporarily reduced. In a shame-oriented personality, therefore, there is a bias in favor of both maximizing positive affect and minimizing negative affect, since the occurrence of shame is an unwelcome intrusion in an otherwise positively rewarding experience.

In a contempt-oriented personality, however, the strategy of minimizing contempt can assume sufficiently monopolistic influence so that the strategy of maximizing of positive affect is radically attenuated in favor of avoiding contempt for the self. Such a personality is haunted by the imminence of contempt, and such excitement or enjoyment as is experienced is limited to those occasions when there is a prospect of avoidance or escape from contempt. Like the prisoner who has been given a last-minute reprieve, his zest for life is entirely derivative of rescue from or minimizing of the primary negative affect which is his concern. This is not to say that it is any less real or any less intense than any other excitement or enjoyment, but it is to say that it is an unintended and often unexpected by-product of the central strategy, which is the minimizing of the negative affect of self-contempt or humiliation.

Anti-pleasure philosophies, personal and formal, as a consequence of minimizing contempt

One consequence of such a strategy is the heightening of outwardly directed contempt when others unashamedly pursue positive affect for its own sake. In socialization this is reflected in the concern lest in sparing the rod one spoil the child. It is better to terrorize and humiliate the child than to run the risk that the child will be encouraged to maximize his positive affects.

In philosophy, the naked pursuit of pleasure and happiness has been rejected as a value theory again and again on two somewhat contradictory assumptions. It has been argued by Broad and many others that one cannot, in fact, pursue happiness directly because it is a by-product of interest in something other than happiness, and the direct pursuit of happiness is therefore self-defeating. The wish is here father to the thought. It is not difficult to pursue the pleasures of the palate or of the genitals, so long as one can wait for the cyclical promptings of the drive mechanism. Indeed, for the Romans, regurgitation short-circuited even this delay for the pleasures of eating.

The kernel of fact in such a stricture derives from the innate structure of joy and excitement. One depends on a rising level of density of neural stimulation and the other on a falling gradient of neural stimulation. This complicates the self-conscious cultivation of excitement and joy, but it does not present an insuperable barrier to an individual who would self-consciously seek to maximize excitement or joy. Such a one has only to court uncertainty, risk and danger in order to heighten his sense of excitement, and to suddenly reduce these same risks to produce the smile of enjoyment.

One cannot escape the impression that this belief is powered by a Puritanism which is concerned lest human beings too successfully achieve pleasure and positive affect. Rather than disbelieving in the possibility of the pursuit of happiness, such theorists appear more concerned lest such a pursuit become monopolistic. This is a more subtle form of the hell-fire theory of the consequences of the direct pursuit of enjoyment.

The second argument, originating with Plato, is that the pursuit of pleasure violates the dignity of the human being. All anti-hedonistic theories of value betray a thinly disguised contempt for pleasure, for positive affect and for the strategy of maximizing positive affect. Indeed, all normative theories of value derogate not only positive affect but human beings as such, insofar as they fail to embody in their behavior those norms which are postulated to be prior to, more real than and more valuable than the human being, who, it is asserted, must be governed by such norms if he is to become good. We will examine ideological postures and their relationship to affect in Volume III. At the moment we wish to show some of the consequences of the strategy of minimizing negative affect, and of minimizing contempt in particular.

Consequences of minimizing contempt by turning it outward

It is a short step from minimizing contempt for the self to maximizing contempt for others as a derivative of the primary strategy. If you are contemptible and if I am the one who makes this judgement, then I am less likely to be measured and found wanting. In part, this posture of reversal is not only defensive in intent but is also a consequence of identification with the source of contempt.

The personality which contains an internalized oppressor is governed in large part by the wish to minimize the experience of humiliation, by the wish not to hear the rasping, tongue-lashing voice of the internalized shamer and condemner; but, it may also be governed by identification with that not so small voice. The same process whereby the parent who humiliates one takes up permanent residence in the self of the derogated one powers the derogatory thrusts not only against the self but against others as well.

The personality governed by the strategy of minimizing self-contempt may fail, nonetheless, to minimize negative affect entirely, insofar as it is committed to the frequent resort to contempt of others. Although it is more comfortable to be disgusted by others than by the self, it is nonetheless an experience of negative affect. To be continually outraged and disgusted by the shortcomings of others is not to lead a rewarding life.

What frequently happens when contempt is turned outward is that positive affect is also activated. The rescue from self-derogation and the identification with the internalized humiliator combine to activate excitement or joy or both along with contempt, so that piety is bathed in self-satisfaction. Under these conditions the individual can pursue both strategies of maximizing positive and minimizing negative affect at the same time. He is the evaluator of others who enjoys self-inflation through the deflation of others and who enjoys self-purification through sullying the selves of others.

It should be noted, however, that in many personalities the turning of contempt outward permits neither the maximizing of positive affect nor the minimizing of negative affect. Such individuals are truly outraged and disturbed by the evidence, to which they are especially sensitive, that human beings are worthy only of contempt. The continually outraged piety of such a one need not be much less uncomfortable than finding the self forever worthy of self-contempt.

To the extent to which the parent was unrelenting in the humiliation of the child, unrelieved either by smugness or by self-satisfaction in piety, the individual so socialized will be forever vulnerable to the harshest kind of unrelieved self-contempt as from an alien self within the self. Such an unrelenting humiliator within the self forever defeats the strategy of minimizing negative affect as well as the strategy of maximizing positive affect. No one who has learned to loathe himself can ever completely succeed in the pursuit of positive affect nor in the avoidance of negative affect.

More generally, any normative philosophy which polarizes the realm of essence and value in sharp opposition to man must of necessity seriously attenuate both strategies of maximizing positive and minimizing negative affects. In such philosophies, man, it is supposed, can attain his full stature only through struggle toward and conformity to a norm, an ideal essence basically independent of man. Both positive and negative affects are conceived as relatively unimportant considerations, as derivatives and by-products of the progress toward or the failure to conform to ideal norms and values. It is proper for man to suffer and to be humiliated for his sins and his failures. It is appropriate, but not important, that he be rewarded if he has been good. Virtue can be its own reward, even if sin requires punishment. But good and evil are essentially independent of both positive and negative affect in normative ideology.

In tradition- and norm-oriented societies, too, behavior is often rigidly prescribed independent of the feelings and wishes of those who are members of this society. There are negative sanctions for norm violation and positive sanctions for conformity, but these sanctions are quite independent of the strategies of maximizing positive affect and minimizing negative affect. Only in modern democratic societies are the rights of man, his "life, liberty and pursuit of happiness," affirmed as primary aims of the society.

THE CONFLICT BETWEEN MINIMIZING AFFECT INHIBITION AND THE FIRST TWO GENERAL IMAGES

The third General Image is that affect inhibition should be minimized. The inhibition of the overt expression of any affect will, under certain conditions, produce a residual form of the affect which is at once heightened, distorted and chronic and which is severely punitive. Such inhibited affects may sometimes be effectively suppressed without residual intensification, and may be reduced by avoiding or escaping from the circumstances which might reactivate them. But frequently they simply persist as affects which are experienced in intensified but muffled form, along with the responses which are designed to prevent or attenuate the overt expression of the affect. Thus the cry of distress may be experienced in the distorted form of the stiff upper lip, which is calculated to interfere with the trembling crying mouth.

The hanging of the head in shame may be experienced only as it is distorted by the posture of the chin up and head back, the specific defense against the shame response.

These defenses are not always effective and sometimes the muffled cry breaks through the stiff upper lip, and the lowered eyelids break through the defiant raised chin and head thrown back. When this happens we see simultaneously the original affect and the specific defense. Ordinarily these two are not seen simultaneously at the overt level, even though they may be felt covertly as feedback by the individual who is struggling to inhibit the overt expression of affect.

The inhibition of the overt expression of any affect can be punitive. To feel excited but not to be able to show it, to feel like smiling but to be unable to smile, to feel like crying but to be unable to cry, to feel enraged but to swallow it, to feel terrified but to have to hide it, to feel ashamed but have to pretend that all is well, to feel disgust but have to smile—any and all of these are punitive experiences which produce affect hunger, the wish to express openly the incompletely suppressed affects. Alcohol has for centuries provided therapy for affect hunger of all kinds, releasing the smile of intimacy and tenderness, the look of excitement, sexual and otherwise, the unashamed crying of distress, the explosion of hostility, the intrusion of long-suppressed terror, the open confession of shame, and the avowal of self-contempt.

The General Image of minimizing affect inhibition conflicts with the General Image of maximizing positive affect and with the General Image of minimizing negative affect. Any chronically but incompletely suppressed negative affect produces what appears to be a quest for maximizing rather than minimizing negative affect. Ultimately such a strategy reduces the suffering which the suppression of the overt expression of affect entails. At the outset, however, it increases rather than decreases negative affect.

When an intoxicated person insists on a full avowal of his shame with a detailed confession of his past sins and failures to someone he has just met at a bar, he does not appear to be either maximizing his positive affect or to be minimizing his negative affect. He is indeed increasing his overt expression of shame and self-contempt because, when alcohol reduces the dreaded consequences of the overt expression of affect, the inhibition of these feelings seems to become unnecessarily punitive. The morning after he may be seized with shame at his alcoholic shamelessness, but at the time of intoxication the promise of relief from the communication of shame overwhelms the impulse to hide it.

The General Image of minimizing affect inhibition, especially when it is negative affect which intrudes and explodes into overt expression, creates an alien force deep within every self. To the extent to which all societies call for the muffling and sedation of the uninhibited and free expression of affect, self is divided against self. Each self will in varying degrees be committed to conflicting general strategies with respect to the expression of negative affect. The human being will strive to minimize the experience of negative affect at the same time that he longs to express overtly the affect which grows stronger just because of his effort to suppress and minimize it. There will be much suppression and avoidance of affect which will be successful, and under these conditions the second general strategy will provide a clear directive. There will also be failures of suppression which will grow to intolerability until they are released and reduced by overt expression. The self which is so overwhelmed is necessarily a divided self, siding both with and against the affect within, which was his own but which has become alien.

It is the discovery of this basic ambivalence which constitutes Freud's most significant contribution to our understanding of human nature. He mistakenly identified this conflict as one between the drives and the threat of castration which produces anxiety, rather than between the affects themselves. Nonetheless the image of man, passive and overwhelmed, at the intersect of forces over which he has little control is an aspect of the human condition which requires courage to confront steadily. Man's propensity to deny his own self-defeating impulses is a consequence of the power of the General Images of maximizing positive affect and of minimizing negative affect. He would generally prefer to completely suppress his negative affects than to be overwhelmed by them, rewarding as it may be to give free expression to long-suppressed feeling.

Alcoholic intoxication is not the only de-inhibitor of suppressed affect. For many, the intensity and intimacy of sexuality provides an isolated island for the free avowal of affects otherwise overcontrolled. It may be that I can be openly tender only in the arms of one who holds me, that I can express excitement only when sexual pleasure forces me into the open display of excitement, that I can be angry only in beating my sexual partner, that I can cry only when I throw myself at the mercy of one who nurtures me sexually. It may be that I can be openly afraid only when I cheat sexually, that I can hang my head in shyness and shame only when I am naked and sexually excited and that I can avow my self-contempt only when passion has forced me to violate my own image of myself in sexual fantasies and behavior which is as humiliating as it is exciting.

Sexual shamelessness has two different sources. First, it can provide a channel for the overt expression of shame or self-contempt which otherwise is suppressed and hidden lest the burden of humilitation grow even more intolerable. But as we shall see later in this chapter, it can also provide a vehicle for the maximizing of power—the fourth General Image. In this case the focus of shamelessness is not simply to relieve the pressure of suppressed humiliation but to reduce the power of the other to humiliate.

Affect promiscuity

The General Image of minimizing affect inhibition has among other consequences the effect of producing *affect promiscuity* which in turn may produce sexual promiscuity. By affect promiscuity we mean such an intensification of any affect that objects for affect investment are sought indiscriminately. If I must cry, then I will seek out tragic objects. If I must experience terror, I will court danger. If I must express anger, I will pick fights. If I must feel ashamed, I will expose myself to certain defeat. If I must feel self-contempt, I will seek humiliators, provoke contempt or do what is disgusting. Sexual promiscuity is but one vehicle of affect promiscuity. Nor is affect promiscuity restricted to negative affects and their open display. I may be as indiscriminate in the avowal of tenderness and excitement, e.g., in sexuality, as I am in the avowal of self-contempt, if joy and excitement are affects which I must suppress in my everyday world.

Affect promiscuity may itself be focal or diffuse. If I can revel in humiliation only in sexuality, this is focal affect promiscuity. However, I may perpetually seek objects which will humiliate me. In this case my affect promiscuity becomes diffuse. The distinction is similar to one between two types of sexual promiscuity. I may seek sexual experience any time, anywhere, with any object, in diffuse promiscuity, or my promiscuity may be more focal, in which case I am rarely promiscuous with respect to the type of sexual partner I require, but occasionally I am overwhelmed by the impulse to experience sexual excitement with a perfect stranger.

The distinction between focal and diffuse promiscuity is, however, a relative one, in that what is diffuse in one respect may be regarded as focal in another. For example, if I am sexually promiscuous in the sense of being ever ready for indiscriminate sexual experience, this may be considered diffuse promiscuity with respect to the focal promiscuity of an individual for whom such experience is only occasional. However, if such diffuse sexual promiscuity occurs in the context of an otherwise integrated personality, deeply committed to other long-term goals, then we would regard this diffuse promiscuity as more focal than if it constituted the major style of life. Similarly with affect promiscuity. An individual may look for trouble which will permit him to experience humiliation constantly, or often or only occasionally under very special circumstances. In each instance he is nonetheless his own agent provacateur when he is governed by affect promiscuity.

While affect promiscuity is associated with the strategy of minimizing affect inhibition, it also occurs as a consequence of the strategy of maximizing positive affect. One who has become addicted to a high degree of excitement may require perpetual objects which will pay off in thrills. He may be a scientist who must continually solve problems, because this is the only way in which he can maintain his required level of excitement. Such a one may be forced to solve crossword puzzles or read detective stories or science fiction stories whenever there is satiation or a lull in the ordinary demands on his intelligence. Another who is also addicted to excitement may split his sources between problem solving and sexuality, or art or skiing or gambling.

In such circumstances it is the affect payoff which governs the pursuit of objects, rather than the objects which govern the affects. Thrills are sought, and, when the object or activity ceases to provide such rewards, the pressure of affect promiscuity forces liquidation of affect investment and the renewal of the incessant quest for a particular level of excitement. When there is such excitement promiscuity with respect to the sexual life, the individual may be forced into sexual promiscuity despite strong ties of enjoyment and tenderness experienced in the intimacy of more enduring love and marital relationships. When there is such excitement promiscuity with respect to the intellectual life, the individual may be forced into becoming a dilettante by virtue of his craving for novelty, which does not permit him to tolerate the boredom which is sometimes the price of the continuing commitment of the specialist.

We have so far considered alcoholic intoxication and sexuality as vehicles for the minimizing of the inhibition of shame and self-contempt as well as other affects. Let us now examine other circumstances in which the individual resorts to the overt expression of suppressed affect, rather than to its complete suppression or rather than to counter-action against the source of the inhibited affect.

Displacement of affect: a generalization of Freud's concept

Displacement of affect is one such circumstance. Freud sensitized us to the importance of the displacement of both fear and anger. We wish to generalize this concept since it seems clear that whenever any affect, positive or negative, must be suppressed, for whatever reason, and whenever such overt suppression produces an intolerable intensification of this affect, that appropriate objects will be sought upon which the suppressed affect can be displaced and overtly expressed.

Freud made it quite clear that if anger could not be safely expressed against a superior, it might be displaced with less risk against an inferior. He also showed us what is less obvious, in his classic examination of a phobia in a five-year-old: if little

Hans could not show his fear of his father to his father or to himself, he might openly express his fear displaced to a horse.

Let us now examine the same mechanism with respect to shame and self-contempt. If I have been humiliated by someone whom I hate, my pride may not permit me to openly show my feelings of humiliation in his presence lest my defeat be further exaggerated and his victory become complete. But if afterwards my self-contempt deepens, by virtue of its overt suppression when it was first experienced, then I may be forced either to provoke contempt from a person before whom I may more easily show my humiliation or to find some other audience for the avowal of my humiliation.

Our earlier analysis of *l'homme escalier* has focused on the fantasies of revenge and counter-humiliation provoked by insult under such circumstances. These are important affects provoked by enforced humiliation, and we will consider them at length under the power strategy, and as this classic situation was analyzed by Dostoevsky. Now we wish rather to emphasize a neglected type of displacement—the displacement of the oppressor and the vicarious overt show of humiliation which it permits.

The resort to alcohol, which permits either the open avowal of self-contempt and/or the picking of a fight with a strange adversary who will defeat and humiliate one, vicariously, is one way in which such displacement operates. The channeling of a humiliating defeat into sexual experience which degrades and humiliates is another instance of displaced, vicarious humiliation. Alcohol and sex, though both permit the emergence of suppressed affect, are not, however, necessarily restricted to the function of enabling specific displacement in which a substitute object is sought as a vehicle for affect which had to be suppressed in a particular situation.

Apart from alcohol and sexuality there are numerous ways of seeking vicarious outlets for the display of any inhibited affect. Anna Freud has described a governess whose entire life style could be understood as the vicarious living of her life through her identifications with the children she cared for, and through her identification with her friends. Our concern at the moment, however, is more specific. It is to trace the displacement of either insult, humiliation or both to more acceptable oppressors and more propitious circumstances for the avowal and display of feelings of humiliation.

We have seen children who, having suffered humiliation at the hands of one parent, respond with an outburst of defiant anger toward that parent, and then seek out the other parent before whom they hang their head in shame and literally ask to be spanked and further humiliated. A child humiliated by a bully before whom he is too proud to show his feelings will hang his head in shame before his loving mother. A husband humiliated by his boss may avow his full sense of defeat only to his wife. In these latter cases the vicarious experience appears to be limited to the feeling of humiliation without the necessity of a vicarious oppressor. Frequently, however, this is more apparent than real. The recital of the insult to the sympathetic listener frequently includes such magnification of the original oppression that it may be regarded at the least as a thoroughly revised and expanded edition of the original outrage. Not uncommonly the insulted needs no further audience but withdraws from punitive combat to lick the wounds to his pride privately. Again this is vicarious expression of humiliation when it occurs after defiance or apparent indifference to the antagonist, but it may also contain magnification of the insult which provides a vicarious oppression greater than the original affront.

Magnification need not, of course, result in displacement. It may lead to such an intensification of the humiliation, contempt and anger that there is a direct counter-attack on the provocateur.

Vicarious, displaced humiliation frequently is shown in an unusual sensitivity to insult. The individual who fights his real oppressors tooth and nail may nonetheless hang his head in shame and self-contempt frequently over the slightest affront to his dignity. The smallest sign of failure on his own part may become the occasion for vituperative self-contempt, magnified and displaced by virtue of its suppression in the face of original insult. It has too often been supposed that the suppression of anger is necessarily the primary problem in the handling of humiliation. In the case of those who are too proud to be humiliated and who *are* capable of responding to insult with anger against the antagonist, it is the muffled feelings of humiliation which are magnified and ultimately cry out for open avowal. It also of course happens that the defeated one shows his humiliation but suppresses his anger, which later increases in intensity and presses for expression.

This over-sensitivity to insult may lead to open displaced self-contempt to even small signs of slight or indifference by the other. The same individual who would try to destroy one who tried to humiliate him will vicariously complain bitterly that he has been humiliated by someone who did not say hello to him, when that one might have been so involved in a conversation with a friend that he did not see the easily wounded one. It is possible for such sensitivity to be openly displayed either to the self or to others, because, although the self may be injured by such apparent indifference, it does not appear to be such a total defeat for the self as would be involved in openly avowing self-contempt before someone who is obviously intent on humiliating one.

Just as it may be safer to vent anger on an inferior rather than on a superior, there are numerous critical differences between situations which make it more or less tolerable to the self to openly acknowledge and avow its humiliation. There are important idiosyncrasies in respect to the differential conditions under which the individual must hide his humiliation and the conditions under which it may be possible to show these feelings even if somewhat painful, and so permit the displaced overt expression of shame and self-contempt.

Thus, it has been noted frequently that children who are aggressive in the presence of their parents are quite well-behaved at school, or with strangers. It is equally commonplace that husbands and wives may have better manners in company than when they are at home by themselves. In both cases, strangers restrain both the behavior that might lead to shame, guilt or contempt and the open expression of whatever humiliation might have been provoked by the stranger. The child is not only on his good behavior lest he invoke reprimand which might humiliate him. He is more likely to take reprimand or even suggestions from a stranger relatively gracefully with a minimum of crying, anger or hanging the head in shame, because he cannot tolerate what he considers public humiliation. When this child returns home he may give vent to anger, to distress, to shame and to self-contempt, full of complaint about the outrages to which he had to submit; or he may hide these outrages and give displaced displays of tantrum and humiliation to the slightest hint of parental control.

Conversely, the child who is held under such a tight rein at home that he is not permitted the luxury of sulking in humiliation, but required immediately to mend his ways without expression of either distress, anger, or shame or self-contempt may express all of these suppressed affects outside the home in his interactions with peers, teachers or strangers. Both extreme psychopathy or the avowal of shame and self-contempt or both are occasionally noted among children and adolescents who are model children at home.

Effects of intimacy on the avowal or suppression of shame—humiliation and self-contempt—disgust; consequences for intimacy

The same dynamic appears among adults. Husbands and wives may have impeccable company manners, neither giving nor taking offense even under provocation. The rude guest receives the other cheek, but the head is not hung in shame, lest the guest experience the discomfort of knowing he has insulted his host. After the dinner party the offended one may openly avow his deep shame as well as his vicariously expressed anger at the guest's thoughtlessness.

Less frequently, the individual cannot tolerate the avowal of humiliation to his mate. Particularly is this likely to be the case when the mate tries or is believed by the other to try to humiliate the other. In such a case the suppressed humiliation may be carried to the office or to friends and either confessed, properly identified as to source, or displaced to a new source which is more tolerable than the original source even though painful. Thus a husband humiliated by his wife, whom he will not permit the satisfaction of realizing how much he has been hurt, may be too readily wounded by his boss towards whom he either expresses his displaced humiliation or further displaces both experiences onto yet another associate towards whom he has a sufficiently positive relationship to express his wounded pride, either directly through reference back to his wife and boss, or again indirectly and vicariously so that he is easily offended by what he takes to be an instance of unusual thoughtlessness on the part of an associate who is ordinarily friendly.

It should be noted that the confession and open avowal of humiliation in the presence of a sympathetic other not only presupposes intimacy but also deepens it. The mutual avowal of past humiliations can produce a tie that binds. At the social level, too, the power of the oppressed has come from the mutuality of avowed humiliation. "You have nothing to lose but your chains" is a modern statement of the ancient covenant of martyrs, Christian and otherwise.

Minority groups who must suppress both anger and humiliation in face-to-face interaction with the majority group characteristically find substitute oppressors. The American Negroes who live in the South in some cases displace both anger and humiliation to safer oppressors, by shifting first to the cognitive level away from the action level and by shifting the source of oppression to members of their own group or to other minority groups rather than the majority group. On the other hand, affect on the cognitive level may be as threatening, and for some even more threatening, than on the action level.

Intimate relationships sometimes begin in a mutual confession of feelings of inadequacy, shame and self-contempt. Indeed the test of another person's feelings may take the form of his reaction to the avowal of shame. One of the most critical changes in the status of romantic love, from the honeymoon to disenchantment, is that from the shared avowal of shame which is responded to with love, disbelief and a shared sense of outrage that anyone should have humiliated the beloved, to contempt for each other's inferiority, shame and avowed self-contempt and the defensive suppression of shame and self-contempt by each mate in response to disenchantment and possible humiliation by the other. When the idealized image of the other is shattered, mutual love and respect often turns to mutual contempt. Thereupon every vestige of inferiority, of shame and self-contempt must be suppressed and eventually expressed vicariously, if at all.

Whether humiliation is more easily tolerated at the hands of a stranger or intimate, whether in public or privately, whether from a superior or inferior or equal, whether from within the self or from another person, whether the other intends to humiliate or does it unintentionally, whether the source is in an area where one feels competent or in area in which one is totally ignorant, whether it is because another is truly superior or because he is not superior but acts arrogantly, whether it is because there are invidious comparisons or because no one pays any attention—whether it is one or another or some or all of these conditions depends upon the whole affect matrix in which humiliation has developed. One or another of such alternative conditions may sufficiently intensify or attenuate shame so that one condition is the goad which forces incomplete suppression, and its alternative provides an outlet for vicarious expression of the intensified negative affect. The complex mixtures of other positive and negative affects as these interact with shame and contempt are critical in such ultra-labile equilibria.

Humiliation must often be suppressed not only because the other is hostile but because he is loving and beloved. Thus, husbands and wives and friends and associates may be forced into the suppression of humiliation and into its vicarious avowal not because the other is hostile but because the other idealizes one or is dependent on one. A mother or a father may feel constrained to hide inferiority or immorality because his child either idealizes him or depends on his show of strength or both. An individual ordinarily overwhelmed with feelings of guilt or shame or self-contempt may indeed find new inner resources with which to build a strong personality because he knows that his child must have such support or because he thinks that he could not tolerate the disrespect of his child who has idealized him. Such a parent may borrow strength from such demands, but he may also find such demands so oppressive that the suppressed humiliation renders him extraordinarily vulnerable to vicarious humiliation with others. Such a mother may be forced into fantasies of prostitution by way of relief from mother idolatry which she cannot sustain indefinitely.

The over-idealized role as a source of shame—humiliation or self-contempt—disgust which must be displaced

More generally, the over-idealized role and its strain are ubiquitous. The feelings of shame or guilt or self-contempt must constantly be suppressed lest the mask of the actor fall from the face. There are no roles, in any society, which do not sometimes or for some individuals create acute awareness of discrepancy between the demands of the role and one's ability to meet these demands.

Goffman's *The Presentation of the Self in Everyday Life* spells out the sense in which the total social enterprise is a play of actors on a stage before an audience. The self is, we think, much more than a concatenation of assumed roles, more or less well played before other actors who happen also to sometimes play the role of the audience. Nonetheless, the self is to *some* extent an actor in a play in which he is not always perfectly cast.

To the extent to which his ineptness in playing his role evokes shame or guilt or self-contempt, each actor is further constrained to hide these feelings lest he be unmasked. The husband who is not a model husband, the wife who is not a model wife, the father who is not a good father, the mother who is not a good mother, the educator who cannot know as much as he would like or thinks he should know, the student who fails to understand or wishes to play rather than to study, the soldier who does not want to kill or who wishes to run away, the doctor who cannot save his patient, the psychiatrist who increases the suffering of a neurotic, the judge who is not certain the law he applies is just or that he is himself without sin, the executive or business man who finds his competition overwhelming or the ethics of the market place troubling, the artist who is not sure of his creative powers or of the significance of the way of life he has chosen, the politician who is not certain he can lead or, if he can, where to lead those who will follow him, the priest who is not sure of his own saintliness or of God's existence—all of these are actors who do not know their lines perfectly or who cannot speak them with complete conviction.

Because of this, shame, guilt or self-contempt must not be

displayed, lest all be lost. Such actors are forever vulnerable to the lure of abandoning the mask and crying out their humiliation. Failing this, they will detect vicarious grounds for the avowal of these feelings. Still others are caught by their too-complete commitment to a role so that they suffer excessive specialization of identity with its eventual satiation and alienation from other aspects of the self. Others may be caught by role diffusion, being cast in so many different roles that they have lost the sense of identity which might have been found in a more integrated and specialized way of life.

Endopsychic shame–humiliation and contempt–disgust

We have stressed the insult-humiliation sequence which originates in relatively recent interpersonal relationships, which proceeds from an outside source to inner magnification and eventually returns to vicarious external expression. Much more subtle and confusing to both victims is the vicarious expression of humiliation and contempt which is ultimately endopsychic in origin. If the individual is host to a severe inner critic, whose origin is lost in the mists of time and who now speaks with his own authority, the self which is his primary target may find his strictures much too harsh to hear.

He responds with pride and not a little defiance to the inner critic, keeping him at a distance by insisting on the sanctity of the self, so far as that inner voice is concerned. But such a self wearies of its unequal struggle with itself and readily succumbs to criticism from others, or from their indifference, through which the incompletely suppressed insult and humiliation from within may be vicariously experienced in high intensity, but with somewhat less pain than if it were the voice of the inner critic.

Such relief as the vicarious expression affords under these circumstances is likely to be brief, because of the continuing presence of the hated inner voice. More permanent relief from his tyranny requires that he be permitted to speak and to be heard, until he can speak no more or until he has lost the power to humiliate.

When an individual with such a personality structure is forced to directly confront the internal oppressor, and to become aware of the full measure of contempt in which he holds his other self, the dialogue of the two selves has the characteristic unrelenting ferocity of civil war. Two caricatures of the self now compete openly for permanent possession of the self. One is a derogating, unrelenting critic, and the other is an arrogant affirmer of the glory of the self. Both selves have been hardened by the protective armor of mutual distrust to such an extent that there can be no experience of unity within such a personality. Only if neutralization of both self-contempt and arrogance can be achieved through sustained painful confrontation of self before self can can civil war surrender to self-government. Failing this, the arrogant self will be forever vulnerable to vicarious insult and humiliation from without.

Expression of shame—humiliation and self-contempt—disgust through abstractions

Finally, the quest for vicarious expression of shame and self-contempt may shift away from interpersonal relationships to the cognitive level. The oppressor may be displaced and sought at the cognitive level, in quite remote ways. "Life" or the "human condition" may be cast in the role of the oppressor before which one can abase oneself and give full vicarious satisfaction to the intolerable humiliation suffered at the hands of a despised or feared antagonist.

Cynicism in general may function not only as an outlet for counter-contempt but as vehicle for expressing some of the self-contempt generated by the presumably oppressive conditions under which men live. In such a case the individual asserts simultaneously that human beings in general are no good and that he himself is no good.

As we will presently see, the repeated experience of humiliation at the hands of a self-righteous parent who casts himself in the role of the representative and defender of the norm of civilization may encourage a masochistic displacement of oppression, and humiliation, to the ideological realm of objective norms towards which the individual can abase himself without total surrender to the one who originally imposed the norms. Such self-flagellation can be understood as vicarious oppression and humiliation in which the internalized norms act as the vicarious oppressors, and self-abasement becomes the vicarious avowal of humiliation.

The same dynamic appears in art. The dramatist and the novelist may displace the original oppressor to the hated antagonists of his plays and novels and displace his avowals of self-contempt to the hapless victims of these antagonists.

So much for displacement as a technique of expressing and so reducing feelings of humiliation which can neither be counteracted directly against the oppressor nor completely suppressed.

AFFECT MAGNIFICATION

Let us now consider affect magnification as a stimulus to the minimizing of affect inhibition through evoking the open avowal of humiliation.

By affect magnification we refer to any systematic increase in intensity and/or duration of affect, with or without suppression of the overt expression of affect. Thus, an individual may grow more and more angry as he expresses his anger in words and action until finally he has exhausted both himself and his adversary. But he may also suppress the outward display of anger and yet also continue to grow more and more angry until it erupts into an explosive display. Affect magnification can feed equally well on expression as on suppression, and affects can also be minimized and reduced either through overt expression or through suppression. There is no necessary relationship between expression and intensity or duration of affects, or between suppression and intensity or duration of affects. We shall concern ourselves in this section primarily with affect magnification and suppression. We have already examined displacement as a technique of reducing affect which has been magnified to the point of intolerability.

Magnification is one of the prime reasons for the vicarious expression of humiliation. After insult and incomplete suppression of humiliation the inability to suppress self-contempt or shame can be reinforced by a circular intensification of humiliation and the nature of the insult as this is re-experienced again and again upon review. The smouldering ashes of humiliation recruit images and re-interpretations of the antagonist so that he grows more and more offensive. As this happens, the embers of shame and self-contempt are fanned into hot flames which in turn recruit cognitive reappraisals that provide fresh fuel for the magnification of the negative affect. Just as individuals fall in love at a distance, so may they fall in hate with one who has humiliated them. The mutual, circular magnification of humiliation and insult following humble withdrawal from insult is a prime condition for producing a level of humiliation such that the individual is forced into the vicarious avowal of his feelings. It, of course, also happens that the individual fortified by righteous indignation and incensed by the monster of his own imagination now returns to vanquish his original antagonist.

The painter who destroys his work and the gambler "who takes a bath"

We will now examine magnification as it provokes the direct expression of suppressed affect. This phenomenon is centuries old, but it has not been adequately conceptualized. We refer to a species of masochistic behavior the aim of which is to increase negative affect to such a point that it produces an explosive overt eruption of affect which ultimately thereby reduces itself.

Consider the following examples:

A painter has labored long on a canvas—it has been difficult but he has made progress up to a certain point. Then everything he does seems to be wrong. The painting goes from bad to worse, and the painter, feeling more and more incompetent and disgusted with himself, struggles against the feeling of hopelessness until at a critical moment he dips his brush into his palette indiscriminately and disfigures his painting in an explosion of anger and humiliation. The feeling of humiliation is profound and complete. Ultimately he recovers and begins again.

A professional gambler is successful for many years because he has learned everything there is to know about horseracing or the stock market. His self-discipline is not unlike that of yester-year's sterner martyrs. He skillfully avoids all the common snares of his profession. He arises early every morning the better to prepare for the struggle with uncertainty which daily tries his soul. His immersion in and concentration on the data which chart the past performances of horses or market investments is total. Finally, he confronts the moment of truth and somehow out of the blooming, buzzing confusion of possibilities forges a decision to which he commits himself with the resources which he has slowly accumulated by exactly the same risk-taking, day by day for many years. When he sustains an unexpected and heavy loss, he becomes a man of steel. Knowing the possible impact of a wildfire of shame, anger, distress and fear on his judgment, he may take a brief holiday until his dangerous negative affect has burned itself out at a safe distance from the competitive arena. When he has assimilated the chagrin and anger and humiliation of what was either his bad luck or his poor judgment or both, he re-enters the arena to recoup his losses. Such threats are part of the way of life of the professional risk-taker. He becomes a professional by meeting and coping with such challenges to his self-esteem and to his resources.

Despite iron self-discipline among professional gamblers, there are few who have not experienced what is known in the profession as "taking a bath." If the loss is both apparently un-merited and exceptionally heavy, as when a horse wins a race easily, as expected, but is disqualified for interefering with another contestant in the race who would not have won in any event, then the gambler may succumb to the classic trap of an attempted quick recoup. Such an attempt at undoing the damage which has been sustained ordinarily prompts the defeated gambler to make a still heavier investment in what appears to be an exceptionally safe venture. He is prepared either to make a very large investment on a venture which promises a very slight return, or a small investment on a venture which promises a very large return.

At the race track this means that he will invest in a top-heavy favorite to come in at least in third place, seeking to recoup his loss by doubling his bet. Or he may invest a small amount of money in an extreme outsider who will return such favorable odds that he will recoup his loss with relatively little risk of money. He is classically driven to excess of boldness or caution, or to oscillate between such extremes, whenever his negative affect begins to exert monopolistic influence on his judgment— when he can tolerate loss no more and is driven to undo his loss and recoup immediately. If this strategy is successful and he does immediately recoup his loss, the affect storm subsides, and he vows never again to permit himself to be seduced by his inability to tolerate his own negative affect. The next day he is again entirely in command of the situation.

The phenomenon of "taking a bath" depends upon the failure of the reparative strategy. If the gambler, having invested very heavily on an apparently safe venture in his attempt at a quick reversal of loss, should now a second time suffer an unexpected and in his view unmerited loss, he may now be overwhelmed with shame, with self-contempt, with anger and with distress, compounded not only by the new loss but by the breakdown of his self-control and his deteriorating judgment. It is at just such a moment that he is a candidate for "taking a bath," which will "clean" him and purify his soul by bathing him in total defeat. He is driven now to magnify his humiliation so that he may wallow in it that eventually he may be purified.

At this point he will take all of his money, which it may have taken him years of hard work to accumulate, and invest it in what appears, even to him, to be at best only a remote possibility, in order to "get it over with." If he wins now, which he regards as improbable although desirable, he will not only recoup his losses but make a very large profit. He will have turned defeat into the greatest of his victories. If he loses, which he expects, and in part hopes he will, his humiliation will be magnified, his defeat total.

He resorts to such an extreme, self-defeating tactic because he feels he cannot reduce his feelings of humiliation and loss otherwise than by magnifying them so that he is utterly consumed and finally purified, "cleaned," "bathed." It is as though he said to himself, "If I have been stupid, I may as well go the whole way." After this complete loss many gamblers report a feeling of peace, that the struggle is over, that they have hit bottom and can suffer no longer. Some gamblers, however, do not attain the nirvana state until several hours later, after having immersed themselves completely in their despair.

Psychological addictions; smoking

Consider next the phenomenon of psychological addiction. By psychological addiction we mean a commitment to the familiar which has the following characteristics.

A particular psychological object or set of objects activates intense positive affect when it is present, and intense negative affect when it is absent. This needs to be qualified, inasmuch as it also activates intense positive affect even when absent if the future presence of the object or the individual's past commerce with the object is entertained in awareness, and it activates intense negative affect to the extent that the individual is aware at the moment of the possibility of its absence in the future, or of its having been absent. Further, any absence of the object becomes the occasion for awareness of the object.

Let us consider the plight of any individual who attempts to free himself of a psychological addiction, e.g., of smoking cigarettes. The motive for attempting such a breakthrough is not our present concern. Let us assume that, for reasons of health or because of self-contempt from the inability of the self to modulate the habit, an individual embarks on a program of stopping his smoking of cigarettes. As in the case of the painter and gambler, great self-discipline is required, and the one who has the strength to initiate the renunciation of his addiction ordinarily is capable of withstanding the painful longing and shame of the initial period of abstinence.

The withdrawal symptoms ordinarily include not only distress, ambivalent longing and shame, but also anger and fear and humiliation at the impotence of the self in not being complete master of its own destiny. If this complex of negative affects can be tolerated through the long initial period when it is likely to grow in intensity and become increasingly difficult to tolerate, eventually these negative affects will burn themselves out and recruit supportive auxiliary positive affects by virtue of the apparent ability of the self to withstand the temptations of backsliding.

If, however, the negative affect accelerates too steeply to be tolerated, so that the individual is confronted with the prospect of an indefinitely increasing intensity of longing and suffering, he may become panicky and humiliated at his inability to control or tolerate his own withdrawal affects. At such a moment humiliation, fear and distress seem to be accelerating in intensity, with no end in sight. He feels his longing to be endless and is frightened by the prospect of unending and accelerating misery and humiliation. It is an altogether intolerable state, and he must act to reduce it at once. If he breaks his resolve, he may reduce the misery and fear of infinite longing, but at the same time he knows he will increase his shame and self-contempt because of his surrender. As this conflict grows in intensity and intolerability, he reaches a moment when he cries "Enough!"—and greedily and ashamedly surrenders to his longing.

But he smokes not one but many cigarettes, one after another until his defeat and humiliation are complete. He will wallow in his surrender and degradation, doing whatever is necessary to guarantee complete humiliation, much as the painter destroys his canvas and the gambler needlessly wastes his entire reserves. As in these cases, he acts so that he will magnify and accelerate his feelings of humiliation because they have already become intolerable, and they can be reduced only by first magnifying them until they reach their peak intensity.

The case of Jack

Finally, consider the case of a child, Jack, whom I treated. Because of the birth of a sibling, Jack had experienced the classic fall from grace. His golden age of unlimited love and attention from his mother and father came suddenly to an end one day with the birth of another child. Jack was angry, confused and humiliated by his toothless rival. By the time I saw him, he had become an intensely angry, defeated agent provocateur who, at the slightest provocation attacked and denounced himself and others with complete abandon.

For example, when I engaged him in a game of ball, all went well until he made the mistake of failing to catch the ball, or, having caught it, dropped it. At this moment his head dropped in shame. In rapid succession he bit his hand savagely and then hit me. When this failed to evoke a reply he returned to hitting himself until he cried himself into utter exhaustion and defeat, with his head hung low. In a while, however, he was ready to resume the game.

The details of this case and the therapy which was successful in changing him we will present later. We are concerned now with the dynamics of his masochistic self-humiliation. As an aftermath of the trauma of the birth of the sibling, Jack oscillated between attempted self-control over his anger, disappointment, humiliation and self-conscious magnification of his negative affect by explosive attacks against others and himself, which would evoke punishment. These increased his rage and humiliation until it reached such a frenzy that it subsided, leaving him exhausted but free of the intolerable jealousy and humiliation.

It should be noted that the slightest provocation was enough to initiate shame, which in turn initiated a set of tactics designed to accelerate and magnify what was initially much less intense humiliation. When, for example, he dropped the ball, his initial shame reaction was moderate; if this had occurred to a child with a different past history, it would have subsided rather quickly. But for Jack this momentary shame was similar to the shame of the gambler who has unexpectedly and unjustly just lost his second investment after trying to recoup his first loss. It was experienced both as intolerable and as growing in intolerability, so that it had to be made even more intolerable very quickly to reduce the whole expected sequence of humilating experiences. The slightest experience of shame became in effect a sign of more humiliation to come, and so Jack would take the initiative and accelerate the process rather than wait passively for the dreaded magnification.

Masochistic self-humiliation: a summary

In all of these instances, and others similar in structure to these, the individual is caught in the grip of humiliation and other negative affects in such a way that he must not only openly avow these feelings to reduce them, but he must also do whatever is necessary to magnify them in intensity and duration so that they are finally spent, their fire burned out. Sometimes, as in the case of Jack and in the breaking of the addiction of smoking, this represents a short circuiting of a sequence whereby the accelerating negative affects are seen as inevitable in any event. Sometimes, as in the case of the painter and the gambler, it seems to the individual to be possible to avoid further intensification of humiliation if restraint can be exercised by the individual, but he feels he cannot exercise this restraint because he cannot tolerate the slow decline of humiliation.

In contrast, the smoker who is suffering withdrawal affects is more likely to feel that these will simply grow in intensity and intolerability independent of his behavior, and so he chooses to break his resolve, by which he reduces the suffering of endless longing but immediately pays the price of intensified shame at his loss of control. He then magnifies his humiliation by smoking one after another cigarette so that his defeat is total and he wallows in his loss of control.

For the individual who cannot tolerate the feeling of humiliation either because it promises only to increase in intensity and never to end, or because it promises to be relieved but too slowly for him to tolerate its afterglow, there must be resort to heroic measures to speed the process—to accelerate both the anabolism and catabolism of shame. Like the dental patient who inflicts pain on himself to mask the lesser pain but greater anxiety of being the passive victim of oppression, he is caught between two evils and chooses what he regards as the lesser.

Whenever human beings fail to learn to tolerate their own negative affects, they may be forced into the masochistic strategy of reduction through magnification. This inherent vulnerability to masochism argues strongly for the importance of the rewarding socialization of affects and against the punitive socialization of affects. The punitive socialization of affects has as one of its consequences the ever present imminence of an intolerable experience of rapidly accelerating negative affect which overwhelms. In the rewarding socialization of shame, self-contempt, and the other negative affects, the individual's experience with overwhelming negative affect is minimized, and he is taught techniques of coping with unavoidable negative affect by neutralization and counteraction.

THE GENERAL IMAGE OF POWER

The human being inevitably develops the strategies of maximizing positive affect, of minimizing negative affect, of minimizing affect inhibition and finally of maximizing his power to implement these strategies. He wishes not only to maximize his experience of excitement and enjoyment but to be able to guarantee that he has the power to continue to do so. He wishes not only to avoid the experience of shame, of fear, of distress and of anger, but also to be able to guarantee his power to continue to do so. He wishes not only to minimize the inhibition of the feelings of shame or fear or anger which he cannot successfully avoid or suppress, but to be able to guarantee his power to continue to do so.

This is to say, whenever human beings wish ends in themselves, they sooner or later recruit the auxiliary wishes to be able to command the means, whatever they may be, that are necessary to achieve those ends. On the face of it this would appear to be a strategy entirely complementary to the ends that it serves. Frequently this is so, and it is entirely appropriate that human beings become as interested in the means to ends as they are in the ends themselves. Indeed, without such auxiliary investments of affect, the fires of affect metabolism would be banked and the major affect strategies would wither. For example, if one wants much excitement but does not want to do anything to achieve such experience, that is, if one does not develop the General Image of power with respect to excitement, then the strategy of maximizing positive affect remains at the level of wish, where one hopes for propitious circumstances but cannot actively pursue excitement.

We regard the General Image of power as one that all human beings in all societies will sooner or later inevitably develop. We say sooner or later because of the possible delay in the generation of such an Image by virtue of interference from some of the other General Images. Thus, a monopolistic interest in positive affect as such might lead to an idyllic but primitive way of life, in which life was so easy and so rewarding that the investment of affect in the means of guaranteeing the future never developed to any significant extent. Further, the conditions of life might be so harsh that only the reduction of present suffering and negative affect monopolized the consciousness of an entire community. Under such conditions neither the maximizing of positive affect nor the power to do so might develop as influential strategies. Not even the power to minimize future suffering would be pursued if the present were sufficiently harsh and demanding.

The idea of God

Indeed, the delay in the development of a generalized Image of power may be seen in the gradualness of the historical evolution of the idea of a single God. In the beginning there were multiple gods, because the multiplicity of human wants and demands competed chaotically for the attention of man. Now he wanted excitement and enjoyment and then he wanted relief from fear and distress. Different gods were generated as each need arose. Before man could conceive of the idea of a single, omniscient, omnipotent God, he had first to conceive the ideal of himself as all-powerful, as one who could maximize his positive affects, minimize his negative affects, minimize his affect inhibition, and maximize his power to achieve each of these strategies.

After attaining such General Images, he was ready to appreciate both the infinity of his craving and the finitude of his power. He craves perpetual excitement and joy and everlasting freedom from fear, from distress, from shame, from anger. For these he requires immortality and omniscience, the endless power which would guarantee that life would meet the heart's desire.

The idea of God is a derivative construct. If and when man first conceives the power strategy, and then surrenders to fate and renounces the idea that he can help himself as much as he wishes, and that his parents can, and that his society can—it is a short step to the creation of one God who can and will. It is for this reason that secular revolutionary movements must destroy the image of God and restore omniscience and omnipotence to the new government to guarantee the complete commitment of the governed to the state and its revolutionary governors.

The idea of progress

Given the development of the power strategy, each of the other strategies could then be pursued with increased commitment. After the idea of God came the development of another derivative of the power strategy, the idea of progress, with its derivatives—the conquest of nature and the rights of man. The control of nature made possible by the development of science and technology and the great rise in the standard of living in modern industrialized societies have not entirely attenuated either religious or utopian ideology.

Monopolistic image of power: self-defeating concentration on the means rather than the end

If the three major affect strategies wither without the power strategy, neither are they maximized easily when the power strategy becomes monopolistic. Nothing is more commonplace than the self-defeating investment in the means to any end. In the attempt to guarantee the power to maximize positive affect or to minimize negative affect or affect inhibition, positive affect may be surrendered, negative affect maximized, affect inhibition exaggerated. The excitement of the quest for knowledge can be transformed into the drudgery of scholarship and the shame of the scholar lest his knowledge be incomplete or found wanting. The enjoyment of intimacy between parents and children can be surrendered by the effort of the breadwinner to guarantee the economic future of that family against the humiliation of poverty. The enjoyment of the intimacy of family can be contaminated by attempts to guarantee that children not shame their parents but grow into certain kinds of adults. In the name of minimizing negative affect, it is possible to distress a child excessively by attempting to guarantee an invulnerability to future distress by hardening a child, by teaching him to tolerate severe discipline. In the investment of affect in the acquisition of money, the universal means to ends of many kinds, original affective investments in ends in themselves may become liquidated or attenuated so that the pursuit of the means becomes an end in itself.

The transformation of means into ends is a perennial liability of human beings because affect which is the major psychological currency of the human being is the same affect whether it is invested in ends or means. Excitement about the means is the same excitement as it is experienced at the attainment of the end.

To the extent to which the means to any end is extended in time while the end itself is brief in duration or continually moved into the future, the individual must be more and more engaged by the means in which his most enduring affects are daily invested. A man becomes most of all what he is trying to do. Despite the importance and the ubiquity of means-end behavior, the corruption of ends by means is a continuing liability generated by the General Image of power, which engages affects in the quest for guaranteeing the future maximizing of positive affects and the future minimizing of negative affects, regardless of the present cost of such preparations. At the national level, in many countries we find the same wholesale sacrifice of a generation to future generations in the name of rapid modernization.

Perhaps the most serious unintended consequences of the monopolistic influence of the power Image are those which proceed from the wish to minimize affect inhibition. Consider the circumstance in which socialization is exploitative and repressive. In such a case the parent imposes serious restraints on the maximizing of positive affects by forbidding particular behaviors which may delight the child. If the child then shows his feelings of distress and humiliation at this constraint, he is further constrained to hide and suppress these negative affects. "Stop crying, don't sulk, lift up your head" are directives which may follow rapidly upon the initial constraints. The machinery of affect suppression has been set in motion. The price for failure to suppress negative affect is as severe as the sanctions invoked to constrain the original behavior. The child can be no less disgusting to the parent because he cried and sulked and hung his head in shame than because he was too noisy and flamboyant. And so humiliation and distress are heaped upon humiliation and distress, except that the second dyad of negative affects must be muffled and hidden from the offended parent.

When any negative affect is produced by another person in a position of control, then denied overt expression by the controlling person who produced the affect and yet cannot be completely suppressed, it is likely to become magnified and cry out for expression. As such magnification occurs, the oppressor grows more oppressive in imagination, and the humiliation is deepened.

The general power strategy which emerges under such conditions depends upon the duration and severity of such suffering. The minimal power strategy which will develop will be to violate the constraint on the suppressed negative affect. In this case the tears that are held back with difficulty, and the shame with which the head is held up with difficulty are both permitted free expression. An otherwise model child, who has long accepted severe restraints both on his exuberance and on the expression of his negative affects, may on the occasion of a slight increase in demands on him, or on the occasion of a sudden relaxation of demands for restraint, dissolve in tears of shame. The open avowal of humiliation and distress can be deeply rewarding to the individual who has had to struggle lest they escape his tight control. Such a minimal power strategy may produce fantasies in which such breakdown of the control over humiliation occurs.

If the recovery of communion is what is critical for such a child, the emphasis on breaking through the original taboo on behavior may be minimized, but the wish to openly avow the humiliation and distress without surrendering the love and respect of the parent may become the dominant power strategy. "Love me even though I sulk" is one such formula. A variant is "Love me because I am so miserable and ashamed." The fantasies of such power strategies include a tearful reunion of the relenting parent and the tearful, ashamed child. Such a strategy may arise either from the imagination of the child or from his memory of actual reconciliations with his parent who was equally anxious to re-establish communion after having ruptured the relationship with his child through his excessive harshness.

The fantasy of running away from home

If the power strategy under these circumstances includes also a revenge component, the fantasy which is generated will have the child turn the tables on the parent as well as reverse the harsh judgment before both parties are united in tearful reconciliation. The classic example is the fantasy of running away from home. By this the parent is brought to his knees in sorrow, self-reproach, forgiveness and, above all, love, longing and a new respect for the missing one who is now appreciated for the first time as the paragon that he is.

Mark Twain in *The Adventures of Tom Sawyer* portrayed the universal fantasy of the glorious flight and return of the oppressed, noble child. In such a fantasy the child wishes not only to be reunited with the parent and not only to minimize his past humiliation but also to minimize the power of the parent to humiliate him in the future. This is achieved by teaching the parent a truer appreciation of the child's worth by giving him a taste of what his loss would mean. Although this contains a component of revenge, this is nonetheless a relatively minor component since the ultimate aim is communion with mutual respect. Such a fantasy is a testament to the predominantly positive character of the parent-child relationship.

Royal birth, Cinderella and prophet-without-honor fantasies

As the experience of humiliation deepens and as the possibility of counter-action against the parent declines, unrelieved by balancing positive affects in the parent-child relationship, the imagination is likely to turn to the fantasy of royal birth. Here the child is still concerned with the love of the parent as well as with the parent's respect and the minimizing of the experience of humiliation. The fantasy that he was really the son of better parents offers some satisfaction in the derogation of his present parents compared with his real parents. It also elevates the child himself over his inferior present parents. Finally, it preserves a possible love object who can be loved without fear of humiliation.

The Cinderella fantasy we take to be a variant of this power strategy. At the adult level, the fantasy of the prophet who is without honor in his own country is another instance of a power strategy that is designed to minimize both humiliation and the inhibition of humiliation since the prophet experiences humiliation in his own country; but this is converted into a counter-humiliation by the honor which the more discriminating world outside his country lavishly bestows on him. It should be noted that in this circumstance the individual conceives that it is impossible for him to influence his oppressor directly; that the oppressor cannot be won over to either love or respect, and that he can at best only be counter-humiliated by the example of those who pay their respects to the prophet.

In all of these strategies the individual is trying not only to undo the humiliation but to recover the positive relationship which has been ruptured by the insult. This is true even in the fantasy of royal birth and the prophet without honor in his own country. In these latter cases the original relationship is surrendered and a vicarious positive relationship is sought.

Flaunting, reversal of roles and revenge

We will now consider a less benign consequence of the power strategy to minimize humiliation inhibition. Whenever this strategy operates exclusively, without benefit of leavening by the image of maximizing positive affects and when the only positive affects experienced are consequences of reducing his humiliation, expressing it or humiliating others, the individual is then caught up in the most deadly of human aims.

Depending upon the intensity and depth of humiliation, and the feelings of helplessness which grip him, the individual will struggle to express his humiliation, to undo humiliation, to turn the tables on his oppressor and at the extreme to destroy him to recover his power to deal with intolerable humiliation. The individual can be pushed into such a corner whenever humiliation looms large in socialization and is unrelieved by love or is reinforced by other negative affects.

The paranoid we suppose is created by a socialization in which both terror and contempt are exercised with a minimum of love. Excessive humiliation or contempt alone, without terror and without balancing positive affect, can create a humiliation power strategy this side of the paranoid posture. Let us now examine the varieties of humiliation power strategies which are unrelieved by love for the source of humiliation.

In these circumstances the individual characteristically has suffered at least a double restraint: he suppresses particular behavior which offends and also inhibits his humiliation and anger at this constraint. His minimal power strategy is to break through both of these constraints. He therefore does the shameful or disgusting act and wallows in his degradation, flaunting both the act and his self-contempt in the face of the oppressor. Such children delight in tormenting their oppressive parents by doing everything which they have been forbidden to do and at the same time take a perverse enjoyment from the exhibition of their own self-contempt.

As we will see in the case of Dostoevsky's "underground man," this strategy may remain underground because the individual is too fearful and too humiliated openly to avow his vengeful feelings, but it nonetheless represents his basic strategy even though he lacks the courage to translate the fantasy into open defiance. The overly submissive husband or wife may, with the help of alcohol, find the courage to disgrace his mate by flaunting behavior which particularly offends the other and at the same time flaunts the feeling of self-disgust, which also offends the other. The individual may compound his offense by sexual promiscuity which is conjointly offensive to the spouse, to the sex object and to the self.

The next stage in the power strategy has the aim of violating the constraint on shameful or disgusting behavior but also of freeing the self of the humiliation which was forced on the self by the original oppressor. The formula now is "I will do as I wish and I will *not* be ashamed of it, no matter what you say." Shameless, psychopathic behavior serves the function of defiance in such a bolder strategy only if the individual can free himself from the price of shame, or guilt or self-contempt.

In the early days of Psychoanalysis this was a common construction put upon Freud's discoveries. The individual was thought to be needlessly shackled by convention and that he was not mature until he could violate without guilt the outworn superego constraints inherited from his childhood. Groddeck in his *Book of the Id* defended the view that the emancipated human being should be able to fly in the face of pre-genital taboos without shame or remorse.

It is probable that some of the psychopathy of adolescence is motivated by such a power strategy, since the need to individuate the self from the parent may produce intolerable humiliation when the negative impact of the socialization process has not been sufficiently balanced by love and identification. If this strategy is generally inhibited, it may nonetheless press for occasional expression in the sexual life. In this case the aim is to indulge in the most shameless of sexual exploits without paying the price of shame or guilt.

As the oppressor grows more formidable and the role of positive affects diminishes even more, the power strategy takes the form of pure revenge and reversal of roles. The formula now is "You cannot humiliate or condemn me, but I can humiliate and condemn you." This is a classic reply to insult and is seen most clearly between children. When one has just called the other an insulting name, the other replies in kind—"*You* are a dirty thingumabob." In its adult form it is less obvious but may occupy the fantasies and energies of the insulted one for much of his life. No animal other than man is capable of so long sustaining a grudge or wounded pride, and a biding of time for the appropriate moment for turning the tables on the oppressor.

This strategy is not limited, however, to indirection and delay. It is seen frequently in disturbed marital relationships in which a cumulative score is kept by each party, and every attempt is made to settle accounts daily. Whenever this strategy is conceived but is somewhat inhibited in expression, it may seek occasional expression in the sexual life. When this happens, sexual excitement is generated only by the humiliation of the sex object. In contrast to the prior stategies it is not mutual degradation nor obscenity without shame which is the aim, but rather the reversal of roles in which the self achieves revenge by humiliating the humiliator or by feeling contempt for the condemnor.

Finally, when humiliation reaches a maximum, whether in fact or in the imagination of the oppressed one, and no relief is in sight and anger is recruited by the continuing high level of negative stimulation from the feelings of humiliation, it may appear to the individual that there is no alternative but to destroy the oppressor.

Such a strategy may be interfered with by a competing consideration, namely the fear of reprisal. As soon as the threat of
fear is reduced, we should expect the overt emergence of this
extreme strategy from those who have been humiliated and
terrorized to the breaking point. All the oppressed over the
centuries have at one time or another risen to slay their oppressors. We must expect that all those who have suffered chronic
humiliation will nurture a deep wish to humiliate the other, that
those who have suffered chronic fear will nurture a deep wish
to terrorize the other, that those who have suffered chronic distress must nurture an enduring wish to frustrate the other. When
these are combined in the form of an oppressor who conjointly
exploits and distresses as he humiliates and terrorizes—these are
the conditions in which we may expect the emergence of the
ultimate strategy which powers the blood baths of rebellion
and revolution.

Such a strategy ordinarily remains at the level of fantasy,
however, unless and until there is some reduction of fear and
some basis for hope of success in the minds of the revolutionary.
This is why revolutions characteristically appear when conditions
are improving. These are the times not only of hope but of the
reduction of terror for resistance to oppression. This is also why
in the present world-wide revolution, we may expect the emergence of counter-humiliation, counter-terror and counter-distress
in repayment of the former colonial powers for past suffering,
past terror and, above all, past humiliation.

We have previously contrasted shame and contempt as negative affects which differ in their ambivalence, and in their com-
pleteness and finality. Contempt, we argued, was total, complete
and final rejection in contrast to shame which was a partial,
incomplete and temporary barrier to positive affect. In this
section we have been dealing with affect compounds involving
a larger component of self-contempt than of shame. We see here
that the same kind of distinction that we drew between shame
and contempt can be drawn between contempt when it is balanced by love and contempt when it is reinforced by fear and
hate. When contempt is neutralized by positive affect, it has
radically different properties than when it is reinforced by anger
or terror. In the former case there is a way back to the object

as an object of love. In the latter, there is no way back other than defiance, reversal or destruction of the oppressor.

This is not to say that the one who has the former posture may not harbor an encapsulated kernel of hatred, nor that the one who has the latter posture may not harbor an encapsulated kernel of love—indeed they do, as a price of their renunciation of either hate or love. Nonetheless humiliation and love, and humiliation and hate or fear, are fundamentally different syndromes which produce disorders as distinct as depression and paranoia. We will return later to a closer examination of the combinations of shame and self-contempt with the positive affects in one class and with the other negative affects in the second great class of sets of feelings.

We have in this section restricted ourselves to a discussion of the more general properties of, and some relationships between, the four strategies of dealing with affect. We defer the more specific question of the individual's option of emphasizing one or another strategy, and the balance between these strategies within a particular individual. Different types of socialization characteristically favor maximizing of positive affect over minimizing of negative affect, or favor minimizing affect inhibition over maximizing power. Other types of socialization favor a more balanced set of strategies. We will consider these particular options later.

Chapter 20

Continuities and Discontinuities in the Impact of Humiliation: The Intrusion and Iceberg Models

In this and the following chapters on continuities and discontinuities in development, we shall discuss, in connection with the affects of shame—humiliation and contempt—disgust, certain general developmental trends which apply to all affects.

We shall describe the nature and development of affect theories (differing organizations of affective experiences), the nature of weak and strong affect theories, the basic models for affect theories in human beings and those elements of our theory of memory which are necessary to explain the development of these differing organizations of affective experiences.

Specific to the affects of shame—humiliation and contempt—disgust are the descriptions of what child-rearing practices may be considered rewarding socializations of these affects. Also specific to shame and contempt is the description of the dynamics of a common type of manic-depressive personality. Inasmuch as these dynamics are direct derivatives of the theory of memory, they illustrate the retardation of psychological theory which has resulted from the separation of the study of the "dynamic" and the study of the "cognitive" aspects of human function.

As in the preceding chapter, we shall again use the word humiliation as a generic term to include both the affects of shame—humiliation and contempt—disgust.

In the preceding chapter some of the universal consequences of the impact of humiliation on human beings have been considered. We wish now to consider some of the gross differences in the impact of humiliation. We will therefore examine the general structure and varying scope and influence of the affect

301

theories by which individuals organize their experiences of shame and contempt, and the continuities and discontinuities of the impact of such theories in development. How influential is humiliation in governing the personality, and does this influence vary or increase or decrease over time? We will defend the proposition that the pervasiveness of any affect theory at any moment in time is relatively independent of its influence over time.

THE BASIC MODELS OF AFFECT THEORY

We distinguish four types of interrelationships between affect theories at any moment in time and four types of interrelationships between affect theories across time. At a moment in time an affect theory may exemplify the monopolistic model, the intrusion model, the competition model or the integration model. Across time monopolism has the analog of the snowball model, intrusion has the analog of the iceberg model, competition has the analog of the coexistence model, and integration has the analog of the late bloomer model. These relationships hold for any type of affect theory, whatever the specific affect. We will in this chapter, and the following two chapters, however, limit our discussion to shame and contempt theories.

In the monopolistic theory, shame or self-contempt dominates the affective life of the individual. Its developmental analog, the snowball model, is the case in which early experience, whether monopolistic or not, continues to snowball and more and more dominates the personality. It is entirely possible for early monopolism not to snowball but to atrophy, and for an early minor, weak and uninfluential theory to gather strength over the years and snowball into a late monopolism.

In the intrusion model, shame theory is a minor element in the general structure of personality, but capable under specific, limited conditions of intruding and displacing dominant affects. In its analog across time, the iceberg model, the adult personality is vulnerable under specific, limited conditions to intrusions from the past, which are alien to the affective life of the adult. What intrudes from the past is not limited to what was intrusive in the child's personality. The shame theory which intrudes into adult life may have been a monopolistic theory in the life of this individual in his childhood. Further, there may be intrusive shame theories developed in adulthood for the first time which are alien to the dominant affect theories of the adult.

In the competition model, shame theory is one theory among others and is in perpetual competition with other theories for the interpretation and disposition of information. In its analog across time, the co-existence model, there is a relatively unstable equilibrium between the adult personality and the earlier personality with continuing competition between early and later types of belief and reaction to shame and contempt. Such a personality constantly surprises by its lability and swings from adult to childish responses to shame. It is also possible in the co-existence model that the early competition is simply maintained with some further strengthening of all the competitors. It is further possible that two monopolisms, one deriving from childhood and the other from adulthood, constitute the co-existing competitors in a battle of giants. Finally it is also possible for two major adult interests to compete for attention.

In the integration model no single affect theory is permitted to dominate the personality monopolistically, to be suppressed or relegated to the mode of intrusion or permitted to oscillate in competition with alien affect theories. Instead, a modus vivendi is achieved in which there is mutual accomodation between the affects in the interests of a harmonious personality integration. In its analog across time, the late bloomer model, the elements of the past personality may have continued to compete with each other unhappily, in an early competition model which continued into a co-existence model. At some later point in development there is a confrontation of the warring affect theories out of which a harmonious integration is achieved by the late bloomer. If the individual early achieves integration which continues as he develops, we characterize him as exemplifying the integration model. Further, the integration may not be achieved in a single effort but may be piecemeal over a considerable period of time and even over a lifetime, so that the individual increases in integration with increasing age. Finally, such integration as is achieved may be a finite solution which breaks down under the stress of new circumstances that produce a series of crises, each of which is met by a new integrative solution.

Any affective experience, then, prompts the formation or transformation of an ideo-affective organization which will determine the future role of that experience in the life history of the individual. That role may be described by three dimensions: magnitude, independence and direction of interdependence. Differences in magnitude are the differences between a minor role as in the intrusive or iceberg model, a medium role as in the competition or co-existence model, and a major role as in the monopolistic and snowball models. Differences in independence are the differences between on the one hand the competition and co-existence models in which each role is relatively segregated from its competitor and the iceberg model which preserves the intrusive and major elements independent of each other, and, on the other hand, the integration and late bloomer models in which the segregation of each organization is penetrated and syntheses are achieved.

Differences in the direction of interdependence are those between the monopolistic, snowball models and the integration, late bloomer models. In the snowball model the core experience continues to grow by assimilating new experience to itself, and in the integration, late bloomer model past experience is assimilated to and reinterpreted and transformed by new experience.

The intrusion and iceberg models

The phenomena we have labeled intrusive are so commonplace that neither everyman nor psychologists would seriously dispute their existence. The intrusion model assumes only that in the realm of affect, some affects assume a much smaller importance than other affects but that these latter are nonetheless capable under specific, limited conditions of intruding and displacing dominant affects.

It is a commonplace observation that some individuals, ordinarily very friendly, can become mean after a few drinks. An otherwise courageous individual grows faint with fear if he has to speak in public or visit the dentist. An otherwise happy individual becomes morose whenever he finds himself alone. In these instances anger, fear and distress are intrusive affects which enjoy only a minority status in personalities which are primarily governed by the positive affects of excitement and enjoyment. Those who know others reasonably well frequently learn to pinpoint the specific conditions under which their children or friends or wives display atypical affect—their "idiosyncrasies."

Everyman, contrary to Freud, has not assumed that these intrusive affects are under continual tension ready to burst forth at the slightest relaxation of defensive vigilance. Rather, he has assumed there is something about certain kinds of situations which inflame and activate certain otherwise dormant affects. It is our belief that both Freud and everyman are correct. Intrusive affects may indeed be continually activated but also continually warded off, to overwhelm the individual when defenses are less vigilant; there are also intrusive affects which do not come alive except under conditions which are both rare and specific. These latter are consequences of truly weak affect theories which play only a secondary role in the personality. With respect to shame or contempt or self-contempt, this can arise whenever such experiences are infrequent enough so that the individual does not dwell upon them, does not magnify them and does not elaborate them cognitively. They remain isolated memories capable of reactivation in memory, by any repetition sufficiently similar to the initial experience to recruit such a memory, but are otherwise dormant.

In general, if the socialization of shame and contempt is rewarding rather than punitive, shame and contempt remain secondary affects. In order for shame and contempt to play minor roles in the personality of the child, the socialization of these affects must attenuate and minimize them rather than amplify and maximize them. In the next section we will examine what we have called the rewarding socialization of these affects, which is a precondition of a weak shame theory that is only occasionally activated to become intrusive in the experience of the child.

Rewarding socialization of shame—humiliation,
contempt—disgust and self-contempt—disgust

By a rewarding socialization of shame and contempt we mean one in which the arousal of these affects is minimized, attenuated

if aroused, sympatheticially recognized and reduced by helping
the child to cope with the sources of these affects. The parent is
concerned about reducing both the suffering of the child and its
source. We shall now present the essential components of a rewarding socialization of shame and contempt.

CONTEMPT—DISGUST AND SHAME—HUMILIATION
ARE BOTH MINIMIZED

The parent rarely shows contempt for the child or for others.
When the child offends him, the parent is likely to express distress or anger. If he wishes to shame the child, he expresses
empathic shame by hanging his own head in shame with an
accompanying expression of regret or disappointment or shame:
"I'm very disappointed you did that" or "I'm ashamed of you."

ANTI-CONTEMPT, ANTI-SHAME IDEOLOGY

The child hears the parent defend an anti-contempt, anti-
shame ideology, that one should respect others generally and
that one should not humiliate others. Further, he hears this
ideology applied to a wide range of objects and circumstances.
Those who have failed, those who have violated laws, those who
hold unpopular opinions, those whom one employs, those who
are unattractive, those who are old, those who are ill—these and
many others who incur the contempt of others are included in
the golden rule. The ideology which is against humiliation is
made vivid and spelled out in numerous circumstances by the
editorial commentary of the parents. Such commentary ranges
from expressions of regret for the plight of the weak and the
defeated to condemnation of those who are responsible and of
those who respond to the plight of others with contempt.

ANTI-HUMILIATION AND ANTI-CONTEMPT
IDEOLOGY IS EXPRESSED IN ACTION

The child is exposed not only to the verbally expressed belief
that one should treat others as ends in themselves but sees the

parents act consistently with these beliefs. Numerous good works for the underprivileged and the oppressed are initiated and sponsored by the parents, and the child is encouraged and rewarded for doing likewise. Those occupying lower status roles, such as maids in the home, are treated with respect and kindness. Concern for all men who are less privileged is translated into action. Stray animals are given asylum. Minority group members are given help. Employees are treated generously and sympathetically. Help is sent to underdeveloped nations as well as to disaster areas. The mentally ill and the retarded are given time, energy and money. Such translation of belief into action minimizes the impact of humiliation both for others and, by example, for the child, since he is taught that the sources of shame and self-contempt not only should be, but can be and are reduced by his parents and by others.

ANTI-HUMILIATION AND ANTI-CONTEMPT IDEOLOGY IS EXPRESSED IN AFFECT

Not only does the child hear the parent express an anti-humiliation ideology and translate it into action but he also sees the affective empathy and identification of his parents with the humiliated one. He sees the wincing of the parent at the humiliation of the other because of identification with the other. Indeed, without such facial and non-verbal communication the espousal of a formal ideology, even when accompanied by action, can be cold and sterile and without impact on the child, since both belief and action require amplification by affective display to entirely capture the imagination of the child. It is even possible to communicate the ideology almost entirely through such non-verbal communication of facial affect. Thus a parent who looks tenderly at a stray dog communicates his sympathy with the weak and the lowly and his reverence for life as much or more than a parent who tells his child to be kind to dumb animals.

THE CONFLUENCE OF IDEOLOGY, ACTION AND AFFECT

It is, however, the confluence of ideology, affect and action as the child witnesses these in the avowals of the anti-humiliation ideology, in the display of appropriate affect and in the translation of ideology into action, that most powerfully reinforce the socialization of shame and contempt. Important as the impact of the direct parent-child interaction is, its significance has been somewhat exaggerated in current theory by the usual understatement of the significance of the example of the parents' beliefs, affects and actions toward others.

We do not wish at this point to examine the complexities of the effects of gross discrepancies between the ideological, action and affect levels, but rather to stress the significance of their consistency and integration in the life and personality of the parent, for the rewarding socialization of shame and contempt. It is not possible for the parent to build a wall around his general social relationships which will isolate them from the scrutiny of his wide-eyed child. If shame and contempt are to be minor and, at most, intrusive elements in the personality of the child, they cannot be major experiences in the relationships between the parents and other adults. Nor can there be gross discrepancies between action, affect and ideological postures with respect to humiliation and contempt without exaggerating rather than minimizing the role of contempt and shame for the child.

THE INNOCENT ARE FAVORED OVER THE GUILTY

The anti-humiliation ideology avows that it is preferable that hundreds of the guilty should not be punished than that one innocent individual should be unjustly punished or humiliated. In part this is a derivative of the larger ideology which argues that even the guilty should not be humiliated or punished. Should it become necessary to restrict the freedom of anyone, the anti-humiliation ideology tends towards a greater concern for the possible miscarriage of justice for the innocent than for the possible injustice of letting the guilty go unpunished.

The consequence of such a generally permissive ideology, as the child hears it expressed by the parent, is to further minimize in the mind of the child the possibility of experiencing humiliation at the hands of his parents or at the hands of other adults who might share this ideology.

ATTENUATION OF EVALUATION AND RESPONSIBILITY

Not only does the anti-humiliation ideology favor the protection of the innocent over the punishment of the guilty, but wherever possible, evaluation which might lead to the blaming of human beings is minimized. The evaluation function is restricted to approbation. The parent attempts to maximize positive affects and minimize negative affects. He avoids wherever possible any assessment of behavior which might be derogatory either to his child, to himself, to others or to the human race. As a consequence there is a loss of clarity in the evaluation of behavior and a loss of clarity of the responsibility for shameful behavior. The child is thereby taught to attenuate humiliation, to avoid and to evade both evaluation and responsibility whenever humiliation is possibly involved for himself or for others.

EXTENSION AND FORGIVENESS ARE FAVORED
OVER HUMILIATION, CONTEMPT AND PUNISHMENT

Another aspect of the anti-humiliation ideology concerns the strategy of dealing with the true offender, whether it be child or criminal. When the parent who avows and lives by an anti-humiliation ideology is confronted with behavior which truly and deeply offends him, when evaluation and responsibility cannot be avoided or attenuated, then he looks for and usually finds extenuating circumstances. These are then the grounds for forgiveness, and the offender is given yet another chance to redeem himself. If he has offended many times before, so much more were the circumstances extenuating and so much more does he need forgiveness and yet another chance. Again the ultimate strategy is that of maximizing positive affect and minimizing negative affect. Given such permissiveness, the child's experience with shame and contempt is minimized.

ATONEMENT AND RESTITUTION FOR SHAMING THE CHILD

Shame and humiliation may be minimized and yet not reduced to zero. If the parent who occasionally humiliates his

child is governed by an anti-humiliation ideology, he characteristically attenuates the severity of such experience, and its
consequences for their relationship, by making resitution. Such
a parent will follow the alienating experience by a display of
unusual warmth in which he throws his arms around the child
and so re-establishes their intimacy.

If the parent feels that he has been unnecessarily harsh
toward the child for reasons which are unrelated to the child,
he will apologize for the affront to the child. He will make
excuses for the child which absolve the child of total responsibility
if the punishment does not truly fit the crime but is in part the
consequence of other harassment of the parent. Thus a parent
returning tired and angry from a trying day at the office may
humiliate his child for the most trivial offense. If, however, he
is governed by an anti-humiliation ideology, he will subject himself to further punishment by assuming some of the blame for
scapegoating for a somewhat trivial offense. Thereby the child's
experience of shame is minimized, and he is also taught to
minimize the expression of contempt toward others by the
example of his parents' governance of his contempt.

TOLERANCE AND SYMPATHY FOR THE
FEELING OF SHAME—HUMILIATION

The shame response is both visible and contagious. When
the child who feels defeated hangs his head in shame, the parent
through empathy and identification can also be made to feel
defeated. Whether the impact of the child's humiliation will be
magnified or attenuated depends in part on the tolerance of the
parent for the experience of shame and defeat. If the parent
is not completely crushed through empathic identification, then
he can communicate his own tolerance of shame and defeat to
the child. Then he can show the child that the experience of
shame, while not pleasant, need not be disastrous and that
counter-action is possible. In such socialization, sympathy and
empathy ultimately enable mastery of shame and defeat, and
so attenuate the role of shame.

The role of shame can be reduced by not requiring that the child hide the shame response. He is not further humiliated or otherwise punished for shyness, discouragement or the expression of guilt. On the other hand, neither is it insisted that the child accentuate his humiliation by a public confession or display of his shame against his will. The shame which is displayed and acknowledged is quickly dissipated in contrast to the same feeling which must be hidden from public view or which becomes the occasion for further amplification by the enforced confession and avowal of shame.

*Child is helped to cope with shame—humiliation
and self-contempt—disgust and their sources*

Shame is often experienced by children on the occasion of their numerous failures. These are failures to do what parents can do, what peers can do, or what children themselves spontaneously wish to be able to do. On such occasions, the child is offered sympathy and help to overcome his discouragement and shame and to cope with his problems. As this is done again and again the child grows in self-confidence, learns how to tolerate his own shame responses whenever he meets failure and learns how to cope both with the sources of defeat and with shame and discouragement. The impact of the numerous and somewhat inevitable experiences of failure and discouragement is much attenuated whenever parents utilize such experiences to teach the child both to have courage in the face of defeat and despair and to learn the skills necesssary to minimize failure.

Since the experience of shame is all but inevitable in the development of human beings, a critical part of the rewarding socialization of shame and self-contempt must consist in teaching the child the double skills of tolerating his own shame and in overcoming the source of it. As in the rewarding socialization of distress, it is not enough to simply sedate the negative affect or to teach tolerance of it. There must also be taught the skills of dealing with whatever is responsible for activating the negative affect. We have seen before that these are two quite independent aspects of affect socialization. Parents may teach or insist that the child learn to cope with the sources of shame or distress but be intolerant of the expression of these affects; or parents may be tolerant of the affects, sedate them but not teach or encourage the child to learn to deal with the sources of his misery.

Some general consequences of the rewarding socialization of shame—humiliation, contempt—disgust and self-contempt—disgust

In general the rewarding socialization of shame and contempt has the consequence of producing a weak shame theory. A weak shame theory is like any other weak theory. It accounts for little more than itself. It is developed to account for and organize very specific experiences which are neither intense enough nor recurrent enough to prompt the generation of more than a crude general description of the phenomena themselves. (In the next chapter on monopolistic affect theory we will examine in more detail the characteristics of a strong affect theory.)

When a shame theory is weak, it accounts for little and is activated relatively infrequently, since it is in competition with the more complex, stronger affect theories of other positive or negative affects. Since this competition is between theories which are continually being differentially activated and confirmed or disconfirmed, a weak theory can either grow weaker in time or it can grow stronger depending upon its growth relative to the growth or atrophy of its competitors.

A weak theory is not as readily strengthened in the presence of strong competitors as it may be further weakened. Ordinarily, the weak theories become weaker and the strong theories become stronger. The exceptions to this rule we will consider later. Let us consider now those aspects of a weak shame theory and of its competitors which are the consequences of the rewarding socialization of shame and contempt.

ATTENUATION OF SHAME—HUMILIATION, CONTEMPT—DISGUST, AND SELF-CONTEMPT—DISGUST

Because shame, contempt, and self-contempt were minimized by the parent, the experience of these affects was not permitted to last very long, or to become very intense. Further, because such shame as was experienced more frequently became the occasion, ultimately, of intimacy and help from the parent, there is a radical attenuation of suffering for the child who is socialized in this way. In contrast with the doubling of penalties for all offenses in the punitive socialization, here penalties are halved, even when it is the parent himself who has shamed the child. Having shamed the child and given expression to his own negative affect, the parent is now likely to be ashamed of the suffering he has inflicted on the child and to rush to the aid of his own victim. The parent will then offer not only sympathy but help in how the child is to govern himself in the future so that he does not again provoke unnecessary shaming.

MULTIPLE SHAME—HUMILIATION AND SELF-CONTEMPT—DISGUST FREEDOMS

In contrast to the multiple binds produced by the punitive socialization of shame and contempt, rewarding socialization enlarges the freedom of the child to express, deal with and reduce his shame and self-contempt. This freedom is a function of the lack of secondary binds, such as the necessity to hide these feelings and from the repeated experience of successful remedial action in coping with numerous sources of shame and self-contempt.

INCREASED TRUST IN HUMAN HELP

The repeated experience of help from parents in coping with shame and contempt and their sources produces not only an enlargement of freedom to cope with shame and contempt but an increased general trust in the parents and in human beings. This makes possible both a deep and strong interdependence and a confidence in the efficacy of the remedial action taken by others on one's behalf. Basic trust has these two somewhat independent components. First, that my shame concerns you; second, that you can help me or that you can help me to help myself.

INCREASED WILLINGNESS AND ABILITY TO OFFER SYMPATHY AND HELP TO OTHERS

Inasmuch as the parents' response to the shame of the child provides a critical identification model for the child, rewarding shame and contempt socialization produces in the child an empathic shame at the shame of the parents and others, a willingness to communicate felt sympathy, a willingness to help the other and a belief that it is possible to do so. As in the case of distress, these attitudes towards the shame, the defeat, the feelings of discouragement, and the feelings of alienation of others, combined with the belief that there is reciprocity, is necessary if enduring and intense social ties are to be generated and maintained.

Depending upon the nature of the socialization, these elements may be fragmented. Through identification the child may be taught to feel shame at the shame of the other but be unable or unwilling to communicate it. He may be willing to communicate his sympathy, but unwilling or unable to offer remedial help. He may offer help but in a way which is punitive toward the experience and expression of shame itself, derogating the affect of shame as spineless or stupid.

Sympathy and helpfulness for the defeated, the oppressed and the alienated is a consequence not only of identification with a parent who showed such sympathy and helpfulness towards the child. It is also a consequence of two kinds of enjoyment which arose from the past experience of shame. First, it has been learned to be an occasion of the deepest intimacy and affirmations of love and concern. Second, it has become an occasion of additional enjoyment when something has been done to reduce shame. Since the sudden reduction of shame is an innate activator of the smile of joy, this incremental reward may become linked with the affect of shame, which then becomes a sign of enjoyment that is to come. These two sources of enjoyment reinforce identification as a source of increased willingness and ability to offer sympathy and help to others.

INCREASED WILLINGNESS AND ABILITY TO OFFER HELP TO THE SELF

In rewarding shame and contempt socialization the child is taught through identification to feel sorry for himself as well as for others. Such self-sympathy is a sufficient, though not a necessary, condition of the reduction of shame through habituation and through a direct attack on its source. Such sympathy for the self is also a sufficient condition for the repair of self-respect, since a self which can sympathize with its own suffering can more readily forgive its failures. Self-reliance and self-respect may also be bred by adversity and by punitive shame and contempt socialization, though not without other serious costs.

A complete and truly rewarding shame and contempt socialization necessarily involves guidance and help to help the self, as well as balm. Given such a socialization, the individual not only sympathizes with himself but also has achieved self-trust in his ability to help himself out of his shame and discouragement.

GENERATION OF RESONANCE TO THE IDEA OF PROGRESS

In addition to personal and interpersonal trust and confidence, the rewarding socialization of shame and contempt generates a resonance to the general idea of progress. Tradition-bound societies feel none of the necessity to be inventive that man in modern society cannot escape. It is the repeated experience of progress in coping with shame, discouragement and alienation which generates the idea of the possible—and progress. To the extent to which one has confronted failure and shame and has had the experience again and again of remaking the world closer to the heart's desire, the idea of progress is born, takes root and grows.

Neither meliorism nor revolution grow out of unrelieved defeat and humiliation, in the nursery or in society. The invest-

ment of positive affect in achievement and in progress depends
in part on the attenuation of that shame and self-contempt which
are the great internal barriers to the counter-actions against
defeat. If victory is to be achieved in the face of defeat, the voice
of the inner enemy must be silenced. A rewarding shame socialization cannot in itself give the child the sense that he was
chosen by his parents and that he has a destiny to fulfill. This
requires a rewarding excitement and enjoyment socialization
which we will describe later. But a belief in progress and in his
own destiny nonetheless does require a minimal sense of shame
and self-contempt, a weak shame theory.

FAVORS THE DEVELOPMENT OF PHYSICAL COURAGE

Physical pain innately activates distress and is commonly
learned to be feared. Both distress and fear of pain are controlled by contempt and shame in the typical socialization of
American men. American women are characteristically more
tolerant of physical pain, and make better patients in a hospital
than do American men, because, we think, their socialization
with respect to the tolerance of distress and fear is less punitive.
They are more courageous because they have not been shamed
into bravery too early and too severely.

FAVORS THE DEVELOPMENT OF SHAME—HUMILIATION
TOLERANCE IN PROBLEM SOLVING

Since the rewarding socialization of shame teaches tolerance
for shame, the individual can learn to continue to try to solve
problems despite the fact that he feels discouraged and ashamed
and hopeless. Not only is the frequency of the experience of
shame radically reduced by rewarding shame socialization, but,
when the feeling cannot be avoided or attenuated, the individual
has been taught to live with it and to act in spite of it. Just as
physical courage is bravery in the face of fear, so persistence is
counter-action despite the feeling of shame, self-contempt, of
discouragement and of hopelessness.

This is a critical feature of the socialization of shame and
self-contempt because the reduction in the frequency of shame,

coupled with the help and guidance which attenuates the experience of defeat, could nonetheless seriously cripple the individual's ability to cope with severe shame over long periods of time when he can neither escape the problem nor count on help. In the truly rewarding socialization of shame the child is encouraged to develop just such tolerance of unrelieved despair, on his own, until he has coped successfully with its source.

FAVORS INDIVIDUATION AND THE ACHIEVEMENT OF IDENTITY

Individuation and the achievement of an identity require that the individual tolerate his loneliness, his aloneness and his uniqueness. To the extent to which he must hang his head in shame whenever he is alone, whenever his difference from others becomes visible and whenever he loses the love of others or is rejected by them, he cannot become individuated and he cannot achieve a firm sense of his own identity. The individual whose shame socialization has been rewarding is better able to tolerate the pain of loss of love, of the separateness which is occasioned by the confrontation of real differences between oneself and one's identification figures and love objects, by virtue of maturation and the assumption of adult responsibilities or by the death of loved ones. It is easier to become individuated when shame has been softened by linkage with sympathy rather than suppressed by contempt and loss of love.

RELATIONSHIP BETWEEN THE INTRUSION
AND ICEBERG MODELS

In the intrusion model a weak shame theory is a minor element in the personality but capable under specific, limited conditions of intruding and displacing dominant affects. In its analog across time, the iceberg model, the adult personality is vulnerable under specific, limited conditions to intrusions from the past, which are alien to the affective life of the adult.

The relationship between those two models is somewhat complex. If shame is a minor element for the child, why should it not play an even smaller role in the personality when the

individual reaches adulthood? Why should it intrude into adulthood because it may have intruded into the experience of the
child? The question is a critical one, and the answers are not
simple.

It is true that what is minor in childhood may vanish altogether from the experience of the adult if what began small
does not grow and if its numerous competitors do grow. Clearly,
also, what may have been minor and intrusive in childhood may
grow and become a major or even monopolistic force in the
adult personality. What is intrusive in childhood may therefore
disappear from the experience of the adult or it may become
much more important. But what was a minor element in childhood may also continue as a minor element in adulthood. This
can happen in one of two ways. Either the minor element grows
proportionately and retains its strength relative to its competitors,
or it becomes relatively weaker but still capable of intrusion
into the experience of the adult.

In the first case, an individual may continue in his adulthood
to be touchy about a small class of situations which are analogous
to the same class to which he was sensitive in his childhood.
Thus, if as a child he became ashamed if and only if his peers
teased him, he may continue to respond with shame as an adult
when, and only when, adults who constitute an analogous group
tease him in an adult way. The critical point here is that there
has been limited growth and generalization, but also attenuation
and weakening of earlier sources of shame. If an adult friend
were to tease him as he was teased as a child by calling him a
"big doo-doo" or a "scaredy cat," such derogations may well
have lost their sting though their later analogues have not.

In the other mode of intrusion, the individual's vulnerability
to shame from teasing by his peers may not have generalized,
and therefore one might not guess that there still remains such
a sensitivity. In this case the shame theory has grown relatively
weaker by its failure to generalize to adult analogues, but it is
nonetheless capable of intruding suddenly as an alien response
in the experience of the adult if and when an adult unwittingly
uses the childhood term of derogation.

In one such case an adult who had been teased by the nickname of "baloney" outgrew his general sensitivity to teasing by

his peers, but whenever any adult used this word he would blush with shame despite the fact that it was not being used as a nickname or necessarily being used toward him personally.

In both of these cases, the vulnerability to an adult analog to the weak shame theory in childhood, and in the more restricted vulnerability, we are dealing with the temporal analog of the intrusion model, the iceberg model.

The iceberg model is, however, not restricted to shame theories which were weak in childhood. Just as a weak shame theory in childhood may grow into a monopolistic theory in adulthood, so a monopolistic theory in childhood may be sufficiently weakened by the relative growth of competitors that its status becomes only intrusive in the personality of the adult. In this case a shy, easily discouraged child grows into a tenacious, lion-hearted adult, who nonetheless can be suddenly overwhelmed with shame under particular conditions which are very similar to those to which he could respond as a child only with shame. The intrusion from the past, in the iceberg model, then may represent a fragment which has grown steadily weaker, a fragment which has maintained its relative strength, or a very large but submerged chunk of what was once the major component of the personality. The iceberg model is the developmental analog of the intrusion model, since in it the thrust of the past is relatively weak into the present, regardless of its relative strength in the past.

CHARACTERISTICS OF A WEAK AFFECT THEORY: A WEAK FEAR THEORY

It should be noted that a weak shame theory is not necessarily an ineffective ideo-affective organization. We do not mean to imply that the strength of a shame theory is equivalent either to the successful avoidance or to the passive sufferance of shame. This is because the ideo-affective organization we have called affect theory includes two quite distinct components. First, it includes an examination of all incoming information for its relevance to a particular affect, in this case, shame and contempt. This is the cognitive antenna of shame. Second, it includes a set of strategies for coping with a variety of shame and contempt contingencies, to avoid shame if possible or to attenuate its impact if it cannot be avoided.

A weak theory does not necessarily guarantee successful avoidance, or even successful escape or attenuation, for all possible contingencies, but it does guarantee a sensitization to particular threats of shame and some strategies for coping with these particular threats. If the conditions which actually confront the individual are sufficiently different from those for which his strategies are contrived, then they may be inadequate and fail either to avoid shame or soften its blow. After such an experience the theory may be revised to include such contingencies in the future, but at any moment in time one cannot easily detect the structure of an affect theory by the extent to which it avoids the activation of affect or fails to do so.

A commonplace example is the pause of the individual at a curb before he crosses the street. It is certain that most of us at the curb learn to anticipate not only danger but fear. Few individuals experience fear at the sight of automobiles on the street. One of the reasons for this is an ideo-affective organization which informs the individual of the relevance of a broad band of contingencies for danger and for fear, and a set of strategies for coping with each of these contingencies. Thus on the curb of a city street, if automobiles do not exceed 35 or 40 miles an hour and do not deviate from relatively straight paths by more than a few degrees and if the individual allows a few hundred feet between himself and the oncoming automobiles, he characteristically crosses the street without the experience of either danger or fear.

The affect theory (a fear theory) here operates so silently and effectively that it would surprise everyman if the question of fear about crossing the street were even to be raised. He would say, quite self-persuasively, that he uses his common sense so that he doesn't need to be afraid. This is one of the major functions of any negative affect theory—to guide action so that negative affect is not experienced. It is affect acting at a distance. Just as human beings can learn to avoid danger, to shun the flame before one is burnt, so also can they learn to avoid shame or fear before they are seared by the experience of such negative affect.

This is one of the primary functions of affect theory. Without such ideo-affective organization the individual could at best escape after the dreaded experience like the child who can only pull his finger from the flame. The individual's affect theory enables him to act *as if* he were afraid or ashamed, so that he need not in fact become afraid or ashamed.

Contrary to Freud, we do not think such defense necessarily entails an activated affect which is warded off at a high cost. The beauty of such an organization is that so long as the theory is adequate to anticipate the possible dangers and to provide appropriate strategies for coping with them at a distance, then the affect need never be activated nor experienced.

It is only when the situation violates the boundaries of the affect theory that the individual is exposed to the affect proper. If there is some uncertainty about the nature of the danger or about the adequacy of the defenses, the individual may suddenly be overwhelmed with the affect in question. If an automobile appears to be coming at 70 miles an hour or so and if the car careens from one side of the street to the other, the fear theory now activates fear and also prompts the individual to run for cover. We do not believe that the panic which is now experienced is "breaking through" the customary defensive strategies. The fear which now overwhelms is, we think, peculiar to this situation in which new threats have appeared and in which old successful strategies have broken down.

We have chosen the commonplace example of the man at the curb to highlight three phenomena: First, affect theory can successfully anticipate and avoid the experience of affect. Second, it need not be successful in avoiding the experience of affect. Third, whether it succeeds or fails it is nonetheless a weak theory, since it accounts for a very restricted domain, whether it succeeds or whether it fails.

Individuals who vary widely in their vulnerability to fear in general may all nonetheless possess a weak fear sub-theory by means of which they calmly and effectively face the crossing of streets. This is a weak fear theory because it provides neither information nor strategies to deal with a hundred other potential sources of fear. The individual who has a strong fear theory is an anxiety neurotic or a schizophrenic, for whom fear is an ever-present threat which must be anticipated and dealt with. Even the neurotic or the psychotic may nonetheless suffer no fear in crossing the street. Within the strong general affect theory, there may be special, weaker theories which do not differ in structure from the weaker fear theories of the normal individual.

We have employed this example of a weak theory because it is so widely held in our society despite the substantial numbers of pedestrians killed annually in traffic accidents. We have chosen this example also to illustrate another aspect of what we mean by the weakness of an affect theory. This is the independent variability of the frequency of the phenomena described by a weak theory and its general extent. A theory may be weak because it is relevant to phenomena which are very infrequent, but it may also be weak when it accounts for a phenomenon which is frequently repeated but is nonetheless restricted in scope.

An individual may cross a street once a year or twice a day and yet despite this variance remain the object of a weak theory. If a drop of water is a small part of the ocean, so too are a thousand drops. The sea of experience in the lifetime of a human being involves large numbers; therefore weak, medium and strong theories must be understood not with pseudo-precision but with a capacity for the rounding of numbers.

Psychoanalytic theory had the unfortunate consequence of undermining the sense of proportion. The difference between the significance of weak, medium and strong affect theories was washed out in the excitement of the discovery and detection of traces of affect in the so-called psychopathology of everyday life. All affect theory was endowed with the properties of strong affect theory. If an individual showed signs of some break-through of fear or anger in an interpersonal relationship, then it seemed likely that there must be much more behind these slips. If negative affect was experienced only occasionally, then it was often supposed that only by the most heroic efforts did the entire ocean not pour through the hole in the dike.

Such phenomena are real and of the greatest significance

when they are truly symptomatic of a strong negative affect theory, but they are readily misinterpreted when they arise from the temporary breakdown of otherwise adequate avoidance strategies of weak negative affect theories. In short, the individual who carelessly steps into the street too close to an oncoming car may do it only once and do it from insufficient anxiety rather than from excessive anxiety. In the case of dogs conditioned to jump from one place to another at a signal to avoid a shock, Solomon found that the continuing successful avoidance of both fear and shock eventually interfered with the maintenance of the avoidance response. The dogs eventually forgot to be careful enough and would fail to successfully avoid the shock. Again, as in the case of the individual, such error tends to be self-limiting. Punished once, the successful avoidance strategy is again reinstated.

AFFECT THEORY MUST BE EFFECTIVE TO BE WEAK

Let us return to our discussion of weak shame theory and its relation to the rewarding socialization of shame. The rewarding socialization of shame is one which results in few collisions in which the child is humiliated and in which the techniques of either avoiding humiliation or coping with it if it is unavoidable are well taught. The result is a weak theory with successful strategies for dealing with the traffic of shame. The individual's daily encounters with the few possibilities of shame are handled so silently and effectively that he rarely knows that he was even in potential danger. He stands at the curb of shame, confident that he knows when to commit himself to the risks of passage, while at the same time he enjoys the passing traffic which is colorful and exciting even though it could be dangerous.

We can now see more clearly that although a restricted and weak theory may not always successfully protect the individual against negative affect, it is difficult for it to remain weak unless it does so. Conversely, a negative affect theory gains in strength, paradoxically, by virtue of the continuing failures of its strategies to afford protection through successful avoidance of the experience of negative affect. As we will see in our examination of the growth of monopolism in affect theory, it is the repeated and apparently uncontrollable spread of the experience of negative affect which prompts the increasing strength of the ideo-affective organization which we have called a strong affect theory.

Despite the fact that a strong affect theory may eventually succeed in preventing the experience of negative affect, it is usually only through the repeated failure to achieve this end that the ideo-affective organization grows stronger. If the individual cannot find the rules whereby he can cross the street without feeling anxious, then his avoidance strategies will necessarily become more and more diffuse. Under these conditions the individual might be forced, first, to avoid all busy streets and then to go out only late at night when traffic was light; finally, he would remain inside, and if his house were to be hit by a car, he would have to seek refuge in a deeper shelter. Under such conditions both the anticipation of negative affect and the strategies of avoiding it must grow, so that the affect theory becomes stronger as the strategies become less and less effective.

A weak theory then must be a relatively effective one to remain weak. If it breaks down only occasionally, it can be revised and yet remain relatively weak. There is, we think, a critical rate of acceleration of breakdown at which a weak theory begins to gallop and gather strength. We will examine this later in connection with the development of a monopolistic shame theory. Now we wish rather to examine the structure of a weak theory which permits it to play only an intrusive role in childhood, and the structure of a theory which either continues to be or becomes weak enough to become intrusive from the past into the experience of the adult.

Strong childhood affect theory becoming a weak adult affect theory: a non-Freudian possibility

Let us examine the crossing-the-street example from the point of view of the iceberg model. It is clear enough that such a theory will not gain in strength as the individual grows older, if he is never endangered, because he observes the appropriate avoidance strategies. However, we can envision a strong theory growing weaker and thereby fitting the iceberg model.

Let us suppose that the individual had in fact been hit by automobiles not once but several times in his childhood, while crossing the street. Such a child might develop a strong fear theory, in which he became afraid not only of passing auto- mobiles but of moving through space and of other human beings in general. Let us further suppose that gradually such a child is persuaded that human beings can be trusted, that mobility can be exciting, that even the dread automobile is not as danger- ous as it appeared and that his experience had been truly atypical. As his positive experience grew in scope and he de- veloped stronger and stronger excitement and enjoyment theories, the relative strength of his fear theories grew weaker and weaker. If now, as he stepped off the curb to cross a street, a prankster were to blow his horn unexpectedly, we might expect an intru- sion from the past and a momentary panic lest he be hit again.

It would be intrusive in the present, despite the massive reactivation of former affect, so long as the further consequences of such reactivation were limited and constituted a minor episode in the life of the adult. It is, of course, always possible that such a reactivation would produce a major regression to the earlier monopolistic status of the strong fear theory, or an ultra-labile oscillation between this state and the adult personality. In the latter case there would be a transformation from the iceberg to the coexistence model in which two relatively strong medium affect theories are in enduring competition between the present and the past.

Let us return now to shame and contempt. It would be readily admitted that if the child experienced little shame or self-con- tempt because of a rewarding shame socialization, the shame theory which would be developed under such circumstances would be a weak one. This is not to say that he might not be an anxiety neurotic, but shame as such would play a minor role in his personality. A weak shame theory can co-exist with strong affect theories concerning other affects, positive or negative. It would also be readily admitted that such a weak shame theory would play at most a weak or, more likely, an even weaker intrusive role in the adult personality in the manner of the iceberg model.

The critical case concerns the relationship between the strong monopolistic theory and its subordination to a minor intrusive role in the adult personality. Freudian theory and much contemporary theory does not entertain such a possibility very seriously. Radical discontinuity in development appears unlikely and is generally abhored as a theoretical model. Further, those like Allport who have sponsored the principle of functional autonomy as an anti-Freudian protest have introduced so great a discontinuity that one cannot go home again—the child is forever lost in the man.

This question cannot be answered apart from a general theory of memory, and of thinking and learning. We shall present our understanding of memory and learning in some detail in Volume III. At this point we wish only to outline such general features of our theory of memory as are necessary to account for the iceberg model. We will defer our account of thinking and learning until we discuss the monopolistic and snowball models.

THEORY OF MEMORY

We will argue that the human being employs two radically different strategies in the processing of information. In the strategy of memorizing, the aim is to create a unique object. In the conceptual strategy, the aim is to create, ideally, an infinite set of objects. In terms of class membership, memorizing aims at the construction of a class with a single member or, at the least, to minimize the number of members of a class; whereas the conceptual strategy ideally aims at maximizing the number of members of a class.

The aim of memory is to duplicate and preserve information as exactly as possible, to create a unique object. The aim of the conceptual strategy is to so transform information that class membership is maximized. If I ask you whether you remember a particular telephone number, the criterion by which your memory is evaluated is whether you can reproduce one particular set of numbers correctly. It is a matter of indifference that you might be able to generate an infinite set of numbers, one of which might be the set of numbers I wish. If, however, I were to ask you to guess the number I was thinking of and that happened to be the same telephone number, the conceptual strategy would be involved; and the strategy by which the same number would be found would be a radically different one than that used by the memory system. If I will only answer yes or no to your number guesses, then you must generate a very large set of numbers to find the needle in the haystack. One may either remember the number, or one may generate it along with numerous other numbers until the criterion is met. We have used this as an example that two correct responses may be identical, but the underlying mechanisms and strategies may yet be radically different.

Let us now consider the nature of the memory mechanism. No cumulative learning would be possible without the ability to duplicate the past. Without memory the individual would face the world with a permanent *tabula rasa,* perpetually innocent and surprised. By an as yet unknown process every conscious report, we think, is duplicated in more permanent form. Not all the information which bombards the senses is permanently recorded but only that information which in the competition for consciousness has succeeded in being transmuted into reports.

An equally critical but different type of duplication process is that of information retrieval. We have distinguished sharply the storage process, as automatic and unlearned, from the retrieval process which we think is learned. Both are duplicating processes, but one is governed by a built-in, unconscious mechanism, the other by a conscious feedback mechanism. The individual may not choose what he is to store or not store, but he may choose to "memorize" or not to memorize, i.e., to learn how to reproduce past experience, to retrieve information which has been permanently stored, without reliance on sensory input.

Whether we accept an automatic registration trace theory or not, the greatest burden must be placed not on the passive registration of traces but on the later activity which finds the prior information in the labrynthine networks of the brain. The problem of accessibility and retrieval of stored information is so great that the assumption of a trace theory necessarily requires a retrieval theory in order to make the traces at all useful. It is analogous to the problem of retrieval of books in a very large library. A theory of the nature of the retrieval process is a critical requirement for any theory of memory because what is stored would be entirely wasted if one did not learn how to retrieve specific memories.

The details of our theory of retrieval will be presented in Volume III. There we will examine as an example how an individual teaches himself to remember a telephone number. We conceive of this as a process of informational compression in which the individual produces more and more miniaturized copies of the original information. This he does by using the original to produce a more miniature copy, and then using this compressed copy to produce a still more miniaturized copy, which in turn is miniaturized in a series which, for example, may begin 5——9——2——3 as it is first read from the telephone book. Then it is speeded up in the first internal reproduction to 5—9—2—3, which is then reverberated in immediate memory and further speeded up on the second internal reproduction to 5–9–2–3. On the next repetition it is said still more quickly as 5923, until finally it is so abbreviated that it is unconscious; but one knows that one knows it and can reproduce it from within.

This miniaturization, however, involves more than simply speeding up the performance, since the sounds of the digits has to be clipped and abbreviated without destroying their essential message. Otherwise such a series of increasingly compressed equivalents might be like the blurred feature of a person seen from an increasing distance. They would be of no use unless they were recognizable as compressions of the original model rather than equivalents of the just-preceding miniature. It must be possible not only to recognize the original from the miniature but also to reproduce the original exactly from the miniature. The compression relationship must be reversible—and expandable. This is achieved in teaching oneself to remember by applying the inverse of the compression transformation, for example, using the operation "decreased speed" on the miniature which had been produced from the original by the operation "increased speed." In this way one can learn to reverse what one has just done.

But miniaturization involves, as we have said, more than speeded performance. In addition to increased speed the sounds must be clipped without destroying their essential message. The relationship between the various parameters of any performance which is to be compressed is complex. In attempting to operate on one parameter, it will often happen that other parameters will also be transformed unintentionally. For example, in speeding up our handwriting we may lose legibility. Increased speed may, however, improve certain performances by so altering the relationships between the parts that it becomes easier to duplicate. This is the case in learning to ride a bicycle. It takes much more skill to ride a bicycle slowly and expertly than to ride it moderately fast. Any operation, including miniaturization, on any message ensemble can vary from a comparatively simple bit of neurological trial and error to a very complex process in which the original model may be transformed in a variety of unintended ways.

By using the inverse transformations one learns to expand and thus recover the original from the miniature compressed copy which is the equivalent of the original in some but not all respects. It should be noted that among other things, the compression process reduces the density of reports to messages, that is, the ratio of the messages actually transmuted into conscious awareness to the total pool of messages available; the result is that consciousness increasingly legislates itself out of representation. For example, the individual may become aware of the remembered telephone number for the first time only as he hears himself talk to the operator. Also it should be noted that in the process of this learning of retrieval skill the individual progressively frees himself from dependence on the external stimulus as a necessary support for his reproductive memory skill and teaches himself how to retrieve the information from within rather than from the external stimulus. Not only is information being stored in increasingly compressed form at different sites in the brain, but he is learning these addresses—where and how to find the stored information and reassemble it.

The concept of "name" and of "name oɟ a name"

At this point we wish to introduce the concept of a "name," which in ordinary usage is commonly conceived to be a relatively unique symbol for something. It is a symbol of limited expansion characteristics, but this is its chief virtue. You and I may both have the same first name; but if we share the same first, middle and last name, it is an awkward coincidence. A brand name may refer to as many as a few million automobiles of the same kind, but the intent of the name is to differentiate the automobile made by one manufacturer from that made by a competitor.

We will define a "name" for the purposes of our theory of memory as any message, conscious or unconscious, which is capable of activating a particular memory trace at a particular neurological address. We will assume that a name itself may or may not have an address, and that this address itself may therefore have a name.

In recognition, as with reproduction, the sensory input itself may constitute the name of the appropriate address, insofar as it initiates retrieval processes which activate a specific trace at a specific address. Often such stimuli are the only names of specific addresses. Unless the individual encounters this stimulus, he may not be able to remember because this name itself has no brain address.

The name may be any part of the original message, any compression of that message or any part of any compression of that message. A name however may be no part or bear no resemblance to the original message. Thus "my friend's telephone number" may be the name of the original message if this enables recovery of the original message.

A natural name by this definition is similar to a symbolic name. Thus, if a particular restaurant is located one mile before one crosses a bridge it may become a sign of the bridge and by our definition a "name," if the person remembers that the bridge is a mile away whenever he sees the restaurant.

A name then may be a natural sign, a symbol, something similar to the information stored in the trace, any part of that information or similar to part of that information, any compression of that information or similar to any compression of that information, or any part of any compression or similar to part of any compression.

By a "name of a name" we will mean a message, conscious or unconscious, which is capable of activating a name. An example is the tying of a string around the finger to serve as a reminder to do something. Another is a sequentially organized skill, in which there is no direct access to any particular part of the set of traces except by retrieval in order, as when one first learns the alphabet.

Next we will define three sub-types of names. "Alternative names" are any set of equivalent names for the same address. (For the benefit of those who are familiar with logical notation, this may be expressed as a v b ⊃ x. It should be noted that this is simply a restatement of what has already been stated verbally. The reader who is unfamiliar with logical notation may safely skip the statements in this notation without loss of information.)

Examples are: the presence of either John or Mary as "names" of "a child of mine." Different parts of the same stimulus may be recognized as parts of the same object by activating the same trace. Different synonyms may be alternative names of the same trace.

A "distinctive name" is a name which is the only name of a trace and the name of that trace only. That is, there is a one-to-one relationship between a distinctive name and its trace. (The logical form is a ⊃ x . ~ (a ⊃ x'). ~ (a' ⊃ x) — a and only a implies x and only x). An example might be "the stimuli a moment ago which assembled the present moment of awareness," which in all probability will never again be retrievable in exactly the same way.

A "conjoint name" is any set of messages which, when they occur conjointly, are capable of activating a particular trace at a particular address. (The logical form is a . b ⊃ x. Both a and b together activate the trace x.) Thus, when a child learns that large four-footed furry animals are dogs and smaller four-footed furry animals are cats, he is learning conjoint names. Sentences in a language also have the structure of a conjoint name, since it is a set of symbols in a particular order which may be uniquely ordered to one trace rather than another.

Retrieval ability

The retrieval ability which is being learned under the conditions of miniaturizing we have described consists then not only in the deposition of miniaturized information in traces at specific addresses but also in the central assembling of names for each address and the storage of these names at still other addresses. These names, and names of names, will be somewhat fragile and unreliable once the reverberation and continuing self-stimulation is interrupted by other central assemblies. If the telephone number is a new one for an old friend, then there are many older names and names of names which can be recruited to assist in the extension of the fragile new skill in retrieving the number from storage. But let us suppose that the person was looking up the number as a favor to a friend, but the individual himself had never before heard either the telephone number or the person's name whose number it happened to be. Under such conditions the name of the number would itself have no well-established name or names of names, and these latter would also have to be learned to be retrieved just as much as the telephone number itself.

How limited the retrieval ability in general may be is still uncertain. Underwood has shown that the classical Ebbinghaus curve of forgetting is primarily a function of interference from materials learned previously in the laboratory. When this source of intereference is removed, forgetting decreases from about 75 per cent to about 15 per cent over 24 hours. Thus, similarity of past names and names of names to later names, and names of names, interferes with the recovery of present names on retest 24 hours later. If the subject is rehearsed in only one series, this source of interference is removed and the names, and names of names, are almost as good 24 hours later as they were originally in enabling retrieval of the stored information. It seems clear that the interpolation of more or less similar material before the critical learning is not changing the storage process nor the immediate retrieval, since the subjects do not stop the learning trials until they can reproduce all the stimuli, but is influencing the retrieval process on retest.

Returning now to our example of memorizing a telephone

number, the stability of this retrieval skill will depend on several factors. First, it will depend on the number of alternative and conjoint names for each member of the set of compressed traces. Second, it will depend on the number of ways (names) for retrieving each compressed trace from every other more or less compressed member of the set of compressed traces. This enables the individual to retrieve an unrecognizable compressed trace and use it to support equally rapid and unrecognizable performances (such as in touch typing) or to support slower, more conscious expansions in which the density of reports to messages is as high as in the original reading of the model, as in telling an operator a telephone number by expanding a compressed trace. Third, it will depend on the number of names of names for each member of the set of compressed traces.

Relationship between early and late experience

The requirements of name formation and reversible compression-expansion transformations must take much time, and this will have two somewhat antithetical consequences: 1) any human being deprived of the opportunity to do this work will be relatively incompetent when first given the opportunity and will then at the later date require a long period of experience before elementary perceptual and motor skills will be achieved; 2) by virtue of the necessarily long period of incompetence enforced by the slowness of learning how to remember, the impact of experience in early infancy on later life will be limited.

Much of early experience will not be remembered and will not influence later personality development except a) insofar as the infant is kept under continuous restricted stimulation resulting in a condition equivalent to 1) above, so that the effect on later life is incompetence or retarded development; and b) insofar as the infantile experience is continuous with that of childhood and adolescence. The longer the conditions of infantile experience are continued into later life, the more massive an effect will the earliest experience have. There is now evidence that deprivation of early sensory experience does impair recognition and perceptual development. There is also evidence, which we will review later, that if early experience is not either continuous or periodically reinforced, its influence on later experience is radically attenuated.

The relationship between early memories and later memories may be continuous or discontinuous. New learning may proceed by transformations on older memories or by the assembling of relatively new components which result in the deposition of relatively independent traces and names of traces. Accessibility of these traces will vary as a consequence of the relative continuity or discontinuity of learning and of the degree of independence of the stored traces resulting from learning. Before continuing with the exposition of our theory, we will present an experimental test of a derivative of the theory in which we were successful in the prediction of retrieval of early memories.

RETRIEVAL OF EARLY MEMORIES NO LONGER AVAILABLE:
TWO EXPERIMENTS AND A PARADIGM

One experiment was as follows: the subject is required to write his name very slowly, at a rate approximately three seconds per letter. Under these conditions the handwriting closely resembles that of childhood rather than his present handwriting, if he is now an adult. Long forgotten ways of forming letters are reproduced. Second, there is a decreased variability of handwriting between all subjects. Many of the idiosyncratic characteristics which distinguish one adult's handwriting from that of another are lost.

In a second experiment of this type, a subject is asked to shout at the top of his voice the phrase, "No, I won't!" Not all subjects are willing or able to do this, but most comply. The consequences are somewhat varied. On the faces of most adults the lower lip is protruded immediately after speaking, giving the appearance of a defiant, pouting child. Spontaneously emitted reports from many subjects indicate a re-experience of childish affect of distress and anger, with recollection of long forgotten, specific incidents in which such affect was evoked. Other subjects whose faces expressed the smile of triumph rather than a pout reported feelings of joy and anger rather than distress and anger.

Let us now examine further that part of our theory of memory upon which these experiments were based. In the case of both handwriting and speech, there are at least two aspects of both early and late performance which co-vary, so that early performance is characterized by one value of each parameter and the later performance by a different value of each parameter.

In the case of handwriting the early performance is slow, the late performance more rapid. The co-varying other parameter is in fact a set of parameters, which produce in one case the more regular script of childhood, or in the other case the more idiosyncratic adult signature.

In the case of speech, the early performance is louder than the late performance. Pitch appears to be one of a set of co-varying, other parameters which together constitute speech. If the early and late performances varied in one aspect alone, this might be used to retrieve the early performance but this would then be the only difference between the two performances. Thus, if early handwriting resembled late handwriting except for a difference in speed, we would not have been able to demonstrate that retrieval was involved.

For our experiment to work, one of the two values of one parameter must be characteristic of early performance, and the other value must be characteristic of late performance. The differential speed instruction is an essential part of the distinctive name which will retrieve the early handwriting, but it is not a distinctive name in that it is not a sufficient name.

A sufficient name in this case is a distinctive conjoint name which includes at least three components a) write, b) slowly and c) your name. Whereas b) is the critical part of the distinctive name, a) and b) are also necessary components. This conjoint instruction happens to be the name of a name. The instruction "slowly" is used by the subject as an operator on the distinctive conjoint name for the *late* performance, since he ordinarily starts to write as he usually does, but more slowly.

If the subject is asked to write his name as he did when he first learned to write, he characteristically disclaims knowledge of how to do this. He is entirely surprised at the outcome of his slow handwriting. This conjoint instruction is a name of a name. He did not as a child use this type of instruction at all, since he did not then know how to write fast and certainly did not know how to write his present adult signature.

A more accurate description of our instruction is that it is a conjoint distinctive name of a name. The subject interprets the instruction not as an instruction to write his name as he did when he was a child but as an instruction to write as he now writes, except to do it more slowly. This modification of the adult performance constitutes the name of the name, i.e., it produces a retrieval of the name of the earlier performance. Since the early handwriting is slow and the late handwriting is fast, our particular instruction is effective in retrieving the only set of traces which are stored which have a program for guiding the slow movements of the hand in writing the name.

Such an instruction applied to speech does not work because speed in speech is variable, whether the speech is early or late. One has learned to speak both slowly and rapidly as a child and as an adult. The critical discontinuity in early and late speech is loudness or intensity. While children speak at varying levels of intensity, the intensity is required to be much reduced in adulthood. Children's loud speech is under steady negative pressure from parents and teachers who insist that the child lower his voice. Eventually this produces an adult who rarely shouts. Because of this discontinuity, the instruction to shout at the top of the voice is effective in retrieving early speech, whereas instruction to speak more slowly or more rapidly is not. It is, however, not effective for those who continue to shout as adults.

Degree of independence of earlier and later experience: the inter-name distance

One of the outstanding characteristics of these two sets of early and late performances is their almost complete segregation one from the other. The debate about primacy versus recency, about early versus late experience, is a mistaken polarity, since it appears that the nervous system is quite capable of supporting two independent sets of traces under certain conditions. Given the specific conditions under which we learn early and late handwriting, two quite independent organizations may exist side by side with little interaction in either direction. Early memory here does not influence later memory, nor does later memory alter early memory. There is neither pro-active nor retro-active interference. Each address has its own name, and each name has its own address. The subject continues to be unable to write as he wrote early at a rapid rate, nor does he appear to be able to write his adult signature slowly. The primary cause of the state of segregation of the two sets of traces and the skills they program is the number of transformations which would be necessary to build a set of bridges between one set of traces and the other set of traces. This is what we have defined as the "inter-name distance," the number of transformations upon a name which is necessary to enable the formation of a modified trace with a modified name, which combines characteristics of both sets of traces.

Consider that each signature is guided by a set of conjoint messages which guide the fingers of the hand how to move from moment to moment to create the unique tracings which constitute the two signatures. Let us simplify the problem and represent the first set as composed of a series of three sub-sets of instructions, one of which, q, is a constant slow speed; the other, x, is a set of instructions to proceed to a particular set of points with respect to an abcissa; the third, y, is a set of instructions to proceed to a particular set of points with respect to the ordinate. The second set we may conceive as another program composed of q' which is a faster constant rate and x' and y' analogous to x and y but systematically different. The subsets of x and y, and x' and y' are very numerous, and each individual instruction has a speed marker tightly linked to a particular xy or $x'y'$ reading.

The empirical correlations between the distinctive components of each signature is critical for how many information transformations will be required to learn the new skills $q'xy$ and $qx'y'$; i.e., to write a fast childlike and a slow adult signature. If a very small change in speed produces a large and inappropriate change in an x reading or a y reading or in both, and if a small change in an x reading produces a very large change in a y reading and conversely, then a great deal of work will be required to build a series of bridges between qxy and $q'x'y'$ and $q'xy$ and $qx'y'$.

If, on the other hand, one could change q, say half way to q', without disturbing the xy part of the program, and change q' half way to q without disturbing $x'y'$, then in only a few more transformations one might achieve $q'xy$ and $qx'y'$, that is, fast early writing and slow late writing. The number of intermediate transformations which will be necessary to achieve the new programs and their traces, the inter-name distance, will depend on how much distortion in early writing is caused by how much speed-up, and how long it will take to learn to correct these distortions at each new intermediate speed. The number of such intermediate transformations which would be required to achieve handwriting skill which was free of speed effects would be a function of the strength of the correlation between all components of the set.

If the correlations between components of the distinctive sets are weak, then relatively simple transformations will bridge the small inter-name distance, and the intrusion of early memories will be short-lived. If it were in fact easy to learn to write early handwriting rapidly and late handwriting slowly, the instructions we used would not provide a stable regressive phenomenon. Sometimes, for some subjects who shout "No, I won't!" this does prove to be an unstable regressive phenomenon, just because it is readily transformed into a variant of adult speech and therefore no longer recovers early memories or affects.

The introduction of negative affect into the distinctive, discontinuous behavior enormously complicates the inter-name distance. The very thought of using a specific parameter such as very loud sounds, which were once relinquished under the threat of negative sanctions, is itself often sufficient to reactivate the same negative affect. Every time the possibility of so behaving is imminent and negative affect is aroused, the segregation and discontinuity between the two types of speech is heightened. Under such conditions, the initiation of a set of transformations which would reduce this distinctiveness must contend not only with the potential inter-name distance which would be there even if there were no anxiety or shame to discourage the work of transformation, but in addition must be motivated to tolerate the punishing negative affect involved.

APPLICATION OF THE THEORY OF MEMORY
TO THE ICEBERG MODEL

This theory of memory has implications for the iceberg model of development. Whenever affect experience is distinctively discontinuous from early to late experience, there may be a name which will retrieve early memories in a manner which is intrusive to the dominant adult personality, as early handwriting is intrusive to adult handwriting. Second, this name itself, or a name of this name, may or may not be activated during adult life. Most adults live their adulthood without ever writing as they did as a child, except under the very special conditions of our experiment. The same personality organization will support either an iceberg organization with relatively infrequent intrusions, or a co-existence organization in which there is frequent oscillation between the early and late ideo-affective postures, depending on such differences in the adult environment as the number of names of earlier sets of traces in that environment. Thus, much of our posture as adults is achieved and maintained by radical discontinuities in the behavior of others towards us and by the discontinuities of the behavior expected from us as we play the adult role.

The rites de passage in many societies are designed to segregate childhood from adulthood and accentuate just such discontinuities, so that after puberty, for example, the child is expected to act as an adult, and he is treated by others as though he were an adult.

It has not always been appreciated by personality theorists just how dependent our adult personality is upon the fact that other adults act toward us as though we were adults. The difference between the way in which a child is treated and the way in which an adult is treated is as radical and distinctive a discontinuity as the change in speed in handwriting

Earlier affective responses can be readily activated if another adult fails to treat us as an adult. So long as we are treated like adults, we act and feel like adults; but many adults can be made to feel like ashamed children by an overly authoritarian police officer who speaks to them as they might have been spoken to by their parents when they transgressed. It is always possible to activate earlier feelings by acting toward the adult as though one were his parent and he was the child. This is the power of all who exercise hierarchical authority in a democratic society which is otherwise non-hierarchical in organization. The doctor, the judge, the educator, the general and all those who display and use their expert knowledge before the inexpert and the relatively untutored evoke in them the wonder of the child before his parents.

It is not only through role differences that the distinction between the childhood self and the adult self is maintained. It is also buttressed through the taboo on the use of the eyes. The child is taught not to stare too directly into the eyes of the other and adults cooperate in maintaining this taboo on the overly intimate interocular experience, so that there may be no adult experience of interocular intimacy. When two adults' eyes meet, therefore, and they are suddenly lost in each others' eyes, they can fall in love because they are returned to the earlier, more intimate, more intense communion which they enjoyed as children. They can also now baby-talk as well as baby-look. Romantic love is a return to early love. Eyes meeting eyes is the name of these early feelings.

But if eyes meeting eyes can return the individual to early love, they can also return him to early shame. If a police officer, judge, educator or doctor fixes his eyes sternly and directly on the adult he is talking to, as though speaking to a child, the adult will drop his eyes in shame, acutely aware that the eyes of the parentlike figure are upon him. The expertise and the parental-like tone of voice can become overwhelmingly similar to the socializing parent when the eyes are also used as a parent's eyes may be used, to penetrate to the center of the child's being. Whenever one adult fixates his eyes on those of another adult, in violation of the taboo on the use of the eyes, and the look is not reciprocated and mutual, it can be similar enough to the prerogative of the parent with his erring child to reactivate shame.

The parent's treatment of the child is distinctly different from an adult's treatment of that same individual grown to adulthood and so makes possible an iceberg relationship by providing two distinctive names, one for early and the other for late experience.

Another discontinuity that makes for the intrusive reactivation of early experiences of humiliation are all those situations in which adults are rendered relatively helpless and incompetent. Failure, illness, hospitalization, surgery, the prospect of death, the loss of a love object, loss of status or money are some of the occasions when any active, ordinarily competent adult may suddenly feel like a humiliated, helpless child. Helplessness need not necessarily redintegrate humiliation. This depends in part on how the child's helplessness was treated by the parent. To the extent to which being an adult is distinctively associated with competence and being helpless is distinctively associated with being humiliated as a child, the adult is vulnerable to such intrusions whenever he is confronted with situations which are beyond his immediate control.

Re-experience of isolated childhood affects upon becoming a parent

A third general situation which is likely to reactivate early affects, including humiliation, to the extent to which these were experienced as a child and not experienced as an adult, is through the vicarious reliving of childhood as a parent. As a parent, every adult is vulnerable to massive intrusions from early affects long forgotten. Many a parent is hurled back into his past and held as in a vise. If this was a discontinuous period of positive affect, the adult may find himself reliving a golden age. If it was a discontinuous period of *Sturm und Drang* he may have to suffer through it again. If it was a golden age with a sudden decline at the birth of a sibling, this too may be relived.

The parent may relive not only the role of himself as a child but also the roles of his own parents. Thus the now emancipated but once humiliated adult may suddenly become as contemptuous a parent as was his parent, if there was a sharp polarization between the child and parent in which each played complementary roles and then followed by a sharp break in the developmental sequence. Most frequently under such conditions the

parent is forced to relive both his own childhood and the role
of his parents, if there was a sharp break with both roles in the
developmental sequence. Under these conditions the adult's
relationship with his own child can become a distinctive name
for the entire earlier relationship which becomes intrusive to
his adult personality and his adult interpersonal relations.

TRANSFORMATION OF A CHILDHOOD
MONOPOLISTIC SHAME THEORY INTO AN INTRUSIVE
ADULT SHAME THEORY: AN ILLUSTRATIVE CASE

Let us return now to the question from which we started.
How may a strong shame theory, monopolistic in early experience, become no more than intrusive in the adult personality?
If the parents treat the child in one way but later others treat
him differently, this difference may so transform his personality
that the older personality appears only intrusively under conditions which are similar enough to constitute the name of the
earlier monopolistic shame theory.

Let us consider one such case we have observed. This individual was excessively humiliated by both parents. He responded
to this with submission and self-contempt and a strong shame
(and self-contempt) theory assumed monopolistic status in his
early personality. Gradually, however, he found in books a great
excitement and enjoyment. As his positive affects grew in
strength, he found a great friend who turned his positive affect
back toward human beings. There were now in his adolescent
personality two competing affect theories, one of humiliation and
the other of excitement and enjoyment.

At this point the positive affects were radically reinforced
by the mechanism of resonance, which has been somewhat
neglected in contemporary theoretical discussions. So deep and
strong were his feelings for human beings who did not humiliate
him that his positive affect evoked very strong positive affect
from others through resonance. Because he was so grateful for
the excitement and enjoyment, which he wrested first from books
and then from his good friend, his positive feelings radiated out
to others so transparently that he evoked from them the positive

feelings which he needed so that these positive feelings of his own would be nurtured and grow. Ultimately he developed sufficiently hardy positive feelings so that he was not so dependent upon immediate resonance from others. He became a well-integrated, warm, effective personality.

Nonetheless he remained extremely vulnerable to the contempt of others, which was a name for the shame and self-contempt with which he had responded to parental contempt. The radiance and luster of this personality could, however, be dulled in an instant by the open contempt of another, who thereby reduced him to the humiliated child of his past. Because of the adult monopolistic excitement and enjoyment ideo-affective organizations, these intrusions were, however, ordinarily of brief duration, depending somewhat on the nature of the affront to his self-esteem.

Transformation of a weak shame theory into an intrusive, then monopolistic, shame theory: a paradigm for one type of manic-depressive personality

If a previously monopolistic shame theory can be reduced to the level of an intrusion into the adult personality which has been transformed by a competing monopolistic affect theory, it can also happen that a previously weak theory can become intrusive into the adult personality and finally become monopolistic at any time, but frequently late in the life of the adult.

Such is the case of an individual who is deeply rewarded by the respect and love of his parents for every show of independence, activity and achievement and who is punished by contempt for any show of shame and passivity or discouragement, admitted defeat or quitting in the face of challenge. Whenever he hangs his head, feels beaten, discouraged and wants to give up, he is further humiliated. If he then resumes the struggle, he is encouraged and rewarded, and when he wins, his cup runneth over.

This child begins with a relatively sharp differentiation between affects of his own which elicit positive affects and those affects which elicit humiliation. If the balance and clarity of reward and punishment is such as to evoke determination to maximize positive affect and minimize negative affect, in this case primarily shame and self-contempt, then such a child characteristically develops high achievement motivation. He will tend to have a continuous history of successful achievements through childhood and adolescence, marred only by occasional experiences in which he yields momentarily to the intrusive shame and passivity. These serve only to strengthen counter-active efforts to maximize his positive experiences. As he enters adulthood, this individual has a firm sense of his own identity as the master of his own destiny, as one capable of achieving what he wants, of eliciting respect from others for his efforts and of generally enjoying his interpersonal relationships.

Because this individual always counteracted passivity and shame, he never experienced protracted shame or self-contempt; consequently, he developed neither gradations of humiliation nor any tolerance of it. If such an individual is now suddenly confronted with enforced passivity which he cannot counteract, he is vulnerable to deep shame and self-contempt.

This is the distinctive name for his humiliation. Such would be the case if he suffered a long siege of enforced passivity through the loss of his savings and business through an economic depression, which did not permit his customary counteraction, or by senility and retirement, which undermined his customary activity and productivity and confronted him with the imminence of his death.

In the case of the individual whose adult humiliation was intrusive but limited in duration, the contempt of the other, which was the distinctive name for his shame and self-contempt, could be escaped; and sooner or later the positive affects he evoked from others reasserted the adult monopolistic excitement and enjoyment theories, but in this case the passivity or weakness could not be escaped.

In our present paradigm, what begins as an intrusion will end as a new monopolism if two conditions are met. First, if passivity is enforced and customary counter-action is blocked, then the name of humiliation, though it was always a minor name, now gains in strength because of lack of competition. Second, the experience of humiliation itself is a name for the expected further humiliation from the parents and from the internalized parent within. Because this individual always experienced intense though brief humiliation and because he never experienced protracted shame or self-contempt, he developed neither gradations nor tolerance nor immunity for these affects. Consequently, these feelings now deepen and grow more and more disturbing until they become monopolistic. The once unconquerable one is now defeated by passivity, and the shame and self-contempt which feed on each other, recruiting cognitive elaboration so that the self learns more and more to hold itself in utter contempt with a strong humiliation theory.

Such a one can ultimately become deeply depressed, or may become manic in a desperate reassertion of the worth of the self. The characteristic lability and self-limiting characteristic of the depressive psychosis is in part due to the dependence of such affective growth upon names which activate intrusive affect only so long as the individual cannot or feels he cannot counteract them.

This and the prior case illustrate how much the iceberg model depends upon the structure and variable nature of the environment. In the first case, the monopolistic shame theory of the past remained intrusive only because of the relative infrequency of the open display of contempt in adult interactions and because the personality radiated such positive feeling toward others as to minimize even these contingencies. In the present case, the past shame theory was weak but eventually becomes monopolistic only because enforced passivity is a name for the weak shame traces which continue to activate shame in adulthood so long as the name remains active. If the enforced passivity had been of brief duration, as, for example, in the case of minor surgery, then the iceberg model would have continued to be an accurate description of the relative status of early and later personality. We do not mean to suggest that the iceberg model and its transformation into either a co-existence model or a monopolistic model depend entirely on environmental contingencies. This is surely not the case. However, we do mean to stress the importance of environmental contingencies for personality theory.

STABILITY AND CHANGE IN PERSONALITY
STRUCTURE AS A FUNCTION OF ENVIRONMENT,
TOLERANCE FOR NEGATIVE AFFECT AND
MOTIVATION TO CHANGE

Any personality theory which does not include the relationships between the variable structure of the environment and the
variable structure of the personality, in a unified theory, must
remain seriously incomplete. Personality is not only a structure
which is capable of transforming its environment. It is also a
structure which is in part formed by and transformed by its
environment. To deny either its constraints or its freedoms is
to caricature the human condition.

Nor is this to affirm that all personalities are equally free or
equally constrained, for they are not. Nor is it to view the environment as essentially constraining since it contains opportunity,
challenge and reward as well as constraint and punishment. It
is rather that we avoid the perennial vulnerability of personality
theory to characterize the structure of personality as an
ultra-stable nucleus, which once fixed necessarily continues
to display relatively constant properties independent of the field
in which it moves. Our snowball, iceberg, co-existence and late
bloomer models are paradigms of person-field relationships which
may vary radically from ultra-stable to ultra-labile transformations.

This leads us to the third implication of our theory of memory
for these developmental models, and for the iceberg model in
particular. As we have seen in the case of handwriting, the early
and late names of memory traces organized as theories or programs can remain relatively independent of each other during
the lifetime of the individual, so that the relationship of intrusion is itself ultra-stable. The stability of the intrusion phenomenon in the iceberg model depends, as we have seen, on two
factors: the inter-name distance and the tolerance for the negative affect in question. We will examine this problem in more
detail in our discussion of the integration and late bloomer model,
since the destruction of the vulnerability to alien intrusion is a
large part of the problem of integration. At this point we wish

only to note that the intrusive phenomena of the iceberg model may remain ultra-stable throughout the lifetime of the individual, as in the case of early and late handwriting, in which the individual either writes as a child slowly or as an adult more rapidly; he never learns the intermediate transformations which would make it possible for him to write slowly as an adult or rapidly as a child, so that the speed instruction continues to be a distinctive name for the intrusive appearance of early handwriting.

However, such a relationship need not continue to be intrusive. In the case of loud speech many individuals learn to tolerate the negative affect which was responsible for the discontinuous speech of childhood and adulthood. These are, for example, actors before audiences, housewives calling children and others who must for one reason or another raise their voices louder than is customary for adults. In this case the inter-name distance is small and easily bridged, if the negative affect which prompted the inhibition can be tolerated by the adult long enough to adapt to it and learn new adult names free of shame for either loud or soft adult speech. Further, there must be not only tolerance of the intrusive affect, but a wish to confront, master and integrate these alien elements of the personality.

There are many intrusive phenomena for which there exists neither strong positive wishes to transform them nor strong enough negative motives to reduce the intrusions. For example, most of us have no motive for learning the skill of writing slowly as an adult, or rapidly in our childish signature.

We have already seen that there are numerous instances of residues of the past which humiliate us, which we would wish not to re-experience. But it often happens that we would rather tolerate such occasional unwelcome intrusions than confront these alien experiences steadily and long enough to achieve control over them. If the wish for self-knowledge and integration is not strong, the punishment during the confrontation necessary to reduce the inter-name distance will not be tolerated, even though it could be tolerated if the wish for integration were stronger. This situation is similar to the reluctant patient in psychotherapy. If the pain of neurosis is not very severe, and the wish for integration is weak, the patient is unlikely to pay the price of the greater temporary pain of self-confrontation. The problem of the balance between the toxicity of therapy and the toxicity of the disease is a general one in medicine; it is also a problem in psychotherapy.

Chapter 21

Continuities and Discontinuities in the Impact of Humiliation: The Monopolistic and Snowball Models

A monopolistic, snowball theory of humiliation is common only among those human beings whom we ordinarily consider severely neurotic or psychotic. It is particularly common among those bearing the diagnosis of paranoid schizophrenia. This chapter examines the conditions that lead to the development of such a theory.

We shall begin by describing in detail that kind of punitive socialization of the child with respect to shame, contempt, and self-contempt which forms the basis for a monopolistic humiliation theory. But, unlike Freud, we shall argue that a punitive socialization is, in itself, not sufficient to account for the continuance and snowballing of that theory. We shall derive the necessary and sufficient conditions for the development of a monopolistic snowball humiliation theory from our general view of the nature of memory and thinking, of class and symbol formation by human beings, and of the mutual re-shaping of present and past experience. The role of shame in Freud's "most common perversion"; the difficulties in present-day theories of personality measurement that result from ignoring the partial independence of sub-systems in the human being; the possibility of growth through discontinuity; the nature of traumatic experiences; the possibility of benign trauma as psychotherapy; the typically American crisis of identity—all will be explored in the course of the discussion.

A monopolistic affect theory is one in which one affect comes to dominate the entire affective life of the individual. The developmental analog of the monopolistic model, the snowball model, is the case in which the early experience, whether monopolistic or not, continues to snowball and more and more dominates the personality. As we have said before, it is entirely possible for early monopolism not to snowball, but to atrophy or to become intrusive, as in an iceberg model; and for an early minor, weak theory to gather strength over the years and snowball into a relatively late monopolism.

An individual experiencing monopolistic shame—humiliation, contempt—disgust, self-contempt—disgust or any combination of these is one governed by a strong humiliation theory which organizes his ideas and feelings into a tight pervasive program for the interpretation of all information for its relevance for humiliation and prepares numerous strategies for coping with a wide variety of threats of humiliation.

We shall also describe as governed by a strong humiliation theory an individual who does not experience shame—humiliation, contempt—disgust, self-contempt—disgust in isolation but who, as is more usual, monopolistically experiences an amalgam of these humiliation affects with other negative affects, namely, distress—anguish and/or fear—terror.

Punitive socialization of shame—humiliation, contempt—disgust and/or self-contempt—disgust

In order for humiliation to play a monopolistic role in the life of the child, and later to snowball into the life of the adult, the socialization of these affects must amplify and maximize them. In this section we will examine the punitive socialization of shame and self-contempt which is a pre-condition of a strong humiliation theory in the personality of the child, recognizing that while it greatly increases the probability of a strong humiliation theory in the adult, it is not sufficient in itself to produce such an adult theory. Punitive socialization occurs under the following conditions:

CONTEMPT—DISGUST, SELF-CONTEMPT—DISGUST AND/OR SHAME—HUMILIATION ARE MAXIMIZED

Shame or contempt or self-contempt may become monopolistic if the parent frequently shows contempt for the child and others. The child appears to the parent to be a continual offender whom he must therefore continually humiliate by tongue lashing, by facial expression of contempt, by teasing and by derogation.

THERE IS A CONTEMPT—DISGUST IDEOLOGY

The child hears the parent frequently expound an ideology which asserts the worthlessness of man. Men are asserted to be contemptible unless proven otherwise. He hears this ideology applied to a wide spectrum of objects and circumstances. Those who have failed, who have violated the law, who hold unpopular opinions, those whom one employs, those who are unattractive, who are old and who are ill are all dwelt on as deserving of contempt. In addition, however, such a parent is quick to point the finger of scorn at the feet of clay of heroes, those of the child and people in general. The impact of such derogation is further amplified by the claim that it is realistic, whereas the respect for many idols is based upon myth.

THERE IS AN ANTI-ANTI-CONTEMPT—DISGUST IDEOLOGY

Not only is the child exposed to the frequent and systematic derogation of human beings in general but he is also exposed to an anti-anti-contempt ideology. The greatest contempt is reserved for those who are self-consciously soft on the use of contempt and humiliation. These individuals are described as lacking in basic integrity, who do not know the difference between good and evil, between what is of value and what is worthless and contemptible.

CONTEMPT-DISGUST IDEOLOGY IS EXPRESSED IN ACTION

The child is exposed not only to the verbally expressed belief that human beings are contemptible and worthless, but he also sees the parents act consistently with these beliefs. Those occupying lower status roles, such as maids in the home, are treated with contempt and are exploited as much as possible. Those occupying upper status roles, such as one's employer, are not only derogated but exploited, cheated and opposed whenever possible. No opportunity is missed to derogate others and to attack and to humiliate them either in face-to-face relationships or in conversations about them. Their motives are questioned, their reputation and their competence undermined, their work ridiculed. No contributions or good works are undertaken. Charity is said to begin at home, if at all. The child is also discouraged from helping those who need or ask for help on the ground that God helps those who help themselves.

Stray animals are thrown out of the house if they are brought into the house by the child. The friends of the child are derogated, and he is asked not to entertain them at home nor to visit them, since their parents are contemptible or suspect. Minority groups are discriminated against, and the parents express satisfaction whenever life becomes harder for them. Underdeveloped nations, disaster areas, appeals for help in the fight against disease, these and numerous other appeals for time, money and energy are ostentatiously and piously declined. Civic and other duties are declined on the ground that they are not worthy of support.

If the child identifies with the parent, he has been taught how to have and act on contempt frequently and for many causes, institutions, activities and persons. If he does not, he has learned to have contempt for himself insofar as he identifies himself with any other person or institution or activity. He has been taught to help or respect himself and others with great reluctance and to question the value of human beings generally.

CONTEMPT-DISGUST IDEOLOGY IS EXPRESSED IN AFFECT

Not only does the child hear the parent express derogation in his contempt ideology and see him translate this into action, but he also sees the parent frequently display the affect of contempt through the sneer of the raised upper lip as well as the tone of the voice.

It is possible for a parent to lecture a child on the sins of others, on their utter unworthiness, and yet to display no contempt affect. This is a cold contempt which hides itself in a verbal piety which purports to present an objective analysis of the nature of things. Indeed such an individual may display a minimum of any affect, despite the fact that his language is highly suggestive of affect. We have noted this phenomenon before in the pseudo-affective help response to distress. In this case the offer to help is designed to muffle the distress of the other, because it is too disturbing to be responded to with empathic distress.

A contempt ideology which is expressed without affect may or may not have an affective impact on the child. Much will depend on how the parent ultimately responds to violations of such an ideology. When the child of an upper-class parent brings home a lower-class playmate, the parent who has consistently expressed misanthropic ideas without feeling may or may not display the affect of contempt toward the child's choice of a friend. If he does not, the strength of the sanctions which are imposed is much reduced.

Ultimately, however, the affects of the parent are likely to become engaged and overtly expressed, no matter how general the inhibition of parental affect. Nonetheless there are numerous circumstances in which the lack of affective display would attenuate the impact of the parental ideology. In such cases the child may respond to the parental ideology as though this was one opinion among many, but not an opinion which he had to share, particularly if it concerns objects remote from the child's immediate interests. An example might be the opinion, delivered without affect, that do-goodism in government is not only wasteful of money but that it further undermines the character of those who deserve no help in the first place. If that opinion, and others in the contempt ideology, are expressed with deep scorn, however, there is likely to be an amplification of the impact of such messages on the child through the more certain arousal of the child's affect in response to the affect of the parent.

This is not to say that the child is incapable of responding to ideas as such without affect. The child can and does respond to general ideas, misanthropic or otherwise, with affect, but usually in direct proportion to their immediate relevance to his own somewhat limited experience. Thus, if he has a colored boy playmate, he is likely to respond with affect to the general idea that Negroes are inferior, whether or not this opinion is accompanied by affect. However, he is much less likely to respond with affect to the previously cited message concerning dogoodism in government if the parent does not display affect as he utters this opinion.

In any event the accompaniment of the contempt ideology with the affect of contempt in a wide variety of circumstances in which the child observes the parent responding with scorn to individuals, places, institutions and activities radically reinforces the impact of contempt and shame on the personality of the child.

THE CONFLUENCE OF IDEOLOGY, ACTION AND AFFECT

It is the confluence of ideology, affect and action as the child witnesses these in the avowals of contempt ideology, in the display of contempt and in the translation of ideology and feeling into action that most powerfully reinforces the socialization of shame and contempt. We are here referring primarily to the parents' beliefs, affects and actions toward others. Although this is an even more powerful influence when the child is also one object among many objects of contempt, it is important to note that even where the child is treated with love and respect, shame and contempt can become important affects if the parent expresses much contempt in word, action and feeling towards others.

LACK OF CONFLUENCE WITHIN THE ANTI-HUMILIATION IDEOLOGY

Another source of monopolistic shame, contempt and self-contempt is the lack of confluence within the parent of action and feeling with the anti-humiliation ideology. When the parent gives eloquent voice to a humanistic, anti-humiliation ideology but visibly violates or fails to act on his beliefs or fails to display the appropriate affect in critical situations, the child is not only confused but may also experience contempt and shame at such discrepancies between the ideological, action and feeling levels.

If a parent who verbalizes a humanistic ideology turns away someone who asks for help, albeit with regret, or expresses contempt for him even though he offers help, the child who has taken the ideology seriously is not only troubled by such a discrepancy but also suffers a similar cleavage within the self which has identified with such a parent. Exposures to such experiences are in part responsible for the numerous discontinuities in the later personality structure of the adult and for the cleavages between feelings, ideas and actions which radically complicate the achievement of a firm sense of personal identity. Such confusion arises not only from the inconsistencies in the parent-child interactions, and from the discrepancies between these parent-child interactions and the interactions of the parents with others, but also from the discrepancies within these latter alone.

VICARIOUS HUMILIATION: THE HUMILIATED FATHER

A related source of shame and contempt which arises from the relationships between the parent and others is vicarious humiliation. Regardless of the ideology of the parent, the child is very likely to idealize the parent if for no other reason than that he appears to be an extraordinarily competent giant. When the child discovers the feet of clay of the hero, there is likely to be a deep disenchantment, with contempt for and shame of the parent, and self-contempt and self-shame by virtue of identification with the parent.

All children are vulnerable to such disenchantment as they grow, first into equality with the parent, and then into some superiority as the parent becomes older and possibly senile. However the children of the lower classes, of immigrant families and of minority groups are particularly vulnerable to such sudden and deep shame experiences. Thus we have observed the son of an American Negro intensely humiliated through the witnessing of the humiliation of his father at the hands of a white who would not serve him in a public eating place. A classic instance among Jews is the incident recounted by Freud.

In the *Interpretation of Dreams* Freud tells of an incident recounted to him by his father, in which a fur cap is knocked off his father's head into the mud by a Christian; his father simply picked up the cap without protest. The young Freud was humiliated and would have avenged the insult. "That did not seem heroic on the part of the big, strong man who was leading me, a little fellow, by the hand. I contrasted this situation, which did not please me, with another, more in harmony with my sentiments — the scene in which Hannibal's father, Hamilcar Barca, made his son swear before the household altar to take vengeance on the Romans. Ever since then Hannibal has had a place in my fantasies.

"When I finally came to realize the consequences of belonging to an alien race, and was forced by the anti-Semitic feeling among my class-mates to take a definite stand, the figure of the Semitic commander assumed still greater proportions in my imagination. Hannibal and Rome symbolized, in my youthful eyes, the struggle between the tenacity of the Jews and the organization of the Catholic Church."

Despite the centrality of the affects of shame and contempt in Freud's personality, he failed to analyze them fully; and, as we shall see, projected them (in order to attempt to come to terms with them) into the concept of castration anxiety, which implicitly symbolizes humiliation as well as anxiety.

THE GUILTY ARE MORE IMPORTANT THAN THE INNOCENT

Returning now to the contempt ideology, there is an expressed unwillingness to let a single guilty individual escape detection and punishment, no matter what the cost to the innocent. The offense to the zealous that the guilty should go unpunished is much more painful than that some innocents should be humiliated or punished as a by-product of the reign of zeal.

In part, this is justified on the ground that there are no purely innocent human beings. If they are humiliated or punished unjustly, there is a presumption that there have been other offenses which they have committed for which punishment is appropriate, and at the very least it will act as deterrent to them and other potential future offenders. If an individual is innocent now, the presumption is against his continued innocence.

Therefore the punishment of the guilty should not be attenuated by any undue concern for possible injustice to the innocent. The consequence of such a generally repressive ideology, as the child hears it expressed by the parent, is to maximize in the mind of the child the possibility of experiencing punishment and humiliation at the hands of his parents or at the hands of other adults who might share such an ideology.

CLARITY OF EVALUATION AND RESPONSIBILITY FOR SHAMEFUL BEHAVOIR IS AMPLIFIED: THE SHAMING PARENT

Rather than anticipating the possibility of shame and blame and attenuating the clarity of responsibility by backing away from the evaluation of behavior, the parent employs a shame microscope. He is continually on the alert for possible offenders. He is a witch hunter. He illuminates and amplifies the possible occasions for shaming by evaluating others as his way of life. He is a professional critic. Just as a non-shaming parent is concerned lest he find another inferior or guilty, so this one is concerned lest he find another superior or innocent. The evaluation function is restricted to derogation.

PUNISHMENT SHOULD BE SWIFT, CERTAIN AND SEVERE

The child may be exposed to a parent whose ideology, action and feelings are integrated and who metes out humiliation and punishment which is swift, certain and severe. He believes that it is better to err on the side of severity rather than leniency, since the child, like all human beings, is presumed to have within him the potentiality for more future offenses. It is expressed verbally as the ideology that nothing is more important than clarity about fundamentals and appropriate action immediately following shameful behavior. The child, like others, is thought to need and want structure in his life. If he does not want it, he needs it; and if he does not need it, at the very least he deserves it, since he is at heart contemptible. As such a parent is confronted with recurrent offenses, there is an exponential

growth in the severity of humiliation and punishment which is
meted out since the repeated flouting of authority compounds
the sin.

ATONEMENT AND RESTITUTION ARE REQUIRED OF THE CHILD

The monopolistic growth of shame and contempt in the child
is accelerated by parents who not only humiliate him but who
require him to confess his unworthiness or to promise to reform
or to make some kind of restitution. For this further humiliation
of the child, there is no reciprocal effort made by the parent to
soften the blow. More often the case is not permitted to be
closed, but is recalled from time to time as a reminder of the
child's fallibility. If there is to be any atonement by the parent,
it is for any failure of nerve by him to uphold the norm, out of
sympathy for the child. Occasionally the parent may be soft in
his shaming of the child. These are the occasions for which the
parent holds himself, and others in analogous situations, most
accountable. The failure to be harsh enough in the defense of
standards is the most serious offense for which the representative
of authority should atone.

INTOLERANCE AND CONTEMPT—DISGUST FOR THE FEELING OF SHAME AS SUCH

The monopolistic growth of the humiliation complex is favored by any parent who responds to his own shame with disgust and
contempt. Such a parent can tolerate even self-contempt since
that part of the self can then be rejected. But shame, which is
an ambivalent response of the self as a whole to the self as a
whole, cannot be so readily tolerated by the parent who is
governed primarily by a contempt ideology. It would be dangerously close to having to reject the self as a whole completely.
The child is taught by such an adult that his display of shame,
quite apart from its sources and its appropriateness, is itself a
response which arouses contempt in the parent, so that he is
ashamed to show that he feels ashamed. Shame itself then must be

hidden as an ugly scar is hidden, lest it offend the one who looks at it.

The role of shame can be amplified by requiring that it be hidden, so that shame inhibition is not minimized as in the rewarding socialization of shame. The child's parent may require that the child hide his shame response not only because of an intolerance of the display of shame as such, as described above, but also because the display of shame means that the child has accepted defeat. Such a parent may wish his child to become independent, competent, to have high achievement motivation as well as to achieve much. When the child who feels defeated hangs his head in shame, this evokes contempt, not for the affect of shame as such but as a sign of quitting or of lack of motivation or both. This child must hide shame lest he betray his lack of persistence and lack of will to achieve and to succeed.

Again, some parents require that shame be hidden because it is a sign of general unhappiness and discouragement, and the parent requires the child to appear happier than he is. There is a taboo on depression, which ordinarily requires that energy level be kept high and any sign of distress or shame be hidden.

A taboo may be communicated by parents who do not wish to interfere with the display of shame by their discouraged and defeated children. When the child who feels defeated hangs his head in shame, the parent through empathy and identification can also be made to feel defeated. For example, if a child comes home with a very poor report card from school, which indicates a serious failure and this is now public knowledge, the parent may suffer humiliation at his child's defeat. He hangs his head while the child hangs his head. Such an experience in which the child's own shame is further amplified by seeing that the parent too is deeply ashamed may so radically increase the impact of shame that the child feels constrained to hide his shame out of love and respect for the parent. Such pressure, even though unintended, may nonetheless exaggerate the impact of shame.

The necessity of hiding shame and its sources enormously increases the stress of adolescence. When the increase in the strength of the sex drive evokes guilt in the adolescent who has an over-empathic parent, the adolescent feels he must hide both his sex drive and his guilt (which, according to our view, is a variety of shame) lest he increase his and his parents' humiliation, and thus forfeit the love and respect of his parents who would be shocked by the disclosure. The common difficulty in feeling tenderness and lust toward the same person, which Freud attributed to the Oedipus complex, we think is rather a consequence of shaming the child than of terrorizing him. The child whose libido is split between love and sex and who grows into an adult who distinguishes sharply between sacred and profane love is, we think, one whose mother and/or father characteristically expressed intense shame not only at the child's display of sexuality but also at other offenses against the parents' norms; the parent responded to the shame response of the child with empathic shame regardless of its source, and nonetheless responded to most of the child's displays with love and respect. Under these conditions the child is motivated to hide his shame and his sexuality as well as his other sources of shame.

One consequence of inhibiting these responses is a rapid luxuriant growth of shame in connection with sexuality, and thence the limitation of the expression of shameful sexuality to shameful sex objects and the limitation of the expression of love to beloved and loving objects who do not evoke or satisfy or respond to the sexual impulse.

HUMILIATION IS HEAPED UPON HUMILIATION

The monopolistic growth of shame and self-contempt is produced by the compounding of shame and self-contempt. When the child feels ashamed and discouraged after failure, his shame is increased by heaping shame or contempt upon shame. He is shamed because he has failed or because he has surrendered or both. Further, he may be shamed into trying again. In this way shame and failure are used to amplify each other. In such a socialization self-confidence may be either utterly destroyed or consolidated in the crucible of compounded humiliation. If he is defeated by the severity of such a socialization, he is consumed with shame or self-contempt. If he survives, he may learn to tolerate considerable shame and self-contempt and to come back for more until finally he overcomes his defeats. In such a case it is contempt and the dangers of possible self-contempt which become monopolistic. He learns to have contempt for those who surrender too easily and to avoid defeat at any cost lest he suffer self-contempt. In contrast to the rewarding socialization, he has not been trained to swim in the sea of risk, but he has been thrown in and left to sink or swim.

Relationship between the intrusion, iceberg models and the monopolistic, snowball models

In general, it is a rewarding socialization of shame and contempt which prompts the formation of a weak, intrusive shame theory and its developmental analog, the iceberg model. The iceberg model can also, as we have seen, develop after a childhood in which the same theory was monopolistic but which in later conditions becomes more benign, so that a rewarding socialization is not always necessary for the iceberg model.

But the monopolistic model of shame theory, whether it eventually leads to the iceberg model or to the snowball model, is primarily produced by a punitive socialization of shame and contempt, which we have just examined. Whether a punitive shame socialization leads in the long run to the developmental snowball model will depend as much on the child's resources, native and environmental, and on the vicissitudes of development as on the earlier parent-child interactions.

In all of our models, the relationship between socialization and the childhood personality must be assumed to be much closer than that between either of these and the later personality. It is in the snowball model par excellence that the impact of socialization has the greatest magnitude, the greatest continuity and the greatest one-way interdependency. The Psychoanalytic model has so stressed the snowball and iceberg models that the co-existence and late bloomer models have been somewhat discounted as alternatives.

In our view, the influence of any experience on the total personality depends primarily on how it is processed; that is, upon the transformations which the ideo-affective organizations make upon it, the ideo-affective organizations which it may initiate or the transformations which it may initiate on the dominant ideo-affective organizations within the personality. Any experience, in short, may initiate theories, change them or be changed by them. It is primarily the ideo-affective organization which is formed or transformed by any particular experience which will determine the future role of that experience in the life history of the individual. That role may be described by three dimensions: magnitude, independence and direction of interdependence. In the iceberg and intrusion models the magnitude is weak, and there is relative independence of minor and major elements in the personality. In the monopolistic and snowball models the magnitude is strong, there is great interdependence rather than independence of organization and the interdependence is in the direction of the time arrow, from past to present. In the snowball model the core experience continues to grow in influence by assimilating new experience to itself as a special case of what has been established and apparently repeated again and again.

At every moment of his life a human being is bombarded with information which is in numerous ways similar to his past experience and in equally numerous ways quite different from his past experience. He is therefore continually confronted with the possibility of stabilizing his world by interpreting it as essentially repetitive. He also enjoys the option of responding to the present as largely new and independent of his past experience. Finally, he has the option of responding to much of the novelty in his later experience without entirely surrendering his past experience, but continually reinterpreting the latter in the light of recent experience so that a higher integration is achieved. This latter represents the strategy of the integration and late bloomer model. The interpretation of new experience as independent of early experience is one mode of the competition and co-existence models, and the continual reinterpretation of the present in terms of the past is the dominant mode of the monopolistic, snowball models.

RELATIONSHIP BETWEEN MEMORY, THINKING AND LEARNING

If a theory of memory was necessary to account for the intrusion, iceberg model, a theory of thinking and learning is necessary to account for the monopolistic snowball model. In the iceberg model we were concerned primarily with the retrieval of information at a specific address by a specific name. This is a memory function in which the same information may be used over and over again. In the theory of memory, the information stored at a specific address was a compressed analog of a past experience in which enough unique information was preserved so that an expansion transformation could be learned to recover that past experience to any desired degree of precision.

Thinking, however, is a technique of dealing with classes of objects rather than with unique objects. It will clarify the discussion if we replace the word memory, which as ordinarily used refers to a complex function involving thinking, with more specific terms—storage, retrieval and compression-expansion transformations.

Storage is an automatic, unlearned process. Retrieval must be. learned, usually through compression-expansion transformations. Such transformations are as flexible and active as conceptual transformations but have an aim which is different from the transformations involved in thinking and concept formation. Storage and retrieval are organized to minimize class membership, and thinking is organized to maximize class membership. The difference may be seen at the level of the most elementary concepts. It is one thing to recognize or remember the appearance of my dog and quite another to know what the concept dog means, whether we refer to the intensive or extensive definition of the concept. If an individual remembers his dog as though it were no more than *a* dog, he has erred as much as if he responds to the concept dog as though it referred exclusively to *his* dog. Not only is there a difference between minimizing versus maximizing class membership in storage and retrieval versus thinking; retrieval involves a part-whole synthesis, while thought requires a whole-part analysis.

In reproduction, as well as in some recognition, the name is something less than the original, and from this something less, which may be a part of the original (or a sign or something similar), the unique original whole can be recovered through expansion of the compressed analog.

If storage and retrieval involve the recognition or reproduction of a whole from a part, the formation and utilization of a symbol involves the detection or generation of a critical, communal, non-unique part from the whole. What is an instance of the concept in the particular whole object is embedded in the object and often hidden by other characteristics which may be more salient. The aim of thinking is to construct a class with a symbol, rather than a unique object with a name. The difference between a *name* and a *symbol* is a critical distinction within our theory of cognition.

The symbol is the neurological structure which enables the detection of the similarity between members of a class and an indefinite number of new instances of members of a class, which may differ radically from previously identified members of the learned class. As such, a symbol is a means not only of detecting similarities in otherwise disparate entities but also of creating similarities where none may have existed before as, e.g., in drawing new kinds of dogs. We will define a symbol as any learned technique for maximizing the repetitions within a class, and this information is stored at a specific address.

In memorizing, the non-unique characteristics of the object which are common to that object and other objects are compressed, e.g., the speed and volume of speech is compressed in memorizing the telephone number, whereas what is selected for permanent storage is only what is unique in the information. It is similar to a microfilm library which can be used with a magnifying glass. So long as the shape of the letters and their order is preserved in an analog, size and other non-unique aspects of the information can be compressed and then recovered through expansion. In contrast, when a set of objects is conceptualized or symbolized, that aspect of a set of objects which they share in common is detected, compressed and miniaturized; the other, relatively unique information about each object is disregarded. That which is unique in the object is preserved in one compression-expansion transformation (storage and retrieval); whereas that which is common in the object relative to other objects is preserved in the other set of transformations (thinking).

It should also be noted that compression-expansion transformations are used both in storage-retrieval and in concept formation. The major differences are, first, in whether it is the unique or the common features of the object which are compressed; and second, in the scope of such transformations. Whereas the model to be compressed is given in storage, and can be continually used to monitor the adequacy of retrieval, such is not the case in concept formation. Not only is it the non-unique aspect of the object which must first be detected and then compressed as a symbol, which will enable the detection of other instances of class membership, but this aspect is never immediately given in experience. Any experience can be memorized, so long as it can be experienced, no matter how piecemeal memorization may have to be, and no matter how long it may take to memorize. It may be hard work and the compression-expansion transformations may be complex, but the criterion by which these efforts can be evaluated is usually clear. In the concept formation underlying the construction of a symbol, there is no such clarity or certainty. The concept itself has first to be learned, and it is never certain that the concept has in fact been adequately understood until it has been detected in objects other than the original object.

Symbols and names

The distinction between a symbol and a name is a distinction between two types of relationships between neurological traces and other messages. A name is any message which has the property of activating information stored at a specific address in the nervous system. A symbol is a type of information stored at a specific address which has the property of operating on

messages so that a particular class of information is either detected or generated. If a computer program were stored at a
specific address within the computer, it would constitute an
instance of a symbol. A symbol therefore may have a name, but
a name need not be the name of a symbol, since it can also be
the name of a specific memory.

A name activates specific traces at which there may be stored
either a compressed analog of the name or a symbol, a stored
strategy for further transforming messages to extract symbol-
relevant information. One has attained a concept to the extent
to which one can reproduce or recognize any and every instance
of the concept in a series of objects. One has attained a memory
to the extent to which one can reproduce or recognize a particular object as distinct from other particular objects.

It should be noted that in the case of both names and symbols
we are dealing with learned phenomena. We are dealing with
memories and thoughts, rather than with memorizing and thinking. Names and symbols refer to neurological structures which
have been stabilized after much learning and numerous transformations have occurred. Memorizing (storage and retrieval)
is as active and problem-solving a process as is thinking. It
utilizes internal feedback circuitry. By the same token, congealed thoughts are as structural and stable phenomena as
congealed memories or their inherited analogs, the genes. Many
of our learned skills are as "remembered" as the simplest rote
memories, despite their greater complexity. In this sense a
symbol resembles a program in a computer, which, no matter
what its complexity, does not generate more information than has
been built into it. This is not to say that there are any inherent
restrictions on how much complexity can be built into a program
or a symbol.

The distinction between the processes of memorizing and
thinking and their products, memories and thoughts, should not
be blurred because of the lack of theoretical restriction on the
magnitude and complexity of information which may be handled
by either memories or thoughts. This distinction, as we shall see,
may become quite critical in the option between the monopolism
of the snowball model, the competition of the co-existence model
and the integration of the late bloomer model. The latter, for

example, places a particularly heavy burden on thinking rather than on previously acquired thoughts, and on thoughts (symbols) rather than on memories.

Whereas we could give a somewhat detailed account of the process of memorizing as a set of compression-expansion transformations, no such general paradigm exists for thinking because of the great increase in degrees of freedom in thinking. Thinking, indeed, necessarily involves so many false starts relative to successful problem solution that the latter is a relatively minor part of the description and understanding of the dynamics of thinking. Indeed, the analysis of thinking would no doubt be much further advanced than it is today had it not been seduced by the lure of the problem solution as constituting the major part of the phenomenon of thinking. To understand thinking, we need to return to an analysis of what we have called transformation dynamics, which will be discussed in more detail in Volume III in the chapter on transformation dynamics.

We will examine at this point, however, some of the interrelationships between thoughts and thinking, as we consider how a shame theory becomes monopolistic and then snowballs during the developmental process.

The symbol as unfinished business

Because a symbol is a stored learned technique of maximizing repetitions within a class, it is a continually unfinished business, with the properties of an open rather than a closed system. Whether the next object will be co-ordinated to one symbol or another will depend in part on the competition between symbols and the monopolistic power of one symbol over another as well as on the nature of the object. Because of the competition between symbols and between symbols and unique objects, they characteristically grow stronger or weaker. Every new encounter with the same object as well as with new objects has within it the potentiality of destroying the symbol which was once achieved in commerce with it.

Because the neurological symbol which underlies conceptual activity is a strategy for detecting or generating similarities, it is not only an unfinished business but also an unfinishable business, inasmuch as new information will necessarily present new challenges for the detection of the symbol, and other symbols will also provide competition. A one-tracked mind, possessed by a monopolistic theory, however, minimizes such competition. Such an individual is regularly confirmed in his theory despite the greatest improbabilities. Such a mind continues to find theoretical needles in every haystack.

SYMBOLS AND SHAME THEORY: SOME CLARIFIED DEFINITIONS

Let us now consider the relationship between this theory of thought and thinking to the ideo-affective organization we have called shame theory. Symbols vary not only in their complexity but also with respect to their domain. The invariances whose detection or generation is controlled by symbols occur within or between the perceptual, affective, ideational or motor domains. A monopolistic affect theory is a symbol which organizes the interpretation of perceptual input, co-ordinates it to a particular affect, prompts ideational elaboration about this affect as well as alternative action strategies to cope with different types of affect arousing or threatening situations. This is why we have frequently used as synonyms the terms affect theory and ideo-affective organizations. The latter would indeed more properly have been expanded to "perceptual-ideo-affective-motor organizations." We have used the briefer designation for convenience, and we have also used the word theory as an abbreviation of an organization which in its monopolistic form includes every subsystem of the personality. This is an idiosyncratic use of the word theory. We have used the word theory rather than system because we wish to use it to correspond to the neurological structure we have defined as a symbol. Since symbols vary in complexity from the simplest concepts to the most elaborate sets of concepts, such as systems, we have compromised and used the word theory to refer to symbols of any degree of complexity. We have used the word theory to refer to symbols, as we have used the word names to refer to memories stored at specific addresses.

Since most affect theories have a degree of complexity well above that of simple concepts, the word does not do violence to the systematic nature of the symbols involved even when it is a minor, weak affect theory as in the intrusion model. Further, we have used the word theory to stress the high-order inferential processes which are inevitably involved when a human being is engaged by affect. The co-ordinations of percepts, ideas and actions which are prompted by even the most transitory affects are of the same general order as those involved in science in the co-ordination of empirical evidence and theory. The individual whose affect is engaged is inevitably thereby confronted with such questions as: "What is happening?" "What is going to happen?" "How sure am I of what seems to be happening and what will happen?" "What should I do?" These are theoretical questions in that they involve the interpretation of empirical evidence, the extrapolation into the future, the evaluation of both interpretation and extrapolation and the application of knowledge to strategy.

We are using the word theory to refer to the neurological symbol which activates particular affects in response to such interpretations, which activates further cognitive elaborations and transformations in response to both these interpretations and the affect thereby aroused, and finally which programs alternative decisions and actions in the light of these combined sequences of perceptual, ideo-affective experiences.

The problem of relative independent sub-systems

It is clear that a theory is an organization of sub-systems and sub-theories, each of which may enjoy considerable freedom from each others' influence, and vary also in their degree of differentiation and complexity. Thus, if the individual could distinguish five different degrees of inferiority, ranging from slight to very serious, he might nonetheless not be capable of responding with five matching degrees of shame or self-contempt. He might be capable of responding only with slight shame or with utter humiliation. There would be several different combinations possible, given 5 discriminations of inferiority and 2 intensities of shame. One individual might respond to values 1, 2 of inferiority with slight shame, and to values 3, 4, 5 with intense shame. Another might respond to values 1, 2, 3, 4 with slight shame, and to 5 with intense shame. Still another might respond to value 1 with slight shame and to 2, 3, 4, 5 with intense shame.

Given these varieties of combinations of interpretation and aroused affect, there may also be significant differences both in the number of alternative strategies for either avoiding shame or reducing shame, as well as in their relative effectiveness. Thus two individuals who respond to all inputs in terms of five degrees of difference of interpreted inferiority or moral culpability, and who agree in responding to 1, 2, 3 with weak shame and to 4, 5 with intense shame might differ radically in how many strategies they have learned for avoiding shame, and in the differentiation of strategies for dealing with weak shame compared with intense shame.

Further, there can be gross differences between the number of alternative strategies available and their relative effectiveness. One individual has at his disposal numerous strategies, none of them effective in either avoiding or reducing shame; another has only one strategy but it is very effective in avoiding shame, and still another has numerous effective strategies. Differences in the degree of differentiation between sub-systems and the programs which govern them is the rule rather than the exception. As a consequence, inconsistency, conflict and incomplete integration within personality is much more common than integration. Monopolism as a very special type of integration is the rarest type of personality organization. If it is possible for an individual to respond with intense humiliation to a broad spectrum of circumstances but to believe an ideology of the glory of man, to what shall we refer as a monopolistic humiliation theory? If an individual has Machiavellian beliefs but is in fact not contemptuous but kind to human beings, what shall we mean by a monopolistic contempt theory? Given such potential critical heterogeneity in the structure of perceptual-ideo-affective-motor organizations, what are we to mean when we speak of a monopolistic humiliation or contempt theory?

Is it to be considered monopolistic whenever every perceptual interpretation is in terms of humiliation, whenever every thought concerns humiliation, whenever shame is the only affect which is ever experienced, whenever action is perpetually governed by strategies of avoiding or escaping from humiliation, whenever action is perpetually effective or ineffective in avoiding or escaping humiliation? Unfortunately these criteria are not identical.

Assumed homogeneity and simplistic theory in psychology

This relative independence of sub-systems and the sub-theories and sub-programs which govern them has been a source of continual embarrassment to personality theorists and experimentalists. The quest for generality of explanation has again and again prompted the assumption of more homogeneity between sub-systems than is usually warranted. Generalizations have often been reminiscent of the efforts of the pre-Socratic philosophers to deal with nature—that all is one or two or three or four substances, such as air, earth, fire and water. Today they may be called factors. The mind is either open or closed, authoritarian or democratic, concrete or abstract, field-independent or dependent, overconforming or independent, very anxious or not anxious. Once the skeleton of the personality has been laid bare at either the action, perceptual or ideological level, the flesh which is then put on this skeleton is assumed to be consistent with and derived from this skeleton.

So if an individual has an authoritarian ideology, it is assumed and proven that he also has an authoritarian personality in general, and that he acts, feels and perceives as an authoritarian. If he has an open mind, it is assumed and proven that he wears the flesh which will cover these structural bones. When it happens, as it does, that an authoritarian ideology is the ideology of an individual whose behavior is somewhat permissive or even democratic, and conversely, that the democratic ideology is passionately affirmed by an individual who is in fact authoritarian in most of his interpersonal relationships, these are regarded as embarrassments to the theory.

Again, many investigators have begun at the action level. Will the individual yield or not yield in a conformity experiment? Yielders and non-yielders then form the bare bones of the skeleton, and appropriate flesh is postulated and found at the ideological and perceptual level. Again, the skeleton may be perceptual. Does the individual orient himself with respect to his body or to his surroundings? If he does one or the other, the effort is made to account for the remainder of personality on a two-way classification. It should be clear that if one begins with a dichotomous or trichotomous classification of either ideology, action and/or perception, one will be constrained, insofar as generality of explanation is sought, to impose the same categorization on the residual sub-systems.

We may be judged to have fallen into the same trap in connection with our theory of ideology and affect in the chapter on Ideology and Affect. Since we postulate an historical polarization of ideology into right, left and center positions, and since we suggest a family of programs for the socialization of affect which bias the individual in one direction or another, the critic may find us guilty of what we are here accusing others of doing. We have, however, attempted to cope with this radical reduction of complexity at the ideological level by the concept of resonance. By resonance we refer to the process whereby two individuals with otherwise different personality structures may be attracted to the same ideology for somewhat different reasons, as two individuals may fall in love with the same person for somewhat different reasons.

GROWTH FROM DISCONTINUITY: A POSSIBILITY OBSERVED BY PSYCHOANALYSIS

Discontinuities between perception, cognition, affect and action are the rule and not the exception. They are a source not only of stress and strain but of development, as we will see in connection with the integration and late bloomer models. It is just because there is relative independence of perception, ideology, affect and action that human beings can be influenced to change. If one can persuade an individual to believe something other than he now believes, one may eventually influence his feelings and his actions. If one can arouse particular affects within an individual discrepant with his ideology, one may eventually influence that ideology and the action which flows from it. If one can induce an individual to act in a way he otherwise would not act, one has the beginning of leverage in changing his ideology and feelings.

Because of Psychoanalytic theory it has been fashionable for some time to consider that there are true motives which are the important entities in personality, and a variety of façades, ideological and behavioral, which primarily serve to conceal the central motives. Thus, Else Frenkl-Brunswik showed that those who were most strident in the proclamation of the nobility of human nature were in fact the most self-centered individuals. But the distinction between these individuals and their more consistent misanthropic brothers tended to be lost. Again, it was considered that exposure to an opposing ideological atmosphere in four years of college was essentially trivial when it could be shown that changes were merely intellectual, unaccompanied by affective change; and that when retested after college, the subjects showed ideological regression to the pre-college status.

Quite apart from the oversimplification of the nature of personality structure in such assumptions, it also has the consequence of reducing all developmental models to the snowball model and thereby to blind us to the real contingencies in development. It discourages the attempt to systematically change personality after infancy and early childhood.

It is our opinion that it is just the relative independence of sub-systems within the personality which makes it a perpetually open system whereby the past may be attenuated through the initiation of new perceptual experiences, new affective experiences, new ideas, new decisions and new actions. At the beginning it may be possible only to change one or another of these systems. If one does not take seriously *both* the independence and dependence of each of these sub-systems, one may be misled into either exaggerating or underestimating the significance of the change which has been effected when one succeeds in introducing such segmental novelty into the individual's experience.

Such new experience is akin to the beachhead, hard won by the landing of the first wave of troops invading a continent in a major war. The beachhead may be repulsed entirely when reserves are brought up, it may be contained or it may overrun and overwhelm the entrenched forces. Because of Psychoanalytic theory, the posture of contemporary personality theory resembles that which assumed the impregnability of the Maginot line rather than the strategy of the highly mobilized army which broke that line, or of the strategy of the Allied invasion of Europe which in turn broke the German fixed line of defense.

The practical consequences of assuming more homogeneity of personality structure than exists is the discouragement produced by the self-fulfilling prophecy. Since many beachheads will be pushed into the sea, and since many will be entirely contained within a small pocket of the personality, the monopolistic and snowball models will be confirmed again and again as entirely appropriate cognitive maps for the study of personality. Important beachheads which might have been extended to finally reorganize the personality will not be exploited when it is assumed, on theoretical grounds, that the probabilities are too small to justify the sustained and costly effort which is involved in the transformation of any personality.

Development is necessarily both continuous and discontinuous. This means that the quantal jumps from one moment to the next are not likely to influence every sub-system with equal force. One will be more influenced in his modes of thinking when one is learning logic in a classroom than at the action and feeling level, as when one is mountain climbing.

Commonplace and nineteenth-century-ish as the distinctions are, between the "faculties," it is our belief that they must be reintroduced (in the form of sub-systems) and taken seriously in personality theory if we are to understand the complex structure of personality.

THE MEASUREMENT OF PERSONALITY CHANGE

These considerations are relevant not only to the developmental problem of the transformation of personality, but also to the measurement of any personality change. Thus the measurement of the impact of four years of college cannot be assessed either by measures of changes in information alone, or by measures of changes in conceptual skill alone, or by measures of changes of perceptual skill alone, or by measures of changes in responsiveness alone, or by measures of changes in decision making alone, or by measures of changes in action alone. The impact may be very slight on all of these sub-systems, or more substantial on a few of them, or major in one sub-system and zero in all other sub-systems. It is quite possible that three such outcomes can be exactly equivalent in terms of the ultimate impact of such an experience as four years in college. If a college experience produces a small but reliable set of changes in what is perceived, what is learned, how one thinks, the objects towards which one makes decisions, and the kinds of actions one takes, this set of changes may in the long run produce radical changes in the future personality by steady attrition on the dominant structures.

A future transformation of the same scope may be the outcome of a more substantial change which during the college years is restricted to the area of conceptual skill and the acquisition of information. In such a case the individual learns, for the first time, how to evaluate evidence and how to solve problems, and he also acquires a large store of new information. When he leaves college, the application of his new knowledge and his new techniques of handling information may eventually significantly change his ideology, his affective investments and his overt behavior.

Finally, the individual who is changed in only one way, but that a radical change, may also later generalize and exploit this beachhead so that his whole personality is transformed. This may happen if he is converted to any organized ideological movement. In the college years this may be restricted to the ideological level. He may shift, for example, from a strong belief in the ideology of one political party to an equally strong belief in the ideology of an opposing political party. After graduation he may become more actively involved in leadership in this party and so his affects and thoughts become integrated and committed to a way of life which would not have been possible except for the change at the ideological level during the college years—this despite the fact that the change was at that time only an "intellectual" change. If we assume that significant development is, in fact, always possible, then it is clear that the measurement of the impact of any experience, whether it occurs in

childhood, in adolescence or in adulthood, must include measures
of the delayed, long-term effects, and that development must
be measured until death.

Implications for the interpretation and validation of projective tests

The same problem of the complexity of measurement of
independent sub-systems is also involved whenever we subject
an individual or group to an experimental or clinical treatment.
Nothing is more commonplace than the discrepancies revealed
by the studies of the effects of psychotherapy on neurotic and
psychotic individuals. A psychotic who is very much improved
by psychotherapy in terms of clinical status often shows no
change in his Rorschach record. He may now be a relatively
tranquil individual whose feelings and behavior both suggest
that he should be discharged from the hospital. His Rorschach
record, however, frequently shows no change from that taken
upon admission when he was in an acute phase of the psychotic
reaction.

How is it possible for the "basic" personality structure revealed by these responses to be so inert while the individual
seems to have made a recovery? We would suggest that in many
such instances what has taken place is a deceleration of growth
of the monopolistic theory. It is not unlike the affective storms
of terror or shame which may seize an otherwise normal individual under extreme provocation. When the acute affective
storm has subsided the person is "himself" again. The arousal
of terror or humiliation in the normal individual may well overwhelm anyone and will produce defensive phenomena which
would otherwise never appear. When the individual is no longer
in the grip of such affect, his dominant personality reasserts
itself. In the case of the psychotic whose Rorschach shows no
change despite radical change in feeling and behavior, the
"normal" personality is not normal, but is pre-psychotic in the
sense that the thresholds for psychotic perception, affect, cognition and behavior are lower than in the normal. Nonetheless this
state of latent psychosis is sufficiently distinct from the acute

state to produce the discrepancy between the Rorschach record which taps potential as well as manifest feeling and behavior.

The supposed invalidities of projective material depend in large part on the failure to take seriously the distinctions between perceiving, expecting, thinking, feeling, and deciding and acting. Further, there has been a failure to consider the much more subtle distinctions between specific "names" which are activated only under the most particular circumstances, as in the intrusion model, and the more general names, as in the monopolistic model. Finally, there has been a failure to take seriously the distinction between the state of the individual when specific affects are in a state of activation and when they are dormant, but with variations in general threshold values from individual to individual.

The multiplicity of similarities

Finally, the relative independence of sub-systems poses a problem for the definition of similarity and psychological class formation. Because similarity has so often been defined in "behavioral" terms, it has skirted dangerously close to circularity of definition. When an individual responds alike to two apparently different stimuli, this has often served as a criterion of perceptual similarity. Circularity is, however, not the most serious problem with such a definition of similarity. It is the multiplicity of similarities which is the more serious ambiguity. The ambiguity of such a definition of similarity is not exposed until one tries to specify what is a stimulus and what is a response. Thus, if the individual is asked to describe a stimulus at two different times and the descriptions are reasonably similar, one may suppose that the perceptions are similar. But if one asks the same individual to describe his feelings about the same stimulus at two different times, these may or may not be similar, and if they are different these differences may or may not be correlated with the descriptions of the percepts. Clearly, I may find a person more or less exciting the second time I see him, as I may find a joke more or less amusing the second time I hear it. It is also clear that the percepts may change along with these changed feelings, or they may not.

Further, if the individual were asked to freely associate or think about the stimuli, his thoughts might well vary with or without variation in the percepts which acted as the "stimuli" to these thoughts. Again, if the stimuli did produce exactly the same percepts and feelings on two separate occasions, there is no reason to suppose that the further thoughts aroused need be similar. A second unexpected contact with a person who is equally exciting as on the first meeting might well activate ideation about the fortunate accident and to plans for yet another meeting. The person who was equally interesting on second contact might clearly activate action calculated to effect a third meeting, even though the first contact had not produced a decision to effect a second meeting. The same feeling, in short, may or may not lead to the same decision or action.

The same action twice taken need not produce the same feeling. One may become habituated or sensitized, so that the third meeting and the fourth meeting evoke increasing interest or extinguish interest altogether. All of these examples are commonplace enough. They have not obtruded themselves into the discussion of psychological similarity because the problem seems difficult enough when it is limited to the domain of perceptual invariances. Theorists have been content to let sleeping subsystems lie.

There are, nonetheless, as many different types of similarity as there are combinations of sub-systems. A percept may be different or similar to another percept, holding its stimulus constant. Holding a percept constant, it may evoke different or similar affects on different occasions. Holding a percept constant, it may evoke different or similar ideas on different occasions. Holding a percept constant, it may evoke different or similar actions on different occasions. Holding a feeling constant, it may evoke different or similar actions on different occasions. Holding a feeling constant, it may evoke similar or different ideas on different occasions. Holding ideation constant, it may evoke similar or different action on different occasions. Holding ideation constant, it may evoke similar or different feelings on different occasions.

The same logic holds for the varieties of triads as the independent variables. Thus, given the same stimulus, the same perception, the same feeling, the individual may or may not respond with the same ideas and the same actions on two or more occasions. Further, similarity on two occasions does not guarantee similarity on three occasions and least of all on *n* occasions. The problem of similarity, when scrutinized closely, mushrooms into what we have called the problem of "affect theory," the complex interrelationships between stimuli, percepts, memories, concepts, affects and actions.

A RETURN TO THE QUESTION OF WHAT IS A MONOPOLISTIC HUMILIATION THEORY

How then shall we define a monopolistic humiliation theory? The possible types of definition are numerous. We might say that humiliation theory is monopolistic when any one or any combination of sub-systems is entirely and continuously captured by this affect. We might say humiliation becomes monopolistic when the individual never experiences humiliation because he is forever vigilant and so always successfully avoids the feeling of shame. We might consider humiliation monopolistic whenever the individual is perpetually humiliated, as we define an anxiety neurosis by the presence of chronic anxiety. We might define it by the exclusive interpretation of stimuli in terms of their relevance for humiliation, independent of whether this leads to humiliation or to successful avoidance of the affective experience. Any one of these, or any combination, might be an appropriate way to define monopolistic humiliation theory.

The question is, however, not altogether a semantic one. It is in part a psychological question. One must ask what special states of sub-systems or what relationships between these must occur for monopolistic humiliation theory to take roots and grow. Monopolistic organization is, at the beginning, a fragile beach-head phenomenon. The probability that any beachhead will mushroom into a monopolistic organization and then grow into a snowball organization is in general extremely low. The cognitive and affective apparatus does not lend itself readily to monopolism. Indeed, whenever any negative affect assumes a monopolistic form, it is certain that we are dealing with psychopathology and highly probable that psychosis is involved. Before we address ourselves to the problem of the definition of monopolistic theory and to the analysis of its structure, it will help to examine in greater detail the nature of class formation, since any theory, monopolistic or otherwise, involves a class of classes.

Memory, class formation and the increase of humiliation

How does experience "grow"? Under what conditions will a single experience of humiliation make it more probable, first that I may be more readily humiliated in the future, and second that if I am humiliated again that these two or more separate experiences will initiate the formation of an ideo-affective organization in which these experiences become special cases, as members of a larger class?

If the initial experience has been stored as an isolated experience, then the probability that I will be humiliated again in this way depends in part on the nature of the name of this memory and its relation to later experience. As in the case of the recovery of early handwriting, if later experience is uniquely distinctive it will re-activate the earlier memory and with it the accompanying affect. How distinctively similar future experience may be to the first humiliation experience depends, in part, on how similar competing experience has been. To the extent to which a parent uses a particular tone of voice when he derogates the child, the probability of other tones of voice serving as names of the earlier humiliation is very low. By the same token there is a very high probability under such circumstances that, when the parent does use that particular tone of voice again as in the initial humiliation experience, the latter will be re-activated.

Conjoint versus alternative names for humiliation

To the extent to which the humiliation was accompanied by a relatively unique posture of the parent, and about a relatively unique type of behavior as well as by a unique tone of voice of the parent, the probabilities of re-activation are now further reduced unless these conjoint names are re-experienced. This is particularly so if the same tone of voice is often used without the particular posture associated with contempt, and this particular posture is often used in a non-derogatory way so long as the tone of voice is non-derogatory and finally if the type of behavior derogated is not always derogated. Thus if everytime the child turned on the TV very loud, the parent shook his finger and expressed his scorn in a loud tone of voice, it would in general require this triple conjoint behavior to re-activate his initial experience of shame at offending his parent. If, however, the parent often gesticulated with his fingers, often shouted when he was excited and happy as well as when he was angry and if, further he did not shout whenever the child simply turned on the TV, so long as it was not too loud, then the name would be a triple conjoint one in which each of the three characteristics of the parent's behavior would have to be emitted together to re-activate the earlier humiliation.

If however, the triple name was a triple alternative name (that is, if each name by itself was associated only with shame or contempt), this would increase the general probability of re-activation of humiliation by the parent or by a parent surrogate, for example, a teacher. Thus, if the parent never used this tone of voice except in angry disapproval, and if he never used this posture of shaking his finger except in angry disapproval, and if he never was harsh except about noise made by the child, then any one of these names would have the property of re-activating shame. Therefore when the child encountered a teacher or another adult who spoke to him in a derogatory tone of voice, or who gesticulated with his hands and shook his finger at him, or who talked to him quietly and calmly about the excessive noise he was making, any of these could re-activate the memory of past humiliation.

We may restate this most explicitly in the notation of symbolic logic, for those readers to whom such notation is familiar. (What is being said in these symbols has been explicitly stated in words, so that the symbol notation may be skipped by any reader to whom it is unfamiliar or confusing rather than clarifying.) Any experience of the form $(a \cdot b \cdot c \supset x) \cdot \sim (a \supset x) \cdot \sim (b \supset x) \cdot \sim (c \supset x) \cdot \sim (a' \cdot b' \cdot c' \supset x)$ (i.e., a and b and c together activate shame, but a alone does not, b alone does not, c alone does not, and any combination of non a, non b, non c does not) will restrict the activation of shame to the conjoint presence of a and b and c. Any experience of the form (a v b v c ⊃ x) .(a ⊃ x). ~ (a ⊃ x'). (b ⊃ x). ~ (b ⊃ x'). (c ⊃ x) . ~ (c ⊃ x') (i.e., a and, or b and, or c activate shame and a activates shame and nothing else, and b activates shame and nothing else, and c activates shame and nothing else) will lend itself to more frequent activation and to generalization of activation by parent surrogates, since the latter are more likely to manifest one of these triggers than all three at once, if these three are idiosyncratic to the parent.

Despite this fundamental difference, the conjoint name may change from an intrusive organization to a monopolistic organization if these conjoint conditions are encountered very frequently. If and when this happens, parts of the conjoint name may become alternative names, so that shame is activated by less than the total conjoint name. The part of the original name then becomes a name of the original name.

A closer look at memory and recognition and its relation to perception

So much for the role of memory in the first repetition of an initial experience. What will initiate the more critical transformation from the repetition of a memory of a past experience to an organized class of such experiences and ultimately to classes of classes in complex shame theories?

First is the nature of the initial memory. We have proceeded thus far on the assumption of detailed, exact reproduction of earlier experience. We have emphasized the storage and retrieval functions in such skills as handwriting, because rote memory is the most trying test of any thory of memory. It is not, however, a description of the way in which we remember most of our past experience. It is too costly, and would burden us with too detailed and too literal information if it were to be used to remember most of our past experience.

We must distinguish reproductive memory rather sharply from recognition memory. In recognition we may indeed reproduce the past exactly as it was perceived before, as we identify someone correctly when we meet him again. But we may also recognize an object which is only partly the same as we first perceived it. Growing more and more familiar with the same object, i.e., perceptual learning, demands that we recognize what we did before, but also something new each time, as in listening to a symphony repeatedly. The symphony does not change, but we must become more and more adept at recognizing its complexity. Further, if we are to recognize differences in the interpretation by two conductors, we must be able to make even more complex transformations on succeeding inputs.

We will now examine the nature of the original coding of experience (i.e., perception) and its relation to reproductive memory, to recognition, to symbols and to later theory formation. To the extent to which the original name formation in an experience of humiliation is detailed and specific, it has the possibility of remaining as an isolated experience, retrievable under very specific conditions, but it may also remain locked in memory for a lifetime, if the appropriate name is never again encountered. Its very detail and specificity provides the possibility of its preservation in isolation. This is a very improbable fate for any isolated experience because of the dependence of the access to memory on learning how to retrieve. Rote learning is essentially learning how to retrieve for reproductive memory. But, if rote memory is only occasionally the strategy for retrieval of past experience, how does one ordinarily learn to remember when one recognizes rather than reproduces information?

We ordinarily learn to recognize in two or more steps. First, the percept which is to be recognized is not given, but must be achieved by matching information already retrievable, with incoming sensory input. This matching we assume is a trial and error process involving an internal feedback circuit in which one first retrieves what is available and then modifies this past information which has been retrieved until the best fit is attained with the incoming information. It is this best-fitting information which becomes conscious and is then automatically stored as a new memory with which one can interpret the same sensory input when it is next received. In this way the tailoring and modification on older recognitions provide the newer recognitions which support increasing perceptual skill to match increasingly fine variations of sensory input. We are learning not only to perceive, but also to recognize more differentiated information and to retrieve this information with increasing skill. Instead of the self-conscious compression-expansion transformations which are required for rote memorizing, here it is the repetition of the challenge of the input to be matched that prompts the conjoint learning of both retrieving whatever is stored in memory and at the same time tailoring this information to better fit the present sensory input.

We use the term tailoring to suggest that the perceiver is like a clothier who has on his racks a number of suits which fit exactly all of last year's customers. He then attempts to fit each new customer this year on the assumption that he is either identical with or not very different from his former customers. If he has now to alter a suit so that the sleeves must be shortened, he then adds a replacement of these measurements to his stock for his next year's supply of suits. He now knows that he has a regular 44 in stock and also a 44 with slightly shorter sleeves.

It is our assumption that the human being would continue to stock or store every variant which his customer, nature, ever asked him to provide except for two considerations. One is that he has to learn where each suit is on the rack—the problem of retrieval. If he does not rote-memorize each sensory customer, a task for which he does not have enough time if he is to wait on each new customer, then he must begin to retrieve fewer suits, but be ready to make more extensive alterations so that these all-purpose models will fit more customers. This is another type of transformation, half way between the names produced by compression-expansion in rote memory in which class membership is minimized and the symbols produced by transformations in which class membership is maximized. These memories we are now considering describe no one past experience exactly, nor a general class exactly, but with minimal further transformation they do enable the generation, and therefore the recognition, of specific new objects.

The phenomenon of recognition, in short, demands neither exact memory of specifics nor the abstract concepts of thinking but an analog or set of analogs which can be altered to fit a variety of objects which are partly new and partly old.

The second consideration is that succeeding encounters with variants of the initial stimuli may not permit, or demand, modification of the past memory to better fit the new input. In terms of the clothier analogy, this would be the case either if all customers were built alike, or sufficiently so that the same suit on the rack fits them all, or if the fit was very crude but the customer did not complain, or the clothier was lazy, uninterested, had no motive to fit suits more closely or had a motive to act as if the suit fit better than it really did. Like a proofreader he may not pick up some errors because, despite his search for lack of fit, he too much expects his stored information to fit the input. Like an escaped hunted prisoner, everyone he sees may look like a guard or a policeman because he must avoid his past. Like a relatively unobservant user of money, he fails to detect counterfeit bills because their general shape and color and numbering is all he has ever had reason to learn accurately. In contrast to customers and the fit of their suits, nature will not inevitably complain about poor perceptual fits.

The mutual transformation of memories and percepts

Earlier memories, in short, must be learned to be retrieved in light of their relevance for succeeding inputs and purposes. How any unique experience will be remembered is a joint function of how it was originally experienced and to what extent succeeding inputs are experienced as similar. This is inevitably so, because of the necessity to match succeeding experience by past stored experience. In the process of such retrieval, there is the conjoint transformation of past memories and present percepts. The present customer can always be sent out with a poorly fitting suit, but it also happens that last year's suits may never be used again as models to be altered but may be displaced by the altered model as the suit to be stocked in abundance. If a clothier moved from a community of short-stouts to long-leans, it would be simpler to stock long-leans and occasionally shorten them in length for the occasional old short-stout customer who insisted on shopping with him than to carry short-stouts and make extensive alterations for the long-leans.

Apart from rote memory then, what we learn to remember

for purposes of recognition depends upon the continuing relevance of the initial experience to related, later experience. There is, however, a difficulty with the clothier analogy. Apart from rote memory the clothier does not have many suits, and he does not know where any of the suits he does have are on the rack. It is only because each new customer describes his needs that he learns to find something that, with considerable additions as well as alteration, may fit. However, to be precise, what he finds is not necessarily a suit but a sleeve, a vest or half of a pair of pants. His second customer may be sent out of the shop with a jacket without arms, or with something which has the shape of a whole suit but which is incomplete.

The individual learns to retrieve, then, not his original experience, but what that experience becomes as he attempts again and again to retrieve information which is relevant to present needs. The only way in which he can isolate past experience so that it is uniquely retrievable is through the complex compression-expansion transformations used in rote memorizing. Otherwise he is dependent on the initial abbreviation or coding by which he became aware of sensory input and by the additions and changes in these abbreviations which are dictated by succeeding experience.

A theory of traumatic experience: it does not exist except in the light of earlier and later experience

One important consequence of such a state of affairs for psychopathology and for the ultimate monopolistic affect theory which develops is that there is no such thing as a traumatic experience. An experience has to become traumatic by being further transformed both in content and in retrievability by succeeding experience. Of course, such succeeding experience may consist of purely conceptual transformation initiated by the individual himself without further environmental support, as a result of earlier experiences. Nonetheless, this work has to be done for the experience to become traumatic.

An important corollary for socialization is that parents had better be sensitized to the signs of traumatization rather than to the shielding of children from the dangers of potential trauma.

What is potentially traumatizing is also potentially enriching. If potential trauma is confronted and mastered, the person has gained a valuable quantum of immunity. If potential trauma is experienced in such a way that succeeding experience becomes more and more humiliating or terrifying, then a trauma is in the making and heroic measures should be taken to decelerate the galloping class formation and theory construction.

Haggard has shown that when subjects are stressed by painful electric shocks, those subjects who are relatively unaware of when they will be shocked are much more disturbed and intolerant of shock than those subjects who are aware of when they will be shocked.

Here we see that how much repetition there is of negative affect may depend upon the initial clarity of the perception of the activator.

The looser the fit between the achieved percept which activates negative affect and succeeding percepts, the greater is the probability that class formation will be diffuse rather than restricted. However, whether an initial coding of experience will lead to an eventual increase in diffuseness of class formation or to an eventual increase in specificity of class formation, i.e., eventual discrimination or eventual generalization, will depend on whether succeeding experiences demand or support further commerce with the more specific aspects of a single object or circumstance, or whether succeeding experiences encourage the individual to group his first experience with more and more examples of a broader class of objects. Thus, if a child is shamed for turning up the volume of the TV set, succeeding experience can dissociate the total shame experience from its possible initial meaning that his mother doesn't love him or that he cannot play at all at home, if he is permitted both to play at home and to listen to the TV at a reduced volume. If however there followed, in close succession to his initial experience, a series of tantrums on the part of his mother, first at his playing in the bedroom, and then in the living room, and then to his further protests, the original significance of the restriction on listening to TV at loud volume will be radically transformed as a special case of a much more alarming state of affairs.

It should be noted that, when the later, larger class is formed, the earlier memory of an initial set of related experiences is no longer readily retrievable. It is as lost as is the perception of a once new city or a new person after one has lived for some time in that city and with that person. It is as lost as all innocence may be lost. If I have had an initial experience with someone who seems enchanting upon first impression, I cannot readily recover that memory and that affect, if I later learn that I entirely mis-understood the significance of those impressions. Conversely, if I respond to someone on first meeting with strong negative affect and I later learn that this one is a diamond in the rough, I cannot readily now perceive him as I once did, independent of my present knowledge and feelings. What is live among my memories, and readily retrievable, are the present cumulative totals.

MEMORY AND CLASSES

It is our argument thus far that when memory is not specific rote memory, what are retrievable are incomplete and somewhat indeterminate fragments which can become complete and deter-minate in a variety of ways, depending upon the nature of succeeding demands on retrieval by succeeding sensory inputs. It is not simply that the first experience is changed, but rather that it has to be radically supplemented before it can learn to be retrieved. The first retrievable information should be sharply distinguished from the first stored information. Not all that is first stored may be retrieved unless succeeding inputs demand the learning of such retrieval skill. It may require several ex-posures to the same object to be able to remember what was first seen. If these succeeding trials, however, stress aspects of the object which were not seen at first, then what was seen first may never be learned to be retrieved. It is similar to the embedding of a word in a larger word. If one views letters sequentially, two at a time, then when the presentation is at-te-nt-io-n, the first two letters "at" may be seen as a word, but never retrievable as such from the word attention.

We must now examine some of the different ways in which classes may be learned, and the different ways in which they may be learned to be retrieved as memories. In the last example the whole of a series is neither perceived nor learned to be retrieved until a series of experiences has occurred. Clearly one could not learn to remember such a series until after it had been first perceived. But it may be perceived as a whole well before it can be retrieved as a whole. This is true even when the series of trials is in connection with one object, if each perception gives only a partial glimpse of the object.

There are many different ways in which initial experience may be analyzed and perceieved, and in which such initial analysis may be related to later retrieval. We will restrict our examination to a few of the major types of analysis and retrieval. These we have distinguished as summaries, totals, cumulative totals, averages, cumulative averages, variances, trends and correlations.

SUMMARIES

Let us first consider the summary. The summary is midway between rote memory which preserves the whole object intact and the simple concept of an attribute, such as red, which abstracts only one out of many characteristics of any object. The summary is an abbreviation or compression which refers to and thus preserves the whole properties of an object or a set of objects, while disregarding most of the particulars of the object. As such it is a compression transformation which differs from the compressions in rote memorizing because it is not strictly reversible as an expansion transformation. If I read a book and summarize it as "wonderful," so that I can retrieve only this summary, I may when someone later asks me to describe the book be incapable of retrieving any more from memory than this summary, despite the fact that I understood everything in the book as I read it. In such a case the initial analyses and storages may have been quite detailed, but the most frequently repeated retrievals are limited to exclamations such as "very good!" The summaries may, however, have been more detailed, such as "psychoanalytic," "non-directive," "Hullian" or may even have included the major contours of the arguments of the book.

Whatever detail may be included in the summary, it should be noted that what was perceived and understood as one read is never totally included in what we are defining as a summary transformation. The whole point of such a transformation is to compress and exclude part of the information which is perceived so that it may be more readily retrieved than if it had to be rote memorized. In contrast to rote memory it enables the retrieval of diffuse rather than specific information.

The informational advantage of summaries is very considerable. Information which is much too detailed and complex to be either detected or retrieved can be digested or generated piecemeal if the general outlines can be summarized at the outset. Summaries are resorted to not only to simplify the amount of information so that it can be retrieved more readily but also to enable the individual to perceive in the first place. Although perception enjoys the support of the sensory input which serves as a model for the retrieval, matching process, yet the input may be much too detailed, relative to the information which is stored in memory, to be perceived without some summarizing transformation. In listening to a long speech it would be difficult if not impossible to understand unless there were a concomitant compression of the sentences into summary form. The scientist may also first detect the meaning of his experimental data when he can convert the hundreds of detailed recorded observations into some summary measure which enables him to see the general trends within his data.

Summary: "they will humiliate me"

If succeeding experiences which otherwise differ in many particulars prompt the retrieval of a summary rather than a more detailed perceptual response, the past memories may also be transformed in this way so that both the past and the future become special cases and repetitions of the summary. Thus one may have had a variety of experiences with a variety of human beings. If, due to a critical set of experiences one begins to summarize these varieties of human beings as humiliators, then many initial experiences, which were subtly differentiated when they occurred, may henceforth be transformed and retrieved as humiliating.

If such summarization is part of the initial early experiences, then all future experience may be responded to in terms of such summaries. In this case the summary may be repeatedly confirmed, like a proofreader's error, because it displaces a more detailed perception of new experience which might disconfirm the summary. A child who begins to react frequently to his mother with the phrase "damned women," as one we know did, enjoys the advantage of picking up all the correct instances with minimal effort but at the price of considerable loss of sensitivity. Inasmuch as a summary of "shamer" may govern the initial response to a stranger, such summarization can readily produce the self-confirming prophecy, since the expectation of being humiliated can in fact later activate shame with other strangers and so confirm the summary response.

It should be noted that the summary may itself have quite different sequels. The summary may produce the self-confirming prophecy, so that all strangers and eventually all human beings do in fact become oppressors who humiliate and shame. The summary may however be restricted to individuals who do indeed derogate others. In this case the individual gives a summary response to many who differ from each other in many ways despite their common tendency to derogate.

The summary, however, may be the beginning of a set of transformations which finally enable the most sensitive discrimination not only of degrees of shame evocation but of non-shame evocation. An individual may begin to learn to swim by wildly flailing arms and legs at the same time, in a summary which is like a caricature of swimming; so an individual may begin by over-responding in all directions to derogation as though the world had in it nothing but oppressors. In both cases increasing contact may yield more and more precision and complexity in reproducing the exact nature of the model. In such learning, summaries are combined and refined by successive approximation.

Total: "all this humiliation"

Next we will consider the total as a conceptual transformation which influences the memories which are retrieved in the interpretation of new information. In contrast to the summary, the total is a conceptual transformation in which a series of past experiences is retrieved at a moment in time, reacted to as a unit which thenceforth is retrieved in place of the components of the total. Thus, if a child has been humiliated a dozen or more times, each experience may be responded to as an isolated experience until a critical moment when in the nursing of present wounded pride all past grievances are reviewed at once, and the child's awareness of the total generates a new experience which thencefore is retrieved whenever he is again shamed by his parent or by others.

Cumulative total: "more and more humiliation"

In the cumulative total, the same transformation which we have just described is continually repeated so that the sense of defeat and outrage grows with every repetition. Whereas a summary repeatedly confirms the same retrieval that one has again been humiliated in the same way, in the cumulative total there is a perennial freshness to each new outrage which is experienced as on the point of breaking the back of the oppressed one because of the intolerable growing total of insult. Again, with the changing cumulative total the earlier memories cease to be retrieved as such, except insofar as they are reflected in the total outrageous sum.

The average: "I will be somewhat humiliated, more or less"

In the class of transformations we have called averages, it is the central tendency of a series of experiences which is retrieved as a model to fit the present sensory input. Whereas a summary of past experience may produce an interpretation of a series past, or future, on the basis of one experience of humiliation, in which all others then become repetitions of this summary, in the transformation we call averaging it is the central tendency of a series which becomes the model by which future instances are judged. If the individual has been sometimes respected, sometimes deeply humiliated and sometimes only moderately shamed, and he applies an averaging transformation, he may thenceforth confront the future with a standard model whereby it is his expectation that he will be made only slightly uncomfortable.

This stored, now readily retrievable information may function in one of two ways. It may be used exclusively as an interpretation of every variety of derogation by the other, so that the individual is confirmed again and again in his mild feeling of shame and the accompanying summary that others are to be kept at arms length. It may however be used as a standard model which will need varying amounts of tailoring if it is to fit each new instance of the class. If he is like the clothier who now expects all customers to be long-leans, he will tend to assimilate small differences and send the average customer out with a small misfit, but he will also tend to exaggerate the shortness and portliness of the occasional short-stout whose suit must be radically altered if it is to fit at all.

Assimilation and contrast effects will appear whenever the new instance deviates only a little or very much from the standard, but for most new instances the standard is used in conjunction with alteration. Like the clothier he does not expect every customer to be fitted exactly with a suit out of storage, but he does expect that he knows what the average customer will need and how much alteration will be necessary in the long run.

The cumulative average: "This is how I will be humiliated from now on"

In the cumulative average, the same transformation is repeated so that it is kept up to date. The cumulative average necessarily places a higher weight on recent experience than does the average. Some averages may be employed for a lifetime despite the increasing burden of transformations required to make them useful. In this sense they resemble the endless additions which an outmoded theory requires to account for exceptions, such as the relationship between the Ptolemaic and Copernican theories.

An outmoded average is like a clothier whose customers change from predominantly short-stout to long-lean who continues to stock mostly short-stouts. He may fit all of his new customers, but he will have to rely less and less on the average which is stored and more and more on extensive alteration. He will have to think more than remember if his retrieval of the average is to be at all suitable for the interpretation of new experience. Primacy will dominate over recency in retrieval, and the cost of this will be either distortion or extensive tailoring if he is to continually make the accurate fit. In the cumulative average there is also a continuing need for alteration if the fit is to be close, but less so than in the case of the average which is not cumulative.

Further the individual may learn to retrieve both averages and cumulative averages, as well as averages based on specific, recent series of past experiences. Thus, if the individual has achieved an average expectation of mild shame to be expected from derogating others, and a cumulative average of the same kind, he may also, upon exposure to a series of intensely humiliating encounters, generate a new and competing standard which remains dominant only for a short period of time and eventually is assimilated to and attenuated by the larger cumulative average. He may become atypically touchy for a short while and then becomes himself again. Recent effects may under such conditions be dramatic but short-lived if they run counter to the dominant, monopolistic theories.

Helson's theory of the adaptation level is a special case of what we are calling the cumulative average, since Helson's theory was constructed to account primarily for the shifting assimilation and contrast effects in psychophysical experimentation.

Variance: "I don't know whether they will like me or humiliate me"

What we have called a variance transformation is one in which past experience is co-ordinated to a class referring primarily to the variability of the members of a class. In contrast to the average and to totaling transformations the series is neither converted into its central tendency nor added together but rather converted into a range of variation. After experiencing severe humiliation, intense respect, moderate respect and moderate shame, the individual does not expect an average of these experiences but expects that others will be quite variable and

unpredictable, both collectively and individually. Such a transformation is highly self-confirming since no matter what happens
it was predicted.

In terms of the clothier analogy, the individual either carries
a great variety of suits in stock or carries an average model but
expects to do extensive alterations. Under the special conditions
of a variance transformation, there may emerge the paradoxical
strategy of responding to positive affect by resignation, since
the individual may suppose himself to be incapable of responding to what he sees as a war of nerves by any pattern of shifting
affect on his own part.

Trend: "they are going to really humiliate me soon"

In trend transformations, the individual learns to respond to
a series in terms not of its central tendency, nor its total, nor its
variance, but rather in terms of its directionality. Just as one
learns to drive an automobile by extrapolations of the moving
pathways described by one's own automobile relative to the
movement of the automobiles driven by others, so here the past
memories are examined for suggestions of an order which may
be extrapolated into the future.

In such class formation, it is the repetition of a specific kind
or rate of change which is critical. A child who has been
humiliated several times over a long period of time may at a
critical point detect an increasing frequency or an increasing
severity or both in the series of past memories of humiliation
experiences. He thenceforth may respond to each new experience as confirming or disconfirming an expected extrapolated
trend.

The affective response to an individual experience of defeat
or censure under these conditions cannot be understood in
terms of the severity of the present circumstances but only as
a confirmation of a series which it is now confirmed will grow
worse and worse or better and better. Each individual experience may now have a specific value and a more general value.
The specific value is what it appears to be. Its general value is
what it will become. Just as an automobile driver may become
panicky at the sight of an automobile approaching him on the

wrong side of the road, so an individual may respond with extreme humiliation to any censure or defeat if it has been transformed by trend analysis as a sign of worse to come. Just as the oncoming automobile may be correctly identified as not having yet struck him, but as nonetheless coming closer and closer, so may a trivial derogation or defeat be appreciated as trivial and yet extremely humiliating because of the shape of things to come. After trend analysis the individual is more likely to judge the other's ultimate intent rather than his apparent present purpose.

Correlation: "I know when they are going to humiliate me"

By correlations we refer to those transformations on past experience which attempt to extract a relatively invariant relationship between classes of events. A correlational analysis may begin after a variance analysis.

Consider the relationship between a child and a negativistic parent. He cannot, whatever he seems to do, evoke the kind of behavior he is trying to evoke. Eventually this may be crystallized into a formula of the type "mother will never do what I try to get her to do." The next series of interactions may then be dedicated to the study of what kind of behavior to expect from mother. The first explanation might be in terms of variance: "She is very variable in her behavior. One day she is nice. The next day she may be nice, but she may also be horrid." The concept of variability while it does not enable strict control of her behavior for the child nor even very specific prediction does soften the impact of her behavior by making every unexpected event understandable after the fact by making it fit this low-order theory. The next analysis might be based on the discovery that the behavior is more than variable—since so much of it seems exactly what he least wishes at that particular time. He therefore one day conceives the devil theory of motherhood. She is a malevolent one who simply wishes to frustrate and shame him.

He is excited by the hypothesis since it explains more—much more of her behavior and in fact enables him to begin successful prediction. At a particular time when he would most like to talk to her, she is "busy." Dramatic confirmation of such a sort strengthens the hypothesis immeasurably. The unbelievable is true! This hypothesis may suffice him for a lifetime—since it will work reasonably well for one so prejudiced as our hypo-thetico-deductive child. But let us suppose he harbors a residual love for this monster. Is there, he asks, anything in her behavior which would relieve this dreary picture? One day he notes with special interest that when he is busy and more than happy play-ing with his toys, she is suddenly most solicitous and loving kind. She wants to play with him! He accepts this not entirely unwelcome interest, but is troubled. She is not a full-time devil. Our fable ends with the child eventually controlling his mother through his brilliant discovery of the law of her nature! From complete failure of control, through the theory of variability, to hostility, to negativism, he has been enabled to understand, then to predict, and finally to control more and more of the behavior of the domain of his major interest. The idea of her being a devil, or finally of her negativism, is based upon correlational analysis of the relationships between his wishes and those of his mother. It is the elementary stuff of which higher-order theories may later be compounded.

Correlations are at the boundary between the dynamics of class formation and theory formation. A theory, and particularly a monopolistic theory, ordinarily posits more complex relation-ships between classes, whereas class formation involves the relationships between symbols and individual members of the class. Let us turn now to the dynamics of the more complex theory formation and monopolistic theory in particular.

THE DETERMINANTS OF MONOPOLISTIC SHAME THEORY CONSTRUCTION

We are now in a position to examine some of the major ways in which the complex organization we have termed a monop-olistic shame theory may be produced.

How then is a monopolistic humiliation theory initiated and attained? Ordinarily such theory formation requires equally monopolistic environmental pressure, and because such pressure

is the exception rather than the rule, such personality organization is also exceptional, and limited essentially to the schizophrenic psychoses and some of the more serious neuroses.
Ordinarily a strong humiliation theory never becomes monopolistic because it is countered by competing affect theory formation.

The major mechanisms by which monopolistic humiliation
theory may be initiated and maintained are internalized verbal
amplification, duration of critical density, traumatic defeat, inevitable defeat, depression and total affect shame binds.

Internalized verbal amplification

The first major mechanism by which monopolistic humiliation theory may be initiated and maintained is by learning from
a parent who literally teaches the child how to loathe and
condemn himself by verbal amplification. By verbal amplification we mean the verbal communication of the description and
analysis of the isolated event as a member of a larger class of
events drawn from the past, from the future, from the experience
of the child, from the parent and, indeed, from the experience
of all mankind. Such a parent is already governed by a very
strong or even monopolistic contempt theory, or by contempt
for others as a strategy of protecting the self against a monopolistic self-contempt theory. The slightest offense or suggestion
of the possibility of an offense by the child becomes the occasion
for an extended lecture in which the child is belabored for the
iniquity and weakness of man in general, from the beginning of
time to some remote future date when all will receive their just
and bitter deserts: "You will be the death of me. You're no
good—just like all children. You must mend your ways or you'll
come to no good end, just like your brother Harry. God bless
him, I hope he learns something in the house of detention. I
told his father he'd come to no good end and you mind me
or it will be the same with you. That shiftless father of yours
will spoil you all. Whatever possessed you to knock over that
vase? Must you always be thoughtless and indifferent to the
feelings of others? How do you expect to grow up to be a fine
man if every time my back is turned you do something like

that? I haven't forgotten the chair you spilled the milk on either. You can't just go round needlessly making trouble for others and just forget about it, you know. God calls us all up for a final accounting, you know. Don't look away, pay attention. I'm sick and tired of you not paying attention. You've got a lot to learn—which reminds me that your teacher told me you weren't paying any attention to her either and that you were going to fail for sure if you don't straighten out. Oh, I don't know what I'm going to do with you. God knows I try—but what good does it do? It's the same thing over and over again with you. You're hopeless."

The point of such verbal amplification is that the individual offense is described *sub specie aeternitatis,* so that the child is taught on every occasion that what he is doing is the same as what he has been doing again and again, what others like him have always done, and what he and all others of his kind will continue to do. The child is prompted to initiate further theory construction which readily becomes monopolistic because he has already been taught the fundamentals of class formation and the ordering of classes of classes in a more general shame theory. He ceases to be able to regard an individual shame experience as idiosyncratic or limited in time and scope. Each experience is "another" instance in which the only change recorded may be in the deadly cumulative total of such experiences or in their dismal trend.

Nor is it essential that the parent deliver the full analysis on every trial. After the lecture has been recorded by the child and stored in his library of such tapes, it may require no more than an eyebrow lifted in surprise which says in effect, "not again?" or an upper lip lifted in scorn which says, "you know what I have said, don't make me go through it all again," to start not only the stored tape recording but further commentary in the same style by the child himself. Further, very abbreviated summaries of the fuller versions will carry the same impact. These would be statements of the form "Aren't you ever going to stop that?" "Not again?" "Why do you always make me ashamed of you?" "I'm not going to be patient very much longer." These and similar summaries co-ordinate the present offense not only to past and future offenses, but to the more extended analyses of the past, so that both parties continue to respond to each situation as though it were but a small sample of a much larger dossier on the offender, or more accurately, as though there was a continuing performance of that larger spectacle.

Extended duration of humiliation

The occasion of the initiation of a monopolistic humiliation theory may be the extended duration of the experience of shame, or guilt, or self-contempt. No matter how intense humiliation may be, if it is of relatively brief duration it may be buffered by countervailing positive affects or by repression or both. The parent who has humiliated the child may help attenuate the sting of the experience by heroic displays of positive affect which heal the wounded pride of the child. No matter how frequent the experience of humiliation, it may also escape generalization if the intervening periods offer sufficient competing reward.

If, however, the intensity of humiliation increases concurrently with its continuous duration, the probability of higher-order generalization increases. Parents differ in how unrelenting they are in keeping the child within the humiliation "field." Some cannot tolerate the enforced humiliation of their child except for very brief periods of time, as others cannot tolerate any attempted escape by their child from the field of blame, shame or guilt. In the latter case punishments are contrived to prolong the experience of humiliation or guilt sufficiently long so that the lesson is overlearned and never forgotten.

Why should the duration of the humiliation experience make a difference between the formation of shame theory and the preservation of the separateness of isolated past humiliation experiences? As humiliation is continually renewed, the self is afforded the opportunity to confront itself as a shameful, worthless or guilty object. There is time and there is motive to remember all the occasions on which one not only felt humiliated but on which one might have been shamed and perhaps should have been shamed, and on all the future possibilities for such experience. Nor is this necessarily a totally inner-prompted review. The parent may take this extended occasion of shame and atonement to review in miserable detail the history of all past offenses and the even more calamitous prospects for the future if the child does not reform. In contrast to the general technique of verbal amplification by the parent, such review is neither altogether necessary nor need it be a frequent running commentary on all offenses, major and trivial. The critical feature of the extended duration of humiliation is that the parent uses it in lieu of a running commentary at a high level of generality. The parent may be a strong, silent one who believes that if the child can be made to experience humiliation for a sufficiently extended period of time, the child will inevitably draw the proper inferences from his suffering.

Freudian theory as a self-refuting prophecy: mental hygiene that worked

Such very strong medicine for the purging of evil and shamelessness has been renounced in contemporary America. The disappearance of the major hysterias, and the attenuations of the classical neuroses in which the individual was haunted by intrusions from guilt-laden anger and sexuality are, we think, related to the disappearance of the phenomenon of extended humiliation at the hands of parents who could believe in the utter righteousness of such extreme forms of punishment.

Allen Wheelis in *The Quest for Identity* has given a classic description of the relationship of father to son which created the personal superego which "wore the very image of his father's face." The harshness and length of punishment which Wheelis describes was not uncommon in the nineteenth century, and Freud's Psychoanalytic theory grew out of such a cultural milieu. Paradoxically Freud provided the dominant personality theory for a generation which has changed, in part, owing to the dissemination of this very theory. The theory has had the consequences of a self-refuting prophecy. Most of the hysterical and phobic phenomena for which it accounted so well are harder and harder to find in contemporary America, owing in part to the widespread influence of Freudian ideology on child rearing. We no longer unduly extend the punishment and humiliation of our children to produce the monolithic superegos of yesteryear.

Because of the importance of the duration of the experience of shame or guilt, and because the extended suffering which our parents' parents imposed is well on the way to extinction, we will present Allen Wheelis' account of such an incident, entitled "Grass." We will reproduce his account in some detail in a later section, since it is more pertinent on the whole to the formation of a competition, co-existence model than to the formation of a monopolistic, snowball model. At this point we wish to call attention only to the extended duration of an experience which humiliated and taught a nine-year-old a "lesson"—not to misbehave in school.

When the boy returned home from the last day of school with a report card which showed that he had passed, but with a grade of 75 in conduct, his father taught him to behave himself in school by keeping him at a difficult task of cutting grass all summer long, denying him entirely the opportunity of playing with his friends. As the enormity of the task became clearer, punctuated by punishment for attempting to escape, the child became more and more depressed. By the end of the summer the "lesson had been learned" and when next the report cards were distributed he had a nearly perfect score in conduct.

The extended, imposed experience of shame and guilt during which every avenue of escape from the field is blocked requires a parent of exceptional conviction and character. The consequence of such experience in which the child is forced into daily and continuous confrontation of shame or guilt is the formation of a kind of conscience which is today becoming more and more rare.

THE AMERICAN PROBLEM OF IDENTITY

That type of conscience in which sex and aggression are held in tight check is becoming increasingly rare in contemporary American society, as Wheelis has argued. But it is not true that the affect of shame is becoming less important. It appears to us to have only shifted in its object. Since positive affect is still heavily invested in achievement, in America, shame is now primarily shame about failure rather than about sexual or aggressive offenses. This shame about achievement is, however, not produced by an extended duration of enforced humiliation, as it might have been done in nineteenth-century America.

Further, the increased preoccupation with identity problems arises in part from the multiplicity of kinds of achievement and the multiplicity of criteria which are a consequence of both the heterogeneity within a modern complex society and its rapid rate of change. The modern American is engaged in a quest for his identity because of an embarrassment of riches in his possible identities. This however is not to say that his conscience is weak, but that he has many ideals and therefore many consciences. But if he has many ways of succeeding and failing, he nonetheless learns to pay for his failures just as dearly and in the same currency as he paid for his "sins" of yesteryear.

THE DIFFICULTY IN ATTAINING
A MONOPOLISTIC THEORY

It should be noted that despite a continuing experience of punishment, humiliation and guilt extending over the entire summer, the hero of the "Grass" story does not develop what we would call a monopolistic shame theory. This is because the harshness of this experience was softened by the love of the father and mother. The bonds which tied the child to the punishing father were stretched to the breaking point, but they were never permitted to be entirely ruptured. This, as we will see, is critical for the formation of a competition, co-existence model and it is what makes the monopolistic, snowball model a much rarer phenomenon than it might otherwise be. If a human being is to achieve a shame theory which is truly monopolistic he must be subjected to forces which themselves are in some sense monopolistic, by virtue of their verbal amplification, their frequency, their duration, their intensity, their provocation by multiple affects or by their amplification by a total negative affect matrix, or by some combination of such high pressure forces.

Critical density of humiliation

The occasion of the critical initiation of a monopolistic humiliation theory may be any event, no matter how trivial, if it occurs when a series of humiliation experiences has been suddenly accelerated to have reached a critical density. Given this critical density, the wildfire of humiliation may be ignited through spontaneous combustion or through any trivial event which inflames the imagination. This critical density may have been produced either by a massed series of humiliations, by a massed series of memories of past humiliations, or both. In such a case the individual may suddenly encounter humiliation much more often than he can readily assimilate. These in turn act as names for long-forgotten similar experiences which now increase the density of the total set of such experiences until a critical density is reached which is either self-igniting or requires only the slightest discouragement to accelerate into monopolistic humiliation theory.

Traumatic defeat versus strength from defeat

The formation of a monopolistic shame theory can be also initiated by the traumatic defeat. A defeat may be crushing in one sense and yet remain an isolated memory which, though painful whenever it intrudes, is nonetheless relatively uninfluential in the life history of the individual. Such searing experiences may be walled off and segregated from consciousness, as a focal infection is isolated by a temporary and relatively impermeable barrier which prevents spread of the infection until the sting of the defeat has abated sufficiently to be assimilated without undue magnification and generalization.

Some years ago Alper showed that subjects with strong egos repressed the memories of their failures, when tested immediately after the experience of a series of experimentally induced successes and failures, but were able to remember these same failures when tested somewhat later. In contrast, those individuals initially diagnosed as having weak egos were swamped with feelings of shame and remembered their failures when tested immediately afterwards, but were unable to remember the same failures when tested later. It appeared that those who could generally function more effectively were able to segregate failure, and thus to minimize immediate shame and the generalization of the sense of failure. Later however, when it was more tolerable failure could be remembered. Those whose personalities were less adequately organized were both vulnerable to immediate feelings of shame and to the more permanent, although delayed, strategy of denying both shame and failure.

The truly traumatic defeat, whether it is the defeat of an individual or of a nation, cannot be easily diagnosed at the time it occurs. It may be walled off temporarily, to be assimilated later when it is more tolerable. It may flood consciousness and appear to overwhelm the individual, but in fact it may constitute a source of great future strength as the brooding individual painfully assimilates his defeat and his humiliation and develops greater tolerance and immunity to the stresses which once so humiliated and defeated him. In this respect the severe defeat is like a disease to which one can develop immunity only by surviving early challenge.

As in general immunological procedures, the difference between a series of exposures to an allergen which results in desensitization and a series which results in sensitization may be a very small one. Depending upon the spacing and magnitude of trials, there is a critical zone where small differences either in the magnitude of the allergen or the time intervals between exposures can result either in increased sensitization or in increased desensitization and in immunity. We would suggest that the magnitude and spacing of humiliation and defeat is an analogous phenomenon, in which the individual may be poised on the razor edge of increased tolerance—or increased sensitivity and the formation of a monopolistic humiliation theory.

If the crushing defeat recruits all the past defeats and sources of humiliation and creates expectations of the future in which humiliation is further magnified and the power of the self is further reduced, the will and spirit of this one may be truly crushed by the single overwhelming humiliation, as a nation may be crushed by a critical defeat in war if the defeat has followed a heroic but unavailing effort.

A defeat is traumatic to the extent to which it prompts the individual to create a humiliation theory which will thereafter radically transform his picture of the world and his own role in that world. The sources of the initiation of such a monopolistic humiliation theory from a traumatic episode are diverse. For some individuals it arises because of a lack of strong inner resources, such as strong competing positive affect theories. For others it may be for exactly the opposite reason. Having enjoyed only rewarding experiences, it is the combined suddenness and massiveness of the first encounter with humiliation which overwhelms. For others it is the fact that the most heroic efforts failed to stave off defeat and humiliation. In this case the individual may have strong, competing inner resources, may have encountered humiliation before, but initiates the formation of a monopolistic humiliation theory just because he threw into the battle all of his reserves, counterattacked again and again and this heroic, his best effort proved in the end to be insufficient.

It may thus be the most spirited and the most courageous child whose spirit can be crushed in a heoric but ineffective encounter with an unrelenting parent. Let us consider the structure of such a possibly traumatic encounter.

AN EXAMPLE OF A HUMILIATION TRAUMA

Let us suppose that our drama begins innocently enough in a conflict between a parent and child, in a low key. The child is playing with a friend and together they are creating a minor disturbance and an invasion of the tranquility of the life space of the parent. Again and again the indulgent parent suggests that the children modulate their voices, stop running through the living room, stop accelerating the natural increase of general entropy. Since the parent's irritation burns at a relatively slow rate, it is easy for the child and his playmate to mistake it for acquiescence. Suddenly the parent's impatience has passed a critical density and it explodes in an authoritarian outburst that this nonsense must stop and stop immediately.

The child is shamed not only by the rupture of the relationship with the parent, but he has been made to lose face before his playmate. He therefore counteracts his shame by opposing his will against the will of his parent and he flaunts his shamelessness in exaggerated hilarity and playfulness. The parent's patience is now quite at an end. He resorts to the threat of physical punishment.

Again the child is shamed and not a little frightened. Will he permit himself to be cowed into compliance before his equally frightened and humiliated friend? He must now assert himself even more if he is to call his soul his own. He cannot give in now or he will surrender all. With fear, trembling, and shame, he rushes into headlong defiance of the enemy.

The reserves of pride of the parent have now been thrown into the contest. The child defies not only the sweet voice of reason of a loving parent, but also the stern wrath and most serious threats of punishment which have been held in abeyance until the final extremity. Has a parent ceased to be capable of inspiring fear as Jehovah inspired it in his chosen children? Is he to be limited to identification with God's son and to be able only to turn the other cheek? No, he will smite his child and humble him, as he was once humbled by his parent. With fury in his face and voice and with flailing arms he beats a crushing series of slaps to the face of the offender.

The child collapses in humiliation at the violation of his dignity in being beaten, in fear at this sudden display of overwhelming force, and in anguish at his impotence to meet force with force, to confront pride with pride. He is dissolved in fearful, bitter and humiliating tears. He cannot look either at his enemy or at his true friend. His defeat is complete, and the ruminations which follow in rapid succession are far ranging. He entertains fantasies of revenge, of running away, of finding his true parents or someone who will really love him, of ways and means of avoiding another holocaust.

This can be a self-limiting incident in the life of an otherwise spirited child, but it can also be the beginning of an amplified humiliation experience which rapidly retrieves all his past experience with humiliation and together with his present feelings constructs a theory which will change his life thereafter. He has lost his innocence. He has been driven from the Garden of Eden. He may elect never to entirely trust this parent again, or he may vow relentless revenge, or he may bow his head permanently in shame, or he may seek security in overweening ambition and work.

Whatever his posture, be it submissive, defiant or excessively self-reliant, it is a response to the challenge of humiliation and defeat which is traumatic in initiating a shame theory which thereafter renders him vulnerable to excessive shame or which will forever drive him to counteraction and vigilance lest it happen again, or both. It can be in the life of a child what the loss of a great war can be for a nation—the beginning of an unceasing preoccupation with an intolerable threat in which "the deadly parallel" haunts every aspiration, every effort to break out of the confines of the traumatic experience.

Multiple negative affect bind on shame

The traumatic episode just cited has the structure of the multiple negative affect bind. In the multiple negative affect bind, a particular affect, in this case shame, is controlled and bound by many other negative affects. This is produced by punishing attempts to deny, escape or minimize shame by arousing and imposing distress, anger and fear for every attempt at repeating the shameful act, for every attempt to protest, for every attempt to minimize or escape the shameful situation. In this way any behavior which might have been punished as a shameful act, for which the child was made to hang his head in shame, is reinforced by also making him angry, afraid and distressed for any behavior which has as its aim the minimizing of the experience of shame.

Finally, therefore, he is humiliated and angry and afraid and distressed, so that the original shame is amplified by the simultaneous or sequential arousal of multiple negative affects. In the future, the awareness of the possibility of such a set being reactivated wherever a situation or a wish to do something which seems shameful is imminent, will constitute an extremely powerful bind. Such humiliation is felt as impotent, angry, fearful anguished humiliation rather than as shame *per se*.

For an episode to be traumatic, it is not necessary for the

child to have been challenged to mobilize all of his resources and then have been decisively defeated. Nor is it necessary for the child to have been capable of heroic resistance. An otherwise generally but not completely submissive child can be traumatized into an accelerated monopolistic humiliation theory construction through an episode in which an outraged parent intends to teach the child a lesson once and for all. Similarly an otherwise generally hostile contemptuous child can be stiffened into a more permanent and more monopolistic contempt theory through a similar traumatic episode by a parent who similarly intends to put an end once and for all to his child's insolence.

It is also apparent that the child may be plunged into a rapid shame theory construction by a traumatic episode because he is entirely unprepared for the hostility or contempt of the parent or anyone else. A defeat which might have been tolerated and assimilated by a child more accustomed to the sting of humiliation may crush the pride of the child who has known only love and tenderness. It is then akin to a disenchantment experienced in the full flush of romantic love during a honeymoon. Most marriages survive such shocks, depending on the magnitude of the suddenly discovered discrepancy, but some are quickly dissolved by the first single traumatic humiliation.

"BREAKING THE CHILD'S WILL"

Although the traumatic consequences of the single episode depend on the nature of the personality which is being humiliated, and although one child's defeat is another child's victory, it is also the case that most children could probably be forced into monopolistic shame theory construction by a single episode if the experience were made sufficiently humiliating. Ordinarily today's parents do not maximize humiliation, either at a moment in time or by constantly humiliating their children, and the parent who does grossly humiliate his child episodically may provide immunity against traumatic elaboration by much love and respect at other times. Although socialization in contemporary America rarely involves humiliation in a single episode sufficiently severe to have traumatic consequences, it was not always so. In the popular child-rearing literature of America which was based on Calvinism, it was assumed that the child was doomed to depravity throughout his life unless given careful and strict guidance by the parents and ultimately saved through grace. Complete obedience and submission were thus required, and achieved by "breaking the will" of the child. Sooner or later the child would refuse to obey a command, and the issue of "will" was at hand. It was considered fatal to let the child win out. One mother, writing in the *Mother's Magazine* in 1834, described how her sixteen-month-old girl refused to say "dear Mama" upon the father's order. She was led into a room alone, where she screamed wildly for ten minutes; then she was commanded again, and again she refused. She was then whipped, and asked again. This kept up for four hours until the child finally obeyed. Parents commonly reported that after one such trial, the child became permanently submissive.

BENIGN TRAUMA: AN EXAMPLE OF SUCCESSFUL PSYCHOTHERAPY

If the traumatic origin of monopolistic affect theory construction is possible, then the direction of trauma should be reversible by the appropriate use of countervailing trauma. We have applied the technique of the "good" trauma in a particularly challenging case and succeeded in reversing an accelerating growth of a strong humiliation theory.

Black, seven years old, was referred to me because of a severe sibling rivalry which so disturbed the child that he was failing at school, despite high intelligence, and was more and more hostile toward parents, sibling and friends, and also severely intrapunitive. When I engaged him in throwing a ball back and forth with me, he was quite unable to tolerate his occasional failure to catch or hold the ball. Whenever he failed to catch the ball, or caught it momentarily but dropped it, he dropped his head in shame and immediately thereafter bit his own hand until he cried out in pain. His attitude toward me was generally hostile, hitting me quite hard when he failed and on numerous other occasions. He resisted almost every effort to engage him in play and particularly the form board which was the vehicle through which I intended to give him a traumatic success experience.

When I first asked him if he would try to fit the parts of squares and triangles and other pieces into the correct spaces of a very simple form board, he rejected the task as something he could not do. I then asked him to watch me fit the pieces of the various geometric shapes into the form board. As I proceeded I was able to get more and more participation from him by pretending to be baffled and puzzled. At these points he would leap to the bait. He had everything to gain in defeating me, and nothing to lose. When he succeeded, I showed the proper amazement at his accomplishment and so he was lured into finally accepting my invitation to play the game entirely on his own. This he did very reluctantly, protesting strongly his inability to do it. For fifteen minutes he was rewarded by me for almost everything he did. His eyes and face gradually changed from that of a sullen, angry, humiliated boy to that of a playful, smiling, excited child.

All this while he had been performing against the stop watch which I held in my hand. At first he payed no attention to this, but as he began to master the problem, his level of aspiration increased and he became increasingly concerned with just how fast he was putting the pieces together. As he began to pay attention to time, he was permitted to believe that each performance was a little faster and better then the one preceding it. After twenty minutes of pure success I introduced his first setback. I announced his time as slower than the preceding trial. At this he all but collapsed in humiliation and defeat. The preceding twenty minutes of unalloyed success had provided almost no defense against his very powerful humiliation theory. It seemed as though we would have to start out all over again if we were to make it possible for him to modulate his shame reaction at all, and, once aroused, to tolerate it sufficiently to be able to resume the battle. At this point he wanted to quit altogether. I did not urge him to resume, but kept up a running commentary on his past recent successes: "You know the time before last you did that faster than most boys of your age. You really are very good at this kind of thing. Have you ever done anything like this before?" On and on I inflated the deflated ego until he was prepared, albeit reluctantly, to resume the struggle. I was playing the role of one who was doing battle with the harsh inner man, because Black was at that moment incapable of opposing his own self-contempt. I was an ego who fought back with affirmation against every derogation from within. It was my intention to teach him to love and respect himself just at those moments when every inner voice judged him most worthless. The first step in such teaching is to provide the model which can then be identified with and interiorized. This second step of interiorization demands a gradual elimination of the alter ego and an encouragement to the individual to provide self-love and self-help at a similar critical moments. The combination of the series of recent successes and the words of approbation finally were sufficient to just balance the powerful shame and self-contempt which had been released by the first failure experience.

Black returned to the task with something less than eagerness, but his imagination was once again captured when I announced with enthusiasm that he had once again broken his own best time. I continued him on this pure success program for another ten minutes and then gave him another failure experience. Again he collapsed, but this time I had to supply only a little praise before he resumed. Then I gave him approximately five minutes of pure success experience ending again with a sudden failure. Despite the fact that the time between successive successes and failure experience was being progressively reduced, the amount of praise and encouragement necessary to absorb the punishment of self-contempt steadily declined. This time it was necessary only that I smile sympathetically at him for him to resume his struggle. Then I rewarded him only two minutes before failure was introduced. This time I did not smile but I looked at him and he smiled and immediately resumed.

Next I reduced the success experience to one minute and announced his failure in a non-commital way with a minimum of sympathy, with no smile and without looking at him, I left the room for a minute to observe him. At this complete lack of support his head dropped, and I waited to see if Black could make the critical transfer from the external ally to the interiorized ally. He could not so long as I was absent. However, upon my return he was so lifted in spirit that he resumed immediately. Now I reduced his success experience to thirty seconds, which was just one trial on the form board, and on the second trial he was made to fail. His face showed distress and a quick shame response but then a smile at me, and he was on his way again. I gave him another success experience followed immediately by a failure and then excused myself and left the room again. This time the critical transfer was achieved. He resumed the battle in my absence. Next I began to expand the newly won tolerance for failure and for shame by gradually increasing the number of consecutive failures. The first time he was permitted to experience two consecutive failures, there was a regression to complete humiliation surrender. At this point we again had to start all over again repairing the injured pride. But it took less time to achieve, and when he was again confronted with two successive failures there was no regression. Then I increased his massed failure experience to three consecutive trials and he held on by the skin of his teeth. At this point I attempted as an alter ego to consolidate his newly won gains by recognizing for him the fact that he had been able to snatch victory from defeat again and again, and that he had even done this on his own, while I happened to be out of the room, and that I was proud of his self-confidence in the face of defeat. This was followed with five minutes of pure success experience at the end of which I introduced a most intoxicating idea. Not only had he conquered the enemy within, but he was in fact in sight of the world's record for form board performance of a boy of his age. With subdued excitement I shared with him my fantasy of together surpassing this record this very day, here and now. My excitement was contagious. His eyes were ablaze with the possibility of reaching where no one had been before and together we began to scale Everest.

Now when he failed, I too openly showed my distress and chagrin, but I also sided with him in his successes more openly in an attempt to radically amplify the significance of this frontal attack on a world record. The success of the trauma would depend, I thought, on sustaining an ever-increasing excitement in the face of continually increasing distress and shame and discouragement. As I announced succeeding performance times,

I accompanied this by a running commentary designed to bring his excitement to a fever pitch: "We're getting closer and closer, try it once more as fast as you can." These inspirational analyses were combined with the look of great excitement on my face and in my voice. Nor were these altogether feigned, since the rapid growth of the child's confidence in his own ability and his excitement at the magnitude of his achievement were in fact contagious.

Finally I announced a time just one second slower than the world's record! We both prepared for the last final push. With great determination he started again to storm the barrier. Now I held him at this time reading for five minutes, until Black was ready to explode if he did not succeed. I expressed my chagrin at the great difficulty he was encountering, but further amplified the significance of the final breakthrough by a commentary on the rareness of all excellence.

Before permitting him to resume I insisted that he gird his loins to the limits of his resources because he would certainly not scale the heights unless he gave his all. Then breathlessly I held the stop watch up and gave the signal to begin. As he put the last piece into the form board I shouted out "23 seconds! You've done it! You've done it!" I jumped with joy into the air and hugged Black who wept tears of joy. At that moment he was beloved and respected by himself and at least one other. As he left my office one would not have recognized him as the child who had entered little more than hour before.

In this episode we have engaged all the reserves of the personality in a heroic struggle which is no less traumatic than the tragic total defeat which we delineated before. What was here destroyed was a strong humiliation theory which had been growing to monopolistic proportions. But it may well be asked how permanent this dramatic reversal was. The sequel to this one therapeutic contact was as follows.

The next week Black and his father failed to meet their appointment. When I called and inquired about this, both parents seemed surprised that I expected them to bring Black back. Black's behavior had changed so radically for the better that they had "forgotten," they confessed, all about his series of appointments which I had scheduled at their previous very urgent insistence. It had been difficult for me to schedule seeing their child at all, and I had arranged a series of appointments only because their distress concerning the child had been so acute. I was happy enough that the impact of the therapy had been so massive, that they were no longer concerned about the child, although it made it difficult to evaluate the effectiveness of the therapy. From reports from those who knew the child I learned that he gave no signs of disturbance for at least a year afterwards.

About eighteen months later Black was brought to my office again, by his father. He had been seriously ill for some time, and under the stress of imposed passivity, he had regressed to his earlier hostility and self-contempt. While his father spoke to me, Black went to my secretary and persuaded her to open the glass door behind which the form board was kept. He immediately began, on his own, working with the form board, as though he sensed its therapeutic value for himself. After his father left, I chatted briefly with Black who insisted we play the game together again. This we did, but without the *Sturm und Drang* of the previous series. Black was very subdued throughout the first half hour but gradually recovered some of his *élan*. By the end of the hour he seemed better but had not recovered the gains he had lost. To my surprise the child again was not brought back for another appointment. Every report I have had suggested that his regression had proven temporary and that his development was satisfactory.

One case is of course insufficient evidence to establish the efficacy of a therapeutic method, but it lends some support to the theoretical possibility that the single episode is capable of initiating monopolistic affect theory construction whether the affect be negative or positive, and that traumatic positive affect can be used as a countervailing organization against traumatic negative affect.

The inevitable defeat

The formation of a monopolistic humiliation theory can also be initiated by what we will call the inevitable defeat. Although almost all of the determinants we have thus far considered give rise ultimately to a sense of inevitable defeat or shame or guilt, we here use the term to refer to a somewhat special mode of producing this final set of expectations. This is the case in which the parent's contempt or anger or disapprobation is not used constantly, does not necessarily produce a critical density of humiliation experience, is not verbally amplified, does not terminate in a single traumatic defeat, which thenceforth is followed by a monopolistic shame theory; rather it is invoked only at critical, terminal phases of any confronting of wills. The parent may be generally quite mild in his strictures and in his governance of the child, but when the child opposes the parent he is always ultimately defeated. This gradually generates the awareness that one cannot win the last battle of the campaign.

This is, we think, the structure of British shame and guilt. They lose every battle with the enemy but the last, because in times of national crisis they are British parents who must not let their erring child win an immoral victory. In their films, too, after the hero has played fast and loose with every norm, he inevitably pays the price for this immorality. Unrelenting and dogged insistence that the child always pay the price of punishment, of shame or guilt, when he has critically violated the parental dictates ultimately produces the awareness that winning is an epiphenomenon, and a temporary victory at best. In the end it is the parent who wins.

The kind of superego produced under such socialization may not, on the surface, appear to be monopolistic in structure, but it is our belief that it may be as monopolistic as that produced by the single traumatic episode. It appears not to be, in part, because it frequently includes a playing out of the entire drama, beginning with the flaunting of the parent, or the internalized parent, through the stage of increasing shamelessness until the parent or his internalized surrogate is forced to declare the offender intolerably guilty or shameful in his behavior. Such a monopolistic shame or guilt theory permits a great display and enjoyment of immorality but only because such a child knows at the outset that he is on his way to certain moral defeat and surrender.

Similar in structure to the British shame or guilt is that of the Catholic church. The enforced, required confessional guarantees that no immorality will ultimately go unnoticed. Since confession reduces guilt, there is a periodic attenuation of the sense of sin. Although the devout Catholic may be bathed in a sea of guilt, he may yet be permitted the variations of the high and low tides of guilt. He is sufficiently cleansed after the high tide to be able to sin again at the low tide. But such a pervasive sense of the ebb and flow of guilt and innocence nonetheless protects the Catholic against the monopolistic shame theory.

It is, we think, quite different in the case we are considering. The child in this case is not like a rock which is gently washed over by the high tide and alone at low tide, but rather like a rock which is inevitably worn down every time there is a storm. There may be few storms and they may not be periodic, but when they come the rock surrenders part of itself to the fury of the storm tide. This rock knows that the storms, though infrequent, are inevitable whenever it is tempted to remove itself from the surveillance of the sea around it. Eventually it may come to enjoy a sense of serenity but only at the cost of complete immobility and conformity to the interiorized potential storm within. In contrast to the traumatic episode, no one storm produces such a theory, but a number of storms may finally prove to be an irresistible force.

DEPRESSION

When shame becomes intense and protracted enough to constitute a depressive mood, there may also be a sufficient reduction in reticular and other non-specific amplification to reduce available energy which in turn further discourages and recruits more shame. Such a continuing depressive mood is another condition under which isolated memories of shame from different sources may be retrieved in sufficient density to both sustain shame, to amplify and deepen it and to organize it into a more unified theory. One of the critical consequences of such recruitment is the emergence of a more general feeling of worthlessness in the place of the more specific and previously independent sources of shame about the body, social relationships and about one's work and feelings of competence.

Johnson asked thirty female college students to rate their moods daily for sixty to ninety consecutive days and to serve in two experimental sessions, one in an elated and one in a depressed mood. She found that accompanying depressed moods there were reduced feelings of physical energy, felt loss of power and capacities, reduced outgoing friendliness, indecisiveness, diffidence and withdrawal from social interaction.

We see here that where there is depression the major areas of affect investment are simultaneously involved: the self and the body, one's work and other human beings. The body's energy expenditure is at low ebb. The zest for work is gone and there is a felt loss of "power and capacities." The sociophilia is weakened so that there is withdrawal from social interaction. A deepening depression is at once a sign of the formation of a more powerful shame theory, and a prime condition for deepening that theory and for producing a monopolistic shame theory. Because the energy level of the older individual declines rather steadily, he is more vulnerable to the deeper and more enduring depressions which in turn produce a more monopolistic shame theory.

Binds of multiple affect by shame

The formation of a monopolistic shame theory can be initiated by creating multiple affect binds in which every affect other than shame is bound by shame. In our discussion of the sources of shame we presented a paradigm of such socialization in which the child was first shamed by his peers about his fear and thus shamed into fighting another child, returns home to be shamed by his parents for having fought, then shamed for crying in distress, is then shamed for showing excitement at dinner, then shamed for a too intense display of enjoyment of his favorite food, then shamed further for showing shame and finally is shamed for his apathy.

In such a case every other affect is bound by the same shame affect. This has the consequence that no matter what he wishes to do, no matter what affect is invested in any kind of behavior it activates and is bound by shame or self-contempt. When all roads lead to Rome and one cannot leave Rome, then one becomes a Roman no matter what the origin of one's native wishes. Such an ideo-affective organization is a prime candidate for rapid transformation into a central monopolistic humiliation theory because humiliation is the recurrent common fate of so many different aspirations.

It should be noted that such a basis for monopolism is quite independent of the critical density of humiliation experiences, of their continuous or long duration, of their intensity or of the structure of the massed traumatic single episode. Such experience need not necessarily reach a critical density of humiliation since it may operate at relatively low density until there is a cumulative effect over a long period of time. It need not however go on either continuously nor for long periods of time if the density of separate humiliation experiences from different affects is sufficient to initiate the cognitive insight that he is blocked by humiliation no matter what.

Similarly, the intensity of each experience may be high or low. If the intensity of each humiliation experience is high, the probability at any moment in time of initiating a higher-order humiliation theory increases with intensity. Holding probability constant, if the intensity of each humiliation experience is high, the time necessary to initiate humiliation theory construction decreases. The more intensely humiliated I am in a wide variety of aspirations representing multiple affects, the more likely I am to connect these separate experiences and the sooner I am likely to do so.

This basis for initiating a strong humiliation theory differs also in structure from that of the massed traumatic episode. In the latter case the totality of negative affects was involved rather than the totality of positive and negative affects. Secondly, in the traumatic episode these other negative affects act as amplifiers of humiliation, accompanying it and deepening it, in angry, fearful, anguished humiliation; whereas in the bind of multiple affects by shame it is the ubiquity of shame arousal rather than its concurrent amplification which provides the stimulus to generalization.

In the multiple affect bind, strong humiliation theory construction begins at that critical moment when humiliation changes from that of an isolated single experience to a reconstruction in which it is experienced as a member of a class of similar experiences. From the awareness of the experience as a member of a class of such experiences, it is a relatively quicker step to an enlargement of the class as a class among classes.

If the present incident is experienced as humiliation or guilt because I expressed my anger and this is transformed into an awareness of shame or guilt for the expression of my anger in general, then I am in a better position to transform this into the larger class formation: I am humiliated and made to feel guilty, it seems, whenever I express any feeling. The latter requires a very high-order theoretical construction despite the fact that it is "true."

Stimulus-affect response relationships may in fact be invariant without awareness of such invariance, and there may be "awareness" of such invariance which is initially far from true but which becomes true because it is believed to be true. In the paradigm we are now considering, it is entirely possible if excitement and anger are both curbed by humiliation that the individual may initiate a humiliation theory in which the world seems to derogate his every aspiration, and ultimately every affect is in fact bound by humiliation.

Chapter 22

The Structure of Monopolistic Humiliation Theory, Including the Paranoid Posture and Paranoid Schizophrenia

We are now in a position to examine the nature of a monopolistic, snowball model of humiliation theory, and to examine the over-interpretation and over-avoidance strategies which comprise it, including the paranoid posture and that extreme state of human existence, paranoid schizophrenia.

In the course of this chapter, the defense mechanism of psychotic denial will be subjected to a careful analysis; some evidence will also be presented concerning the surprising role played by the attempt to perceive reality accurately, in the formation of responses that are nonetheless psychotic denial responses.

ESSENTIAL CHARACTERISTIC OF MONOPOLISTIC AFFECT THEORIES: DIFFERENTIAL GROWTH RATE RELATIVE TO COMPETING THEORIES

Let us turn now to an examination of the structure of monopolistic humiliation theory. As is clear from the previous chapter, there is no hard and fast cutoff-point before which one may be certain there is competition and beyond which lies monopolism. Every theory, strong or weak, is in a relatively unstable equilibrium which is constantly shifting. Nonetheless, we will define a humiliation theory as monopolistic or snowballing whenever the rate of its growth exceeds that of its chief competitors, and such a differential growth rate has itself become relatively stabilized. In monopolism and its developmental analog,

421

the snowball model, the strong theory grows stronger as its competitors, the weak theories, grow weaker.

The key to monopolism, as we define it, is not the existence of an organization which has attained an absolute level of strength, or even a dominant level of strength relative to competing organizations. This is because a complete domination of the personality by one or another affect is always vulnerable to the competition of other affects. Even the catatonic schizophrenic who trembles in a corner, terrorized and mute, ceases to be such a monopolistically organized personality the moment another human being establishes even the most fragile contact with him.

It is our assumption that personality structure is continually changing. The monopolistic organization is also changing, but is one in which the change is in the same direction, continually reinterpreting in terms of the past what might have been seen as novelty, continually improving strategies which have broken down, so that they become more and more effective but which break down again and are again improved.

The individual with a monopolistic organization is like a skilled player of a game who is concerned only with playing the game with more and more skill against opponents who are also continually improving. The moment such a game failed to provide risk, error and possible defeat, it would cease to be monopolistic. We have noted before that a weak, intrusive theory must work reasonably well if it is to remain weak. We cease to develop new strategies for crossing the street to avoid automobiles if and when common prudence achieves our purposes effectively. Under these conditions, such a miniature perceptual-ideo-affective-action organization becomes stabilized and thereby grows progressively weaker, relative to its competitors which continue to grow and proliferate. Occasionally, as we noted before in connection with Solomon's experiment, a dog who has learned to avoid a shock may become so careless that it must be shocked again if it is to continue to act *as if* it were anxious.

In a monopolistic theory, as in monopolistic capitalism, the strong become stronger as the weak become weaker or are assimilated by successive mergers. In the snowball model, which is monopolism across time, there is a similar absorption and recruitment to an ever-growing organization. Once a differential growth rate has become stabilized, the further maintenance and growth require only occasional external support for confirmation. This is because the reinterpretation of external circumstance continues to produce self-confirming prophecies. Pro-action more and more dominates over retroaction as the present is assimilated to the past.

CONJOINT UTILIZATION OF MEMORY AND THINKING: LEARNED SKILL, THE BREAKDOWN OF SKILL AND THE LEARNING OF NEW SKILL IN CIRCULAR INCREMENTAL MAGNIFICATION— A THEORY BECOMES MONOPOLISTIC IF IT DOES NOT WORK VERY WELL

Monopolistic theory becomes monopolistic and remains monopolistic through the learning of skills to anticipate, counteract, avoid and escape humiliation, the utilization of these skills as stored programs, followed by their breakdown which leads to further strengthening of the theory which is followed by further breakdown which continues to strengthen humiliation theory by a circular incremental magnification.

Monopolistic theory is a complex theory which requires time for its construction. In addition, it requires motives. Both time and motives are provided by a circular, endless process of construction, destruction and reconstruction. When what has been learned as a mechanism of coping breaks down and humiliation is again experienced, there is motive enough to strengthen the learned techniques of coping with the dread affect. When the improved and stronger techniques also prove unavailing, the task of reconstruction is taken up again. As the cycle of construction, breakdown and reconstruction is repeated again and again, the theory grows in strength until it accounts for more and more of the life space.

As in the growth of theory in science, it is the discovery of error which provides the essential dynamic of the growth of affect theory. An affect theory, to remain weak, must work. We could not possibly become generally concerned about the danger of crossing a street unless there were numerous close calls and unless motorists began to pursue pedestrians wherever they went. Humiliation to become monopolistic must acquire a wild mobility which again and again defeats or endangers the would-be prudent one. It is the repeated failure of defense which uniquely strengthens it. As in any growing science, older theories are continually replaced by newer theories which account both for all the phenomena accounted for by the older theory plus the more recently discovered exception to the older rule.

As a consequence of this dynamic, a monopolistic humiliation theory is characteristically an unstable equilibrium, oscillating between the established, silent skill which operates largely outside of consciousness and the frantic new learning which takes place in the full glare of consciousness. Thoughts congealed into programs, i.e., automatic neurological structures, which support skilled avoidance of humiliation, co-exist side by side with the most hurried improvisation. Nor will this individual ever be caught twice making exactly the same mistake. But although he gets better and better at anticipating and avoiding possible humiliation, he also increasingly experiences humiliation.

CIRCULAR RECRUITMENT BETWEEN HUMILI-ATION, PERCEPTION, COGNITION AND ACTION PRODUCES OVER-ORGANIZATION

In a monopolistic humiliation theory all roads lead from perception, cognition and action to humiliation, and all roads lead back from humiliation to all the other sub-systems. It is an organization in which wherever one looks, whatever one thinks, whatever one does, humiliation may be aroused, and in which perception, cognition and action are commandeered, so that they are reduced to instruments for the minimizing of such affective experience.

As such it closely resembles the modern dictatorship with its ubiquitous monopolistic exercise of power. Whether at any moment humiliation is experienced or avoided or reduced, the pervasive concern of the total personality is with this affect or, as in paranoid schizophrenia, with the combination of this affect and terror. It is the commandeering of all the resources of the personality and their subordination to dealing with one or a set of negative affects which constitutes the most serious pathology. Because of the continual breakdown of defensive strategies and because of the apparent perpetual imminence of humiliation when it is not actually activated and in awareness, the individual has no holidays from the unfinished and unfinishable business of coping with humiliation in the monopolistic organization of a negative affect theory. The only enjoyments he knows are those rare occasions when the burden of humiliation is suddenly reduced, temporarily. The only excitement he knows is the mirage of the hope of such enjoyment.

Such an organization we have defined as an over-organization because the normal pluralism of affects, and cognitive functions, is seriously constricted. Perception is too much concerned with the detection of possible insult. Memory excessively nurses old wounds to pride and adds past burdens to present insult to unduly increase cumulative totals. Thinking is too exclusively concerned with extrapolations of future insult and with strategies for its avoidance. Action is too exclusively instrumental to avoiding or escaping humiliation. Above all, the whole machinery—cognitive, perceptual, motor and affective—is in continuing two-way communication about the same concern, thus binding the personality to a permanent alert.

MAGNIFICATION OF HUMILIATION DESPITE EFFECTIVE DEFENSE BECAUSE OF THE VARIABLE RELATIONSHIP BETWEEN AFFECTS AND THEIR OBJECTS

We have said that, in a monopolistic humiliation theory, there is an equilibrium between a skilled defense which operates so silently and effectively that the individual may not even be aware that he is avoiding humiliation, and a recurring breakdown of these defenses which floods awareness with the dreaded affect and thereby motivates further defensive learning. This is true, but also somewhat misleading in its implication of a clear-cut dichotomy between relatively unconscious skill in defense and helpless vulnerability in the breakdown of defense. It is misleading because it is predicated on a relationship between affects and their objects which is, in fact, only one specific kind of affect-object relationship, namely, that an affect is instigated by an object, which therefore might be avoided.

Everyman and personality theorists alike have exaggerated the dependency of the activation and awareness of affect on an object. While ever since Freud it has been assumed that one may be mistaken about what one is afraid of, and while phenomeno-logically the state of objectless anxiety is assumed to be what it appears to be, there is nonetheless a continuing assumption that there is a true object for every affect. If this true object is not in awareness because the affect is free-floating, or if it is not in awareness because of some error in identification of the true object, it is nonetheless assumed that there really is a true object and that this is the cause of the activation of the affect. We distinguish sharply the cause of an affect from its object. We will argue that every affect arousal has one or more causes but that it may or may not have an object. Second, the objects it does have may or may not be perceived as causes of the affect. Third, the objects perceived as causes may or may not be correctly identified. Fourth, variation in the original causal affect arousal conditions may or may not be perceived as such. Fifth, percep-tion of changes in the original causal conditions may or may not be accompanied by changes in the affect which was produced by the original causal conditions, even when these were correctly identified. It is this latter state of affairs which radically com-plicates the clear dichotomy between effective defense and the breakdown of defense. It is our argument that defense may be effective in many respects and nonetheless not prevent the magnification of the affect which prompts the defense.

Let us briefly consider each of these propositions. First, affect arousal with cause but no object: I may arise feeling ashamed, defeated, discouraged but about nothing in particular. These are usually called moods. They can have any one of a great variety of causes or sets of causes. If I have been humiliated often as a child for the expression of distress so that there is a distress-humiliation bind, then if the temperature or humidity of the room in which I slept was not optimal and my sleep was thereby disturbed and I woke feeling tired rather than refreshed and full of energy, I may respond with humiliation because the low-grade pain would innately activate distress, except for the learned distress-humiliation bind.

Second, the objects it does have may or may not be perceived as causes. Suppose I wake in a mood of discouragement from shame or self-contempt and then begin to think of a very difficult problem which I have still to solve. The on-going despair may now be perceived to be caused or deepened by the overwhelming problem, but it also happens that the individual senses that his mood was prior to his awareness of this problem, and he distinguishes between the cause of the mood, which is unknown to him, and the gloom with which it bathes every demanding task of the day which lies ahead. The task may, however, be identified as the cause of his mood.

Third, such identification of objects as causes may or may not be correct. In our example above, the supposition that the problem created the mood, or deepened it, may be entirely incorrect. If the mood was in fact caused by the awareness of the overly demanding problem, then the individual may well accurately identify both the cause and the object of the affect and recognize that they are one and the same. Identification of cause, however, even under such circumstances, is never entirely correct because the individual usually mistakes the proximal cause for the entire set of determinants. Thus it may be true that if he did not have to deal that day with such a difficult problem, he might not have become discouraged. He will rarely be aware of the possibility that, if his past history had been different, the same problem might not have seemed so difficult; or if it seemed so difficult, it might have excited him as a challenge rather than discouraged him.

Fourth, variation in the original causal conditions may or may not be perceived as such. A child who is constantly humiliated by a parent may not be capable of detecting significant changes in the parent's attitude toward him, once monopolistic theory formation has occurred. We will examine the nature of these distortions presently in connection with the humiliation equation. There may, however, be equally marked contrast effects as well as assimilation effects. Under these conditions any positive affect from the oppressing parent may be perceived as much more positive than it is.

Fifth, perceived changes in the original causal conditions of affect arousal may or may not be accompanied by affective changes. A lovers' quarrel in which each felt humiliated by the other can end in showing increased positive affect for the other and in a complete and mutual reduction of humiliation. However, it also happens, when humiliation theory is snowballing, that the overly offended one may perceive that the other no longer intends insult but yet cannot shake the feeling of humiliation. This may be reinforced by a cognitive transformation which now views the other as a totality of selves across time rather than in terms of a central tendency. The other is now seen as the same but also "different," and so the relationship can never again recover its original innocence despite the fact that the offended one knows that on the whole the other is a loving, lovable object. The God of the Old Testament so regarded Adam and Eve after they had tasted the fruit of the tree of knowledge. The critical question here is how much and what kind of a change a real change is interpreted to be.

In monopolistic humiliation theory there can be an accurate perception of real change in the other, yet it makes no difference in the feeling of humiliation. This very lack of corresponding affective change can itself cause the further cognitive transformation which shifts the view of the other from what he is now to what he is as a totality, or in the extreme case may even reinterpret his apparent shift as yet another deceit and a further example of malevolence. In monopolistic humiliation theory there can be a high inertia of humiliation because of the failure to perceive changes in affect arousal conditions, despite the changes in affect arousal conditions, or in the extreme case because the perception of change is further transformed to support and heighten the original affective response. Such a transformation may be either that the other as a totality is contaminated despite some saving graces, or that the other has no saving graces because what appears to be change is really more evidence for the malevolence of the other.

INCREASED HUMILIATION DESPITE SUCCESS-
FULLY COUNTERATTACKING THE HUMILIATOR

The same phenomena appear when the humiliated one actively defends himself against an offender and so changes the original cause of humiliation. Despite the fact that he has personally counterattacked the other so successfully that the original cause for humiliation no longer exists, he may nonetheless continue to experience humiliation, or humiliation along with joy at having defeated the other. Ordinarily, successful defense, for example, through counterattack against another who has humiliated one will reduce shame or self-contempt and activate joy at having defeated the offender. A thin-skinned individual may find few sources of positive affect more rewarding than deflating a serious adversary. But it is not always so, and it is rarely so when humiliation theory becomes monopolistic. In the latter case there is increasing magnification of humiliation both because of defense and despite defense, even when defense is in many respects otherwise successful.

Consider the paradigm above, in which the censor is humbled in a successful counterattack which completely reverses the original circumstances. Let us suppose that the censor now replies in such a way that insult is compounded, and the feeling of humiliation is re-aroused in our hero and that it is deepened. He then girds himself for yet another attempt to subdue his critic, and again his triumph is short-lived. Now the censor, utterly infuriated, delivers what may be the *coup de grâce* and our hero is crushed. Again, however, he finds what he thinks is *le mot juste* and he throws himself against his adversary. But at this moment, the censor overly confident of ultimate victory laughs in the face of our hero.

Defenses which have been partially successful in subduing the adversary now appear to be less and less effective and because of their mixed effectiveness there is a magnification of humiliation. As a consequence of such magnification the defensive strategies now become more and more primitive and less and less effective, until he is utterly humiliated not only by the

censor but by the ineffectiveness and duration of his unavailing
efforts to escape defeat. In this case there is a substantial increment in the intensity and duration of humiliation due to the
duration and relative ineffectiveness of the efforts to reduce and
escape the initial humiliation. The situation now calls for heroic
defense, and our hero is challenged to a final desperate confrontation with his adversary. He defeats his enemy by a combination
of heroic effort aided by a lucky blow. He unwittingly hits an
exposed psychic nerve which so humiliates the critic that he is
finally silenced.

Does our hero proclaim his revenge and declare a joyous
holiday? He does not. First, the victory is Pyrrhic insofar as he
has suffered much humiliation, and his continuing awareness of
this cumulative total far outweighs whatever joy might have
been released by his victory. Indeed, so long as there is a high
inertia to this negative affect, joy cannot readily be activated,
despite the radical reversal of roles.

Second, in addition to a continuing awareness of the whole
set of the preceding experiences, there can be initiated a re-
hearsal of these which greatly magnifies them and the righteous
sense of outrage. Such magnification may grow every time the
individual rehearses the experiences both when he is alone and
particularly if and when he communicates to others. "Did you
hear what X said to me?" can be the beginning of an account
which grows with each retelling as humiliation is rekindled
again and again.

Third, humiliation may be magnified by the individual's
awareness that he has been provoked into exhibiting the most
primitive and least attractive aspects of himself, and so in part
confirming his adversary's assertion about his worthlessness.

Fourth, humiliation may be magnified by the continuing
awareness that he was defeated again and again despite his
ultimate victory.

Fifth, humiliation may be magnified by the continuing awareness that he repeatedly had to defend himself and that he could
not simply disregard his critic as beneath his contempt. This is
a critical source of magnification of humiliation whenever im-
perturbability is a central part of the strategy of dealing with
humiliation.

Sixth, humiliation may be magnified by the continuing awareness that he repeatedly hung his head in shame and that this was publicly observed and so confirmed his worthlessness. For many, including individuals who do not suffer monopolistic humiliation theory, the display of humiliation is the critical phenomenon sought by one adversary and avoided by the other. According to such a view, an insult does not become an insult unless the other's feeling of shame or self-contempt has been aroused. Thus it would be believed that if one is insulted but can respond with sufficient indifference or amusement, the adversary has failed in his attack.

Seventh, humiliation may be magnified by the awareness that one has in large part transformed a minor criticism which might have occasioned only a brief and inconsequential embarrassment into a major war for all concerned. As such transformations recur over time with an increasing number of individuals, the one who is responsible for such magnification sees himself as the helpless pawn of his own humiliation theory and so deepens his sense of his own worthlessness.

Eighth, humiliation at frequent transformation of minor conflict into major confrontations may be magnified by the conviction that behind the façade of good will there lurks in everyone a wish to degrade and humiliate the other. Once such a conviction has been attained, it accelerates the frequency with which it is confirmed by provoking censorious others into more and more serious conflict. Legal paranoia is but a special case of the litigious personality which provokes increasingly serious censorship and humiliation.

Ninth, humiliation may be magnified rather than reduced when the other is defeated because the offense of the other is viewed as too great to be capable of being repaid in kind. This would be the case, for example, in such crimes against humanity as the extermination of six million Jews by Hitler and Eichmann. The law of talion, an eye for an eye, becomes meaningless when the debt incurred is impossible of repayment. When an individual is possessed by a monopolistic humiliation theory and when he has at the same time excepted one individual or a very small class of human beings from his strictures so that he trusts that one or those few implicitly, he is ultra-vulnerable to humiliation should that one disappoint him or censure him. Under such circumstances the fury of his contempt cannot eradicate his disenchantment or his humiliation, no matter how complete is his destruction of his beloved.

Finally, the defeat of an adversary after suffering severe humiliation at his hands may magnify humiliation because it is the occasion of a sudden expansion of the general possibilities of such humiliation again. The individual may be entirely satisfied that he has subdued his rival, but he is now seized with a concern for the future and for all possible enemies. This is especially probable if the critic is presumed to be weak and the struggle unexpectedly difficult. In such a case the individual is likely to suppose that he will have a much more difficult time with more serious adversaries. It is not unlike the close call of last year's championship team, when in its first game with a weak rival, it is pushed to the limit to eke out a victory. There is small joy in such a victory.

These are some of the reasons why defense which may be otherwise effective in dealing with the source of humiliation may nonetheless be accompanied by magnification rather than by reduction of negative affect. Defense, given a monopolistic humiliation theory, is rarely altogether clean-cut and decisive. Indeed it is precisely this ambiguity in the confrontation of humiliation and terror which may prompt the individual to create such arenas as the bull fight in which every possible adversary is symbolized by the bull and confronted at a moment of truth when the issue is joined decisively.

OVER-INTERPRETATION BY THE HUMILIATION EQUATION

We have said that there is over-organization in monopolistic humiliation theory. By this we mean not only that there is excessive integration between sub-systems which are normally more independent, but also that each sub-system is over-specialized in the interests of minimizing the experience of humiliation. We have just examined some of the ways in which because of monopolistic interpretation, action undertaken to reduce humiliation may yet magnify it. Now we wish to examine over-interpretation in perception, memory, and thinking when they are captured by a dominant affect and subordinated so that they provide information relevant only to that affect and its avoidance. In over-interpretation, every bit of incoming information is scanned for information which is humiliation relevant. The entire cognitive apparatus is in a constant state of alert for possibilities, imminent or remote, ambiguous or clear.

Like any highly organized effort at detection, as little as possible is left to chance. The radar antennae are placed wherever it seems possible the enemy may attack. Intelligence officers may monitor even unlikely conversations if there is an outside chance something relevant may be detected or if there is a chance that two independent bits of information taken together may give indication of the enemy's intentions even though each bit of information might be valueless by itself. But above all there is a highly organized way of interpreting information so that what is possibly relevant can be quickly abstracted and magnified, and the rest discarded. This organized way of interpreting information relevant to humiliation we shall term the humiliation equation. Before describing its characteristics formally, let us see how it works.

Relevance of remote information

Any theory of wide generality is capable of accounting for a wide spectrum of phenomena which appear to be very remote, one from the other, and from a common source. This is a commonly accepted criterion by which the explanatory power of any scientific theory can be evaluated. To the extent to which the theory can account only for "near" phenomena, it is a weak theory, little better than a description of the phenomena which it purports to explain. As it orders more and more remote phenomena to a single formulation, its power grows. The same criterion may be used to evaluate the strength of any ideo-affective organization. A humiliation theory is strong to the extent to which it enables more and more experiences to be accounted for as instances of humiliating experiences on the one hand, or to the extent to which it enables more and more anticipation of such contingencies before they actually happen, or to the extent to which it enables more alternative strategies for the avoidance or escape from such contingencies. Here we shall be concerned with the remoteness of information that is processed by an individual as relevant.

Remote transformations produce a wide variety of over-interpretations, which range from slightly irrelevant distortions to delusions and hallucinations. The line between exaggeration and delusion is not easy to define. There is a continuum of operations on information which produces more or less single-minded interpretations. In monopolistic humiliation theory it is not the case that the individual necessarily favors the most improbable interpretation of incoming information. Indeed he is trying to arrive at an accurate interpretation of the relevance of input to the possibility of humiliation. The major source of distortion in his interpretation is his insistence on processing all information as though it were relevant only to the possibility of humiliation. Granted this initial constriction, however, he still exercises degrees of freedom and indeed great conceptual skill in the interpretation of information.

In contrast to strategies which have as their aim the reduction of cognitive dissonance, these perceptual strategies aim at the detection of dissonance. Ultimately there is a strategy of reduction of such dissonance, but not before it has first been detected and magnified.

Perceptual vs. cognitive distortion: two types of delusions (or misinterpretations)

We will first distinguish two types of remote transformations which on the surface appear to be quite different. These are perceptual remoteness and cognitive remoteness. In perceptual remoteness a stimulus is given what appears to be an extremely improbable interpretation. Thus, if someone is reading a newspaper and does not look up and acknowledge the presence of another who has just entered the room, a remote perceptual interpretation by the latter would be that insult was intended. The most probable interpretation would have been that the first individual did not hear the other enter and continued to read.

If, however, one is restricting perceptual interpretation to relevancy for humiliation, it becomes possible that the other did in fact hear but chose to show his indifference or contempt by continuing to read.

In cognitive remoteness the individual does not necessarily transform the significance of the immediate perceptual information. In the present case he would admit that no insult is intended but nonetheless think that this is the beginning of the end of the relationship. He might argue: In the past the beloved was always looking for me and was hyper-alert to the possibility of my presence. Now he is just as interested if not more interested in other things and other people and that is why he did not hear me. But it is a short step from interest in newspapers to disinterest in me and then to hate of me. He will soon hate me, and I now feel humiliated in his presence. Here it is the extrapolation of a correctly interpreted situation which converts it into a humiliation relevant beginning of the end of a relationship. Although the line between perceptual and cognitive transformations is not a sharp one, it is nonetheless useful in distinguishing between remote transformations which depart from reality immediately in the interpretation of the stimulus and those which do not but which place the stimulus in an extremely improbable future series and thereby distort it.

This distinction is of some consequence for the testing of psychotics. It not infrequently happens that his further cognitive and affective responses to the same stimulus represent delusions. Delusions may be perceptual or cognitive or both. If one restricts the testing to the immediate perceptual level, one may find responses which are indistinguishable from normal responses, despite the fact that the further cognitive and affective responses may be quite bizarre.

In our further treatment of remote transformations we will not distinguish these two varieties, since both are very frequently used together in monopolistic humiliation theory.

The invidious comparison

Consider first the remote transformation of the invidious comparison. When humiliation theory becomes monopolistic, all experience is perpetually transformed into the invidious comparison. The other is a god, and the self is an unworthy, insignificant sinner. "From dust thou art to dust returneth." It is not simply that the self and the other are invidiously compared but rather that the individual is compelled to transform experience which is essentially non-relational into the invidious comparison, to the disadvantage of a predetermined member of the dyad.

If it is the self which is to be humiliated by the transformation, then, first, a comparison object is sought; and second, the comparison object is selected from amongst those who are superior rather than from amongst those who are inferior. Thus, if the individual has been honored, he may import a comparison object rather than simply accept and enjoy the honor which has been extended. Secondly, the comparison object is chosen so that an invidious comparison can be readily achieved in the fewest number of further transformations. If he has been honored as a benefactor of mankind, it is Christ who is the appropriate object for invidious comparison. If he has been honored as a military man, it is Napoleon with whom he must compare himself. If it is as a physicist that he has been honored then it is Newton with whom he must compare himself. Under such conditions it becomes relatively easy to evoke shame and self-contempt despite the respect and love of others.

If the contempt theory is to operate against others, either as a primary theory, or as a strategy instrumental to protecting the self against the same contempt, then it is the other who is to be perpetually compared with superior objects and thereby robbed of his just deserts. It is the other who is no Christ, no Napoleon or no Newton. Further, the other is compared unfavorably with the judging self. The achievement of the other is something which the self envisioned a decade earlier and had the good sense to reject as not worth the effort, or as something which, had the self done it, would have been done right.

In contempt theory, whether primary or defensive, comparison objects are also perpetually sought but now from a field of inferior objects so that the self can be more readily compared to the disadvantage of the other. The weakest competitors are sought, or strong competitors are sought who have weak spots, or strong competitors are sought and transformed so that the self can hold the other in contempt at least in some respect. Thus the other may have done excellent work but the time was so ripe that had he not stumbled upon it a hundred others would, in contrast to one's own real originality. The work of the other is flashy but not solid, like one's own, or solid but pedestrian and not inspired, like one's own.

In contempt theory there is also no restriction on the nature of the objects which are vulnerable to perpetual invidious comparison. Thus science as a human activity may be derogated by comparison either to some other field or to the future state of the same science. "Psychology is in its infancy. It is a pretender. It doesn't know anything. Someday it will be a real science, like physics." Or the activity of science in general may be derogated by comparison with its own shinier future development or by comparison with omniscience. "Physics today, for all its apparent success, will be as obsolete ten years from today as Newtonian physics is today." "Science is an approximation at best—a shorthand way of describing the facts. It explains nothing." By means of such transformations the luster of any type of human achievement is perpetually reduced by the invidious comparison to the disadvantage of the self or the other.

As we will see presently, it is not uncommon either in a monopolistic humiliation theory or in a competition model for the invidious comparison to be used to the disadvantage of the other. In such cases the invariant is the continuing transformation of apparently non-relational situations into invidious comparisons. The individual is compelled to be either judge or defendant. This appears linguistically as a radical increase in the use of comparative, relational words. This one is far wiser, richer, more beautiful, stronger, older than that one. The remote invidious comparison need not be restricted to the domain of human competitors. It is indeed often simpler for the individual haunted by humiliation to compare himself with an ideal specially constructed to defeat him. If he is held in the highest esteem by others, he can nonetheless compare himself unfavorably with an aspiration just this side of omniscience and omnipotence. The idea of God and its philosophic equivalent, Platonism, both have served as ideals by which men could be certain that they could perpetually victimize themselves by comparing themselves to their predetermined disadvantage. The delusion of grandeur in paranoia is nothing more than the strategy of turning the invidious comparison to one's own advantage.

Is what I have done shameful?

We have thus far considered over-interpretation as though it involved only the evaluation of the self in relationship to some external source of information. Perceptual over-interpretation however also includes the monitoring of one's own behavior. "Is what I have done shameful?" is asked as often as "Is he trying to humiliate me?" Often the two questions may both be involved at once, as in the concern that I may be humiliated because of what I have just done or failed to do. Remoteness of transformation of my own behavior frequently involves the detection of inferiority or blame or defeat coupled with censure from others for my failures, moral or otherwise.

Ensured inadequacy and humiliation resulting from the use of multiple criteria

In the invidious comparison which is impersonal, the activity of the self is devalued not only by the utilization of very demanding criteria but also by the excessive use of multiple criteria. Whereas an individual with a relatively high level of aspiration might keep himself under high pressure from a considerable discrepancy between his attainments and his aspirations, in monopolistic humiliation theory there is frequently constructed an ideal distant from present attainment but which also combines numerous criteria, each of which is capable of generating a victimizing invidious comparison and which together guarantee a crushing burden of humiliation. The excessive burden usually began as a more modest burden which grew in pretentiousness as the successive defeats of the individual deepened the sense of humiliation and so generated more and more heroic claims which had to be met if the individual was ever to throw off the yoke. We will consider these multiple claims in more detail in the section on over-avoidance and over-escape strategies. Here we wish only to note that the individual in the grip of a monopolistic humiliation theory is governed by remoteness of perceptual and cognitive transformations insofar as he necessarily constructs a multiple criterion, every component of which is capable of generating humiliation whenever it is used in the invidious comparison.

The individual lives in a field with many fences, as far as the eye can see, and on the other side of each there can be seen the deepest of green grasses, each so much greener than where he stands. Given such multiple criteria, any significant progress toward one is devalued by a transformation which exposes the failure to satisfy one or more of the residual set of criteria.

Thus if such a one has ventured far into the unknown, in a bold and imaginative exploration there is a nagging self-criticism that there is uncertainty about some details which were bypassed because of the velocity of exploration. Or if one has with the greatest care and meticulousness cultivated a small garden, the same individual will be haunted with the awareness that he has missed what is beyond the horizon, that he has subordinated his imagination to an over-disciplined use of his powers. If he has achieved success as an artist, his latent wish to be a scientist comes to the fore as a source of defeat and longing. If he achieved great wealth, he is aware that he has not achieved equal political power; if he has achieved political power, he is aware that his personal wealth leaves something to be desired. If like Chekhov, he has achieved fame as a writer of short stories, he must struggle to show that he can also write novels, which he could not do and which he never did despite the most heroic struggles. If he is a great tragic actor, he is defeated because he is not a comic; if he is a great comic like Chaplin, he must culminate his career by showing that he too can be a great tragic hero.

This is, of course, not to say that all great achievement necessarily generates devaluation and discontent, but rather how in monopolistic humiliation theory, the multiple criterion guarantees continuing defeat by remote transformations in which the present actual attainment of one ideal is compared invidiously with the failure to attain the remaining ideals of the set by which the individual governs himself.

A special case of the multiple criterion is that in which the standard is essentially defined by the distance between the aspiration and the attainment. In such a case if there should be goal attainment, there is an immediate redefinition of the goal which serves at once to devalue the present attainment and to re-establish a discrepancy between this and the goal to be achieved. Attained success is bitterly disappointing to such individuals because it reveals the hopelessness of their strategies for escaping defeat and humiliation. Such a one is lured by the carrot of ambition which dooms him to failure whether he can eat it or not. If he eats it, it will turn to ashes in his mouth and he will need a new carrot. If he cannot reach it, he is defeated by its wondrous promise which he can never reach. There are no fruits of his labor.

Interpretations of the attitudes of others which ensure humiliation

These are some of the ways in which one's own efforts can be remotely transformed by the invidious comparison. Let us turn now to types of remote transformations other than the invidious comparison, for the interpretation of the attitudes of others rather than for the interpretation of the behavior of the self by the self.

Thus if someone attempts to instruct or give advice to an individual with a monopolistic humiliation theory, this is transformed into the humiliating belief that the other recognizes that one is desperately in need of help, or that one is childlike, or that one is inexperienced or that one is stupid.

In the case of advice, it is transformed into a condescension as if the other had said something of the form "If I were you, I would put on my rubbers, child, because it has just started to rain as I was coming in." In the case of dominance, the transformed statement is of the type "Put on your rubbers, stupid." The remote transformation of instances of domination is usually similar to that performed upon instances of advice, but with the added insult that it appears there is even less choice to the helpless one.

Remote transformations are applied to any positive request

for action. Thus the statement "Give me the newspaper, please" may be translated into the form "Do as I say, you are my servant." If advice is converted into dominance, dominance is converted into tyranny. Whenever the self is in a process of rapid growth and individuation, as in adolescence, the slightest suggestion of advice or dominance can thus be translated into an unholy war of extermination through a transformation in the humiliation equation which detects and amplifies the sources of inferiority which humiliate.

Consider next the opposite state of affairs. I ask a stranger if he knows the time, and suppose he replies that he doesn't carry a watch. In monopolistic humiliation theory the failure to give trivial information may be transformed into something like the following: "I showed him that I needed something from him but he rejected me." "He could have said 'I'm sorry, but I don't have a watch' instead of such a cold reply." "Why did he look at me as though I were imposing on him. I only asked him for the time."

The failure of the other to communicate is remotely detected even when the interaction does not concern the self. Thus if someone asks another for an opinion this is transformed into the form: "He asked *him* his opinion rather than me because he knew that my opinion was worthless."

Similarly with distant advice giving and dominance. These may be transformed into: "He is asking that person's advice because he thinks I am too worthless and hopeless to justify his efforts to instruct and dominate me."

Next is the case in which anyone else is rewarded. This individual may be unknown to me, may be in a field unrelated to mine and yet a remoteness transformation is capable of converting his reward into my punishment: "He really deserves the recognition he is receiving, and it makes it all the more evident how unworthy I am."

Next is the case in which anyone else is criticized, punished or humiliated. I am made acutely aware, through identification with him, how unworthy we both are.

Next, consider the case in which someone expresses a great longing for a particular object or type of experience. This may humiliate by the following remoteness transformation: he is really inferior because he does not have what he wants, because he has never experienced what he most wants out of life, and I am reminded that I too am like him in this respect.

Humiliation is also the consequence when anyone expresses great satisfaction with his self and his life. The transformation here is of the form: he is really superior because he is satisfied with himself, but it makes it so much clearer that I am different from him and truly inferior.

Next consider the consequences of the dependency of others on the self. If someone shows his dependency on one by asking a favor, humiliation is a consequence by the following transformation: he thinks that I can help him. He does not know how incompetent I am, but he will soon find out.

If others are independent of me, it is because they understand that there is no point in relying on one so incompetent as I am; or they are trying to assert their superiority over me and to flaunt their contempt of me.

If others try to impress me with the excellence of what they are doing, it is transformed into: "He takes me for a fool whom he is trying to deceive. He is trying to pull the wool over my eyes and he thinks I cannot see through it."

If others do not try to impress me, it is insulting because they don't take me seriously enough to try. Educators not infrequently respond to the poor examination performance or to the indifference of their students as though it were an intended insult to their own persons and their chosen profession.

The integration of negative evidence: converting benign experiences into humiliation

The second important characteristic of a monopolistic affect theory is its capacity to integrate negative evidence, to account for apparent exceptions to the theory. In contrast to remote transformations, these may concern obvious instances which rather than being only remotely related to humiliation are rather clear-cut instances that one is not being humiliated.

Let us suppose the individual to be richly praised. What transformations can convert such positive evidence into its opposite? First, the sincerity of the judge may be questioned.

He cannot really believe what he is saying and indeed he is using exaggerated praise to mock me. Second, he praised only this work because he knows that everything else which I have done is trash, and he is praising this work because there is nothing else to praise. Third, he may be sincere, but he is probably a fool to be taken in like this—and he is thereby exposing me all the more to the ridicule of those who can evaluate properly. Fourth, this is a temporary lapse of judgment. When he comes to his senses and sees through me, he will have all the more contempt for me. Fifth, the judges have incomplete information. They do not really have all the evidence which they would need to see the worthlessness of the work of the self. Sixth, this is a fluke. It is truly praiseworthy, and the judges are not mistaken but it was a lucky, unrepresentive accident, which will probably never occur again. Seventh, others are trying to control me, holding out a carrot of praise. If I eat this I am hooked, and I will thenceforth have to work for their praise and to avoid their censure. Eighth, they are exposing how hungry I am for praise and thereby exposing my inferiority and my feelings of humiliation, even though they do not intend to do this. Ninth, they are seducing me into striving for something more which I cannot possibly achieve. Ultimately this praise will prove my complete undoing by seducing me into striving for the impossible and thereby destroying myself. Tenth, he is acting as though he alone is the only judge of my work, as though I am incapable of correctly judging its worth and so I must forever be dependent upon his or their judgment.

So may genuine respect be transformed in the monopolistic humiliation equation.

Integration of contradictory evidence

A powerful affect theory accounts not only for remote evidence and for negative evidence but also for what is apparently contradictory evidence. Thus if someone important and close to me is praised, this separates us and highlights how unworthy I am, but if he is criticized or humiliated, I feel close to him and I am also humiliated. Thus the spouse who is easily humiliated by the mate who makes a fool of himself or herself is just as easily humiliated if the mate should be especially honored by others.

If someone praises me it shows only how little they know, but if they censure me they are astute critics.

If others are attracted to me they are fools, but even they will soon be disenchanted; if they are repelled by me, this will be contagious and soon no one will speak to me.

If the same person praises me sometimes and censures me at other times, he shows good judgment in the latter cases but a lapse of judgment in the former. He may be sincere in his censure but insincere in his praise. He knows all the facts when he censures but he usually does not when he praises.

If others try to impress me they are trying to deceive me, and they think I am fool enough not to understand their strategy. If they do not try to impress me, they also show their contempt for, since they should take my opinion more seriously.

If others are dependent on me this will expose my incompetence because I really cannot help anyone. If others are independent of me it is because they know my worthlessness.

If the other advises or dominates me, this demonstrates lack of respect by the other who realizes I need his help. If the other fails to give advice or even to give information or advises or dominates someone else, it is also because the other has no regard for one, that one is not worth the trouble. In one case the transformation is that the other realizes the incompetence of the self; in the other it is that there is no use in trying to help because it is hopeless.

If the other expresses his humiliation, or great longing for something which is missing in his life, this arouses self-contempt through identification with the defeated other. If however the other expresses great satisfaction with himself, this also humiliates by arousing envy of the other and a heightened awareness that one is dissatisfied with oneself.

A MORE FORMAL DISCUSSION OF
THE HUMILIATION EQUATION

These transformations by which remote information is made relevant, by which benign experiences are illusory and by which exactly opposite events are found to have the same meaning, all with the consequence that the individual suffers humiliation, are examples of what we term the humiliation equation.

In the last chapter, using terms borrowed from statistics, we examined some of the more common ways in which large quantities of information can be conceptualized so that central tendencies, totals, trends, variabilities and other general properties of series can be detected. We will now examine the more complex type of cognitive analysis which we call the equation.

We have borrowed the term equation from mathematics to express an organization of information involving some information which is known in advance, and a general form which governs the solution of the problem. In a mathematical equation, such as $10x + 5 = y$, the constants 10 and 5 represent information known in advance; the unknowns represent information not known in advance, and the total direction of the final solution of the problem is given by the form of the equation.

To state the humiliation equation in its most general form, we need to introduce the mathematical concept of operator, which is simply a letter that stands for a set of operations to be performed. For example, if the operator k stands for "take the square root and add five" or "add 1,667 and find one-half the logarithm," then $k(x)$ would mean $\sqrt{x}+5$ in the first case and $\frac{1}{2} \log(x+1,667)$ in the second. There is no limitation of how complicated or extensive are the operations which one may choose to denote by a single operator.

In our theory we have contrasted the name, which is a message that can retrieve information about a specific object stored at a specific address, with the symbol, which is a learned technique of compressing the non-unique or similar characteristics of a set of objects that maximizes rather than minimizes class membership. In the equation the constants represent names and the operator represents a symbol which will enable the equation to be solved so that, for example, in humiliation equation, the present circumstance becomes one more instance of a possibly humiliating state of affairs.

The humiliation equation is one form in which a humiliation theory may be organized. Its most general form is $k(x)+i=h$, in which i is a constant quantity of inferiority, h is experienced humiliation, x is an experience and k is an operator which can transform x into a quantity of inferiority which, when added to the known, constant background of inferiority, can produce the experience of humiliation. In those cases, where possible operators are given or stored, an equation is essentially a computer program. But the operators in these equations must originally have been learned. Where h, the amount of humiliation, is fixed in advance, the operators must be continually fabricated.

One may usefully make just this assumption, namely, to regard the quantity h to be fixed at a critical value and that the individual solves for k, the operator. Where no operator in the repertoire of the individual yields h, the equation is "unsolvable," so to speak, and the individual does not experience humiliation.

Thus, in a relatively weak shame theory the operator k may be restricted to such a relatively narrow set of values, that the equation is ordinarily not solvable except under unusual circumstances. In this case the individual can not apply transformations beyond a certain value, because, for example, they seem too improbable to him. He might even entertain such extreme possibilities, but discount them in his interpretation of what might be a somewhat shaming experience.

Further, in a weak shame theory the constant base level of inferiority, i, is so low that the operator k would have to be astronomiclly large to produce the humiliation, quantity h. That is to say, that since the individual feels so little inferiority to begin with, any particular experience would have to be transformed into a very great example of inferiority to produce humiliation. Empirically this may be equivalent to phenomena predicted from equations concerning a frictionless plane, or a temperature of absolute zero. This is to be distinguished from the previous characteristic of a weak shame theory, namely, the restriction on the values of k which are permissible to solve the equation. In the present case he may even apply extreme transformations, but the total inferiority thus generated still does not activate humiliation.

In a monopolistic shame theory there may be no restriction on the nature or number of transformations represented by the operator k, and the equation is always solvable. Further, the quantity i, the constant burden of assumed inferiority, is ordinarily so great that the present experience generally requires a small quantity $k(x)$ to add up to an amount equal to h. Even if x is small, if i is large, the operator k need not always assume large values. This means that a very slight indication of inferiority may be sufficient to produce humiliation.

However, x may require very radical transformations by the operator k when the present experience is very remote from providing the necessary evidence. Let us consider the nature of "solving" for the unknown operator k which will so transform any experience that the total quantity of produced inferiority or culpability or defeat will be sufficient to constitute humiliation.

First are those circumstances in which almost anyone, no matter what the strength of the shame theory, would respond with an interpretation that one was either morally in the wrong, or incompetent or inferior. Let us suppose that one is driving an automobile in heavy traffic, and the car unaccountably comes to a dead stop. As other motorists honk their horns in impatience at being held up, most individuals might interpret this experience as one in which they are somewhat in the wrong and giving offense to others by blocking traffic. Again, if one accidentally steps on the feet of someone as one finds one's way to one's seat in a dark theatre, most individuals would interpret this as their responsibility, even though accidental.

If the constant load of assumed inferiority, guilt or responsibility were not too high, neither of these cases would provide sufficient additional inferiority or culpability to add up to an experience of humiliation. One with a very weak shame theory might experience a momentary twinge of shame for his unintended affront to others, but the individual with a monopolistic shame theory would need only this small increment of culpability to constitute a total quantity which would humiliate. It should be noted that in both of these cases, for both the individual with a strong and weak shame theory, the operator k may assume the same value, produce the same interpretation of these experiences, but nonetheless produce a radically different total quantity because of i, the load of assumed inferiority or guilt.

This is a different circumstance than those we have considered, in which the operator k assumed much more extreme values in order to produce a large total quantity $k(x)+i$. In those instances, operators k were found that would make remotely relevant information sufficient for producing humiliation, or for deriving humiliation equally well from an event and from its opposite or from benign circumstances. In the latter case, for example, genuine respect (x) was transformed by an operator k to yield a quantity of inferiority, which, combined with the base line inferiority i, was sufficient to activate humiliation h in the monopolistic humiliation equation.

It should further be noted that because of the nature of the operator k in strong humiliation theory, it is possible to humiliate such an individual even under the circumstance that the quantity i, the base load of presently assumed inferiority, is small, and the nature of the present experience is apparently very remote from an occasion of inferiority.

OVER-AVOIDANCE AND OVER-ESCAPE STRATEGIES

Perceptual reinterpretation as an over-avoidance
or over-escape strategy

In a monopolistic humiliation theory there are two distinguishable, though coordinated organizations, perceptual over-organization and cognitive over-interpretation on the one hand, and over-avoidance and over-escape strategies designed to minimize the humiliation which has been detected by over-interpretation on the other.

Excessive vigilance and defense are not antithetical phenomena to be contrasted with each other. They are part of the larger over-organization which constitutes the entire monopolistic affect theory. Just as over-interpretation is defined by a restriction of interpretation to a particular affect, which thereby magnifies its influence, so over-avoidance or over-escape can be defined as a restriction of strategy to the minimizing of one affect.

Magnification of affect is instrumental to the minimizing of the same affect through strategies based upon the magnified information. It is apparent from our discussion so far that though the perceptual and cognitive interpretation which detects and magnifies humiliation by means of the operator in the humiliation equation is in the service of strategies of avoidance and escape, such co-ordination can also misfire.

Any technique which magnifies negative affect can hinder as well as assist minimizing strategies. They come into clearest conflict in two conditions. First, if avoidance or escape strategies should fail, as we have seen they often do, then the perceptual over-interpretation leaves the individual with an unnecessarily heavy burden to bear. Second, perceptual interpretation and avoidance strategies can come into severe conflict if and when magnification can be avoided or escaped only at the same perceptual level. In such a case the individual must resort to changing the percept. Instead of an interpretation which magnifies the possibility of humiliation, the same stimulus must be reinterpreted to minimize such a possibility.

An analysis of the defense mechanism of denial in psychosis

As Anna Freud noted, such simple denial of danger is a method of defense of a relatively undeveloped and young personality. It is, however, also an adult strategy and a strategy of desperation, a consequence of the failure of direct action strategies which sustains the belief that there is no possible way in which avoidance or escape can be achieved except to deny that there is any danger. Whenever we find extensive employment of perceptual denial, it is probable that there is also a deep pessimism concerning more effective escape or avoidance strategies.

The aim of such secondary reinterpretation of the stimulus is no different in motive than any direct counterattack on the obvious source of humiliation. He so reinterprets his initial interpretation that he is partially spared the experience of humiliation. This reinterpretation may itself be upon an original interpretation of incoming information which is either near or remote, accurate or distorted. Thus if a psychotic detects in the other an intent to humiliate, and this is in fact delusional, he may further transform this information by now seeing in the other extreme good will, since this is the only way in which he thinks he can avoid the consequences of the initial delusion.

The secondary delusion is a remote transformation designed

to cope with the primary delusion. The reinterpretation may, however, operate on a stimulus which is perceived alike in some respects by normal and psychotic, except that the consequences attributed to the stimulus by the psychotic are so disturbing that he must reinterpret and deny the obvious. The initial interpretation is also in some respect very remote and delusional, but it nonetheless is close to the stimulus despite cognitive exaggeration of the interpretation.

Thus in the PAT (Tomkins-Horn Picture Arrangement Test) we have found that a psychotic who sees a picture of a bleeding finger may identify it as such, but also think that this has consequences which are so horrible that he cannot continue to look at it and so he is prompted to reinterpret what he sees. This reinterpretation which appears so obviously delusional to the normal, because it denies that the finger is bleeding, is however no more delusional than the original perception which prompted the reinterpretation. The delusional aspect of the latter is often masked by the fact that both normal and psychotic might agree that the finger is bleeding. Identical identification of a stimulus may be a normal interpretation for one individual and part of a delusional interpretation for another. If the secondary delusional over-interpretation is in response to some of the imagined consequences of what is perceived, then it should be possible to present the same stimulus to a psychotic so that he reports it reasonably accurately in one condition and distorts it seriously in another. We have demonstrated this in connection with the interpretation of a given picture in the PAT. On Plate 16 a worker is shown standing in front of a machine with his finger bleeding. In one other scene of the same plate he is shown working, uninjured at the same machine, and in the third scene he is shown in a hospital bed. The modal interpretation by normals is that the man was working at the machine, that he injured himself and is then hospitalized. About a third of paranoid schizophrenics interpret the scene of injury as something other than injury. The worker is said to be oiling the machine and the drops of blood are seen as dripping oil; or the worker is said to be working with wood and the drops of blood are seen as wood shavings. Occasionally these are interpreted as semen ejected during masturbation.

If, as we suppose, there has been an initial perception of the bleeding finger by these psychotics which was so exaggerated in its consequences that it prompted a secondary reinterpretation to reduce the possibility of humiliation and terror, then these same subjects should in fact respond with this initial interpretation if they could be reassured about the seriousness of the consequences.

On Plate 21 of the PAT two of the three scenes are repeated exactly. The worker is shown at the machine, uninjured in one, and in the other he is shown injured, with his finger bleeding. The third scene shows a doctor, with a medical bag, taping up the finger of the worker. Under these conditions the same psychotics, who thought the drops of blood were oil drippings, now correctly identify the blood as due to an injury. The critical difference appears to be that because the doctor has taken care of it, it is a tolerable stimulus to perceive. This does not necessarily mean that the total interpretation is identical with the normal one, but it does mean that the psychotic, under these safer conditions, need not resort to secondary perceptual reinterpretation to deal with the threat.

ACCURACY OF REALITY PERCEPTION
IN PSYCHOTIC DENIAL

Not only does the psychotic not necessarily resort to remote secondary reinterpretation of a stimulus which arouses severe negative affect as in the case above, but it can also be shown that even when there is perceptual distortion, there is also an attempt to keep this transformation within bounds.

Psychotic perceptual distortion is a compromise between what the stimulus truly appears to be and the avoidance of this interpretation. The sight of injury and blood may be too disturbing to be tolerated, but the schizophrenic does not then plunge heedlessly into the least likely, most bizarre interpretation possible. He attempts to be as accurate as possible, to stay as close as possible to the apparent nature of the stimulus, subject to the restriction that he must not see or report that the finger is bleeding and that the worker is injured. The reinterpretations of bleeding as a dripping oil can, or wood shavings, or semen are *Umweg* solutions to the problem.

We ordinarily assume that when a direct path to a desired object is blocked the individual will take a detour, or substitute path, but that this substitute does not constitute an abandonment of the original goal. Perceptual over-interpretation may be viewed as a special case of substitute behavior. If we assume that the goal of the psychotic is to interpret the stimulus as accurately as possible consistent with tolerable affect, then if the primary over-interpretation arouses intolerable affect we may think of this as a barrier to the original goal. If he were completely to relinquish his original goal, he might refuse to continue with the test, as indeed some do. But if he continues to want to describe the stimulus with precision but at the same time avoid severe negative affect, he could best achieve both aims by reinterpreting the stimulus as the next most probable thing it might be.

If such is the case then it should be possible to simulate this state of affairs in normals by asking them to play the game according to the same rules. If one asks a normal to look at the picture of the man standing over the machine with his finger bleeding, and to forget what it really looks like and try to see it as something else, as the most likely something else it might be, then the normal will also give, among others, the same responses which psychotics have given. It is not that normals act like psychotics so much as that psychotics act like normals under the special circumstance that the most likely perceptual response is blocked by the consequences of initially magnifying the possibilities of humiliation and terror in the stimulus.

CONSCIOUSNESS AND DENIAL

It should be noted that the initial magnification need not attain full consciousness to prompt a secondary reinterpretation which reverses the initial interpretation. By this we do not mean either that it is entirely an unconscious defense nor that it is entirely conscious. It is similar in conscious status to that in any over-learned skill. Just as a skilled driver may take appropriate action in meeting possible dangers while he continues to speak to someone who claims most of his attention, so the initial magnification of humiliation may lead to perceptual reinterpretation with only the dimmest awareness of what he has done. It is in the very nature of skill that the density of reports to messages is so reduced that the individual can no longer say how or even that he has used his skill. If and when perceptual denial becomes a customary mode of defense, then it may become relatively unrecognizable to the individual himself.

THE PARADOX OF DENIAL OF
THE SELF-CREATED THREAT

One of the paradoxes of such an extreme defense is that it is in large part produced by the very magnification which it is calculated to cope with. Had it not been for the original magnification, the humiliation would not have been so intolerable and so there would have been less need to deny that experience. Even extremely intense humiliation might be tolerated if the initial perceptual and cognitive over-interpretation did not so exaggerate its probable density, i.e., the product of its intensity and duration. Over-interpretation sometimes makes it appear imminent that what is about to happen will be extremely humiliating and that this feeling will never abate but grow with time. If, added to this, there is a belief that there is no possibility of avoidance or escape, then perceptual reinterpretation may be forced. If the individual cannot avail himself of such a defense either because of his character structure or because others will not permit such a defense to work at all, then there may be recourse to suicide, as happens, for example, in cases of bankruptcy and in suddenly discovered behavior which promises humiliation as in fraud and embezzlement by individuals.

The over-interpretation humiliation equation generates an action equation of strategies of over-avoidance and over-escape

As previously mentioned, in a monopolistic humiliation theory there are two distinguishable, though co-ordinated, organizations, each of them representing over-organization. One is the perceptual and cognitive over-interpretation organized into the humiliation equation which magnifies humiliation and alerts the individual to the remotest possibility of its imminence. The other is a hyper-vigilance concerned with over-avoidance and over-escape strategies to minimize the humiliation which has been detected by over-interpretation. Together, the over-interpretation of the humiliation equation, and the over-avoidance and over-escape strategies constitute the monopolistic humiliation theory. Just as over-interpretation is defined by a restriction of interpretation to a particular affect which thereby magnifies its influence, so over-avoidance or over-escape can be defined as a restriction of strategy to the minimizing of one affect. These are necessarily co-ordinated organizations, but as we shall see, co-ordination can also misfire. Magnification of humiliation, though it generates action strategies to minimize humiliation, can, under specific circumstances, hinder as well as assist minimizing strategies.

As also noted before, in monopolistic humiliation theory, there is a circular recruitment between humiliation, perception, cognition and action which produces over-organization of the entire personality. When the humiliation equation magnifies the nature and the imminence of dread possibilities, the individual is driven to act to minimize these possibilities just as he was driven to magnify them in the first place. Because avoidance and escape are prompted by over-interpretation which has grossly magnified the threat, decisions and actions to minimize humiliation assume the same inflated, desperate proportions as the perceptions and expectations which prompt them. For these reasons we have called these over-avoidance and over-escape strategies. These titanic struggles necessarily generate heroic strategies, lest all be lost. André Gide described the phenomenon in *The Counterfeiters:* "This self-contempt, this disgust with oneself that can lead the most undecided to the most extreme decisions."

THE PARANOID POSTURE

Just as monopolistic interpretation seizes upon the most remote possibilities, including even negative evidence, and twists it into supporting evidence, so there are equally extreme analogs at the strategy and action level. In the final extremity a trivial remark can become the occasion for the suicide of the self or the destruction of the oppressor or both. Ordinarily under such circumstances, the interpretation of the apparent triviality is radically magnified and thereby produces an intolerable burden of humiliation, which in turn threatens to detonate a mushrooming chain reaction of nuclear magnitude within the self.

Equally extreme action strategies which are prompted by monopolistic affect theories are those of complete withdrawal, mutism, and complete immobility, as in catatonic stupor. These, however, represent terminal phases of monopolistic affect theory organization in which the individual has been essentially totally defeated. Before this terminal phase of organization of monopolistic humiliation theory, however, there is unrelenting warfare in which the individual generates and tests every conceivable strategy to avoid and escape total defeat at the hand of the humiliating bad object. This we have called the paranoid posture. When the contempt of the other is unrelieved by love, and when no other love object exists, then monopolistic humiliation theory necessarily turns to defense of the self against the oppressor at any cost.

This is not to say that the self is suddenly held in high esteem and completely relieved of its burden of humiliation. On the contrary, the over-interpretation of the malevolent contempt of the other results in frequent misfiring of over-avoidance and over-escape strategies which expose the self to humiliation from the over-inflated insult, which add fuel to further over-interpretation and more desperate strategies of defense.

The reader will recall that we are using humiliation theory as a generic term, to refer not only to the affects of shame—humiliation, contempt—disgust, and self-contempt—disgust but to amalgams of these with other negative affects. In the paranoid posture, it is particularly the affect of fear—terror which is conjoined with the humiliation affects.

OVER-ESCAPE AND OVER-AVOIDANCE ARE CONJOINTLY GENERATED BY OVER-INTERPRETATION

In normal avoidance learning, as we noted in our analysis of a man learning to cross the street in safety, the individual ultimately learns to act both without fear and at the same time *as if* he were frightened at the potential danger. He learns to avoid both the fear and the danger at the same time. As he selects the moment to cross the street he is characteristically affectless. In the case of monopolistic affect theory such double avoidance strategies can never be learned because of the continual breakdown of defense and the continual reconstruction of avoidance and escape strategies which continually magnify the potential threats and the affects they activate. In the case of the man on the street he would have been again and again hit by drivers who seemed intent on hurting him so that there were fewer and fewer possible islands of safety.

In monopolistic humiliation theory avoidance learning and escape learning are necessarily conjoined. Avoidance learning is always accompanied by present humiliation from which he must escape. Present humiliation is always experienced while avoidance is attempted, and at the same time escape learning is always accompanied by avoidance learning because the combination of over-interpretation and presently experienced affect guarantees that the individual who is escaping present humiliation is at the same time trying to avoid a future contingency which would promise an even more humiliating experience. If the future always represents an accelerating deterioration of circumstances, then it becomes impossible merely to escape present humiliation, since this is overshadowed by the dread of things to come of which the present is only the beginning.

This is the kind of imagination which is represented in the admonition: "If you think this is bad, wait." Such over-interpretation guarantees that there is always present negative affect with which to cope, thus requiring constant escape learning, but that, in addition, such escape is always conjoined with a future contingency which must also be over-avoided at the same time that one copes with present threat.

In terms of the man on the street, he has always to escape his present fear and present dangers of drivers and at the same time be careful lest in escaping present dangers he fail to avoid a fleet of drunken truck drivers who are coming down the highway at a rapidly accelerating rate careening towards both sidewalks in random fashion.

It is for these reasons that over-organization necessarily involves conjointly both over-avoidance and over-escape. Theoretically it would have been possible for over-avoidance to have been so successful that escape strategies would have become superfluous.

The pluralism of apparent threats generates a pluralism of over-avoidance and over-escape strategies

Not only does overinterpretation produce heroic, intense preoccupation with ways and means of avoiding and escaping humiliation, and alternative strategies in depth to counter possible strategies of the other; the pluralism of apparent threats generates a pluralism of defensive strategies. If everything under the sun, no matter how remote, how negative or contradictory it may appear, nonetheless is so interpreted, so transformed that it threatens the individual with humiliation, then numerous different strategies must be generated to cope with each individual threat of such a pluralism of threats.

Strategies are developed for remote as well as contradictory apparent threats

The individual generates a pluralism of strategies, first, because over-interpretation makes it appear that the most innocuous contingencies must be dealt with harshly. If the other is reading a newspaper when I come into the room, he must be humiliated so that he will not again insult me by his indifference. If the other expresses a mild difference of opinion from mine, it is blown up into a life-and-death struggle in which I must defeat him or be forever humiliated. If the other receives an honor, I must find as many ways as possible to minimize its significance. If the other should praise me, I must expose his stupidity or his insincerity. I must not be seduced by love any more than I will permit myself to be beaten by contempt. I must keep everyone at arm's length just as desperately as I must guarantee that no one is indifferent to me or rejects me. People must not be permitted to become either dependent on me, because they make demands on me which I cannot meet, or independent of me because then they do not need me and thus expose me. I detest and reject all those who are humble and lowly, or who complain of their troubles or their inadequacy, because they make me feel the same way and I do not wish to be identified with them.

But I also reject and derogate those in high places, those who are successful, those who are self-confident, those who are happy, because I envy them; and if they were to be permitted to enjoy their status, their success, their life, then I would be so much more humiliated. Both the humble and the proud must be further humbled. I cannot tolerate the existence of beauty in the world because I am thereby consumed with envy. Nor can I witness or tolerate ugliness because it degrades and humiliates me.

In short, the humiliation equation guarantees that I oppose every one of the most remote bits of evidence of possible insult with as urgent action as if it represented a real and present danger. Obvious evidence and remote evidence, as well as evidence which appears to be negative, are all responded to in a variety of ways but with the same underlying assumption concerning the nature of their consequences.

Such pluralism of response to threat is, however, not restricted to passively meeting the unwelcome thrusts of the other. The other is actively pursued and attacked in a general offensive calculated to elevate the self and derogate the other. Further, the self is actively over-inflated to ward off deflation. In the monopolistic paranoid posture the self is over-inflated by the delusion of grandeur while at the same time a holy war is waged against the over-inflated persecutor.

ABANDONMENT OF THE IMAGE OF POSITIVE AFFECT

With respect to over-interpretation we have said it is defined by the limitation of perception and cognition to one affect and that the same is true for over-avoidance and over-escape. Because the affect involved is negative, one of the four major affect strategies is necessarily radically attenuated and frequently completely excluded. The strategy of maximizing positive affect has to be surrendered by any person who lives constantly under the shadow of negative affect. The only sense in which he may strive for positive affect at all is for the shield which it promises against humiliation.

The paranoid posture sees in the delusion of grandeur some protection against persecution and humiliation. It is not that he would not or could not enjoy positive affect, in the abstract, but it is a luxury he cannot afford while he is engaged in warfare. To take seriously the strategy of *maximizing* positive affect, rather than simply enjoying it when the occasion arises, is entirely out of the question.

The power image and the paranoid posture

Of the three remaining affect strategies, minimizing negative affect, minimizing affect inhibition and maximizing power, it is the power strategy which ultimately becomes dominant. This is because of the perpetual breakdown and repair of defense. If an individual could in fact successfully avoid or escape negative affect, he would be prepared to adopt as dominant the strategy of minimizing negative affect. In the case of fear he might be willing to become overly timid so long as cowardice returned security. In the case of humiliation he might be willing to become excessively humble and submissive so long as his tormentors ceased to torment him in return for his compliance. Under these conditions he would swallow his pride and his humiliation, thus renouncing the strategies of maximizing positive affect and of minimizing affect inhibition. He would also not need to maximize his power to achieve any of the three affect strategies since he would have achieved a stable solution to his dominant strategy of minimizing his negative affect.

But since the monopolistic humiliation theory construction involves not only a continuing contempt from the other for some period of time, unrelieved by positive affect, or by let-up, and since the over-interpretation of the humiliation equation ultimately accelerates the pace of insult independent of actual insult, the individual cannot achieve an island of security long enough to achieve even a semblance of minimizing negative affect. He is therefore driven to the power strategy—to try to guarantee some future security against the slings and arrows of outrageous fortune. He is prepared to fight for peace. He is willing to be psychologically hurt now so long as it increases his power to reduce insult in the future.

There is a parallelism of structure between the power strategy in monopolistic humiliation theory and Freud's formulation of the primacy of the Reality principle over the Pleasure principle in which maximum present pleasure is surrendered to an optimal balance of pleasure and pain on the average and in the future. Similarly with the dominance of the power strategy over the strategy of minimizing negative affect, and affect inhibition, optimizing techniques dominate maximizing and minimizing techniques.

The individual is prepared to suffer *some* humiliation, and to suppress rather than express his bitterness, if he can thereby guarantee a more optimal status over the long run, and especially in the future. This is not to say that in monopolistic humiliation theory the strategies of minimizing humiliation, and of expressing it rather than inhibiting it, are entirely surrendered, for they are not. Rather it is to say that they are generally subordinated to the power strategy.

Such an individual may frequently avoid situations which threaten to humiliate him, and frequently express his feelings of being persecuted and humiliated, but these cannot become stable and dominant modes of accommodation because the frequent breakdown of defense mobilizes continuing efforts to guarantee that future defenses will not break down, and this requires an increasing power over the sources of his misery. Because there is no place to hide he cannot settle into a permanent posture of avoidance and so minimizing negative affect.

Indeed one of the major techniques which Rosen used for accelerating movement in the therapy of the paranoid patient was to continually ridicule the power strategies of grandeur, to maximize awareness of the bad mother while at the same time offering a good mother substitute in the person of the therapist. The major differences between this technique and what would happen naturally are the acceleration of breakdown of defense and the offering of a non-persecuting other at the very moment of breakdown of defense. That other appears to be powerful enough to penetrate the patient's defenses but does not further press his advantage except to offer the possibility of positive identification with him rather than hostile identification and maximal conflict.

THE PARANOID POSTURE AS A WAR BETWEEN THE SELF AND THE OTHER

Let us return now to the nature of the pluralism of defenses against humiliation. This is a multiple strategy, as in any warfare, in which every effort is made to build up the self for the purpose of defeating the other, and to defeat the other so that the self may be saved. No one reaches the extremity of a monopolistic humiliation theory without a past history of actual, prolonged bitter attack by a parent and/or others against the integrity of the child. Further, despite the basis in reality for the paranoid posture, it is also true that the later awareness of these malignant contacts is always radically exaggerated.

Although the self is characteristically over-inflated in importance, as in the delusion of grandeur, the primary means by which the self is defended is by a variety of attacks and derogations of the other in which contempt is thrown back at the other. The other is bitterly blamed for a variety of offenses as in the delusion of persecution. The other is also defied, so that one will act shamelessly to outrage the other and to prove that one does not care what the other thinks. But one also tries in every way to prove that the other is totally wrong and that his contempt is based on delusion.

One also tries to punish the other by counter-humiliation, by interpreting the behavior of the other in terms of the hyper-vigilance of the humiliation equation. Thus I may say to you that you are entirely narcissistic—that whatever you do is utterly self-centered—that you can love only an extension of yourself, so that what appears to be generous and noble to others is nothing more than concealed pride and self-love. I can attenuate the significance of all your good works further by showing that you were ashamed or afraid to do otherwise lest others humiliate you. Your apparent sympathies are at best sentimentality. I will use the genetic method as a technique of insult in the sudden insight that at last I have decoded the mystery of your personality—"Now I understand why you are the way you are," in which the assumption is implicit that you are not only contemptible, but surprisingly so.

When the other displays behavior similar to my own, it is interpreted to reveal exactly its opposite. Thus if I have been humiliated for exhibitionism, I say to the other on the occasion of his modesty, "I wouldn't have thought an exhibitionist like you would be troubled with modesty," thereby derogating both the moral and the imputed immoral wish at the same time. I will expose the other's personality as inadequate, spelling out in detail his internal inconsistencies, exaggerate his sensitivities into delusions, predict confidently that his apparent adequacies will have unexpected miserable consequences, interfere as much as possible with his efforts at constructive activity, attribute as much as possible of his success to others or to luck.

I will use multiple criteria in evaluating the other, so that if he cannot be found wanting in one respect he will surely fail by another criterion. He has not done enough, or if he has, it is work of poor quality; or if the quantity and quality are good, then he had to work too hard—he is an over-achiever, a person of limited talent who could be surpassed with little effort by anyone with superior talents. If he has not achieved enough he is flayed for his waste of talent, for his laziness or his playfulness. If he has been energetic, he is condemned for his incompetence and lack of talent. If the other pursues a career in which he fulfills himself, I contaminate his enjoyment by placing it into relationship with some other activity which is more worthwhile, or which should preclude the legitimacy of his enjoyment. Thus, if he is an artist I speak of the irony of one man expressing his miserable self on canvas while millions die of starvation and disease. Better he had been a soldier in the war against disease and starvation—a doctor or a farmer who deals with the problems of the real world rather than the feelings and fantasies of one person. If he is a successful capitalist, I speak of his spiritual bankruptcy. If he is a scholar, I speak of his alienation from the world. If he is an actor, I speak of his narcissism and the fact that he produces nothing. If he is a psychiatrist, I dwell upon his exclusive concern with the negative aspects of personality and with his lack of surety. Of invidious comparison between the other and the self and between one person and another there is no end when there is a will to save the self in warfare with others.

RECURRENT BREAKDOWNS OF DEFENSE PRODUCE UNIFICATION OF OVER-AVOIDANCE AND OVER-ESCAPE STRATEGIES

We have said before that the breakdown of defenses prompts the learning of new defenses in circular incremental magnification. The recurrent cycle of theory construction, destruction and reconstruction we have likened to the growth of theory in science. We believe the analog to be exact and we are now in a better position to examine some of the details of the process.

A pluralism of strategies, each one of which was effective, would not produce a unification of strategies. Even in science two quite different theories may continue to co-exist side by side for some time so long as each accounts for different aspects of the same domain. Such for a time was the status of the wave and corpuscular theories of light. The essential dynamic of unification in theory construction, in science and in affect theory construction alike, is error and inconsistency. Whenever any strategy of defense ceases to work or is visibly contradictory to another strategy, repair and unification is forced upon the individual. The strategy ceases to work whenever the individual experiences humiliation despite the attempted defense. Thus if a child insulted by another child says, "Stop that, or I'll hit you" and the other child responds by laughing and ridiculing the possibility of such a counter-defense, that verbal defense is a failure if the insulted one now feels just as bad as he did before he responded with his verbal counteraction.

Breakdown of defense due to retroflexive over-interpretation

The strategies may become visibly contradictory whenever the individual becomes humiliated just because he has employed a mechanism of defense which creates more new humiliation than the humiliation it was intended to minimize. If an individual strives excessively hard to overcome his feelings of inadequacy, he may suffer secondary humiliation because his own defense is overinterpreted by him. He now feels humiliated because he has unwittingly revealed to others how overwhelming his feelings of humiliation are.

In a case of paranoid schizophrenia cited by R. W. White, there are numerous instances of such retroflexive breakdowns of defense. Thus: "Ambition. This word used to be my nickname, I was called 'Ambition.' This slur applies to my striving to make something of myself in spite of attempts to make me weaken and give up trying to progress intellectually." Here we see that insult is added to insult by the very defense which reveals how hard he is trying to overcome his initial inadequacy. This is then re-projected outward as another "slur" which his attempts to better himself evokes from others.

There are many reasons why monopolistic defenses against humiliation characteristically misfire. Not the least of these is the principle just cited—that what the individual does to defend himself can easily become, through over-interpretation, a further source of humiliation. Thus if in over-avoiding humiliation an individual cooperates with others lest he seem uncooperative, he may then feel humiliated because others may regard him as too compliant. But if he acts steadfastly independent as a defense against being overcooperative, he is vulnerable to humiliation because he is now concerned that he is unreasonably stubborn and willful.

Contamination vs. insufficiency: obsessive vs. depressive inadequacy

There is a similar bind in the strategy of overinflating the value of the work of the self. There are two distinct competing criteria by which work may be evaluated. One is the criterion of quality and freedom from contamination, and the other is the criterion of plenitude and freedom from insufficiency. The obsessive, and all those who have been over-socialized by contempt for deviations from exactness and excellence, is forever concerned lest he make a mess, that his work lack precision and orderliness. The depressive, and all those who have been the recipients of both love and contempt and thereby made very vulnerable to shame, is ordinarily governed in his work by the principle of plenitude. Have I done enough to capture and hold the interest and love of the other, or will he be disappointed, or turn away? This product must excite, and continue to excite, so that the product must be rich, deep and ever-changing lest the other look away.

The paranoid system

Each of these criteria, the principle of quality or contamination and the principle of plenitude or insufficiency, can be tyrannical enough. But in the case of monopolistic humiliation theory as it is found in the paranoid posture, the individual is under the double bind of both principles. His work must be both orderly and full. These are the criteria which are responsible for the extraordinary combination of logical coherence and breadth of vision which one may find in a fully worked out paranoid system. Here there is nothing left out, and the whole must fit together tightly, an intellectual achievement which is beyond the tidiness of the mind of the obsessive and beyond the luxuriant showiness of the mind of the depressive. It is the difference between richness, on the one hand, and precision and organized complexity on the other, in evaluating the self and others.

The depressive is satisfied with suggestiveness, with depth, with brilliance, with exciting the self and the other. The obsessive is satisfied with clarity, certainty, freedom from error and economy, so that he is sure that the internalized contemptuous other will not be offended. But the paranoid's work must combine both criteria because it must be perfect in every way. It must be rich and deep, but with no loose edges, no sacrifice of rigour or precision. It must at once avoid the contempt of the internalized other and also excite the envy of the other by its perfection. It must in short support the delusion of grandeur, the identification with God.

Clearly, as the paranoid attempts to meet one criterion, he must necessarily risk humiliation by violating the other criterion. If his reach is too great, he exposes himself to the contempt of the specialist. If he concentrates all his expertise in one area, he is vulnerable to the humiliation of lack of scope, of triviality, of overspecialization. A passion for generality is of course not inherently paranoid, but paranoids do share this passion with the immortals.

For some years I have interviewed those ambulatory paranoids who came to Princeton in the hope that Einstein would see them and bestow his blessing upon their system. More often than not the individual had indeed created an extraordinarily ingenious system which accounted for his personal concerns writ large, along with many other phenomena. In some cases these were authors who had paid to have their ideas privately published as books which they had hoped to persuade Einstein to sanction. These paranoids could not be satisfied with a merely personal delusion. They were driven to account for their personal predicament in terms of the universal, in terms of the eternal, in terms of the general human condition. They were, in short, philosophers, who must exteriorize and universalize their own personal tragedy if they are to understand it.

The communalities between the motivation of the paranoids which drives them in the same general direction as Newton, Marx, Freud, Einstein were driven we do not wish to examine further at this point, except to note one historical communality among them. Three of these four revolutionary innovators were Jews, a people who have both suffered considerable persecution and discrimination but who have also managed to cling tenaciously to their identity and their heritage.

Let us now return to the breakdown of defense due to retroflexive over-interpretation. If he is excessively proud and hides his humiliation lest he be ridiculed, his defense makes him dread further humiliation because he appears overly arrogant. In the case of the paranoid schizophrenic cited before, who was plagued with humiliation, his façade of defense evokes the same humiliation it was designed to minimize. Thus: " 'I'll tell the world!' This remark insinuates that I had been in the habit of telling the world what to do, or telling the world defiantly where to go to. This remark insinuates that in my supreme arrogance I had been telling the world some of my opinions held by me to be of more importance and consequence than the opinions of all the rest of humanity put together." Just as Christianity and Judaism alike found over-identification with God no less sinful and heretical than underidentification and defiance of God, so the paranoid is also caught in the bind of creating more humiliation by either defense. If he pretends to grandeur through identification he is not humble enough, but if he is an antichrist he is sure this pride too goes before a fall because of its heresy.

Breakdown of defense due to conflict between different strategies

Breakdown of defense is occasioned not only through over-interpretation of the defense itself producing additional humiliation but it is also generated by real conflict between the pluralistic strategies which have been generated in response to a wide variety of different kinds of threats, all of which however evoke humiliation. Thus if you combine insult with hostility, I may be tempted to reply in kind so that I express defiant scorn for you. But if you insult me by assuming an attitude of condescension and amused indifference, I may reply in kind with shameless behavior calculated to demonstrate that I care as little for you as you do for me. If, however, you insult me by blaming me for all your troubles, I may respond by humiliating you by recounting in detail how again and again you disappointed me when I was counting on you. If your mode of insult is to reveal my hopeless incompetence, I may respond by trying to prove that you are utterly mistaken. I may do this by a heroic effort in which I accomplish all of those things which you said I was incapable of doing. If, however, you complain bitterly of my incompetence, combining distress with contempt—that you are regretfully disgusted with me—I may confirm your judgment by abasing myself before you, expressing my hopeless despair about myself.

These are but examples of a very great variety of possible defenses against a great variety of threats of humiliation. Insult rarely occurs in pure form. It is characteristically combined with hostility or distress or surprise or even love. These compounds tend to evoke somewhat different strategies in the same individual and from individual to individual.

Let us now assume that one parent offends the child in these various ways, at different times, and sometimes collapses all of these varieties within a single episode, so that he begins, for

example, in an attitude of condescension and amused indifference: "Don't be a slob all your life, pick up your clothes like a
good boy." Let us suppose the child responds by throwing some
more of his clothes on the floor, thus demonstrating that he
cares as little for this haughty parent as the latter is concerned
for him. Now that one becomes angry as well as self-righteous:
"I said, pick up those clothes and do it now, you miserable
thing." The child may now switch from shamelessness to counter-
hostility and contempt: "I won't! I won't! I hate you. You're
awful." Now the parent combines distress and contempt: "You'll
be the death of me—as if I didn't have enough to do—without
going around the house all day picking up after you—because
you're so thoughtless." The child, not to be outdone, matches
pious anguish with a recital of his own grievances at the hands
of his even more despicable parent: "You never let me play!
You won't buy me anything! Harry's mother lets him go swimming. You're a kill-joy!"

At this the scope of argument is opened still further, and
the parent turns to an examination of his general posture toward
life: "I don't know what will ever become of you. You just don't
seem to be as responsible as other boys." Having questioned his
general worth she then dissolves into tears: "What will ever
become of you?" At this the child is overcome with remorse
and humiliation: "I'm sorry, mom. I guess I'm just no good."
Our drama ends with the child picking up not only his clothing
but straightening up most of the house to prove to himself and
his mother that she was mistaken.

Since affects do not always come in tidy packages, one to a
package, defenses against them are necessarily varied. If the
variety of insults and the variety of defenses which they generate
are all focused on one person, then some defenses must necessarily defeat some other defenses. I cannot at one and the same
time defy you, prove that I don't give a damn about what you
think, prove that you are wrong, submit to you and confess my
defeat, turn the tables on you, and destroy your power over me
by destroying you. If I care enough about what you think to
wish to convince you, others or myself that you were wrong,
then I cannot do this by acting shamelessly and thus confirming
your low opinion of me. If I wish to defy you I cannot act as

though I were indifferent. If I wish to minimize affect inhibition and cry out my unworthiness, promise to atone and reform, clearly I cannot at the same time further insult you or try to destroy you, or act shamelessly so that I minimize your power to make me feel ashamed.

The strategies of minimizing humiliation, humiliation inhibition and the power to do either can come into direct conflict again and again. Insofar as these strategies were forced upon me in monopolistic humiliation theory, I will be vulnerable to continuing breakdown of each of these defenses insofar as other defenses are violated every time I employ one defense rather than another. If I strive desperately to maintain the façade of superiority, I must violate the wish to express my feelings of humiliation. If I continually express these, I must violate the power strategy of minimizing the experience of humiliation.

One of the most poignant phenomena in psychopathology is the confusion produced in the neurotic and particularly in the psychotic by the labile, rapid transformation of defenses as each breaks down in radical conflict with other defenses, to be replaced by another defense, which in turn breaks down and thus prompts an accelerating rate of breakdown and repair.

In the acute phase of the schizophrenic reaction, we have noted a common defense against this phenomenon and its attendant terror, despair and confusion. This is the self-conscious attempt to order the kaleidoscope of conflicting thoughts and feelings by writing them down and attempting to organize them so that their rate of change is decelerated and the individual recovers control over their appearance and disappearance. This state of confusion is ordinarily preceded by an accelerating rate of change of affect and defense against negative affect. The pre-psychotic feels hurled violently between confrontation of the bad object, being overwhelmed by it, acting as though one were indifferent, trying to disprove its insults and threats, abasing oneself before it and confessing, hiding lest it destroy one, determined to destroy it and rid oneself of it once and for all.

Such a rapid rate of breakdown and repair is due in part to the very pluralism of strategies themselves. If the individual could have sustained either aloofness, over-achievement, counter-contempt or psychopathic shamelessness, he might have kept humiliation at bay; but the pluralism of strategies is at once a cause and an effect of the ineffectiveness of each of these strategies.

A similar dynamic has been noted by Saul in psychosomatic hypertension in that these individuals are permanently enraged and therefore hypertensive because they are too proud and angry to be openly dependent and too dependent to be openly hostile and rejecting. In this case anger interferes with dependence and dependence interferes with anger.

In the case of monopolistic humiliation over-organization the dynamic is somewhat similar, but also different. The similarity consists in the barrier which each wish constitutes for the other wish. The difference is that, whereas in hypertension neither wish is overtly expressed, in humiliation over-organization the contradictory strategies are all expressed but thereby increase the humiliation they were designed to minimize.

The desperate effort of the decompensating schizophrenic to save himself from drowning in the whirlpool of his own defenses, in his ultra-labile thoughts and feelings, frequently results in his writing, night and day, the whole tumultuous sequence of the affects and ideas which threaten to consume him—to organize them so that they will slow down enough for him to recover his feeling of unity and identity. To wish desperately one moment to kill the oppressor and the next to abase oneself completely before the same persecutor is not only to be incapable of warding off the dread affect of humiliation—it is also to lose the self. What kind of a self can it be which oscillates wildly between the fear of persecution, the affirmation of grandeur and counter-contempt and anger and the panic of self-enforced confession and submission to the oppressor?

Breakdown of defense due to continuing insult and threat from the other

The paranoid posture requires for its elaboration not only a luxuriant growth of defense, but for some time a continuing source of real threat which is capable of puncturing and penetrating the over-defended ego of the oppressed one. Unification and proliferation of defense, we have said, depends upon re-current breakdown and repair. The latter in turn requires at the beginning a real enemy if an over-inflated imaginary one is to be finally constructed in response to the numerous painful deflations at the hands of the oppressor.

If and when the pre-psychotic terminates his relationship with his original oppressor, parent or parent surrogate, he continues to evoke from others similar threats of humiliation which also make his defenses misfire.

If I act toward you, whom I have just met for the first time, as though you were my enemy, as though what you said insulted me, then there inevitably follows a conflict in which you will confirm my assumptions and humiliate me. Thus if the other makes a casual remark about the abominable weather today, and I interpret this to mean that he dislikes the town I live in and all its inhabitants and especially me, I may respond with an invitation to the stranger to go back to where he came from, if the weather there is so superior. At this the stranger is unlikely to leave town but he is likely to tell off our suspicious hero, thereby confirming his interpretation and at the same time puncturing his defense.

As avoidance becomes over-avoidance it becomes a more and more self-confirming prophecy. If I am overly arrogant, overly identified with God, you are more likely to increase my humiliation. If I am shameless, overly ruthless in my ambition, overly defiant or overly pious, I will inevitably evoke from others exactly what I am trying to avoid—the contempt of others which further humiliates me. The more I criticize you so that my ego may be saved, the more likely you are to respond in kind so that my ego will then need further and more heroic defense. The tragic paradox of the paranoid posture is that the better an actor the paranoid is, the more convincing his assumed superiority, the more crushing the hostility and counter-contempt he will evoke from others.

THE PHENOMENON OF POLARIZATION

The relationship between the paranoid and the innocent stranger becomes very much more complicated when the other is also somewhat paranoid. Under these conditions interpersonal relations and intergroup relations, when each group is unduly suspicious, can become self-confirming in a more subtle fashion. This same phenomenon, of course, like all the phenomena in this chapter, may be readily found to a lesser degree in individuals not close to psychosis.

I first became aware of the phenomenon of polarization in my graduate seminars. It may, for example, begin innocently enough with a statement on my part that the central problems of psychology are those of affect and cognition. A behavioristically oriented student upon hearing these weasel words immediately rises to do battle: "Sir, do you mean to say that what a person *does,* how he acts, has no importance whatever in psychology?" I did not say that, but the poorly concealed contempt and hostility in his voice is bait to which I must rise. If this is what he is ridiculing and since he is ridiculing *me*—then I must surely defend it! "Behaviorism was a blight which wasted the energies of a generation of psychologists" I hurl back at him, flogging a dead horse whose praises, in a calmer moment, I might even have sung.

The critical point here is that I have been forced, by his contempt, into the defense of a proposition which I did not originate, and which I do not really believe, and most important —I do not know that I did not say this in the first place. I have been seduced into believing something I did not say and do not believe simply because someone who irritates me has attributed it to me and I must justify myself and humble him.

Now let us turn to our young Behaviorist. When he originally challenged me he was not really sure what I meant, and so he put his suspicion in the form of a question, albeit poorly concealing his scorn. Upon hearing my arrogant reply his suspicion has been confirmed! "Tomkins is a muddlehead! I cannot let him get away with that brand of idiocy," he mutters inaudibly. Audibly he continues, "I suppose you would have us return to Introspectionism."

I did not say that, but if he is against it, that is more than enough for me to defend it. I throw the full weight of my scholarship against the tenuous shibboleths he has learned from reading the philosophy of science of amateurs. "If you will trouble yourself to read some of the earlier introspective reports, and particularly the German phenomenologists, you will find there some extraordinarily interesting things."

My antagonist can scarcely believe his ears. How did he happen to wander into this museum? Hasn't Tomkins ever seen a rat, or a Skinner box, or even a T-maze? "I know what it means when a rat presses a bar, and how many times he does it when he has just eaten and when he hasn't eaten for 24 hours, but I don't know what it means for the rat to be conscious."

I too can be obtuse: "I don't know what it means when a rat presses a bar—whether he's hungry or not—except that he's pressed the bar—which is not terribly interesting in and of itself."

Now my antagonist rises to the bait and is forced to defend something he did not say and does not believe: "There just aren't any other kinds of facts in psychology than how many times did a rat press a bar when he was deprived of food 24 hours, compared with after he has just eaten. That's science—all the other things—like 'I don't like spinach' are just words. You don't really know whether he likes it or not till you give him spinach after he presses a bar."

And so on and on until two hours are spent in which I have communicated none of the ideas I intended to discuss but during which I have defended more and more absurd propositions in the mistaken belief that I had uttered them and had to defend them, all the while forcing my suspicious antagonist into an identical posture.

The essential dynamic in polarization is that the negative affects of each antagonist are aroused and prompt the testing of attitudes attributed to the other, which the other confirms as his own and defends because he must counter the attack by the other and does not recognize the distortions which the other at first subtly, and unconsciously, introduces into his rewording of the initial proposition of the other. As the ball is thrown back and forth, the distortions which are successively introduced become more and more grotesque, but they are not recognized because these have been produced in steps of just unnoticeable differences. It ends in mutual recrimination and an uneasy awareness that one has been seduced—just when and how, neither party understands. He is certain only of the waywardness of the other whom he dimly realizes is somehow responsible for the whole mess.

Breakdown of defenses due to insight into their nature: guilt and atonement

Last and not the least of the reasons for the inadequacy and recurrent breakdowns of defense is the small, soft voice of the intellect—periodically insistent and intrusive. In the quiet between the affective storms, the paranoid cannot forever escape honest self-confrontations. At these moments his self is exposed in its naked ugliness. His pretensions, his insincerity, his alienation from himself and from others, his inconsistencies, his essential powerlessness, the wrongs he has unjustly inflicted on others, the misery and ugliness which he has introduced into the lives of others, his inability to love or evoke it or accept it when it is offered—all conspire to turn the entire burden of humiliation and guilt against the self.

This is not an irrational self-loathing. It is an appropriate response in the face of the erosion of the human potentiality for dignity and fulfillment. The fact that there was an original oppressor who was in part responsible for the intransigency of the paranoid posture cannot relieve oneself of the burden of humiliation and guilt for the role he too played in his own destruction and in the destruction of others.

It is in part the awareness of the essential irrationality and immorality of his defenses which forces the paranoid to the realization that his fantasies of revenge are both impossible to achieve and unjustified. His sudden awareness of the extent to which his ideas of grandeur are over-inflated force him to confront the truth that fame and the respect of others is neither possible nor deserved. His true vision of himself at such moments will from time to time generate visions of an ideal world, which for him is one free of hate and humiliation and fear. If he is a playwrite like Strindberg, who ultimately succumbed to paranoid delusions, he will during this period write an utterly idyllic love story as white and pure as his other plays are black with envy and malice. If he is like Dostoevsky in *Notes From Underground*—a defiant, sullen, unrelenting mouse—he will also generate an ultra-Christian solution to the problem of love and hate.

We believe it is an all but inevitable consequence of the union of human affect and intelligence that negative affect will be the response to anyone, including the self, who is responsible for the undeserved and unprovoked production and evocation of negative affect in the self or the other. I must be distressed, angry, fearful and ashamed at anyone who willfully inflicts any of these affects upon myself or upon others. If I am the one who is primarily responsible for producing or increasing the misery of myself or others, then I must ultimately distress, anger, fear or loathe myself.

Our position in this respect is midway between Psychoanalysis and that of Hobart Mowrer. While we have expounded at length on the human potentiality for experiencing guilt where it does not belong, we do not regard the guilt and humiliation of the paranoid at the awareness of his over-inflated pride, anger and shamelessness simply as another part of his illness. Rather this is the voice of the intellect which insists it will be heard. This is one of those rare moments when the accelerating over-organization temporarily halts, and the individual, becalmed, sees clearly that he has embroiled himself and others in needless warfare and misery.

What we have called neurosis and psychosis must periodically be illuminated by the truth of the matter, and when this happens it must evoke further humiliation and guilt as well as other negative affects. Under these conditions the individual is properly ashamed and guilty for the fact that he is sick, because he has wronged himself and others. Guilt and shame are not, under these conditions, part of illness but rather an inevitable and characteristically human response to human misery.

If however there is no restitution and no atonement, then the defenses must ultimately become more rigid just because of this flash illumination.

THE FURTHER UNIFICATION OF DEFENSE BY
SECONDARY LOSS: THE THREAT OF IDENTITY
LOSS: AN EXPLANATION OF SOME PSYCHO-
THERAPEUTIC FAILURES

Unification of defensive strategies is motivated and maintained not only by the breakdown of defense but by the threat
of the loss of identity after defensive strategies have been
stabilized for several years.

The concept of secondary gain in Psychoanalysis refers to a
phenomenon of minor significance. If a hysteric becomes bedridden and wins new attention by her enforced passivity, this
gain was presumed secondary because it had little to do with
the origin of the hysterical paralysis, had little import for its
perpetuation and constituted at best an unexpected bonus as a
by-product of the primary phenomena of hysteria.

In monopolistic over-organization, however, there is a related
phenomenon which we have defined as secondary loss, which
does constitute a major motive for the growth and maintenance
of the strategies of over-avoidance and over-escape. Consider
the example of the bedridden hysteric. Whatever the original
motive which literally paralyzed the legs, how can such a person
tolerate the humiliation of being unmasked as a fraud? Simply
to get up one day and walk would expose the hysteric to great
ridicule. The loss of secondary gain from much attention might
not be altogether welcome, but it would seem trivial in comparison with the humiliation she would suffer from the exposure
of her having gone to bed with nothing "really" the matter. Such
loss of esteem, or secondary loss, as we have defined it, would
constitute a major embarrassment. We can call it a secondary
loss only in the sense that it is derivative and comes after monopolistic over-organization has occurred, but not in the sense
in which secondary gain is secondary.

In Psychoanalytic theory the binding power of defensive
strategies is presumed to derive primarily from the original
state of affairs which was responsible for the individual's hurried
and desperate manoevers. If the threat of castration was awful
enough to panic and humiliate the child into repression or some

other mechanism of defense, it never ceased to be a major threat during the lifetime of the individual and could account entirely for the maintenance of the original defensive repression. The individual was represented as simply continuing to be afraid of what he originally feared.

We do not wish to quarrel with this possibility *per se*, but the failure to appreciate the massiveness and independence of the new motivation provided by the monopolistic over-organization is in part responsible for a certain percentage of the failures of orthodox Psychoanalytic therapy. Not only is the contemporary over-organization a radically different set of defenses from the original defenses, but the price of relinquishing them, the price of secondary loss, ordinarily appears excessive.

It is not our point that the neurotic or psychotic wants to be sick, or that he is necessarily afraid of being without defenses or defense-less, though these are not unimportant resistances to change; rather, having assumed a defensive posture toward a dread affect for many years, the person has become this set of defenses. Just as a normal person would not readily give up the totality of his addictions which in large part constitute his personality, his characteristic speech, his wife, his children, his friends, his profession, his native land, his native food, so will the monopolistically over-organized individual not readily surrender his identity, painful as it may be. As he becomes sicker he may feel his identity slipping away. He may suffer violent intrusions which transform him so grotesquely he does not know who he is, but through all of this he clings tenaciously to the only self he has. To threaten to strip him of this self, his identity, is to expose him to the most violent panic and humiliation.

It is no less humiliating when an ordinarily honest bank clerk is discovered to have stolen money than when an individual who has spent his life as a confidence man is suddenly discovered to have gone straight. I have known professional gamblers who have opened a small grocery store in order that their children might have fathers like other fathers, but who have tried to keep this secret from other members of the fraternity lest they be ridiculed for their sudden bourgeois respectability.

Similarly, we think, an individual whose paranoid posture

has become stabilized as deeply oppositional cannot easily act as a friendly trusting human being without radically surrendering his hard-won identity. Further this would expose him to others and to himself as never really having had an identity —as a paper tiger—a lamb in wolf's clothing. As Dostoevsky expressed it in *Notes From the Underground*: "But do you know, gentlemen, what was the chief point about my spite? Why, the whole point, the real sting of it, lay in the fact that continually, even in the moment of the acutest spleen, I was inwardly conscious with shame that I was not only not a spiteful but not even an embittered man, that I was simply scaring sparrows at random and amusing myself by it. I might foam at the mouth, but bring me a doll to play with, give me a cup of tea with sugar in it, and maybe I might be appeased. I might even be genuinely touched, though probably I should grind my teeth at myself afterward and lie awake at night with shame for months after. That was my way."

DIFFERENT TYPES OF UNIFICATION OF DEFENSIVE STRATEGIES IN MONOPOLISTIC HUMILIATION THEORY

As monopolistic humiliation theory deepens and becomes unified and stabilized, the general direction in which such unification necessarily moves is analogous to warfare between nations. A permanent state of vigilance is created in which every precaution is taken lest the self be overwhelmed. The assumption of the complete malevolence of the other no longer needs documentation. The unified strategy tends toward an unrelenting hostility and counter-contempt in which every attempt will be made to save the self by destroying the power of the other. To the extent to which the other is seen as too powerful to be defeated at a particular time, this strategy will be modified by a more prudent tactic, but the main strategy will not be altered or surrendered. The military distinction between the general strategy and the shifting means, or tactics, to attain the ultimate aim is as relevant to an understanding of the unification of monopolistic humiliation theory as it is in warfare generally.

When over-interpretation and over-avoidance and over-escape strategies attain a more unified form, the individual is rescued from the wild swings of both strategy and tactics as well as the intervening breakdowns of defense which flood consciousness with humiliation. This is not to say that the unified strategy works perfectly but only that it spares the psychotic the disturbance of the acute phase. It is the difference between an individual who is debating with himself whether another person is malevolent, how malevolent he is, and what one should do about it, which of several alternative interpretations and strategies he should adopt.

In the more terminal phases of over-organization, alternatives of interpretation and strategy drop out and only the alternatives of tactics remain. The question now becomes what must be done to insure final victory over an enemy who must be destroyed?

The dynamic of the homosexual panic

In this phase, the most dangerous threat ceases to be the oppressor but rather anything which would threaten the solid front of the unified strategy. Just as a nation at war is likely to deal more harshly with its own pacifists or deserters than with its captured prisoners, so the paranoid is most alarmed by anyone who would raise a question about the malevolence of the enemy on the one hand, and by his own inner temptations to cry out his humiliation and guilt and abase himself before his enemy. This is the essential dynamic of the so-called homosexual panic in paranoia—the fear of the enemy within who would offer the self in complete abasement to the enemy one has sworn to destroy.

Paranoid schizophrenia

Although unrelenting opposition defines the final phase of the paranoid posture, there are nonetheless different types of such over-organization. We have to this point used the terms paranoid posture and paranoid schizophrenia almost interchangeably. We wish now to distinguish paranoid schizophrenia as a special case of the paranoid posture.

As we have noted before, insult does not always come in tidy single packages. One child may be humiliated and at the same time terrorized by the anger of his parent. Another child may be humiliated by a parent but be angered by the anger which accompanies the parent's insult. Another child may be humiliated without any other affect than contempt from a parent. A child may be primarily terrorized by his parent, and suffer humiliation only secondarily, just because he has been terrorized and is afraid to counter-aggress against his parent. Another child may be humiliated by the indifference or scorn of a parent who is, was before, and will be again, full of love for the child. Another parent will humiliate the child for transgressions of various kinds but stop if the child will atone or make restitution.

Not all of these patterns of humiliation and other affects constitute the paranoid posture. The last instance constitutes what we have defined as the depressive posture, which we will consider later. Any unrelenting posture against the oppressor who humiliates, whether or not he also terrorizes, or angers, or whether he humiliates secondarily because he angers or terrorizes but successfully defeats counter-offensives, we will define as constituting the paranoid posture.

Paranoid schizophrenia is that special case of the paranoid posture in which the individual is both terrorized and humiliated at the same time, and in which the only level on which the individual can respond is in his beliefs and fantasies, delusions of persecution and grandeur. There are those who have also been terrorized and humiliated who do not develop paranoid schizophrenia, because anger is strong enough and fear is sufficiently weaker, so that although direct counteraction is blocked, fantasies of revenge are more open and delusions of persecution and grandeur do not develop. In the next chapter we will consider a classic example of this type of paranoid posture in Dostoevsky.

Chapter 23

Continuities and Discontinuities in the Impact of Humiliation: Some Specific Examples of the Paranoid Posture

Up to this point, our discussion of humiliation theories has tended to be somewhat abstract; in this chapter we shall describe some illustrative examples of strong humiliation theories—some flesh-and-blood embodiments of these abstractions.

We shall discuss first a literary genius, Dostoevsky, whose writings indicate that he suffered an extreme form of the paranoid posture. We shall also examine a special kind of strong humiliation theory produced, in our view, by the fact that there are minority groups who have been subjected by society at large to the same pressures to which the paranoid schizophrenic has been subjected by his parents in the process of socialization. The resultant humiliation theories in the oppressed, and through the fear of the weak in the oppressors as well, will be examined with respect to Jews, Negroes, and Southern whites; and also with respect to the social phenomenon of witchcraft.

Then we shall return to Freud, whom we also discussed in the chapter on Interest—Excitement, as a case history of radical intellectual creativity, illustrating our theory of creativity. We shall re-examine him in terms of the nature of his strong humiliation theory. He will be contrasted with another gifted individual, August Strindberg, similar in many respects to Freud but whose paranoid posture took a more malignant turn, eventuating in paranoid schizophrenia. To illustrate the process of malignant growth of humiliation theory, we shall examine the case of Strindberg at some length.

Finally, we shall consider that most monopolistic form of all humiliation theories, the functional psychosis of paranoid schizophrenia as such. We shall also note the differential nature of schizo-affective, simple, catatonic and hebephrenic types of schizophrenia.

DEPRESSIVE VERSUS PARANOID POSTURES: CHEKHOV AND DOSTOEVSKY

The posture of terror and humiliation in paranoid schizophrenia is not the only humiliation complex which may assume monopolistic status. Humiliation may also lead to anger and contempt with some fear, in a monopolistic paranoid posture of the sullen, defiant mouse, so well described by Dostoevsky.

Corporal punishment of serfs by their masters was a commonplace in nineteenth-century Russia. No less commonplace was the beating of children, particularly sons, by their fathers. Chekhov was beaten daily by his father. Dostoevsky's father was murdered by his serfs for his drunken cruelty. This laying of heavy hands upon the body of the weak and helpless provided the soil for the nagging preoccupation with the problem of servility, not only for serfs but for the intelligentsia as well. Chekhov said he required his entire life to free himself of his slavishness. The problem of the insult and its affront to human dignity haunts the literature of nineteenth-century Russia. The reactions to being beaten by a parent are numerous, but the common affect of the complex of affects aroused is humiliation. It may result in the depressive posture of shame and anguish as in Chekhov, the paranoid schizophrenic posture of shame and terror, or the defiant posture of shame, anger, fear and contempt, as in Dostoevsky.

In the depressive posture the beating is responded to as an insult which alienates those who otherwise love each other. "How could you?" is the question which the beating raises for the child who loves the one who so offends him, and who is confident enough of the love of the other so that he is not frightened by the physical attack. This was the response of Chekhov to daily beating by his father. The lack of fear and the hurt pride from such insult is nowhere clearer than in the dramatic turning point in the relationship between the young Anton Chekhov and his older brother.

Following a beating at the hands of his older brother, he

elected not to inform their father of it. To have done so would, both of them knew, have called down the wrath of the father on the older brother who would have paid many times over in the coin of physical punishment for his offense. Both of them also knew that the father would thus guarantee the future physical safety of the young Chekhov. The older brother describes his chagrin at the courage and pride of his younger brother when he elected not to inform the father. That day he said he realized that his hold on his younger brother was broken. He was later to become an alcoholic, and Anton was thereafter to repay him in contempt for the beatings he had suffered from him. But such a solution was not possible toward the beloved father. Chekhov was tortured with the oscillation between shame and love in this relationship, and this theme is recurrent in his work.

Another common reaction to the beating is humiliation and terror, the paranoid schizophrenic's posture which we will examine in some detail presently. The third reaction is that of Dostoevsky—the introverted, defiant posture of shame, anger, fear and contempt restricted primarily to the level of fantasy. In contrast to the depressive posture, there is not so much love that contempt is suppressed. In contrast to the paranoid schizophrenic, there is not so much fear that anger is completely suppressed. There is sufficient fear to restrict revenge primarily to the level of fantasy but not so much fear as to crush revenge fantasies or bar them from consciousness or to generate the paranoid fantasies of grandeur and persecution. In fantasy the individual plans to turn the tables on his oppressor, to humiliate him as he has been humiliated.

MONOPOLISTIC SHAME, CONTEMPT, SELF-CONTEMPT, ANGER AND FEAR: THE SULLEN, DEFIANT MOUSE OF DOSTOEVSKY

Let us examine the anatomy of this conflict as Dostoevsky explicitly elects to "stick out his tongue," come what may.*

* I am indebted to a stimulating study by Robert Louis Jackson, *Dostoevsky's Underground Man in Russian Literature,* for his analysis of the relationship between *Notes from Underground* and other works and writings of Dostoevsky. In the following pages, the quotations of Dostoevsky, except those from *Notes from Underground,* are Mr. Jackson's translations.

First, from *The House of the Dead,* is the affirmation of the necessity of self-expression of the humiliated, imprisoned, impotent self: ". . . the anguished, hysterical manifestation of individuality, the instinctive yearning to be oneself, the desire to express oneself, one's humiliated personality, a desire which suddenly takes shape and reaches the pitch of malice and madness, of the eclipse of reason, of fits, of convulsions. Thus, perhaps, a person buried alive in a coffin and awakening in it would thrust at the cover and try to throw it off, although of course, reason might convince him that all his efforts were in vain. But the whole point here is that this is not a question of reason: it is a question of convulsions."

Again in the same work the plight of the imprisoned, humiliated one leads to impotent defiance. He describes the convict who is fond of playing the bully and braggart: ". . . that is, of pretending to his comrades and convincing even himself, if only for a while, that he has a freedom and power incomparably greater than it appears; in a word, he can carouse, storm about, crushingly insult somebody and prove to him that he can do all this, that all this is in 'our hands,' that is, he can convince himself of something of which it is out of the question for the poor fellow even to dream. . . . Finally, in all this blustering about there is a risk, which means that all this has at least the semblance of life, at least a distant semblance of freedom. And what will one not give for freedom?"

All the circumstances which permit the full expression of anger and contempt and the full awareness of impotence at the hands of the aggressor save Dostoevsky and others like him from the twin paranoid delusions of grandeur and persecution. He knows who his persecutor is and in contrast to the paranoid he knows that he feels impotent in his presence. But the line is a fine one, and the philosophy of love which it generates as an antidote to hate may be perilously close to that generated in the paranoid schizophrenic posture to deal with overwhelming fear of the aggressor as well as fear of the counter-aggression it mobilizes, again because of the fear of reprisal.

But there is nonetheless a difference between the philosophy of love, as in Christianity, and the secondary philosophy of love of the schizophrenic who conceives of a world in which human beings are utterly safe from attack from others and from the fear and hate within. Strindberg is the classic case of the paranoid posture which from time to time generates a completely idealized love affair which is as white a portrayal of human nature as the majority of his plays present the completely black world of the paranoid.

But if Strindberg (who in fact suffered delusions of persecution) is able to generate a fantasy of light and love, another whose posture was paranoid, Nietzsche, gave the classic answer of the paranoid to the philosophy of love: it is a misreading of human nature and it is weak and dangerous. Anyone whose life and dignity are at stake cannot be indifferent to an injunction to turn the other cheek.

For Dostoevsky, as we shall see, his freedom to hate also eventually gave him a freedom to love, which the paranoid schizophrenic either explicitly rejects, as in the case of Nietzsche, or is enjoyed only as a third delusion, the delusion of love, a momentary intrusion permitted only when the delusion of grandeur and persecution is in temporary eclipse.

The trouble begins for Dostoevsky with a slap on the face for a violation of paternal authority. To quote from *Notes from Underground*:

" 'Possibly,' you will add on your own account with a grin, 'people will not understand it either who have never received a slap in the face,' and in that way you will politely hint to me that I too, perhaps, have had the experience of a slap in the face in my life, and so I speak as one who knows, I bet that you are thinking that."

In another section we can recover the next step: "I could never endure saying 'Forgive me, Papa, I won't do it, again'—not because I am incapable of saying that—on the contrary, perhaps just because I have been too capable of it."

Because he has been too capable of apology when confronted with paternal authority he feels he is a mouse, but a defiant, sullen, brooding mouse. He contrasts the mouse with ordinary people:

"With people who know how to revenge themselves and to stand up for themselves in general, how is it done? Why, when they are possessed, let us suppose, by the feeling of revenge, then for the time there is nothing else but that feeling left in their whole being. Such a gentleman simply dashes straight for his object like an infuriated bull with its horns down, and nothing but a wall will stop him. (By the way: facing the wall, such gentlemen—that is, the "direct" persons and men of action— are genuinely nonplused. For them a wall is not an evasion, as for us people who think and consequently do nothing; it is not an excuse for turning aside, an excuse for which we are always very glad, though we scarcely believe in it ourselves, as a rule. . . .

"Well, such a direct person I regard as the real normal man, as his tender Mother Nature wished to see him when she graciously brought him into being on the earth. I envy such a man till I am green in the face. He is stupid. I am not disputing that, but perhaps the normal man should be stupid, how do you know? Perhaps it is very beautiful, in fact. And I am the more persuaded of that suspicion, if one can call it so, by the fact that if you take, for instance, the antithesis of the normal man, that is, the man of acute consciousness, who has come, of course, not out of the lap of Nature but out of a retort (this is almost mysticism, gentlemen, but I suspect this, too), this retort-made man is sometimes so nonplused in the presence of his antithesis that with all his exaggerated consciousness he genuinely thinks of himself as a mouse and not a man. It may be an acutely conscious mouse, yet it is a mouse, while the other is a man, and therefore, et cetera, et cetera. And the worst of it is, he himself, his very own self, looks on himself as a mouse; no one asks him to do so; and that is an important point."

It is clear that having violated paternal authority he is slapped in the face to which he responds with anger and a wish to hurt his father, smash things and stick out his tongue. His father insists on an apology, to which he cannot bring himself. Neither can he express his full resentment like a "real normal man" so he feels himself a mouse, but an insulted, brooding mouse, who is not without doubts about the righteousness of his cause, who evokes more contempt and laughter from his father because of this, who creeps into his mousehole and becomes absorbed in cold malignant spite:

"Now let us look at this mouse in action. Let us suppose, for instance, that it feels insulted, too (and it almost always does feel insulted), and wants to revenge itself, too. There may even be a greater accumulation of spite in it than in *l'homme de la nature et de la vérité*. The base and nasty desire to vent that spite on its assailant rankles perhaps even more nastily in it than in *l'homme de la nature et de la vérité*. For through his innate stupidity the latter looks upon his revenge as justice pure and simple; while in consequence of his acute consciousness the mouse does not believe in the justice of it. To come at last to the deed itself, to the very act of revenge. Apart from the one fundamental nastiness, the luckless mouse succeeds in creating around it so many other nastinesses in the forms of doubts and questions, adds to the one question so many unsettled questions, that there inevitably works up around it a sort of fatal brew, a stinking mess, made up of its doubts, emotions, and of the contempt spat upon it by the direct men of action who stand solemnly about it as judges and arbitrators, laughing at it till their healthy sides ache. Of course the only thing left for it is to dismiss all that with a wave of its paw, and, with a smile of assumed contempt in which it does not even itself believe, creep ignominiously into its mousehole. There in its nasty, stinking, underground home our insulted, crushed, and ridiculed mouse promptly becomes absorbed in cold, malignant, and above all, everlasting spite. For forty years together it will remember its injury down to the smallest, most ignominious details, and every time will add, of itself, details still more ignominious, spitefully teasing and tormenting itself with its own imagination. It will itself be ashamed of its imaginings, but yet it will recall it all, it will go over and over every detail, it will invent unheard-of things against itself, pretending that those things might happen, and will forgive nothing. Maybe it will begin to revenge itself, too, but, as it were, piecemeal, in trivial ways, from behind the stove, incognito, without believing either in its own right to vengeance, or in the success of its revenge, knowing that from all its efforts at revenge it will suffer a hundred times more than he on whom it revenges itself, while he, I dare say will not even scratch himself. On its deathbed it will recall it all over again, with interest accumulated over all the years. . . ."

Here Dostoevsky accurately describes the essential mechanism of monopolistic theory construction: remembering every-

thing "down to the smallest, most ignominious details" and then
magnifying this further—"invent unheard-of things against itself,
pretending that those things might happen, and will forgive
nothing." He adds to this monopolistic theory construction his
perceptive insight into the consequences of such magnification.
The sullen mouse can believe neither in the moral righteousness
nor in the possibility of vengeance because his grievance has
been inflated into a monstrosity. He contrasts this with the direct
action of the normal man who when he becomes angry "simply
dashes straight for his object like an infuriated bull with its
horns down, and nothing will stop him."

The mouse can neither apologize for affronts to others, nor
revenge himself because shame, anger, contempt and fear have
all been over-inflated and so a lifetime will be wasted till "on
its deathbed it will recall it all over again, with interest accumulated over all the years."

Even when one can only beat oneself there is some satisfaction to the mouse who would like to challenge those he
cannot defeat.

Further, his very moaning in suffering is calculated to achieve
revenge and hurt those who must listen:
". . . I ask you, gentlemen, to listen sometimes to the moans
of an educated man of the nineteenth century suffering from
toothache, on the second or third day of the attack. . . . His
moans become nasty, disgustingly malignant, and go on for
whole days and nights. And of course he knows himself that he
is doing himself no sort of good with his moans; he knows better
than anyone that he is only lacerating and harassing himself and
others for nothing; he knows that even the audience before whom
he is making his efforts, and his whole family, listen to him with
loathing, do not put a ha'porth of faith in him, and inwardly
understand that he might moan differently, more simply, without
trills and flourishes, and that he is only amusing himself like that
from ill-humor, from malignancy. Well, in all these recognitions
and disgraces it is that there lies a voluptuous pleasure. As
though he would say: 'I am worrying you, I am lacerating your
hearts, I am keeping everyone in the house awake. Well, stay
awake then, you, too, feel every minute that I have toothache.
I am not a hero to you now, as I tried to seem before, but simply

a nasty person, an imposter. Well, so be it, then! I am very glad
that you see through me. It is nasty for you to hear my despicable moans; well, let it be nasty; here I will let you have a nastier
flourish in a minute. . . .' You do not understand even now,
gentlemen? No, it seems our development and our consciousness
must go further to understand all the intricacies of this pleasure.
You laugh? Delighted. My jests, gentlemen, are of course in
bad taste, jerky, involved, lack self-confidence. But of course
that is because I do not respect myself. Can a man of perception
respect himself at all?

Though the mouse loses further respect by his suffering, he
nonetheless makes others suffer and this is some revenge.

This hateful way of life is not without its charms. Some
enjoyment can be wrested from the fantasies of smashing things,
from the rehearsals and magnifications of insults, and the crushing retorts which are delivered at the level of fantasy. Indeed
Dostoevsky equates destruction and chaos with suffering:

"Whether it's good or bad, it is sometimes very pleasant too,
to smash things . . . I am standing for my caprice, and for its
being guaranteed to me when necessary. . . . I think man will
never renounce real suffering, that is, destruction and chaos.
Why, suffering is the sole origin of consciousness. Though I
did lay it down at the beginning that consciousness is the
greatest misfortune for man, yet I know man prizes it and would
not give it up for any satisfaction. Consciousness, for instance,
is infinitely superior to twice two makes four. Once you have
mathematical certainty there is nothing left to do or to understand. There will be nothing left but to bottle up your five
senses and plunge into contemplation. While if you stick to consciousness, even though the same result is attained, that is, there
is nothing left to do, you can at least flog yourself at times, and
that will, at any rate, liven you up. Reactionary as it is, it is
better than nothing."

Dostoevsky had in 1862 visited London's Universal Exhibition
with its famed Crystal Palace on Sydenham Hill, and referred
to it in his parody of Chernyshevsky's Fourierist vision of the
future in *What Is To Be Done*, which was aimed at creating a
new morality. In Chernyshevsky's work, self-interest is presented
as identical with the common good. These heroes are rational

egotists. Chernyshevsky's vision of the future includes a "huge building" never before seen—"no, there has been one hint of it; the palace which stands on Sydenham Hill: iron and glass, iron and glass."

Because of his unrelenting hatred and indirect mouselike defiance, Dostoevsky rejects the "crystal palace":

"You believe in a crystal palace that can never be destroyed —a palace at which one will not be able to put out one's tongue or make a long nose on the sly. And perhaps that is just why I am afraid of this edifice, that it is of crystal and can never be destroyed and that one cannot put one's tongue out at it even on the sly."

The attack on Chernyshevsky was also an attack on the humanism of the 1840's with its faith in the goodness of man.

In *Winter Notes on Summer Impressions*, Dostoevsky criticizes the utopian socialist ideal in his own name. He argues that man must reject the Fourierist utopia if in exchange he is asked to give "a tiny drop of his personal freedom for the common welfare. No, man does not want to live even on these conditions, even a little drop is too much. He keeps on thinking, foolishly, that this is a prison, that it is better to be independent, because there is complete (free) will. And even if in his freedom he is beaten, unemployed, starving and without any (free) will, the queer fellow still feels that his own will is better. Of course, the socialist will have to spit and say to him that he is a fool, has not grown up, not matured and does not understand his own self interest; that an ant, any old inarticulate, insignificant ant is cleverer than he is because in the ant hill everything is so good, everything so ordered, everyone is replete, happy, each knows his own task, in a word: man has a long way to go before he can measure up to the ant hill."

In *Notes from Underground* he pursues his disbelief in the possibility of being "rational":

"But these are all golden dreams. Oh, tell me, who was it first announced, who was it first proclaimed, that man only does nasty things because he does not know his own interests; and that if he were enlightened, if his eyes were opened to his real normal interests, man would at once cease to do nasty things, would at once become good and noble because, being enlightened and understanding his real advantage, he would see his own advantage in the good and nothing else, and we all know that not one man can, consciously, act against his own interests, consequently, so to say, through necessity, he would begin doing good? Oh, the babe! Oh, the pure, innocent child! Why, in the first place, when in all these thousands of years has there been a time when man has acted only from his own interest? What is to be done with the millions of facts that bear witness that men, consciously, that is fully understanding their real interests, have left them in the background and have rushed headlong on another path, to meet peril and danger, compelled to this course by nobody and by nothing, but, as it were, simply disliking the beaten track, and have obstinately, willfully, struck out another difficult, absurd way, seeking it almost in the darkness. So, I suppose, this obstinacy and perversity were pleasanter to them than any advantage. . . . Advantage! What is advantage? And will you take it upon yourself to define with perfect accuracy in what the advantage of man consists? And what if it so happens that a man's advantage, *sometimes*, not only may, but even must, consist in his desiring in certain cases what is harmful to himself and not advantageous? And if so, if there can be such a case, the whole principle falls into dust. What do you think—are there such cases? You laugh; laugh away, gentlemen, but only answer me: have man's advantages been reckoned up with perfect certainty?"

Finally rationality and the crystal palace must be rejected if for no other reason than that it would be "frightfully dull":

"Then—this is all what you say—new economic relations will be established, all ready-made and worked out with mathematical exactitude, so that every possible question will vanish in the twinkling of an eye, simply because every possible answer to it will be provided. Then the 'Palace of Crystal' will be built. Then . . . In fact, those will be halcyon days. Of course there is no guaranteeing (this is my comment) that it will not be, for instance, frightfully dull then (for what will one have to do when everything will be calculated and tabulated), but, on the other hand, everything will be extraordinarily rational. Of course boredom may lead you to anything. It is boredom sets one sticking gold pins into people, but all that would not matter. What is bad (this is my comment again) is that I dare say people will be thankful for the gold pins then. Man is stupid, you know, phenomenally stupid; or rather he is not at all stupid, but he is so ungrateful that you could not find another like him in all creation. I, for instance, would not be in the least surprised if all of a sudden, apropos of nothing, in the midst of general prosperity a gentleman with an ignoble, or rather with a reactionary and ironical, countenance were to arise and, putting his arms akimbo, say to us all, 'I say, gentlemen, hadn't we better kick over the whole show here and scatter rationalism to the winds, simply to send these logarithms to the devil, and to enable us to live once more at our own sweet foolish will!' That again would not matter; but what is annoying is that he would be sure to find followers—such is the nature of man. And all that for the most foolish reason, which, one would think, was hardly worth mentioning; that is, that man everywhere and at all times, whoever he may be, has preferred to act as he chose and not in the least as his reason and advantage dictated. And one may choose what is contrary to one's own interests, and sometimes one *positively ought* (that is my idea). One's own free unfettered choice, one's own caprice, however wild it may be, one's own fancy worked up at times to frenzy—is that very 'most advantageous advantage' which we have overlooked, which comes under no classification and against which all systems and theories are continually being shattered to atoms. And how do these wiseacres know that man wants a normal, a virtuous choice? What has made them conceive that man must want a rationally advantageous choice? What man wants is simply *independent* choice, whatever that independence may cost and wherever it may lead. And choice, of course, the devil only knows what choice. . . ."

As one might suppose, there are also residual positive affects which press for something more than the rodent estate. Indeed there is clear evidence of a golden age fantasy of the state of innocence.

Dostoevsky ideally would like not to feel defiant:

". . . I know myself that it is not the underground that is better, but something different, quite different, for which I am thirsting, but which I cannot find! Damn the underground!. . .

Destroy my desires, eradicate my ideals, show me something better, and I will follow you. . . .

"But while I am alive and have desires I would rather my hand were withered away than bring one brick to such a building! Don't remind me that I have just rejected the palace of crystal for the sole reason that one cannot put out one's tongue at it. I did not say that because I am so fond of putting my tongue out. Perhaps the only thing I resented was that of all your edifices there has not been one at which one could not put out one's tongue. On the contrary, I would let my tongue be cut off out of gratitude if things could be so arranged that I should lose all desire to put it out. It is not my fault that things cannot be so arranged, and that one must be satisfied with model flats. Then why am I made with such desires? Can I have been constructed simply in order to come to the conclusion that my whole mechanism is a cheat? Can this be the whole purpose? I do not believe it."

He cannot be consistently defiant because there lurks a wish for infantile innocence and love. This wish will later be rationalized in favor of Christianity.

In another section of *Notes from Underground* there is a hint of what he is thirsting for:

"But do you know, gentlemen, what was the chief point about my spite? Why, the whole point, the real sting of it, lay in the fact that continually, even in the moment of the acutest spleen, I was inwardly conscious with shame that I was not only not a spiteful but not even an embittered man, that I was simply scaring sparrows at random and amusing myself by it. I might foam at the mouth, but bring me a doll to play with, give me a cup of tea with sugar in it, and maybe I might be appeased. I might even be genuinely touched, though probably I should grind my teeth at myself afterward and lie awake at night with shame for months after. That was my way."

He wishes to return to the state of innocence of the pre-defiant child, to be fed tea and to play with dolls.

How much the lure of love and the state of innocence which preceded insult and hate has attenuated and inhibited the latter compared with the inhibiting effect of fear cannot be easily assessed, but it is clear that *Notes from the Underground* occupies a shifting position in Dostoevsky's consciousness. When he wrote it there is no doubt his own anger and distress was at a peak.

The conditions which surrounded the writing of *Notes from Underground* were very trying. His consumptive wife was dying and he was suffering illness which permitted him neither to "stand nor sit" because of hemorrhoids and a disease of the bladder.

Dostoevsky was never able to entirely associate himself with or disassociate himself from "Notes." In *Winter Notes on Summer Impressions,* he affirms that the voluntary self-sacrifice of the individual in favor of others is "in my opinion, the mark of the highest development of the individual, of his greatest power, his highest degree of self-determination, his greatest freedom of his own will."

In a letter to his brother, this idea was in the original manuscript of *Notes from Underground*:

"The swinish censors let pass those places where I ridiculed everything and blasphemed for show, but where I deduce from all this the need for faith and Christ—this is forbidden. Just who are these censors, are they in conspiracy against the government or something?"

Despite this criticism of the cuts of the censor, he did not restore them when he subsequently republished the work.

Dostoevsky ten years later wrote: "It is really too gloomy. Nowadays I can write in a brighter, more conciliatory vein." Yet in a notebook he later remarked: "I am proud that I was the first to depict the real man of the Russian majority and the first to expose his disfigured and tragic side. The tragedy consists in the consciousness of disfigurement. . . . I alone depicted the tragedy of the underground, consisting in suffering, self-punishment, the consciousness of something better and the impossibility of achieving that something, and chiefly consisting in the clear conviction of these unhappy ones that it is like this with everyone and therefore it is not even worth while trying to reform. What is there to sustain those who are trying to reform? A reward faith? There are rewards from no one, there is faith in no one. But another step from here and one comes upon extreme depravity, crime (murder). Mystery."

That Dostoevsky cannot entirely accept his underground man nor forget him is further seen in the later identification of defiance with reason. It is again the voice of the underground man in Raskolnikov's cry: "Freedom and power, but chiefly power! Over every trembling creature and over the whole ant hill! That is the goal! Remember that!"

It is "reason" which leads him to destruction as it does all "spirits endowed with reason and will."

In *Crime and Punishment* the basic polarity is love, self-sacrifice, religious reconciliation with reality as opposed to rationalist rebellion. In contrast to *Notes from Underground*, he joins the rebel and rationalist in Raskolnikov; and, continuing his attack on the rationalists, in effect withdraws his support from the rebel.

In *The Brothers Karamazov*, Ivan Karamazov "doesn't love anybody," Fedor Karamazov observes. Ivan's "Euclidian reason" does not disregard suffering as did the rationalists of the *Notes from Underground*. He cannot accept a world harmony that is based upon the tears and suffering of children that are unatoned for. "I do not want harmony, out of love for humanity I do not want it."

However, Dostoevsky regards Ivan's uncompromising idealism as ultimately destructive. Ultimately the demand for independent will "whatever this independence costs and wherever it may lead" is a tragedy for Dostoevsky, which leads to catastrophe for both the individual and society. Dostoevsky insists elsewhere that society must renounce its tyranny over the individual and the individual must renounce his demands upon society, and that Christianity is the only way out of the underground.

Few have looked at the humiliation-hate complex so long and so hard. It corrodes and sears the spirit unless it is neutralized, and love is one of the few alkalies for such an acid, Dostoevsky knew. Heroic counter-measures are required in the world of Dostoevsky, because his affects run so deep and strong.

We have examined Dostoevsky's *Notes from Underground* because we regard it as a classic statement of a universal problem, the defiant mouse in the man who walks erect. If a man cannot respect himself, he must hate himself and those who humiliate him. However, the solution to this problem is not love after the fact, but the prevention of such erosion of the spirit *before* the human being is engulfed.

PARANOID POSTURE IN THE EXPLOITED AND THE EXPLOITERS: THE JEWS AND THEIR OPPRESSORS

From the beginning of time groups of human beings have exploited other groups of human beings. The exploiting group has ordinarily subdued the exploited by the same affects we still find in the paranoid schizophrenic—terror and humiliation. The oppressed have been characteristically frightened into submission at the same time as they were shamed into submission. The oppressed have been kept in a subordinate position by the twin strategy of assigning them a lower status and threatening to kill them if they rebelled. Terror is heightened in the oppressed by the awareness of his helplessness and humiliation, as humiliation is intensified by the awareness of the impotence to rebel against either the terror or the insult of the oppressor.

Not infrequently have oppressed groups responded with the paranoid's fantasies—persecution and grandeur. In the most notable case—that of the Jews—God's chosen people have most often been persecuted by those with similar paranoid postures: recently by Hitler who proclaimed himself and the Germans the true super-race, persecuted by the false super-race—international Jewry. The Jews have again and again become targets for groups just emerging from oppression into individuation and independence themselves. The most recent instance is the anti-Semitism of the revolutionary Negro movement, the Black Muslims.

Under Hitler, Jews were not only terrorized and humiliated but were in fact killed by the millions. Whenever Jews have suffered oppression, they have responded as the oppressed have always responded, with anger, with terror, with humiliation, with contempt for the self and for the oppressor, and with distress and misery—in short, with one or other of the variants of the paranoid posture, with tactics which varied according to circumstance but with the universal strategy of all the oppressed —to smite their enemies.

Freud supposed that the unconscious root of anti-Semitism was castration anxiety, since in the nursery, according to Freud, the child learns that something has been cut off and "this gives him the right to despise the Jew." Freud is saying in a symbolic way what we believe to be generally true: that the strong fear the envy of the weak; that the oppressor fears the oppressed because he is weak and oppressed, and so envious, vengeful, with nothing to lose but his chains.

Freud has equated the status of Jews with that of women, whom he supposes are also oppressed because they lack the penis and therefore envy men. We will presently examine the concepts of castration anxiety and penis envy in Freud, and suggest that this was his way of conceptualizing a relationship involving both terror and humiliation. At this point we wish only to note the relationship which Freud posited between Jews and Christians was identical with that he posited between men and women.

Man and the Christian fear woman and the Jew, respectively, because they are inferior and therefore envious of what man has (symbolized by the intact penis) and therefore might rob him of what is most precious to him. So the paradox that there is in the relationship of oppression, and, in the mind of Freud, in the relationship between men and women, the same affects of fear and envy on both sides. The strong fears the envy of the weak and is fearful and envious because he may be robbed; the weak envies the strong but fears reprisal for his wishes against the strong one.

The classic expression of this mutual fear and envy is Shakespeare's portrayal of Shylock and Antonio:

"If you wrong us, shall we not revenge? If we are like you in the rest, we will resemble you in that. If a Jew wrong a Christian, what is his humility? Revenge. If a Christian wrong a Jew, what should his sufferance be by Christian example? Why, revenge. The villainy you teach me, I will execute; and it shall go hard but I will better the instruction."

Shylock wants "an equal pound of your fair flesh, to be cut and taken in what part of your body pleaseth me."

Antonio is prepared to be mutilated by Shylock, because he feels inadequate:

"Most heartily do I beseech the court to give the judgment. . . . "I am a tainted wether of the flock. Meetest for death, the weakest kind of fruit drops earliest to the ground, and so let me."

The Jews in the United States today, however, enjoy relative freedom from discrimination and persecution. Where oppression becomes attenuated the paranoid posture—both the hate and the love of suffering—also becomes attenuated. Both the oppressor and the oppressed can become less fearful and less envious of each other under these conditions.

The fear of the weak

We have once before examined the universality of the fear of the envy of the weak in our review of the history of the evil eye. It is the weak and crippled, the old ugly women, the impoverished and the humble who historically have constituted the chief threat from their envy through the evil eye.

The history of the fear of the weak begins with the myth of the Garden of Eden. The Garden of Eden was the state of innocence before the experience of shame. It is God's pride in the knowledge which he alone possessed which made it possible for him to love. When God was shamed by his children who competed with him by learning what he knew, he no longer loved them completely and drove them by the sword out of Paradise.

There is a sense in which the God of the Old Testament is not only a jealous God who punishes his children for worshiping other Gods, but he is also one who needs to be reassured that his children do not hate him. Thus in the Kaddish (the prayer for the dead), the faithful must reaffirm their love of him despite the fact that he has taken away their loved ones. This God knew that there was bitterness toward him from the weak whenever he hurt them, his chosen people.

Cain and Abel, Joseph and his jealous brothers are further instances in the Old Testament in which the envy of the weak threatens the favored one.

WITCHCRAFT

Witchcraft and the fear of witches is a special case of the fear of the weak and the envious, and it seems to appear when individuals or groups feel their status and power to have been undermined and weakened and there is no way of socially controlling and punishing those who are responsible—the weak and the envious.

As Swanson has suggested: "Witchcraft, with its objective of harming some individual or group, implies that the reason underlying its use is hatred of others—others whose purposes toward one are close, important, persistent, and uncontrolled by legitimizing social arrangements."

By unlegitimated contacts Swanson refers to social relations which have all of the following characteristics: "People must interact closely with one another for the achievement of common ends. . . . These relations were not developed with the consent, tacit or explicit, of all concerned, or the relations are not such that persons with conflicting objectives and desires can resolve their differences through commonly agreed upon means such as courts or community councils."

In a study of twenty-four societies, Swanson found a strong relationship (at the .0005 level) between the prevalence of witchcraft and the presence of important but unlegitimated relations among people.

Among the societies in Swanson's sample, the close and important but unlegitimated contacts were equally related to the prevalence of witchcraft whether these were between ultimately sovereign groups or within such groups.

According to Swanson, it was the absence of legitimate political procedures in any society where black magic was considered possible that was responsible for the widespread fear of witches.

The widespread use of black magic suggests a serious lack of legitimate means of social control and moral bonds. It implies that people need to control one another in a situation where such control is not provided by means which have public approval.

There was a rise in black magic at the close of the Middle Ages and the beginning of the Renaissance. There was also a rise in witchcraft in Salem, Massachusetts, in the late seventeenth century. Swanson believes that all of these were cases in which there was a breakdown of legitimate political procedures.

The periods of the Renaissance and the Enlightenment, from 1500 to 1750, both saw radical political change from government by small local and regional units to government by national states. The allegiance of the governed and the legitimacy of political power were uncertain throughout these years. The middle class was emerging and achieving power and Protestantism challenged Roman Catholicism.

In Salem, Massachusetts, the government of the Colony was chaotic. Under Cromwell an autonomous Puritan theocracy had ruled, but this had been curbed by Charles II who had appointed a royal governor in 1683. After Charles' Catholic successor, James II, was deposed in 1688, William of Orange, a Protestant, removed the governor but provided no new form of colonial government until 1691. The new charter was unpopular and did not enable the maintenance of a stable regime.

In the year 1692, the year of the witchcraft hysteria, the village of Salem was disorganized by the general confusion which prevailed consequent to the removal of the English governor and the weakening of the Colony's theocracy. In contrast to other towns in Massachusetts, there was in Salem a disruption of orderly judicial processes. The local judges disregarded the customary procedures in connection with accused witches, abandoning customary rules of evidence. Under these conditions the accusation of one person grew to the indictment of hundreds, and the execution of twenty.

Kluckhohn has noted that witchcraft among the Navaho Indians was especially prevalent at the time of their decisive defeat by the whites and in the years following when they were creating a new way of life under white supervision from 1875 to 1890. The second period of marked prevalence of witchcraft among the Navahos came in the 1940's, when the United States government forced them to reduce their holdings in sheep in order to preserve the range lands, and when there was a great increase in the number of them forced into the American economic system if they were to survive.

According to Kluckhohn witchcraft appears when there are strong deprivations of unknown or uncertain origin, which occur under social conditions which provide neither non-aggressive means of discharging anger nor means which are not socially disruptive and where at the same time there are beliefs in the efficacy and availability of magical procedures. Under these conditions the formerly strong have in fact been weakened by their enemies. Nonetheless their response is to fear not their enemies but the weaker—the witches.

THE SOUTHERN NEGRO IN THE UNITED STATES

There is still within this democracy an exploited, lower-caste group, the Southern Negro. Though he is on the march, there is impressive evidence that he suffers the paranoid posture of impotent anger at the terror and humiliation which have been imposed by heavy caste sanctions, punctuated by violence of the lynch mob. (We are using the term lower caste, as did Karon as well as the classic writers, to refer to an hereditary, endogamous subdivision of a society with an ascribed inferior status. We do not follow the practice of some recent writers of defining caste as implying acceptance by the lower caste of lower status as fully appropriate, since this is an empirical question. What evidence there is suggests that such a caste system has never existed anywhere.)

The definitive study is that of Karon, *The Negro Personality.* What does it feel like to live as a member of a caste in an otherwise democratic society? Karon has illuminated the world which the white American has created for the colored American. It is revealed as a world of threat—the threat of violence and humiliation to which the Negro has responded by muting his own feelings. The expression of his hostility is delayed, indirect and remote. The Negro of today is no less afraid of his own feelings of hostility than of the threat of violence which instigated them.

Although he suffers massive discrimination and implicit threat, the Northern Negro enjoys freedom from fear relative to the Southern Negro, and freedom from the consequences of fear; but the Southern colored American lives continuously with the fear of violence, and with humiliation from without and from within.

The severity of the humiliation complex varies consistently with the uniformity and severity of the caste restrictions and the degree of terrorization. Massive humiliation complexes not only are more frequent in the South than in the North; within the South, the more malignant humiliation complexes were found in the more terrorizing as opposed to the less terrorizing areas.

As we have seen with Dostoevsky, the freedom to know that one is being oppressed and to be angry at one's oppressor is not trivial.

Karon's study

Karon used the PAT (Tomkins-Horn Picture Arrangement Test), starting with the representative sample of the United States population which Gallup has obtained for the standardization of this technique. He then gathered additional data on high-school students from various parts of the country to check on the adequacy of the norms for that group. It was possible, therefore, to choose two Northern and two Southern communities from those in which high-school students had been tested; ninth-grade Negro students in the selected communities were used as the final sample for his studies.

The high-school samples had been gathered by group administations, generally carried out by the local school authorities. A rural area of the Deep South characterized by severe caste sanctions was chosen as one of the Southern communities and an urban ara where the caste sanctions are relatively benign by Southern standards was chosen as the other.

Karon found that Northern Negroes differ from Southern Negroes on precisely the same personality characteristics as do Northern Whites, and on no others (after the effects of differences in age, sex ratio, education, vocabulary, rural-urban residence, population density and degree of industrialization are controlled statistically). Thus, these characteristics are the result of the impact of the caste sanctions.

These characteristics are primarily concerned with anger and aggression; the denial that others are angry; the denial that there is fighting; the denial of symbolic anger; consciously suppressed anger; and, in the deep South, weak affect.

For example, on PAT Plate 13, Southern Negro subjects will deny that the hero is being aggressed against. Picture L of that plate is commonly described as "The boss is bawling him out" or "The foreman's giving him hell." If, instead of this, a subject describes the action as "The mechanic is telling him everything is OK" or "The boss comes and helps him again," the response is scored as a denial of aggressive press.

On Plate 4, the fact that there is a fist fight occurring is more frequently denied by Southern Negroes. Plate 4 is commonly described as "(L) having a hot argument, (O) someone breaks it up, (V) all friends now" or "(V) telling jokes, (O) someone gets mad, (L) gets into a fight." If, instead of this, the action is described as "(O) looks to me like they're on a dance floor, (L) I don't know what to give here, (V) looks like they are at a party and are dancing and singing" or "(V) the men are talking, (O) the men are working, (L) the rest of the men are working, too," the response is scored as a denial of physical aggression.

Not only is the press of anger from others denied, and the fact of physical aggression denied, but so too is the feeling of anger itself. Even the feeling of anger and the thought of being angry may become so frightening that the impulse to be angry is subjected to a massive repression. In order to safeguard this repression, the defense mechanism of denial may then be invoked against any situation which is too closely related to the repressed impulse.

Thus, on Plate 13 the subject may deny that the hero feels angry. Picture O of that plate is commonly described as "He's just telling the supervisor where to go" or "He is hot under the collar and is thumbing his nose at the boss." If, instead of this, the action is described as "He is blowing his nose" or "He has cut his finger and can picture that guy bawling him out," the response is scored as a denial of symbolic aggression.

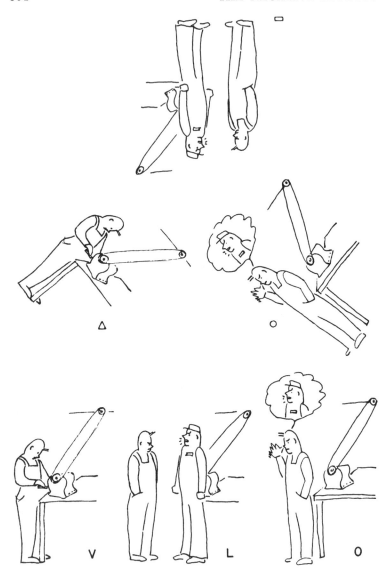

Plate 13 of the PAT is shown at top, in the form in which it is presented in the test itself. Below it are the same pictures arranged as a sequence, identified by the letters V, L, O (which are those used in keying and scoring the test). Picture L, center, is commonly described as "The boss is bawling out" the workman; irrelevant descriptions, for example, "The mechanic says everything is OK," indicate a denial of aggression.

L   O   V

Plate 4 of PAT, arranged in a commonly chosen sequence. (L, "a hot argument"; O, "someone breaks it up"; V, "all friends now.") The fact that a fight is in any way occurring is frequently denied by Southern Negroes.

Pictures V and L of Plates 25 are identical with pictures V and O of Plate 13, respectively. The remaining picture of each set provides a context which influences the subject's reactions to the other two pictures. Picture L of Plate 13 shows the foreman "bawling out" the hero; this is usually seen as the instigation for the hero's feeling angry. Plate 25 has no such instigation included in the pictures. For some subjects it is less frightening to express anger when there is no one around to retaliate; for others it is more frightening inasmuch as there is no obvious instigation to the aggression (and the feeling of anger therefore seems "irrational"); and for many it is equally frightening (or not frightening) irrespective of whether anyone else is around. Typical descriptions of picture L of Plate 25 are "To heck with the foreman" or "Thumbs his nose at the foreman." If, instead of this, the picture is described as "He is waiting on somebody to come help" or "A friend is looking at him," the response is scored as a denial of symbolic aggression.

According to Karon: "The reason for the increase in these characteristics would seem simply to be that the caste sanctions are, in fact, ways in which people are making trouble for the Negro; this trouble may mean not only inconvenience, discomfort, or humiliation, but also real physical danger. Against these problems, he may have no defense: any attempt to fight back seems likely to lead to vindictive and inescapable retaliation. He must therefore fight a continuing battle with his own feel-

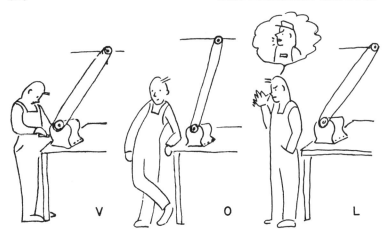

Plate 25 of the PAT in a commonly chosen sequence. Pictures V and L are identical with pictures V and O in Plate 13, but in Plate 25 the third picture does not include an instigation to anger. Picture L, above, is typically responded to with "Thumbs his nose at the foreman." But if this picture is described, for example, as "A friend is looking at him," denial of aggression seems obvious—a kind of response frequent among Southern Negroes.

ings of anger, lest he lose control. In a rural deep South area where physical security for the Negro is minimal, all of the aggression traits seem to increase. On the other hand, in a Southern city, where the Negro enjoys a good deal of physical security, this greater physical security is reflected in the fact that only two of the characteristics which concern aggression show striking increases over the North: strong but consciously suppressed anger, and denial of the idea of being angry without provocation. The increase in the latter seems to represent the fear of losing control and endangering the relative security he enjoys in this urban area."

The strong but consciously suppressed anger which is elevated in a Southern city compared with a Northern city are composed of responses such as LVO and VLO on Plate 13. The former is an example of a delayed expression of anger, and the latter is an example of a negativistic response. Insofar as the Negro suppresses his anger, we would expect the reactive increase in aggression to be reflected in the PAT not on the high general aggression scale but as an increase in delayed expression of aggression (aggression is aroused or expressed in the picture placed first, and then not expressed in the second, and finally expressed) or in negativism (mediation of another person stops work or leads to aggression).

WEAK AFFECT

Karon's summary of his findings continues: "Another characteristic which reflected the increased physical security of Negroes in the urban area as opposed to the rural deep South area was weak affect. One of the consequences of choking back one's anger may be a complete deadening of one's emotions. This seems to occur only in the rural sample where the Negro is most insecure, but not where he enjoys the relative physical security of the urban southern area studied. The avoidance of male-male contacts is still another characteristic which showed a more striking increase for the rural sample than for the urban. This supports the notion that close contacts between men are avoided because these contacts are most likely to erupt in physical aggression."

Weak affect is manifested on the PAT by sequences which end with no emotion where it was possible to end with a strong emotion. Responses VOL, VLO, OVL, and LVO on Plate 11 are examples of the kind of sequences which made up this scale.

Again to cite Karon: "It is striking that . . . these characteristics . . . indicate disturbed individuals. What this implies is that the impact of the caste sanctions on human beings is destructive, and the destructiveness varies with the severity of the sanctions. . . . The difference between the North and the South is considerable in terms of the human cost. Indeed, even within the South the difference between an area of severe sanctions and an area where they are less stringent is paralleled by an appreciable decrease in the human cost."

Postscript on the Southern American

What about the Southern whites? If we are correct that the strong fear and envy the weak, as much as the weak fear and

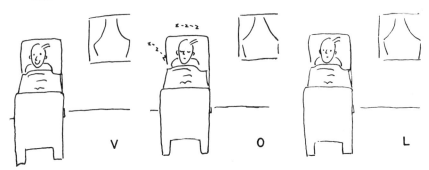

Plate 11 of the PAT, with pictures in the VOL sequence. This arrangement, ending with a picture indicative of no emotion, is typical of weak affect.

envy the strong, then the Civil War must have very much exaggerated an already untenable position.

Even before the defeat of the Civil War, Southern writers were viewing man as limited, and fallible "with evil as an active force in life," according to C. Hugh Holman. After the Civil War this was deepened.

As C. Vann Woodward has written: "The inescapable facts of history were that the South had repeatedly met with frustration and failure. It had learned what it was to be faced with economic, social, and political problems that refused to yield to all the ingenuity, patience, and intelligence that a people could bring to bear upon them. It had learned to accommodate itself to conditions that it swore it would never accept and it learned the taste left in the mouth by the swallowing of one's words. It had learned to live for long decades in quite un-American poverty, and it had learned the equally un-American lesson of submission: For the South had undergone an experience that it could share with no other part of America—though it is shared by nearly all the peoples of Europe and Asia—the experience of military defeat, occupation, and reconstruction. Nothing about this history was conducive to the theory that the South was the darling of divine providence."

Contrast this with De Tocqueville's classic account of the American dream, as of 1840:

"I have shown how the ideas of progress and of the indefinite perfectibility of the human race belong to democratic ages.

Democratic nations care but little for what has been but they
are haunted by visions of what will be. . . . [Americans'] eyes
are fixed upon another sight: the American people views its
own march across these wilds, draining swamps, turning the
course of rivers, peopling solitudes, and subduing nature. This
magnificent image of themselves does not meet the gaze of the
Americans at intervals only; it may be said to haunt every one
of them in his least as well as in his most important actions and
to be always flitting before his mind."

C. Hugh Holman has urged: "Such a series of experiences
as that undergone by the South is in sharp conflict with a view
of life dedicated to inevitable success, to plenty, to progress
and perfectibility, or even to the doctrine of individualistic
strenuosity in which man is master of his fate and captain of his
soul. The Southern writer's message has often seemed to be:
Acknowledge your own evil, plumb the depths of darkness
possible to you, and then let us join in trying to save ourselves
from disaster."

The Southern American, defeated and humiliated in the
Civil War, must necessarily have struggled against identification
with the Negro. He was caught between this identification with
the Negro as a fellow sufferer and the need to differentiate
himself from this symbol of shame. But the very attempt to
preserve the lower status of the Negro added to his own shame.
The Negro as the symbol of the weak was a many-dangered
thing.

Listen to William Faulkner:

"A race doomed and cursed to be forever and ever a part of
the white race's doom and curse for its sins. . . . The curse of
every white child that ever was born and that ever will be born.
None can escape it. . . . And I seemed to see the black shadow
in the shape of a cross. And it seemed like the white babies
were struggling, even before they drew breath, to escape from
the shadow that was not only upon them but beneath them too,
flung out like their arms were flung out, as if they were nailed
to the cross."

Joe Christmas in *Light in August* believes that he has an
infinitely small trace of Negro blood, a symbol of his shame and

guilt with which he is obsessed until he must die in expiating it.
In "The Wolves" Allen Tate describes the guilt and shame
of the Southern American as threatening

". . . wolves in the next room waiting
With heads bent low, thrust out, breathing
As nothing in the dark

The protagonist must go in fear to open the door and confront
the evil

—and man can never be alone."

In Robert Penn Warren's poem "Original Sin: A Short Story,"
the persecution of the persecutor, of the white by his bad conscience about the Negro, is expressed:

"But it never came in the quantum glare of sun
To shame you before your friends, and had nothing to do
With your public experience or private reformation:
But it thought no bed too narrow—"

Postscript on international relations

So much for the Jew, the Negro, the evil eye and witchcraft.
What of our own relationships with Russia and with the emerging nations all over the world? We live in a revolutionary period,
as a powerful nation which cannot help but excite fear, anger
and envy of those who would if they could equal us and surpass
us. Shall we provide an identification figure or will we too succumb to the paranoid posture, and like countless empires before,
fear and envy the weak who threaten us? Two individuals or
two groups who both assume the paranoid posture are engaged
in a *folie à deux* which can only end in mutual destruction and
fulfillment of each other's darkest prophecies.

Intransigence in such conflict seizes the weak and strong
equally. The strong can feel as weak as he supposes his oppo-
nent to be. The king is as paranoid as the son; in all the myths
of the birth of the hero, it is the king who is ultimately destroyed
by his son despite the best efforts of his father to kill him. The
weak and envious generate as much hate, contempt and fear
from the strong as they feel toward and from the strong.

Our fear of Russia is in large part a fear of the weak who are
becoming stronger. As Russia establishes her actual strength, our

fear abates and is transferred to the more primitive rival—
China. China is now pictured as utterly indifferent to human
life and more than willing to sacrifice millions of lives to defeat
us. The "yellow peril" is now invested with most of the characteristics once assigned the Russians in the "Red scare" following the First World War.

If our analysis of the paranoid fear of the weak is correct,
then our witchcraft should abate as our rivals grow in actual
strength. They should therefore be invited to our country, and
Americans should be invited to Russia and China and Africa
so that mutual respect might be strengthened and so dissipate
mutual fear.

THE PARANOID POSTURE IN THE BETRAYED: FREUD AND CASTRATION ANXIETY AND PENIS ENVY: THE STRONG PARENTS ARE WEAK AND TAKING, NOT STRONG AND GIVING

Humiliation and the paranoid posture which it may generate
do not issue from oppression alone. Hell hath no fury like a
human being scorned—and so it happens that fantasies of persecution and grandeur follow in the wake not only of oppression
but also of betrayal and infidelity. The goddess who once loved
her prince ceases to be a goddess when another prince or
princess arrives, and when it is the king to whom she must
have turned in her infidelity. The idealized strong mother and
father who give turn out to be weak and not strong, threatening
to take rather than continuing to give unlimited love.

We shall examine the relationship between Freud's personality and his theory, but first let us examine Freud as Freud
would have examined himself had he been a patient.

Freud was a first-born. As he wrote later, "A man who has
been the indisputable favorite of his mother keeps for life the
feeling of a conqueror, that confidence of success that often
induces real success."

Freud was born in a caul, which was believed to guarantee
future fame and happiness. One day an old woman whom the
young mother encountered by chance reinforced this by telling

her that she had brought a great man into the world. This story was repeated often enough so that Freud later had to deal with it and minimize it. He wrote, "Such prophecies must be made very often, etc."

It is clear that Freud was his mother's favorite and that the relationship between them was intense. When he was four, on the journey from Leipzig to Vienna, he saw his mother naked, which so impressed him that he revealed it forty years later in a letter to his friend Fliess—but in Latin.

Sibling rivalry was to play the major role in his relationship to his mother. His first rival was his brother Julius, who died when he was only eight months, when Freud was nineteen months old. Freud never ceased to reproach himself for being, through his hostile wishes, responsible for the intruder's early death.

Although he had admitted in a letter to Fliess his jealousy of his rival and the guilt this occasioned after his death, twenty years later, Freud wrote it was impossible for a child to be jealous of a newcomer if he is only fifteen months old when the latter arrives. Jones says of this discrepancy, "In the light of this confession it is astonishing that Freud should write twenty years later how almost impossible it is for a child to be jealous of a newcomer if he is *only* fifteen months old when the latter arrives." As we shall see later, Freud wavered on this point even in his later writings.

But Freud did not feel betrayed by his mother alone. When he had to account for his sibling, he would not believe it was his father who could have done such a thing. Rather he supposed it was his half-brother Philip who had made his mother pregnant. He suspected his half-brother Philip of having been responsible for the birth of the unwanted sibling and tearfully begged him not to make his mother again pregnant.

When Freud was three years old his family moved from Freiberg, in Moravia, to Leipzig where they lived a year before moving to Vienna. This move was in response to a rising anti-Semitism among the Czechs.

On the way to Leipzig the train passed through Breslau, where Freud saw gas jets for the first time; they made him think of souls burning in hell. This train ride marked the beginning of a phobia of traveling by train, which he suffered for about twelve years. He was able to rid himself of it through analysis which revealed it to be a fear of losing his home and ultimately his mother.

Freud remembers, at the age of seven or eight, of having urinated deliberately in his parents' bedroom, and being reprimanded by his father, "that boy will never amount to anything." Freud wrote about this fall from grace: "This must have been a terrible affront to my ambition, for allusions to this scene occur again and again in my dreams, and are constantly coupled with enumerations of my accomplishments and successes, as if I wanted to say: 'You see, I have amounted to something after all.'"

Freud's interest in his mother and in his father were later to be displaced to Rome. This interest began in his boyhood, and as he expressed it "became the symbol for a number of warmly cherished wishes." Years later in a letter he said he was spending his spare time studying the topography of Rome, and four months later he spoke of a secret wish that would mature if only he could get to Rome. Freud's interest in Rome was intense and enduring. When finally he overcame his inhibitions—"I discovered long since that it only needs a little courage to fulfill wishes which till then have been regarded as unattainable," he called it "the high point of my life"—which he had so long yearned for.

According to Jones' account of Freud's inhibition about going to Rome, there are at least two apparent sources. Freud quoted Rank's study of the symbolism of cities and Mother Earth in which the following sentence occurs: "The oracle given to the Tarquins is equally well known, which prophesied that the conquest of Rome would fall to that one of them who should first 'kiss' his mother." Freud cites this as one of the variants of the Oedipus legend. As Jones suggests, this is a reversal of the idea that one must conquer the enemy, the father, before one can sleep with the mother. It is rather that if one can kiss the mother, the father is thereby vanquished.

For Freud, as we shall see, the Eternal City, the mother, was as formidable to enter for the father as for the son because of her assumed penis envy and her assumed wish to castrate both

father and son. We have noted before Freud's disenchantment
with his father when he did not respond aggressively to insult
and how he compared his father invidiously with Hamilcar's
insistence that Hannibal take revenge. But even Hannibal's
attempt to enter Rome, the Mother of Cities, had been thwarted
by some inhibition. For years Freud too could get little nearer
to Rome than Trasimeno, the place where Hannibal had finally
stopped.

Freud's father by all accounts was not a stern patriarch, but
generally a loving father who took great pride in his son and
in all his children. When Freud wet his bed at the age of two
his father reproved him, but how harsh this and other reproof
must have been can be gleaned from the young Freud's nurturant response: "Don't worry, Papa. I will buy you a beautiful
new red bed in Neutitschein." Freud as a youngster regarded
him as "the most powerful, wisest and wealthiest man."

Another memory of Freud's was that when he was five years
old his father handed him and his little sister a book with the
mischievous suggestion that they amuse themselves by tearing
out its colored plates. As Jones comments—"certainly not an
austere father."

Yet he demanded respect from the young Freud. Moritz
Rosenthal tells the story of how when he and his father were
arguing, Jakob Freud laughingly reproved him: "What, are you
contradicting your father? My Sigmund's little toe is cleverer
than my head, but he would never dare to contradict me!" Here
again we see pride in his son, good humor attenuating the sting
of reproof. We have also noted before that it was Freud who
ultimately rejected and became ashamed of his father's lack of
aggression rather than that he was frightened of a stern patriarch.

If Freud's relationship with his mother and father was as
benign as in general it seemed to have been, how could he have
arrived at the dictum that life was not a nursery—with its implicit
nostalgia combined with not a little bitterness?

The key to this is to be found in his relationship to his
mother, who generated in him an unrelenting hatred and disenchantment for her betrayal of his love. She betrayed him to
sibling after sibling and to his father. Because she gave love
promiscuously she also betrayed his father, as he in turn had

betrayed his son in accepting the love of his mother. This results in a state of warfare between son, mother and father which is quite different than the family romance as Freud represented it in the Oedipus Complex. The villain in the piece is the mother and not the father. Rome will fall to that one who will first kiss his mother.

An analysis of Freud, using "The Psychology of Women" as a projective instrument

Where can we find Freud then in his theories? He is to be found, not too surprisingly, in his account of the psychology of women. His views of female development have often been regarded as trivial and somewhat mechanical—as indeed they are. They mask, however, Freud's most intense feelings.

Freud had confessed to Marie Bonaparte: "The greatest question that has never been answered and which I have not been able to answer, despite my thirty years of research into the feminine soul, is 'what does a woman want?' "

If we but assume that what anyone does not understand but will labor thirty years to find out and yet continue not to understand, is himself, then, the key to understanding Freud is in his portrait of women.

Although he professes not to understand women in general, he was nonetheless sure about the relationship between mother and son during the "golden age." The relationship between a mother and her son is, Freud thinks, "quite the most complete relationship between human beings, and the one that is the most free from ambivalence." We may presume that both Freud's mother and Freud were completely fulfilled in their earliest relationship.

Penis envy is a symbol for the mutual disenchantment after the golden age when innocence was lost through infidelity and betrayal.

If we assume that there is projection operating in Freud's understanding of women, then we have a much more accurate picture of Freud's development as he describes the relationship between a girl and her mother than in his portrayal of masculine development. Listen to Freud's account of female development in the *New Introductory Lectures*:

"You will remember that interesting episode in the history of analytical research which caused me so many painful hours? At the time when my main interest was directed on to the discovery of infantile sexual traumas, almost all my female patients told me that they had been seduced by their fathers. Eventually I was forced to the conclusion that these stories were false, and thus I came to understand that hysterical symptoms spring from fantasies and not from real events. Only later was I able to recognize in this fantasy of seduction by the father the expression of the typical Oedipus complex in woman.

"And now we find, in the early pre-oedipal history of girls, the seduction fantasy again; but the seducer is invariably the mother. Here, however, the fantasy has a footing in reality; for it must have been the mother who aroused (perhaps for the first time) pleasurable sensations in the child's genitals in the ordinary course of attending to its bodily needs."

Note that Freud is now satisfied that he has found the real thing—not the quicksands of fantasy which deceived him before.

"The turning away from the mother occurs in an atmosphere of antagonism; the attachment to the mother ends in hate. Such a hatred may be very marked and may persist throughout an entire lifetime; it may later on be carefully overcompensated; as a rule one part of it is overcome, while another part persists."

"The complaint against the mother that harks back furthest is that she has given the child too little milk, which is taken as indicating a lack of love."

"But whatever may have been the true state of affairs, it is impossible that the child's complaint can be as often justified as it is met with."

"It looks far more as if the desire of the child for its first form of nourishment is altogether insatiable, and as if it never got over the pain of losing the mother's breast."

Notice next that Freud now forgets that he is speaking about the development of girls and slips into a reference to a masculine primitive. It is of interest that the thought of insatiability of the neutral "it" of the last sentence now turns Freud's thoughts to a greedy but primitive overfed male child. "I should not be at all surprised if an analysis of a member of a primitive race who must have sucked the mother's breast when *he* could already run and talk, brought the same complaint to light.

"It is probable, too, that the fear of poisoning is connected with weaning. Poison is the nourishment that makes one ill. Perhaps, moreover, the child traces his early illnesses back to this frustration."

"One discovers the fear of being murdered or poisoned, which may later on form the nucleus of a paranoic disorder, already present in this pre-oedipal stage and directed against the mother."

Notice that when the mother turns away Freud supposes that not only does the child fear being poisoned by unwanted food and attention but also fears being attacked by the mother.

Next, Freud is reminded by this poisonous event of the difficulty in believing in chance, and guilt for the death of a rival and then the problem of sibling rivalry. Weaning, poisoning, hatred for the sibling who steals the mother's love and guilt when he dies follow in orderly succession and represent essentially Freud's early development. As Freud continues:

"It requires a good deal of intellectual training before we can believe in chance; primitive and uneducated people, and certainly children, can give a reason for everything that happens. Perhaps this reason was originally a motive (in the animistic sense). In many social strata, even to this day, no one can die, without having been done to death by someone else, preferably by the doctor. And the regular reaction of a neurotic to the death of some one intimately connected with him is to accuse himself of being the cause of the death."

"The next accusation against the mother flares up when the next child makes its appearance in the nursery. If possible this complaint retains the connection with oral frustration: the mother could not or would not give the child any more milk, because she needed the nourishment for the new arrival. In cases where the two children were born so close together that lactation was interfered with by the second pregnancy, this complaint has a real foundation. It is a remarkable fact that even when the difference between the children's ages is only eleven months, the older one is nevertheless able to take in the state of affairs."

Note that Freud's reference here is unmistakably personal in the reference to eleven months, since Freud was eleven months old when his younger brother Julius was born, and he was nineteen months when his brother died at the age of eight months.

Freud then goes on to give a more persuasive account of the jealousy of sibling rivalry than simply the frustration of weaning:

"But it is not only the milk that the child grudges the undesired interloper and rival, but all the other evidences of motherly care. It feels that it has been dethroned, robbed and had its rights invaded, and so it directs a feeling of jealous hatred against its little brother or sister, and develops resentment against its faithless mother, which often finds expression in a change for the worse in its behavior. . . . All this has been known for a long time, and is accepted as self-evident, but we seldom form a right idea of the strength of these jealous impulses, of the tenacious hold they have on the child, and the amount of influence they exert on its later development. These jealous feelings are particularly important because they are always being fed anew during the later years of childhood, and the whole shattering experience is repeated with the arrival of every new brother or sister. Even if the child remains its mother's favorite, things are not very different; its demands for affection are boundless; it requires exclusive attention and will allow no sharing whatever."

Again the personal reference of the repeated trauma is clear. There were five daughters and one more son to contend with in the next ten years. Anna, the next after Julius, was born when Freud was two and a half years old. This is approximately the differential which produces maximal sibling rivalry according to empirical studies. Further, the fact that the sibling was a girl cannot have diminished his impression of the infidelity of the sex he was later to accuse of penis envy.

Freud now addresses himself to the problem of why the girl is alienated from the mother while the young boy is not. The ground is "that the girl holds her mother responsible for her lack of a penis, and never forgives her for that deficiency. . . ."

Next Freud claims that not only is the little girl consumed

with penis envy, and holds her mother responsible, but because her mother is also without a penis she ceases to be a love object. "With the discovery that the mother is castrated it becomes possible to drop her as a love object, so that the incentives to hostility which have been so long accumulating get the upper hand. This means, therefore, that as a result of the discovery of the absence of a penis, women are as much depreciated in the eyes of the girl as in the eyes of the boy, and later, perhaps, of the man."

One might ask at this point why the young boy does not also turn against the mother as a love object—since she has no penis. Freud does not take this logical step, though as we shall see he does use this argument to account for anti-Semitism. Freud wrote: "The castration complex is the deepest unconscious root of anti-Semitism, for already in the nursery the child learns that something has been cut off the Jew's penis, and this gives him the right to despise the Jew."

Notice that in Freud's mind there is the trinity of fear, hatred and contempt aroused by the Jew's absence of a penis. Freud's anti-feminism is based on the same dynamic. But he will not admit that the young boy might hate and fear this penisless goddess. Instead he accounts by the same discovery for the origin of castration anxiety in the male rather than anger and contempt as well for the mother.

"In the boy the castration complex is formed after he has learnt from the sight of the female genitals that the sexual organ which he prizes so highly is not a necessary part of every human body. He remembers then the threats which he has brought on himself by his playing with his penis, he begins to believe in them, and thence forward he comes under the influence of castration-anxiety, which supplies the strongest motive for his further development."

If we add to the weaning and poisoning, the infidelity and the succession of rivals whom she feeds and loves, the discovery that she has no penis and that she might therefore want to take this from him too, all of this could not have made the young Freud's lot so much more enviable than that he attributes to the disenchanted little girl. Nor could the attachment to the mother, even when "the child remains its mother's favorite"

("mein goldener Sigi" as she referred to him to Ernest Jones)
remain entirely free of the hate, fear, contempt and suspicion
which he thought the girl never entirely outgrew as a woman.

But the repressed returns in his account of the after-effects
of disenchantment on the personality of women. Consider the
dismal outcomes of penis envy for the development of women.
First is narcissism:

"We attribute to women a greater amount of narcissism so
that for them to be loved is a stronger need than to love. Their
vanity is partly a further effect of penis envy, for they are driven
to rate their physical charms more highly as a belated compensa-
tion for their original sexual inferiority."

"Modesty, which is regarded as a feminine characteristic par
excellence, but is far more of convention than one would think,
was, in our opinion, originally designed to hide the deficiency
in her genitals."

"It must be admitted that women have but little sense of
justice, and this is no doubt connected with the preponderance
of envy in their mental life; for the demands of justice are a
modification of envy, they lay down the conditions under which
one is willing to part with it. We say also of women that their
social interests are weaker than those of men, and that their
capacity for the sublimation of their instincts is less."

Finally, "a man of about thirty seems a youthful, and in a
sense, an incompletely developed individual, of whom we
expect that he will be able to make good use of the possibilities
of development, which analysis lays open to him. But a woman
of about the same age frequently staggers us by her psychological
rigidity and unchangeability. Her libido has taken up its final
positions, and seems powerless to leave them for others."

Women then are more envious and narcissistic than men,
modest only to hide their inferiority, over-rate their physical
charms, have little sense of justice, have little social interest,
less capacity for the sublimation of their instincts and are more
rigid in personality structure.

Had Freud himself suffered disenchantment at the hands of
his mother, these qualities would not have been too remote from
what any wounded lover might have said about his once beloved.

But what of the good qualities of a woman? There are

residues of her pre-Oedipal attachment, the golden age before disenchantment. This "paves the way for her acquisition of those characteristics which will later enable her to play her part in the sexual function adequately, and carry out her inestimable social activities. . . . The only thing that brings a mother undiluted satisfaction is her relation to a son; it is quite the most complete relationship between human beings, and the one that is the most free from ambivalence. The mother can transfer to her son all the ambition which she has had to suppress in herself and she can hope to get from him the satisfaction of all that has remained to her of her masculinity complex. Even a marriage is not firmly assured until the woman has succeeded in making her husband into her child and in acting the part of a mother toward him. . . . In this identification, too, she acquires that attractiveness for the man which kindles his oedipal attachment to his mother into love. Only what happens so often is, that it is not he himself who gets what he wanted, but his son. One forms the impression that the love of man and the love of woman are separated by a psychological phase-difference."

One cannot escape the impression that the golden age for both man and woman, according to Freud, was that period before the birth of a sibling when the mother loved "mein goldener Sigi" and he in turn loved her equally passionately. After this there is disenchantment. The disenchanted boy must look for another mother, the disenchanted girl can ultimately become a loving mother if and when she has a son who heals her penis envy. But her husband who looks for his mother will be out of phase and in rivalry with his own son for the love of his wife.

Thus it is that the mother gives herself completely neither to Freud nor to his father, but rather to the succession of children each of whom are in turn disenchanted according to the female developmental sequence as it is portrayed by Freud.

If we turn now to Freud as an adult, and examine his relationship with Martha Bernays who was to become his wife, we do not have to search long to find that he is involved in a titanic struggle to recover the faithful mother but that he cannot easily still his doubts that he may be or has once again been betrayed.

Jones tells us that during his engagement to Martha Bernays he had an "immense capacity for jealousy . . . and [an] inordinate demand for exclusive possession of the loved one."

Jones tells us that Freud was "tortured by periodical attacks of doubt about Martha's love for him and craved for repeated assurances of it. . . . Special tests were devised to put the matter to the proof. . . . The chief one was complete identification with himself, his opinions, his feelings, and his intentions." Jones comments: "Even in his relations with the woman he loved so much one has the impression that he often needed some hardness or adverse criticism before he could trust himself to release his feelings of affection. . . . Towards the end of his engagement he told Martha that he had never really shown her his best side; perhaps it was never fully revealed in all its strength."

The focal point of conflict was whether Martha would side with him against her mother and brother. It appeared that in Martha he might reclaim the good mother—if only she would renounce her own mother—who more and more was cast in the role of a witch by Freud.

According to Jones, "the demand that gave rise to the most trouble was that she should not simply be able to criticize her mother and brother objectively and abandon their "foolish superstitions," all of which she did, but she had also to withdraw all affection from them—this on the grounds that they were his enemies, so that she should share his hatred of them. If she did not do this she did not really love him."

Once he wrote a strong letter to Martha's mother and then another to Martha: "I have put a good deal more of my wrath in cold storage which will be dished up some day. I am young, tenacious, and active: I shall pay all my debts, including this one." Here we see the imagery of cold, hard food—the weaned one will repay in kind. He will dish out to the bad mother what she dished out to him, and then some.

At more than one point, his testing of Martha's fidelity seriously threatened the relationship: "If that is so, you are my enemy: if we don't get over this obstacle we shall founder. You have only an Either-Or. If you can't be fond enough of me to renounce for my sake your family, then you must lose me, wreck my life and not get much yourself out of your family."

Again in connection with a possible rival, Martha's former art teacher, Fritz Wahle, he threatened: "When the memory of your letter to Fritz and our day on Kahlenberg comes back to me I lose all control of myself, and had I the power to destroy the whole world, ourselves included, to let it start all over again— even at the risk it might not create Martha and myself—I would do so without hesitation." This is not far removed from an end of the world fantasy—such, for example, as Hitler toward the end of World War II promised if Germany were defeated.

There are residues of physical fear of women in a humorous fragment on overly robust women: "A robust woman who in case of need can single-handed throw her husband and servants out of doors was never my ideal, however much there is to be said for the value of a woman being in perfect health. What I have always found attractive is someone delicate whom I could take care of."

There are also residues of the traumatic sibling rivalry in Freud's attitude toward children. Before his marriage and the birth of his own children, he had written: "It is a happy time for our love now. I always think that once one is married, one no longer—in most cases—lives for each other as one used to. One lives rather with each other for some third thing, and for the husband dangerous rivals soon appear: household and nursery. Then, despite all love and unity, the help each person had found in the other ceases. The husband looks again for friends, frequents an inn, finds general outside interests. But that need not be so."

And indeed it was not to be so for Freud. As Ernest Jones has commented, Freud was "not only monogamic in a very unusual degree, but for a time seemed well on the way to becoming uxorious." Freud had doubts about both Martha and the possible rivalry from their children. Nonetheless he was able to transform both Martha and his children into ideal mothers.

Although Martha was to supply him with almost the unconditional love he had demanded but never won from his mother, it was his daughter Anna who was cast by Freud in the role of the utterly faithful mother. Her love for her father and her lifelong commitment to him which excluded even marriage must have been encouraged by her father. Of their relationship, Jones wrote: "She it was who a quarter of a century later was by her loving care to reconcile him to the inevitable close of his life."

Jones refers to Freud's letter to Ferenczi indicating that his interest in the themes of love and death in his essay, "The Theme of the Three Caskets," must have been connected with thoughts of his three daughters, particularly the youngest, Anna. His second daughter Sophie was then about to be married.

The essay begins with a comparison between Basanio's choice of the leaden one in the scene of the three caskets in *The Merchant of Venice* and Lear's demand for love from his three daughters, the muteness of the lead being equated with Cordelia's silence. Freud's analysis of the number three is that it refers to the three aspects of womanhood: the mother who gives one life; the loving mate who is chosen by influences dating from the mother; and Mother-Earth (the goddess of Death) to whom we return at the end.

Freud, like Lear, wondered whether he would find the mother in the daughter. It is in this context that we must understand Jones' belief that it was his daughter Anna "who . . . by her loving care [was] to reconcile him to the inevitable close of his life."

But Freud felt not only vulnerable to humiliation by women and betrayed by them; he was also deeply puzzled. As we noted before, he said that he had "not yet been able to answer, despite my thirty years of research into the feminine soul . . . 'What does a woman want?'"

Insofar as Freud was deeply identified with his mother, we think this means that he never relearned exactly what it was he had wanted from a woman, as well as what she wanted, which would have preserved the golden age forever.

What of his relationship to men? It is our impression that contrary to what one might have expected from Freud's theory of the Oedipus complex, there is no fear of being castrated by the male, but rather an oscillation similar to that in his heterosexual relationships between passionate devotion and alienation at "betrayal."

Freud's sensitivity to insult was not restricted to his relationship with Martha Bernays. That Freud was unduly sensitive to insult in general may be seen in an incident he reports about a patient who left the door to his office open as he entered. He interpreted this as an indication of the patient's contempt for him—that he thought him much inferior to other physicians and wished to humiliate him.

If we piece together Freud's reflections on his general interpersonal relationships, we find a statement that there was something in him which seemed to repel others on first acquaintance, but that this is compensated for by the number of very close friendships he ultimately established, and finally that he has been "betrayed" by his closest friends: "I regard it as a serious misfortune that Nature did not give me that indefinite something which attracts people. If I think back on my life it is what I have most lacked to make my existence rosy. It has always taken me a long time to win a friend, and every time I meet someone I notice that to begin with some impulse, which he does not need to analyze, leads him to underestimate me. It is a matter of a glance or a feeling or some other secret of nature, but it affects one very unfortunately. What compensates me for it is the thought of how closely all those who have become my friends keep to me."

To Abraham he wrote: "I have always sought for friends who would not first exploit and then betray me." In his later years Freud often complained of the times he had been "betrayed" by his friends. Breuer, Fliess, Adler, Jung had promised to help him and then deserted him. Several times in his writings Freud spoke of his need for a loved friend and a hated enemy.

As Freud himself remarked, his dependence and overestimation of men proceed from what he called the feminine side of his nature. He once remarked to Ferenczi that the overcoming of his "homosexuality" had brought him a greater self-dependence.

The same motives which would not permit him as a child to imagine that it had been his father who had impregnated his mother continued throughout his adult life to make him overidealize his masculine friends and then to be wounded again and again by their "betrayal" and desertion of him.

Indeed it was the double quest for the good mother and the good father, the vision of the age of innocence, the secret belief that the world might really be a nursery which prevented the paranoid posture of hate, contempt and disenchantment from snowballing into a more malignant humiliation theory. The paranoid posture while always strong never became entirely monopolistic because of the weaker but still tenacious quest for the good mother and the good father. We will presently see, in the case of Strindberg, that the same dynamic readily lends itself to psychosis and to delusions of grandeur and persecution if the dynamic balance between innocence and betrayal shifts only slightly.

The reader may question why we consider Freud as a representative of a monopolistic humiliation theory if it is held in check by a competing quest for the good parent. We do so not because we consider Freud a paranoid schizophrenic, which he clearly was not, but because his thoughts and feelings were so exclusively caught up with the threats of danger and humiliation which he thought were inherent in the family romance, and because he was ever vigilant for what he regarded as the inevitable betrayal and attack by the love object. The world is in debt to Martha Bernays for the peace and tranquility which she brought to Freud that permitted him to wage his warfare outside his castle, his home. If Freud had had to wage warfare on two fronts, the paranoid posture might have assumed a more malignant form, as it did late in the lives of two others with a similar personality structure, Strindberg and Nietzsche.

PSYCHOANALYTIC THEORY AND
THE PERSONALITY OF FREUD

Let us turn now to an examination of Psychoanalytic theory and its relationship to the personality of Freud as we have interpreted it.

Psychoanalytic theory, in its central concepts of the Oedipus complex, castration anxiety and penis envy, is an expression of Freud's paranoid posture. In Freud's world there is humiliation and terror, and the threat of castration is an extraordinarily appropriate symbol not simply of anxiety as Freud represented it but of the conjoint threats of terror and humiliation.

Consider that castration is not simply a punishment which

terrorizes, but a symbol of an emasculated, inferior male who has been forced into a permanent, irreversible submissiveness to male and female alike. It is certainly not the most extreme punishment which we find in Freud's mythology. In the Oedipus myth it is the son who exacts the most extreme punishment against the father. He kills the father. If the father threatens the son, it is not to kill him but rather to humiliate him as much as to frighten him. Castration, actual or psychological, cannot, in fact, kill the son. To have called it castration anxiety concealed from Freud and others the dual nature of the threat of castration. It concealed also the dual source of the dual threat. If Freud was more aware of the role of anxiety than humiliation in his and others' relations to their mother and father, he was also more aware of the threat from the father than from the mother.

If the mother will not continue to give her son her undivided love because she gives birth to another child and thus turns away from her favorite, the favored son is castrated by his mother. If she was unfaithful even in bringing him into the world, she was a whore even while she appeared to love only her son. The discovery of the primal scene was doubly painful for Freud, for he had half convinced himself that it had been his half-brother Philip rather than his father who had impregnated his mother. He had deliberately urinated in his parents' bedroom at the age of seven or eight, and his recollection of his father's displeasure as we have noted was his father's statement, "That boy will never amount to anything." It will be remembered that Freud's dreams concerning this incident revolved about disproving his father's prophecy: "You see, I have amounted to something after all."

It would seem that the shock of the primal scene for Freud was the witnessing of a double betrayal which deepened the already severe feelings of humiliation. This was further reinforced by the nature of the reproof from his father. Freud's reaction, as ever, was counteractive—he *would* amount to something. Freud's recollection of the primal scene is, however, noteworthy in its absence of feelings of betrayal, when one considers his general intolerance of any kind of rival and his interpretation of its significance for others.

The meaning of the concepts of castration anxiety and penis

envy must be understood in the context in which they originated for Freud. They did not originate at the age of five, when the young hero contested the king for the love of the queen. They originated when the mother turned to the infant intruder, weaning and "poisoning" her first-born. This is how he was "dethroned" and emasculated. He now develops castration anxiety for the first time—not because his mother has no penis, but because she has no breast—she has withdrawn the milk of human kindness and poisoned him.

Now he knows both terror and humiliation. She has betrayed him because she is not a good mother who always offers the good milk of human kindness but a narcissist, a whore who takes from the father, as from her son, as from the infant, what she must have, because she is empty of love and therefore envious of her son and her husband who have offered her their love for what they thought was her love.

You, my mother who have taken from me, must have some terrible lack in you which consumes you with envy of me. The mechanism is common among children. If one child calls another a "thingumabob" with intent to derogate, it is only a moment before the other child, stung to the quick, replies in kind, "You're a thingumabob." I am not bad because you rejected me—you are the bad one. I am not envious of the newborn infant. It is you, and all women who betray the love of their sons who are envious of their sons, and wish to rob them of everything which is precious to them. Thereafter it will be a war between the sexes, in which I must suffer castration anxiety lest your penis envy devour and poison me. You will not again seduce me to betray me, to castrate me and humiliate me.

We do not believe with the English school of Psychoanalysis that because the pre-Oedipal early years are critical in development that they are therefore necessarily "oral" in nature. The prominence of oral imagery in Freud and others we take to be symbolic of the positive affects of excitement and enjoyment and of negative affects of distress, shame, anger and fear occasioned not only by hunger but by the varieties of discomforts which infants and children suffer, not the least of which is the absence of the familiar and exciting face of the mother.

Castration anxiety and penis envy are not, to our way of

thinking, genital masks for oral dangers; both are symbols of the threat to positive affect from negative affect—in short, the danger to love from hate.

THE PARANOID POSTURE AND MUTUAL
ADMIRATION AMONG MEN OF GENIUS

Those who share the paranoid posture resonate to each other's rediscovery that the world is not a nursery. Thus, Shaw, Nietzsche, Strindberg, Dostoevsky, Freud, Sean O'Casey, Eugene O'Neill among others constitute a mutual admiration society. We will leave for another publication the exploration of the communalities between a dozen or more creative artists who shared the same dark vision of oppression, betrayal and eternal warfare.

Each of these men "discovered" the others with great excitement. Nietzsche wrote to Strindberg: "Such as I am, the most independent and perhaps the strongest mind living today . . . it is impossible that the absurd boundaries which an accursed dynastic nationalist policy has drawn between peoples should hold me back and prevent me from greeting those few who have ears to hear me." Of Strindberg's *The Father* he had said, "I read your tragedy twice over with deep emotion: it has astonished me beyond all measure to come to know a work in which my own conception of love—with war as its means and the deathly hate of the sexes as its fundamental law—is expressed in such a splendid fashion."

Strindberg wrote back to Nietzsche in Italy telling him that in *Also Sprach Zarathustra* he had "given mankind its most profound book." However he advised Nietzsche against translation into Swedish: "You can judge our intelligence from the fact that people want to shut me up in an asylum on account of my tragedy." On second thought he also advised against translation into English since that country was much concerned with "a library for girls of good family" and such domination by women was "a sure sign of decadence."

Strindberg wrote to Edward Brandes: "My spirit life has received in its uterus a tremedous outpouring of seed from

Friedrich Nietzsche, so that I feel as full as a pregnant bitch. He was my husband."

Nietzsche said of Dostoevsky that he was "the only psychologist, by the way, from whom I learned something." Nietzsche had read Dostoevsky's *Notes from Underground* in 1887 and wrote: "I did not even know the name of Dostoevsky just a few weeks ago. . . . An accidental reach of the arm in a bookstore brought to my attention *L'esprit soutterain,* a work just translated into French. . . . The instinct of kinship (or how should I name it?) spoke up immediately; my joy was extraordinary."

Freud, according to Ernest Jones, said of Nietzsche "that he had a more pentrating knowledge of himself than any other man who ever lived or was likely to live." Of Dostoevsky Freud said, "As a creative writer he has his place not far behind Shakespeare. *The Brothers Karamazov* is the greatest novel that has ever been written, and the episode of the Grand Inquisitor one of the highest achievements of the world's literature, one scarcely to be overestimated." On the other hand he was disappointed in him as a man because he was a docile reactionary rather than a revolutionary leader.

Eugene O'Neill with the help of a German grammar and dictionary read the whole of *Also Sprach Zaranthustra.* Another favorite was Strindberg.

Shaw said of Strindberg, "The only genuinely Shakesperian modern dramatist." Sean O'Casey said, "Strindberg, Strindberg, Strindberg, the greatest of them all."

Strindberg had also been extraordinarily attracted to another who shared the paranoid posture, Edgar Allan Poe. He saw so much of himself in Poe's work that when he discovered he had died in 1849, the year of his own birth, he wondered if he were not a reincarnation of Poe.

THE PARANOID POSTURE IN STRINDBERG:
BETRAYAL AND THE BATTLE OF THE SEXES

Let us now consider Strindberg, a man in many ways like Freud, also a truly creative genius, also oppressed by a monopolistic humiliation theory. But his early life was somewhat more stringent, and he was never able to find in reality, particularly in the relationship to his wife and child, possibilities for softening his paranoid posture, as Freud was able to find. Rather, that posture eventuated into a paranoid schizophrenic psychosis.

Strindberg's relationship with his mother was similar to Freud's relationship in its intensity, and in the experience of betrayal. There was, however, a critical difference which may account for the more malignant development of paranoid ideation in Strindberg. Strindberg was a fourth child, and he never did succeed in winning his mother's love as completely as he wanted. So far as we can tell the golden age in which he enjoyed exclusive possession of her love was brief. He has said "his desire for his mother was an incest of the soul." Strindberg was very jealous of his mother's favorite, Axel, the eldest son. August tried in every way to win his mother's heart—did everything she asked, and more, without success. Whatever he did seemed wrong. Whatever he most enjoyed was always stopped with, "What will Father say?" "What will people say?" "Remember God can see you."

According to Elizabeth Sprigge he thought his mother very beautiful and kind. She bound up wounds and dried tears, although she was also false and gave the children away to their father who punished them. When they were beaten it was their mother who comforted them, and though Strindberg loved his mother and her comfort he could not forget her perfidy.

As a child Strindberg considered himself ill-treated and unloved—he thought he was always hiding from adult wrath. In fact, according to Elizabeth Sprigge, he did everything possible to attract attention. His love for his mother was as tormenting as hatred. When he was away from her he was sick with longing, but when they were together there was no communion between them. She was dying because she had had too many children. When his mother spoke to him of the humility of Christ and the vanity of worldly wisdom and warned him to remain "simple," he remembered she had had no education and detected in her the hatred of the ignorant for the cultured.

When Strindberg was thirteen his mother died. He had never won her and he shrieked in despair. He was sure that the others had not loved her as well as he, although his own conscience hurt him since at the very moment of her death he had been thinking of the golden ring she had promised her sons when she was dead.

When his father announced his intention to marry the house-keeper, Strindberg could not understand how his father, a Pietist, could do such a thing. It seemed to him that their religion was only a cloak for their sin. He saw himself now as Hamlet. He thought that to be given a stepmother was an even worse fate than to have a stepfather. He was now obsessed with sexual fantasies. Soon he became equally obsessed with science and knowledge and he was consumed with an interest in how things worked. He wished to become a scientist.

Strindberg's view of women was that on the one side were bad women whom he must avoid and, on the other, women like his mother who must be worshiped and protected. He did not love his father but at times he was sorry for him. Even though he was the master who must be obeyed, Strindberg felt that he seemed like an intruder in the home.

August came to be looked upon as the scholar of the family and was given a better education than any of his brothers. He was for the first time grateful to his father and experienced intense joy at seeing his mother proud of him. At the same time he wondered if it were not for their own honor rather than for his good that his parents wished him to be well educated.

Without his father the family would be destitute, yet he could feel no gratitude toward him. He observed that every creature fed its young, and resented being asked to treat his parents' care as a special favour. Since he had not asked to be born, he could not see that he owed anyone gratitude.

In *To Damascus* he wrote, "Even in childhood I began to serve my sentence." Like Freud he was intensely vulnerable to humiliation from his peers. For Freud it had been anti-Semitism which had wounded his pride. For Strindberg it was his lower-class status. In school he became even more unhappy. He tried to escape attention because attention meant pain and humiliation. His clothing drew sneers of contempt from the aristocratic bullies. Young Strindberg envied their clothing. Despite the punishment and the humiliation he suffered in school and although his lessons seemed meaningless, yet he liked learning and was eager to explore the world.

His pride was greater than his fear. If he were alone he crept into the lake from the bank, but if any one watched he hurled himself from the roof of the bathing hut. He was like the girls in many ways but pride kept him from their babyish games but also from rougher ones of the boys. The older boys "weighed him down" so that he spent much of his time alone.

Presently he read a book on the serious consequences of masturbation—death or insanity. His body would decay, his spinal marrow and his brain would melt, his hair and teeth would drop out. Religion was proclaimed the only salvation—but it would not save his body. The young Strindberg stared in the mirror watching in panic for the first symptoms of decay. He determined to renounce the gaiety of the world, to fast and suffer so that he might become one of God's elect. If by a miracle God spared his life he vowed to become a priest. At his first communion the Spirit had not descended, and he realized that his wish to be a priest had arisen more from fear than from a desire to serve God, that his faith was based on fear, and that fear had shut his eyes to the truth.

Strindberg and Freud were both tormented lovers of their betrothed. Strindberg, however, carried the same intensity and the same tortured doubts into marriage and into three marriages. His first wife was the tempestuous Siri von Essen. After much dissension and recrimination they were divorced in 1891. He then married the young Austrian novelist Frida Uhl in 1893. They separated a year later and were formally divorced in 1897. In 1901 he married the actress Harriet Bosse with whom he lived long enough to have a child and from whom he separated before the child was born.

All of Strindberg's relationships are marked by passionate over-idealization accompanied by great jealousy which ultimately destroys the relationship so that the image of purity, love and innocence is transformed into infidelity, hate and betrayal. To Siri von Essen he had written: "I love you!!! And I walk in the streets as proud as a king and look compassionately at the crowd —why don't you fall on your dirty faces before me? Don't you know that she loves me? . . .

"Mine, my beloved—and she loves wretched me—if she doesn't soon throw me over I shall go mad with pride.

"Thank you for yesterday. Wasn't I dignified? I'm making progress. I was meant to be born a woman.

"Why am I cold and sarcastic with you? I love you and sometimes want to leap into your embrace but am held back by fear of being driven out of Paradise. That's why. Oh, see for once my tenderness!"

Siri begged Strindberg to declare his love to her husband: "O, sacrifice your pride for once to your love! You'd let me die. . . . Haven't you the courage to say 'I love your wife—our love is pure?' " Strindberg could not bring himself to this. He finally wrote him a formal letter and an "Epistle" in six chapters.

"You have his friendship, I have that too and as my friend he is the finest, the best, the noblest I have ever known and I love him. But as your husband, as my love's cruel tyrant I hate him. Now I'm going crazy! . . ."

"Oh, how I hate, detest, despise my friend Carl! How deeply he has offended me! How dare to stop adoring my love! He can't see her for a harlot! O my God! She who loves me is so superior to him. He, with the aid of the law and religion and the consent of her parents, stole her beauty and youth and favours, and then threw her away like a withered flower, he denies me the right to gather up what he has thrown away. God in heaven, I shall go mad!"

Strindberg had always hated dogs. His wife's spaniel appeared to him to be an orally demanding pet that got all the tidbits and at the same time a slobbering dirty animal which made messes, for which it was not punished but rewarded. The love and nourishment he craved from his wife she seemed to squander on this dirty, unworthy animal. His wife Siri detested Nietzsche because he seemed to encourage Strindberg to think he was God. Supported by Nietzsche, he called Christianity a religion for "women, eunuchs, children and savages."

"Now I'll stop—don't kill me—read all my letter—don't despise me—I have really suffered intolerably. . . . Forgive me—believe in me steadfastly—however I behave believe in me. . . . Oh, oh, save me and I will save you—forgive me all this—I love you, love you, love you!!!"

The last years of their marriage were as stormy as the beginning had been. Then he married for a second time. His second wife, Frida Uhl, was a journalist. It is one of the tragedies of Strindberg's life that he insisted on marrying professional women who essentially would not relinquish their individuality and their careers for him. We have seen that Freud was wiser in this respect, although he too had insisted that Martha give up her identification with her mother and brother. It is not unlikely that Strindberg was attracted to professional women because they provided the ultimate test of whether his mother could be persuaded to give up everything for him.

Like Freud he was a man of deep and intense feeling, but with strong feelings that only Reason and the Truth could save man from self-deception betrayal. In his introduction to *Miss Julie* he wrote, "I myself find the joy of life in its strong and cruel struggles, and my pleasure in learning, in adding to my knowledge."

The disenchanted, the betrayed who are gifted with high intelligence have always turned to nature, to unlock the secrets of Mother Nature from one who will not cheat or deceive. Freud, Strindberg and Einstein alike have insisted on the Truth in part because they felt they had been betrayed. Einstein, the gentlest of these, nonetheless has said he turned to the study of nature when he became convinced that interpersonal relationships were too heavily laden with deception and deceit.

Einstein, Freud and Strindberg form a graded series with respect to the intensity of their feelings of betrayal and disenchantment, but there are few who insist on the "Truth" in a belligerent mood who do not in part mean that they are seeking to undo the wrongs of the past, to expose the betrayer, and perhaps ultimately to recover the innocence of a golden age— the Garden of Eden before it was necessary to eat the fruit of the tree of knowledge.

To Edward Brandes, who had written Strindberg that he would become the great reformer of Swedish literature, he wrote: "I have scarcely anything left but my big beautiful hatred for all oppression and all gilded rottenness. Added to which I am swift in attack, but then comes my humanity and I suffer for having scourged my fellow beings, even when they deserved it.

Therefore I cannot be a trustworthy friend nor an enduring enemy." After the great success of *The Father* in Paris he was lionized. At once, however, he became indifferent to the theatre. He must continue his chemical research until he had found the single origin of all matter.

All literature now seemed to Strindberg concerned with woman's infidelity and with madness. During this period his literary work came to a standstill and he pursued a variety of scientific experiments through which he imagined that he would overthrow many scientific theories and attain world fame. He engaged in alchemic experiments and believed he had solved the riddle of making gold.

Indeed he considered himself a greater scientist than dramatist, despite the fact that he was enjoying great success at that time with *Miss Julie, Creditors,* and *The Father.* To find unexpected traces of one substance in another thrilled him. He was breathless with anticipation, feeling that at any moment he might make a discovery that would solve the riddle of the universe. In reply to the question, "What power would you most like to possess?"—Strindberg answered, "Power to solve the riddle of the world and the meaning of life." He distilled for himself some drops of prussic acid, and it gave him an extraordinary pleasure to know that under the glass stopper of the little phial, he had imprisoned death. Then he turned to occultism. He said that it was as if he had died and been born into another world where none could follow him.

In *Married,* Strindberg attacked the upper classes and particularly the Church. He told of his fear after reading the yellow book, that his masturbation would lead to insanity. He attacked the Church for advocating celibacy because this perverted the virility of youth. Confirmations and communion he attacked as superstitions by which the Church kept the lower classes subjugated.

For this book he had to stand trial for blasphemy. Frightened as he was he would not recant. His only defense was that he was in earnest, that he told the truth. He wrote that "people were more afraid of me than I of them." He was acquitted, but he felt humiliated rather than triumphant. He would rather have become a martyr because now he felt that as a result of his attack on the upper classes he was threatened with poverty and was made more dependent on his "natural enemy," the capitalist. He complained that "Albert Bonnier is so persecuted that he dares not publish my work."

During this period he wrote:

"What fate now awaits me, I do not know. But I feel 'the hand of the Lord' upon me. Some change is coming, upwards or straight down into the bowels of the earth. Who can tell?

"I am once more a victim of superstition. I hear the voices of crows at night in my garden and children weeping on the further shore of the Danube; I dream of days gone by, and have a longing to fly in some warmish medium, neither air nor water . . . to have no more enemies neither to hate nor be hated any more. . . .

"Prison might have some attraction, but what comes before—brutal lawyers, probing my soul and asking questions I will not answer—No!"

During his trial he returned to his early love for his wife, wrote her love letters and expressed his gratitude for her loyalty. Immediately after the trial, however, he was quick to believe she had gone over to the enemy if she seemed at all indifferent. After winning the trial both his terror and his hate grew. His belief in a benevolent deity crumbled. He began to be concerned also with his own powers for evil. Two of his enemies towards whom he had strong hate died quite unexpectedly. He remembered that during his trial one man had call him Lucifer.

He feared his children would starve to death—that he himself was more dependent on his enemies, the capitalists, than ever before. About his children, after the trial he wrote "At night he heard the threat of hunger and want rising like a flood to engulf them." His friend Bjornson suggested that Strindberg submit to his wife's judgment before he published anything more.

Strindberg began to rehearse the meaning of the trial for blasphemy in connection with *Married*. He became more and more convinced that it was not really blasphemy for which he had been tried but rather his unveiling of women. It was women then who were behind the attacks on him. Strindberg then wrote a series of stories on women in which his hate and fear were given full expression. The depth of his hate frightened him. He tried to explain it to a friend as "only the reverse side of my fearful attraction towards the other sex." He wondered whether his wife was not really an old witch brewing potions and wondered whether his headaches were not really due to her intention to poison him. He became consumed with doubt about his wife. He now was sure she had lovers of both sexes. Worst of all, he wondered if his children were his own. He became more and more certain she wanted him to be weak, believed him insane and was planning to put him away.

As his second marriage deteriorated Strindberg wrote to an old friend: "My marriage is about to be dissolved. The cause: much the same as the first time. All women hate Buddhas, maltreat, disturb, humiliate, annoy them, with the hatred of inferiors, because they themselves can never become Buddhas. On the other hand they have an instinctive sympathy for servants, male and female, beggars, dogs, especially mangy ones. They admire swindlers, quack dentists, braggadocios of literature, peddlers of wooden spoons—everything mediocre. . . . English physicians have recently established that when two children of a family sleep in the same bed, the weaker draws strength from the stronger. There you have marriage: the brother and sister bed."

To his second wife he wrote:

"What is the use of a comedy of love, since we hate each other? You hate me from a feeling of inferiority; I am a superior who has done you nothing but good; and I hate you as an enemy, because you behave like one.

"If I wanted to go on fighting you, I should have to use the weapons of your decadent morality, but I won't do that. So I'm leaving you—and going never mind where. As soon as you're alone, deprived of the urge to humiliate me, your energy will desert you too. Your strength is rooted in cruelty, you need an eternal victim to play the part of the eternal fool. I don't want the role any longer.

"Look for another man. Adieu!

"P.S. . . . I was bewitched into a marriage in which I've been treated as a beggar, worse than a servant, and have fallen so low that my children curse me."

As Strindberg sailed away in a steam ship on the Danube,

from his second wife, he felt such longing for his wife and child that he was tempted to jump overboard and return to them. But as the steamer drew away he felt the bond between himself and Frida Uhl "stretch and stretch until at last it broke." Attracted as he was to the safety and warmth of the womb-like love of his wife but repelled by any suggestion of dominance and control, he alternately felt overcome with grief and longing, and euphoric and triumphant at his freedom.

During this period came the crisis in which Strindberg struggled with psychosis. When he feared insanity, he left instruction either to be poisoned by a skillful doctor or sent to an asylum in Belgium where he had read patients were allowed freedom. He explained the possibility of his insanity "as it would be scarcely surprising for a sane man to be driven out of his wits by seeing the world run by knaves and fools."

Strindberg shared the fear of the eyes of the other with all those who are in the grip of the paranoid posture. He complained that the eyes of the audience in a theater "harpooned" him. From the staring, rough faces which he found increasingly malevolent he shielded himself by withdrawing to solitude and by alcohol to deaden the impact. He avoided restaurants in which the light was "too bright for him." He never attended premiere performance of his important plays. In his early twenties he began to notice that people often looked queerly at him, and wondered if he were going mad and sometimes became panicky when he thought that others might be planning to have him shut up.

Strindberg had noted with some alarm evidence of Nietzsche's insanity in his signatures such as "Nietzsche Caesar" but he had assumed these to be jests. When Nietzsche was sent to a mental hospital, Strindberg became panicky since he felt infected by him. His mind already felt like "an overcharged Leyden jar." How was he to retain his own sanity? In a letter at that time he complained of being "frightfully nervous, and mild persecution mania after stormy days and sleepless nights. Walk about with revolver and mankiller to protect my blond boy from the gypsies' kidnapping plans."

Stanislav Przybszewski, the Polish pianist, adored Strindberg, called him "Father" and "Master" and kissed his hands. But

Strindberg came to believe he was his enemy, partly because of his intimacy with a woman to whom Strindberg was attracted and partly because of his jealousy of what he regarded as the pianist's superior mind. Strindberg believed this man had tried to rob him of his subsistence but that since he had failed he had come to kill him. Strindberg in terror "reversed the spear" and willed his enemy's destruction, for which he felt like a murderer. When he heard that Prybyszewski had been arrested on the charge of murdering his mistress and their two children he was as first relieved and then frightened at the thought that his wish for revenge was responsible for this crime.

Later when Przybszewski was released for lack of evidence Strindberg considered killing himself. He smelled the fumes of a vial of potassium cyanide but did not go through with it. He began to think his persecutor was in the next room and was sending poisonous gases through the wall. He thought of reporting this to the police, but didn't because they might think him insane.

Shortly thereafter he felt an electric current passing through his room and he fled in terror. He hid from his persecutor in another hotel. Then he recovered enough to let his whereabouts be known, but at once an old man with wicked eyes seemed to have moved next door. This time he prepared for his death. One night he was awakened by a pump drawing out his heart lifting him from his bed. Then as the clock struck two an electric current seemed to strike his neck and press him to the ground. On succeeding nights, at the same hour an electric current seemed to shoot through his body.

He went to see a psychiatrist, whom he thought might torture him, poison him and steal his secret of making gold. This doctor thought the Bible unsuitable reading for one with a religious paranoia and gave him Victor Rydberg's *German Mythology* as a soporific. The following passage seized Strindberg's imagination: "As the legend relates, Bhrign, having outgrown his father's teaching, became so conceited that he believed he could surpass his teacher. The latter sent him into the underworld where, in order that he might be humbled, he had to witness countless terrible things of which he had no conception."

From this point on Strindberg changed. He saw his suffering

as penance and that God wished him to stop exploring the secret of the universe. He therefore renounced his scientific studies. The theme of atonement appears again and again until his death. In Gustavus Vasa, Strindberg made the tyrant who was nonetheless the loving father of his people end by saying "Oh God, Thou hast punished me, and I thank Thee!"

Strindberg was to die of cancer. As the illness progressed, the doses of morphia were increased. One evening as the end approached he took the Bible from the table beside his bed, pressed it to his breast and murmured, "Everything is atoned for."

In Strindberg and others, in whom the hate of the paranoid posture overwhelms the love from the age of innocence, there is generated a fantasy of complete salvation from hate. In answer to George Brockner's question, "What would give you the greatest joy?" Strindberg replied, "To hate no one and have no enemies." In answer to the question, "What social reform would you most like to see accomplished in your lifetime?" his answer was, "Disarmament."

His third wife he had described as "the white dove who, unafraid because she had never provoked the heavens, could give the frightened eagle peace." To her in the days of their courtship he had written:

To Harriet!
(Written with the eagle pen)

Fear not the eagle, pure white dove!
Never—oh beloved!—will he rend you. . . .
Should you tire of your life on earth,
He will take you on his mighty wings,
Lift you high above the clouds!
Dove of mine so pure, the eagle is your friend. . . .
He protects you from the gray winged hawk.
Guard him—and protect him from your arrows!"

"I embrace you, I kiss your eyes and thank God for sending you, little dove, with a branch of olive, and not with a birch rod.

"The deluge is over, the old swallowed up, and the earth will be greening once more!

"Peace be with you, my beloved."

The following is another letter written in the beginning of their relationship:

"You ask me if you can impart something good and beautiful to my life! And yet—what have you not already given me?

"When you, my dearly beloved, my friend, stepped into my home three months ago, I was grief-stricken, old and ugly—almost hardened and irreclaimable, lacking in hope.

"And then you came!

"What happened?

"First you made me almost good!

"Then you gave me back my youth!

"And after that, you awakened in me a hope for a better life!

"And you taught me that there is beauty in life—in moderation . . . and you taught me the beauty of poetic imagery—*Swanwhite!*

"I was sad and grieving—you gave me happiness!

"What, then, is it you fear?

"You—young, beautiful, gifted—and what is much more: wholesome and good!—There is so much more you can teach me! And you are rash enough to say that you would like to learn!

"You have taught me to speak with purity, to speak beautiful words. You have taught me to think loftily and with high purpose. You have taught me to have reverence for the fates of others and not only my own.

"Beloved! Who can tear us apart, if Providence refuses to separate us?

"If it is the will of Providence—well, then we shall part as friends for life; and you will remain my immortal faraway Love, while I shall be your servant Ariel, watching over you from afar! I shall warm you with my love and my benevolent thoughts. . . . I shall protect you with my prayers!

"Let us now wait until the sixth of May and see whether Providence desires to separate what He has joined together!"

The savior for Freud and for Strindberg is a woman, not a man. He conceived of Harriet Bosse as a female Christ:

"Yes—this is what I fear: that you will tire of sharing my painful, peculiar fate. . . .

"As I sit before your Eleonora picture, I am aware of how

much you have already suffered for my sake. . . . It is a female Christ image—the suffering for others!

"But, beloved, do not try to change my fate, either from good will or love, for that would be dangerous. Through patience I have finally succeeded in bringing about a change for the better. Support me in these efforts and do not embitter me against Providence or mankind.

"Stand by me now until my fate is completed . . . I do not think it will be long now.

"Never be angry with me . . . be compassionate! What you see is not temperament or disposition—it is my fate you witness. . . .

"Help me bear it! I will never be able to overcome it. . . ."

To Strindberg, as for Freud too, his home was his castle—outside was the enemy. To Harriet Bosse he once wrote: "As long as I stay peacefully at home, I have calmness; the moment I go out and mingle with people, the Inferno begins. That is why I long for a home of my own!"

After his first quarrel with Harriet he wrote:

"Last night I felt as if God was angry with me and as if everybody hated me. And I wreaked my anger on all and everything.

"Then I read your lovely letter, in which you thanked me for giving you light!

"Can I, like Eleonora—herself so unhappy—provide happiness for others? Can my sufferings be transformed into joy for others? If so, then I must continue to suffer. . . .

"I am thinking of the dark, ghastly electricity machine that reclines down in the cellar on Grev Magnigatan. It lies somber in the darkness, grinding out light for the entire block. . . .

"What happened last evening I today realize was my fault. Last night I fell—downward, downward, pulling you down with me.

"During the evening my ill-nature drew to me only the malicious and mean!

"That was all!

"Therefore: again upward! Will you?"

Harriet Bosse tells the following story about Strindberg's jealousy:

". . . He even forced himself to dine with me at Hôtel Rydberg, although he abhorred appearing in public places. But that dinner had an unhappy ending, for an unfortunate army officer, seated at an adjoining table, gave me a few glances—I was just beginning to be known as an actress. But the poor officer should never have done that! The hairs on Strindberg's upper lip stood on end, and with a snarl in the direction of the officer, he said to me: 'Come! Let us go—I can't stand this!' This was our first and last visit to a public restaurant. We did, however, dine at Bellmansro and Djurgardsbrunn, but invariably in a private room."

The incident is reminiscent of Freud's refusal to let Martha go ice skating because she might be touched by another man who would support her on the ice.

When Strindberg's doubts about his beloved began to overpower his love, Harriet left him: ". . . And if I should come back to you again, then you would naturally feel still more contempt for me. And the next time you were angered over one thing or another, you would again—and then even more viciously—heap over me such words as I can't imagine any man could use, even to the foulest street walker—least of all to his wife."

In reply Strindberg wrote:

"I stretched out my hand to you yesterday. . . . But you did not accept it. . . .

"How often during the nights . . . have I not taken your outstretched little hand and kissed it, even though it had clawed me—merely from mischievous, childish whim to claw! . . .

"Do you recall what it was that set it off? You wanted to deprive my child of my name. . . . But long before this you had played with the poison." Note that it was the threat of his child becoming her child which arouses the idea of being poisoned—just as Freud had explained the paranoid delusion in women.

"If the child is not mine [Strindberg wrote], then it must be someone else's. But that was not what you meant to imply. You merely wished to poison me; and this you did unconsciously. To bring you back to your senses, I awakened you with a shock.

"Are you awake now? And can you resolve not to play with crime and madness in future?

"You write me that you have not had a happy life. What do

you think I have lived through? Having seen what I considered
sacred treated as buffoonery, having seen the love between
husband and wife after so short a time exposed to public view—
I came to regret that I had ever taken anything seriously, was
driven to believe everything in life to be colossal farce and
fakery! . . .

"And now you ask: How can I, in spite of all this, still love
you?

"You see: Such is love! It suffers all—but it will not tolerate
humiliation and debasement!

"And at the very moment that our marriage was to be
cleansed and ennobled through our child—you take leave of
me!"

In his next letter he continues in this vein:

"In this spook tale, which is called our marriage, I have sometimes suspected a crime. Will it surprise you that I momentarily
have believed that you have been playing with me, and that you
—like Emerentia Polhem—had sworn you would see me at your
feet. . . .

"I presume you know it to be true that there was wickedness
in your eyes and that you never gave me a friendly glance. But
I loved you and hoped unceasingly that I would finally meet
with love in return. . . .

"This—our marital relationship—is to me the most inexplicable
thing I have ever experienced: the most beautiful and the
ugliest. At times the beautiful stands forth by itself—and then
I weep, weep myself to sleep that I may forget the ugly. And
in such moments I take all the blame upon myself alone! When
I then see you, melancholy, agonized—in May and June— in
your green room, sorrowing over your lost youth, which _I_ have
'laid waste,' then I accuse myself, then I cry out in pain because
I have been wicked to you and wronged you. . . . I kiss the
sleeve of the garment from which you stretched out your little
hand, and I plead with you to forgive me all the misery I have
inflicted upon you!"

As we have noted before, the paranoid posture is characteristically punctuated, especially when the individual is alone, by
shame and guilt for the wrongs he has inflicted on the other.

We now approach the description of the greatest affront—

the birth of the child which will be the moment of betrayal:

"When I have shed all my tears and the Angel of the Lord has consoled me, I can think a little more calmly . . . this is the way all young girls have grieved over their youth and through these portals of grief have entered into the domain of motherhood, where woman comes into the greatest joy of life, the only true joy—and which she divines instinctively beforehand."

Note that Freud and Strindberg are both convinced that there is no greater joy or fulfillment than in the bond between mother and child. Strindberg wished to become his mother through having her child. Indeed he had said, "To love a child was for a man to become a woman, it was to feel the heavenly joy of sexless love." He wished to impregnate not only women but other men. About Ibsen he wrote, "See now how my seed has fallen in Ibsen's brain pan—and germinated. Now he carries my semen and is my uterus. This is *Wille zur Macht* and my desire to set others' brains in molecular motion."

To return to the letter to Harriet Bosse:

"You have already sensed and experienced it!

"But I—who was a partner in this grief—I am not permitted to share the happiness!

"Is it my fate to give life to children, to be weighted down by worries and ingratitude, and then to have all the joy torn from me? Then do not say that it is I who flee from happiness!"

Jones has said of Freud's marriage, "Freud was not only monogamic in a very unusual degree, but for a time seemed to be well on the way to becoming uxorious. But when the thought of children entered his mind he became troubled." As Jones put it, "Freud's great fondness for children had not yet become manifest." Freud had second thoughts on his marriage in connection with children.

But Freud resolves his doubts when as the husband he played the role of father and mother along with his wife. As Jones has told us, Freud was not only a loving but an indulgent father. He was able to act out the fantasy of the golden age by recovering the indissoluble bond through his children—notably Anna who in fact never "betrayed" him since she never married but collaborated with her father throughout his life. Had Freud suffered separation from wife and children or Strindberg been able to have an Anna, the destinies of these two would not have been too dissimilar. It is clear, however, that the element of hate and the fear of betrayal was a self-fulfilling prophecy in the case of Strindberg whereas it was held more in check by Freud, though as we have seen, Freud was hardly unaware of the potential danger from the nursery.

Indeed Harriet Bosse many years later also had second thoughts about Strindberg:

"Today—after having passed through much in life—I can see how unreasonable and foolish I was, not to settle down in peace with this man, who asked for nothing better than to be given the opportunity to care for me. Unquestionably it was occasionally somewhat of a hardship to accommodate myself to his changing whims and moods, and to accept his views of life. But if I had erased my own personality and tried to adapt myself to his demands, this might have been possible. Yet, even so, it would be questionable whether things might have been better that way. . . . I have a feeling that Strindberg reveled in meeting with opposition. One moment his wife had to be an angel, the next the very opposite. He was as changeable as a chameleon. . . .

"Strindberg was kind and warmhearted. He was never ill-natured and fierce as he sometimes depicts himself in his writings. Only when he took pen in hand did a demon take possession of him . . . and it was this demon that helped to release his genius."

Notice that Strindberg, like Freud, was in fact a loving, gentle man in many of his interpersonal relationships. The paranoid posture, like paranoid schizophrenia, may be played out entirely in the realm of cognition and feeling rather than in direct action in interpersonal relationships.

Nor is the paranoid posture always even an accurate portrayal of the feelings of the individual as these may be later described in writing. Thus Hariet Bosse recalls:

". . . I can recall one time, when he had persuaded himself to attend a dinner party, given for us both, at the home of an acquaintance of his, incidentally not a friend.

"The entire gathering was in excellent humor, Strindberg not least. In other words, a most agreeable company; and Strindberg seemed very contented with the evening on our return home. Imagine my astonishment when I, several years later, read in a book of his then just published [*Black Banners*] with what infernal spite this dinner party had been arranged: Everyone present was a malicious person and the party a complete failure! I presume he wrote this in his loneliness, changing the mood of that evening to suit his own feelings at the time."

Strindberg's jealousy was diffuse. It was in no way restricted to the fear that his wife would betray him. He was equally concerned lest he betray his wife. Thus Harriet Bosse tells:

"Strindberg had such fear of a woman's power over him that he would refuse to see a lady caller, if he knew she was beautiful. I recall one time when Marika Stiernstedt was coming to visit him—the visit somehow did not take place! He was afraid she was too beautiful! Nor did he dare face Olga Raphael (Mrs. Linden) who at that time was quite young. She also was too dangerously beautiful! I believe that Strindberg was afraid he might be unfaithful to me, even in thought; and in order not to risk that, he chose to shield himself against any possible temptation."

But it was not the strength of women which alone frightened him. Toward Bjornsterne Bjornson he wrote he had felt "a tumult as if a storm had gone over the city, as if a magician had passed by." He admired and feared this man because he wrote as he wished, and had been successful despite this and above all he was a robust and virile man. Strindberg, according to Sprigge, "shrunk in the presence of the strong male."

Thus a woman for Strindberg is a creature wondrous fair, who will, however, not be molded and controlled by him but will ultimately betray him and "poison" him. Strindberg's imagery comes straight from Freud's account of the disenchantment of the girl with her unfaithful mother. On the one hand he must have someone to adore; on the other he wanted to revenge himself for the misery women caused him—reminiscent of Freud's repeated statement that he must have both a friend and an enemy. The war of the sexes which permeates his plays is taken directly from his own life. In play after play a man and a woman torture each other, unable to live with each other or without each other.

In *The Road to Damascus* The Stranger says: "We made a

mistake when we were living together, because we accused each other of wicked thoughts before they'd become actions; and lived in mental reservations instead of realities. For instance, I once noticed how you enjoyed the defiling gaze of a strange man, and I accused you of unfaithfulness."

To which The Lady replies: "You were wrong to do it, and right. Because my thoughts were sinful."

In *The Father* the Captain is victimized by the heroine Laura:

Laura: And as to your suspicions about the child, they are quite groundless.

Captain: That's the most terrible part of it. If there was an foundation for them, at least one would have something to catch hold of, to cling on to. As it is there are only shadows that hide in the undergrowth and thrust out their heads to laugh. It's like fighting with air or . . . with blank cartridges. The deadly reality would have roused resistance, nerved body and soul to action. But, as it is, my thoughts dissolve into mists and my brain grinds in a vacuum until it catches fire.

When you were young, Laura, and we used to walk in the birch woods . . . glorious! Think how fair life was, and how it is now. You didn't want it to become like this, nor did I . . .

In *The Ghost Sonata* the tender love story of the student and the hyacinth girl is contaminated by a huge, sinister vampire cook—the bad mother who takes away, as she poisons.

"She belongs to the Hummel family of vampires. She is eating us. . . . Yes we get many dishes, but all the strength has gone. She boils the nourishment out of the meat and gives us the fibre and water, while she drinks the stock herself. And when there's a roast she first boils out the marrow, eats the gravy and drinks the juices herself. Everything she touches loses its savor. It's as if she sucked with her eyes. We get the grounds when she has drunk the coffee. She drinks the wine and fills the bottles up with water."

But it is not only the old, fat cook who is orally dangerous. The student in the last scene reflects: "To think that the most beautiful flowers are so poisonous, are the most poisonous. The curse lies over the whole of creation, over life itself. Why will you not be my bride? Because the very life-spring within you is sick . . . now I can feel that vampire in the kitchen beginning to suck me. I believe she is a Lamia, one of those that suck the blood of children. It is always in the kitchen quarters that the seed leaves of the children are nipped, if it has not already happened in the bedroom. There are poisons that destroy the sight and poisons that open the eyes. I seem to have been born with the latter kind, for I cannot see what is ugly as beautiful, nor call evil good. I cannot. Jesus Christ descended into hell. That was his pilgrimage on earth—to this madhouse, this prison, this charnel-house, this earth. And the madmen killed Him when He wanted to set them free; but the robber they let go. The robber always gets the sympathy. Woe! Woe to us all. Saviour of the world, save us! We perish."

The first play Strindberg wrote, a two-act domestic comedy, was written in a frenzy of creative activity in four days. He was much relieved "as if a long pain were over, an abcess lanced at last." He felt that he had made love at last to the woman of his dreams. In A Dream Play Strindberg had written:

"Why are you born in agony
Why do you give your mother pain,
When, child of man, you bring her joy,
Joy of all joys, a mother's joy?"

According to Sprigge, nothing moved him more than a woman sitting at home with her children. Yet he had fallen in love with a woman who had insisted she was unfit for domesticity, and he had encouraged her to believe he would rescue her from the boredom of domesticity. Strindberg's child was born prematurely and died. His wife though distressed was somewhat relieved since she could once again pursue her career as an actress. Strindberg agreed to this but yearned for the child. He thought it was a crime not to welcome any new soul to this earth. He had never forgiven his parents for their not welcoming his arrival.

Like Freud, too, Strindberg was captivated by the dream. He began to write A Dream Play in 1901 shortly after his third marriage, at the age of fifty-two. He had now emerged from the long period in which he had struggled only with scientific and alchemical treatises. He was reborn with "new productivity, with faith, hope and charity regained—and absolute conviction."

In his note to A Dream Play, he, like Freud, explored the

dream as a revelation: "In this dream play . . . the Author has sought to reproduce the disconnected but apparently logical form of a dream. Anything can happen; everything is possible and probable. Time and space do not exist; on a slight groundwork of reality, imagination spins and weaves new patterns made up of memories, experiences, unfettered fancies, absurdities and improvisations. The characters are split, double and multiply; they evaporate, crystallise, scatter and converge. But a single consciousness holds sway over them all—that of the dreamer. For him there are no secrets, no incongruities, no scruples and no law. He neither condemns nor acquits, but only relates, and since on the whole, there is more pain than pleasure in the dream, a tone of melancholy, and of compassion for all living things, runs through the swaying narrative. Sleep, the liberator, often appears as a torturer, but when the pain is at its worst, the sufferer awakes—and is thus reconciled with reality. For however agonizing real life may be, at this moment, compared with the tormenting dream, it is a joy."

Although we have stressed the inevitability of the self-fulfilling prophecy of betrayal, it should not be forgotten that had Strindberg been blessed with less actual censure, his paranoid posture might have been combined with more happiness than he ever enjoyed, and the contrast between his life and that of Freud might have been markedly attenuated. We are led to believe this from an examination of those relatively rare occasions after he had enjoyed the love and respect of others. He had worked on *Master Olof* for nine years and he felt that this play represented him more than anything he had written since then. He was too anxious to attend its first performance. When it was acclaimed, he was reborn, and in fourteen days wrote a romantic fairy play, *Lucky Peter's Journey*. Reflecting his deep joy at the success of *Master Olof*, his hero's sufferings led to ultimate achievement of the heart's desire. Suffering was due to lack of understanding between people rather than to their viciousness. Success had for the moment attenuated his bitterness.

At another time he fell in love with Switzerland. Strindberg so fell in love with Switzerland that he sometimes felt that the good Swiss air was softening him. He was tempted to give up his destructive mission and to stop hurting others, but then he

would recognize that it was truly his mission to destroy everything false.

PARANOID SCHIZOPHRENIA: CONJOINT
TERROR AND HUMILIATION

Paranoid schizophrenia is a monopolistic over-organization
in which terror has been added to extreme humiliation so that
the individual, like a Jew in Nazi Germany or a Negro at a
lynching, feels he is at once humiliated and in mortal danger.
The paranoid has been humiliated and terrorized at once, by a
parent who combined shaming with attempts to dominate and
control, and who was quick to threaten punishment for resistance.

There is also reason to believe that this combination of affects
may be produced by both parents, in which one parent shames
and the other terrorizes. This appears to have happened in both
Strindberg's and Freud's family. It was a pattern of shared
responsibility which has become much rarer in the United States
in recent years. Strindberg's mother would threaten her children
with physical punishment by the father. Strindberg reacted to
this as a betrayal but also was frightened by these beatings.

The consequence of such a split is that there may be much
greater fear in the face of the male avenger, and humiliation in
the face of the female betrayer. Indeed the Oedipus complex
necessarily presupposes a father with some vigor. Despite the
fact that the critical relationship with the mother is laid down
long before the conflict with the father, the pre-Oedipal drama
of renunciation of the mother cannot be re-enacted as an Oedipus
drama with any novelty or new danger introduced, unless the
father can to some extent frighten the male child as well as
provide a masculine model whom the mother might conceivably
respect and love—and prefer to her son.

When, as in the United States in recent years, the mother
becomes both love object and punisher at once, and the father
is emasculated by his dominant wife, then paranoid schizophrenics, as Singer and Opler have shown, become the overly submissive good boys of over-idealized dominant mothers.

I was made aware of this critical change in American socialization in a most indirect way. For some years I had used the following demonstration of the power of projective techniques to my undergraduate classes. I would predict to a group of a few hundred undergraduates exactly what they would collectively write to a few TAT cards. Thus to card 1, I would say, "Thirty percent of you will see the boy as involved in conflict with his parents who want him to practice the violin. Of these, one third will comply and another third will passively resist and another third will openly flout parental authority, etc."

This worked very well until about 1949 when for the first time my predictions failed to account for a third of the stories written to the picture of a young boy looking at a violin. I could not guess what had gone askew and asked for help from the audience. It appeared that about 100 out of the class of 300 Princeton undergraduates had introduced into their stories the theme of a weak father. When one considers that their average age was about eighteen, they would have been born in 1931 and grown up during the last major economic depression, in a house in which the father had been shorn of his status and self-respect.

It is still an open question whether the conjoint terror and humiliation which appears in paranoid schizophrenia more commonly derives from severe treatment at the hand of one or both parents, and if one parent, which one. It is also an open question whether there may not be two variants of the paranoid syndrome—one based upon oppression, unrelieved by love, and one based upon the fantasy of betrayal, with or without auxiliary reinforcement from a threatening father.

It is highly probable, though we do not as yet have evidence enough to be certain, that when the disorder stems from betrayal (either from the mother or father) rather than unrelieved oppression, that what is produced is a so-called schizo-affective schizophrenia. This would account for two critical features of this disorder. First, its episodic quality—its characteristic sudden onset and brief acute duration; second, its resemblance to the manic-depressive disorder which is responsible for its having been given the hyphenated name. Like the depressive, these individuals cling tenaciously to the overidealized love object despite betrayal and the dangers of persecution from either parent, but like the paranoid there is also an unrelenting hostility to one or both parents. In one patient whom I had the opportunity of attending continuously for the first few days of onset, the entire drama centered around the dangers from a male who would kill the loving son who was trying desperately to achieve contact with his mother. This mother had reared three sons who were depressives, two of whom had committed suicide. This son also was a depressive who suffered one and only one acute paranoid-like episode, towards the end of his life.

Another critical question is whether paranoid schizophrenia is simply an exaggerated form of the paranoid posture or whether there are significant discontinuities between the two syndromes. It will not be an easy question to answer. We have seen in the case of Strindberg that he suffered a psychotic episode for a few years. His third wife (Harriet Bosse), many years later, said of him in this connection: ". . . If a person during life's trials should become highly sensitive, shy and suspicious, this need not come under the heading of what is commonly called mental illness. . . . I have never seen any indication of mental illness in Strindberg; but I was conscious of his individual eccentricities. . . ." Yet there can be no doubt, either of his distinctly paranoid-like feeling and ideation throughout his life, nor of his great achievement as a dramatist.

What of those like the Southern Negro whose social environment is at but one remove from the conditions which might produce paranoid schizophrenia? Malzberg's data on psychosis rates in New York state show that Negroes have a much higher psychosis rate than whites, but this increase is due entirely to high rates among migrants. Negroes born in New York state have the same psychosis rates as do whites. The Negro-white ratio in schizophrenia for those Negroes who have migrated from the South is 2 to 1. We also have evidence from our studies, which we will discuss later, that there is among Negroes a significant increase in the number of paranoid schizophrenics who are concerned with the danger of aggression.

It would appear that when social conditions in general are similar to those which produce paranoid schizophrenia within the single family, there is produced a paranoid posture which needs relatively little additional stress to push it over into paranoid schizophrenia. Similarly an individual, like Strindberg, who has been socialized in such a way as to generate a paranoid posture may be more readily precipitated into paranoid schizophrenia, should he be subjected to further undue pressure, than an individual who does not face such pressures with a fully formed paranoid posture.

If, as we are proposing, there is nonetheless a real and significant difference between the paranoid posture and paranoid schizophrenia, wherein does this difference lie?

It lies, we think, primarily in the degree of competition which the monopolistic organization encounters. Strindberg we have seen could be joyous, could love his wife deeply, could immerse himself in his work so that he found partial fulfillment there all of his life and intense fulfillment for brief periods, many times. It is these experiences of intensely rewarding positive affect, extraordinarily amplified for all of those who like Strindberg suffer so much rage and terror, anguish and humiliation—which heal and close the psychic wounds sufficiently so that psychosis is held at bay.

Because the monopolistic negative affect organization of terror and humiliation encounters the competition of the positive affects of excitement and enjoyment, not only are the perceptual cognitive over-interrpretation and over-avoidance strategies kept within check, but the experience of negative affect itself is attenuated by the competition from positive affect.

It should not be forgotten, however, that just as the reduction of negative affect heightens the experience of positive affect, the converse is also true. Strindberg more than once was tormented by just the contrast between the joy he had experienced with the beloved and the agony of what he felt to be betrayal. Nonetheless without these islands of excitement and enjoyment there can be little doubt that he would have been very much more vulnerable to paranoid schizophrenia. The same argument we believe holds for Freud. Freud was able to create, much better than Strindberg, exactly the conditions under which he could wage warfare against his "enemies" without surrendering his sanity.

There is a critical difference between paranoid postures and these and paranoid schizophrenia, which we have failed thus far to stress sufficiently. This is the peculiar power of terror added to humiliation. As we noted in our analysis of Dostoevsky, it is possible to be humiliated and angry and defiant, and even a little afraid too, without being terrorized at the same time. Dostoesky's "underground man" is bitter, but he is not a paranoid schizophrenic. He knows who is his persecutor, he knows his own feelings of humiliation, he is not forced either into terror or into delusion. When terror is added to humiliation, the individual is forced to fight for his life as well as his identity. The word anxiety has become debased and over-generalized to include all negative affect. It has lost the original intensity which Freud meant to express. We therefore suggest that it be replaced by the word terror, which more accurately conveys the panic of this state.

The syndrome of terror and humiliation which is paranoid schizophrenia should also be distinguished from other types of schizophrenia, some of which appear to be pure terror states, as in the catatonic stupor, and some of which appear to be pure humiliation states such as in simple schizophrenia or as in hebephrenia in which the spirit has been humilated and crushed by parents who are over-controlling, and over-protective or cold and aloof or alternately over-controlling and aloof.

These are also types of monopolistic humiliation syndromes in which resistance has been crushed through main force or through the disappointments of repeated inconsistency or withdrawal, without necessarily producing panic and counteraction. Not only is the paranoid schizophrenic terrorized and humiliated, but he is among schizophrenics much the most intact because he has been pushed into a posture of counteraction and fighting back. His cognitive capacities are stretched to the limit to account for the world in which he seems to live.

If the psychotic paranoid is the victim of terror and humiliation, he should be distinguished not only from those with paranoid posture who are utterly humiliated but not terrorized, but also from another group of psychotics, the manic-depressives, who we believe also to be utterly humiliated but not terrorized, but rather so distressed as to suffer anguish along with their feelings of worthlessness. The head is bent as they cry. We will present our view of this psychosis in the next volume.

It is the paranoid schizophrenic, par excellence, who suffers castration anxiety. As we have noted before, this concept of Freud's should properly have been called castration humiliation and anxiety, since the concept of castration is an extraordinarily appropriate symbol of the combination of terror and humiliation. Freud, we think, over-generalized both the terms anxiety and castration to include not only all anxiety and all threats but all negative affect—it was, he thought, the "real" danger behind all other threats.

The paranoid danger we have said had its real origin in the case of Freud in the betrayal by his mother. The paranoid image of the unloving oppressor, however, did not come from his father, who in fact he came to think was not proud and aggressive enough, but from the daily anti-Semitism which outraged him deeply. He could not and would not submit either to the physical threats or to the humiliation of being treated as an inferior. His hatred of the anti-Semitic oppressor was unrelenting, and it is our belief that the hostility which he posited between the son and the father was an amalgam of the hate generated by his mother's betrayal and that generated by the anti-Semitism which offended him so deeply.

This amalgam of hate and fear and humiliation, first from the mother and then from the anti-Semites, finally found a condensed expression in the concept of castration anxiety. The anti-Semites will attack and rob you of your manhood and humiliate you again before your mother, as she herself once did.

Further, in the choice of the term Oedipus complex, Freud also expressed his contempt for his father, his hatred for the anti-Semites and his confidence that he really was his mother's favorite. In the Oedipus myth it is after all the son who kills the father, not the other way around. The Oedipus myth is the paranoid's response to the threat of a father (for Freud the anti-Semite) who makes every attempt to kill the son in his infancy, but who is foiled and who ultimately is killed by the son. Freud did not wish to kill his father, but he did wish to kill his anti-Semitic enemies, as we saw in his identification with Hannibal.

Because Freud was a Jew, an oppressed member of an oppressed people, his concept of castration anxiety is entirely appropriate to an understanding of the paranoid schizophrenic, who does indeed feel in danger of physical attack and of humiliation by his oppressors. It is much less relevant to an understanding of many other disorders unless one uses the term metaphorically. Indeed, there is metaphor even in its use in connection with paranoid schizophrenia, inasmuch as the latter may feel in danger of being killed rather than simply castrated. Castration is nonetheless an appropriate symbol for representing the paranoid's deepest fears because it does unite both his feelings of impotence and terror.

Castration, actual or psychological, does not kill the son. It hurts, frightens and shames him. The son is now permanently an inferior man who has been terrorized and shamed into submission and subordination to the omnipotent father. Further, the myth of Oedipus also represents the wish of the son who will avenge himself on this father who tried to kill him in his infancy. The deepest hope of the paranoid is to be able to turn the tables, to control, frighten and humiliate the father—to castrate him. Pending such a final victory, he must forever be vigilant lest he be further controlled, frightened and humiliated. The staring eyes of other human beings frighten him and shame him.

Paranoid schizophrenia: an investigation using the PAT

Some of the evidence on which this theory is based comes from our normative studies on the Tomkins-Horn Picture Arrangement Test. We compared approximately eight hundred pathological cases with a representative normal sample of fifteen hundred cases. Our paranoid group numbered one hundred and seventy-three and our manic-depressives one hundred. Since then we have gathered more records of both normal and abnormal subjects. We will now present some of these findings in support of our theoretical position.

First, the paranoids are reliably elevated over normals on

Low Self-Confidence such that they believe the hero will fail
to win approbation from the group (Key 168). In a set of
situations showing a man talking to a large audience, the paranoid ends more frequently being booed than applauded and
also ends with smaller rather than larger audiences. This indicates an expectation of being humiliated and censured rather
than being praised. Indeed, some of the paranoids are apparently
so threatened by a picture of the hero exposed to so many
human beings at once that they deny the nature of crowd
situation altogether. Thus, the faces of the audience may be
interpreted as apples and oranges which are on the hero's push
cart.

PAT Plates 14, 19 and 24 are shown in the sequences characteristically chosen by paranoid schizophrenics with a frequency
reliably greater than the normal control group.

Further evidence for the difference in the nature of the
interpersonal relationships of paranoid patients comes from the
elevation of Key 142, Dependence, Continuing Support as End
State, Dominance or Instruction. In these plates the hero is
placed in a final situation in which he is either told how to do
something by a foreman, and in another case hypnotized by a
psychiatrist or hypnotist. This is shown in Plates 9, 17 and 23
in the sequences characteristic of the paranoid schizophrenic.

Taken together, these two findings tell us that the paranoid
sees himself not only over-controlled but also censured and
humiliated. His reply to this is to counteract it through work
and achievement.

Consistent with the importance of humiliation and the
counteractive work interest is an elevation of work motivation
for paranoids. It is our supposition that achievement supports
the individual wish for independence from others' control.
Plates 3, 7 and 18 are given in sequences that are characteristic
of the High Work Interest of the paranoid schizophrenic.* In
all of these the hero is placed in a final situation in which he
continues to work rather than to stop working.

Next is an elevation of general Lability of Affect (Key 202).

* PAT Plates 1, 5, 6, 13, 15, 16, 20, 21 and 25 also are shown at the end
of this chapter, in the sequences indicating High Work Interest as arranged
by paranoid schizophrenics.

Plates 14, 19 and 24 of the PAT, in the sequences characteristically chosen
by paranoid schizophrenics.

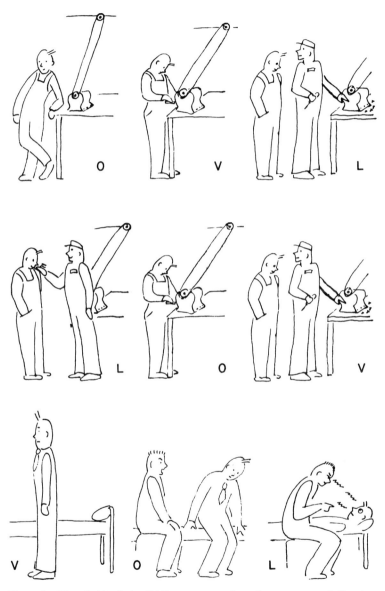

Plates 9, 17 and 23 of the PAT, as arranged in the sequences indicating Dependence, Continuing Support as End State, Dominance or Instruction—characteristic of the paranoid schizophrenic.

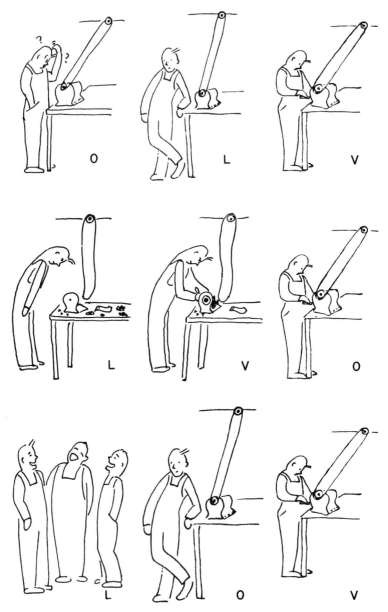

Plates 3, 7 and 18 of the PAT, as arranged in sequence by paranoid schizophrenics showing High Work Interest.

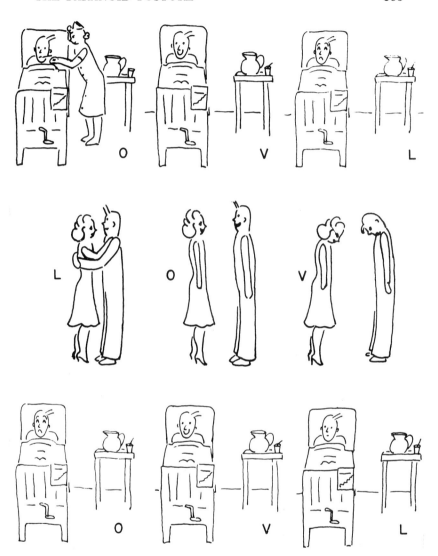

Plates 2, 10 and 12 of the PAT, in sequences that indicate Lability of Affect among paranoid schizophrenics.

This is indicated by the selection of a sequence in which the hero is presumed to oscillate directly between strong negative and strong positive affect rather than to go from one to the other more gradually through an intermediate neutral state. This is shown in the sequences of Plates 2, 10 and 12.

This lability of affect appears to exert sufficient pressure so that paranoids are also elevated on General Restlessness—the tendency to move from one environment to another (Key 200) and on Social Restlessness Sociophilic (Key 150). This latter is indicated by the sequence together-alone-together, the former by such sequences as the hero together with a group, at home alone, and then walking somewhere. Both findings taken together indicate a restlessness which moves the individual toward and away from social interaction with an inability to sustain either being alone or with people or to stay long in one place together or alone. General Restlessness is indicated in the sequences of Plates 8 and 20 which are selected by paranoid schizophrenics. Social Restlessness is indicated in the sequences of Plates 17, 22 and 23 which are selected by paranoid schizophrenics.

We come now to our evidence for the fear of aggressive attack. In the paranoid the significance of the increased distance which he wishes between himself and others is illuminated by a very marked denial of physical aggression. On Plate 4 of the PAT a group of men are shown in a free-for-all fight.

This picture is unambiguous to most people. Denial, which is scored only when this picture is described in a manner which clearly does not involve physical aggresion, occurs in only 4 per cent of normal subjects. The paranoid more than any other group radically distorts this situation. He may interpret it as "talking it over, or telling a joke or planning a fishing trip." Approximately 20 per cent of paranoids deny the aggression in this extreme way.

Other schizophrenics deny this aggression 10 per cent and manic-depressives deny it 5.9 per cent, which does not differ from the normal frequency. The denial by paranoids is reliable at the .01 level. There is no necessary relationship between this denial and an inhibited or very low degree of aggression *per se.* The neurotics as a group are distinguished by their very low

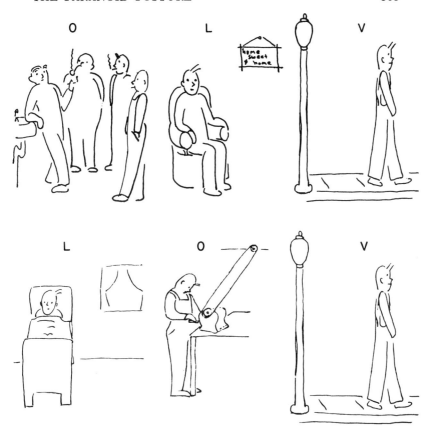

Plates 8 and 20 of the PAT, arranged in sequences indicating General Restlessness of paranoid schizophrenics.

aggression on the PAT but they do not deny aggression in this way on Plate 4. The significance of the elevation of denial of aggression is more a fear of an aggressive situation and of an aggressive attack than of a wish *per se*.

If such is the case, we should expect such denial to occur more frequently in normals who are exposed to more physical violence and who cannot fight back. As we noted before, Karon's study of the Northern and Southern Negro bears out this expectation. He reports the increased frequency of denial with respect to every aspect of aggression when the Southern sample is

Plates 17, 22 and 23 of the PAT, as arranged in sequences indicating Social Restlessness of paranoid schizophrenics.

Plate 4 of the PAT (set in right-side-up order for the reader's convenience).

drawn from an area of markedly severe caste sanctions, which exposes the Negro to physical danger.

Further, our first studies of paranoids were conducted in New Jersey state hospitals which have a very high percentage of Negro relative to white paranoids. We found an unusually high frequency of denials of aggression (70 per cent) in these early studies. It was only when our nation-wide testing showed a lesser elevation which failed to confirm this figure that we began to inquire into the possible reasons for the discrepancy from our initial findings and discovered that the combination of the status of being Negro and developing the disorder of paranoid schizophrenia was responsible for an even more extreme elevation of denial than among paranoid schizophrenics from a groups with a lower base rate of denial of aggression.

It should also be noted that perceptual distortion may be the consequence of factors other than defense mechanisms. In general, low education and low intelligence produce misinterpretation of even the most obvious stimuli. Old age, too, with its failing acuity, will usually produce an increased frequency of perceptual distortion on Plate 4 and throughout the test.

In order to control for these factors we divided our total normal sample into two groups—those with an I.Q. of ninety or more and six or more years of education, aged sixteen to sixty-four, and those with an I.Q. of under ninety, less than six years of education, aged sixteen to sixty-four. We also divided our abnormal population into two such matched groups.

The low I.Q. and low education-normal group are scored as denying aggression almost as frequently as the high I.Q.-and-education paranoid schizophrenic group is; but the low-I.Q., low-education paranoid schizophrenic group has still higher frequency of denial than either group. This group of low intelligence and undereducated paranoids deny aggression 30 per cent on Plate 4 and deny injury 44 per cent on Plate 16. The low I.Q., low-education normal groups deny 11 per cent on Plate 4 and 21 per cent on Plate 16. The difference between paranoids and normals is still reliably different, for high or low I.Q. and education samples, although the magnitude of the difference is reduced for the low I.Q. and education samples.

In addition to the denial of aggression, paranoids also deny physical injury. On Plate 16 of the PAT a man is shown working on a machine, having injured himself so that his finger is bleeding, and in a hospital lying in bed. We scored denial when there was no reference, direct or indirect, to bleeding or cut or injury, for example, "going to work, oil dripping."

Denial on Plate 16 is most elevated in the paranoid group; 25 per cent compared with a normal frequency of 6 per cent. As with the denial of aggression, the remainder of the schizophrenic group is intermediate with 19 per cent. It is unexpectedly high in our manic-depressive group with 17 per cent, which is reliably elevated above the normal frequency. It is also reliably elevated among the Organics with 18 per cent. Neurotics give

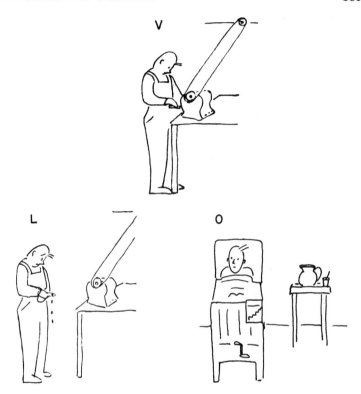

Plate 16 of the PAT (set in right-side-up order for the reader's convenience).

4 per cent and Character Disorders 10 per cent, neither of which is reliably different from the normal frequency.

Fear of the bleeding finger may signify specific castration anxiety or a more generalized hypochondriasis about the body as a whole, inside and out. Paranoids are elevated on Key 171, General Hypochrondriasis, above every other pathological group. This is indicated in the sequences on Plates 12, 16 and 21 which are selected more frequently by paranoid schizophrenics.*

This is indicated, first, by a selection of poor outcome from hospitalization or medical treatment, second, pessimism when

* PAT Plates 2, 11 and 15 also are shown at the end of the chapter, in sequences indicating General Hypochondriasis as arranged by paranoid schizophrenics.

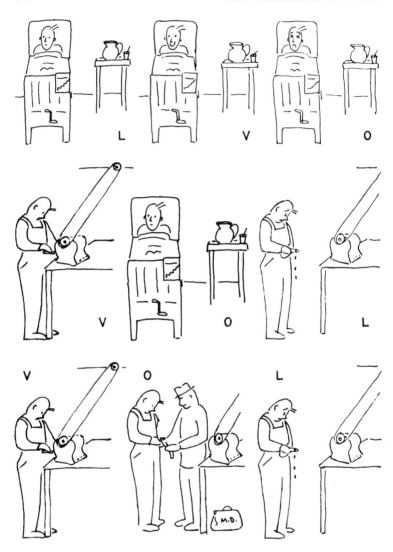

Plates 12, 16 and 21 of the PAT, arranged in sequences indicating General Hypochondriasis of paranoid schizophrenics.

alone in a bed (not in a hospital) or third, low energy at work when recovery from low energy is possible. The first case is indicated by ending on unhappy or neutral affect in the hospital

situation when it is possible to end on happy affect; or it is
indicated by ending on hospitalization following a more serious
rather than a less serious injury, indicated by the injury-work-
hospital sequence rather than the work-injury-hospital sequence
with a second more serious injury or unexpected complication
in the former injury usually being introduced; finally, by ending
on injury after hospitalization or medical attention rather than
injury before hospitalization or medical attention. The second
case is indicated by ending on a neutral affective state rather
than a happy state when the choice is posssible in a situation
depicting the hero alone in bed but not in a hospital. The third
case is indicated by a sequence which begins on energetic work
followed by less energetic work and ends on being tired and
not working. We had originally related both this denial of
injury and hypochondriasis to the fear of aggressive attack and
the denial of aggression.

Our assumption was brought into question by two findings.
First, the failure of the manic-depressives to be elevated on
denial of aggression, combined with their unexpected elevation
on denial of injury, made the assumption that fear of injury
was a consequence of fear of aggressive attack less probable.
Second was the converse finding by Karon that among the
Southern Negroes there was denial of aggression without denial
of injury. Nonetheless, even though manic-depressives deny injury, its significance may be quite different than its denial by
paranoids. Thus although both paranoids and manic-depressives
are elected on general hypochondriasis that specific sub-key
(174) Hypochondriasis-Injury Proneness is elevated only in paranoid and other schizophrenia and not among manic-depressives.

This is indicated by those sequences on Plates 16 and 21
described under poor outcome from hospitalization or medical
treatment. It appears probable that a hospital can be dangerous
to the paranoid because he feels he will be hurt and possibly
castrated or killed there; whereas the depressive feels he may
be nurtured, or abandoned, there, because there is something
the matter with him. We will examine this problem further in
the next volume.

While there is still reasonable doubt concerning the significance of the denial of injury as it is related to the denial of aggres-

sion by paranoid schizophrenics, such denial seems central to paranoid schizophrenic pathology. Not infrequently among our intellectually superior cases these denials are the only evidence for psychotic disturbance, so far as the PAT record is concerned. Indeed, one of the most striking findings among our intellectually superior paranoids is the combination of a very high level of functioning throughout the PAT, combined with extreme perceptual distortion of situations which are peculiarly threatening to the paranoid. Thus, if we removed two such responses from the record of a paranoid who was a college professor, the remainder of the record would certainly have been identified as that of an individual functioning at a very high level.

We interpret this conjoint denial of stimuli connected with physical aggression and with physical injury as evidence of a massive effect of terror and humiliation, and of an equally massive organization of the individual's cognitive capacities to produce such gross but specialized perceptual distortion.

"A new theory": an introspective account of paranoid schizophrenia

We will now present parts of an anonymous account, by a 34-year-old man, of the experience of paranoid schizophrenia which was written in a closed ward of a mental hospital. It purports to be "A New Theory of Schizophrenia." We offer it here as further support for our own view of the nature of paranoid schizophrenia. It begins as follows:

"I propose that the motive force of schizophrenic reactions is fear, just as fear motivates, according to Freud, neurotic mechanisms—but with these differences: in 'the case of schizophrenia, the chronic fear is more properly called terror, or concealed panic, being of the greatest intensity; and second, as is not the case in neurosis, the fear is conscious; third, the fear itself is concealed from other people, the motive of the concealment being fear. In neurosis, a sexual or hostile drive, pointing to the future, is defended against. In schizophrenia, by my view, detection by others of a guilty deed, the detection pointing to the past, is defended against. . . .

"My hypothesis may be called the Dick Tracy theory loosely in honor of that familiar fictional, human bloodhound of crime.

"Motivated in the very first place by fear, the schizophrenic psychoses originate in a break with sincerity, and not in the classically assumed 'break with reality.' The patient's social appetite (an instinctive drive in primates, I believe), including love and respect for persons and society, is consciously anticathected or forsaken and ultimately repressed with the passage of time, since full satisfaction of sociality entails, more or less, communicative honesty, faith and intimacy. Also, the tension set up in interpersonal intimacy by the withholding of emotionally important (although perhaps logically irrelevant) information causes unbearable pain. This repression of sociality accounts for the well-known 'indifference' of schizophrenics. But if safety can be achieved by means of 'perjury' alone without great discomfort, then no further defenses are adopted. . . .

"Paranoiacs specialize in 'proving' that they are not guilty, could not be guilty because of natural loftiness. But even most paranoiacs avoid responsibility like the plague. Those who accept responsibility see to it that they fail in a big way—like Adolf Hitler.

"I believe schizophrenics tend to adopt any means which promise to interfere with the examiner's understanding of them—despite all appearances to the contrary. In order to conceal misdeeds for the long run, with minimum disadvantage, very subtle means of uncooperation must be employed. . . .

"A large amount of the damage to the schizophrenic's self-esteem results from his contemplation of his own vicious insincerity, which damage is more an effect than a cause of his disease. His unethical defense mechanisms cause him deep shame and fear of loss of others' esteem. In addition, the primary deeds—whose exposure and punishment are avoided by the disease—are shameful. Insincerity involves using people always as means, never as ends. . . .

"A primary danger which is defended against is detection by other people of the patient's anti-social deeds, past or present (varying from, say, murder and treason to petty emotional dishonesty and masturbation), of which the patient remains conscious throughout any degrees of progression of severity of his disease. A second primary danger defended against is the patient's own guilty conscience, which self-demands his own punishment. Also, the severing of 'genuine' social ties is a kind or treason against the human race, and itself brings secondary guilt. Thus, guilt which is always present in schizophrenia, complementing the danger of externally threatening punishment, explains Clifford Beers' discovery that in psychosis there is a serious impairment of self-esteem.

"More broadly speaking, schizophrenia shares with all functional mental illness the ultimate danger of punishment meted out by men, demigods or gods. Common punishments feared are the being deprived of love of kith or kin, loss of social status, financial security, etc., and especially in the case of schizophrenia the more violent punishments such as being abominated by kith or kin, bodily mutilation, imprisonment, lynching, execution.

"This abandonment of social ties and good feeling, in the interest of personal safety, is sometimes starkly simple, as in mutism, but is usually supplemented by the development of 'phony' social behavior, that is to say, designedly cryptic or misleading expressions of interests, sentiments, opinions: designedly unfriendly 'friendliness'; asking only questions to which the answers are already known; the limitation of speech to severely pre-censored statements; the limitation of conduct to carefully self-criticized, self-rehearsed stratagems, etc. The patient has aggressed, ultimately in self-defense, by means of an undeclared, passive, preventive 'war' against his fellow men, and in the interest of preventing defeat (positive victory is soon sensed to be hopeless attainment) most of his knowledge and sentiments, and indeed his spontaneous behavioral tendencies, have been classified 'top secret.' Whatever words he actually uses are employed, thus, as self-defensive weapons. . . .

"The proximate goal is to avoid being understood. The ultimate goal is to avoid punishment. They 'non-want' punishment. . . .

"Only after this more or less conscious process of social insincerity and disaffection has become well established does the psychosis proper begin. . . . Pre-psychotic schizophrenia is, I believe, related to 'psychopathic personality' (a kind of arrested stage of preschizophrenia), some cases of alcoholism, and even what may sometimes be diagnosed as 'obsessional neurosis' or 'anxiety neurosis. . . .

"Delusions are but weakly believed by the patient himself when alone or unthreatened. Delusions are dormant except in interpersonal relationships, where they are trotted out and strongly advanced as weapons of defense. . . .

"So what is a schizophrenic? In brief, he is a terrified, conscience-striken crook, who has repressed his interest in people, unavowedly insincere and uncooperative, struggling against unconscious sexual perversion. He is of no mean Thespian ability. And his favorite Commandment is that which one nowadays facetiously calls the Eleventh Commandment, 'Thou shalt not get caught.'

"Attempts to expose him may only drive him further 'underground.' But a knowledge of his true nature will surely lead, someday, to someone's discovering a sure, quick, effective, and enduring cure."

The paranoid schizophrenic: in brief

In this account, as in ours, it is conscious terror and humiliation which are the dominant affects. Humiliation here is called guilt because it is immorality which is the source of the humiliation. We have not stressed immorality as a source of humiliation, not because it is unimportant but because guilt has been well analyzed by Freud and others, whereas the same affect when it is concerned with inferiority rather than immorality has been relatively neglected. Further, the relative importance of humiliation about immorality and about inferiority has shifted towards inferiority and away from immorality, since the nineteenth to the twentieth century.

We do not mean to say that there are today no paranoids who are concerned with the guilt, or humiliation, which attends the possible detection of their sins. The account we have just presented is evidence enough that not all shame and self-contempt in paranoid schizophrenia today centers exclusively on the problem of inferiority. We have been concerned rather to offer further evidence that the paranoid is involved in unceasing warfare with his enemies who primarily both terrorize and humiliate him and who must therefore be warded off lest the self be destroyed and humiliated. Further, we have seen here that when the paranoid is alone and unthreatened he does not necessarily believe his delusions.

We are not, however, entirely persuaded that the immoralities which he fears may be detected should be called simply guilt. When one fears detection of an immorality as much as this individual does, it is altogether possible that what he calls guilt would more properly have been labeled terror lest I be hurt, exposed and degraded for sexual behavior. The issue is largely a semantic one, however. What is critical is that he experiences this disorder as the conjoint presence of terror and humiliation lest he be exposed.

PAT Plates 1, 5 and 6 as arranged by paranoid schizophrenics in sequences indicating High Work Interest.

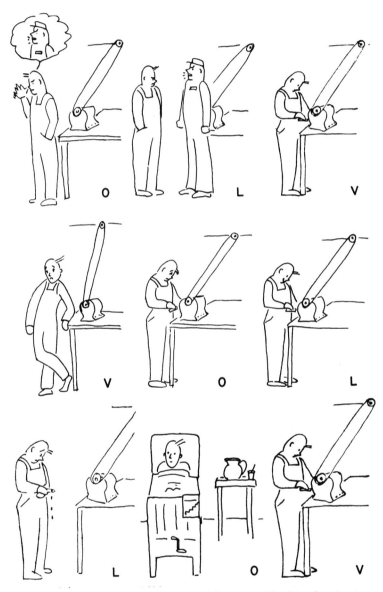

PAT Plates 13, 15 and 16 as arranged by paranoid schizophrenics in sequences indicating High Work Interest.

PAT Plates 20, 21 and 25 as arranged by paranoid schizophrenics in sequences indicating **High Work Interest.**

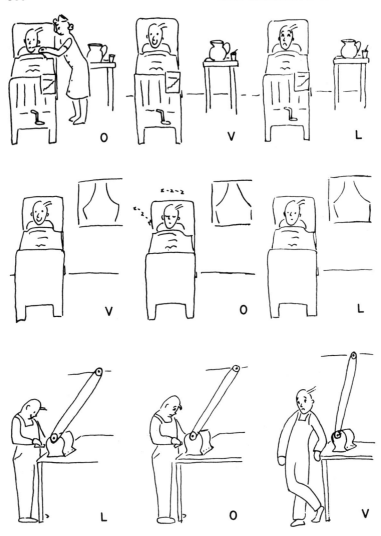

PAT Plates 2, 11 and 15 as arranged by paranoid schizophrenics in sequences indicating General Hypochondriasis.